CADOGANguides

NORMANDY

'Victor Hugo called Rouen the city of a hundred bell towers, Monet was so entranced by its cathedral that he painted it over 30 times, and Flaubert's Madame Bovary bumped along its cobbled streets with her illicit lover in their horse-drawn cab.'

Clare Hargreaves

About the Guide

The **full-colour introduction** gives the authors' overview of the region, together with suggested **itineraries** and a regional **'where to go' map** and **feature** to help you plan your trip.

Illuminating and entertaining **cultural chapters** on history, food and drink, art and architecture give you a rich flavour of the region.

Travel covers the basics of **getting there** and **getting around**, plus entry formalities. The **Practical A–Z** deals with all the **essential information** and **contact details** that you may need, including a section for disabled travellers.

The **regional chapters** are arranged in a loose touring order, with plenty of public transport and driving information. The authors' top **'Don't Miss'**  **sights** are highlighted at the start of each chapter.

A short **language guide**, a **glossary** of cultural terms, ideas for **further reading** and a comprehensive **index** can be found at the end of the book.

Although everything we list in this guide is **personally recommended**, our author inevitably has her own favourite places to eat and stay. Whenever you see this **Authors' Choice** ⭐ icon beside a listing, you will know that it is a little bit out of the ordinary.

Hotel Price Guide

Luxury	€€€€€	€230 and above
Very Expensive	€€€€	€150–230
Expensive	€€€	€100–150
Moderate	€€	€60–100
Inexpensive	€	€60 and under

Restaurant Price Guide

Very Expensive	€€€€	€60 and above
Expensive	€€€	€30–60
Moderate	€€	€15–30
Inexpensive	€	€15 and under

About the Author

Clare Hargreaves' first experience of France was a day trip to Boulogne on her 10th birthday, when she was particularly impressed by a cheese omelette dished up by a man in a beret. She's been ferreting out France's hidden corners and gastronomic delights ever since. When she isn't writing and researching travel books and articles, she works for BBC Magazines. This is her fourth book, and her second on France.

2nd Edition Published 2007

01

INTRODUCING NORMANDY

Above: Apple blossom; calvados, p.64–5

Normandy is the land of the apple. In spring, when the apple trees blossom, it dons a petticoat of pretty pink and white lace; in autumn the intoxicating smell of fermenting cider apples permeates its countryside and half-timbered barns (Balzac was apparently so addicted to the aroma that he could only write if he had a rotten apple on his desk). These apples are transformed into cider or made into rich, cream-drenched puddings. Best of all, Normandy is the only region of France to produce the tipple of the gods – a smooth apple brandy called calvados. The drink even managed to give its name to one of the five *départements* into which Normandy is divided.

There are countless other goodies in the Norman basket too, from pungent cheeses, fresh oysters and ruined abbeys shrouded in mists that rise off the Seine, to the exquisitely carved façades of medieval houses and the towering milk-white cliffs that sent the Impressionists wild. There are sights that make your hair stand on end, like the abbey of Mont-St-Michel, gaunt and proud on its rock surrounded by racing tides, salt flats and quicksands that have carried away many an unwary pilgrim. The Bayeux tapestry – the oldest and longest comic strip in the world – still amuses and intrigues with its exuberant depiction of medieval life and the Norman invasion of England. For almost a millennium, academics have argued about exactly how Harold died – an arrow in the eye, or a sword in the thigh? Then there are Normandy's horses, which you can see somersaulting through the Bayeux tapestry. Today they are put to the test not on the battlefield but on racecourses, such as the one at ritzy Deauville, where the world's rich and famous congregate each August. The rest of the year you will see the sleek

Opposite:
Mont-St-Michel,
pp.368–75

beasts quietly grazing in Normandy's manicured stud farms, like the Haras du Pin, near Argentan, in the region's deep south.

A word about what you won't find in Normandy. There are no vineyards: Normandy's last attempts at producing wine were throttled by the vine disease phylloxera, so the region returned to what it does best, fermenting apples. You won't find constant sunshine – why do you think it's so green? – nor crowds, with the exception of the busloads that descend on Mont-St-Michel and Normandy's coastal resorts during July and August. Another thing you won't find is effervescent rural folk of the type familiar in Mediterranean climes. The Normans have a reputation in France for being guarded, shrewd and horribly stubborn – hence the phrase *têtu comme un Normand* (stubborn as a Norman). But once you've penetrated their taciturn exterior and won their trust, they can be as genuine and kind as anyone else in France.

One thing every inhabitant of the region knows is its history – which is everywhere. Four dates stick, limpet-like, in every Norman's mind. First, there is the Conquest of England in 1066, which changed the face of England and Normandy for ever. Normandy's best-known celeb, William the Bastard (later to turn Conqueror) had associations with many parts of Normandy: he was born in Falaise, married at Eu, died in Rouen and buried in Caen. Next comes 1204, when, after the Duchy of Normandy had effectively maintained complete independence from outside interference for 300 years, its Anglo-Norman rulers finally admitted defeat after King Philippe Auguste of France smashed his way into Richard the Lionheart's castle of Château-Gaillard on the Seine. In 1789 it was all change again when the Revolution struck and historic abbeys were gutted and closed down, and their inmates sent packing. Then, on 6 June 1944, Normandy witnessed its latest event to change the course of history: the biggest amphibious invasion of all time, known as the D-Day landings. For two grim months armies of more than a million men fought in the green fields of Normandy to decide the fate of Europe. The carnage would be some of the bloodiest of the Second World War, but it was a carnage that would liberate France, and eventually the Continent, from the tyranny of Hitler.

Whether you are in Normandy to commemorate those historic landings, or to follow up family connections and revisit the sites of so many private and terrible dramas – whether you have come in search of a piece of unspoiled rural France that's not too far from home, or to marvel at the region's architectural jewels – you'll soon catch the Norman bug and find yourself returning time and again.

Above: Water lilies, Giverny, pp.175–9

Below: Honfleur, pp.214–20

Opposite: Cider cave, pp.64–5; WWII museum, p.289

Where to Go

In landscape and architecture, Normandy is not one region but dozens. This guide carves the region up not into its huge and rather arbitrarily defined *départements*, but into areas that have a shared history, character and landscape. It starts on the northeast coast, whose great alabaster-coloured cliffs – as well as inspiring the coast's common label, the **Côte d'Albâtre** – attracted Impressionist painters like Monet, and whose historic, easy-going port, Dieppe, has always been a favourite hangout for English travellers dipping into France. Just south of this coast and the plateau of the **Pays de Caux** – dotted with placid villages, and atmospheric, venerable châteaux – is the cheesy, charming and very rural **Pays de Bray**, on Normandy's eastern border.

The next two chapters focus on the mighty Seine, the highroad holding it all together. 'Paris, Rouen and **Le Havre** are a single town,' Napoleon declared, 'the Seine is their main street'. We walk the other way from Napoleon, starting in war-smashed but spectacularly rebuilt Le Havre, then stopping in lovely half-timbered **Rouen**, where Normandy was born and which later became the birthplace of its most famous novelist, Flaubert, and the setting for Emma Bovary's amorous wanderings. We end up at Monet's gardens at **Giverny** – an Impressionist painting in themselves – and the placid **valley of the Eure**, one of the great river's most attractive tributaries.

Less well known but equally intriguing are the Risle Valley and the **Perche**, for a taste of untouched – and largely unvisited – Normandy. The highlight of the Risle is **Le Bec-Hellouin**, whose magical abbey spawned Lanfranc, first Norman archbishop of Canterbury; there are hidden jewels too in the Perche, a remote, wild area of rambling fortified manor houses and thick forests, known above all for two products – black pudding (*boudin noir*), and the huge, placid, immensely strong and hardy Percheron horse – and with a lovely old medieval town in **Mortagne-au-Perche**. Next we move on to the sedate, self-styled **Norman Riviera**, where we visit such gems as **Honfleur**, whose stunning 17th-century skyscrapers look as if they could topple into the harbour at any minute, before ambling west along the coast with its 1900s villas with pepperpot towers, ornate balconies and mock half-timbered façades. Passing through ever-well-heeled **Deauville**, where movie stars still sport their tans each summer, we reach Cabourg, beloved of Marcel Proust, via little Dives-sur-Mer, where long ago William the Conqueror spent four nail-biting weeks waiting for a fair wind to transport his army to England.

The lush and undulating **Pays d'Auge** is what most people consider quintessential Normandy: apples, cows, cheese, tiny medieval churches, ramshackle half-timbered barns and cider

presses, and thatched cottages that sprout strings of purple irises. It is here that the most esteemed of Normandy ciders and calvados are made, as well as the most famous Norman cheeses – in the south of the region, the little village of Camembert still churns out its gooey offering.

Returning to the coast, the next chapter tours historic **Caen**, with its 'his' and 'hers' abbeys, built by William and his wife Matilda in the diaphanous white stone known as *pierre de Caen*. Caen's impressive Mémorial museum is good preparation for a tour of the 'D-Day Coast' the 60-mile (96-km) strip of huge, golden-sand beaches – Sword, Juno, Gold, Omaha and Utah – where Allied troops landed in June 1944. We end up in lovely **Bayeux**, whose precious tapestry tells the story, in glorious technicolour, of another invasion, that of England by William 'the Bastard'. Bayeux also has one of Normandy's most comprehensive Second World War museums.

Plunging south again, the next stop is the **Suisse Normande**, 'Norman Switzerland', which may not look quite like real Switzerland but is nonetheless an outdoors-lovers' and kayakers' paradise, with fast-flowing rivers running through lovely steep, rocky gorges. From there, we pass through **Falaise**, William's birthplace, before wandering along the **Valley of the Orne**, with

Chapter Divisions

English Channel

Jersey/Guernsey

Newhaven · Le Tréport · Eu

St-Valéry-en-Caux · Dieppe

Cherbourg

Fécamp · Etretat · **08 DIEPPE, THE ALABASTER COAST AND THE PAYS DE BRAY** · Neufchâtel-en-Bray

SEINE-MARITIME · Forges-les-Eaux

Caudebec-en-Caux · **09 LE HAVRE AND THE LOWER SEINE VALLEY** · Rouen

Le Havre · Trouville-sur-Mer · Deauville · **12 THE NORMAN RIVIERA** · Cabourg · Houlgate · Pont-Audemer

St-Helier

Carentan · **14 THE D-DAY COAST, CAEN AND BAYEUX** · Bayeux

10 ROUEN TO GIVERNY · Les Andelys

MANCHE · St-Lô · **Caen** · CALVADOS · **13 LISIEUX AND THE PAYS d' AUGE** · Lisieux · Bernay · EURE · Vernon

Coutances · **16 CHERBOURG AND THE COTENTIN** · Livarot · **11 RISLE VALLEY AND THE PERCHE** · Evreux

Iles Chausey · Granville · Vire · Falaise · **15 THE SUISSE NORMANDE AND SOUTHERN NORMANDY** · L'Aigle · Verneuil-sur-Avre

Mont-St-Michel · Avranches · Mortain · Argentan · ORNE · Mortagne-au-Perche

Alençon · Bellême

N

20 km
10 miles

its rugged good looks, little-known châteaux and aristocratic horse studs.

The **Cotentin Peninsula**, on Normandy's border with Brittany, is saved until last. Its tiny granite villages, giant, windswept beaches and dramatic rocky coastline often make it look more like Britain's West Country than rural France. One of the first, early heartlands of medieval Normandy, the Cotentin also contains many of the most spectacular creations of Norman architecture from nearly 1,000 years ago – Coutances cathedral, abbey churches like Lessay, Hambye and La Lucerne, castles that seem lost in time such as Pirou and Gratot. The last stop on our voyage around Normandy is its most awe-inspiring: **Mont-St-Michel**.

Below: Coutances cathedral, pp.350–52

Time for a Tipple

The only region in France to have not a single vine, Normandy's tipple is cider. Or, if you like something stronger, calvados or *calva*, an apple brandy which is so central to the Norman palate that it gave its name to the *département*. There are as many types and qualities of cider as there are farms, and one of the joys of travelling in Normandy is stopping off by the roadside to sample and buy the stuff. The most picturesque area to indulge in some cider-tasting is the Pays d'Auge, the only region with an AOC (*appellation d'origine contrôlée*) for cider, where you can follow the well-signposted *Route du Cidre*. Some of the best calvados is produced here, too. Visit in autumn and you can join in the harvesting and pressing of the apples at individual farms or at one of Normandy's many genial cider fairs.

From top: Cider Bar, Honfleur, pp.214–20; Cider, Pays d'Auge, pp.239–43

Above: Livarot cheese pp.249–50; cheese labels

Say Cheese

Gooey, rich and gorgeous, Normandy's cheeses are not for slimmers. The region is best known for its Big Four – Neufchâtel, Pont-l'Evêque, Livarot and Camembert – but there are countless other types produced on individual farms, advertised by signs saying *'fromages fermiers'*. The best place to sample them is at weekly markets, such as those at Pont-l'Evêque and St-Pierre-sur-Dives, where mountains of the pungent cheeses are displayed and sold, or at cheese fairs like the one at Livarot.

Horse Play

Horses are as much a part of Norman life as cider and cheese. Everywhere you'll find immaculately maintained studs, or *haras*, with sleek smooth-coated inmates worth fortunes. They include the stud owned by descendents of the Aga Khan and the elegant Haras du Pin in southern Normandy, which was the brainchild of Louis XIV's minister Colbert. In William the Conqueror's time mounted horses fought it out on the battlefield – you can see them tumbling out of the Bayeux tapestry – and subsequently they were bred to

Above: Haras du Pin, p.309; Deauville races, pp.221–7

Right: Percheron horse, p.205

work the land, but today most are thoroughbreds that thrive on Normandy's fine grazing. The most important horse sales and races are at Deauville in August, attracting the world's rich and famous and offering an entertaining spectacle for visitors.

Above: Rouen, pp.151–66;
Villa Strassburger, p.224

Architecture

From medieval half-timbered farmsteads to Gothic abbeys and ancient castles, the variety and richness of Normandy's architecture is staggering. Each region has its individual architectural style and materials. Typical black-and-white half-timbered farms are found in the Pays d'Auge. The best collection of timber-framed townhouses is in medieval Rouen, where pressure on space meant that houses were built taller and taller still. In Honfleur, too, you'll find 17th-century skyscrapers that look as if they will topple over at any minute. For Gothic gems, the cathedrals of Bayeux, Coutances, Rouen and Caen all vie for supremacy, and the ancient abbeys of the Seine provide medieval magic. Or for something completely different, on the coast you'll find what's known as *anglo-normand* architecture, extravagant mansions with mock-traditional half-timbering and fanciful Japanese-pagoda roofs.

William the Conqueror

Normandy's best known celeb, William the Bastard (later to turn Conqueror) has left his indelible mark on numerous parts of the region. Born in Falaise of an illicit liaison within the castle walls, he was married in Eu on Normandy's northern border, and died in historic Rouen. He was buried – somewhat unceremoniously – in Caen, whose 'his' and 'hers' cathedrals had been built by the Conqueror and his wife Matilda. Though his grave was routinely plundered, a dignified stone now marks the place where his thighbone rests, in Caen's Abbaye aux Hommes. William's invasion of England is told in fascinating detail by the tapestry at Bayeux. Further east is Dives-sur-Mer, where William and his men waited for a favourable wind before setting sail for Hastings.

From top: American Military Cemetery, p.275; Omaha Beach, p.273

The Legacy of the D-Day Landings

The Second World War changed the face of Normandy forever. The most dramatic event was the landing by allied forces on Normandy's northern shores on 6 June 1944, which left around 10,000 dead or wounded. Some of the bloodiest fighting took place northwest of Bayeux on Omaha Beach, whose exposed dunes afforded little or no shelter from German gunfire. The trim white lines of white crosses in the region's cemeteries are a grim reminder of the war's terrible toll.

01 Introduction | Itineraries

Itineraries

Normandy in Two Hectic Weeks

Day 1 Sample a *marmite dieppoise* (fish stew) in Dieppe, and spend the afternoon at Lutyens' Bois des Moitiers at nearby Varengeville. For a treat, eat at La Buissonière. Alternatively, head south to the Château de Miromesnil (now a B&B), where writer Guy de Maupassant lived as a child.

Day 2 Drive south to half-timbered Rouen and enjoy its narrow medieval streets, Gothic cathedral, museums and Michelin-starred restaurants.

Day 3 Head south along the Seine to Les Andelys, dominated by Richard the Lionheart's Château Gaillard, then continue to Giverny to enjoy Monet's house and garden.

Day 4 Head back northwest along the Seine, taking in the abbeys of St Georges de Boscherville, Jumieges and St-Wandrille and enjoying the thatched cottages and birdlife of the Marais Vernier.

Day 5 Cross the state-of-the-art Pont de Normandie into Honfleur, drink in the arty vibes, pop into the Maisons Satie and the church-cum-boat of Ste-Catherine. For a taste of modern Norman cooking, treat yourself to dinner at Le Breard.

Day 6 Relax on the white sands of Trouville, enjoy the over-the-top Anglo-Norman architecture and look out for film stars in snooty Deauville. Then head south through attractive Beaumont-en-Auge to chocolate-box-pretty Beuvron-en-Auge.

Day 7 Starting at Pierre Huet's *cidrerie* in Cambremer, follow the *Route du Cidre* through the Pays d'Auge for some serious cider and calvados tasting.

Day 8 Now it's time for cheese: head for the tiny village of Camembert, where the famous cheese was invented, and visit the only farm that still makes it. Returning north, stop at the quirky Château de Vendeuvre to enjoy its museum of miniature furniture and gardens packed with sedate surprises.

Day 9 Visit the Norman abbeys in Caen, pop into the city's art museum with its wonderful restaurant-café, then devote the rest of the day to the Memorial de Caen.

Day 10 Spend the day lapping up the riches of Bayeux, including its gothic cathedral, its stone streets, its D-day museum and its world-famous tapestry.

Day 11 Starting from Bayeux, take a tour, organized or self-guided, of the D-Day landing beaches. Fortify yourself with freshly caught *moules* at Port-en-Bessin, or if you want a fishy extravaganza, try the port's Michelin-starred L'Ecailler.

Above: Notre–Dame Cathedral, Rouen, p.153; Cider apples ready for harvesting in the Pays d'Auge, pp.239–43; Camembert cheese

Day 12 Moving northwestwards, divide your day between the granite ports of Barfleur and St-Vaast on the Cotentin peninsula, sampling the seafood, watching the fishing boats, and soaking up the sea air.

Day 13 Drive south through the Cotentin peninsula, stopping to admire Coutances' magnificent Gothic cathedral and the bell foundry at Villedieu-les-Poêles, before arriving at the bay of Mont-St-Michel. Stay in one of the gorgeous B&Bs listed in this book, and ask for a room with a view of the mount.

Day 14 Get up early and hit Mont-St-Michel before the coaches get there. Enjoy the austere peace of the monastery and when the crowds arrive, retreat to La Mère Poulard for an omelette. If the history of the place has gripped you, pop over to Avranches and its new *Scriptorial*, which houses the Mont-St-Michel manuscripts.

Artists' and Writers' Normandy (9 days)

Day 1 Sail into Dieppe, beloved of Camille Pissarro, and English painter Walter Sickert, and get your fill of local art at the Château-Musée. Maupassant fans should drive south to the Château de Miromesnil where the writer lived as a child. If Impressionist art is your thing, head west to Pourville, whose jagged chalky cliffs were painted countless times by Claude Monet in 1892.

Day 2 Head 6km west to Varengeville, whose Maison du Douanier and church were painted by Monet. The church, facing the sea, was also a favourite haunt of Georges Braque; he's buried in the cemetery and you can see windows by him inside the church.

Day 3 Potter west along the Côte d'Albâtre (Alabaster Coast) to Fécamp, whose pebble beach and cliffs were painted 22 times by Monet, and then to tiny Yport, the setting for Maupassant's novel *Une Vie*. The highlight of this stretch of coast, though, is Etretat, a few miles on, whose famous rock arches were captured in so many different lights by Monet and Gustave Courbet. Maupassant was schooled here, too.

Day 4 Continue west to Le Havre, stopping first in the outskirts at Sainte-Adresse, often painted by Monet. His most celebrated work, painted around 1873, is *Impression, Soleil Levant* whose title is said to have given rise to the name of the Impressionist movement. Le Havre was also the home of Eugène Boudin, Camille Pissarro, Raoul Dufy and Otthon Friesz, and their works are displayed at Musée Malraux.

Day 5 Cross the elegant Pont de Normandie to Honfleur, the birthplace of Boudin, whose works are displayed in the Musée Eugene Boudin. On the cliffs overlooking the city you can visit

Above: Foundry, Villedieu-les-Poêles, pp.357–8; Honfleur pp.214–20; Etretat, pp.124–7

the Ferme Saint-Simeon, now a hotel, but once a farm where Impressionists like Corot, Courbet and Jongkind exchanged ideas and produced some of their finest works.

Day 6 Continue west to Cabourg, whose Grand Hôtel was the holiday hideaway for Marcel Proust. Stay here and enjoy madeleines for breakfast. Head southeast inland to Rouen, stopping en route at Villequier, whose Musée Victor Hugo recalls the tragedy that befell the novelist when his daughter drowned in the river here.

Day 7 Follow in Emma Bovary's footsteps with a tour of the interior of Rouen's Gothic cathedral, and admire the exterior, painted in myriad lights by Monet. See his and other artists' portrayals of the city in the fine Musée des Beaux-Arts. Visit the house, now a fascinating medical museum, where Flaubert was born.

Day 8 Head to Ry, the one-street town, used by Flaubert as the setting for *Madame Bovary*, and pop into its Bovary museum. Drive cross-country to Gisors, whose marketplace was depicted by Pissarro, and finish up back on the River Seine at Les Andelys, birthplace of 17th-century, classical painter Nicolas Poussin.

Below: Monet's Garden, Giverny, pp.176–7

Day 9 Last but not least, savour Giverny, whose oriental willow-laden gardens with their waterlilies were painted so many times by Monet. Tour Monet's house, now a museum, then head across the road to the Musée d'Art Americain, which houses works by fellow Impressionists. Round off your tour with a drink at the atmospheric Hôtel Baudy (now a café), where many artists once lodged.

The Bayeux Tapestry

1 *Edward the Confessor of England sends Harold Godwinson, his heir, to Normandy to meet with Duke William*

2 *Harold rides off with his hawk and hunting dogs towards Bosham, near Southampton*

3 *Before sailing, Harold and his knights enjoy a meal in the upstairs of his seaside house. Note the drinking horns, and the man bearing a knife on the stairs*

4 The border scene at the bottom of the tapestry depicts medieval life: ploughing and harrowing the fields. The scene probably shows Aesop's fable of the swallow and the birds

5 William entertains Harold at his palace, probably in Rouen, where they have a heated discussion. Their entourages are armed and carry shields

6 Harold's men get stuck in the quicksands of Mont-St-Michel

7 William makes Harold his vassal by giving him arms

Details from the Bayeux Tapestry – 11th century by special permission of the City of Bayeux

8

UBI HAROLD:SACRAMENTUM:FECIT:~ HIC HAROL
VUILLELMO DUCI:~

9

:IN:EO:ALLOQUII:EIDE

ET HIC GODEFUNCTUS
EST

10

OWARDI:REGIS:AD:ECCLESIAM:S
PETRI

11

OO:
EGIS

HIC RESIDET:HAROLD
REX:AN GLORUM:
STIGANT
ARCHI:EPS

8 Touching two reliquaries, Harold makes an oath to William (it's not known what the oath was, but it is assumed he promised to support William's claim to the English throne)

9 Edward the Confessor falls ill and dies. A cleric stands on the far side of the bed, his wife Edith at the foot, and a man, presumably Harold, stands on the near side touching the king's fingers, symbolising Edward's bequest of his kingdom

10 Edward's funeral

11 Harold becomes King of England with crown, orb and sceptre. Stigand, the archbishop of Canterbury, stands beside him

12 The sighting of Halley's comet, seen as an ill omen, causes consternation. A messenger whispers secret intelligence (possibly the news of the impending Norman invasion?) to King Harold

13 William's woodcutters fell trees and split them into planks to make ships to invade England

14 William's men load arms and provisions. Note the four-wheeled wagon drawn by two men

Details from the Bayeux Tapestry – 11th century
by special permission of the City of Bayeux

...VENIT AD PEVENESÆ :-

15

hIC EXEVNT:CABALLI DE NAVIBVS :- ET hIC:

16

HIC:COQVI TVR:CARO ET hIC: MINISTRAVERVN
MINISTRI

17

hIC FECERVN: PRANDIVM : ET hIC EPISCOPVS:CIBV E
POTV: BE NE DIC IT

18

15 William's fleet crosses the Channel and lands at Pevensey

16 William's men and horses disembark; they are beached with the aid of a fork-ended pole.

17 William's cooks set to work preparing a feast that includes kebabs and hot pot cooked over a brazier

18 A blast horn summons guests to the feast, attended by William, his barons and Bishop Odo. Note the shields turned into makeshift trays

19 The Normans set fire to an English house; a mother and her child flee

20 Battle commences. The Norman cavalry charges the English infantry near Hastings

21 Both sides suffer losses. Note the dismembered corpses and broken weapons in the lower border

Details from the Bayeux Tapestry – 11th century by special permission of the City of Bayeux

22, **23** Horses and bodies in battlefield chaos

24 Harold is killed by an arrow in the eye; without their leader the Saxons are defeated and William wins his prize, the English throne

For the story of the Bayeux Tapestry, see pp.284–7

Details from the Bayeux Tapestry – 11th century by special permission of the City of Bayeux

CONTENTS

History

02

[Normandy] is a land which is very fruitful, with fertile fields, abundant pasture for flocks, rich woods and meadows, which support many kinds of wild animals and birds. It has an abundance of rivers and sea ports, is well-stocked with fruit-bearing trees, and is distinguished by noble towns protected by strong fortifications. Its metropolis is Rouen, an ancient town made powerful by its wealth and numerous population, which is situated on the river called Seine.

Robert Blondel, 15th-century historian

Early Beginnings: Celts and Romans

Once upon a time there was a river. This river, vast and sinuous, was the Seine, and on its banks in around 1000 BC small pockets of people were ekeing out a living. The river was their main highway, and tin was transported along it from Brittany and Cornwall to the depths of Europe. Around this time the first **Celts** arrived from central Europe, setting up *oppida* (trading centres) that grew into little towns as trade increased. By the 1st century BC, the Seine and its trading routes had attracted the interest of the **Romans**, who saw Normandy as a springboard for their designs on Britain. The Roman Emperor **Diocletian** (AD 245–313) christened it *Gallia Lugdunensis Secunda*, or 'Lyonnaise II', reflecting the region's second-rank status among the 17 Roman provinces in Gaul. Roman roads provided a new form of communication, and former Celtic strongholds were turned into walled cities, such as *Rotomagus* (modern Rouen), *Caracotinum* (Harfleur) and *Mediolanum* (Evreux).

The civilizing effects of the Romans would be cut short, however, by the **barbarian invasions**. Germanic tribes had trickled across the Rhine as early as the 1st century BC; Saxon pirates landed in the Bessin, near the site of present-day Caen, in the 2nd and 3rd centuries, and the flood began around 400 with the arrival of Franks, Burgundians and Visigoths, as Rome's empire disintegrated. One Frankish tribe was led by a formidable chieftain named **Merovech**, and he and his sons managed to unify the Franks under their rule. **Clovis** (481–511) thrashed the Gallo-Romans at Soissons and incorporated the old *Lugdunensis Secunda* into a kingdom called Neustria. He also became a Christian, under the influence of his pious wife Clotilde, Christian daughter of the king of Burgundy. However, the reign of the Merovingians (descendants of Merovech) was short, and by the middle of the 7th century real power in the Frankish kingdom was held by the king's minister, Pepin II of Herstal. His great-grandson, **Pepin III the Short**, disposed of the last feeble Merovingian and had himself proclaimed king in 751, but he is overshadowed in the history books by his son and successor, the mighty, seven-foot-tall **Charlemagne**.

The one thread of continuity through these chaotic goings-on was the Christian church. The first Christians had arrived in Normandy under Roman rule, though large-scale monastery-building did not begin until the arrival in 640 of **St Ouen**, a high-ranking official in the Frankish court, who was influenced by the monastic fervour spreading from Italy. He built the abbey of St-Ouen in Rouen, and then went on to found two more large monasteries downriver along the Seine, at Jumièges and St-Wandrille. By the 8th century they had become two of Europe's greatest centres of learning. And so they would have continued, had a group of tough warriors from the north not rudely interrupted their studies.

Normandy's Creators: The Vikings

These warriors, whose fearsome longboats first sailed up the Seine around 800, were *normannus*, Latin for Norseman or Viking, and it was they who would give Normandy (*normannia*) its name and identity as we know it today. There was plenty to attract these rugged Scandinavians to the Seine valley: excellent transport links, the busy city of Rouen, and defenceless abbeys, crammed with treasures. As word got around, they descended in their hordes. Normandy was plunged into decades of pillaging and destruction. In 841 the wooden houses of Rouen were razed, and Jumièges was plundered and burned. Ten years later, St-Wandrille met the same fate.

Poacher Turned Gamekeeper: Rollo

In among one of the later waves of Vikings was a warrior called **Rollo** (Rollon in French), son of Earl Rognwald of More in Norway, who had been booted out of his homeland for stealing the king's cattle. Followed by his ragged crew, from 876 Rollo marched across Normandy, starting in Rouen, where he set up his headquarters, and then sacking St-Lô and Evreux. In 911 the king of France, **Charles the Simple** (which was not a derogatory term but meant only that he was straightforward rather than a schemer), decided enough was enough, and that the best way to contain Rollo was to put him in charge of the lands he'd wrecked. Under a treaty agreed at St-Clair-sur-Epte, on the southernmost borders of Normandy, Rollo was recognized as Duke of Normandy and he and his men were given the lower Seine valley around Rouen and Evreux – the area now known as Haute-Normandie – in the hope that they would keep other Scandinavian raiders at bay and leave Charles in peace. In addition, Rollo would have to convert to Christianity.

Now that they owned the land, the Vikings had to protect rather than pillage it. Rollo made Rouen his capital, transforming it into one of the largest markets in northern Europe, and in 924 added the Bessin (around Bayeux) and the land around Sées to his dukedom. Little by little he established his hold over the more long-established Franks, and a common language and customs began to emerge. The Vikings bequeathed numerous words to French, like *bec* (river), *ville* (estate or domain) and the points of the compass – *nord*, *sud*, *est* and *ouest*. Under Rollo's often ruthless rule, peace and stability slowly returned. This new order is illustrated by a legend in which a golden ring, left hanging on the branch of an oak tree, was left untouched. Christianity too continued to put down tentative roots: clergy who had fled during the Viking raids returned, and Rouen's monastery of St-Ouen again resounded to the chanting of monks. Among the Norman masses, though, Christianity could still run second to traditional paganism. In the 920s an exasperated archbishop of Reims wrote to the Pope asking 'what should be done when they have been baptised and rebaptised, and after their baptism continue to live in pagan fashion, killing Christians, massacring priests, and offering sacrifices to idols?' Even Rollo was torn between the two: it is said that on his deathbed, having made a generous donation to the Church to save his soul, he then ordered that some Christian slaves be taken out and slaughtered as sacrifices to the gods Odin and Thor.

A New Nation Takes Shape

Rollo was succeeded by his son **William Longue-Epée** ('Longsword'), who, as good as his name, managed to extend his conquests as far west as the Cotentin peninsula, the Channel Islands and the Avranchin, sketching the shape of the Norman border with Brittany. Longsword proved an astute politician, offering his services to one side and then another in France's many internal wars, and by a series of treaties with other magnates, sealed by marriages, expanded the dukedom to its fullest extent.

Now that the Vikings were established in Normandy, further hordes of Norsemen arrived from Scandinavia, Ireland and England, and intermarried with the locals. As a result French fast became the region's main, and official, language. The power of the Church was growing too: the abbey at Jumièges had revived, and was becoming one of the richest and most powerful in France. But danger and anarchy always lurked in the wings, and in 943 William Longsword was murdered after being lured into a meeting with Count Arnulf of Flanders, his oldest enemy.

Independent Normandy finally took shape under Longsword's son, **Richard the Fearless**. Given that Normandy had no natural geographical or ethnic boundaries, the Duchy's wealth and strength was astonishing, providing the springboard for conquests across Europe. In 987, when the house of Capet replaced the Carolingians as supposed 'kings of France' – with scarcely any real power – Richard was acknowledged as able to do what he wanted in Normandy, in return for recognizing Hugues Capet as his theoretical overlord. Rouen continued to grow and flourish. The historian Orderic Vitalis described the 'fair city set among murmuring streams and smiling meadows, abounding in fruit and fish and all manner of produce... strongly encircled by walls and ramparts and battlements, and fair to behold with its mansions and houses and churches.' As Normandy's secular power grew, its spiritual strength blossomed as well. Monasteries such as St-Wandrille and Mont-St-Michel flourished, and a new large abbey was established by Richard at Fécamp.

Church expansion continued under **Richard II 'the Good'** (996–1026), Richard the Fearless's illegitimate son. His most important move was to invite William of Volpiano, a monk from the great monastery of Cluny, to reform his father's abbey at Fécamp along Benedictine lines. Yet more abbeys mushroomed all over Normandy, including Bernay, Cerisy-la-Forêt and Holy Trinity in Rouen. Their magnificent buildings displayed a new style of architecture, Norman Romanesque, which would become famous across Europe. Norman monasteries like the one at Bec-Hellouin became outstanding centres of scholarship and learning, especially under Lanfranc, one of the foremost scholars of his age, who would go on to become Archbishop of Canterbury. As bishops were appointed by the Duke, the expansion of the Church also bolstered the power and unity of the Norman state. Richard's ambitions started to expand. His eyes began to focus on England, and in 1002 he secured the marriage of his daughter Emma to King Ethelred II ('the Unready') of England.

Richard II was progressive in other ways too. He broke with Norman tradition by marrying Judith, the mother of his children, instead of settling for a concubine (so that two of their children, the future Richard III and Robert I, were actually the only legitimate dukes of Normandy before 1066). The reign of **Richard III**, however, was cut brutally short by a quarrel with his brother over Falaise, which left Richard 'mysteriously' dead from poisoning just two years after his accession, in 1028.

Robert, despite his skulduggery, has become known as **Robert 'the Magnificent'**. He's best known for his fling with a tanner's daughter by the name of Arlette (or, more probably, Herlève), whom he spotted from the window of his castle in Falaise. She, just 16, was paddling in the River Ante below, but her charms were apparently irresistible. Robert invited her to look at his etchings, but Arlette, instead of furtively sneaking in the back entrance, rode in for her assignation triumphantly through the main gate. During their night of passion Arlette had a dream, in which branches sprouted from her body to cover the whole of Normandy and England. Nine months later, in 1027, a bastard son, William, was born.

Robert's passion proved shortlived. He cast Arlette aside, marrying her off to Herluin de Conteville. She bore him two sons, Odo and Robert, both of whom would play big parts in Norman history. Robert the Magnificent would get a taste of his own medicine (or poison) while travelling back from pilgrimage to Jerusalem in 1035. Mortally ill, he was carried on a litter by slaves when he met a Norman who was returning home. Asked if he wanted any messages taken back, Robert said 'When you return to Normandy, say that Duke Robert was taken to paradise by four devil slaves'. He collapsed and died, and the epithet 'Robert the Devil' has largely stuck, in place of the title he preferred of 'the Magnificent'.

William the Conqueror

William, Robert's bastard son, was just eight. Fortunately for William, before his father Robert had gone travelling he had secured the French king's approval for William to succeed him as Duke of Normandy. But it was a tender age to embark on such a job, and it's a miracle the duchy survived at all as it cascaded into blood feuds and civil war. Robert had astutely surrounded the boy with the pick of his companions, like the all-powerful Archbishop Robert of Rouen and a monk called Ralph Moine, who was William's principal tutor and schooled the boy in Latin, military strategy and hunting. On his deathbed William is said to have declared 'I was schooled in war since childhood.' Handling arms was a much-needed skill, for the knives were out. Three of his guardians and a tutor were assassinated by pretenders to the throne, and when William was barely 20 he foiled an assassination plot by Guy of Burgundy, the legend goes, by riding for 16 hours through the night to Falaise, and only survived after the French king, Henri I, came to his rescue. More plots and counterplots followed, as his neighbours tried to swallow Normandy up into their possessions.

With this background it's perhaps not surprising that as an adult William could be something of a control freak, with a puritanical disdain for food and drink and an unstoppable craving for wealth and power. His cruelty is shocking: he chopped off the hands and feet of prisoners at Alençon because he thought – probably mistakenly – they'd insulted his mother. What marks out William from other chiefs, though, is the softer side of his character, brought out by his wife **Matilda**, daughter of Count Baldwin of Flanders, to whom William remained remarkably faithful (some say from his own trauma of having being labelled a bastard all his life).

Politically, too, Matilda was a good bet: not only did an alliance bring powerful Flanders on side, she was also descended from Alfred the Great of Wessex.

The battle for Matilda's hand in marriage, though, was almost as tough as those against his many enemies. Apparently she wasn't too keen, declaring she'd 'rather be sent to a convent than be given to a bastard!', and William only got his way with her by dragging her by her hair across his bedchamber. Whether William's illegitimacy or the fact that they were cousins was the obstacle isn't clear, but Pope Leo IX forbade the union, possibly egged on by the Duke's enemies. With characteristic obstinacy, William defied the pope and got married anyway, in the château in Eu, in around 1050. In 1059 the papal interdiction was finally lifted, on condition that William and Matilda both build abbeys in Caen, Normandy's newly created second capital, in atonement.

In the meantime, William was busy building the foundations of what would for a time be the richest, most powerful and best-organized state in the western Christian world. He assembled a personal bodyguard of knights as the nucleus of a Norman army, and like his father and grandfather realised the importance of co-opting the Church as an ally, naming friends and relatives as bishops, including his truculent half-brother and comrade-in-arms **Odo de Conteville**, whom he made Bishop of Bayeux. With stability restored, and an abundance of idle aristocracy hungry for land, adventure, and experience in warfare, the time was ripe for Normandy to expand. Many knights headed for Italy and Sicily. In 1066, however, William's ambitions were focused far closer, across the grey waters of *La Manche*.

1066 and all that

William was hunting in his park at Quenilly when news reached him that **Edward the Confessor**, the King of England, had died and that the Saxon **Earl Harold** had grabbed the English crown. According to legend, the Duke abandoned his bow and arrows and sat in silence for hours. Finally he summoned a council of his nobles and sent an envoy to England claiming that Edward had previously promised him the throne. Rebuffed by Harold, William took the matter over his head by appealing to the Pope in Rome, who gave his blessing to William's marauding expeditions. With this stamp of approval, a conquest of England could be portrayed as a holy war. Normandy, however, had no significant navy, and a fleet had to be built from scratch. Throughout the spring of 1066 forests rang to the sound of axes. Landless Norman knights and mercenaries from all over Europe rolled up in Dives-sur-Mer, on the coast near Caen, lured by the promise of good wages, fiefdoms in England and high adventure – all with papal approval.

Both sides saw the passing of Halley's Comet in April as a portent. By 12 September William had mustered between 8,000 and 14,000 men (no one knows the exact figure) who embarked, it was said, in some 2,000 to 3,000 vessels (although many modern historians believe the figure was nearer 400). They sailed, though, only as far as St Valéry-sur-Somme in Picardy, where for two agonizing weeks William watched the weathercock on the church spire, waiting for the northerly winds to change. On 27 September the winds turned and William and his men set sail in their primitive wooden ships, so beautifully depicted in the **Bayeux Tapestry** (*see* colour feature). In mid-Channel, William stopped for breakfast, washed down with wine. According to the chronicler William of Poitiers he was so relaxed he looked 'as if he was in his chamber at home.' The next day the Normans landed at Pevensey in Sussex. William stumbled as he stepped ashore. His superstitious entourage wondered if this was a bad omen, but William laughed it off, saying, so the story goes, 'My lords, by the glory of God have I seized this land with my own two hands. As long as it exists it is ours alone.'

Harold, who had been distracted by Norwegian enemies in the north, rushed down to Hastings, and pitched camp on a hill. On 14 October William launched an assault. A terrible struggle ensued, which ended only when Harold was killed – probably not by an arrow, and probably not in the eye, although arguments still go on about it. By Christmas, William was crowned at Westminster Abbey, and by March 1067 he felt confident enough to return to Normandy and his wife, whom he apparently missed awfully. Although it was still Lent, great parties were thrown to welcome home the man who'd turned from William the Bastard to William the Conqueror. For the next 140 years, England would be united with Europe.

William encouraged Norman families to settle in England, and began cataloguing the riches of his new kingdom in the **Domesday Book**. Art and architecture were exported across the Channel, as the great cathedrals at Canterbury, Winchester and Durham testify. Back in Normandy, the dukedom's new wealth funded the building of magnificent monuments such as the cathedrals of Bayeux, Coutances and the abbey church of St Pierre-sur-Dives, many stuffed with treasures seized in England. There was money left over to pay for the making of the world's most famous embroidery, the Bayeux Tapestry. Norman French became the administrative language of England, and Anglo-Norman literature was born, as in the writings of Robert Wace, a clerk from Caen who wrote *Brut d'Angleterre*, a history of the kings of England, and the *Roman de Rou*, chronicling the dukes of Normandy. The only fly in William's ointment was the death of Matilda; the tough old warrior, we are told, wept for days after burying his beloved in her Abbaye-aux-Dames in Caen.

After William

When William died in a riding accident in 1087, the waters of the Anglo-Norman empire were muddied by squabbling among his sons as to who should succeed him. Since no one could agree, the union was split, with his eldest son **Robert Curthose** given Normandy and his second son, **William Rufus** ('red-face'), awarded England. William's youngest, **Henry Beauclerc**, had silver but no land, but cunning, luck and a fair dose of dirty dealing would in the end make him the most powerful of the three. The villainous William Rufus, stouter and even more ruthless and avaricious than his father, was loathed by his own subjects and most later historians. Few tears were shed in 1100 when, while hunting in the New Forest, he was struck by an arrow and died. 'A few of the peasants carried his corpse to the cathedral at Winchester on a horse-drawn wagon, with blood dripping from it the whole way,' wrote William of Malmesbury. Given William's reputation as a devil-worshipper, few were surprised when the tower of the cathedral, where he had been buried, collapsed a year later.

The ambitious Henry, who had been with his brother on the hunting expedition, lost no time. With a speed that some saw as suspicious he galloped off ahead of the body to Winchester to secure the royal treasure, and within three days of his brother's death he was seated on the English throne, eager to beat his other brother Robert – away on Crusade – to the prize. When Robert returned Henry decided to settle things once and for all, and did so in a pitched battle at Tinchebray, in the Vire. He defeated his older brother, locked him up and seized his duchy of Normandy. The Conqueror's inheritance was united once again, with Henry I as both king and duke.

But bad luck lay around the corner: in 1120, the *White Ship*, in which Henry's heir William Atheling, his brother, and the flower of the Anglo-Norman nobility were travelling, hit a rock off Barfleur and sank, drowning all its passengers bar a butcher from Rouen, who lived to tell the story (*see* p.333). It's said that Henry, who was sailing in the ship behind them, never smiled again. The dynasty founded by Rollo thus ended, as Henry had no more sons; hence, he named his daughter **Matilda** as heir. At Henry's death in 1135, however, **Stephen of Blois**, his dashing nephew, claimed the Anglo-Norman throne, and squabbles between his followers and those of Matilda dogged the next decades. After years of anarchy a compromise solution was found whereby Stephen would hang onto the crown, but on his death it would pass to Henry, son of Matilda and her husband Geoffrey of Anjou. In 1154 he became **Henry II**, first of the House of Plantagenet, so-called as his father sported a sprig of broom (*genêt*) in his cap. With Henry's marriage to **Eleanor of Aquitaine**, whose dowry included the whole of the southwest of France, Normandy became the heart of the great Angevin empire, stretching from the North Sea to the Gulf of Gascony.

Now that Normandy was part of a larger, more powerful empire, though, it presented a still greater challenge to France's Capetian monarchs, eager to at last exert their authority over their over-mighty 'vassals'. The most important French king of the era, **Philippe Auguste**, had been on Crusade with his friend (and by some accounts, lover) **Richard the Lionheart**, who succeeded Henry II. Philippe had promised Richard that the land along Normandy's border would be demilitarized, but Richard doubted the King's intentions and built a massive castle, Château Gaillard, at Les Andelys to keep his Norman possessions safe. While Richard was in charge Philippe Auguste held off, but the Lionheart's death left a far less threatening man at the helm, his brother **King John 'Lackland'**. It was only a matter of time before Philippe Auguste stormed Château Gaillard and forged up to Rouen, conquering the whole of Normandy in 1204. The Duchy of Normandy was no more.

The War of a Hundred Years

By the 1300s the English monarchy's connection with Normandy was fading into the past. But a few years later the English were back, dragging Normandy into the Hundred Years' War (1328–1450), after **Edward III** decided to make a play for the throne of France. Edward and his sons had a go at Caen and Rouen, returning home with boatloads of fabulous booty; then, in the 1360s the French gained the advantage thanks to a general called **Bertrand de Guesclin**, whose ugliness apparently matched his military genius. In 1415 **Henry V** decided to do the job thoroughly and conquer the whole of France. The image of him storming Harfleur –

'Once more unto the breach, dear friends, once more...' – has of course been immortalised by Shakespeare. It was an uphill struggle, but his victory at Agincourt in Artois spurred him on to complete his conquest, capturing Caen, Bayeux, Falaise and Rouen in quick succession. By 1420 the French Crown lay within his sights, and Henry's dying words to his brother, the Duke of Bedford, were to hold onto Normandy at all costs.

Eight years later the French were hanging on by a thread, defending their last stronghold at Orléans on the Loire, but were saved at the eleventh hour by a peasant girl who heard saintly voices in her head, **Joan of Arc**. Dressed in gleaming white armour, and leading 4,000 French soldiers,she managed to relieve the six-month siege. Bolstered by victory, Charles VII of France advanced to Reims, where he – rather than the English king – was crowned in 1429, his unlikely female comrade beside him. Determined as ever, Joan went on to attack Paris, which was a disaster, and then to relieve Compiègne, besieged by the Duke of Burgundy, England's ally. Her luck, however, had turned. She was captured by the Burgundians and sold for a fat sum to the English, who attributed her victories to witchcraft and spells. In 1430 Joan, now 19, spent Christmas imprisoned in the castle at Rouen, and was later tried and burnt at the stake, her ashes scattered on the Seine. In 1449, though, French troops marched into Rouen, and in 1450 they secured permanent control of Normandy through the battle of Formigny, in the Bessin. From 1468 Normandy was a part of the French Crown, but with a large degree of administrative independence up until the Revolution.

While France and England slugged it out, Norman seafarers were chasing even greater spoils. In 1362 a band of sailor-adventurers set out from Dieppe to sail down the African coast as far as what is now Sierra Leone, where they founded a colony called Petit-Dieppe. The greatest seafarer of them all was **Jean Ango**, born in 1481. He became so rich that even King François I borrowed cash from him, and named him Viscount of Dieppe; the magnificent house he built in Dieppe was, alas, destroyed by Anglo-Dutch bombardment in 1694, but his Renaissance-style country house, the Manoir d'Ango, survives (*see* p.108). Two Florentine brothers, Giovanni and Girolamo da Verrazano, whom Ango commissioned to explore North America, were the first Europeans to stumble across New York harbour, where a bridge is now named after them. In 1517 Le Havre was founded as France's new Atlantic port, and in the next two centuries Norman colonies would be set up in Brazil, Canada, Florida and Louisiana.

The Wars of Religion

Normandy's frequent contact with England and, through its ports, with the world at large, meant that it had a large number of Protestants, especially in the university cities of Caen and Rouen. Led by Eude Rigaud, the Archbishop of Rouen, the Protestants – or **Huguenots**, as they were known in France – were openly critical of the corruption of the **Catholic Church** and by the mid-16th century posed a serious challenge to its hold on the French establishment. Normandy was therefore in the front line when the Wars of Religion, between Catholics and Huguenots, flared up in the 1560s. In 1572 thousands of Huguenots were butchered in the notorious **St Bartholomew's Day Massacre** in Paris, prompting an orgy of reprisals and counter-reprisals. The Huguenots were finally placated by the Edict of Nantes in 1598, which granted them freedom of worship, judicial protection and privileges.

Less than a century later, though, in 1685, **Louis XIV** revoked the Edict of Nantes. This devastated Normandy's economy, as the Huguenots packed their bags and left, taking their skills with them. Fields in which the Huguenots excelled, like the textile trades and the navy, nose-dived, and Rouen, the Huguenot stronghold, faced an economic disaster from which it would take nearly a century to recover.

In the countryside, meanwhile, there were other rumblings of discontent. While France's kings and their court lived it up at Versailles, peasants were made to pay for the country's debts through taxes. In 1639 the *Va-nu-pieds* (literally 'those who go barefoot') of Avranches had gone on the rampage to protest against higher salt taxes, holding the towns of Mortain and Pontorson to ransom. Peasants rebelled over food shortages and the cost of bread, and a wider uprising came in the 1670s when Louis XIV's minister **Colbert** put new taxes on tobacco, pewter and legal documents to raise money for the king's wars. Riots began in Brittany but spread across Normandy and the rest of France, in a dress rehearsal for the Revolution a century later.

The Revolution and After

In July 1789 France's National Assembly demanded that King Louis XVI grant the country a constitution, and when no sign of cooperation came from the monarch, the Paris crowds stormed the Bastille prison, unfurled the tricolour and effectively ended the *ancien régime*. In 1791 Normandy officially ceased to be a legal entity, when the Revolutionary government divided the old province into the *départements* of Manche, Calvados, Orne, Eure, and Seine-Inférieure (now Seine-Maritime). Normandy generally supported the Revolution, but drew the line when it came to the execution of the King; in Rouen 30,000 people turned out to voice their opposition. In a region riddled with abbeys, there was unhappiness too about the Revolutionary government's attack on religion and the clergy.

Counter-revolutionary murmurings began, and many Normans voiced their support for the **Girondins**, a middle-class faction, originally from the Gironde in southwest France, who opposed the abolition of the monarchy and called for moderation. In May 1793 the radical Jacobins expelled the Girondins from the National Convention and ordered their arrest; leading Girondins fled Paris to try to continue resistance, but their improvised army was defeated at Pacy-sur-Eure. Many Girondins took refuge in Caen, where their cause fired the imagination of 25-year-old **Charlotte Corday**, who had been closeted in the Abbaye-aux-Dames with the works of Voltaire and Jean-Jacques Rousseau. On hearing of the butchery of the Revolutionary Terror in Paris, she slipped into the capital to wreak her revenge and, she hoped, put an end to the slaughter with one dramatic act. Her target was **Jean-Paul Marat**, the radical Jacobin leader and the Girondins' chief tormentor. After several tries she finally got an audience with him as he lay in his bath; once alongside, she whipped out a kitchen knife hidden in her skirts, and plunged it into the heart of the naked revolutionary. Marat's body with its wound was exhibited in public the next day. At her trial, Charlotte was unrepentant: 'I have killed one man to save a hundred thousand,' she said. She lost her head on the guillotine for her pains.

Some Normans in the conservative rural fringes also actively supported a Royalist counter-revolutionary movement known as the **Chouannerie** (from *chouan*, meaning screech owl), which had begun in Brittany. Their great hope was that when a force of aristocratic exiles landed to help them, with British support, sympathizers would flock from all over France and the pagan Republic would be tossed aside. In the event, however, the invasion attempt in 1795 was a flop, and its leaders met a sticky end. Dissenting voices rumbled on in the Cotentin and the Bocage, often echoed by those of young peasants who resisted enlistment for the Revolutionary and Napoleonic wars. By the 1800s, though, no one realistically believed the *ancien régime* would return.

Normandy in the 19th Century

The political turmoil that racked France from Napoleon's declaration as Emperor in 1804, through a succession of regimes in an impossible search for consensus and legitimacy, was scarcely felt in the fields and orchards of rural Normandy. Its inhabitants' worries were not political but economic. Under Napoleon, its ports were crippled by the British blockade. Compared to the rest of France, Normandy was still a wealthy region, but when protectionist tariffs were removed from grain in 1828, and Normandy had to compete with other producers, widespread rioting broke out.

The early 19th century was a period of grand architectural schemes, notably the completion of the huge naval port at Cherbourg, begun under **Louis XVI** and only finished in the 1850s during **Napoleon III**'s Second Empire. In 1858 a brand new railway between Cherbourg and Paris allowed transatlantic passengers to step off their liners and jump straight onto a train to the capital. The grand station on Cherbourg harbour where they disembarked is currently being restored.

Elsewhere, the coming of the railway gave added impetus to a new industry that had made its first appearance in Dieppe: tourism. Queen Hortense of Holland, Napoleon's sister-in-law, had declared that sea water was good for the constitution, and was one of the first celebrities to dip her toes in the chilly Channel. She was followed by the arch-royalist **Duchesse de Berry** in 1824, who, following a trend she had observed in exile in Brighton, was carried in a sedan chair to the water's edge to indulge in the new pastime of bathing. It seemed risqué, but others followed suit and resorts sprang up in Trouville and Deauville, their beaches lined with hundreds of changing huts. After the Paris–Trouville railway opened in 1846, enabling Parisians to reach the sea in less than three hours, beach tourism became big business.

The limpid light of Normandy's coast attracted another type of visitor too: painters, and above all the Impressionists. The great forerunner of Impressionism

Eugène Boudin, and later Claude Monet, Pierre-Auguste Renoir and many others, set up their easels on Normandy's beaches, and painted their visitors in their hats and parasols. The novelist Guy de Maupassant, another local, compared Trouville in his 1888 novel *Pierre et Jean* to a 'long garden full of brilliantly coloured flowers,' covered in 'sunshades of all colours, hats of all shapes, dresses of all shades.'

World Wars

The First World War was fought far from Normandy, but its physical, emotional and economic impact was still huge, as in the whole of France. From 1914 the well-heeled Le Havre suburb of Ste-Adresse, beloved of the Impressionists, became the seat of the Belgian government. By contrast, the effects of the Second World War would be very direct, and devastating, in every part of Normandy.

The Germans entered Normandy at Forges-les-Eaux on 7 June and Rouen on 9 June 1940, days that local inhabitants have never forgotten. In 1942, the Allies conducted a large-scale amphibious raid against Dieppe with disastrous results: of the 6,000 men involved – most of them Canadians – more than half were killed, captured or wounded, and over 900 Canadians lost their lives (*see* p.104). This debacle made it clear that a heavily defended port could not be attacked head-on. Instead, they would choose the vast sandy beaches of western Normandy to launch an amphibious invasion of Europe. Normandy had seen nothing like the campaign that began on 6 June 1944 since the Hundred Years' War. For a full overview of the D-Day Landings and the Normandy battles, *see* the following chapter, pp.39–46.

Modern Normandy

Devastated by the war, Normandy spent the late 1940s and the 1950s slowly rebuilding its towns and cities. In some, like Le Havre, avant-garde architects were given free rein to experiment with new styles and materials; in others, new buildings sought to replicate traditional ones, using local stone or half-timbering. The construction boom provided much-needed employment for agricultural workers weary with working on the land or faced with increasing mechanization, spurring an exodus from the countryside that has continued ever since. The dead, meanwhile, were given solemn resting places in the many war cemeteries. It would be a full 20 years, however, before the region was anything like back to normal.

Near-total destruction of the region's infrastructure also gave Normandy the chance to start again, with a network of bridges, roads and railways that is now superior to that of many other regions of France. Economically, while Normandy has remained predominantly an agricultural region, it has also diversified into new industries, especially in the Seine valley around Rouen and Le Havre. Nuclear reprocessing plants also appeared, including the La Hague plant near Cherbourg, the largest of its kind in the world. In farming, large-scale cereal production outstripped the output of the traditional livestock farms whose dairy cattle produce the rich cheeses and creams for which Normandy is famous. In recent years, though, traditional agriculture, such as cattle and cider farming, has been boosted by Normandy's new major growth industry, tourism, whether in the form of Parisians flocking to second homes in coastal resorts like Deauville and Honfleur or foreigners flooding in to visit treasures such as Mont-St-Michel and Bayeux. More than ten million people visit Normandy every year. One of its biggest attractions is the D-Day landing beaches; since the 50th anniversary of the invasion in 1994, in particular, these beaches have changed from being the symbol of Normandy's devastation to a major source of its present prosperity.

D-Day and the Battle of Normandy

03

'Once the green light had come on everyone yelled "Go, go, go" and nearly fell over each other to get out of the plane. We had to get out fast, fast, fast. My gear, which was strapped to my leg, was so heavy I knew that all I had to do was to swing my leg out and the slipstream would pull the rest of me out. My turn came. Out I went into the night. I whirled around with my eyes shut, feeling a delicious freedom – no more engine roar, no more sickly smell of aircraft fuel or cigarettes. I was gently coming down, my canopy was extended and the earth was rushing up to meet me.'

After a year of secret preparations, the D-Day landings had finally begun, and Private Hugh Mowat, of the 3rd Brigade of the British 6th Airborne Division, would be one of the first Allied troops to touch down on French soil. The time was a few minutes after midnight on 6 June 1944, and the Division's mission was to secure the crossings over the River Orne and the canal between Caen and the sea before Allied troops landed by ship on the beaches just to the north later that morning.

Land they did, in their thousands, spewed ashore by landing craft like plankton from the stomachs of massive whales. Supported by a vast air umbrella and naval gunfire that had begun hours earlier, they landed on five invasion beaches stretching from Caen to the Cotentin peninsula. American troops landed on two beaches, codenamed Utah, at the southern end of the Cotentin, and Omaha, in western Calvados, while British and Canadian troops landed on Gold, Juno and Sword beaches between Arromanches and Ouistreham. Many troops suffered desperately from seasickness after their journey across a stormy Channel, some were dragged down by the weight of their equipment as soon as they tried to wade ashore, and all faced a rain of German fire. For two grim months more than a million men fought in the lush fields of Normandy to decide the fate of Europe, in some of the bloodiest carnage of the Second World War.

The D-Day Landings

The decision to launch the invasion, codenamed Overlord, had been confirmed at the Eureka conference of the Western allies in November 1943, when flesh was put on the bones of a plan by Churchill, Roosevelt and Canadian prime minister Mackenzie King. The American **General Dwight 'Ike' Eisenhower** was named Supreme Allied Commander, while **General Sir Bernard Montgomery**, 'Monty' to the British public, fresh from the North African and Italy campaigns, was to be Land Forces Commander.

The most direct invasion route was across the Strait of Dover to the Pas-de-Calais, but German defences were strong there, so Normandy was chosen as the best option. It gave an added advantage of surprise, as the Germans were sure the Allies would land near Calais. Moreover, the disastrous 1942 attack on Dieppe had shown that a head-on assault on a well-defended harbour was out of the question. Instead, the invasion troops would land near a major harbour – Cherbourg – and establish a firm hold on the beaches before seizing the port and advancing inland. Until a port had been captured, supplies and men would be brought ashore using a novel concept: floating prefabricated harbours codenamed 'Mulberries', which would be towed across the Channel in sections. One harbour would be assembled at Arromanches in the British sector, the other off Omaha Beach.

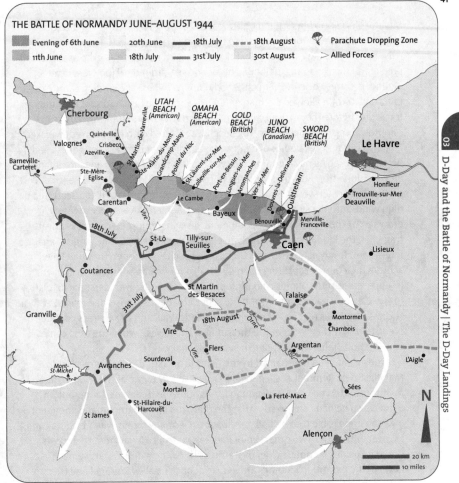

THE BATTLE OF NORMANDY JUNE–AUGUST 1944

Legend:
- Evening of 6th June
- 11th June
- 20th June
- 18th July
- 18th July
- 31st July
- 18th August
- 30st August
- Parachute Dropping Zone
- Allied Forces

For a year, troops, including many who had never seen a gun before, trained on the beaches of England. British troops were joined by nearly two million US and Canadian servicemen, plus contingents from other Commonwealth countries and occupied nations such as Poland or Belgium. No one who took part in the exercises knew exactly where they were going, or when. Aerial photographs and holiday postcards were studied avidly to familiarize troops with the beaches they were about to land on. When the big day finally came, the crossing had to be postponed for a nail-biting 24 hours because a freak storm was whipping the Channel. Mowat recalls the tension as the men attended a farewell religious service and their 'last supper'. 'Nobody could eat much – most of the food got thrown away,' he remembers. Within minutes his 6th Airborne Division were winging their way across the water to hold the eastern approaches to the landing area, while the US 82nd and 101st Airborne flew to the Cotentin Peninsula to secure the exits from Utah Beach (one of these US soldiers, Private John Steele, famously dropped into history by impaling his parachute on the spire of the church in Ste-Mère-Eglise).

Meanwhile, 12,000 aircraft and 5,200 vessels carrying 135,000 men and 20,000 vehicles had started their voyage into the unknown.

By the end of D-Day, the casualty toll was grim – if not quite as grim as some had predicted. Of 156,000 troops landed by air and sea, around 10,000 were dead or wounded, some 2,000 of them on 'Bloody Omaha', where the landing came close to failure. Its terrain allowed German defenders above the beach to spot the landing force long before they arrived, and to rake them with murderous fire. Within minutes of the 6.30am landing, the beach was littered with the debris of wrecked landing craft and the bodies of dead and wounded. Nonetheless, toughness and heroism, backed by naval gunfire, allowed those who survived to advance inland, and on 8 June they linked up with the British 50th Division from Gold Beach at Port-en-Bessin. Further west, US Airborne troops had a tough time of it too, scattered by high winds into the swamps of the Douve and Merderet rivers. Many were drowned by the weight of their equipment. Elsewhere, despite countless private tragedies, the landings went largely to plan. By darkness on 6 June, Anglo-Canadian forces were firmly established on their three beaches, although they had failed to achieve their aim of capturing Caen. On Utah, American troops were virtually unopposed. Months of meticulous preparation, combined with personal heroism, massive air and naval support, and the achievement of surprise, had made D-Day a success. The Allies had breached Hitler's 'Atlantic Wall', and the *Führer*'s confident prediction that they 'will get the thrashing of their lives... when the time comes it will be a huge relief' was looking increasingly shaky.

Surprise had been maintained by the Allies to an astonishing degree. **Field Marshal Erwin Rommel**, the legendary 'Desert Fox', was one of the few German military minds who believed Normandy might be the threatened zone, but on 4 June even he had been so sure that the tides and bad weather made imminent invasion impossible that he had gone back to Germany for his wife's birthday and to meet with Hitler. Two other senior generals were also away from their posts, and General Speidel, Rommel's chief of staff, was throwing a dinner party when first news of the paratroop landings arrived. He at once recalled Rommel and tried to get German tanks on the road, as orders and counter-orders flew back and forth between himself and Hitler. The *Führer* was in cocky mood: 'The news couldn't be better,' he declared. 'As long as they were in Britain we couldn't get them. Now we have them where we can destroy them.' Expecting the beach defences to achieve that task, Hitler cancelled orders for the panzer (tank) divisions to move north. By the time he changed his mind it was too late to intervene that day, and the panzers would have to wait until 7 June to attack the Allied bridgehead.

The Battle of Normandy

Successful as the landing was, though, the weeks that followed were long and bloody. Little went according to plan. From Gold Beach the British liberated historic Bayeux on 7 June, which miraculously escaped virtually intact. Plans to seize Carpiquet airport and Caen, however, proved more elusive. Montgomery's advance towards Caen stalled when German armoured reserves converged on the city. His forces repulsed these counterattacks, but without gaining much ground. The struggle for Caen would be a grim six-week battle of attrition, during which British bombers unleashed more than 2,500 tons of bombs on the city. Only after two days of bitter fighting in the rubble-strewn streets were the northern part of the city and the airport captured. Even then, he Germans still controlled southern Caen, the gateway to the Caen-Falaise plain.

American plans had equally chequered results. The Germans temporarily slowed the advance of General 'Lightning' Joe Collins' VII Corps from Utah towards Cherbourg along the Quinéville Ridge. The advance of Major-General Leonard Gerow's V Corps on St Lô from Omaha fared no better. After Isigny fell on 9 June the way to St-Lô – vital for controlling the roads of western Normandy – seemed open, but the treacherous 'waffle-like' terrain of the Norman *bocage* made progress slow, as every hedgerow provided the Germans with natural defensive positions. Collins

03 D-Day and the Battle of Normandy | The Battle of Normandy

Retracing the Battle

Virtually every area of the Normandy battlefields has its museum or memorial. For those interested in following the course of the D-Day landings and the battles that followed, eight itineraries have been identified by local tourist authorities. They're clearly signposted on roads with signs with a gull logo and *Normandie Terre-Liberté*, and a free booklet on the routes is available from all local tourist offices. Also, anyone who visits one of a long list of World War II museums in Normandy is entitled to reduced-price admission at all the others for 30 days after the date of the first ticket (this applies to all museums except those in Port-en-Bessin, Falaise and L'Aigle; you must show the first ticket). For anyone visiting the battlefields for the first time, it's a good idea to start with one of the big museums that give an overview of the campaign, at Caen, Bayeux or Arromanches.

Useful local websites include *www.normandie memoire.com*, *www.dday-overlord.com* and the site of the Pegasus Bridge and Arromanches museums, *www.normandy1944.com*. All are available in French and English.

Listed here are the main 1944-related museums and exhibits in Normandy:

On or Near the Beaches
From east to west. Most sites are dealt with fully in chapter 14, pp.264–83.

Merville-Franceville: Musée de la Batterie de Merville, *see p.230*.
Ranville-Bénouville: Mémorial Pegasus, Pegasus Bridge, *see p.264*.
Ouistreham: Le Musée du Mur de l'Atlantique *and* Musée No. 4 Commando, *see p.266*.
Caen: Mémorial de Caen, *see p.262*.

Douvres-la-Délivrande: Musée Radar, *see p.266*.
Courseulles-sur-Mer: Juno Beach Centre, *see p.267*.
Ver-sur-Mer: Musée America–Musée Gold Beach, *see p.268*.
Arromanches: Musée du Débarquement *and* Arromanches 360, *see pp.268–9*.
Longues-sur-Mer: Batterie de Longues, *see p.269*.
Bayeux: Musée-Mémorial de la Bataille de Normandie, *see p.289*.
Port-en-Bessin: Musée des Epaves Sous-marines du Débarquement, *see p.273*.
Omaha Beach (St-Laurent-sur-Mer, Vierville-sur-Mer): Musée D-Day Omaha *and* Musée-Mémorial d'Omaha Beach, *see p.273–5*.
Pointe du Hoc, *see p.275*.
Grandcamp-Maisy: Musée des Rangers, *see p.276*.
Utah Beach (Ste-Marie-du-Mont): Musée du Débarquement d'Utah Beach, *see p.280, and* Dead Man's Corner Museum, *see p.278*.
Ste-Mère Eglise: Musée Airborne, *see p.282*.
Azeville: Batterie d'Azeville, *see p.282*.
Quinéville: Musée de la Liberté, *see p.335*.

Elsewhere in Normandy
In the order that they appear in the guide:

L'Aigle: Musée Juin '44, *see p.203*.
Tilly-sur-Seulles: Musée de la Bataille de Tilly, *see p.294*.
St-Martin-des-Besaces: Musée de la Percée du Bocage, *see p.302*.
Falaise: Musée Août 44, *see p.305*.
Montormel: Mémorial de Montormel, *see p.306*.
Cherbourg: Musée de la Guerre et de la Libération, Fort du Roule, *see p.331*.
Avranches: Musée de la Seconde Guerre Mondiale, *see p.367*.

was forced to abandon the idea of a direct advance on Cherbourg, so instead struck west on 15 June and cut off the Cotentin Peninsula, isolating the port. Only on 22 June did Collins launch an all-out attack, entering the city on the 26th. The Americans had finally captured their much-needed harbour, six days behind schedule, but the Germans had left the port in such a ruined state that it would be unusable for many weeks.

There were other obstacles too. The greatest was the weather – the precise factor that Hitler had expected would thwart the Allied invasion. On 19 June a freak summer storm, the worst in living memory, smashed the floating harbour at Omaha and severely damaged the Mulberry at Arromanches, seriously obstructing the Allies' ability to land supplies. One witness recalled how '...the DUKWs (amphibious trucks) wallowed like hippopotamuses between the coasters and the shore. In places... a few landing craft beached. Some broke their backs, crushed by the surf as a dog crushes a bone'.

Despite reinforcement, General Omar Bradley's US First Army made painfully slow progress when it renewed its offensive towards St-Lô on 3 July. Eventually the US 29th Division managed to seize the ridge north of the town, and advanced across the St-Lô–Bayeux highway. On 18 July the hard-pressed Germans abandoned St-Lô.

On the same day Montgomery launched 'Operation Goodwood', a massive and much-criticized operation to shatter German defences south of Caen and open the way to the Falaise plain. German resistance was still intense, despite the fact that their commander, Rommel, had been seriously wounded while inspecting his defences (ironically, the village where he was taken to get first-aid was Ste-Foy-de-Montgommery). Only heavy bombing and artillery fire enabled the British and Canadians to crash through German defences below Caen, eventually reaching the Bourguébus ridge on 18 July. But German counterattacks stopped the British advance, causing heavy losses in tanks and men that Britain could ill afford. Among the casualties was the painter Rex Whistler, whose whimsical decoration of a room in Brighton Pavilion had only been completed on the eve of the invasion.

On 24 July, though, US forces launched 'Operation Cobra' against German positions southwest of St-Lô. Two armoured divisions broke the German front and pushed their way into open country. The break-out from Normandy had begun. Cobra was only the start of a larger campaign aimed at seizing the ports of Brittany and bursting out into central France. As the US First Army was rupturing the German line, General Patton's Third Army moved up behind it. Once the German front began to collapse, Patton's armoured spearhead passed through the US infantry and raced into the enemy rear. They seized the gateway to Brittany at Avranches on 30 July and reached Nantes and the Loire by 12 August, before swivelling eastwards towards Paris. This was one of the fastest armoured thrusts of the war, covering over 200 miles in less than a week.

Desperate, Hitler ordered a German counteroffensive to retake Avranches and seal off the American break-out. His commanders were flabbergasted at his unreal demands, and this great blunder would complete the decimation of German forces in Normandy. At Mortain on 6–7 August the Americans smashed German efforts to push through to Avranches. Refusing to look defeat in the face, Hitler dug his heels in deeper and demanded that his troops try harder, stating that 'the greatest daring, determination, imagination must give wings to all echelons of command. Each and every man must believe in victory.' On 16 August his demoralized commander Field Marshal von Kluge told him that the only feasible strategy was to withdraw behind the Seine. He was rewarded for his troubles by being sacked on the spot, and later committed suicide.

The Germans were being strangled by a noose the Allies were forming around the 'Falaise Pocket' between Argentan and Falaise, in a pincer movement from the north and south. From the north, Montgomery's troops – British, Canadian and Polish – were pushing down towards William the Conqueror's home town of Falaise, 32km south of Caen. The US First Army was moving eastwards from Mortain towards Flers, while Patton's Third Army was heading north from Le Mans towards Alençon and Argentan. Bradley then controversially ordered part of the

War Cemeteries of Normandy

The cemeteries with the graves of those who died in Normandy are naturally some of the most moving – and most appreciated – memorials to the 1944 battles. Countries differ in their approaches to their war dead. The US government repatriated large numbers of the Americans who had died to be buried at home, and gathered the remains of others – including men killed in all the battles in northwest Europe, not just in Normandy – to be buried together in the two cemeteries listed below. In contrast, the practice of the Commonwealth War Graves Commission (responsible for the British, Canadian and Polish cemeteries) has been that men should normally be buried as close as possible to where they fell, so that graves are distributed among several smaller, more intimate cemeteries. The Commission is also the only authority that customarily enables relatives to place personal messages on gravestones.

American
Colleville-sur-Mer, behind Omaha Beach: 9,387 graves.
Saint-James (Montjoie-St-Martin), between Avranches and Fougères: 4,408 graves.

British
Banneville-Sannerville, between Caen and Troarn: 2,175 graves.
Bayeux: 4,868 graves (and 1,837 names on the nearby Memorial).
Bazenville-Ryes, east of Bayeux: 987 graves.
Brouay, between Caen and Bayeux: 377 graves.
Cambes-en-Plaine, between Caen and Courseulles: 224 graves.
Chouain (Jérusalem), between Bayeux and Tilly-sur-Seulles: 40 graves.

Douvres-la-Délivrande, between Caen and Luc-sur-Mer: 927 graves.
Fontenay-le-Pesnel, west of Caen: 520 graves.
Hermanville-sur-Mer, near Sword Beach: 986 graves.
Hottot-les-Bagues, between Caen and Caumont-l'Eventé: 965 graves.
Ranville, near Pegasus Bridge: 2,151 graves.
St-Charles-de-Percy, near Bény-Bocage: 792 graves.
St-Désir-de-Lisieux, near Lisieux: 469 graves.
St-Manvieu, west of Caen: 2,186 graves
Secqueville-en-Bessin, between Caen and Bayeux: 117 graves
Tilly-sur-Seulles, between Caen and Bayeux: 1,224 graves

Canadian
Bény-sur-Mer–Reviers, near Juno Beach: 2,048 graves.
Cintheaux, between Caen and Falaise: 2,959 graves.

French
Nécropole des Gateys, north of Alençon: 17 graves.

German
La Cambe, near Isigny: 21,300 graves.
Huisnes-sur-Mer, near Mont-St-Michel: 11,956 graves.
Marigny, between St-Lô and Coutances: 11,169 graves.
Orglandes, south of Valognes: 10,152 graves.
St-Désir-de-Lisieux, near Lisieux: 3,735 graves.

Polish
Urville-Langannerie, north of Falaise: 650 graves.

Third Army further eastward, towards the Seine. This left the 'Falaise Gap' open, and allowed many Germans to escape.

Montgomery finally reached the august ruins of William's castle in Falaise on 17 August. The last decisive and bloody act of the Battle of Normandy was played out on 19 August at Montormel, near Chambois, where the heroes were the 1st Polish Armoured Division. The Poles formed a key obstacle on the German armies' escape route out of the pocket, and came under heavy attack. Corpses of men and horses carpeted the normally picturesque valley below the hill defended by the Poles, and at one point it appeared they could not resist any longer. Then, at the eleventh hour, the sound of Canadian tanks was heard. The battle of the Falaise Pocket had been won, and Hitler's Army Group B almost annihilated. Three days later the Allies crossed the Seine and entered Paris, less than three months after landing on French shores.

Victory in Normandy was hard-gained. Allied casualties numbered some 209,672, of which 36,976 had been killed. Thousands of French civilians had lost their lives and homes. German casualties numbered around 300,000. The war still had to be won, as Allied troops moved on into Belgium and Holland. In Normandy, the long, painful process of rebuilding lives, homes and cities – which still goes on – had just begun.

Art and Culture

04

Art in Normandy

'Do as I do: learn to... value the sea, the light, the blue sky,' advised the painter Eugène Boudin. His 'pupil' was the 15-year-old Claude Monet, struggling to establish himself as a caricaturist in his home town of Le Havre. Following Boudin's advice, he set up his easel on the beaches, turning them into a great outdoor *atelier* where he could follow the fleeting effects of light. 'It was like a veil tearing,' Monet famously declared later. '[Now] I understood. I knew what painting might be.' Impressionism, as it would become known, had been born, and its birthplace was Normandy.

The key was the region's wonderful light, reflected on clouds scudding over its sandy beaches, chalky cliffs, the façade of Rouen cathedral, or the mirror-glass waters of the Seine. This light, of course, was ever-changing, which meant that brush strokes had to be dashed down to give an 'impression'.

Artists drawn by the light flocked to Normandy, braving the elements to paint on beaches, clifftops and riverside meadows. Many, like Pissarro, Renoir, Degas and Sisley, arrived from Paris. Others, such as JMW Turner, Richard Bonington, John Sell Cotman and later Walter Sickert crossed the Channel from England, while Johann Jongkind – sometimes dubbed 'the first impressionist' – arrived from Holland. Later, American painters such as Theodore Robinson, Willard Metcalf and Lilla Cabot Perry made a pilgrimage to Giverny to seek inspiration from Monet, who had set up home and garden there.

Poussin to Millet

They were not, of course, the first artists to discover Normandy. **Nicolas Poussin**, born near Les Andelys in 1594, became the most influential painter of his time – Voltaire even claimed that French painting was born with Poussin. However, his greatest works were produced not in Normandy but in Italy, where he spent most of his life, painting religious scenes and themes from Classical antiquity. Several of his works are now in the Musée des Beaux-Arts in Rouen, and there is one large painting by him proudly on show in the Musée Poussin in Les Andelys. The early 19th century saw a growing interest in Normandy, especially from English landscape artists such as **Charles Eastlake** and Romantics like **Turner**, who was introduced to the area by the Anglo-French painter **Richard Bonington** and whose paintings of Dieppe and Rouen would strongly influence the later French Impressionists. This period's chief native-born artist was **Théodore Géricault**, born in Rouen in 1791 and credited with launching Romantic painting in France. His great passion was for horses, and his equine paintings fill an entire room of the museum in Rouen.

More rustic and naturalistic, some say political, subjects were portrayed by **Jean-François Millet**, born in 1814 in tiny Gruchy, near Gréville-Hague on the wild Cap de la Hague in the Cotentin (*see* pp.340–43). From a poor farming family, Millet spent his boyhood working in the fields, and peasants formed the subjects of many of his paintings. His insistence on showing peasant life as it really was, rather than churning out the idealized country scenes his audience were used to, prompted critics to label his art as subversive. However, many of his paintings became enormously famous, such as *Les Glaneuses* (The Gleaners), showing three women scraping up leftover corn after the harvest, which still decorates biscuit tins and Camembert boxes today. His works greatly inspired the young Van Gogh, who produced his own versions of the same scenes. Although Millet studied in Cherbourg (whose art museum houses many of his paintings), much of his life was spent in Barbizon near Paris, where he died in 1875 in circumstances almost as impoverished as those of his subjects. Millet also produced often-sombre portraits; one of the most touching is of his consumptive wife, Pauline Ono, a Norman-style Mona Lisa that is now in the Cherbourg museum.

Millet paid frequent visits to Le Havre, where he met **Eugène Boudin**, a sailor's son who was struggling to make a living as an artist. After years in Paris copying classical masterpieces for rich patrons he had returned to the beaches of his childhood, declaring that 'nature remains far richer than I can paint her.' Using the sands, cloud-studded skies and parasol-equipped lady visitors as his subjects, Boudin grew obsessed by light and space, and the restless motion of the elements. 'Three brush strokes from nature,' he added, 'are worth more than two days' studio work at the easel.'

Impressionist Normandy

Boudin's preference for painting *en plein air* proved catching. **Courbet**, **Whistler**, **Monet** and the maverick Dutch watercolourist **Jongkind** all joined him on the beach at Trouville or at the Ferme St-Siméon (now an exclusive hotel) outside Honfleur. In 1872 Monet hurriedly produced *Impression, Sunrise*, a Turneresque painting of ships in a foggy Le Havre that accidentally gave Impressionism its name, after art critic Louis Leroy dismissed its 'impressionist' style. The tag always irritated Monet, who said he'd only called the painting 'Impression' because 'it could not pass for a view of Le Havre.'

Whether Monet liked the name or not, a movement had been born. It was formed by artists such as **Manet**, **Degas**, **Renoir** and **Sisley**, all of them fed up with academic teaching and the rejection of their works by the stuffy Paris Salon. **Pissarro** and **Cézanne** followed, and in 1874 these artists organized their own show to rival the official Salon, which included Monet's sunrise at Le Havre. As more artists abandoned studios for beaches and riverbanks, they earned grudging acceptance from the critics.

Unspoilt Normandy, conveniently near Paris and rich in tranquil rivers reflecting ever-changing skies, was the perfect outdoor studio. The lengths to which artists would go to capture nature's dramas could be extreme. On the coast, Monet would often sit painting for so long that icicles formed on his beard and snow settled on his head, and while painting Etretat's famous rock arches he was once swamped by a huge wave – because, he said, he'd misread the tide tables.

Another reason why artists like Monet painted in hostile weather was to flee another type of visitor that was then arriving on the Normandy coasts: tourists. By the end of the century, neo-urban villas had pretty much ousted rustic fishermen's cottages around many towns. Artists and tourists were also a source of mutual fascination: tourist guides would point out which artist was painting where and which villa they were staying in; the artists, for their part found the visitors fertile fodder, leaving a legacy of paintings of parasols and petticoats, polo and poodles. Occasionally there was conflict. The reclusive Monet often pretended the holiday-makers weren't there, and to look at his paintings of already-fashionable Etretat from 1883–6 you'd think it was still a sleepy village. Only one of his Etretat paintings has human figures in it, *Boats in Winter Quarters*, and they are fishermen, not tourists. Boudin produced more paintings of Parisian beach toffs than you can shake a stick at, but was caustic about the beach at Trouville, 'a frightful masquerade' peopled by 'a bunch of do-nothing poseurs', and almost felt bad about painting these 'gilded parasites who have so triumphant an air.' But, like them or not, artists made good use of these paradings. Even Monet's beaches became peopled with the flowers of Parisian fashion, as in his 1870 painting the *Hôtel des Rôches Noires*, of Trouville's grandest hotel, opened in 1866.

Later, as Monet became ever more obsessed with capturing light, his paintings became more abstract. Just one painting of a subject didn't really capture its essence. The light was always changing. Hence, from around 1890 he began to paint series of paintings on a single subject in different lights. He depicted Rouen cathedral's west façade, for example, no fewer than 18 times. After his move to Giverny (*see* p.150), Monet's paintings became more abstract still, often with contrasting areas of pure colour, as in his extraordinary series of waterlilies.

Meanwhile, other artists were equally busy. The Ferme St-Siméon, where Mme Toutain produced superb dinners, attracted Pissarro, Cézanne, Corot, Courbet, Sisley and the poet Baudelaire. Another centre was Dieppe and neighbouring Pourville and Varengeville, frequented by Monet, Degas, Renoir and Pissarro, whose 1902 *Dieppe Harbour* and painting of the *Eglise St-Jacques* are among his finest works. The English always had a soft spot for the historic port: Whistler was a frequent visitor, as was **Walter Sickert**, who lived there from 1899 to 1905 and was a regular at the Café Suisse (some say because he was actually Jack the Ripper and took refuge in Dieppe to avoid being identified in Britain, but this theory is a matter of personal taste). Rouen was a popular spot too, and not just Monet but also Renoir and Pissarro painted there.

Fauves, Cubists and Duchamp

In the first decade of the 20th century the spotlight moved to Le Havre, where an avant-garde movement called Fauvism was taking off. *Fauves* means 'wild beasts', which is what one critic compared the movement's proponents to for their untamed, primitive use of colour. Fauvism had been started in Paris in 1905 by Henri Matisse and others, inspired by the intense, pure colours of Van Gogh and the 'Nabis' group, which followed Gauguin. Fauvism did not last long, but it was enough to inspire three painters in Le Havre: Emile-Othon Friesz, **Raoul Dufy** and **Georges Braque**.

Dufy, son of an accountant, was taught in Le Havre by Charles Lhullier. In Paris he followed an Impressionist style for a while, before discovering Matisse and the Fauves. Matisse's 1904 *Luxe, Calme et Volupté* was inspirational: 'I understood all the new reasons for painting,' Dufy wrote, '...as I gazed at this miracle of imagination translated into design and colour.' Imagination played a key part in his ebullient, voluptuously colourful paintings, many of which depict Havrais festivals with fluttering flags, bathers and boats. Later Dufy dabbled in Cubism, and developed a passion for blue. There's an excellent collection of Dufys in Le Havre's Musée Malraux, although his lovely *Old Houses at the Harbour in Le Havre* is in Caen.

Georges Braque's family had moved to the port in 1890, when he was eight. Having begun as a decorator, he also studied art under Lhullier before going on to Paris. After experimenting in Fauvism in 1906–7 he went on to formulate Cubism, liberating form as much as Fauvism had liberated colour. By 1910 the term 'Cubist' was being applied to Braque's friend Picasso, who would make the movement famous. From the 1950s Braque spent his last years in Varengeville-sur-Mer outside Dieppe, whose *château-musée* houses a good collection of his later works (*see* p.105). Braque and his wife are buried in the churchyard of Varengeville's tiny clifftop Norman church, which has wonderful stained glass designed by the artist; their grave is marked by a solitary dove.

In the midst of the Cubist revolution, Normandy produced another clutch of hugely influential modern artists, the **Duchamp** brothers, born in Blainville-Crevon near Rouen. The eldest, Gaston, was an early Cubist who, under the pseudonym Jacques Villon, spawned a provocative new style mixed with neo-Impressionism. **Raymond Duchamp-Villon** was a sculptor who, before dying in World War I, worked in a Cubist, abstract style. One of his most famous pieces is *The Horse*, brimming with movement. Most famous of all was **Marcel Duchamp**, who dabbled in Fauvism, Cubism and Orphism before becoming a prime mover in Dadaism. He never stayed still long enough to be exclusively identified with any one group, but a common thread in his ideas was that they challenged every traditional definition of art. Some of his most controversial works were everyday objects that he exhibited as art, called 'ready-mades', such as a urinal signed with the pseudonym 'R Mutt'.

Norman Architecture

The Explosion of Romanesque

The flowering of Norman architecture began with the arrival of Benedictine monks. They were the only real stabilizing force in the area at a time when, under the Franks, the region was forever torn by strife. A key player was **St Ouen**, Bishop of Rouen from 640; he established the abbey of **St-Wandrille**, while his protégé St Philibert built the magnificent abbey at **Jumièges**, helped by handy connections with King Clovis II. These two pre-Romanesque jewels became potent symbols of Frankish civilization.

The arrival of the Vikings brought havoc and destruction. This lasted until peace was agreed and the Norsemen were given their own Duchy under Rollo in 911 (*see* p.29), which, in contrast, allowed a flowering of Benedictine architecture and ushered in the great age of Norman Romanesque. Great abbeys such as Jumièges were rebuilt (in 1037), while new cathedrals and abbey churches, like **Mont-St-Michel**, **Coutances**, **Fécamp**, **Bayeux**, and **Bernay**, and **St-Etienne** and **La Trinité** in Caen, went up amid a frenzy of enthusiasm. The chronicler Ralph Glaber remarked in the year 1000 on a 'white crown of churches' that covered the country like a mantel of snow. Large-scale pilgrimages, which soared in popularity at this time, helped to spread ideas and influences. The close links that existed between Normandy and the English throne (Edward the Confessor lived in Normandy from the age of 13 to 40) meant that similar architectural styles were followed in England, before and after the Conquest of 1066. Westminster Abbey, rebuilt by Edward, and Durham, from the 11th–12th centuries, were strongly influenced by Norman counterparts.

The style known as Norman Romanesque – or just Norman – is so-called because its architects borrowed many elements from Gallo-Roman buildings, still standing at the time. Other influences included the court architecture of Charlemagne, eastern Christian churches in Syria and Armenia, and Islamic buildings. The Benedictine abbey of Cluny in Burgundy, begun in 910 and often considered to be France's first Romanesque abbey, was immensely influential, as it was throughout the whole of Europe. In Normandy Cluny's influence can be seen in the abbey at Bernay (1017–55) and many other monuments.

Typically, Romanesque buildings were built on a cross-shaped plan and vaulted entirely in stone, adapting the Roman barrel vault. In Normandy, however, because churches were built so tall, the barrel vault was often abandoned in favour of a wooden roof over the nave, and groined vaulting (where two semicircular arches cross) was developed for the aisles. Jumièges and the two abbey churches in Caen all had wooden roofs, although in Caen they were later replaced with stone groin vaults. Romanesque churches are characterized by rounded arches, stout round pillars and decorated capitals, but the decoration is mostly abstract and geometrical rather than figurative. Zigzags and chevrons are common motifs: however, look carefully and you'll often find monsters and men hiding on top of them, allegorical figures that defy explanation but give these churches a quirky, irreverent charm. Abbey churches usually have towers either side of the west front, giving them an H-like look, and a square 'lantern' tower over the central transept with tall windows to give more light inside. The nave was usually divided into three storeys, which broke up the monotony of the massively thick walls: the nave at the bottom, consisting of great semicircular arches – buttresses not yet having been invented – then a gallery or *triforium*; and finally, on the top, a narrower clerestory.

This was also the great age for building castles, strategically placed on isolated hills or loops in rivers. As well as housing the lord of the manor, a medieval castle defended the village beside it and in times of trouble was a refuge for the local population. Early Norman castles were of a motte-and-bailey type, with a simple, wooden tower within a larger enclosure ringed by a moat. From about 1050 they were built more solidly of stone, and acquired comforts like latrines. The most formidable was Château-Gaillard, built by Richard the Lionheart in 1196 to keep Normandy out of the hands of the French king Philippe Auguste (*see* p.171). Its remains are now a precious relic.

Norman Gothic

With sweeping vertical lines soaring towards heaven, Gothic architecture expressed another wave of spiritual enthusiasm, and marked the transition to the High Middle Ages. As Europe entered a newly wealthy era there was time and money to spare for things spiritual: building techniques had also advanced, with innovations such as rib-vaults, pointed arches, naturalistic ornamentation and flying buttresses. The result was a dazzling explosion of luminosity: never before had so much space and height been enclosed by so little stonework, allowing light to flood in. Slim walls, no longer required to carry so much weight once it was taken by the new buttresses, could now show off another medium: stained glass.

The development of the new style is normally credited to Paris, whose cathedral of St-Denis, begun in 1136, is considered the first complete 'Gothic' church. However, Normandy had experimented with rib-vaulting long before that; in the late 11th century, in the cathedral of **Bayeux**, there were already two arches resembling rib-vaults in the north bell-tower. The Normans probably took their cue from England, where Durham cathedral, whose choir, transept and nave were all vaulted, was begun in 1093. At **Jumièges**, the chapterhouse was rib-vaulted in the early 1100s. The most perfect examples of Norman rib-vaulting, though, were the **Abbaye-aux-Hommes** and **Abbaye-aux-Dames** at Caen, which both had vaults with six ribs instead of the usual four. Gothic and older Norman styles merged with apparent ease, as in **Lisieux** and **Coutances** cathedrals and Rouen cathedral's **Tour St-Romain**, all from the late 12th century. Superb belfries housed in tall stone spires sprang up too, and ornamentation evolved with acanthus and clover leaves decorating capitals and cornerstones.

In the 13th century architects played with the decoration but not the structure, producing, between around 1230 and 1350, a sophisticated version of earlier Gothic known in France as *Rayonnant* (radiating) **Gothic**. Pinnacles and window traceries were ornately decorated, and churches acquired great rose windows. In Normandy, fine examples of *Rayonnant* Gothic can be seen in the cathedrals of **Sées** and **Rouen**.

With the Hundred Years' War, the era of great cathedral-building shuddered to an end. Only a taste for virtuosity remained, and the last phase in French Gothic made its appearance during and after the war: *Flamboyant* **Gothic** (1350–1500). It takes its name from its window tracery patterns resembling leaping flames, but it is also characterized by far more complex vaulting, and depressed instead of pointed arches. Normandy was one of the richest provinces in France in Flamboyant architecture. Outstanding examples include **St-Maclou** in Rouen (1436–1521), Rouen cathedral's **Tour de Beurre**, **Notre-Dame** in Alençon, the choir at **Mont-St-Michel**, and the belfries of **Notre-Dame** in Caudebec (1426) and **La Madeleine** in Verneuil-sur-Avre.

In non-religious architecture, castles ceased to be purely military constructions, and developed into increasingly elaborate residences. Originally only the keeps were inhabited, but from the 14th century interlinking courtyards and mansion-like apartments were added to castles such as those in Alençon and Dieppe.

The Renaissance in Normandy

At the end of the 15th century the Italian Renaissance made its mark on French architecture, and Italianate arabesques, medallions and shell and urn motifs began to adorn the façades of Norman buildings. Normandy became a major centre of the new French Renaissance style, second only to the Loire, thanks to the well-travelled

Cardinal d'Amboise, archbishop of Rouen and chief minister to Louis XII. In 1502–10 his **Château Gaillon**, near Vernon, was rebuilt with the help of Italian craftsmen and sculptors, creating a remarkable mixture of *Flamboyant* and Renaissance styles. It is the most important Renaissance building in Normandy, although only a few parts of it are still intact today (*see* p.173). Another blending of styles took place in the Lady Chapel of **St-Pierre** in Caen. Although structurally it's late Gothic, from its ribs and bosses hang stalactites of exuberant Italianate decoration. The finest Renaissance carving in Normandy, however, is in **La Trinité** at Fécamp, whose screens were created around the year 1510 by Italian sculptors. The three chapels built at **St-Jacques** in Dieppe by the merchant adventurer Jean Ango date from this same period as well, as does Ango's country home outside Dieppe with its bizarre blend of Norman-traditional and Italianate ornamentation. Elsewhere, stunning stone mansions like Caen's **Hôtel d'Escoville** replaced half-timbered buildings, while surviving old structures acquired delicately decorated new wings as fortifications made way for parks and gardens, as at **Château Fontaine-Henry**, outside Caen.

Baroque and Classical

The 17th century was France and Normandy's *grand siècle*. Inspiration came not just from Italy but also from Holland. Initially, under King Henri IV (1589–1610), domestic châteaux were made from brick – far cheaper than stone – with stone dressings. By 1650 the majestic symmetrical façades of mansions like **Cany**, **Beaumesnil** and **Balleroy** studded the Norman countryside. Balleroy, near Bayeux, was the work of **François Mansart**, France's greatest Baroque architect. With its multiple flights of steps, the château makes an imposing sight towering above a huge entrance courtyard and Balleroy village. Mansart would use his design for the internal staircase as a model for even finer ones at the châteaux of Blois, on the Loire, and Maisons-Lafitte.

In church-building, a similar revolution was underway: the emphasis was on lofty domes, rather than skilful vaulting, and soaring verticality gave way to balanced horizontals. Decoration was reduced to a minimum, producing an austere nobility. Benedictine abbeys discovered new inspiration after the founding of the reforming Congregation of St Maur in 1621, and this Maurist late revival in monasticism was reflected during the 18th century in the renovation and rebuilding of many large parts of Normandy's major abbeys – notably the living quarters at the Abbaye-aux-Hommes in Caen and Le Bec-Hellouin – in neoclassical style, often under the direction of the monk-architect and sculptor Guillaume de la Tremblaye.

Seaside Architecture and the *Belle Epoque*

When spending time at the seaside caught on as a fashionable pastime in the 1850s, accommodation had to be built to house the leisure-seekers who flocked to the coast from Paris. Seaside villas, each grander and more exuberant than its neighbours, replaced fishermen's cottages, while some resorts were built up from scratch, with a casino, theatre and racecourse. Since the new resorts were built at more or less the same time, their builders tended to follow a particular **Anglo-Normand** (or 'Neo-Normand') style. Characterized by multicoloured façades, often with mock half-timbering imitating the cottages of the Pays d'Auge, their villas bristle with pepperpot towers, pagoda roofs, balconies, bow windows and other fancies. Wealthier owners topped them off with ceramic finials, known as *épis de faîtage*, in the shape of cockerels, monkeys or other creatures. Styles were mimicked from anywhere: English cottages, Japanese pagodas, Swiss chalets, art nouveau palaces. The speed at which the Côte Fleurie and other similar resorts mushroomed was phenomenal. In Deauville some 250 mansions were built in three years, including the magnificently over-the-top **Villa Strassburger**, built to amuse the Rothschilds.

Post-1945

Rising out of the ashes of 1944, scores of Normandy's cities and towns had to be rebuilt in the 1950s. Some, such as **Le Havre**, had been almost totally obliterated, providing architects with a tabula rasa on which to try out brave experiments. Two very different architects, Frenchman **Auguste Perret** and Brazilian **Oscar Niemeyer**, set to work to remould the port with spectacularly radical innovations that stand in stark contrast to each other (*see* p.134). Upstream in Rouen, Basque Louis Arretche built the Ste-Jeanne-d'Arc church with a wooden roof in the shape of an upturned ship's hull – although, clever as it is, the soulless concrete bowl around it is a sad replacement for the ancient market square and church that once stood here. Equally controversial has been the restoration of William the Conqueror's castle in **Falaise**, where architect Bruno Décaris deliberately avoided repeating the style or materials of the original. By contrast, everyone seems to admire the three giant, graceful **bridges** over the Seine, which are not only feats of engineering but also striking works of art.

Literary Normandy

Whether cheese and calvados stimulate literary inspiration may be debatable, but it's extraordinary how many writers and poets have flourished in the rich Norman soil – and particularly in the triangle between Le Havre, Rouen and Dieppe. Flaubert, Proust and Maupassant were all directly inspired by Norman landscapes and settings, and many others visited the region from other parts of France, such as Hugo, Zola and Sartre.

The Rouen of Flaubert and Corneille

Rouen, Flaubert's home town, is seen in a gritty light. Emma Bovary scampers through medieval backstreets smelling of absinthe, cigars and oysters to meet her lover Léon. This grimy area was largely destroyed in the Second World War, but Rouen's cathedral, where Emma and Léon are reunited, is mercifully intact. Here the novelist is at his most irreverent – the passage would be a prime cause of the prosecution of Flaubert for 'offending public morals' on the novel's first publication, in 1857 – as the magnificent temple is transformed in the couple's minds into a 'gigantic boudoir' whose 'arches leaned down into the shadows to catch her confession of love.' The sexual tension only gets stronger as a loquacious verger gives them a tour during which Emma's 'tottering virtue cling[s] for support to the Virgin, the sculptures, the tombs, whatever offered', knowing deep down that she will inevitably yield to Léon's charms. Léon finally extricates Emma from the verger and gets what he has been waiting for. The couple bump through the city's streets in their horse-drawn cab, its blinds tightly sealed, 'buffeted about like a ship at sea'.

Flaubert knew Rouen well, having been born in a house attached to the Hôtel-Dieu hospital, where his father was chief surgeon. A museum now occupies the house, which as well as plenty of gruesome medical exhibits has a stuffed parrot claimed to be the inspiration for *Un cœur simple*. Like Julian Barnes in *Flaubert's Parrot*, however, you may be sceptical, as another Flaubert museum, at Le Croisset outside Rouen, has another similar green parrot for which the same historic claim is made.

Two centuries earlier Rouen had been the birthplace of another of France's greatest literary figures, the playwright **Pierre Corneille**. Both his family's main Rouen house off Place du Vieux Marché and the Corneille 'country residence' in the former village – now a Rouen suburb – of Petit-Couronne are now museums dedicated to his memory, although neither has many original furnishings. Corneille was set to be a lawyer when, chancing his luck, he handed an ink-blotched manuscript to some visiting players in 1629. It was for a comedy called *Mélite*, based on a love affair of his own, and its success transformed both Corneille's life and French theatre. In 1637 *Le Cid*, his classical tragedy exploring the conflict between love and duty, proved another great success, and was followed by further tragedies, *Horace*, *Cinna* and *Polyeucte*, all majestic exaltations of man's power to shape his own destiny and rise above circumstance. Unfortunately another playwright, Racine, later eclipsed Corneille, and the Norman dramatist died an embittered man.

The Setting

These writers weren't always flattering. In *Madame Bovary*, **Gustave Flaubert** describes Normandy's eastern borders as a 'bastard region whose speech is as without accentuation as its scenery is without character. It is here they make the worst Neufchâtel cheese in the whole district.' Ry, the one-street village that inspired the fictional Yonville-l'Abbaye, is described as the dullest place on earth, helping to drive Emma Bovary into the arms of her lovers. Today, the village nevertheless happily cashes in on this tedious reputation (*see* p.166).

A more attractive landscape is evoked in his *Un cœur simple*, set in Pont-l'Evêque, his mother's home town. The tale centres around stalwart Félicité, who passes the days babbling with her parrot. Flaubert's most lyrical passages, however, were saved for Trouville, where he had spent many childhood holidays and did much of his writing. His routine was strict: 'I rose at eight, went swimming, ate, smoked, stretched out in the sun, dined, smoked. Read Ronsard, Rabelais, Horace, but not too much, as with truffles.' It was in Trouville that Flaubert, aged just 14, met his first love, the considerably older Elisa Schlesinger, on the beach. He rescued her cloak from the rising tide, and was mesmerized by her dark looks and totally smitten when he spotted her breast while she fed her baby. Their friendship would endure his whole life. Much of his *Sentimental Education* is based on his experiences with Elisa, and memories of her almost certainly coloured his vision of the town when he wrote that 'the greatest events of my life have been some thoughts, readings and a few sunsets on the sea at Trouville.'

On the Coast: Proust, Maupassant and Sartre

If Rouen is Flaubert and Corneille's city, the old-fashioned seaside town of Cabourg belongs to **Marcel Proust** – as its tourist officials aren't shy to remind you. The once-fashionable resort is dominated by its stately white Grand Hôtel, where Proust spent many childhood summers with his grandmother, and where he later returned to write. Dainty *madeleines* are still served for breakfast and tea, and the dining room is called 'Le Balbec' after the fictional town Proust modelled on Cabourg in his *Du côté de chez Swann*. One can picture the sickly young Proust – prevented by his asthma from going outside – gazing through the huge windows at the shimmering sea.

After the death of his mother, Cabourg became a refuge where Proust sought to recover from depression and knuckle down to writing. Every summer between 1907 and 1914 he locked himself in his hotel rooms, shunning the sunlight that aggravated his asthma, and the other guests, whom he found intolerably vulgar. In the evening he would descend to take a whiff of fresh air from the hotel door, watching ladies walking their little dogs along the seafront – now Promenade Marcel Proust – or tennis players in their whites, before repairing to the magnificent chandeliered dining room. Later he'd invite hotel staff – some of whom became his lovers – up to his room to feed him gossip about the other guests.

Further east, the fishing ports of Fécamp and Dieppe are most closely associated with **Guy de Maupassant**. He was born at Miromesnil, a château just south of Dieppe, which his unhappily-married parents had rented. Maupassant spent much of his childhood, though, at Les Verguies, a villa in Etretat, where he first attended school before completing his education in Rouen. The little town of Etretat is the setting for one of his saddest stories, *Miss Harriet*, about an elderly English spinster who dies of thwarted love, while nearby Yport is the location for the equally depressing – but brilliant – *Une Vie* (A Woman's Life), about a woman suffocated by a miserable marriage. Maupassant's sardonic vision of 19th-century Norman life is often bleak, but his appreciation of the region's green landscapes shines through, as in *Nos Coeurs* (Our Hearts) where he describes the '...undulating countryside, with fertile valleys with the peasants' dwellings, their pastures and orchards, all enclosed by rows of massive trees whose heads shone tufted in the rays of the sun.'

Another of Maupassant's haunts was Le Havre, where Jeanne's son in *Une Vie* slides into depravity. His 1888 novel *Pierre et Jean* portrays the port in its most confident days, with 'numberless masts along kilometres of quays', which made the harbour in the very centre of the city 'look like a great dead forest.' However, even before the Second World War Le Havre's decline had begun. For **Jean-Paul Sartre**, who taught there during the 1930s, it was a quite different place. When he wasn't visiting Simone de Beauvoir in Rouen, or writing his first novel *La Nausée*, Sartre spent his time in the bars and cafés of the port area, musing on industrial ugliness and the horror of the human condition.

Other writers: Hugo, Gide, Barbey and Medieval Chroniclers

Equally sombre but in a very different way are the Norman writings of **Victor Hugo**. His 19-year-old daughter Léopoldine moved to a villa in the pretty Seine-side village of Villequier after marrying the young son of a Le Havre shipowner; however, the couple drowned in a boating accident on the river just six months later, in 1843. Hugo, devastated, never really recovered. His grief inspired *Les Contemplations*, extracts from which are exhibited at the Musée Victor Hugo in the Villequier house, while the famous line '*Il faut que l'herbe pousse et que les enfants meurent; Je le sais, ô mon Dieu!*' (Grass must grow and children must die; I know it, my God') adorns a stone by the spot where Léopoldine drowned (*see* p.142).

Villequier was not the only village in Normandy frequented by the restless Hugo. Virtually every town and monument received a visit from the celebrated poet, and in Veules-les-Roses the grand old man gave a party for the village's poor children.

Other outsiders inspired by Normandy include **Zola** and **Stendhal**. Zola set his bleak, ironically titled *La joie de vivre* in the fictional coastal town of Bonneville, reflecting his fascination with the sea. Stendhal was also entranced by Normandy's sea, which, he declared, 'overcomes trivial nastiness.' By contrast, the settings of the novels of **André Gide** are solidly landlocked. Having spent part of his childhood in Rouen, home of his mother's family, Gide inherited a manor house at Cuverville, between the city and the coast at Etretat, and spent many summers there. A tiny gate at the bottom of its kitchen garden leading to a bench by some beech trees was immortalized in his *La porte étroite*, where it takes on religious and sexual significance (*see* p.126). Another of Gide's novels, *Isabelle*, is set in the Pays d'Auge, at La Roque-Baignard northwest of Lisieux, where his mother also owned an estate.

The most obscure, and most thoroughly Norman, of Normandy's writers was **Jules-Amédée Barbey d'Aurevilly**, who, perhaps appropriately, came from the rugged and wind-blown Cotentin Peninsula. Despite being an aristocratic dandy with a love of the macabre, he was greatly attached to local people and their traditions, aiming to be a kind of Norman Walter Scott. There is a tiny museum in his memory in his home town of St-Sauveur-le-Vicomte, in the middle of the peninsula.

Centuries earlier the Cotentin was also home to a poet, **Turold**, who may – it's impossible to confirm – have been the author of the *Chanson de Roland*, the oldest epic poem in the French language. In the same period Normandy produced two great historians whose writings are vital to our understanding of medieval England and Normandy: **Guillaume** (or William) **of Poitiers**, born near Pont-Audemer, who was William the Conqueror's chaplain; and **Robert Wace**, who wrote his chronicle *Roman de Rou* in Caen around 1160. Between them they started a tradition of writing in Normandy that continues today.

Food and Drink

05

On the table were four sirloins, six dishes of fricassees of chicken, some stewed veal, three legs of mutton, and in the middle a nice roast suckling-pig flanked by four pork and sorrel sausages. Flasks of brandy stood at the corners. A rich foam had frothed out round the corks of the cider-bottles, and every glass had already been filled to the brim with wine. Yellow cream stood in big dishes, shaking at the slightest jog of the table, with the initials of the newly wedded couple traced on its smooth surface in arabesques of sugared almond. For the tarts and confectioneries they had hired a pastry-cook from Yvetot.

Charles and Emma's wedding feast, from Flaubert, *Madame Bovary*

It was a long, peasant-style meal with a succession of ill-assorted dishes, chitterlings following roast lamb and an omelette after the chitterlings. Livened up by cider and a few glasses of wine, old Duroy trotted out all his best jokes.

Maupassant, *Bel-Ami*

Take some apples, a dollop of cream, a knob of butter and a generous dash of calvados, and you have the key to Norman cooking. Slimming or cholesterol-free it might not be, but, prepared by a good chef, Normandy's cuisine is not nearly as overpoweringly rich as it might sound, and can be exquisite. Quantity, admittedly, can be a problem: Normans do seem to have Gargantuan appetites (they are descended from Vikings, after all), although you probably won't be expected to wade through quite as much as the guests at Charles and Emma Bovary's wedding. Normandy's trump card is its abundance of wonderful natural ingredients – creamy milk and cheese, the superb fish and shellfish that abound in its coastal waters, and delicious lamb from sheep reared on the salt marshes around Mont-St-Michel. In such a garden of plenty, there's little need for embellishment, and spices and herbs are used sparingly.

The Norman Table

Creams and Cheeses

The Vikings apparently brought their cattle with them from Scandinavia, and the Norman cows that you see grazing in the region's lush fields today, with their characteristic 'sunglass' markings, produce a milk that's exceptionally rich. Most of it is swiftly transformed into cream or cheese, both of which Normans take extremely seriously. In the old days, bowls of cream adorned every dinner table, and today crème fraîche from Isigny, on the Calvados coast, is the only French cream with an *appellation d'origine contrôlée*. In cooking, *à la Normande* means any dish flavoured with cream.

There are different cheeses all over Normandy, but the traditional hub of cheese-making is Calvados, which boasts no fewer than three *appellation contrôlée* cheeses. The most famous, but not the oldest, is **Camembert** – the proper variety of which is not to be confused with the plastic stuff found worldwide under this name – which in its modern form was supposedly invented by a milkmaid in the tiny village of the same name shortly after the Revolution (*see* p.251). The real thing,

Camembert de Normandie, must have a 45 per cent fat content, be made from raw milk, and be cured for at least three weeks. A good one should have a rind with some browny-red colour in it, and be bouncy-firm in the middle. **Pont-l'Evêque**, in the Pays d'Auge, produces a square cheese with an orangey crust. It's far older, as the first were made by monks in the 12th century, who called them *angelots* ('little angels'). A variant that's similar in flavour but stronger and with a darker rind (and does not enjoy an AOC) is **Pavé d'Auge**. One of Normandy's oldest cheeses is pungent **Livarot**, strongest of the Calvados cheeses. With a thick yellow-orange rind, it's made in rounds that are bound in raffia in military-style stripes, giving it the nickname *Le Colonel*. Normandy's fourth AOC cheese, **Neufchâtel**, comes not from Calvados but from the Pays de Bray north of the Seine. This savoury, short-lived, white-crusted cheese comes in a range of shapes, but the dinkiest of them are the hearts. It's much the oldest of all Norman cheeses, and supposedly was a favourite of William the Conqueror. All these cheeses can be tasted in most restaurants: traditional Norman cheeseboards are zealously maintained, and often huge.

Fish and Seafood

With a long and varied coastline at their disposal, Normandy's fishermen haul in a dauntingly wide variety of fish and seafood. Visitors can expect spectacular displays of lobsters, spider crabs, scallops, oysters, mussels and other seafood they perhaps never knew existed. Some of the best comes from the Cotentin peninsula: the oysters of St-Vaast-la-Hougue – sometimes called 'horses' feet' – are famous across France, and lobster-lovers will want to head for the western Cotentin coast – although they shouldn't miss the lobsters served up in St-Valéry-en-Caux, on the Côte d'Albâtre. Mussels – often cultivated semi-artificially on *bouchots* (posts driven into mud-flats offshore) – are produced all around the Norman coast, while Dieppe is famous for its sweet *coquilles St-Jacques* (scallops), which star on restaurant menus throughout winter. Whichever part of the coast you are near, excavating your way through a laden *plateau de fruits de mer* is one of Normandy's unforgettable experiences.

Seafood is also frequently used to flavour fish dishes, most traditionally with sole. This is particularly popular in the Seine-Maritime, where you'll find old favourites like *sole normande* and the similar *marmite dieppoise* – variations on a theme of fish, seafood, cider or wine, and cream. Other popular fish are turbot, *turbotin* (small turbot), sea bass and sea bream (*daurade*). If you're self-catering during your stay, one of the greatest things about Normandy is that in virtually every coastal town you can find wonderfully fresh fish and seafood on sale on the quayside each morning, straight from the sea. And believe it or not, much of the marine produce in Norman markets has actually been brought over from British waters.

Poultry

Another of Normandy's most popular dishes is *poulet Vallée d'Auge* – chicken flambéed in calvados and doused with cream. Rouen and the Seine-Maritime, however, are better known for duck, often a cross between a domestic duck and a wild one. It's gamier and more flavoursome than normal duck, partly because of its

Sole Normande

Controversy surrounds this famous Norman dish. Normans say it has always been a local speciality, and was merely adapted by Parisian kitchens to take its place in the repertoire of French cuisine. A conflicting theory, propounded by Elizabeth David in her *French Provincial Cooking*, is that *sole normande* was created in Paris by the great chef Antonin Carême, who was not Norman, in the early 19th century.

Ingredients (*serves 6*)

300ml/½ pint fish stock
150ml/5 fl oz dry white wine
2 tablespoons finely chopped shallots
6 sole fillets, each of around 200g/7oz
1 dozen mussels, scrubbed and without their 'beards', but still in their shells
180g/6oz peeled prawns
6 large mushrooms
24–36 oysters
2 tablespoons beurre manié, *of equal parts of butter and plain flour*
225ml/7½ fl oz crème fraîche or heavy cream
2 egg yolks
salt and pepper

Method

Pour the fish stock and white wine together into a small saucepan, and bring to the boil. Then reduce the heat to low, and keep warm.

Sprinkle the chopped shallots across a large baking dish, then roll the fillets lightly in the shallots and lay them around the dish, with at least half an inch between each fillet. Season lightly with salt and pepper. Distribute the mussels, the whole mushrooms and the prawns around the fillets, then pour in the hot stock and wine mixture. Bake uncovered in an oven preheated to 220° C/425° F/gas mark 7 for about 15 minutes. The mussel shells should open; throw away any that stay closed.

Remove the fillets from the dish and arrange them on a serving dish with the mussels, mushrooms and prawns. Strain the broth from the baking dish through a fine sieve into a small pan, bring to the boil, and simmer over medium heat for approximately 5 minutes. Add the oysters while there are still 2 minutes to go. Then reduce the heat and whisk in the *beurre manié* until smooth, and simmer for another 10 minutes. While the sauce is simmering, mix together the crème fraîche and the egg yolks, and then pour into the sauce, while it's off the heat. Return the sauce to the heat, and stir constantly over a medium heat for 4–5 minutes until the sauce thickens. Don't let it boil. Season to taste, pour the sauce over the fillets, and serve.

breeding, partly because it's killed by suffocation, a method that retains its blood in the carcass. The famous *caneton rouennais* is made by pressing the carcass to extract the blood, which forms an important ingredient (with wine and foie gras) in the divine sauce that's essential to the dish. Often finely-minced duck liver is stirred into the sauce at the last moment, in *caneton rouennais à l'ancienne*. Duck is also made into fine foie gras; many restaurants make their own, and also common are delicious *rillettes*, minced duck spread.

Lamb, Ham, Veal and Beef

When it comes to meat, the prize must go to lamb grazed on the salt marshes of the Bay of Mont-St-Michel, *agneau de pré-salé*, which carries the reputation of being the finest in all France. Iodine and minerals in the salt water lend a delicate, lightly salty flavour to the tender meat. The Cotentin is also famous for its hams, which are churned in a vat filled with salt to soften their flesh, then left for three weeks before being washed and hung for a month over smouldering elmwood fires. Hams are eaten *cru* (raw) or grilled in thick slices with a cider and apple sauce (*jambon au cidre*).

Cattle in this dairy area are more often served as veal, from male calves, than as beef. Veal escalopes from the Pays d'Auge (served with cream and cider sauce) are legendary.

Sausages and Tripe

They may not be for the squeamish, but tripe, tripe sausages and blood puddings are traditional staples of the Norman diet, and no gastronomic tour of Normandy would be complete without them. Mortagne-au-Perche, in Normandy's southeast corner, is the black pudding capital, hosting an annual *foire au boudin* (black pudding festival) where *charcutiers* vie to produce the best blood sausage. The secret of their tastiness is apparently that the pigs are fed on windfall orchard fruit. For *andouilles*, a slightly-smoked chitterling sausage with a black skin, the mecca is Vire. Slices of *andouille* often rub skins with delicate slithers of apple inside savoury tarts that are served as a delicious starter. *Andouilles* are not to be confused with *andouillettes*, unsmoked sausages made from veal intestines, normally eaten hot, and not so typically Norman.

Beef tripe is another historic Norman favourite. Cooked *à la mode de Caen* ('the Caen way'), beef intestines are cooked for about 12 hours with ox feet, cider, calvados, carrots, onions and herbs. Apparently William the Conqueror loved it. In the old days, pots of tripe were cooked in bakery ovens after the bread had been taken out; nowadays, you can often buy them ready-made in butchers' shops, although many younger Normans now find this very traditional dish all a bit too much, so it's relatively rare on restaurant menus. Down south in La Ferté-Macé, instead of being boiled to death the tripe is wrapped around skewers of hazel wood to produce *tripes en brochette*. Caen and La Ferté-Macé both have tripe promotion societies, to argue as to which method is best. One thing on which they agree: it's best washed down with a hearty slug of Calvados.

Desserts

It's no surprise that apples dominate Normandy's desserts. They come in *tartes* glazed with apricot jam, in puff-pastry turnovers or as delicious *confitures*. The variations are endless, and every restaurant has its favourite. Other sweets worth trying are butter brioches, especially from Evreux or Gisors; *roulettes* from Rouen (small rolls of croissant dough); and Proustian *madeleines*. Bayeux and Mont-St-Michel are famous for *sablés* biscuits, Isigny produces *caramels d'Isigny*, and Fécamp has truffes and chocolates *à la Bénédictine*. On a more stodgy note, a dessert that virtually every part of Normandy claims as its own is *teurgoule* (literally, 'twist your gob'), a thick rice pudding traditionally baked in bakery ovens after the bread was done, as the ovens cooled down.

Drinks: The Wonderful Possibilities of Apples

There is not a single vineyard in Normandy (the last attempts to create them were strangled by phylloxera, a vine disease, in the early 1900s), but thousands of cider-apple orchards. Their blossoms illuminate the countryside in spring, and in autumn Normandy buzzes with pickers gathering in the shiny fruit to be turned into *cidre doux*, *cidre sec* or *brut*, or, in between, *demi-sec*. Once you have a taste for Normandy ciders, cider-hunting (with obligatory tasting) is an absorbing pastime, taking you to farms that range in size from huge commercial undertakings, like some in the Seine-Maritime, to family smallholdings up country lanes in the Pays d'Auge, the Bessin or the Cotentin. Many still have the wooden wheel-presses used to crush the apples, once driven by horses.

The most prestigious cider region of all is the Pays d'Auge, around Cambremer. This is the only area to boast an official *appellation* (AOC) for its cider, and has a signposted *Route du Cidre* leading to a range of local producers. Pays d'Auge ciders tend to be well rounded, with a slightly more golden colour, and often even *brut* ciders still have a touch of sweetness. The stony Cotentin produces more astringent ciders, with a drier, cleaner flavour. Ciders are, like the weather, unpredictable, but this adds to the fun of trying them out.

Apples are picked from mid-September to mid-December, depending on the variety – Normandy has several hundred of them, of which around 100 are used to make cider (but only 48 in the Pays d'Auge, by the rules of its *appellation contrôlée*). They're then left for three to four weeks to build up sugar and flavour. Once they've been crushed and pressed, the dryness of the cider can be varied by how long it is left to ferment in the barrel. Once cider is bottled, fermentation slows right down. *Demi* and *brut* ciders (around 4–5 per cent alcohol) are ready by March or April, sweet ciders with 3–4 per cent alcohol are ready slightly earlier. The best time to taste and buy ciders is from mid-spring to early autumn.

Few farms produce only cider. Many also make *pommeau*, a two-thirds-cider-one-third-calvados mix that's aged in oak casks to produce a smooth liqueur. Often used in cooking, because of the tangy flavour it gives to meat, *pommeau* has only recently been easy to buy, as an obscure law made it illegal to sell it outside Normandy. Another pleasant, non-apple drink is *poiré*, perry or pear cider, the prime area for which is around Domfront in the Orne. Other fine products made with apples include fine cider vinegar, used by Normandy's top chefs, and of course, superb plain apple juice.

Normandy's pride and joy, though, is calvados, often known just as *calva*, distilled cider slowly aged in oak casks. It makes a wonderful *digestif* after a hearty Norman meal, and also flavours many local dishes. One of the most traditional ways to drink it is to down a slug (known as a *trou Normand* or 'Norman hole') between meal courses to revive the appetite, while many modern Normans pop a dash into coffee to make a *café calva*. Like cognac, calvados improves with age, and good ones are exceptionally smooth and fragrant. As with ciders, the most prestigious calvados comes from the Pays d'Auge, where several famous producers such as Château du Breuil and Pierre Huet are based. In spring, the people of Cambremer gather to taste and grade the recently distilled calvados. Under strict distillation laws the

Pays d'Auge is the only area where cider is distilled twice (in a *double fermentation*), to hold a *Calvados Pays d'Auge appellation d'origine contrôlée* label. Calvados produced elsewhere is distilled just once, and has a *Calvados AOC* or, in the case of calvados from the granite soils around Domfront, a *Calvados Domfrontais AOC* label. The latter uses a mix of apples and pears.

Calvados-making traditions go back a long way. The first known written mention of it is from 1553, in the diary of Gilles de Gouberville, a gentleman from the Cotentin. In one story it's claimed the name stems from a Spanish ship called *El Calvador*, which sailed in the Armada to England in 1588. It ran aground on the Norman coast, and the area inland became known by the name of the hapless ship – supposedly. France's Constitutional Assembly made the name official for region and drink in the 1790s.

In the old days every farmer distilled his own calvados, often on the quiet, but since the 1940s distillation has been strictly controlled (although this didn't stop Normans devising ways of dodging officialdom, such as small sausage-shaped barrels that could be hidden under ladies' skirts while being transported). Despite regulation, though, there are still plenty of small calvados producers, and one of the joys of travelling in Normandy is sampling and contrasting bottles from different farms. To be fully appreciated, calvados must be sipped from a tulip glass.

The process of calvados-making is described in Chapter 13 (*see* p.240). Calvados can be sold after only two years' ageing, but at that point it's only suitable for cooking. Most calvados is a blend of different vintages, the most recent being the one indicated on the label, and has an alcohol content of around 40 per cent. With age its volume decreases (the angels imbibe their share) and tannin-based substances in the wood give it a toffee-like colour and a light, smooth taste. The duration a calvados spends in the barrel depends on whether it's made industrially or by an artisan – the latter tend to leave it far longer. Three-star calvados has spent two years in the barrel, *vieux* or *réserve* at least three (five years for artisan producers). *vieille réserve* is four years old (eight to nine for artisan producers), while calvados *hors d'age* (XO) or *Napoléon* must be at least six years old (12–15 for artisan producers). Some, like Pierre Huet's *Cordon d'Or*, are left for as long as 35 years, and cost serious money – magnums fetch around €135.

Poiré aside, there is just one famous Norman drink not based on apples: Bénédictine, the liqueur made from a secret blend of herbs and spices first devised by a monk at the monastery in Fécamp, and which was the source of an extraordinary fortune for its 'discoverer' Alexandre Le Grand (*see* p.121).

A Calvados Cocktail: *Le Normand*

A vintage calvados would be out of place in this easy cocktail: use one that's two or three years old at most. Mix well, and drink. Recovery time depends on how much.

Ingredients

3 tenths calvados
3 tenths pommeau
4 tenths orange juice
dash of grenadine
1 ice cube per glass

Menu Reader

Hors-d'œuvre et Soupes
(Starters and Soups)

amuse-gueule appetizer
assiette assortie plate of mixed cold hors-d'œuvres
bisque shellfish soup
bouchées mini vol-au-vents
bouillabaisse famous fish soup of Marseille
bouillon broth
charcuterie mixed cold meats, salami, hams, etc.
consommé clear soup
crudités platter of raw vegetables
potage thick soup, usually vegetable
tourrain garlic and bread soup
velouté thick, smooth soup, often with fish or chicken

Poissons et Coquillages/Crustacés
(Fish and Shellfish)

aiglefin little haddock
alose shad
anchois anchovy
anguille eel
bar sea bass
barbue brill
baudroie anglerfish
belon flat oyster
bigorneau winkle
blanchailles whitebait
brème bream
brochet pike
bulot whelk
cabillaud fresh cod
calmar squid
carrelet plaice
colin hake
congre conger eel
coques cockles
coquillages shellfish
coquilles St-Jacques scallops
crabe crab
crevettes grises shrimps
crevettes roses prawns
daurade sea bream
écrevisse freshwater crayfish, or large prawns
escargots snails
espadon swordfish
esturgeon sturgeon
flétan halibut
friture mixed platter of deep-fried fish
fruits de mer seafood
gambas giant prawns
gigot de mer a large fish cooked whole
grondin red gurnard
hareng herring

homard Atlantic (Norway) lobster
huîtres oysters
lamproie lamprey
langouste spiny Mediterranean lobster
langoustines crayfish, langoustines, also called Dublin Bay prawns or scampi
lieu pollack or ling
limande lemon sole
lotte monkfish
loup (de mer) sea bass
maquereau mackerel
merlan whiting
morue salt cod
moules mussels
mulet grey mullet
oursin sea urchin
pagel sea bream
palourdes clams
pétoncles small scallops
poulpe octopus
praires small clams
raie skate
rascasse scorpion fish
rouget red mullet
saumon salmon
saumonette dogfish
St-Pierre John Dory
sole (meunière) sole (with butter and lemon)
stockfisch stockfish (wind-dried cod)
telline tiny clam
thon tuna
tourteau large crab
truite trout
truite saumonée salmon trout
turbot turbot

Viandes et Volailles
(Meat and Poultry)

agneau (de pré-salé) lamb (grazed on coastal salt marshes)
aloyau sirloin steak
andouille chitterling (gut) sausage
biftek, bistek beefsteak
blanc breast or white meat
blanquette stew of white meat
bœuf beef
boudin blanc sausage of white meat
boudin noir black pudding, blood sausage
caille quail
canard, caneton duck, duckling
cassoulet haricot bean stew with sausage, duck, chicken, etc.
cervelle brains
chapon capon
cheval horsemeat
chevreau kid
civet meat (usually game) stew, in wine and blood sauce

cœur heart
colvert wild duck, mallard
cou d'oie farci goose neck stuffed with pork, foie gras and truffles
crépinette small sausage
cuisse thigh or leg
daguet young venison
dinde, dindon turkey
dindonneau young, small turkey
estouffade a stew of meat marinated, fried and then braised
faisan pheasant
foie liver
frais de veau veal testicles
fricadelle meatball
gésiers gizzards
gibier game
gigot leg of lamb
graisse, gras fat
jambon ham
jambon cru salt-cured ham
jarret knuckle
langue tongue
lapereau young rabbit
lapin rabbit
lard (lardons) bacon (diced bacon)
lièvre hare
manchons duck or goose wings
marcassin young wild boar
merguez spicy red sausage
moëlle bone marrow
mouton mutton
museau muzzle
navarin lamb stew with root vegetables
noix de veau (agneau) topside of veal (lamb)
oie goose
os bone
perdreau, perdrix partridge
petit salé salt pork
pintade guinea fowl
pintadeau young guinea fowl
porc pork
pot au feu meat and vegetable stew in a thick stock
poulet chicken
poussin spring chicken
quenelle poached dumplings made of fish, fowl or meat, bound with egg
queue de bœuf oxtail
ris (de veau) sweetbreads (veal)
rognons kidneys
rosbif roast beef
rôti roast
sanglier wild boar
saucisses sausages
saucisson dry sausage eaten cold, like salami
steak tartare raw minced beef, often topped with a raw egg yolk

tête de veau calf's head, fatty and usually served with a mustardy vinaigrette
veau veal
venaison venison

Meat Cuts and Styles
aiguillette long, thin slice
brochette meat (or fish) on a skewer
carré (d'agneau) rack (of lamb)
chateaubriand double fillet steak, usually with a béarnaise sauce
confit meat cooked and preserved in its own fat
contre-filet, faux-filet sirloin steak
côte, côtelette chop, cutlet
cuisse leg or thigh
daube meat slowly braised in a wine and meat stock, with vegetables and herbs; usually beef or veal
entrecote rib steak
épaule shoulder
escalope thin fillet
galantine meat stuffed and rolled in its own jelly
gigot (d'agneau) leg (of lamb)
grillade grilled meat, often a mixed grill
jarret shin or knuckle
magret, maigret (de canard) breast (of duck)
noisette small round cut of meat, especially of lamb
onglet flank of beef
pavé thick, square fillet
pieds feet, trotters
plat-de-côtes short ribs or rib chops
râble (de lièvre, de lapin) saddle (of hare, rabbit)
rôti roast
selle (d'agneau) saddle (of lamb)
suprême de volaille boned breast of poultry
tournedos thick round slices of steak
travers de porc pork spare ribs

Cooking Terms for Steaks and Grills
bleu very rare
saignant rare
à point medium rare
bien cuit well done

Légumes, Herbes, Épices (Vegetables, Herbs, Spices)
ail garlic
aïoli garlic mayonnaise
algue seaweed
aneth dill
artichaut artichoke
asperges asparagus
avocat avocado
badiane star anise
basilic basil
betterave beetroot
blette Swiss chard

cannelle cinnamon
céleri celery
céleri-rave celeriac
cèpes ceps, wild boletus mushrooms
champignons mushrooms
chanterelles another name for *girolles*
chicorée curly endive
chou cabbage
chou-fleur cauliflower
choucroute sauerkraut
choux de bruxelles Brussels sprouts
ciboulette chive
citrouille pumpkin
clou de girofle clove
cœur de palmier heart of palm
concombre cucumber
cornichons gherkins
courgettes courgettes (zucchini)
cresson watercress
échalote shallot
endive chicory (endive)
epinards spinach
estragon tarragon
fenouil fennel
fèves broad (fava) beans
flageolets pale green beans
fleurs de courgette courgette blossoms
frites chips (French fries)
genièvre juniper
gingembre ginger
girolles wild, yellow mushrooms, also known in
  other parts of France as chanterelles
haricots (rouges, blancs) beans (kidney, white)
haricot verts green (French) beans
jardinière with diced garden vegetables
laitue lettuce
laurier bay leaf
lentilles lentils
maïs (épis de) sweetcorn (on the cob)
marjolaine marjoram
menthe mint
mesclun salad of various leaves
morilles morel mushrooms
moutarde mustard
navet turnip
oignon onion
oseille sorrel
panais parsnip
persil parsley
petits pois peas
piment pimento, hot red pepper
pissenlits dandelion greens
poireau leek
pois chiches chickpeas
pois mange-tout sugar peas, mange-tout
poivron sweet pepper (capsicum)
pomme de terre potato

potiron pumpkin
primeurs young vegetables
radis radish
raifort horseradish
riz rice
romarin rosemary
roquette rocket
safran saffron
salade verte green salad
salsifis salsify
sarriette savory
sarrasin buckwheat
sauge sage
seigle rye
serpolet wild thyme
thym thyme
truffes truffles

Fruits et Noix (Fruit and Nuts)

abricot apricot
amandes almonds
ananas pineapple
banane banana
bigarreau black cherry
cacahouètes peanuts
cassis blackcurrant
cerise cherry
citron lemon
citron vert lime
coco (noix de) coconut
coing quince
dattes dates
figue fig
fraise (des bois) strawberry (wild)
framboise raspberry
fruit de la passion passion fruit
grenade pomegranate
groseille redcurrant
mandarine tangerine
mangue mango
marron chestnut
mirabelle mirabelle plum
mûre (sauvage) mulberry, blackberry (wild)
myrtille bilberry
noisette hazelnut
noix walnut
noix de cajou cashew
pamplemousse grapefruit
pastèque watermelon
pêche (blanche) peach (white)
pignons pine nuts
pistache pistachio
poire pear
pomme apple
prune plum
pruneau prune
raisins (secs) grapes (raisins)
reine-claude greengage plum

Desserts

bavarois mousse or custard in a mould
biscuit biscuit, cracker, cake
bombe ice-cream dessert in a round mould
chausson turnover
clafoutis thick, pancake-like batter cake, usually with black cherries
compôte stewed fruit
corbeille de fruits basket of fruit
coulis thick fruit sauce
coupe ice-cream: a scoop or in cup
crème anglaise egg custard
gaufre waffle
génoise rich sponge cake
glace ice-cream
miel honey
œufs à la neige floating island/meringue on a bed of custard
pain d'épice gingerbread
sablé shortbread
savarin a filled cake, shaped like a ring
tarte tatin caramelized apple tart, cooked upside down
tarte tropézienne sponge cake filled with custard and topped with nuts
truffes chocolate truffles
yaourt yoghurt

Other Cooking Terms and Sauces

aigre-doux sweet and sour
à l'anglaise boiled
à la bordelaise cooked in wine and diced vegetables (usually)
à la châtelaine with chestnut purée and artichoke hearts
à la diable in spicy mustard sauce
à la grecque cooked in olive oil and lemon
à la jardinière with garden vegetables
à la périgourdine in a truffle and foie gras sauce
à la provençale cooked with tomatoes, garlic and olive oil
allumettes strips of puff pastry
au feu de bois cooked over a wood fire
au four baked
auvergnat with sausage, bacon and cabbage
barquette pastry boat
beignets fritters
béarnaise sauce of egg yolks, shallots and white wine
bordelaise red wine, bone marrow and shallot sauce
broche roasted on a spit
chaud hot
cru raw
cuit cooked
diable spicy mustard or green pepper sauce
émincé thinly sliced

en croûte cooked in a pastry crust
en papillote baked in buttered paper
épices spices
farci stuffed
feuilleté flaky pastry
flambé set aflame with alcohol
forestière with bacon and mushrooms
fourré stuffed
frit fried
froid cold
fumé smoked
galette flaky pastry case or pancake
garni with vegetables
(au) gratin topped with browned cheese and breadcrumbs
haché minced
marmite casserole
médaillon round piece
mornay cheese sauce
pané breaded
pâte pastry, pasta
pâte brisée shortcrust pastry
pâte à chou choux pastry
pâte feuilletée flaky or puff pastry
paupiette rolled and filled thin slices of fish or meat
parmentier with potatoes
pavé slab
poché poached
pommes allumettes thin chips (fries)
raclette melted cheese with potatoes, onions and pickles
salé salted, spicy
sucré sweet
timbale pie cooked in a dome-shaped mould
tranche slice
véronique green grapes, wine and cream sauce

Snacks

chips crisps
crêpe thin pancake
croque-madame ham-and-cheese toasted sandwich with a fried egg
croque-monsieur ham-and-cheese toasted sandwich
croustade small savoury pastry
frites chips (French fries)
gaufre waffle
pissaladière a kind of pizza with onions, anchovies, etc.
sandwich canapé open sandwich

Boissons (Drinks)

bière (à pression) (draught) beer
bouteille (demi) bottle (half)
brut dry (wine, cider, etc)
café coffee
café crème white coffee

café au lait large, weaker white coffee
carafe d'eau jug of tap water
chocolat chaud hot chocolate
demi a third of a litre; also the usual size of glass in which draught beer is served, so that you ask for *un demi (de bière)*
doux sweet (wine, cider)
eau-de-vie brandy
eau minérale (plat, gazeuse) mineral water (still, sparkling)
eau potable drinking water
glaçons ice cubes
infusion (or *tisane*) *de verveine, tilleul, menthe* herbal tea, made with lemon verbena, lime flower, mint, etc.
jus juice
lait milk
menthe à l'eau peppermint cordial
moelleux semi-dry
mousseux sparkling (wine)
pastis anis liqueur
pichet pitcher
citron pressé/orange pressée fresh lemon/ orange juice
ratafia home-made liqueur made by steeping fruit or green walnuts in alcohol or wine

sec dry
sirop d'orange/de citron orange/lemon squash
thé tea
verre glass
vin blanc/rosé/rouge white/rosé/red wine

Miscellaneous
addition bill (check)
beurre butter
carte menu
confiture jam
couteau knife
crème cream
cuillère spoon
formule à €12 €12 set menu
fourchette fork
fromage cheese
lait milk
menu set menu
nouilles noodles
pain bread
œuf egg
poivre pepper
sel salt
sucre sugar
vinaigre vinegar

Planning
Your Trip

06

When to Go

Climate

Emile Zola wrote that Normandy offers 'superb weather and wild tempests, days when the sun beats down, nights such as make you believe you are in Naples, phosphorescent seas, and every change occurring so brusquely that I have never experienced such swift transformations of the scenery'. The Norman climate is similar to that of southern England – and is similarly unpredictable – except that it is generally a few degrees warmer, whatever the season. The Cotentin Peninsula benefits from the warming effect of the Gulf Stream, but is also sometimes blasted by Atlantic gales too. And yes, it does rain, especially in autumn. But without the rain, Normandy would not be so lush, or its cheeses so creamy.

Perhaps the best times to visit are in spring, when the apple blossom is out, and early summer, when it's warm but not stiflingly hot. July and August are fine in remoter corners, but on the coast and on the roads you'll be jostling for space with hordes of Parisians and other French people who still tend to take their holidays en masse. Avoid driving on 15 August, the Assumption holiday, at all costs. That said, though, there are many great festivals in summer (see below), so don't rule it out.

Autumn, when apples hang heavy in the trees and mushrooms dot the woods, is many people's favourite Norman season; the crowds have gone home, prices return to sensible levels, and the weather can be marvellous until late October.

Outside the main cities, many hotels and restaurants – especially on the coast – close for a few weeks in winter. This is, though, a good time to visit cities like Rouen, Caen and Bayeux, where many hotels offer bargain off-season deals. At Easter, Normandy, like a new-born chick, springs to life and everyone opens their doors once again.

For day-to-day weather information, go to the excellent *Météo France* website, *www.meteo.fr*. For a list of events and festivals, see below, and for national holidays, see p.95.

Average Temperatures in °C (F)

Jan	Feb	Mar	April	May	June
8 (46)	6 (43)	8 (46)	13 (55)	14 (57)	20 (68)

July	Aug	Sept	Oct	Nov	Dec
22 (72)	22 (72)	18 (64)	15 (59)	11 (52)	8 (46)

Calendar of Events

February
Sun before Shrove Tuesday Carnival, Granville.

March
All month *Aspects de la Musique Contemporaine*, a wide-ranging contemporary music festival, in Caen; *Foire aux Arbres* (tree fair), Lisieux.
Last or next-to-last weekend *Foire au Boudin* (black pudding fair), Mortagne-au-Perche; a giant celebration of the Perche's most unusual gastronomic speciality.
Last 10 days Nordic Film Festival, Rouen.

April
Easter (Mar–April) *Foire de Pâques* (Easter Fair), Caen; *Festival de Musique de Pâques* (Easter Music Festival), Deauville; Easter celebrations at the Basilica, Lisieux; *Foire de Pâques* (Easter Fair), Vimoutiers; *Foire des Rameaux* (Palm Sunday Fair), Domfront.

May
May–Dec *Les Concerts de l'Abbaye*, Music Festival, Montivilliers.
Sats May–mid-July Perche music festival, Mortagne-au-Perche.
1 May Mussels Fair, Le Tréport; Branding of cows, Marais Vernier; Geranium festival, Beuvron-en-Auge; Cheese fair, Pont-l'Evêque; Regional Food Festival, Cambremer; Music festival, St-Sever.
Whitsun *Marché de l'Art La Perrière*, Orne; *Bénédiction de la Mer* ('Blessing of the Sea' fishermen and mariners' festival), Honfleur; *Fête des Rhododendrons*, Cerisy-Belle-Etoile (Sun); *Journée des Peintres*, St Céneri-le-Gérci (Sat, Sun, Mon).
Ascension Week *Jazz sous les Pommiers* (jazz festival), Coutances.

June

First week Joan of Arc Festival, Rouen.

Thursdays June–Aug *Les Jeudis du Pin* (horse show) at Haras National du Pin.

6 June and surrounding days D-Day and Battle of Normandy commemorations.

First or second weekend *Festival du Lin* (Linen Festival), Routot; Cherry Fair, Vernon; *Rendez-vous des Becs Fins* (Foie Gras market), Bernay; International Romantic Film Festival, Cabourg; Caen Festival; tractor-pulling, Bernay.

Second or Third Sun The Great Coronation: procession of the Order of Malta, Villedieu-les-Poêles. Held every 4 years, and due in 2008.

Mid-June Model Boat Festival, Le Tréport.

One week in late June Music festival, Flers.

Third weekend *Fête de la Mer* (Sea Festival), Fécamp, Seine-Maritime; *Fête du Moulin*, Hauville.

End June *Fête du Lin* (Linen Fair), Doudeville; *Archéo-Jazz* (jazz festival), Blainville-Crevon.

Last weekend Festival Rock, Evreux.

July

July–Aug *Eté Musical de Bayeux* and *Marché Medieval*, Bayeux; *Les Féeriques de Montgothier* sound and light show, Montgothier, near Mont-St-Michel.

First fortnight Folklore and folk music festival, Alençon; *Les Virevoltés* street festival, Vire.

14 Bastille Day fireworks displays.

14–19 *Festival de la Marionnette* (puppet festival), Dives-sur-Mer.

16 Saint Clair festival and giant bonfire, La Haye-de-Routot.

Late July *Fête du Cheval*, Forges-les-Eaux; Blessing of the Sea, Le Tréport; Music festival, Honfleur; Jazz festival and Festival of the Sea, Trouville; World Bridge Championships, Deauville; Arts and Crafts Festival, Reviers; *Marché Normand*, Gavray; Pilgrimage across the sands from Genêts to Mont-St-Michel.

Last weekend *Fête de la Ste-Anne*, Bricquebec.

Last Sun Pardon of the Corporations of the Sea: Procession of Guilds with banners, open-air mass and torchlight procession, in Granville.

August

All month Early music festival, Dieppe; *Semaines Musicales* music festival and *Grand Prix du Port de Fécamp* sailing race, Fécamp; *Corso fleuri* flower festival, Le Havre; *Fête de la Mer*, Dives-sur-Mer; Music Festival, Lion-sur-Mer; Cheese Fair, Livarot; Harvest festivals, La Colombe, Savigny and other villages in the Manche.

First weekend *Fête de la Grand' St Pierre*, St-Pierre-Eglise; *Foire aux Fromages*, Livarot.

First week *Fête de la Mer et des Marins*, fishermen's festival and yacht races, Barneville-Carteret.

First or second weekend *Fête de la Chasse et de la Pêche*, celebration of country sports at Château de Carrouges.

Second week Normandy Horse Show, St-Lô.

15 Feast of the Assumption: Celebrations around the region, of which some of the largest are the Procession to the Smiling Virgin, Lisieux; fireworks on the lake, Bagnoles-de-l'Orne; *Fête des Marins* sailor's festival, Berville-sur-Mer.

Mid-Aug *Fête de la Mer*, Veules-les-Roses, and Viking Village, Eu, held biennially on odd numbered years.

Third or fourth Thurs Coronation of the Virgin: Procession of the Black Virgin, Douvres-la-Délivrande.

Third week *Festival des Musiques du Large 'Les Traversées Tatihou'*, music festival on the island of Tatihou, off St Vaast-la-Hougue.

Last week Sale of yearlings, Deauville, to complement the *Grand Prix de Deauville*, one of France's most prestigious horse races, on the last Sunday in the month.

September

All month The *Musical de l'Orne* music festival, with concerts in many different venues throughout the Orne *département*.

First three weeks Cheese festival, Neufchâtel; *Fête de la Mer*, combining a traditional seamen's festival with yacht regattas and other events, Le Havre.

First week American Film Festival, Deauville. Generally attracts a few big Hollywood names each year.

First and last Sun in Sept, second Sun in Oct Horse-racing meetings, presentation of new stallions and stock sales, Haras National du Pin.

Second weekend *Foire de la Sainte-Croix* (Holy Cross Fair), Lessay.

Second and third weekends International Kite-flying Meeting, Dieppe (held every even-numbered year).

Third week *Voix du Monde*, world music and walking festival retracing old pilgrimage routes, Genêts and Mont-St-Michel, Bay of Mont-St-Michel.

Sun nearest 29 Sept Feast of the Archangel Michael: Mass held in the abbey church, Mont-St-Michel.

Last week *Grandes fêtes de Ste-Thérèse*, major pilgrimage and commemorations of the life of St Thérèse, Lisieux.

Last weekend *Mycologiades Internationales* (Mushroom Festival), a celebration of local funghi, Bellême.

October

All month Music and Dance Festival, Rouen, Dieppe and Le Havre; *Equi'days* horse festival, throughout Calvados; race meetings, displays, open days, gymkhanas and many other horse-related events in many venues across the *département*. The centrepiece is the Deauville yearling sales, one of the most important stock sales in the world for racing thoroughbreds.

First weekend *Fête de la Pomme*, Sainte-Opportune-la-Mare.

Mid-Oct *Journées Mycologiques* (mushroom fair), La Ferté Macé.

Third week *Foire aux Bateaux* (Ships Festival), Ouistreham; Apple fair, Vimoutiers.

End Oct Cider festival, Beuvron-en-Auge and Cambremer.

November

All month Apple fair, Le Havre; *Foires aux Harengs* (Herring Fairs) in Dieppe, Fécamp, Etretat, Lieurey, Le Tréport and St-Valéry-en-Caux.

1 *Andouille Festival*, Vire. A competitive event for the town's artisan sausage-makers.

First or second weekend *Fête du Cidre à l'Ancienne*, Le Sap; St-Cyr-la-Rosière.

December

Run-up to Christmas Christmas markets are held at Caen, Deauville, Rouen, Falaise, Cherbourg and in several other towns around Normandy.

Mid-Dec Turkey fairs, La Chapelle-d'Andaine and Sées.

Tourist Information

France has some of the world's best tourist information services. Each of Normandy's five *départements* has its own *Comité Départemental de Tourisme* or CDT. They coordinate the local *Offices de Tourisme*, and smaller ones which are sometimes still called *Syndicats d'Initiative*. There's also a regional tourist office (CRT), the *Comité Régional de Tourisme de Normandie*, in Evreux.

All tourist offices have sheafs of leaflets (most available in English) on attractions, accommodation, museums, local produce, farms that sell their produce direct to callers and so on, and their staff can usually answer any and every enquiry on their area. Particularly handy are each *département*'s annual visitor guide (usually called *Loisirs*, *Lieux de visite* or similar) and the excellent *Bienvenue à la ferme* leaflets that list all the farms that provide a range of traditional produce – from cider farms to *ferme-auberges* that offer hearty country meals (*see* p.93) – which are an essential aid in fine-food-hunting. In addition, all the CDTs now have good websites, in English as well as French. Addresses of local tourist offices are given throughout this guide.

Main Tourist Boards in Normandy

CRT-Normandie, 14 Rue Charles Corbeau, 27000 Evreux, **t** 02 32 33 79 00, *www.normandy-tourism.org*.

CDT-Calvados, **t** 02 31 86 53 30, *www.calvados-tourisme.com*.

CDT-Eure, **t** 02 32 62 04 27, *www.cdt-eure.fr*.

CDT-Manche, **t** 02 33 05 98 70, *www.manchetourisme.com*.

CDT-Orne, **t** 02 33 28 88 71, *www.ornetourisme.com*.

CDT-Seine Maritime, **t** 02 35 12 10 10, *www.seine-maritime-tourisme.com*.

French Tourist Offices Abroad

Australia: Level 13, 25 Bligh St, 2000 Sydney NSW, **t** (02) 9231 5244, *www.franceguide.com*.

Canada: 1981 Av. McGill College, Bureau 490, Montreal, Quebec H3A 2W9, **t** (514) 876 9881, *www.franceguide.com*.

Ireland: t (01) 560 235 235, *www.franceguide.com*.

UK: Maison de France, 178 Piccadilly, London W1J 9AL, **t** 09068 244 123, *www.franceguide.com*

USA: New York: 444 Madison Ave, NY 10022,
t (514) 288 1904; Chicago: John Hancock
Center, Suite 3214, 875 North Michigan Ave,
Chicago, IL 60611, **t** (312) 751 7800; Los
Angeles: 9454 Wilshire Blvd, Suite 715, Beverly
Hills, CA 90212, **t** (310) 271 66 65; Miami:
1 Biscayne Tower, Suite 1750-2 Biscayne Blvd,
33131 Miami, Florida, **t** (305) 373 81 77,
www.francetourism.com.

Embassies and Consulates

In France

Australia: 4 Rue Jean Rey, 75724 Paris, **t** 01 40
59 33 00, *www.france.embassy.gov.au*.

Canada: 35 Av Montaigne, 75008 Paris,
t 01 44 43 29 00, *www.amb-canada.fr*.

Ireland: 12 Av Foch, 75116 Paris, **t** 01 44 17
67 00, *www.embassyofirelandparis.com*.

New Zealand: 7 Rue Léonardo de Vinci,
75116 Paris, **t** 01 45 01 43 43,
www.nzembassy.com/france.

UK: Consulate: 18 bis Rue d'Anjou, 75008 Paris,
t 01 44 51 31 00; Embassy: 35 Rue du Faubourg
Ste-Honoré, 75383 Paris, **t** 01 44 51 31 00,
www.amb-grandebretagne.fr.

USA: Consulate: 2 Rue St Florentin, 75001
Paris, **t** 01 43 12 22 22; Embassy: 2 Av Gabriel,
75382 Paris, *www.amb-usa.fr*.

French Consulates Abroad

Canada: Consulates: 25 Rue St Louis, Québec,
QC G1R 3Y8, **t** (418) 694 2294, *www.consul
france-quebec.org*; 1 Place Ville Marie, Suite
2601, Montréal H3B 4S3, **t** (514) 878 4385,
www.consulfrance-montreal.org.

Ireland: 36 Ailesbury Rd, Ballsbridge, Dublin 4,
t (01) 277 5000, *www.ambafrance.ie*.

UK: London Consulate: 21 Cromwell Rd,
London SW7 2EN, **t** (020) 7073 1200,
www.consulfrance-edimbourg.org; Visa
section: 6 Cromwell Place, London SW7 2EW,
t (020) 7073 1250; Embassy: 58 Knightsbridge,
London SW1X 7JT, **t** (020) 7073 1000,
www.ambafrance-uk.org. Edinburgh
Consulate: 11 Randolph Crescent, Edinburgh
EH3 7TT, **t** (0131) 225 7954, *www.consulfrance-
edimbourg.org*.

USA: Consulates: 205 North Michigan Ave,
Suite 3700, Chicago, IL 60601, **t** (312) 327 5200;

10990 Wilshire Bd, Suite 300, Los Angeles, CA
90024, **t** (310) 235 3200; 934 Fifth Av, New
York, NY 10021, **t** (212) 606 3600. Embassy:
4101 Reservoir Rd, NW Washington DC 20007,
t (202) 944 6000, *www.info-france-usa.org*.

Entry Formalities

EU citizens and holders of full valid US,
Canadian, Australian and New Zealand
passports do not need a visa to enter France
for stays of up to three months.

Everyone else should check current require-
ments at the nearest French consulate.

If required, the most convenient visa is the
visa de circulation, allowing for multiple stays
of three months over a five-year period.
Anyone, including those who don't need a
visa for shorter stays, who plans to stay
longer than three months in France should
officially obtain a *carte de séjour* or residence
card (although this requirement will soon
probably be dropped for EU citizens).

Most non-EU citizens should previously
apply for an extended visa through a French
consulate at home, a complicated procedure
requiring various documents – but you can't
get a *carte de séjour* without it. However,
some visas are exempt from the need for a
carte de séjour, so it's best to take advice.

Disabled Travellers

When it comes to providing access for all,
France is not in the vanguard of nations, but
things are changing.

Signs in airports and other public places
indicate meeting points where help is available and specific needs are catered for. The
same symbols appear in leaflets to identify
services and tourist attractions that offer
special facilities.

Travel

The Channel Tunnel is a good option for
disabled people, since you can stay in your
own car. You cannot do this on ferries, but
most ferry companies offer special facilities
provided passengers check in at least one
hour before departure.

On Eurostar trains, disabled passengers can
travel 1st-class for 2nd-class fares. Inside
France, vehicles equipped to transport

Useful Contacts

Access Ability, *www.access-ability.co.uk*. A range of information, including lists of travel companies that provide holidays for disabled people.

Access-Able, P. O. Box 1796, Wheat Ridge, CO 80034, t (303) 232 2979 www.access-able.com. Web-based access and travel information.

Access Travel, 6 The Hillock, Astley, Lancashire M29 7GW, t (01942) 888 844, *www.access-travel.co.uk*. Specialist travel agent for disabled people: flights, car hire, tours and accessible gîtes in all parts of France.

Alternative Leisure Co., 165 Middlesex Turnpike, Suite 206, Bedford, MA 01730, t (718) 275 0 023, *www.alctrips.com*. Vacations for disabled people.

American Foundation for the Blind, 11 Penn Plaza, Suite 300, New York, NY 10001, t (212) 502 7600, *www.afb.org*. Excellent US information source.

Association des Paralysés de France, 17 Bd Auguste Blanqui, 75013 Paris, t 01 40 78 69 00, www.apf.asso.fr. French organization providing in-depth local information.

Comité National Français de Liaison pour la Réadaptation des Handicapés, 236 bis Rue de Tolbiac, 75013 Paris, t 01 53 80 66 66, *cnrh@worldnet.net*. Information on access and facilities for the disabled in France in a handy booklet.

DPTAC (Disabled Persons Transport Advisory Committee), t 020 7944 8012, *www.dptac.gov.uk*. UK government travel and transport website for the disabled.

Emerging Horizons, *www.emerginghorizons. com*. International online travel newsletter for people with disabilities. Also available in print.

Ministère des Transports (Normandy office), Direction régionale de l'équipement, Cité Administrative, 2 Rue Saint Sever, 76032 Rouen, t 02 35 58 52 80.

RADAR (Royal Association for Disability and Rehabilitation), 12 City Forum, 250 City Rd, London EC1V 8AF, t (020) 7250 3222, *www.radar.org.uk*. Produces very useful books and pamphlets on all aspects of travel for disabled people.

Royal National Institute of the Blind, 105 Judd Street, London WC1H 9NE, t (020) 7388 1266, *www.rnib.org.uk*. The RNIB holiday service offers information on a range of issues for blind and visually impaired people and will answer queries.

SATH (Society for Accessible Travel and Hospitality), 347 5th Ave, Suite 610, New York, NY 10016, t (212) 447 7284, *www.sath.org*. Travel and access information.

Tourism for All, t 0845 124 9973, *www. tourismforall.org.uk*; c/o Vitalise, Shap Road Industrial Estate, Kendal, Cumbria LA9 6NZ.

disabled people pay reduced tolls on *autoroutes*; to qualify, drivers must produce a vehicle registration document showing disabled status.

French railways, the SNCF, publish a pamphlet called *Mémento du voyageur à mobilité réduite* on travel by train, available outside France through Rail Europe offices (*see* p.81).

Accommodation

French Tourist Offices have listings of accommodation suitable for the disabled, while *Gîtes de France* has lists of self-catering options with disabled access (*see* p.89).

The Balladins hotel chain has budget-priced hotels throughout France that all have easily accessible public areas and at least one room designated for guests with disabilities.

Insurance and EHIC Cards

All EU citizens are entitled to use the French state health system, but to do so they should have a **European Health Insurance Card (EHIC)**, which replaces the old E111 form. You can pick up an application form for the card at post offices, or you can apply online at *www.dh.gov.uk/travellers* (this website also offers useful information about the French health system) or by calling t 0845 606 2030. Allow a couple of weeks for your card to arrive through the post. Remember that under the French system, you (like most French people) still have to pay upfront for medical treatment – though you can reclaim most of the cost later. For more on this, *see* 'Health and Emergencies', p.94.

The EHIC does not cover all medical needs, though, and to avoid this sort of bureaucracy it can just be better to rely on private **travel insurance**. Standard travel insurance policies often do not cover sports injuries – especially from activities such as horse-riding, diving or rock-climbing – so depending on what you aim to do on your trip you might need extra cover. Canadian citizens can also officially use the French health system in the same way as EU nationals, but in general for North Americans and all non-EU citizens the best option will always be to have a fully comprehensive **travel insurance** policy that covers all eventualities – health matters, theft, loss of property, flight cancellations, emergency repatriation if necessary and so on.

Maps

For driving around any part of France, the best mapbook to have with you is the Michelin 1:200,000-scale *Atlas Routier*. An alternative is to buy just Michelin's yellow-series regional map of Normandy (No. 231), and/or their maps of particular areas: No. 59 covers southwest Normandy, 55 and 60 the centre, 52 the northeast. They can be bought at virtually every service station on French highways, and in map shops elsewhere. Michelin also publishes a special historical map, No. 102, on the Battle of Normandy, while the *Institut Géographique National* (IGN) publishes a D-Day map (No.81104).

If you want to walk or cycle around a particular patch of Normandy, you should stick with the IGN, which is the French equivalent of the Ordnance Survey. Their wine-coloured R02 map (1:250,000) covers the whole region, while their pale green maps (1:30,000 and 1:100,000) cover regional national parks. The best maps for walkers are the *TOP 25* and *Série Bleue* (1:25,000) maps, which show the GR long-distance footpaths.

Money

Dealing with Normans who belong to the older generation you might not know it, but since 1 January 2002 the currency of France has been the **euro**, the symbol for which is €. One euro is divided into 100 cents; there are coins for 1, 2, 5, 10, 20 and 50 cents and for 1 and 2 euros, and notes for 5, 10, 20, 50, 100, 200 and 500 euros.

Exchange rates vary, but at the time of writing the pound/euro rate was £1 = €1.51

(so €1 = 66p), while the euro had risen against the US dollar to around $1 = €0.77 (so €1 = $1.30).

French **banks** are generally open Mon–Fri 8.30am–12.30pm (or 9–12 noon) and 1.30–4pm. Some branches open on Saturdays, in which case they will be closed on Monday. All banks close early on the day before a public holiday, and on the holiday itself will be firmly shut. All banks displaying the '*Change*' sign will exchange foreign currency, generally at better rates than *bureaux de change* (and far better than at railway stations and in hotels); you will need your passport for any transaction. The cheapest places of all to exchange cash are the main post offices, which don't charge commission. Traveller's cheques are the safest way of carrying money, but there can be problems getting them exchanged in small bank branches. Very rarely will you be able to use traveller's cheques directly in payments, as you would in the USA.

However, the widespread presence of ATM cashpoint machines often makes using them with a credit or debit card the most convenient – and sometimes most economical – way of getting money. Card companies charge a fee for cash advances, but rates can still often work out better than bank commission rates. Major credit cards such as Visa and MasterCard are very widely accepted in France, but American Express and Diners Card less so. However, in smaller hotels and restaurants, especially in rural areas, and *chambres-d'hôtes* (bed and breakfast), owners may not accept cards, so it's advisable to have some travellers' cheques, cash or other source of money as well, and not rely on cards alone. All French credit cards now work on the chip-and-pin system, and shops sometimes have trouble reading old UK-style magnetic strips. Self-service petrol stations and bridge tollbooths (but not motorway tollbooths) also reject foreign cards.

Credit Card Emergency Numbers
MasterCard: t 0800 901 387
American Express: t 01 47 77 72 00.
Visa (Carte Bleue): t 0892 705 705.
Barclaycard: t (00 44) 1604 230 230.

Getting There

By Air from the UK and Ireland

Normandy has airports in Caen, Deauville, Le Havre, Cherbourg and Rouen. The only direct flights from Britain are with Flybe from Southampton to Cherbourg, or with Skysouth from Shoreham (Brighton) to Le Havre and Caen. Otherwise, you need to fly to Paris and continue your journey by train (*see* p.82). Air France, British Airways and British Midland all have frequent flights from the different London airports and a number of other UK cities, and a number of low-cost carriers now ply this route as well. Flying time from London to Paris is about 50 minutes. For general information on all airports in France, check the website *www.frenchairports.com*.

Fares have become far more competitive in the last decade. On no-frills, low-cost airlines such as Ryanair and easyJet a flight from the UK to Paris can cost anything from around £20 one-way. Many bargain flights are also available from student travel and flight-only agencies. For the best offers, check out the Sunday newspapers, or the websites listed below.

By Air from the USA and Canada

There are frequent flights to Paris from many parts of North America, and from there you can travel on to Normandy by train (*see* p.82). Outside peak seasons (such as any time in fall and winter), you can usually expect to get a scheduled economy flight from New York to Paris from as little as $320–$460. In summer scheduled prices go up, but there are many more nonstop charters available.

It can, though, work out cheaper to fly to Britain – for which there is a bigger range of flights – and then continue your journey to Paris from there. In which case, consider using a low-cost carrier such as easyJet or Ryanair for the last leg (*see* opposite).

A big choice of charters and discount tickets to France and the UK is available year-round. Check Sunday newspaper travel sections for the latest deals, or the specialist flight websites listed on p.79.

Airline Carriers

UK and Ireland

Aer Lingus, t IR 0818 365 000, *www.aerlingus.com*. Daily flights to Paris-Charles de Gaulle from Dublin.

Air France, t 0870 142 4343, *www.airfrance.com*. Daily to Paris-CDG from Heathrow, London City, Birmingham, Edinburgh, Glasgow, Aberdeen, Manchester, Newcastle and Bristol. Also from London City to Paris-Orly. Some routes are operated directly by Air France, others by partner airlines.

bmibaby, t 0871 224 0224, *www.bmibaby.com*. The low-cost offshoot of British Midland has flights to Paris-CDG from East Midlands, Leeds-Bradford, Durham Tees Valley and Heathrow.

British Airways, t 0870 850 9850, *www.britishairways.com*. Direct flights to Paris-CDG from Birmingham, Bristol, Edinburgh, Glasgow, London City, Gatwick, Heathrow and Manchester.

British Midland (bmi), t 0870 607 0555, *www.flybmi.com*. Direct flights to Paris-CDG from Leeds-Bradford and London Heathrow.

easyJet, t 0905 821 0905, *www.easyjet.com*. Several flights daily between Paris-CDG and Liverpool, Luton, Newcastle and Bristol.

Flybe, t 0871 700 0535, *www.flybe.com*. A low-cost airline with flights to Cherbourg from Southampton, to Paris-Orly from London City, and to Paris-CDG from Aberdeen, Bristol, Edinburgh, London City, Heathrow, Manchester and Southampton.

Ryanair, t UK 0871 246 0000, Ireland 0818 303 030, *www.ryanair.com*. Flights to Paris-Beauvais from Glasgow, Dublin and Shannon. Note that Beauvais is about 60km north of Paris, which makes it a convenient arrival-point for approaching Rouen and eastern Normandy by train and bus (without the need to travel via Paris itself).

Skysouth, t (01273) 463 673, *www.skysouth.co.uk*. Flies twice daily Mon–Fri from Shoreham (Brighton) to Le Havre and Caen in an eight-seater plane (flying time 50mins). Free parking at Shoreham.

USA and Canada

Air France, t US 1 800 237 2747, **t** Canada 1 800 667 2747, *www.airfrance.com*. Flights to Paris from Philadelphia, Cincinnati, Atlanta, Boston,

Chicago, Houston, Miami, San Francisco, Los Angeles, New York and Washington DC in the US, and from Montreal (3 flights daily), Toronto (1 daily) and Ottawa in Canada.

American Airlines, t 1 800 433 7300, *www.aa.com.* Flights to Paris from Boston, Chicago, Dallas, New York JFK and Miami.

Continental, t US 1 800 231 0856; **t** Canada 1 800 525 0280 *www.continental.com.* Flights to Paris from Houston and Newark.

Delta Airways, t US 1 800 241 4141, **t** Canada 1 800 221 1212, *www.delta.com.* Direct flights to Paris from Atlanta, Chicago, Cincinnati, Los Angeles, New York, Philadelphia and San Francisco.

Northwest Airlines, t 1 800 225 2525, *www.nwa.com.* Flights to Paris from Detroit.

United Airlines, t 1 800 538 2929, *www.united.com.* Direct flights to Paris from Chicago, San Francisco and Washington DC.

Students, Discounts and Special Deals

UK and Ireland

Students with ID cards can get reductions on flights, trains and admissions.

STA, Priory House, 6 Wright's Lane, London W8 6TA, **t** 0870 163 2226, *www.statravel.co.uk.* Specializes in student travel. Branches all over UK.

Trailfinders, 194 and 215 Kensington High St, London W8 7RG, **t** 0845 050 5940, *www.trailfinders.com.* Branches across the UK.

Useful websites
www.buzzaway.com
www.cheapflights.com
www.ebookers.com
www.expedia.com
www.flightcentre.com
www.flightmapping.com
www.lastminute.com
www.opodo.com
www.studentflights.co.uk
www.traveljungle.co.uk
www.travelocity.co.uk

USA and Canada

If you are able to be flexible some great budget deals are available on stand-bys or as courier flights (which usually only allow you to take hand luggage). Check out *www.xfares.com* for stand-by tickets, or the *Yellow Pages* for courier companies. For discounted flights try the newspaper travel pages or the websites listed here.

Air Brokers International, USA **t** 1 800 883 3273, *www.airbrokers.com.*

STA Travel, t 1 800 777 0112, *www.statravel.com.* Student and charter flights, with branches across the USA.

StudentUniverse, t toll free from US & Canada 1 800 272 9676, from elsewhere **t** 617 321 3100, . *www.studentuniverse.com.*

Travel Avenue, USA, **t** 1 800 333 3335, *www.travelavenue.com.* Discount flights.

Travel Cuts, t Canada 1 866 246 9762, **t** US 1 800 592-CUTS (2887), *www.travelcuts.com.* Canada's largest student travel specialist, with branches in most provinces of Canada and across the USA.

Vacations to Go, t US 713 974 2121, *www.vacationstogo.com.* US discount travel site, based in Houston.

Useful websites
www.bestfares.com
www.cheaptrips.com
www.courier.org
www.eurovacations.com
www.expedia.com
www.flightcentre.com
www.flights.com
www.fool.com/travel
www.hotwire.com
www.lowestfare.com
www.orbitz.com
www.priceline.com
www.ricksteves.com
www.traveldiscounts.com
www.travelnow.com
www.travelocity.com
www.tripadvisor.com

By Sea

Crossing to France by ferry – or the competing 'road route', the Channel Tunnel (*see* p.81) – has many advantages for anyone travelling from Britain, especially with children. The main ones naturally are that you can take your own car, and as much baggage as you need. Children aged 4–15 often get reduced rates, and under-4s go free. Modern ferries are far more comfortable than they used to be; they are also far faster: the high-speed ferries will get you to Normandy in as little as 2hrs 15mins on the Poole–Cherbourg crossing, or 55mins on the

Dover–Calais route. On the longer routes, such as those overnight to Norman ports, it's worth overnighting it with a cabin (for an extra charge), especially if you have kids in tow.

Ferries run direct to four ports in Normandy: **Dieppe** (from Newhaven), **Le Havre** (from Portsmouth and Newhaven), **Caen** (from Portsmouth) and **Cherbourg** (from Portsmouth, Poole and Rosslare in Ireland). Standard ferries on the longer routes take about 4–6hrs by day, 6–8hrs on overnight sailings. However, by sailing direct to Normandy you avoid a drive of at least 3hrs from the busiest cross-Channel route, Dover–Calais, or the Tunnel; also, in April–Sept P&O, Brittany Ferries and Condor run 'fastcraft' to Cherbourg that take under 3hrs. Dover–Calais sailings last about 1hr and there are several each hour, daily.

The downside of ferry travel can be the cost – fares are often expensive, and vary wildly according to season and demand. Annoyingly, all the ferry company brochures now only give rough price guides, and all the companies now prefer you to book online, and give discounts if you do so; however, none of the websites present their company's fares entirely clearly, so this is one case where it's best to phone, get through to a human being and ask for details of the cheapest fares available at any particular time (you can still then book online, to get the discount). The most expensive period runs from the first week of July to mid-August; other pricey times include Easter and school holidays. Book as far ahead as possible, and look out for special offers. Weekdays are cheaper than weekends. Most companies also offer good-value mini-breaks for a car and a varying number of passengers. You pay extra to bring a caravan or trailer, but charges are lower off-season. Brittany Ferries also do good-value day trips to Cherbourg or Caen.

Ferry Companies

Brittany Ferries, t UK 08705 360 360, *www.brittanyferries.co.uk*. Sailings from Portsmouth to Caen (Fri–Sun end-March–end-Oct; 6hrs, or 3½hrs on high-speed ferry) and to Cherbourg (twice daily end-March–end-Oct; 180mins on high-speed ferry), and from Poole to Cherbourg

(end-May–Oct; 4hrs, or 135mins by high-speed ferry). Contact numbers at their French ports are: Caen (Ouistreham) **t** 02 31 36 36 36, Cherbourg **t** 02 33 88 44 88.

Celtic Link Ferries, t UK 0870 600 6054, France 02 33 43 23 87, *www.celticlink ferries.com*. Sailings between Rosslare and Cherbourg (18hrs) three times weekly all year round except mid-Dec–mid-Jan.

Irish Ferries, t UK 08705 17 17 17, Ireland **t** 0818 300 400, Northern Ireland **t** 818 300 400, *www.irishferries.com*. Ferries between Rosslare and Cherbourg (17hrs) approx. three times a week Mar–Dec.

LD Lines, t UK 0870 428 4335, **t** France 0825 304 304, *www.ldlines.co.uk*. Sails once daily Le Havre–Portsmouth and (May–Sept once daily) Le Havre–Newhaven (7½hrs overnight Portsmouth–Le Havre, 5hrs daytime crossing Newhaven–Le Havre).

P&O Ferries, t UK 08705 20 20 20, *www.poferries.com*. Has 3–4 sailings hourly in each direction between Dover and Calais (1hr 15mins; or 55mins on Seacat).

Transmanche Ferries, t UK 0800 917 12 01, France **t** 0800 650 100, *www.transmanche ferries.com*. Year-round three-times-daily services (4hrs, 5hrs for overnight crossing) between Newhaven and Dieppe.

By Train

The most civilized way to get to Normandy is by high-speed **Eurostar** train from London (or Ashford, in Kent) to France, and then a local train to your destination. The best options are to catch a Eurostar from London Waterloo to Paris (Gare du Nord; 2hrs 35mins; from £59 return, from £50 under-12s), or to Lille (1hr 40mins) or Calais (1hr 25mins). The best way to get to Cherbourg, Caen or Le Havre is to take the Eurostar all the way to Paris-Gare du Nord, then cross Paris to the Gare St-Lazare to catch a train for Normandy. This is faster than going cross-country from Lille or Calais, although Lille is a good point to pick up connections to Dieppe or Rouen.

With a standard ticket you need only check in on Eurostar at least 30mins before departure, but in Paris, allow at least an hour to transfer between different stations. To get the cheapest Eurostar fares you must book

Rail Passes

If you expect to travel a lot by train in France or Europe rail passes can be a good investment. They must be purchased in your home country, and cannot be bought in France. For discount fares obtainable within France, see p.57.

Available in the UK and Ireland

All available from Rail Europe UK, see p.56.

France Railpass. This excellent-value pass allows UK residents unlimited rail travel in France for between 3 and 9 days. The cost ranges from £117 for a 3-day adult standard pass, to £222 for a 9-day adult standard class pass. Savings can be made for two or more adults travelling together. Child, youth and senior fares are also available, and under-3s travel free. The pass is available to anyone who has been resident outside of France for six months before purchase.

InterRail. The InterRail pass is open to people of any age who have been resident in one of the participating InterRail countries for more than six months. You can travel in one, two or all 'zones' of Europe covering 28 countries (consult www.raileurope.co.uk to see the zones). The cheapest InterRail is a 16-day pass for one zone, which costs £145 for under-26s, £215 if you're older. A pass covering all the zones costs £285 for under-26s, £405 for over-26s.

Available in the USA and Canada

All available from Rail Europe USA, see p.56.

Eurail. Available to North Americans only, the Eurail pass allows unlimited 1st-class travel through up to 17 European countries for 15-day, 21-day, 1-month, 2-month or 3-month periods; it saves the hassle of buying numerous tickets, but will only pay for itself if you use it a lot. It is not valid in the UK or countries outside the EU. Two weeks' travel costs $414 for those under 26; those over 26 can get a 15-day pass for $588, a 21-day pass for $762, or one month consecutive for $946. Children aged 4–11 pay half the adult fare, and under-4s go free. The more limited Eurail Selectpass gives you unlimited travel through 3–5 adjoining Eurail countries for 5, 6, 8, 10 or 15 days in a 2-month period for $356–$794 (1st-class), or $249–$556 (2nd class).

France Railpass. Gives 4 days of unlimited travel throughout the country in a 1-month period for $218 (reduced to $186 per person for 2 people travelling together). You can travel 1st or 2nd class.

France Youthpass. Under-26s get the same benefit for $189 (1st class) or $164 (2nd class).

France Seniorpass. Similar benefits to the over-60s for $228 (1st class).

France Rail 'n' Drive. A 6-day pass giving 4 days' unlimited rail travel through France and 2 days' car rental, and which costs from $215.

well in advance or include a Saturday night in your stay. Eurostar also offers day-return tickets for the same rate, and at off-peak times there are sometimes good promotional fares that are worth looking out for (they're widely advertised). Eurostar also offers Eurostar Connections, a package that includes a Eurostar ticket and one internal French railways train trip (these can be booked up to 50 days in advance, but no later). You can stop off for up to 24 hours en route. A Eurostar Connections fare to Cherbourg, for example, costs around £89 return; for Caen, the fare is from £79.

Rail Companies

Eurostar, t 08705 186 186, from outside UK **t** 44 1233 617 575; www.eurostar.co.uk.

Rail Europe (UK), 178 Piccadilly, London W1J 9AL, **t** 08708 304 862, www.raileurope.co.uk. Information and bookings on French and all European railways.

Rail Europe (USA), 226 Westchester Av, White Plains, NY 10064, **t** 1 877 257 2887, www.rail europe.com. Take your passport.

By Coach

Eurolines (owned by National Express; **t** 08705 143 219, www.eurolines.co.uk) operates regular coach services from London Victoria to more than 60 French destinations, including Paris, Caen and Cherbourg. The journey to Paris takes 7hrs and costs from £36 return. It's always cheapest to book in advance. Peak-season fares are slightly higher. There are discounts for pensioners, disabled travellers, under-26s and under-12s.

By Car

Putting a car on a Shuttle train through the **Channel Tunnel** has become the most popular way of getting to France from Britain. It takes only 35mins to get from

06 Planning Your Trip | Getting There

Folkstone to Calais and there are up to 4 departures an hour (at peak times) 365 days of the year. There is hot competition between the Tunnel and the ferries so fares are comparable, but the Tunnel has the added convenience of speed, and that it's not affected by the weather. The basic price for all tickets is for a car no more than 6.5m in length, plus the driver and all passengers. A return ticket for a car and passengers starts from as little as £98 with the best deals being available to those who book in advance and out of peak times. The flexible booking system on Eurotunnel's website allows you to view available travel times and prices before making a reservation. There are also frequent special-offer day returns and 2-3 day deals and, of course, you can still turn up on spec, although this is the more expensive option. Eurotunnel also has an accommodation booking service and runs specialist ski packages through the winter.

Whether you arrive in Calais by Tunnel or ferry, you are led pretty painlessly onto an ample network of motorways and trunk roads for your onward journey. To get to Normandy, you have a fairly long drive: approximate driving times from Calais (using autoroutes where possible) are: Eu-Le Tréport, 1hr 45mins; Rouen, 2hrs 15mins; Honfleur, 2hrs 30mins; Bayeux, 3hrs 30mins; Granville, 4hrs 15mins. For information on driving in France, see p.83.

Eurotunnel, t bookings 08705 353 535, information 08705 388 388, www.eurotunnel.com.

Via Michelin, www.viamichelin.com. For road information.

Getting Around

By Air

Air France domestic services fly from Lyon to Rouen, Caen and Le Havre, and there is an independent service between Cherbourg and Paris-Orly (see p.294).

For Air France reservations within France, call t 0820 820 820, or visit www.airfrance.fr.

By Train

Travelling by rail in France is a joy: French Railways (**SNCF**) trains are sensibly priced and

Discount Rail Fares

Many of the rail cards listed below also include other perks like discounts on car hire or hotels. *Découverte* tickets are free.

Carte 12–25. Young people aged 12–25 who travel frequently by train can buy this card for €48 or €36.50: it lasts a year and gives a 25-50% discount on TGVs and sleeper (*couchette*) trains (subject to availability) and travel on other trains if the journey begins in a blue period.

Carte Enfant+. Issued in the name of a child aged 4–12, this allows the child and up to 4 other people a 25–50% discount on TGVs and sleeper trains, subject to availability, and on other trains if the journey begins in a blue period. Valid for one year, this rail card costs €63 or €50.50.

Carte Senior: Over-60s can buy this card, which gives the same discounts as the previous two for a year, for €49 or €36.50. Plus, the *carte* gives 25% off train journeys from France to 25 countries in Europe.

Découverte Séjour. If you set out in a blue period with a return ticket, travel more than 200km and stay at least a Saturday night, you get a discount of up to 35%.

Découverte 12–25. A 25% discount for young people on TGVs and couchette trains (subject to availability) or on other trains if they begin travel in a blue period.

Découverte Enfant+. Up to 4 people travelling with a child aged 4–11 qualify for a 25% discount on TGVs and *couchette* trains, and on other trains departing in a blue period. Also gives discounts on Avis car hire.

Sénior Découverte. 25% off fares (subject to availability) for the over-60s, travelling on TGVs and *couchette* trains or on other trains if they begin travel in a blue period.

generally clean – and they move. The sleek **TGV** (*train à grande vitesse*) allow you to nip, for example, from Rouen to Marseilles in a mere 5½hrs. Inter-City trains are also efficient and quick – Paris–Rouen takes just over an hour. If you're venturing off the main lines, there's also a decent network of slower local trains, and in some areas SNCF buses have taken over former train routes. Train and bus services are linked, so that you can move painlessly from one to the other, rather than finding that the last bus left 5mins before your train pulled in.

Fares are very reasonable, even more so if you take advantage of the many discounts (*see* p.82). When you board a train, you must stamp (*composter*) your ticket in the odd-looking orange machines by the platform entrances. This date-stamps your ticket, and if you forget to do it you'll be liable to a fine; also, if you break your journey you must re-*composter* the ticket. You can book train tickets and rail cards online inside or outside France, and pay by credit card. For non-high-speed trains SNCF fares vary according to whether you travel in off-peak (*période bleue*, blue times) or peak periods (*blanche*, or *période de pointe*): Friday and Sunday evenings, and national holidays, nearly always fall in white periods. All stations dish out little calendars with the cheaper 'blue periods' clearly marked.

SNCF information, in France t 08 36 35 35 35, *www.sncf.com*. The English-language site is *www.voyages-snef.com*.

By Bus

Bus services are less extensive than the rail network. The bus network is just about adequate between major towns and cities, but can be hopeless in rural areas. An exception though is the Calvados *département* whose *Bus Verts* local buses are useful for linking towns, and they run a daily bus between Caen and Le Havre that takes 1hr30mins. They also offer a *Carte Liberté* which allows unlimited travel for 1, 2, or 7 days, and a *Tarif Jeune* for under-26s during school holidays, bank holidays and weekends. In summer the company runs a **D-Day Circuit 44**, which departs from Bayeux and Caen, and tours the landing beaches between Honfleur and Bayeux. A map of all their routes is on their website under *Plan du Reseau*. In the Seine Maritime, there is a reasonable bus route along the coast either side of Dieppe. Elsewhere though buses are sporadic, often timed to fit in with markets and school schedules, so leave a village at the crack of dawn and return late afternoon. Some bus routes are run by the **SNCF** (replacing discontinued rail routes), and rail passes are valid on SNCF buses. Most larger towns have a central *Gare Routière* (bus station). Tickets can be bought on the bus or at a *tabac* or *presse* near the stop. For details of local bus services, ask at the local tourist office.

Bus Verts, t 0810 214 214, *www.busverts.fr.*

By Car

Unless you are prepared to stick to major towns, cycle or walk, a car is the only way to see the remoter parts of Normandy. This has some snags: the local accident rate is double that of the UK, and French drivers often behave like a small winged animal departing hell, especially when in a hurry to get anywhere. Tailgating as an immediate preliminary to overtaking is common, and drivers who dither about where they're heading (i.e. many tourists) are treated with noticeable impatience. The great plus of driving in France, on the other hand, is that traffic densities are low outside cities, so congestion is remarkably absent much of the time. And French drivers have one particular redeeming virtue: if there are *gendarmes* lurking on the road, oncoming drivers warn you by flashing their headlights at you.

Drivers must have their driving licence, vehicle registration document and up-to-date insurance papers in the car with them. Drivers with a valid licence from any EU country, the USA, Canada or Australia do not need an international licence to drive in France. If you take a car to France, you should of course make sure you are properly insured. Under European law all UK motor insurance policies now include basic third-party cover for all EU countries, but it's advisable to get an extension to give you fully comprehensive international cover, which most insurance companies will provide for a limited extra premium. It's also strongly advisable to have breakdown assistance, which many insurance companies can also arrange. Cars from the UK or Ireland require headlamp adjusters. All cars in France are required to have rear seat belts, which must be worn, but note that French law also requires you to have in the car some things that are not usual in Britain: spare bulbs for the car's main lights, and a warning triangle for breakdowns.

There are a few points to note when driving in France. First, watch out for *priorité à droite*, an archaic system whereby traffic coming

06 Planning Your Trip | Getting Around

from streets to your right, unless halted by a stop sign and/or a thick white line (and sometimes even these are ignored), automatically has right of way (this is rigorously observed in Le Havre). This old rule no longer applies at roundabouts, where you give way to cars already on the roundabout. In general the best rule of thumb is to watch out for *Cédez le passage* (Give Way) signs, and treat every intersection with care. Secondly, French drivers rarely respect pedestrian crossings.

Petrol stations can be scarce in rural areas, and many keep shop hours, and are shut at night, on Sunday afternoons, on Mondays or for lunch. Unleaded fuel is *sans plomb*, and diesel may be called *gazole* or *gasoil*. The cheapest places to buy fuel are the petrol stations attached to supermarkets; the most expensive are on motorways. They are often self-service out of hours, but don't usually accept foreign credit cards. At motorway toll stations foreign cards will generally get you through while the tolls are staffed, but they're not accepted on the bridges over the Seine. It's easier to have cash.

Speed limits are 130kph/80mph on *autoroutes* (toll motorways); 110kph/69mph on main highways; 90kph/55mph on other roads; and 50kph/30mph in urban areas. There are few speed cameras, but the police often set up radar traps in lay-bys. Fines are payable on the spot, and begin at about €90 but can be far more, especially if you fail a breathalyser test. A campaign against drink-driving has been going for some time (although attitudes have some way to go in rural areas), and police traps are often set up after Sunday lunch. If you have a breakdown (*une panne*) on major roads or motorways, use the orange emergency phones to contact rescue services or the police. If you're a member of a motoring organisation affiliated to the Touring Club de France, ring them; if not, ring the police, **t** 17.

Autoroute information, *www.autoroutes.fr*. Has the current toll rates.

Road and traffic information, *www. bison-fute.equipement.gouv.fr*. The site of the French National Traffic Centre has an amazing range of information on all aspects of driving in France, in French and English.

Route planning, *www.viamichelin.com*.

Car Hire

UK

Avis, t 0870 606 0100, *www.avis.co.uk*.
Budget, t 0844 581 9998, *www.budget.co.uk*.
easyCar, *www.easycar.com*.
Europcar, t 0845 722 2525, *www.europcar.co.uk*.
Hertz, t 08708 44 88 44, *www.hertz.co.uk*.
Thrifty, t (01494) 751 600, *www.thrifty.co.uk*.

USA and Canada

Auto Europe, t 1 888 223 5555, *www.autoeurope.com*.
Avis, t 800 331 1212, *www.avis.com*.
Europcar, t 877 940 6900, *www.europcar.com*.
Europe by Car, t 800 223 1516, *www.europebycar.com*.
Hertz, t 800 654 3131 (USA), **t** 800 654 3001 (international toll free), *www.hertz.com*.

Hiring a Car

Car hire is relatively expensive in France – an added incentive to bring a car from Britain. If you're travelling from North America, there are big pluses to booking a car in advance through one of the major agencies or online booking services, or looking for a fly-drive travel package with car included. All the major car-hire chains operate in France.

The minimum age for hiring a car in France varies from 21 to 25, and the maximum is 70, depending on the company. Some companies impose surcharges for drivers under 25. Rental conditions are now fairly standard, but check that the price you're quoted includes tax, full insurance and unlimited mileage. Addresses of car hire agencies in Normandy's main cities are given in the relevant chapters of this guide.

By Bicycle

Normandy is the perfect place to cycle: there's plenty of space, countless quiet minor roads, lovely places to stop off for a drink, and a huge diversity of landscapes, smells and terrains. April and May, when the apple blossom is out, are especially spectacular. You'll also join in a national sport: bikes are an important part of French culture, and thousands don their lycra on summer weekends. Tourist offices supply cycle touring guides, and the official French IGN mapping agency publishes maps specifically for cyclists. Look out for *voie vertes* – cycle and walking routes which follow disused railway lines.

Getting a bike to your starting point requires a little thought. If you want to take it by air, check with the airline whether it needs to be boxed and if it will be part of your total baggage weight. British Airways and Air France take bikes free from Britain, as do some ferry operators (others charge £5 per bike one way). From the USA, Canada or Australia most airlines will carry them as long as they're boxed and included in the total baggage. In all cases, phone ahead. On Eurostar, bikes can be stored in the guards' vans, which have cycle-carrying hooks, with advance reservation and for an extra charge.

Once you're in France, some trains (with a bicycle symbol on the timetable) carry bikes for free, sometimes in a designated carriage. Alternatively you can send them as registered luggage, and they will be delivered to an address within three working days. To find out which trains accept bikes check the SNCF website, *www.sncf.com* (click on *guide du voyageur*).

If you don't want to take a bike yourself, bicycles can also be hired from most SNCF stations in larger towns, and then dropped off at a different station, as long as you specify where this will be when you hire the bike. Many towns also have bike-hire shops, usually with rates of around €10 a day, although hirers might also have to leave a hefty deposit or a credit card number.

The common French word for a *bicyclette* is a *vélo*, and a *vélo tout terrain*, or VTT, is a mountain bike. If you rent, ask about insurance against theft, or check if your travel insurance covers you for theft or damage. Bike shops are plentiful, so it's easy to get spare parts.

Useful Contacts

See also below under 'Tour Operators and Special Interest Trips'.

Cyclists' Touring Club, in UK, **t** 0870 873 0060, *www.ctc.org.uk*.

Fédération Française de Cyclotourisme, 12 Rue Louis Bertrand, 94207 Ivry-sur-Seine, **t** 01 56 20 88 88, *www.ffct.org*. Supplies information and maps.

Stanfords Bookshop, 12-14 Long Acre, London WC2E 9LP, **t** (020) 7836 1321, *www.stanfords.co.uk*. Maps, guidebooks and French touring, walking and cycling maps.

On Foot

With over 60,000 kilometres of clearly-marked long distance footpaths or *sentiers de Grandes Randonnées* (GRs), and a fantastic variety of landscapes, France is a superb country in which to walk. GR paths, indicated by red-and-white striped signs, are easy to find, and there are some in every part of Normandy. You can walk a stretch of one, and then cut off onto other paths to make a circular walk.

As well as the GRs there are shorter *Petites Randonnées* (PRs), usually signalled by single yellow or green stripes, plus *sentiers de Grandes Randonnées de Pays* (GRPs), marked by a red and yellow stripe, and any number of variants of the original GR routes which eventually become paths in their own right. Another recent development is the *voie vertes*, a network of traffic-free routes which follow abandoned railway lines – good for people who don't like hills.

Some of the most beautiful walking routes in Normandy are the coastal footpaths: the GR21 between Le Tréport and Le Havre (120km) takes in the spectacular cliffs of Fécamp and Etretat, and the GR223 goes around the edge of the Cap de la Hague and the northern Cotentin. Between them, another coastal path takes you past the landing beaches, and there's a particularly good circular walk around Arromanches.

Inland, the great forests of Andaines, Ecouves and Bellême offer unlimited opportunities, as does the Suisse Normande, with its rugged valleys and meandering rivers. Normandy's natural parks, such as the Parc de Brotonne, are well equipped with well-marked paths too, and last but not least you can stride along the banks of the Seine itself – particularly around Les Andelys and Château Gaillard.

These paths are lovingly maintained by the *Fédération Française de la Randonnée Pédestre* (FFRP), which also produces excellent walking guides (*topoguides*). The best maps for walking in France are the IGN's 1:25,000 *Série Bleue* and *Top 25* series.

Tour Operators and Special Interest Trips

If you want to combine a holiday with study or a special interest, contact French tourist offices or the relevant French Embassy's Cultural Department (23 Cromwell Rd, London SW7, t (020) 7073 1300; 4101 Reservoir Rd, NW Washington DC 20007, t 202 944 6400). On the Net, *www.tourisme.fr* has a list of unusual ways of seeing Normandy, while *www.savoir faire.com* lists courses on the arts and cookery across Normandy. For a full list of tour operators, check *www.franceguide.com*.

From the UK

Battlefield Tours, The War Research Society, 27 Courtway Ave, Birmingham B14 4PP, t (0121) 430 5348, *www.battlefieldtours.co.uk*. D-Day battlefield tours every year.

Belle France, Spelmonen Old Oast, Goudhurst, Kent TN17 1HE, t 0970 405 4056. Independent cycling and walking holidays.

British Tours, 49 Conduit Street, Mayfair, London W1S 2YS, t (020) 7734 8734, *www.british tours.com/normandy*. One-, two-, and three-day aerial and land tours of the landing beaches.

Canvas Holidays Ltd, East Port House, Dunfermline KY12 7JG, t 0870 192 1154, *www.canvasholidays.com*. Self-drive camping and mobile home holidays.

French Golf Holidays, The Green, Blackmore, Essex CM4 0RT, t (01277) 824 100, *www.french golfholidays.com*. Tailor-made golf holidays: mainly self-drive trips to impressive courses such as Deauville, Rouen and Dieppe.

Holts Tours Ltd, HiTours House, Crossoak Lane, Redhill, Surrey RH1 5EX, t (01293) 455 356, *www.battletours.co.uk*. D-Day beach and battlefield tours.

InnTravel, nr Castle Howard, York YO60 7JU, t (01653) 617 949, *www.inntravel.co.uk*. Independent walking trips from hotel to hotel, with luggage transported and self-guided walking notes. Accommodation is in hotels or *auberges*, with an emphasis on fine food.

Le Manoir de l'Aufragère Cookery School, L'Aufragère, La Croisee, 27500 Fourmetot, t 02 32 56 91 92, *www.laufragere.com*. British chef and her French husband run cookery courses and gourmet breaks at their 18th-century manor house in the Risle (*see* p.192).

From the USA and Canada

Backroads, 801 Cedar St, Berkeley CA 94710-1800, t (510) 5271555 or 1 800-GO ACTIVE (462 2848), *www.backroads.com*. Classic cycling and family trips.

Historic Tours, 1281 Paterson Plank Rd, Secaucus, NJ 07094, t 1-877 992 8687, *www.ww2tours.com*. Second World War veterans' tours.

Maupintour, 2688 South Rainbow Blvd, Las Vegas, NV 89146, t 1 800-255-4266, *www.maupintour.com*. Runs an 11-day escorted trip in the Loire, Brittany and Normandy, visiting Mont-St-Michel, the D-Day beaches, Deauville and Giverny.

Battlefield Tours

If you want to take a battlefield tour at short notice, there are a number of reputable Normandy-based companies which are listed below. Note that museum entries (but not lunches) are generally included in the cost of a tour, and the maximum number of people is eight. Tours are bilingual and are usually themed according to the nationality of the landing beaches. A half-day tour is usually around €40, and a whole-day tour €75–80. With the exception of the Mémorial de Caen tours and the *Bus Verts*, all the tours listed below start from Bayeux.

One of the cheapest ways to tour most of the beaches is with the local *Bus Verts* company's D-Day Line, which in most years runs at weekends during June, and daily July–mid-Sept. It leaves Caen around 9.20am, travels along the beaches as far as Pointe du Hoc, and returns to Caen about 6.20pm. It doesn't include Utah, which falls in another *departement* (*see* p.279).

Bus Verts, t 0810 214 214, *www.busverts.fr*.

Battlebus, t 02 31 22 28 82, *www.battlebus.fr*. British-run, Bayeux-based company offering one-day and two-day minibus tours to the British, Canadian and American beaches. Custom-made tours also available. The whole-day tour including lunch costs €80. The 2-day 'American Experience' tour costs €155.

D-Day Tours, t 02 31 51 70 52, *www.d-day beaches.com*. Bayeux-based company running two half-day tours a day, departing daily 8am and 1.15pm, and whole-day tours 8–6.

Mémorial de Caen Landing Beach Tours, t 02 31 06 06 44, *www.memorial-caen.fr*. The Mémorial museum in Caen (*see* p.262) offers a *Journée Découverte* costing around €68 which includes a visit to the museum, a book, and a 4–5 hour minibus tour of the landing beaches. There's also a *Formule Jour J* (€99.50) which includes the above, along with collection from Caen railway station, a guided tour of the Mémorial, lunch and delivery back to the railway station. A two-day *Séjour Découverte* is also available, including hotel accommodation.

Overlordtour, t 06 70 21 43 42, *www.overlord tour.com*. Half-day tours of Omaha or Utah sectors, or you can do both. Private tours also available.

Normandy Tours, t 02 31 92 10 70. Small well-established company providing half-day tours of the D-Day beaches and the Bessin. Tours run Mon–Sat 1–6, cost €39 (inc. museum entry) and depart from the railway station.

Useful Contacts

See also below under 'Tour Operators and Special Interest Trips'.

Comité Départemental de la Randonnée Pédestre de Seine-Maritime, 18 Rue Henri-Ferric, Gruchet-le-Valasse 76210, **t** 02 35 31 05 51.

Fédération Française de la Randonnée Pédestre (FFRP), 14 Rue Riquet, 75019 Paris, **t** 01 44 89 93 93, *www.ffrp.asso.fr*.

Institut Géographique National (IGN), 136 bis Rue de Grenelle, Paris 75700, **t** 01 43 98 80 00, *www.ign.fr*. Maps can be ordered online or by post.

Where to Stay

Hotels

In Normandy you can find a range of hotels from splendid châteaux to fleapits, with most of the rooms available falling somewhere in between. The French hotel classification system awards stars not for charm or warmth of welcome but according to a check list of facilities such as hairdriers and minibars. Hence, star ratings are only a rough guide to real attractiveness (or costs), and hotels (and especially *chambres d'hôtes*, *see* p.88) that have few or no stars can often be just as nice as some that display several. Often they are nicer.

Hotels listed in this guide cover a range from top-scale to budget, and have passed our own charm test. If a hotel was loaded with stars but the receptionist was surly and the rooms soulless it will not have been included, while in contrast a simple place where the welcome was warm, the atmosphere was inviting and the building was oozing with character will often have been added to the list.

Most hotels have a range of rooms and prices, and prices vary in particular according to whether a room has an attractive view. The price ranges indicated with accommodation in this guide are based on average prices.

They don't include luxury suites, but most top French hotels have them – and they can be delightful – so do ask if you're looking for extra opulence. Most two-star hotel rooms in France have en-suite showers and toilets, while one-stars have a choice of rooms with or without.

French hotels charge for the room, not per person, so families can travel pretty cheaply, while people travelling alone, on the other hand, often get a raw deal. Single rooms are relatively rare, and usually cost two-thirds the price of a double. Breakfast is not usually included with the room price in hotels (although it is in *chambres d'hôtes*). Hotel breakfasts can cost anything from €6 to €12 on top of the room prices, and usually consists of coffee or tea, bread, croissants, jam and fruit, although smarter hotels often have ample buffets.

Some other tips. Hotel restaurants are often high quality, and many hotels offer good-value half-board or full-board deals (in summer, some insist on it, especially in seaside resorts). In French hotels wallpaper is an obsession: formerly it had to be floral, usually made of plastic vinyl stuff; nowadays flowers are a little scarcer but the plastic material still seems to be in vogue. It's all part of *la vie à la Française*. Finally, always try to book ahead. It's advisable for all hotels at all times, and essential in July and August.

France's chain hotels (Climat, Formule 1, Mercure) tend to be businesslike and dreary. They are not to be confused with the hotel umbrella associations such as *Logis de France* (*www.logis-de-france.fr*), *Relais du Silence* (*www.relais-du-silence.com*) or the prestigious *Relais et Châteaux* (*www.relais chateaux.fr*) which promote independently-owned hotels and their restaurants. The latter two are at the luxury end of the market, but the *Logis* – all of which have to be independently-owned, family-run hotels, with their owners resident on the premises – are all modest, traditional local hotels, and *Logis* membership is a reliable guarantee of

Accommodation Price Codes

Prices quoted in this guide represent average rates for a double room, with bathroom. In hotels the rates do not include breakfast, but this is included with the basic price in all *chambres d'hôtes* (B&Bs).

luxury	€€€€€	€230 and above
very expensive	€€€€	€150–230
expensive	€€€	€100–150
moderate	€€	€60–100
inexpensive	€	€60 and under

comfort. *Logis de France* has its own grading system, of one to three 'chimneys' (*cheminées*). The annual *Logis* guide is available outside France from French tourist offices. If, on the other hand, you fancy a castle, try *www.chateauxandcountry.com*.

Bed and Breakfasts (*Chambres d'Hôtes*)

B&Bs, *chambres d'hôtes*, have become very popular in France. They're often a better bet than hotels: they are usually much more homely and personal, are often in remote and beautiful locations, and tend to be far better value and more characterful. Most *chambre d'hôte* owners work hard to ensure their guests feel comfortable. You may not have a phone or TV in your room but will probably get home-made jams with breakfast (which is included) and the house is likely to be old and/or furnished with antiques. Almost as much as with hotels, there's a wide range of *chambres d'hôtes*, from baronial châteaux with four-poster beds to rustic cider farms. Tourist offices have lists for each area, but are not allowed to recommend specific ones. The *chambres d'hôtes* listed in this guide have all been individually visited.

Most country *chambres d'hôtes* are affiliated to the same *Gîtes de France* organization as self-catering *gîtes* (*see* below), which publishes informative annual booklets for each *département*. It classifies its members with one to four *épis* (ears of corn), a rating system that, like stars for hotels, is not always enlightening as it's based on gadgets more than character and views. If you like gardens, consult the *Gîtes de France*'s list of *Gîtes au Jardin*, self-catering cottages and bed and breakfasts that have interesting gardens (*see*

below). Another umbrella organization is *Clévacances*, which has more B&Bs in towns, especially on the coast. Anywhere referred to as a *chambre d'hôte de charme* is likely to be, as the name suggests, charming. Both organizations have central booking services, but if you can handle any French it's best to call a B&B directly. Also worth consulting are *Bienvenue au Chateau* (*www.bienvenueau chateau.com*), a book/website which lists bed and breakfasts in chateaux; and *Fleurs de Soleil* (*www.fleursdesoleil.fr*), a website which lists places that have been assessed as *maisons de charme*. Note that all good *chambres d'hôtes* need to be booked well in advance, especially during French holidays.

Gîtes and Self-catering Accommodation

Normandy offers a vast choice of self-catering accommodation, from rambling châteaux to converted cider presses, dovecots and *Belle Epoque* seaside villas. All short-term rented accommodation with its own facilities comes within the French term *gîte*. Most but not all are affiliated to the *Fédération Nationale des Gîtes de France*, whose yellow and green *Gîtes de France* symbol is familiar in every part of the country. Many other rental properties, especially on the coast, are affiliated to another body, *Clévacances*. *Gîte* furnishings vary enormously, from opulent to very basic, so make thorough enquiries before you book. For most *gîtes* there is a minimum rental period of one week, usually beginning on a Saturday (especially in high seasons), but in low season *gîtes* may be available just for long weekends. Prices run from around €110 per week (two people in low season) to €700 (for several people in summer). On top of the rental price quoted you will have to pay tax. Both *Gîtes de France* and *Clévacances* publish illustrated guides and have central booking services, or can be contacted through French tourist offices – although, as with *chambres d'hôtes*, once you've got basic details from the *Gîtes* list it can be easier and save time to contact owners directly.

There is a growing range of other options. The best is word of mouth: once you start asking around in Normandy, you hear of

Self-Catering Agencies and Websites

French Agencies

Fédération Nationale des Locations
Clévacances, 54 Bd de l'Embouchure, BP 2166, 31022 Toulouse, t 05 61 13 55 66, *www.clevacances.com*.

Maison des Gîtes de France, 59 Rue St-Lazare, 75439 Paris, t 01 49 70 75 75, *www.gites-de-france.fr*. The *Fédération*'s central office. In addition each *Département* association has its own office and website, which in Normandy are: **Calvados**, t 02 31 82 71 65, *www.gites-de-france-calvados.fr*; **Eure**, t 02 32 39 53 38, *www.gites-de-france-eure.com*; **Manche**, t 02 33 56 28 80, *www.manchetourisme.com*; **Orne**, t 02 33 28 07 00, *www.ornetourisme.com*; **Seine-Maritime**, t 02 35 60 73 34, *www.gites-normandie-76.com*. In the UK, Brittany Ferries (t 08705 360 360, *www.brittanyferries.com*) acts as agent for *Gîtes de France* and can provide information and make bookings.

In the UK

Allez France, Cutter House, 1560 Parkway, Solent Business Park, Fareham, Hants PO15 7AG, t 0845 330 2056, *www.allezfrance.com*.

Bowhills, Mayhill Farm, Swanmore, Southampton SO32 2QW, t 0870 235 2727, *www.bowhills.co.uk*.

Chez Nous, t 0870 197 6961, *www.cheznous.com*. Brochure of privately owned self-catering homes.

Dominique's Villas, The Plough Brewery, 516 Wandsworth Road, London SW8 3JX, t (020) 7738 8772, *www.dominiquesvillas.co.uk*.

French Connections, *www.frenchconnections.co.uk*.

French Country Cottages, Spring Mill, Earby, Barnoldswick, Lancs BB94 0AA, t 0870 197 6893, *www.french-country-cottages.co.uk*. Part of the RCI Global Vacation Network, which owns several other self-catering bodies including Welcome France and Chez Nous.

Holiday in France, 3 Lower Camden Place, Bath BA1 5JJ, t (01225) 310 623, *www.holidayinfrance.co.uk*.

Inghams/Just France, Gemini House, 10-18 Putney Hill, London SW15 6AX, t (020) 8780 4480, *www.inghams.co.uk*.

Interhome, 383 Richmond Road, Twickenham TW1 2EF, t (020) 8891 1294, *www.interhome.co.uk*. Home exchanges.

VFB Holidays, Normandy House, High St, Cheltenham GL50 3FB, t (01242) 240 340, *www.vfbholidays.co.uk*.

Welcome France, t 0870 197 6959, *www.welcomefrance.co.uk*.

In the USA

At Home in France, PO Box 643, Ashland, Oregon 97520, t (541) 488 9467, *www.athomeinfrance.com*.

Classic Vacation Rental, *www.classicvacationrental.com*.

Doorways Ltd, 900 County Line Road, Bryn Mawr, PA 19010, t 610 520 0806 or 800 261 4460, *www.villavacations.com*.

Drawbridge to Europe, 98 Granite St, Ashland, Oregon 97520, t (888) 268 1148, *www.drawbridgetoeurope.com*.

Villas International, 17 Fox Lane, San Anselmo CA 94960, t 1 800 221 2260, *www.villasintl.com*.

cottages everywhere, and many *chambres d'hôtes* owners also have one or two self-contained *gîtes* on their property. Tourist offices, again, have fairly comprehensive lists of places to rent in their area. At home, try Sunday newspapers, the Internet, specialist guides or the companies listed above. Using the agencies and tour operators will nearly always be more expensive than if you book direct, but preferential rates on ferries, flights and/or car rentals can make up the difference.

Youth Hostels

Most cities have youth hostels (*auberges de jeunesse*) that offer dormitory accommoda-tion and breakfast to people of any age for around €15 a night. Most have kitchen facilities, or provide inexpensive meals. They are a good deal for anyone travelling alone, but for people travelling together a one-star hotel can be just as cheap. Most require a Youth Hostels card to stay in them, but this can often be bought on the spot.

Useful Contacts

UK: YHA, Trevelyan House, Dimple Rd, Matlock, Derbyshire DE4 3YH, t 0870 770 8868, *www.yha.org.uk*.

USA: Hostelling International USA (HI-USA), 8401 Colesville Rd, Suite 600, Silver Spring, MD 20910, t (301) 495 1240, *www.hiusa.org*.

Canada: Hostelling International, 205 Catherine St, Suite 400, Ottawa, Ontario K2P 1C3, **t** (613) 237 7884, *www.hihostels.ca*.

Australia: YHA Australia Inc, PO Box 314, Camperdown 1450, NSW, **t** (02) 9565 1699, *www.yha.com.au*.

Gîtes d'Etape and Refuges

A *gîte d'étape* is a simple shelter with bunk beds and a rudimentary kitchen set up by a village along GR footpaths or scenic bike routes, intended for hikers, school groups or other people travelling light. Lists are available for each *département* and they're also marked on detailed maps. In mountainous areas similar rough shelters along GR paths are called *refuges*, most of which are open in summer only.

Camping

There is a good choice of camp sites in Normandy, from 4-star luxury sites with swimming pools, restaurants and loads of space to one-star sites with basic facilities and prices to match. In addition, virtually every town and village has a no-frills municipal camp site. Camping on farms is popular too, and tends to be cheaper than at other sites; most are designated as *Campings à la Ferme* by *Gîtes de France* (*see* above).

Tourist offices have lists of local campsites, and a nationwide guide, the *Guide officiel camping-caravanning*, is available in most French bookshops. It's very advisable to book camp sites in summer, when even quite out-of-the-way sites fill up.

Useful Contacts

Camping trips can also be booked ahead in the UK through these companies, as well as through Canvas Holidays (*see* 86).

Eurocamp Travel, Hartford Manor, Greenbank Lane, Northwich, Cheshire CW8 1HW, **t** 0870 366 7552, *www.eurocamp.co.uk*.

Keycamp Holidays, 92-96 Lind Rd, Sutton SM1 4PL, **t** 0870 700 0123, *www.keycamp.co.uk*.

Practical A–Z

07

Conversions: Imperial–Metric

Length (multiply by)
Inches to centimetres: 2.54
Centimetres to inches: 0.39
Feet to metres: 0.3
Metres to feet: 3.28
Yards to metres: 0.91
Metres to yards: 1.09
Miles to kilometres: 1.61
Kilometres to miles: 0.62

Area (multiply by)
Inches square to centimetres square: 6.45
Centimetres square to inches square: 0.15
Feet square to metres square: 0.09
Metres square to feet square: 10.76
Miles square to kilometres square: 2.59
Kilometres square to miles square: 0.39
Acres to hectares: 0.40
Hectares to acres: 2.47

Weight (multiply by)
Ounces to grams: 28.35
Grams to ounces: 0.035
Pounds to kilograms: 0.45
Kilograms to pounds: 2.2
Stones to kilograms: 6.35
Kilograms to stones: 0.16
Tons (UK) to kilograms: 1,016
Kilograms to tons (UK): 0.0009
1 UK ton (2,240lbs) = 1.12 US tonnes (2,000lbs)

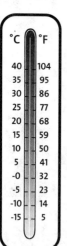

Volume (multiply by)
Pints (UK) to litres: 0.57
Litres to pints (UK): 1.76
Quarts (UK) to litres: 1.13
Litres to quarts (UK): 0.88
Gallons (UK) to litres: 4.55
Litres to gallons (UK): 0.22
1 UK pint/quart/gallon =
1.2 US pints/quarts/
gallons

Temperature
Celsius to Fahrenheit:
multiply by 1.8 then
add 32

Fahrenheit to Celsius:
subtract 32 then multiply
by 0.55

France Information

Time Differences
Country: + 1hr GMT; + 6hrs EST
Daylight saving from last Sunday in March
to the last Sunday in October

Dialling Codes
France country code 33

To France from: UK, Ireland, New Zealand 00 /
USA, Canada 011 / Australia 0011 then dial 33
and the full number including the initial zero

From France to: UK 00 44; Ireland 00 353; USA,
Canada 001; Australia 00 61; New Zealand 00
64 then the number without the initial zero

Directory enquiries: 118 000
International directory enquiries: 3212

Emergency Numbers
Police: 17
Ambulance: 15
Fire: 18
Pan-European no. for emergencies: 112

Embassy Numbers in France
UK: 01 44 51 31 00; **Ireland**: 01 44 17 67 00;
USA: 01 43 12 22 22; **Canada**: 01 44 43 29 00;
Australia: 01 40 59 33 00;
New Zealand: 01 45 01 43 43

Shoe Sizes

Europe	UK	USA
35	2½ / 3	4
36	3 / 3½	4½ / 5
37	4	5½ / 6
38	5	6½
39	5½ / 6	7 / 7½
40	6 / 6½	8 / 8½
41	7	9 / 9½
42	8	9½ / 10
43	9	10½
44	9½ / 10	11
45	10½	12
46	11	12½ / 13

Women's Clothing

Europe	UK	USA
34	6	2
36	8	4
38	10	6
40	12	8
42	14	10
44	16	12

Crime and the Police

France is a pretty safe country, but be aware that thieves target foreigners, especially their holiday homes and cars. Cars that have foreign number plates or are obviously rented are seen as rich pickings. Be extra careful in cities. Any thefts should be reported to the nearest *Gendarmerie* or, in towns, the *Police Nationale*. They will give you an official statement, which will be required for an insurance claim. If your passport is stolen, contact the police and your consulate. It's a good idea to have photocopies of passports, driving licences and other important documents, as this makes life easier if you have to report a loss. By law, the police in France can stop anyone and demand to see an ID. For motoring-related law, *see* p.58.

Eating Out

One thing to get used to when eating out in France – and especially in rural Normandy – is the timing. French restaurants generally take orders between noon and 2pm, and from 7–7.30pm to 9.30–10pm. Arrive later than these hours and you risk being treated as if you've asked for a lift to the moon. The traditional alternative for anyone wanting to eat at more flexible times is the brasserie, and in cities and coastal towns brasseries generally serve meals of all sizes through the day and often until late at night. They are scarce in rural places, though, and many small-town places called brasseries will have nothing much available beyond sandwiches outside the long-established lunch and dinner times.

France has a wide range of restaurant styles, from ultra-formal ones with starched white tablecloths and equally starched waiters to businesslike brasseries, relaxed bistros and country inns where everyone mucks in at the same table. If you're going for the smarter end, dress accordingly. Two particular types of eating place that are very worth looking for – above all for sampling true Norman country cooking made with the best and freshest local produce – are *auberges de terroir* and *fermes-auberges*. The former use only locally-sourced ingredients; *fermes-auberges* are farm-restaurants that predominantly use only produce grown or reared on the farm itself. Plus, you eat in a homely, family atmosphere, getting a true 'taste' of the countryside. Tourist offices have *Bienvenue à la Ferme* leaflets which list all the *auberges* in each area, and there's also one for the whole of Normandy. Be sure to book ahead at *auberges*, as food is prepared fresh according to demand.

The most usual way to order a meal in French restaurants is as a *prix-fixe* set-price menu (also called *a formule*), normally of at least three courses. Virtually every restaurant in France offers them, and they are often great bargains. If you order dishes separately à la carte, this will be considerably more expensive than the menu. The best-value menus are most commonly offered at lunchtime. Many restaurants also have a set-price *menu dégustation* or *gastronomique* – a selection of the chef's specialities, in five or six courses. This is an ideal way to sample the gourmet treats of famous restaurants that would otherwise be unaffordable.

A full-scale French meal consists of an apéritif, *amuse-gueules* (appetisers), a first course, a fish or seafood-based course, a main course (usually meat), then cheese and dessert before finishing off with coffee, petits fours and maybe a *digestif* (in Normandy, often a *petit calva*, a small calvados). Of course French people don't wade through this every day, and it's normally reserved for Sundays and special occasions. On weekdays, if they eat out, meals are usually condensed to a simpler set menu, or single dishes – and perhaps surprisingly, French restaurants rarely ever object if you order only one course. Brasseries offer a variety of one-course dishes, and popular modern alternatives to traditional meals include *salades composées*, mixed salads with a wide range of ingredients.

Restaurant Price Categories

Price of a full three-course meal for one, without wine, based on set menus rather than *à la carte*.

very expensive	€€€€	€60 and above
expensive	€€€	€30–60
moderate	€€	€15–30
inexpensive	€	€15 and under

Non-fish-eating vegetarians have a hard time, although things are improving. Starters should not be a problem, and there will almost always be a salad on offer. For a main course, the best policy can be to ask for a *plat de légumes*, a salad, or an omelette. It's not exciting, but at least you avoid starvation.

It's always a good idea to book ahead, especially at upscale restaurants and in the July–August high season. Most restaurants close on Sunday or Monday nights, and often for a whole day as well (usually Monday or Tuesday). Under French law, service (at 15%) should be included in the price of set menus, indicated by *service compris* or *s.c.* Many people still leave a small extra tip if they are particularly happy with their meal and the service, or if they have eaten à la carte. In choosing a restaurant, a good policy is to look for a place crowded with locals, and not to overlook hotel restaurants. The restaurants listed in this guide almost exclusively serve typical French or Norman food, although exceptions are made when an ethnic restaurant is particularly good. For more on Norman specialities, see Chapter 5, 'Food and Drink'.

Café Drinks

A café is the place to get an essential taste of France. Prices are progressively higher as you move from the bar (*comptoir*) to a table inside (*dans la salle*), or outside (*à la terrasse*). If you order a café you'll get a small black espresso; if you want milk, order un *café crème*; for more than a few drops of caffeine, ask for *un grand*. A decaffeinated coffee is a *déca*. In summer try a *frappé* (iced coffee). The French only order *café au lait* (weaker coffee with lots of milk) at breakfast time, and dunk croissants or bread into it. *Chocolat chaud* (hot chocolate) is usually good. If you order

thé (tea) expect water with a mediocre teabag, unless you are in a *salon de thé*, which should have something better, and may have a whole assortment of unusual teas. Infusions, herbal teas, such as camomile, *menthe* (mint), *verveine* (verbena), or *tilleul* (lime or linden blossom) are very popular. They are kind to the all-precious *foie*, or liver, after over indulgence.

Mineral water (*eau minérale*) comes sparkling (*gazeuse* or *pétillante*) or still (*plat* or *non-gazeuse*). There are all kinds of bottled fruit juices (*jus de fruits*), and some bars offer freshly squeezed lemon or orange juice (*citron pressé* or *orange pressée*). For information on Normandy's own tipples, cider and calvados, *see* p.64.

Electricity

The electric current in France is 220 volts. UK and Irish visitors with electrical appliances from home will need two-pin European plug adaptors, and North Americans with 110v equipment will normally need a voltage transformer as well. Older-style French plug sockets have two round prongs, but there is a new kind of socket with fatter prongs and a third earth prong. Go armed with adaptors for all eventualities.

Health and Emergencies

Fire service (Sapeurs-Pompiers): **t** 18
Ambulance (SAMU): **t** 15

In a medical emergency (*un cas d'urgence médicale*), take the person concerned to the local hospital (which may be called *hôtel-dieu* or *centre hospitalier* instead of *hôpital*). You can also call the local *SOS Médecins*, the number of which will be in the phone book.

Local doctors also take turns to cover night duty. Local papers have details of doctors on call (*médecins de service*) and the addresses of chemists (*pharmacies*) open outside normal hours. In a minor emergency in a rural area, go to the nearest chemist, as pharmacists are trained in first aid. They also have addresses of local doctors (*docteurs* or *médecins*), including lists of those who speak English, and of outpatients' and emergency clinics (*services des consultations externes*).

Restaurant Etiquette: Two Points

Calling for service. Address waiters as *Monsieur*, and waitresses as *Mademoiselle* or *Madame* (according to age). No one calls a waiter *garçon* any more.

Cutting cheese. When cutting a triangular piece of cheese such as Brie, always *garde le point* (leave the tip). Chopping across it is bad form. Instead, cut the cheese at an angle that removes the existing point and makes another.

All EU citizens are entitled to use the French state health system, but to do so they should have a European Health Insurance Card (EHIC) which replaces the old E111 form. For more information on these cards, *see* 'Insurance and EHIC Cards', p.76.

Under the French system you, like most French people, still have to pay upfront for medical treatment and reclaim most of the cost later (around 70% of doctors' fees and 35–65% of medicine and prescription charges). Before consulting a doctor make sure they are *conventionné* – that they work within the French state health system. After treatment obtain a signed statement of treatment given – a *feuille de soins* – as you can't claim a refund without one. The *feuille* should state how much you are being charged for both treatment and any prescribed medicines. You should also hang onto your prescription (the pharmacist will hand it back) and attach it to the *feuille* when you claim a refund. Medicines carry detach-able labels (*vignettes*) showing the name and price of the contents; stick these in the appropriate place on the *feuille*. Note that the cost of medicines marked with a Δ-shaped vignette or 'NR' is not recoverable.

If you need outpatient hospital treatment, you must pay for it, then claim a partial refund from the local Sickness Insurance Office (*Caisse Primaire d'Assurance-Maladie*, or CPAM). If you are an inpatient and show your EHIC, the office will pay 75% or more of the cost direct to the hospital and you pay the balance. You must also pay a fixed daily hospital charge (*forfait journalier*). The 25% balance and the *forfait* are non-refundable.

Internet

France has been peculiarly slow in opening up access to the Internet. Cybercafés are appearing in cities and towns, but they are still far less common (and more expensive) than in other European countries, so don't expect always to be able to check your e-mail with ease. Main post offices in most towns now have perhaps one public Net terminal, but there are often long queues to use them, and they are seriously overpriced.

National Holidays

On national holidays (*jours fériés*), banks, shops, businesses and most museums close, but most hotels and restaurants stay open. If a bank holiday falls on a Thursday or Tuesday, many French people 'bridge the gap' (*faire le pont*) to the weekend and take the Friday or Monday off too.

1 January New Year's Day

Easter Sunday March/April

Easter Monday March/April

1 May *Fête du Travail* (Labour Day)

8 May VE Day, 1945

Ascension Day usually end May

Pentecost (Whitsun and following Monday) end May/early June

14 July Bastille Day

15 August Assumption of the Virgin Mary

1 November All Saints' Day

11 November Remembrance Day

25 December Christmas Day

Opening Hours

If you have a lie-in and aim to contact someone in an office at midday, or do some shopping, think again – or head for the nearest restaurant. Businesses, shops and museums in France – especially in small towns and the countryside – nearly all close their doors between noon–12.30pm and 2–3pm for the all-important business of lunching. Nothing will get a French person to open up shop between these magic hours, with the welcome exception of *boulangeries*, which sell delicious quiches and sandwiches during the lunch break.

On either side of lunch, shops will be open quite long hours, opening at 8–9am and closing around 7.30–8pm. In the bigger cities, of course, it's a little different: larger shops and supermarkets now open continuously Tuesday to Saturday from 9–10am through to 7–7.30pm. The other anomaly is Mondays: nearly all shops are closed, although usually one baker stays open in each town. If you are due to arrive anywhere in France late on a Sunday, bear in mind that most restaurants close on Sunday evenings, and food shops will be closed on Monday. If you expect to be in France over those days, bring some essentials with you, or make alternative arrangements.

Compensations include the fact that food shops open on Sunday mornings, creating a lively atmosphere in villages and towns, and, since shops are open late, it's easy to shop after you've come back from a day's outing. **Markets** (daily in cities, weekly in villages) are held early, usually getting going before 8am and winding up by noon, although in some towns, clothes, flea and antique markets run into the afternoon.

Most **museums** and historic sites close for lunch, and most are closed all day on Tuesdays (some on Mondays). Many close for a whole month (usually November or January) or longer in winter, and some are shut completely from November to March. Most close on national holidays. Hours often change with the season: longer summer hours run from April, May or June to the end of September. Note, however, that changes in hours can be announced at short notice. Most museums give discounts for student card holders and EU citizens under 18 or over 65, and some are free on Sundays. **Churches** are usually either open all day, or closed outside of service times. Sometimes notes on the door direct you to the *mairie* or priest's house (*presbytère*), where you can pick up the key.

Post Offices

Post offices (PTT or *La Poste*) are easily spotted by their blue bird on yellow logo. There is a main post office prominently located in the centre of all French towns, and many villages also have a smaller, local *Poste*. Main post offices in cities open Mon–Fri 8am–7pm, Sat 8am–12 noon; in villages, offices may not open till 9am, often close for lunch, and shut at 4.30–5pm. Ordinary

stamps, though, can be bought in any tobacco shop (*tabac*). You can receive letters poste restante at any post office. To collect them you will need to show a passport or other ID with a photograph, and may have to pay a small fee.

Telephones

Most public phone boxes now operate with phone cards (*télécartes*), although a few still accept coins. *Télécartes* are sold in post offices, newsstands and *tabacs*, for €7.47 for 50 units and €14.74 for 120 units. Most phone boxes also accept credit cards. UK and Irish mobile phones work in France so long as they have a roaming facility, but check on current charges with your service provider. North American cellphones will not work in Europe unless they have a triband facility.

The French phone system has eliminated separate area codes, so that you must dial the whole 10-digit number wherever you are in the country (all numbers in Normandy begin with 02). Mobile numbers begin with 06.

Calling France from abroad, the international code for France is 33, and you then drop the first 0 of the number. To call from France, dial 00, and then the country code (UK 44; US and Canada 1; Ireland 353; Australia 61; New Zealand 64), followed by the area code (minus the first 0 in UK numbers) and the number. For the French operator, dial **t** 13; for directory enquiries, **t** 118 000; for international directory enquiries, **t** 3212.

Time

France is one hour ahead of UK time (GMT) and six hours ahead of North American EST. French summer time runs from the last Sunday in March to the last Sunday in October.

Dieppe,
the Alabaster Coast and the Pays de Bray

Anyone familiar with Impressionist art will recognise the towering white cliffs that characterise the 140 kilometres of coastline between the Seine and Somme estuaries, known as the Côte d'Albâtre *(Alabaster Coast). Where rivers have carved gashes into the cliffs, the coastal centres of Dieppe, Etretat and Fécamp have been created. Inland is the Pays de Caux, a vast limestone plateau studded with* manoirs *equipped with magnificent dovecotes. To the southeast is the Pays de Bray, known in France as* la boutonnière *or 'buttonhole', a sparsely inhabited patchwork of lush pastures and verdant valleys which produces some of Normandy's best cheese.*

08

Don't miss

① A restaurant-lined harbour and grand cafés
Dieppe **p.100**

② A flower-drenched village
Veules-les-Roses **p.115**

③ The grandest distillery in the world
Palais Bénédictine, Fécamp **p.121**

④ Luminous cliffs and dramatic arches
Etretat **p.124**

⑤ Neufchâtel cheese
Neufchâtel **p.128**

See map overleaf

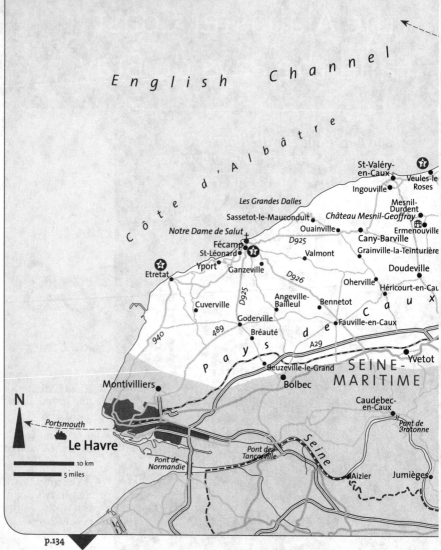

English Channel

Côte d'Albâtre

St-Valéry-en-Caux
Veules-les-Roses
Ingouville
Mesnil-Durdent
Les Grandes Dalles
Château Mesnil-Geoffroy
Sassetot-le-Mauconduit
Ouainville
Ermenouville
Notre Dame de Salut
Cany-Barville
Fécamp
D925
Grainville-la-Teinturière
St-Léonard
Valmont
Yport
Ganzeville
Doudeville
Etretat
Oherville
Héricourt-en-Cau
D926
Cuverville
Angeville-Bailleul
Bennetot
Caux
D925
Fauville-en-Caux
Goderville
940
489
Bréauté
Pays de
A29
Beuzeville-le-Grand
Yvetot
Montivilliers
SEINE-
Bolbec
MARITIME
Caudebec-en-Caux
N
Pont de Brotonne
Portsmouth
Le Havre
Seine
Pont de Tancarville
10 km
Pont de Normandie
5 miles
Aizier
Jumièges

p.134

Painters and writers who visited what has been dubbed the *Côte d'Albâtre* (Alabaster Coast) were captivated by these ancient cliffs, ever-changing in the shifting lights. As you can see from Etretat's famous rock archways, this coastline is continually eroding, and at one point, Cap de la Hève, it does so at an alarming rate of two metres a year. At points along the coast, fishing villages spill down onto shingle beaches beneath the walls of chalk. A surprising

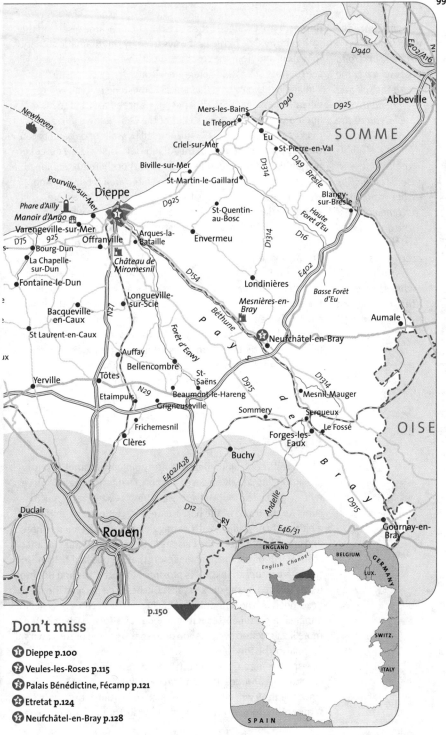

Newhaven

Mers-les-Bains
Le Tréport
Criel-sur-Mer
Biville-sur-Mer
St-Martin-le-Gaillard

D940
D925
Abbeville
SOMME
Eu
St-Pierre-en-Val
Blangy-sur-Bresle
Bresle
Haute Forêt d'Eu

Pourville-sur-Mer
Dieppe
Phare d'Ailly
Manoir d'Ango
Varengeville-sur-Mer
925
D75
Bourg-Dun
La Chapelle-sur-Dun
Fontaine-le-Dun
Offranville
Arques-la-Bataille
Château de Miromesnil
St-Quentin-au-Bosc
Envermeu

D925

Longueville-sur-Scie
Bacqueville-en-Caux
St Laurent-en-Caux
Auffay
Bellencombre
Yerville
Tôtes
Etaimpuis
Grigneuseville
Frichemesnil
Clères

D154
Béthune
Pays
Forêt d'Eawy
N27
N29
St-Saëns
Beaumont-le-Hareng
Sommery

Londinières
Mesnières-en-Bray
Neufchâtel-en-Bray
Basse Forêt d'Eu
Aumale
D1314

D16
E402
D314

D915
Mesnil-Mauger
Serqueux
Le Fossé
Forges-les-Eaux
Buchy

de
Bray
OISE

Duclair
Rouen
E402/A28
D12
Ry
Andelle
E46/31

Gournay-en-Bray
D915

p.150

Don't miss

⭐ Dieppe **p.100**

⭐ Veules-les-Roses **p.115**

⭐ Palais Bénédictine, Fécamp **p.121**

⭐ Etretat **p.124**

⭐ Neufchâtel-en-Bray **p.128**

ENGLAND
English Channel
BELGIUM
GERMANY
LUX.
SWITZ.
ITALY
SPAIN

> *Sometimes the wind would begin to blow in strong gusts which came from the sea and swept across the plateau of the Caux region, filling the whole countryside with cool salt air. The rushes would hiss, flattened against the ground, and the quivering beech trees would rustle loudly while the tops of the trees swayed and murmured.*
>
> Flaubert,
> *Madame Bovary*

number have changed little since they first became resorts in the 19th century. One of the best ways to enjoy this dramatic scenery is to walk it, and from the coastal footpath, with a little luck, you will see fulmars, shags and peregrine falcons.

Inland lies the Pays de Caux, a vast limestone plateau where wheat, rape, sugar beet and most of France's flax, used to make linen, are grown. The farmsteads of the Caux, known as *clos-masures*, were traditionally surrounded by walls of oak and beech trees to protect them from the Atlantic winds, so clearly described by Flaubert. Many expanded into *manoirs* or châteaux, equipped with magnificent dovecotes, for which the area is famous. And where rivers have carved paths across the plateau there are wooded valleys harbouring tranquil, pretty villages where, in summer, you can escape the coast-hugging crowds and uncover delightful hidden corners. In among them are many of France's finest, most original gardens.

Just southeast of the Pays de Caux lies another, equally distinct stretch of countryside, the Pays de Bray – a lush hollow between the stony plateaux of the Caux and Picardy to the east. The Bray country has a noticeable feeling of remoteness, a sparsely inhabited patchwork of flower-filled meadows, verdant valleys and limestone bluffs. It also produces some of Normandy's best dairy produce and cheeses, and to visit here is to sample a piece of rural France that still feels remarkably distant from all kinds of 21st-century bustle.

Dieppe

⭐ Dieppe

With tall, multicoloured 18th-century buildings standing sentry-like around its snugly enclosed old port, Dieppe is a likeable place. A brasserie called *Tout Va Bien* (Everything's Okay) pretty much sums up the mood of the harbour area. By contrast the seafront is a bit scruffy nowadays, with a straggle of car parks, concrete hotels and apartment blocks. The ravages of the Second World War left scant traces of the fashionable resort that Dieppe had become in the 19th century, thanks to its proximity to both Paris and Brighton. Its visitors, led by the ultra-royalist Duchesse de Berry in the 1820s, descended on the long shingle beaches to indulge in a new health-enhancing pastime – sea bathing. Today's visitors to Dieppe are more likely to stop over to shop or to soak up some of the town's fascinating history.

Despite being a Channel port, Dieppe is surprisingly small and easy to walk around. The old town has hardly changed in layout since the time when Dieppe was enclosed within city walls in the 15th century, to keep out the pesky English. Foreigners have been

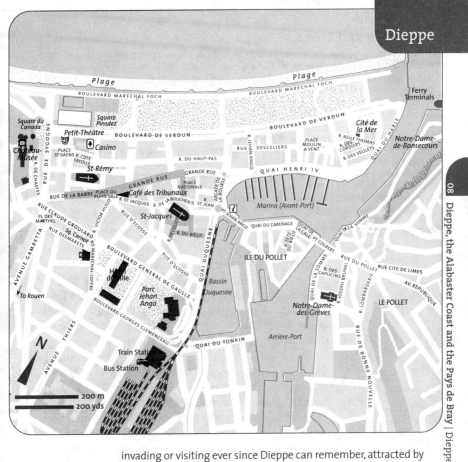

invading or visiting ever since Dieppe can remember, attracted by its deep-water harbour (its name comes from the old Norse for 'deep'). The Vikings found this fishing village and settled here in the 7th and 8th centuries, King Philippe Auguste of France seized its castle from Richard the Lionheart in the 1190s, and throughout the Middle Ages English pilgrims disembarked here en route for Santiago de Compostela.

With sea-salt in their blood, Dieppe's seamen were among the first explorers and exploiters of the New World. One, Jean Cousin, is claimed as one of the discoverers of Brazil. Another, a merchant called Jean (or Jehan) Ango, was given licence by King François I of France to raise a fleet of privateers to challenge the Portuguese and Spaniards in Africa and America. Ango came back loaded with treasures, spices and ivory. Dieppe's most famous pirate, he has been the city's hero ever since. It was on a Dieppois ship that the Italian explorer Verrazano sailed to America in 1524, when he and his men became the first Europeans to enter New York harbour, and more Dieppois were among the first settlers of Canada.

Getting to and around Dieppe

Transmanche Ferries has two or three **ferries** daily each way between Newhaven and Dieppe, with a crossing time of 4hrs (or 5hrs overnight). The ferry terminal east of the harbour has easy access to Dieppe (follow signs for Centre Ville) or routes out of town. For information call **t** 0800 650 100 (from France) or **t** 0800 917 1201 (from UK). For more on ferries, *see* p.79.

There are regular **trains** to and from Paris (2hrs 20mins), via a change at Rouen (1hr from Dieppe), and to Gisors (2hrs) via Arques-la-Bataille (8mins), Neufchâtel-en-Bray (45mins) and Serqueux, near Forges-les-Eaux (1hr).

Stradibus runs local **bus** services to neighbouring villages. To save money, buy packs of 10 tickets from the Café des Voyageurs. In summer there's a No.60/61 bus (various companies) which runs along the coast to Fécamp, via Varengeville, Veules and St Valéry.

An alternative to walking around Dieppe is the **Petit Train**, which makes a 1hr tour around town from the Tourist Office (April–Sept daily).

To phone for a **taxi**, call **t** 02 35 84 20 05. Three **car rental** offices are **Budget**, Av Normandie-Sussex, **t** 02 32 14 48 48; **Europcar**, 32 Rue Thiers, **t** 02 35 04 97 10; **Hertz**, 5 Rue d'Ecosse, **t** 02 32 14 01 70.

In the 17th century Dieppe had one of France's largest Protestant (Huguenot) communities, and one Dieppe Protestant, Abraham Duquesne, played a crucial role in reviving the French navy for Louis XIV. This did not prevent the Sun King from revoking the Edict of Nantes and so ending the relative toleration of French Protestants in 1685, which had a disastrous effect on the town, as Huguenot craftsmen emigrated to England (to Britain's great advantage). A bigger disaster came a few years later in 1694, when an Anglo-Dutch fleet under Admiral Berkeley wreaked havoc on the port, much of which was destroyed by fire. The lovely area around the harbour is the result of the rebuilding that followed.

More than a century later the English returned in more genteel form, with bathing suits and parasols, to visit France's first bathing resort. Alongside the bathers were artists, among them Richard Bonington, Walter Sickert and Aubrey Beardsley. French painters came too, captivated by the limpid light, among them Pissarro, Monet, Renoir, Gauguin and Degas. They were joined by writers, such as Proust and Sickert's friend Oscar Wilde, who came to Dieppe as a refuge immediately after he was released from Reading gaol in May 1897. Depressed and drained of his earlier wit and energy, Wilde sat for long hours in Dieppe cafés like the Suisse and Les Tribunaux writing *The Ballad of Reading Gaol*, his intensely moving account of his time in prison.

The most dramatic moment of Dieppe's recent history was in August 1942, when the Allies sent a predominantly Canadian force of 6,000 men to try to seize the port from the Germans. Tragically, over half of them were killed, wounded or captured, in this 'Dieppe Raid' (*see* p.104).

Exploring Dieppe

Dieppe's focal point is the **Quai Henri IV**, lined with restaurants and cafés that look onto the **Avant-Port**, the inner harbour where the Newhaven ferries used to dock until 1994, giving arriving in Dieppe a charm that was unique among the Channel ports. The ferry terminal has now moved eastwards to the outer harbour, and the inner port turned into a marina. Nevertheless, it's still a working port as well, and fishing boats offload gleaming fish and shellfish every morning onto the quays of the Bassin Duquesne or *Port de Pêche*, to be sold by the fishermen's wives, known locally as *Baladeuses* ('Saunterers'). You can get an even more pungent taste of the town's fishy past by crossing Pont Jehan Ango and Pont Colbert into the 'island' of **Ile du Pollet** and **Le Pollet**, working-class districts that traditionally housed Dieppe's sailors and fishermen. At the eastern end of Le Pollet, you can get lovely views from the point near the sailors' church, **Notre-Dame-de-Bonsecours**.

Back in the harbour and the old town, if you tear yourself away from the *quais* and wander westwards you pass the former Hôtel de Londres, built in 1715, which was popular with 19th-century English travellers and the painter Eugène Delacroix, and still has some striking statuary on its façade. Away from the harbour Quai Henri IV turns into the **Grande Rue**, a lively pedestrianized street with an array of gourmet food shops. A detour southwards leads to the towering buttresses of Dieppe's largest church, **St-Jacques**. Its oldest section is its 12th-century Norman transept, but most of the church was rebuilt in Gothic style after the onslaught by Philippe Auguste. It was dedicated to St James as the patron of the Santiago pilgrims. St-Jacques' chapels were mostly built by Dieppe's wealthy guilds in the 16th century, including one with fine stone carvings of indigenous Brazilians, scantily clad among luscious fruit trees. Looking on from the left is the man whose ships 'explored' (i.e. pillaged) their lands, Jean Ango. Elsewhere, men

Dieppe Ivory

Ivory has been carved and coveted around the world since prehistoric times, thanks to its fine grain, creamy colour and baby-bottom-smooth texture. Dieppois sailors may have brought back elephant tusks from the Guinea coast as early as 1384, but it wasn't until the mid-16th century that the town's ivory trade took off in earnest. Norman produce was traded in far-off lands for ivory to be brought back to Dieppe, where as many as 300 carvers carried out the eye-destroying work. They made model ships, clock cases, sweet boxes shaped like scallop shells, fans, crucifixes, figurines and intricate little snuff graters (apparently the noise of people grating tobacco during Masses became so loud that an edict was passed forbidding them in churches). For local noblemen, ownership of ivory became an important status symbol.

At the end of the 16th century, though, ivory carving was nearly obliterated altogether. The Revocation of the Edict of Nantes in 1685, ending the toleration of Protestantism in France, led Huguenot carvers to flee to England or Holland, and on its heels came the great fire of 1694. By 1731, when Dieppe had been rebuilt, there were only three ivory carvers left. Demand had slumped as well, but it picked up again from the 1820s with the appearance of a new market: the beach tourist, who wanted souvenirs to take home. Ivory, though, was becoming scarcer, and fakes began to appear. Today the import of ivory is banned, and Dieppe's present-day carvers – there are just two (*see* p.105) – use old elephants' tusks, imported long before the ban.

with feathered headdresses squat on top of stone columns, and below the Brazilian carvings you can see a remarkable piece of graffiti, a sailing ship probably scratched out by a thankful sailor. The church also has three wonderful rose windows. Alongside St-Jacques, the **Place Nationale** hosts Dieppe's excellent market each Saturday. Just south on the Rue d'Ecosse is the **Maison Miffant**, a fantastic three-storey half-timbered house that miraculously escaped the fire of 1694.

Winding back to the Grande Rue along Rue d'Ecosse you come to the **Place du Puits-Salé** (so called because a salt-water well once stood here), presided over by the grand, Germanic-looking **Café des Tribunaux**. First built as a cabaret in the 18th century, once it acquired its definitive identity as a café it became a natural hangout for artists and writers, from Monet and Pissarro to Wilde, who wrote at least part of the *Ballad of Reading Gaol* here (although the Café Suisse by the port makes the same claim). Always busy, it's a great place for people-watching or downing an apéritif.

Beyond the 16th-century **Eglise St-Rémy** and pretty **Place Camille Saint-Saëns**, a path leads uphill to Dieppe's most picturesque

The Canadians in Dieppe, 1942

In retrospect, the 'Dieppe Raid' of 19 August 1942 looks so crazy an undertaking it's hard to understand how it ever got approved. The Germans were known to occupy the port in strength, and it was equally well known that Dieppe was flanked by high cliffs that made any assault doubly difficult. However, Lord Mountbatten's Combined Operations staff argued that the capture of a strongly defended French port would be vital to an eventual invasion of continental Europe, and that by raiding Dieppe the Allies would test how well defended these ports actually were. Some 6,000 men – 5,000 Canadians, British Commandos and a few US Rangers – were therefore dispatched to Dieppe. It would be one of the blackest days in British and Canadian military history, a grim price to pay to prove that such an attack was not viable.

The plan involved four flank attacks along 16 kilometres of coastline around Dieppe, followed by a frontal assault on the town itself. However, any element of surprise was lost in the early hours, when a German naval patrol ran into the Allied flotilla just as the first commandos were preparing to land. The Germans, fully alerted, opened fire. At Puys, east of Dieppe, waves of Canadians were mown down as soon as they reached the shore, and by 8.30am every man on the beach was either dead or captive. Of 554 men of the Royal Regiment of Canada who landed at Puys, 227 were killed. At Pourville, two other Canadian regiments found a slightly more protected landing place, and got away with only 100 casualties apiece. But in Dieppe itself disaster was almost as complete as at Puys. The few tanks that managed to get off the beach onto the promenade found further progress blocked by concrete obstacles. At 11am evacuation began, and by night time all fighting had ceased. As heads were counted, the appalling cost became apparent: 907 of the Canadians who had taken part in the raid had been killed, and 1,874 taken prisoner.

Mountbatten claimed that 'For every soldier who died at Dieppe, ten were saved on D-Day.' Two grim lessons had been expensively learned: that a defended port could not be taken by direct assault, and that massive naval and air support would be vital to the success of any attack. Hence, the D-Day plans in 1944 steered well clear of established ports, and the artificial 'Mulberry Harbours' (*see* p.268) were developed. In Dieppe today there's a memorial by the Square du Canada, and the Canadian War Cemetery is at Les Vertus, 5km south. A small museum recalls the raid in the **Petit Théâtre** on Place Camille St-Saëns (*open Easter–April and Oct–mid-Nov Sat–Sun 2–6.30; adm*).

Château-Musée
t 02 35 84 19 76; open June–Sept daily 10–12 and 2–6; Oct–May Wed–Mon 10–12 and 2–5; closed 1 Jan, 1 May, 1 Nov, 25 Dec; adm

monument, the **Château-Musée**. Built in the 14th and 15th centuries, it's a picture-postcard complex of ramparts, towers and turrets, standing amid lawns that enjoy fabulous views. Until the Revolution the castle served as the residence of the governors of Dieppe, and various kings numbered among its visitors. The museum exhibits pay tribute to Dieppe's two recurring themes: seafaring and ivory. The collection of priceless ivories, carved with extraordinary skill by Dieppe craftsmen from tusks brought back by the town's seafarers (*see* p.103), is remarkable. As well as ornate jewellery boxes and mirror-backs, there are oddities such as a sailor's head carved from the tooth of a sperm whale, from 1850, and delightful figurines that give vivid insights into local life, like Pollet fishermen with herrings in hand, and the rat-catcher with a rat carved on his neck. The museum's other strength is its art collection, which includes differing views of Dieppe by many Impressionists and Postimpressionists, including Renoir, Pissarro, Sisley, Boudin and Sickert, and a particularly lovely Renoir portrait of his friend *Madame Bérard*, who owned a château near Dieppe at Wargemont, her face is a picture of quiet serenity. Rounding off the display are some often very fishy Dutch still lives and, in total contrast, a series of late paintings and mosaics by Georges Braque, who lived and is buried at nearby Varengeville (*see* p.107).

Cité de la Mer
t 02 35 06 93 20, www.estrancitedelamer. free.fr; open daily 10–12 and 2–6; adm

At the opposite end of the old town, off the *quais* on Rue de l'Asile Thomas, is the slightly worn **Cité de la Mer**, which also explores Dieppe's relationship with the sea. As well as the usual tanks and aquariums (including a touching pool with baby fish), there are interesting displays on boat-building from Viking times to the present day and on navigation and fishing, and lots to do for children, including a 'Lego space' where younger kids can make their own boats. For older children there are also short mini-boat-building courses (in French, and with advance reservation required) and a range of other activities, especially during summer.

Tourist Information in Dieppe

ⓘ Dieppe ›
Pont Jehan Ango, Quai du Carénage, t 02 32 14 40 60, www.dieppe tourisme.com

Internet Access: @rt au bar Cybercafé, 19 Rue de Sygogne.

Market Day: Sat, Place Nationale (but some stalls are in place and open all week around Eglise St-Jacques).

Post Office: 2 Bd Maréchal-Joffre.

Shopping in Dieppe

Chocolaterie Divernet, 138 Grande Rue, t 02 35 84 13 87. *Pâtissier* and chocolate specialist with a mouth-watering selection of handmade chocolates, sweets and pastries. It also has a small brasserie (*see* below).

Ivory Carvers: Philippe Ragault, 2 Rue J. Ango, t 02 35 82 10 50; Ivoirier Colette, 2 Rue J. Ango, t 02 35 82 36 97. The only two survivors of Dieppe's most traditional craft.

M Pommier, 18-24 Place Nationale, t 02 35 84 14 62. Quirky store selling wines, teas and fine foods.

Olivier, 18 Rue St-Jacques, t 02 35 84 22 55. Superb traditional *épicerie* with excellent cheeses, coffees, fine wines, jams and other delicacies.

Where to Stay in Dieppe

Dieppe ✉ 76200

Villa des Capucins, 11 Rue des Capucins, t 02 35 82 16 52, *www.villa-des-capucins.fr* (€€). This old house, a former nunnery within a walled garden in Le Pollet, is a lovely surprise. The B&B rooms, quite small but imaginatively furnished, are in former outhouses around the garden. Some sleep 3 or 4, and owner Mme Boré takes good care of her guests.

**La Plage, 20 Blvd Verdun, t 02 35 84 18 28, *www.plagehotel.fr.st* (€€–€). Friendly family-run hotel in a modern building on the seafront.

**Windsor, 18 Bd de Verdun, t 02 35 84 15 23, *www.hotelwindsor.fr* (€€–€). A grand old seafront mansion; rooms are clean if unexciting, but sea views make up for it. Older ones have more character, and there's a panoramic restaurant with good *fruits de mer*.

Villa Florida, 24 Chemin du Golf, t 02 35 84 40 37, *www.lavillaflorida.com* (€€–€). A large modern house near Dieppe's golf course and the sea, with smartly furnished, very well-equipped B&B rooms with terraces or mezzanines. To get there, take the D75 towards Pourville and turn left at the golf course.

**Au Grand Duquesne, 15 Rue St-Jacques, t 02 32 14 61 10, *http://augrandduquesne.frec.fr* (€). Venerable family-run Logis hotel in the middle of the old town, with plenty of street life just outside the door. Rooms are basic (and reached via winding staircases), but comfortable, and breakfast is included. The restaurant (€€) serves a famous *soupière de poissons*, topped with flaky pastry.

Eating Out in Dieppe

There is a line of restaurants with harbourside terrace tables all along Quai Henri IV – virtually all specializing in fish and seafood – but quality is variable.

La Mélie, 2/4 Grande Rue du Pollet, t 02 35 84 21 19 (€€€–€€). Dieppe's smartest restaurant, on the main street of Le Pollet. The atmosphere is formal, the portions often modest, but the fish is superb. *Closed Sun eve and Mon.*

La Marmite Dieppoise, 8 Rue St-Jean, t 02 35 84 24 26 (€€€–€€). On a tiny street off Quai Duquesne, La Marmite has long had a high reputation as the town's best restaurant for traditional cuisine, although some doubt whether it's kept up its standards. Specialities – naturally – are Dieppe's famous fish stew of the same name, and other fish variations. A cosy place in winter. *Closed Sun eve and Mon.*

Le New Haven, 53 Quai Henri IV, t 02 35 84 89 72 (€€). The best place along the Quai Henri IV, and good value. Specialities include fish, seafood platters and great *choucroute* (Alsatian sauerkraut).

Bistrôt du Pollet, 23 Rue Tête de Bœuf, t 02 35 84 68 57 (€€–€) A lovely, bustling little bistro on Ile du Pollet, very popular with locals. On weekend evenings you must eat *à la carte*, but at other times there are excellent set menus. Be sure to book. *Closed Sun and Mon.*

Brasserie Divernet, 138 Grande Rue, t 02 35 84 13 87 (€€–€). Attached to the *pâtisserie* (*see* above). There are varied salads for around €7, *plats du jour* (around €8) and good set menus (€10.50), and in the afternoons it's a *salon de thé. Closed evenings.*

Around Dieppe

Dieppe is one of the smallest of the Channel ports, which means it's especially easy to get away from it quickly and drive to villages nearby for lunch, an afternoon or dinner. Anyone feeling more active can walk or cycle out of town almost as easily, following excellently marked GR footpaths. Inland, there are the châteaux of

Getting to Villages in the Dieppe Region

Trains between Dieppe and Gisors stop in Arques (8mins from Dieppe). **Buses** provide more options: from Dieppe Stradibus No.5 runs to Arques-la-Bataille, and No.11 goes to Pourville. Bus Nos.60/61 run between Dieppe bus station and Fécamp (1hr 20mins), via Pourville (15mins), Varengeville (20mins), Veules-les-Roses and St-Valéry-en-Caux. There's no service on Sunday. Cars Denis also have buses to Arques-la-Bataille from Dieppe.

Miromesnil and Arques-la-Bataille; venturing west you come to the coastal villages beloved of the Impressionists, Pourville and Varengeville. The walk below the cliffs along the beach to Pourville takes 50 minutes to an hour, but should be tackled only at low tide.

Pourville and Varengeville

The wild cliffs at **Pourville**, a couple of kilometres west of Dieppe, are another site familiar to lovers of Monet: he spent four months here in 1882, doggedly painting over and over again (18 times, to be precise) a coastguard's cottage on the cliff edge above a ravine. The cliffs are still there, but Pourville's role in the 1942 Dieppe Raid (*see* 'The Canadians in Dieppe, 1942', p.104) destroyed the old village in the larger-than-usual gap in the cliffs, and nowadays it's largely modern. It's a tranquil place, though, to get some fresh air, have a drink or a meal in one of its bars or restaurants, and maybe try the oysters for which it is famous.

Leafy **Varengeville-sur-Mer**, perched on the cliffs another few kilometres west, can look like a well-heeled English suburb, with its expensive homes hidden among trees. Monet painted here too, but its most recent artistic associations are with the Cubist Georges Braque, who lived here for 20 years until his death in 1963. He's buried in the little churchyard, the **Cimetière Marin**, of Varengeville's lovely 12th-century clifftop church. Alongside it, there are stunning views over the sea far below. The grave itself is refreshingly simple – a huge slab of grey marble, illuminated by a mosaic of two white doves against a luminous sky. Inside the church, vivid-blue stained-glass panels by Braque himself mingle magically with the church's early-medieval structure and the wonderful naïve carvings on its pillars, including an engaging seasick sailor.

Bois des Moutiers
t 02 35 85 10 02; house open by appt only, gardens open 15 Mar–15 Nov daily 10–12 and 2–6; guided tours by appt; adm

Another artistic feat in Varengeville is the **Bois des Moutiers**, a remarkable Anglo-French house built in 1898 for a wealthy banker, Guillaume Mallet, by Edwin Lutyens, then only 29 and little known. It is the only English Arts and Crafts-style house in France, and moreover was designed simultaneously with its ravishing and equally English-style gardens, by Gertrude Jekyll. The garden is especially fine in May and June, when the rhododendrons, roses and azaleas are in full flower; the formal walled and hedged gardens surrounding the house were intended as extra 'green

08

Dieppe, the Alabaster Coast and the Pays de Bray | Around Dieppe rooms', extending the mansion outwards. The house is extraordinary, integrating medieval Norman features with exotic touches such as the oriental-style sloping roofs. It was the first foreign commission in Lutyens' career, which culminated years later with the Viceroy's Palace in New Delhi.

There are playful touches too, like the front door at right angles to the great bordered garden pathway, and room corners filled by razor-thin windows. With its bare white walls and brown oak, the tone is typically Arts and Crafts in its simplicity. The exception is the splendid music room, which combines the intimacy of a sitting room on one side with vast concertina-style windows giving panoramic vistas over the gardens and the sea on the other. There's a tea room in the grounds, if you need replenishing.

Several more turns in Varengeville's maze of wooded lanes lead to another house of a very different age and style, the Renaissance **Manoir d'Ango** (closed to the public at the time of writing). If you've walked around Dieppe you'll already be familiar with the legendary 16th-century shipowner-privateer Jean Ango, whose summer residence this was. Between 1530 and 1540, having acquired a massive fortune, Ango employed the finest craftsmen to create this exquisite Italianate villa, which his friend François I dubbed the 'prettiest house in Normandy.' Keen to flaunt his new status, Ango also built a magnificent brick dovecote – a symbol of wealth (*see* p.118) – which is claimed to be the largest in all France. Much of the manor was destroyed in the Revolution and it's in dire need of restoration today. Beside the driveway is the **Shamrock Hydrangea Garden**, a feast for the eyes and the largest hydrangea collection in the world. It's run by a *sympa* member of the Mallet family, the owners of the Bois des Moutiers.

Shamrock Hydrangea Garden
t 02 35 85 14 64,
www.hortensias-hydrangea.com;
open mid-June–mid-Sept daily 10–12 and 2.30–6, Tues pm only, last 2 wks Sept Wed–Mon 2.30–6; adm

Miromesnil and Arques-la-Bataille

Approached via an avenue of ancient beeches near the village of Tourville-sur-Arques, 9km south of Dieppe, the appealing brick and limestone **Château de Miromesnil** was built on the site of an earlier castle in the 1590s. In 1689 it was bought by the Hué family, one of whom, the Marquis de Miromesnil, was Louis XVI's keeper of the seals. Its greatest claim to fame, though, is that from 1849 to 1853 it was rented by the De Maupassant family, and Guy de Maupassant, perhaps France's greatest short-story writer, was born here in 1850. It was by all accounts a turbulent time, as his parents were continually quarrelling, and few artefacts remain from their time at the château, but there are copies of Maupassant's letters and his birth certificate, which ended the debate as to whether he was in fact born here or at Fécamp.

Miromesnil is occupied by its current owners, Nathalie and Jean-Christophe Romatet, whose family photos are dotted about the

Château de Miromesnil
t 02 35 85 02 80,
www.chateau miromesnil.com;
open April–Nov daily 2–6; in July and Aug you can buy separate entry to the park and potager, open daily 10–1 and 2–6; adm

place. They've recently converted five rooms into delightful *chambres d'hôtes* (*see* below), allowing guests to get a feel for this amazing place. You can dine here too, if you stay. Foodies may be interested in attending the cookery courses that are run here all year round.

Just as remarkable as the château itself are its delightful grounds, containing the remains of a 12th-century chapel (all that remains of the original castle), a 250-year-old cedar tree, and an idyllic walled kitchen garden, or potager, which provides the family with flowers and vegetables.

To the northeast of Mirosmesnil, the gaunt white ruins of the Norman castle of **Arques-la-Bataille** dominate the landscape for miles around. The site is open to all, but recently the ruins have deteriorated, so the main structures are now cordoned off. However, there's a pleasant walk around the ruins, with impressive views over the Arques valley. This was the stronghold of Guillaume d'Arques, an uncle of William the Conqueror. In 1038 he rebelled against his nephew, and built the vast moat you see today. William had none of it, blockaded the fortress, and sent his uncle into exile. The walls and keep were rebuilt in 1123 by Henry I, and Arques was the scene of bitter scraps between Richard the Lionheart and Philippe Auguste, who took it in 1204. It's most famous, though, as the site of the Battle of Arques in 1589, during the French Wars of Religion, when King Henri IV and his 7,000 men thrashed the 30,000 soldiers of the Duke of Mayenne. A carved relief on a door depicts Henri's triumphal moment.

Shopping in the Dieppe Region

Lin et L'autre, Route du Phare d'Ailly, Ste-Marguerite-sur-Mer, t 02 35 04 93 37. Linen goods from clothes to home furnishings, all made from local Norman flax, and rolls of material too. Ste-Marguerite is on the west side of Varengeville.

Where to Stay and Eat in the Dieppe Region

Pourville, Offranville and Tourville-sur-Arques ✉ 76550

Château de Miromesnil, t 02 35 85 02 80, www.chateaumiromesnil.com (€€€–€€). Come here for old-fashioned chic, and dream of Maupassant. The rooms are on the upper two floors of the château, reached by twisting staircases. All have superb views of the gardens. If you book in advance, you can dine here, enjoying fresh produce from the potager. Madame also runs occasional cookery courses.

Mme Marchand, Les Hauts de Pourville, t 02 35 84 14 29, www.gite-pourville.com (€). Modern house on the cliffs above Pourville with fabulous views and a heated swimming pool. The *chambre-d'hôte* rooms, decorated with Mme Marchand's paintings, are spacious, stylish and comfy.

Le Colombier, Parc du Colombier, Offranville, t 02 35 85 48 50 (€€€–€€). Elegant restaurant in a delightful old half-timbered house next to a park and a lake in the village of Offranville, a few kilometres inland from Pourville. *Closed Sun eve and Mon.*

Varengeville-sur-Mer ✉ 76119

La Terrasse, Route de Vasterival, **t 02 35 85 12 54, *www.hotel-restaurant-la-terrasse.com* (€). Most of the recently renovated rooms at this traditional family-run hotel have sea views, and guests can also walk in the woods or use the tennis courts. It has a popular restaurant (€€). *Closed mid-Oct–mid-Mar.*

Les Catamurons, t 02 35 85 14 34, *www.catamurons.com* (€). Two B&B rooms in a beautiful *longère* (traditional longhouse) amid large gardens a stone's throw from the Bois des Moutiers. It's bursting with beams and antiques, and the owners are friendly; a stay here needs to be booked well in advance.

(★) La Buissonière >

La Buissonière, Route du Phare d'Ailly, **t** 02 35 83 17 13 (€€€). This neat villa in Varengeville's woods was (and is) owner Mme Colombel's private house.

A few years ago she converted one room into a restaurant; nowadays it has three stunningly furnished dining rooms, a full-time chef and a reputation as one of the best eateries in the area, with innovative cooking with a noticeably light touch, making the very best use of fresh local produce. A lovely place for a treat. *Closed Mon and Jan–Feb.*

Arques-la-Bataille ✉ 76880

Le Manoir d'Archelles, t 02 35 85 50 16, *www.manoir-darchelles.com* (€). A great-value hotel in a stunning 16th-century manor with a walled garden. Half-board deals are particularly well-priced. The beautiful and equally historic stables house the also-very-attractive Auberge d'Archelles restaurant (€€–€), which offers enjoyable traditional Norman cooking.

East of Dieppe: Le Tréport and Eu

I came to Le Tréport in the evening

Unable to resign myself to going to bed so close to the sea

Without first dipping the soles of my shoes in its waters.

I am happy now As the sea froths around my steps.

Victor Hugo

The slate-roofed red-brick houses at the heart of **Le Tréport**, huddled in a steep gap in the cliffs, have scarcely changed since Queen Victoria and Prince Albert disembarked from their royal yacht here in 1843 on their way to Eu, to hobnob with the French monarch Louis-Philippe. A few years later the little fishing port would become one of the most popular bathing spots in Normandy, complete with grand hotels, seafront villas and obligatory casino. Flaubert praised its rocks and its 'blue sky that is almost Asiatic in the bright sun'. This being the north of France, the sun is not always obliging, but Le Tréport's long shingle beach, seaside feel and fabulous seafood still make it a popular spot, especially with Parisians and Belgians. Many of Le Tréport's beachside villas were destroyed in 1939–45, but you can get a taste of how it used to look by popping over the River Bresle into Picardy to **Mers-les-Bains**, whose authorities have had the vision to restore more of their villas in their original, extraordinary, mix of Belle Epoque and Art Nouveau seaside styles.

Fish-lovers are in heaven in Le Tréport. Fishy smells greet you on arrival, fresh fish and seafood can be bought straight off the boat and direct from fishermen most mornings on the quay or at the fish market, and for lunch or dinner you're hard pressed to decide between the great-value fish restaurants that line the harbourside **Quai François 1er**. Le Tréport's maritime and fishing history is

Getting around East of Dieppe

Two **train** lines link Le Tréport to Paris (3–4hrs), via Beauvais/Abancourt and Amiens/Abbeville. All trains stop at Eu. For local rail information, **t** 02 35 86 23 44.

The **Petit Train**, a special tourist ride – pulled by a decorated truck, not a real train – runs around Le Tréport, Eu and Mers-les-Bains (*July–Aug daily from 11, April–June and Sept Sat–Sun only*). It stops outside Tréport tourist office, the casino and the Château d'Eu, and the full ride takes about 1hr. Details are available from tourist offices.

Car Denis runs the No.68 **bus** to Dieppe several times a day (via Eu). CAP runs a regular service to Eu.

Musée du Vieux Tréport
open Easter–Sept Sat–Sun 10–12 and 3–6; adm

commemorated in the **Musée du Vieux Tréport**, in the old jail near the seafront. Among its displays are some amusingly prim bathing suits and beach tents from the 1890s, and an explanation of how it was that for many years one of Le Tréport's main economic activities was the collecting of pebbles from the beach – for use in the distinctive local building styles (*see* p.118).

The town's centrepiece is the 14th–16th-century **Eglise St-Jacques**, perched high above the river and the harbour. As its name suggests, this was a pilgrimage church on the route to Santiago, and there are scallop shells and knots – the pilgrim's symbols – carved over the ornate Renaissance porch. The church was built alongside the Benedictine **Abbaye du Tréport**, founded in 1036. It was closed in the Revolution, and today only a few walls remain. For anyone with the required energy it's worth climbing the 365 steps to the **Belvédère des Terrasses** at the top of the cliffs, for spectacular views as far as the Bay of the Somme to the northeast. There are more fine walks west along the coast (the tourist office has details). At night Le Tréport's 100-metre-high cliffs, claimed to be the tallest chalk cliffs in Europe, are impressively floodlit. Below them there is another attractive walk among the bow-windowed houses of the old fishermen's quarter, the **Quartier des Cordiers**.

A Little Gem: Eu

Its location – just inside Normandy's northern frontier 5km inland from Le Tréport – is almost as obscure as its odd name, so Eu is often overlooked. But the tranquillity of this town beside the River Bresle belies a quiet confidence gained from centuries of royal connections. In the 1840s Eu's château was the place to which Queen Victoria and Prince Albert came to seal a new-born friendship between Britain and France – the first time a British monarch had set foot on French soil since Henry VIII's meeting with François I at the Field of the Cloth of Gold in 1520. Many centuries earlier, William the Conqueror tied the nuptial knot with his Matilda in the abbey next to Eu's castle, even if, the story goes, he only got his wicked way by dragging the poor girl across the bedchamber by her hair. The Duc de Guise, known as *Le Balafré* ('Scarface'), who built the present château with his wife Catherine de Clèves, was no less thuggish, playing a key part in the St Bartholomew's Day Massacre of Protestants in Paris in 1572, and overseeing the murder of many of his wife's lovers.

A superb church, **Notre-Dame-et-St-Laurent**, better known locally as Le Collégiale, faces the château in the centre of Eu. It is dedicated not to a Norman but to an Irish saint, St Laurence O'Toole. He was Archbishop of Dublin at the time of the first Anglo-Norman invasion of Ireland in 1169, and in 1180 was sent by the Irish lords to ask for clemency from Henry II. Henry snubbed him and forbade him from returning to Ireland, but O'Toole, persistent, tried to follow the King-Duke to his Norman court in Rouen. Exhausted by the sea crossing, he stopped at a knoll just north of Eu, where the 19th-century **Chapelle St-Laurent** now stands, and looking down on the town declared 'Here is my place of rest, now and forever.' He died in Eu four days later. Pilgrims flocked to the saintly bishop's shrine almost immediately, and he was canonized in 1225. Soon the crowds were unable to fit inside the old Romanesque church where O'Toole was buried, so a magnificent Gothic church was erected over his grave between 1186 and 1226. It was a major pilgrimage centre throughout the Middle Ages, and the tomb still lies inside the vaulted crypt. The crypt is huge, and in the 1820s Louis-Philippe, Duke of Orléans and later King of France, took advantage of its size to add the tombs of his ancestors, the counts of Eu and Artois. The church above still has its original 12th-century nave, in stark contrast to the choir and south transept, rebuilt in the Flamboyant Gothic style in the 14th century after the central tower was struck by lightning. With its fine proportions and forest of buttresses, the Collégiale resembles the greatest French Gothic buildings, and Viollet-le-Duc, the great Gothic revivalist who restored it in the 19th century, is said to have declared 'I have seen bigger, taller churches, but none more beautiful.' The church also has fine carvings in wood, especially the serious-faced *Notre-Dame d'Eu* (Our Lady of Eu) in the Lady Chapel behind the choir, believed to be the work of Eu's famous 17th-century sculptor François Anguier, who with his brother Michel also worked on the Louvre and the Val de Grâce in Paris.

Joan of Arc passed through Eu on her way to her trial in Rouen in 1430, but little remains of the medieval town as, along with William the Conqueror's castle, it was burned to the ground in 1475 on the orders of Louis XI to prevent the English getting their hands on it. But you can get a taste of the buildings that replaced the old town in the 16th and 17th centuries along Eu's enchanting main street, **Rue Paul Bignon**, with its fine Louis XIII-style merchants' houses, good food shops and the tourist office.

Chapelle du Collège des Jésuites
open Mar–Nov Mon–Sat 10–12 and 2–6, Sun 3–6

By a tiny square on Rue du Collège, just off Rue Paul Bignon, is the magnificent brick and stone **Chapelle du Collège des Jésuites**, originally part of a Jesuit college (next door, and now the town's *lycée*) built by the archly Catholic Duc de Guise in 1582. He didn't live to see it completed, as he was assassinated by agents of King Henri III in 1588, but work was continued by his wife, Catherine de Clèves, between 1613 and 1624. On the façade you can again see the handiwork of the Anguier brothers; the interior is pleasingly simple, its only ornament being vast memorial tombs carved in white marble for Catherine and her husband. Guise's tomb is actually empty, as his remains were burned and scattered over the Loire on the orders of Henri III to prevent him becoming a cult, and his reclining statue looks distinctly uncomfortable in his suit of armour. Across the choir, Catherine appears to be nodding off over a novel. Spurred on by Catherine and the Duc, many other religious institutions sprang up in the town, such as the lovely **Hôtel-Dieu** on Rue de l'Hospice, formerly a convent and a hospital, with its half-timbered buildings and courtyard.

Château d'Eu
t 02 35 86 44 00; open mid-Mar–Oct Mon, Wed, Thur, Sat, Sun 10–12 and 2–6, Fri 2–6; adm

This dynamic duo were also responsible for the rebuilding in 1578 of the **Château d'Eu**, on the site where William the Conqueror's castle once stood. It was intended to be built in a U-shape, but the project was curtailed by Guise's assassination and only one wing and half the central block were completed. The couple did, however, have time to plant a beech tree, *Le Guisard*, which miraculously still stands. The château's lovely gardens (in which you are free to wander) were designed by Mademoiselle de Montpensier, known as *La Grande Mademoiselle*, cousin of Louis XIV, who was banished here in 1660 to keep her from plotting against him. The resident who most cherished the château, however, was Louis-Philippe of Orléans, who inherited it with the title of Count of Eu in 1821 and kept it as a summer residence after the revolution of 1830 catapulted him to power as France's 'Citizen King'. Interested in innovation, he gave the château many Victorian mod cons, including running water, underfloor heating and fine parquet floors crafted by the English engineer George Packham, while an ice house (now a restaurant) was installed in the park to store ice shipped in from Norway. A canal was also built between Eu and the sea at Le Tréport to allow access for the King's yacht. Eu's greatest moment of glory was Queen Victoria's visit, a hectic string of picnics, concerts and outings that was the talk of the town for years. Most of the château's rooms are as Louis-Philippe left them, although some were redecorated in the 1870s for his grandson the Comte de Paris by Viollet-le-Duc, in a style that marries Gothic revival with Art Nouveau. Many of the rooms with Viollet-le-Duc's hand-painted wallpapers and stunning ceilings have only recently been restored, and the château has also retrieved a handsome collection of portraits that was assembled by *La Grande Mademoiselle* and which had been sold in the intervening centuries. They now hang proudly once again in the magnificent *Galerie des Guises*.

The Bresle valley has been famous for glass-making since Roman

Musée des Traditions Verrières

open Easter–end-Oct Tues, Sat and Sun 2.30–6; July–Sept also open Wed; guided tours at 3, 4 and 5pm; adm

times, a tradition well represented in the **Musée des Traditions Verrières**, in an old barracks on the outskirts of Eu. There's a wealth of information on the history of glass-making, and retired glass-workers explain the different processes and the glass-making machines (a written guide in English helps you follow the guided tours, in French only). Perhaps the most interesting part is the collection of fine bottles for the perfume industry, the main outlet for local glass today: the Saint-Gobain Desjonquères factory at Mers-les-Bains produces three million bottles daily for clients such as Chanel, Dior or Saint-Laurent, and the museum has delicate bottles in every conceivable shape from women's bodies to birds.

Glass-makers were first attracted to the Bresle because of its abundant supplies of wood with which to fire the furnaces. The deciduous **Forêt d'Eu** south of the town has plenty of wildlife and is excellent for walking and riding, and details of paths are available from the tourist office in Eu. Just inside the forest at Bois-

Roman site

tours July–mid-Sept Tues 2pm with prior booking from Eu tourist office; adm

l'Abbé, 4km from Eu, a major **Roman site** has been undergoing excavation in the last decade. Thought to date from between the 1st century BC and the 4th century AD, it seems to have been a city of considerable size, with a large Roman theatre, temples, and hot baths reserved for women. It's not officially open to the public but tours are taken around the dig by the archaeologists once a week in summer, bookable through Eu tourist office.

Tourist Information East of Dieppe

At Le Tréport tourist office you can book fishing and boat trips, and in July and Aug there are special night tours of the town.

Market Days: Le Tréport: Tues, Sat; Eu: Fri.

Post Offices: Le Tréport: Rue de Paris; Eu: Rue de la Poste.

ⓘ **Le Tréport >>**
*Quai Sadi Carnot,
t 02 35 86 05 69,
www.ville-le-treport.fr*

Shopping East of Dieppe

Atelier Frédéric Marey, 7 Rue de l'Amiral Courbet, Le Tréport. A colourful shop-workshop producing lamp-worked glass beads and bead jewellery.

Les Trois Clos des Prés, 35 Rue Chantereine, Criel-sur-Mer, t 02 35 86

78 54. Imposing château in Criel, 9km west of Tréport, where M and Mme Tailleux produce *eau de vie de cidre* – a strong variation on calvados. Tours and tastings by appt. They also have a *gîte* for rent, sleeping four. *Shop open Sat 9–12 and 5–7, Sun 9–12.*

Where to Stay and Eat East of Dieppe

Le Tréport ✉ **76470**
Most of Le Tréport's many restaurants are on or near its bustling Quai François 1er, with great-value fresh fish and seafood and outdoor terrace tables.

**Le Calais, 1 Route de Paris, t 02 27 28 09 09, *www.hoteldecalais.com* (€€–€). Imposing old *relais de poste* next to the church, run by the same family for four generations. Guests have included Victor Hugo and Allied soldiers, and Gérard Depardieu shot *Préparez vos Mouchoirs* here. Many of the attractive rooms have fine sea views.

Le Prieuré Sainte-Croix, t 02 35 86 14 77, *http://prieuresaintecroix.free.fr* (€). B&B rooms in a grand manor-farm half-way between Le Tréport and Eu: the oldest parts are 11th century, but most of it was built in the 1840s as the manor farm of Louis-Philippe's Château d'Eu estate. The rooms are full of character, and the ground-floor double has its own sitting room and small kitchenette.

11 Route de Dieppe, t 02 35 86 45 62 (€). B&B in a modern house on the road into Le Tréport, above the church. The delightful owner Mme Bilon has created a colourful garden, which you are free to enjoy, and her rooms are simple but elegant.

Le Saint Louis, 43 Quai François 1er, **t** 02 35 86 20 70 (€€€–€€). Many locals consider this Le Tréport's best restaurant, serving deliciously prepared, impeccably fresh fish in comfortable surroundings.

La Goelette, 57 Quai François 1er, **t** 02 35 86 11 71 (€€–€). Attractive budget fish restaurant that draws a young clientele, with décor that mimics the inside of a ship.

Eu ✉ 76260

Hôtel-Restaurant Maine, 20 Av de la Gare, **t 02 35 86 16 64, *www.hotel-maine.com* (€€–€). Nothing in the ground floor décor at the Maine prepares you for the wacky designs above: room doors are orange with big silver numbers, and inside there are more eclectic colours and striking artwork. They're exceedingly comfortable, too, and the owners give it a distinctively enjoyable feel. The excellent restaurant (€€), in a more conventionally extravagant Belle Epoque dining room with a sinuous Art Nouveau fireplace, is equally special. The food is sophisticated and satisfying: menus are strong on fish, but there are also fine meats. *Closed Sun eve exc July–Aug.*

Manoir de Beaumont, t 02 35 50 91 91 *www.demarquet.com* (€). Fabulous B&B in a renovated hunting lodge with huge gardens in a superb location on a wooded hill south of Eu. There is a Louis XVI-style room for 4 with *toile de jouy* fabrics in the main house, while other rooms are in a newly-built wing. Bikes are available for guests to use.

La Bragance, Parc du Château, **t** 02 35 50 20 01 (€€). A stylish restaurant inside Louis-Philippe's *glacière* (ice house) in the grounds of the Château d'Eu, with a lovely terrace in the park outside. A wood-fired grill dominates the dining room, and the food is light and modern, with good one-course meals such as mixed salads and *tartines. Closed Sun in low season.*

⭐ Manoir de Beaumont >>

ⓘ Eu >
41 Rue Paul Bignon,
t 02 35 86 04 68,
www.ville-eu.fr

The Côte d'Albâtre and the Pays de Caux

Veules-les-Roses and St-Valéry

The outrageously pretty village of **Veules-les-Roses**, 25km west of Dieppe, is one of the Normandy coast's most seductive gems, made up of flint-and-brick and half-timbered thatched cottages, winding sleepy lanes and a glittering, fast-flowing little river, the Veules. Its picturesque charms have long attracted painters and writers, among them Victor Hugo, remembered fondly as the bestower of a lottery for the poor children of the village in which every ticket was a winner – the prize was a great banquet. In

㉒ Veules-les-Roses

Getting to Veules-les-Roses and St-Valéry

The nearest **train** station is at Yvetot (32km) on the Le Havre–Rouen–Paris line. Hangard buses run services to Yvetot to link in with trains (journey time to Yvetot 30mins).

Bus 60/61 between Dieppe and Fécamp stops at both Veules-les-Roses and St-Valéry. There are 3–4 buses daily each way Mon–Sat.

summer the village also draws in so many visitors, especially Parisians, that one alley has been christened the 'Chemin des Champs-Elysées'. Apparently the rush started after a Comédie Française actress, Anaïs Aubert, visited in 1826. She raved so enthusiastically that her friends flocked to see what all the fuss was about, and Veules rapidly became a fashionable location for escapees from the capital to buy second homes. The village still takes its beauty seriously: in a generous gesture one wishes might be taken up in many other places, each resident is supplied annually with a rosebush.

Veules-les-Roses' proudest claim is that it is built along the 'smallest river in France', as the Veules is just one kilometre long. You can see the river rising daintily at the top of the village, just off the main D925 coast road, where watercress beds have flourished since the 14th century; it then picks up enough force in its steep descent to power a string of miniature water mills along the village's leafy ravine (three of which still work), and by the time it gets to the sea it's downright impressive. To best appreciate the village's charms you need to wander along the willow-draped riverside footpaths down the valley, between 19th-century villas and quaint Norman cottages, mostly built, like the whole village, to an unusually small, quaint scale. Veules also has a remarkable Gothic church, **St-Martin**, with some mysterious, deep-relief sculptures inside. The most fascinating appear to show American Indians: some believe they represent indigenous peoples that had been encountered in the New World by Dieppe mariners, but another theory suggests they are imitations of pre-Columbian American carvings seen on the same voyages. At low tide Veules has a reasonable beach with plenty of sand, and its gastronomic delights run from upmarket food shops to lovely tearooms and one of the area's best restaurants, Les Galets.

Just 6km west of Veules is the capital of the Caux Maritime, the busy little fishing and yachting port of **St-Valéry-en-Caux**. Like many ports on the Alabaster Coast it took a severe beating in the Second World War, and the uniform blocks built since then along the seafront and shingle beach are distinctly unexciting. Nevertheless, the town has a pleasing feel; away from the coast much of it escaped destruction, and the charming inner harbour with its expensive yachts is still surrounded by attractive 18th-century houses, while behind them are cobbled streets that are

Maison Henri IV
open July–Aug daily 10.30–1 and 3–7; June and Sept Wed–Sun 10.30–1 and 3–7; April–May Sat–Sun 11–1 and 3–7; Feb–Mar and Oct–Dec Sat–Sun 11–1 and 2.30–6; adm, but free for temporary exhibitions

even older. The port's greatest architectural treasure is the stunning half-timbered **Maison Henri IV**, which also houses the tourist office. Built in 1540 by a rich shipowner, in classic Norman style but with Italian Renaissance details, it now displays a stunning collection of carvings discovered by Caux mariners in the Americas. The house gained its name after Henri IV stayed here in 1593, on his way between Dieppe and Fécamp.

Temporary exhibitions are also held inside, and there's a permanent exhibition on the bitter battle of St-Valéry in June 1940, which left 70 per cent of the town in ruins. It was defended doggedly by French troops and the British 51st Highland Division, which had been cut off from the main British force as it retreated to Dunkirk. There's a monument to the Scottish division on the cliffs above the town, while on the opposite side another pays homage to the French troops who at one point, allegedly, tackled Rommel's tanks on horseback.

Inland in the Pays de Caux

Relatively few people take the trouble to wander inland in the Caux countryside, which on first appearance looks unexcitingly flat. Anyone looking for peace and authenticity, however, will be amply rewarded, and some of its lush river valleys are idyllic. Just west of Dieppe, the **Vallée du Dun** houses a string of pretty villages, such as Le Bourg-Dun (with an ancient limestone church), La Chapelle-sur-Dun and Fontaine-le-Dun. Further west is **Le Mesnil-Durdent**, the smallest municipality in the Seine-Maritime, with just 27 inhabitants. The Caux is also peppered with a bewildering number of châteaux and manors. One of the grandest is the **Château du Mesnil-Geoffroy**, a majestic pile between Le Mesnil-Durdent and Ermenouville. Built in the 17th century in Louis XIII style, it was extended in the 18th, when it was the residence of one of Louis XV's ministers. The furniture is nearly all from the same periods as the buildings. Its delightful current owners, the Prince and Princesse Kayali, are keen to share their enthusiasm for their home with visitors: in summer they organize magical candlelit tours at night through the downstairs rooms. Most visitors, however, come here to see the superb Le Nôtre-style gardens, maze and rose gardens, planted by the Prince, which have over 1,100 varieties. The Princess also takes in bed and breakfast guests, in one of France's most opulent *chambre d'hôtes* (*see* p.119).

Château du Mesnil-Geoffroy
open May–Sept Fri–Sun 2.30–6; adm

To the west, the bucolic valley of the Durdent contains the gorgeous **Château de Cany**. Built by the great François Mansart in 1640–46, the main house and its perfectly symmetrical outbuildings are reflected in the surrounding moat. The château is still owned by descendents of the original family, and many of its furnishings are original: there are impressive Louis XIII parquet

Château de Cany
t 02 35 97 70 32; open July–Aug Sat–Thurs 10–12 and 3–6; closed 4th Sun in July; adm

Caux Architecture: Grès and Dovecotes

Half-timbered houses may be what most people associate with Normandy, but in the Caux you're as likely to see brick, flint and sandstone (*grès*). From the 16th century timber became scarce, so builders turned to the materials at hand: limestone, sandstone and black and white flints. Often used as the base for a structure finished off with timber, these materials were interspersed with red bricks, producing attractive polychrome patterns. A fine example is the checkerwork on the Palais Bénédictine in Fécamp, but others can be spotted throughout the Caux. The flints were mostly extracted from beach pebbles. Collecting them was big business, and in Le Tréport the last pebble collector only retired in the 1990s. In Fécamp, sailors collected pebbles between fishing seasons. This building style disappeared with the arrival of the railways, which brought coal-fired red bricks.

Another of the Pays de Caux's characteristic sights is its giant *colombiers* (dovecotes or pigeon-houses), built of flint, stone or brick in geometric patterns. Outsize dovecotes are found throughout Normandy, but the Caux has the most distinctive of them all. Before the Revolution they were also one of Normandy's most provocative sights, as since medieval times only lords of the manor had been entitled to own them, ensuring a tasty food supply for their household and rich fertilizer for their crops. Hungry peasants looked helplessly on as the aristocratic birds gorged themselves on their newly-planted wheat. Not surprisingly, the *droit de colombier* (right to own a dovecote) was one of the first aristocratic privileges abolished in the Revolution.

From the lord's point of view, the dovecote was the perfect way to show off one's wealth – the equivalent of owning a flash car today. The more pigeons you owned, the richer you were, and by the 16th century, moreover, the rewards for selling their droppings for fertilizer were so great that the gentry turned this trade into yet another privilege that only they could enjoy. Pigeons became such a valuable resource that they were used to settle debts or given as wedding gifts.

Architecturally, *colombiers* were a chance to have a bit of fun. Sometimes matching the architecture of the manor house, sometimes totally different, they were made in all kinds of shapes – round, polygonal or square. Inside, the dovecote was studded with pigeon-holes (*boulins*), one for each pair of pigeons.

After the Revolution, dovecotes fell into neglect. However, some are now finally being restored, and the Seine-Maritime Tourist Board has devised a 55km *Route des Colombiers Cauchois* around several of the most spectacular survivors, starting from Fauville-en-Caux, south of Valmont. At the Manoir d'Auffay in Oherville, whose dovecote has a phenomenal 1,470 roosting holes, there's a **Musée des Colombiers Cauchois** (*open July–Aug Mon, Tues and Thurs–Sun 3–6; adm*).

floors and four-poster beds, doubtless appreciated by Victor Hugo when he stayed here, and the smoking room has an array of portraits of women, which must have kept the gentlemen amused.

Further west again, the Valmont river tumbles down a picturesque valley. The young Guy de Maupassant apparently loved this fish-filled river so much that he was nicknamed Guy de Valmont. The village of **Valmont** itself shot to prominence with the arrival of the Estoutevilles, several of whom fought at Hastings alongside William the Conqueror. In the 12th century they founded the Benedictine **Abbaye Notre-Dame-du-Pré**, which has now been partially restored. After the Revolution it became a private home owned by cousins of the painter Delacroix, who visited them there several times. It now houses a community of 25 nuns, and only the church, the (roofless) choir and the graceful **Chapelle de la Vierge** are open to the public. On the spur above the town, the Estouteville's **château** still preserves its Romanesque keep. The family still live there, but it's closed to visitors.

Abbaye Notre-Dame-du-Pré
t 02 35 27 34 92; open April–Sept Wed–Mon 2.30–5; Mass sung Mon–Sat at 9.45am, Sun at 10am

(i) **St-Valéry-en-Caux ›**

Maison Henri IV,
t 02 35 97 00 63,
www.plateaudecaux
maritime.com.

Tourist Information in Veules-les-Roses and St-Valéry

The Veules-les-Roses tourist office organizes guided tours of the village in July–Aug Mon, Wed and Fri at 3pm. Departs from church. The St-Valéry office has details of local boat trips.

Market Days: Veules-les-Roses, Wed; St-Valéry, Fri, and Sun mornings June–Sept.

Post Offices: Veules-les-Roses, 16 Rue du Docteur Pierre Girard; St-Valéry, 2 Rue de la Poste.

Shopping in Veules-les-Roses and St-Valéry

Veules has an unusual number of speciality food shops and tearooms. Its own local specialities are watercress, and products made from roses: the pharmacy sells home-made *crème de rose* and *eau de rose*.

Les Tourelles, 3, Rue du Docteur Girard, Veules-les-Roses. Village baker whose speciality is a meringue and caramel cream concoction in the shape of a camembert.

★ **Château du Mesnil-Geoffroy ›**

Where to Stay in Veules-les-Roses and St-Valéry

(i) **Veules-les-Roses ›**

27 Rue Victor Hugo,
t 02 35 97 63 05,
www.veules-les-roses.fr

Veules-les-Roses ✉ 76780

Relais Douce France, 13 Rue du Docteur Girard, **t** 02 35 57 85 30, *www.doucefrance.fr* (€€€–€€). A special hotel in a 17th-century *relais de poste*, which now contains stylish modern apartments, sleeping 2–4, around a flower-decked courtyard. Some have views over the river, most have a kitchenette, and some are adapted for disabled guests. The *relais* also has a *salon de thé* (€), with a riverside terrace. Booking is essential. *Closed in Jan.*

Senteurs et Couleurs, 17 Rue Mélingue, **t** 02 35 57 43 88 (€). A lovely old building in the centre of Veules. The three simple B&B rooms, which share a toilet but have their own bathrooms

are decorated in an unusual mix of colours.

St Valéry-en-Caux ✉ 76460 and the Caux Villages

***Château de Sassetot-Le-Mauconduit, 76540 Sassetot-le-Mauconduit, **t** 02 35 28 00 11, *www.chateau-de-sassetot.com* (€€€€€–€€). A country-house hotel in an 18th-century château in its own park, near the coast road between St-Valéry and Fécamp. Empress Elizabeth of Austria, known as Sissi, stayed here in the 1870s, and the most opulent accommodation is the regal 'Sissi Suite'. Standard rooms are on the small side, so it's best to splash out on a *chambre de charme*. The smart restaurant (€€€–€€) in the lovely panelled dining room has decadent desserts.

Château du Mesnil-Geoffroy, 76740 Ermenouville, **t** 02 35 57 12 77, *www.chateau-mesnil-geoffroy.com* (€€€–€€). Perhaps the most sumptuous *chambres-d'hôte* in France, 7km south of St-Valéry. The elegant 18th-century bedrooms have views over delicious rose gardens, and the whole experience is made all the more special by the exuberant presence of the château's owner, Princesse Kayali. One of her passions is 18th-century cuisine, and with advance booking she will prepare you a dinner (€€€) based on historical recipes. The château is also open to visitors (*see above*).

Le Clos du Vivier, 4-6 Chemin du Vivier, 76540 Valmont, **t** 02 35 29 90 95, *www.leclosduvivier.com* (€€). Smart *chambres-d'hôte* in a thatched farmstead whose immaculate garden harbours cats, ducks and bantams. The two bedrooms are snug and colourful, the bathrooms luxuriously large, and the evocative ruins of Valmont abbey are nearby. Self-catering also available. Minimum stay two nights.

Les Courlis, 27 Route du Havre, St-Valéry-en-Caux, **t** 02 35 97 12 79 (€). A grand 19th-century villa in huge gardens by the Le Havre road. It has just two B&B rooms, which share a toilet. Ask for the larger one, with en-suite shower and fine views.

Eating Out in Veules-les-Roses and St-Valéry

Veules-les-Roses ✉ 76780

Les Galets, 3 Rue Victor Hugo, t 02 35 97 61 33, (€€€–€€). A modern, smartly furnished restaurant near the sea, with a grand reputation for its refined variations on traditional Norman cuisine. *Closed Tues and Wed exc. public hols.*

Un Jour d'Eté, 25, Rue Victor Hugo, t 02 35 97 23 17 (€€–€). The tables at this very pretty *salon de thé* are divided between a peaceful courtyard and a characterful inside room. There's a vast selection of teas and coffees to try, and tasty savoury tarts, pastries and homemade cakes. *Open July–Aug daily, Sept–Dec and Mar–June Sat–Sun.*

St Valéry en Caux ✉ 76460 and the Caux Villages

Les Hêtres, 24 Rue des Fleurs, Ingouville-sur-Mer, t 02 35 57 09 30, www.leshetres.com (€€€€–€€€).

Distinguished restaurant in a stunning thatched *longère* amid gardens, 3km west of St-Valéry. The elegant dining rooms have huge beams, chimneys and antiques, and the cuisine is outstanding. It also has five attractive bedrooms (€€€–€€). *Closed Mon, Tues (and Wed Sept–May); also closed mid-Jan–mid-Feb.*

Le Port, 18 Quai d'Amont, St-Valéry-en-Caux, t 02 35 97 08 93 (€€). This intimate restaurant on the quay in St-Valéry is a local favourite; specialities are fresh fish and seafood, stylishly prepared. *Closed Sun eve, Mon, and Thurs eve exc. in July–Aug.*

La Boussole, 7 Rue Max Leclerc, St-Valéry-en-Caux, t 02 35 57 16 28 (€€–€). An attractive old building off the harbour with pretty beams painted baby blue, and stylish dining rooms with exposed stone walls. A good-value option for a light meal, with plenty of salads and single-course choices. *Closed Dec–Feb and Mon–Tues in low season.*

I grew up by the sea shore, the cold grey sea of the North, in a small fishing town, ever battered by wind, rain and spray, ever pervaded by the smell of fish, of fresh fish thrown onto the quayside, their scales glistening on the cobbles, of salted cod rolled up in casks and of fish dried in brown houses, their roofs topped with brick chimneys belching smoke and spreading the pungent odour of herrings far over the countryside.

Maupassant,
Pêcheuses et Guerrières

Fécamp

Cod, a phial of sacred blood and a heady sweet liqueur are the potent ingredients that have made the historic port of Fécamp what it is today. In contrast to many other towns on this coast, it remains a working fishing port, which is an essential part of its gritty charm. Fish has always been part of Fécamp's history, and its ancient name *Fiscannum* comes from the Germanic *fisc*, meaning fish. In a narrow gap between towering white cliffs that so enchanted Monet he painted them 22 times, the town also boasts a pleasant shingle beach.

At the turn of the last millennium Fécamp became famous as the site of one of Normandy's largest abbeys, built by Duke Richard II on the site of a women's convent destroyed by the Vikings. Richard persuaded Benedictine monks to move in, and Fécamp abbey, with Cluny, spearheaded the revival of monasticism across Western Europe. Dukes Richard I and II were both buried there, and William the Conqueror chose Fécamp as the venue for a great celebratory blast at Easter 1067 to mark his conquest of England. It also became one of the most important pilgrimage centres in Normandy, thanks to its shrine of the Precious Blood of Christ. Legend has it that Joseph of Arimathea left a vial of Christ's blood with his nephew Isaac, who hid it in the trunk of a fig tree and then launched it into the sea, entrusting it to God. The log landed in Fécamp, where a chapel was erected in its honour as early as the 7th century.

⭐ Palais
Bénédictine
t 02 35 10 26 10,
www.benedictine.fr;
open July–Aug 10–7;
April–June and
Sept–Oct 10–1 and
2–6.30; Nov–Dec and
Feb–Mar 10.30–12.45
and 2–6; adm

Fécamp's star attraction, however, is its **Palais Bénédictine**, a neo-Gothic extravaganza of pinnacles and stained glass built to make the liqueur of the same name. The man who should really get credit for the drink is a Venetian monk, who invented it as a tonic at Fécamp abbey around 1510. However, the recipe, a secret blend of 27 herbs and spices, was little known until it was discovered in the 1860s by an entrepreneur aptly named Alexandre Le Grand, amid a pile of old papers sold off after the abbey had been dissolved during the Revolution. He turned it into an international bestseller and, keenly aware of the marketing appeal of his 'secret medieval' recipe, used Fécamp's famous Benedictine abbey as his logo, and then built his own still-more 'medieval' Palais to house his distillery and his own personal museum. The palace's grand wood-panelled chambers contain fabulous 15th-century manuscripts, religious statuary, and carved wooden chests, some retrieved from Fécamp abbey, while the liqueur distillery bubbles away in the basement. There are also collections of Le Grand's personal passions, like metal locks, keys and coins, and paintings including a *Virgin and Child* by the Florentine painter Tommaso. It was not all plain sailing

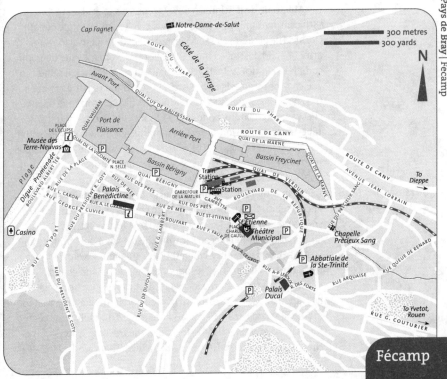

Fécamp

Getting to Fécamp

Autocars Gris run **buses** to Etretat and Le Havre every 1–2hrs, while CNA's bus No.60 runs to Dieppe via St Valery-en-Caux. Information, **t** 02 35 27 04 25.

for Le Grand, however; no sooner had he finished building his factory-palace in 1892 than it burnt down. Undaunted, he is said to have declared 'Bénédictine is not dead, and I shall prove it.' The businessman-cum-Romantic started work the next day on a new palace even bigger than the previous one, but he died before it was finally completed in 1898. His architect was a local man called Camille Albert; he was clearly influenced by Viollet-le-Duc, the godfather of French Gothic revivalism, but his creation also mixes together Renaissance, Gothic and even Baroque. At the end of each guided tour, naturally, there is a moment for the *dégustation* of the liqueur itself, in the Palais's stylish bar-shop.

To explore Fécamp's more distant past, walk through the ancient quarter around the ruins of the **Palais Ducal**, palace of the dukes of Normandy, and the remains of Richard II's **Abbey**. When built in 1001, Fécamp abbey was so dazzling that the Archbishop of Dol described it as 'the celestial Jerusalem, the Heavenly Gate ...' The monastic buildings, rebuilt in the 17th and 18th centuries, now form the town hall. Alongside them stands the vast abbey church, the **Abbatiale de la Trinité**. A new façade was tacked on to it in the 18th century, but inside the church is an elegant example of early Gothic. The church you see today was mostly built in 1170–1219, after fire had destroyed the earlier Norman Romanesque building completed in 1106, which in turn had replaced Richard II's one, but you can see remnants of the 1106 church in the radiating chapels in the choir. The church's treasures include the Romanesque reliquary chest said to hold the bones of Dukes Richard I and II, and the **Tabernacle of the Holy Blood**, on a marble altar built in 1510 by the Italian sculptor Viscardo. The north transept also has a remarkable 1667 clock, which shows not only the hours, minutes, months and seasons but also the tides.

Musée des Terre-Neuvas et de la Pêche
*27 Bd Albert 1er,
t 02 35 28 31 99;
open July–Aug 10–7;
Sept–June Wed–Mon
10–12 and 2–5.30; adm*

Fécamp's main museum, the **Musée des Terre-Neuvas et de la Pêche**, set on the seafront, deals with the port's fishy past, whose smells were described so evocatively by Maupassant. Its illuminating exhibits recall Fécamp's history as a port from as far back as the 12th century, when the abbey's monks were first given the right to salt herrings. Fécamp herrings, tasty and cheap, became a mainstay of the local diet, and were much appreciated by Napoleon, who tasted them in 1802 and immediately asked for more. Later cod became king, and the town's menfolk disappeared for months at a time fishing for cod in the freezing waters of the Newfoundland (Terre-Neuve) Banks, while others worked in shipyards and smokeries. But in the 1970s Fécamp's fishing industry hit the rocks, and the last trawler was beached in 1987. The museum is soon to be expanded and there are plans to move to new premises on Grand Quai (check at the tourist office for details).

The tiny chapel of **Notre-Dame-de-Salut**, perched on the cliffs northeast of Fécamp, is worth the steep climb via an old pilgrims' path, providing stunning views on a fine day. It was built by Duke Robert I in thanks for being saved from a shipwreck, and inside has many ex-votary plaques from sailors who have survived similar tribulations.

Musée Découverte du Chocolat
t 02 35 27 62 02; open July–Aug Mon–Sat 9–12 and 2–6.30, Sun 2–6.30; adm

If you are heading in the direction of Valmont, you may like to stop by at the **Musée Découverte du Chocolat**, which tells the history of chocolate and has an interesting collection of antique moulds, chocolate boxes and grinders. There's a shop selling the stuff too.

Yport

About 8km west of Fécamp, another gash in the cliffs reveals tiny Yport, tumbling down a deep wooded valley into the sea. The beauty of its huddle of steel-grey roofs and red-brick houses drew many writers and painters in the 19th century, including Gide, Corot, Boudin, and Claude-Emile Schuffenecker, whose *Rocks at Yport* is famous. Its remoteness, which today seems so attractive, had its downsides for Maupassant, whose bleak novel *Une Vie* is set here and for whom the village embodied insular attitudes. It has been a fishing port for 2,000 years, which is odd since it has no harbour. Today Yport still has a few picturesque fishing boats, which are pulled up onto the shingle. The beach has no sand, and at low tide algae-clad rocks make swimming difficult, but it's a very pleasant place to take it easy and imbibe the atmosphere from one of its seafront restaurants and bars.

Tourist Information in Fécamp

Fécamp ›
113 Rue Alexandre Le Grand, opposite the Palais Bénédictine, t 02 35 28 51 01, www.fecamp tourisme.com

From June–Sept a second information centre (in addition to the tourist office) opens on the seafront near the Musée des Terre-Neuvas.

Market Day: Sat, Place Bellet.

Post Office: Place Bellet

Shopping in Fécamp

Les Carolines, 44 Rue Théagène-Boufart. A small traditional bakery specializing in exotic breads, including walnut and raisin bread, a delicious variety of fruit tarts and toffees. *Closed Wed.*

Caves Bérigny, 91 Quai Bérigny, t 02 35 27 19 79. Friendly and knowledgeable wine merchant on the harbour quay, with a good selection and competitive prices.

La Fromagerie, Pourtour du Marché. Delightful little market shop selling a vast range of local and non-local cheeses, including some fine goat's cheeses.

Where to Stay in Fécamp

Fécamp ✉ 76400

***Le Grand Pavois, 15 Quai de la Vicomté, **t** 02 35 10 01 01, *www.hotel-grand-pavois.com* (€€€–€€). A brand new hotel with a designer feel is a rarity in these parts, but here is one. Its stylish rooms, especially those with balconies over the harbour, are so soul-soothing you won't want to leave.

***Ferme de la Chapelle, Côte de la Vierge, **t** 02 35 10 12 12, *www.fermedelachapelle.fr* (€€). A heavily restored farm, built around a courtyard and high on the cliffs with wonderful views of the town and the sea. Furnishings are not exciting, but there are all mod cons, a swimming pool, and a restaurant (€€). Next door is the adorable chapel of Notre-Dame-de-Salut (*see* p.123).

Auberge de La Rouge, **t** 02 35 28 07 59, *www.auberge-rouge.com* (€€). The eight rooms attached to this celebrated restaurant in St-Léonard (*see* below) are split-level, with a single bed below and double above. They look out onto a lovely garden.

La Plage, 87 Rue de la Plage, **t 02 35 29 76 51, *www.hoteldelaplagefecamp.com* (€€–€). This friendly family-run hotel is one of the nearest to Fécamp's beach, although only the upper rooms have sea views. Rooms are simple, clean and quiet.

*Vent d'Ouest, 3 Av Gambetta, **t** 02 35 28 04 04, *www.hotelventdouest.tm.fr* (€). The cosy rooms and hallway at this little hotel are furnished on a nautical theme, with portholes and sailors' knots. Friendly, and a good budget option.

★ Auberge de La Rouge >>

★ Le Vicomté >>

Beuzeville La Grenier ✉ 76210

La Chaumière, 590 Route du Carreau, **t** 02 35 38 05 31, *www.la-chaumiere.net* (€). There are two bright pristine guest rooms with great beams in this wonderful half-timbered thatched *chaumière*, just two minutes from the railway station at Bréauté-Beuzeville. There's a sitting room, library and large garden which guests are free to enjoy.

Eating Out in Fécamp

Auberge de La Rouge, Route du Havre, St-Léonard, **t** 02 35 28 07 59, *www.auberge-rouge.com* (€€€). This modest old inn in a village 2km outside Fécamp houses the area's top gourmet restaurant. There's a tranquil and well-tended garden, where lunch is served in summer, and large, welcoming fireplaces inside. The menu highlights fresh local seafood (including lobster), Norman meats and duck: to finish, the warm Benedictine soufflé is hard to match. It also has rooms (*see* above).

La Marée, 77 Quai Bérigny, **t** 02 35 29 39 15 (€€€–€€) A first-floor restaurant above a fish shop, serving exclusively fish, and with good harbour views from its attractive modern dining room. *Closed Sun eve, Mon and Jan.*

Le Vicomté, 4 Rue du Président René Coty, **t** 02 35 28 47 63 (€€). With checked tablecloths, this intimate bistro, run by a husband and wife team, offers one of the coast's best-value and most enjoyable eating experiences. There's just a four-course set menu, using the freshest local produce and superb fish and seafood. *Closed Wed eve, Sun, end Aug and part of Dec.*

Etretat

 Etretat

If you know the seascapes of Monet you'll already be acquainted with the dramatic arches in Etretat's luminous white cliffs, standing like great gateways onto the ocean. Its beaches, though, may be a little different from the deserted ones he portrayed: in summer they tend to heave with Parisians and sandwich stands, as elegant Etretat is one of France's most popular small resorts.

Getting to Etretat

Autocars Gris runs **buses** to Le Havre and Fécamp (No.24) and to the train station at Bréauté-Beuzeville (No.17) to connect with trains to Le Havre or Rouen and Paris. Bus information, **t** 02 35 27 04 25.

From April to Oct a **Petit Train Touristique et Vélo** rail line plies the 6km route to Les Loges. You return by pedalling on the *vélo-rail*.

Monet was actually using a fair amount of artistic licence himself, for the town's great natural beauty had already made it a fashionable spot by his time, and ornate Beaux-Arts-style villas were already replacing fishermen's huts along its harbourless seafront. Aristocracy and minor royalty flocked here for its healthy air and ravishing light, along with painters like Boudin, Courbet and Corot. Maupassant spent part of his youth here, and later stayed at the Villa Orphée, owned by his friend the composer Offenbach. Many mansions and villas from that era still stand, giving the town a genteel olde worlde feel, but you need to visit outside July and August to appreciate them properly. Off-season it's a lovely, charming place to spend a peaceful weekend.

The grandest arch, dubbed the **Manneporte**, and the solitary pinnacle of **L'Aiguille** ('The Needle') are below the cliffs west of the town, known as the **Falaise d'Aval**. On a few days each year you can walk out to the 'Needle' from the beach across the rocks, sometimes without even getting your feet wet. East of the town, below the **Falaise d'Amont**, there is the smaller arch that was most beloved by Monet, and likened by Maupassant to an elephant taking a drink in the sea. There are wonderful clifftop walks in both directions from Etretat (the tourist office has free maps). Heading east from the town along the Falaise d'Amont, you can climb up to the little chapel of **Notre Dame** and a futuristic needle representing the *Oiseau Blanc*, the plane in which French aviators Nungesser and Coli hoped to cross the Atlantic on 8 May 1927. They never arrived, and their plane was last seen flying out to sea over Etretat. The tiny **Musée Nungesser et Coli** recounts the story. The

Musée Nungesser et Coli

open July–Aug Fri–Sun 10.30–12 and 2.30–5.30; April–June and Sept Sat–Sun 10.30–12 and 2.30–5.30; adm

08 Dieppe, the Alabaster Coast and the Pays de Bray | Etretat

Monet in Etretat

By the time Monet came to Etretat in the 1880s it had already become a Parisians' playground. The painter studiously ignored the crowds and remained focused on its alabaster cliffs, the waves, and its ever-changing light. Indeed, looking at Monet's paintings you'd imagine Etretat was still the fishing village it had once been; only one of the paintings he did here has human life in it, *Boats in Winter Quarters*. Monet's portrayal of Etretat was slammed by some critics such as JK Huysmans, who described it as 'savagery seen through the eye of a cannibal'. Unfazed, Monet returned frequently between 1883 and 1886, usually at times when the crowds were fewer and the elements more dramatic. Above all he loved watching – and experiencing – the changing skies, and Maupassant described how Monet 'seized with both hands a shower beating relentlessly on the sea and flung it down on canvas'. When the weather was too inclement, he holed himself up in the now-disappeared Hôtel Blanquet, where he could observe and paint from the window. Monet even painted the walls and furniture of his room, including a wardrobe door now in the Art Gallery of Ontario.

best time to climb the Falaise d'Amont is at sunset, as the view back over the cliffs and Etretat is one of Normandy's most famous and exhilarating sights. There are also good longer walks in both directions along the cliffs, using the excellent coastal footpaths.

The centrepiece of the town itself is the timber-frame **market hall**. Despite appearances it was only built in 1926, albeit using timbers from older buildings in the Eure, from where the design was taken. It houses a series of touristy trinket shops, and on Thursdays hosts an interesting market which spills into the streets around.

For the French, Etretat is also known as the setting for the much-loved detective stories featuring Arsène Lupin, the creation of Maurice Leblanc, who died in 1941. One of them, *L'aiguille creuse* (the Hollow Needle), is centred around Etretat's pinnacle of rock, and has become so integrated into French culture that many visitors arrive believing the real 'Needle' is actually hollow. In Leblanc's book it contains stolen royal treasure, and you can find out how his Robin Hood-style gentleman burglar, Lupin, restores it to its rightful owners by visiting the **Clos Arsène Lupin**, Leblanc's former summer home. Starting off in Leblanc's study, visitors – guided by headphones in the language of their choice – embark on a fantasy detective tour of the house and the dandy detective's secret world, including a whole array of false moustaches, hats and monocles, part of Lupin's 47 different disguises. Images flash up onto walls, voices whisper and doors ominously creak, and it's all highly entertaining.

Inland from Etretat there's a pretty triangle of countryside towards Gerville and Criquetot with many good walks. There is also the village of **Cuverville**, which was once largely owned by the uncle of the writer André Gide. Gide frequently came here for holidays and later married here, and Cuverville is the fictional *Fongueusemare* in his novel *La porte étroite* (*see* p.38).

Clos Arsène Lupin
t 02 35 10 59 53, www.arsene-lupin.com; open April–Sept daily 10–6; Oct–Mar Fri–Sun 11–5; closed mid-Nov–20 Dec and Jan; adm

Tourist Information in Etretat

ⓘ **Etretat >**
Place Maurice Guillard, t 02 35 27 05 21, www.etretat.net

Market Day: Thurs.
Post Office: 25 Rue Georges V.

Shopping in Etretat

Maison Tranchard, 10 Rue Georges V, t 02 35 27 01 56. Outrageously expensive but irresistible *épicerie* with wonderful honeys, terrines, chocolates, coffees, foie gras and excellent wines, Normandy ciders and calvados.

Fromagerie Le Valaine, Manoir de Cateuil, Route du Havre, t 02 35 27 14 02, www.levalaine.com. Goat farm west of Etretat producing fine *chèvre* cheese, ice cream, chocolates, pâté and cider. They also run tours. *Open April–Nov.*

Where to Stay and Eat in Etretat

Etretat ✉ 76790
Château des Aygues, Rue Offenbach, t 02 35 28 92 77 (€€€€–€€€). A remarkable B&B in a 19th-century

fantasy house with grand staircases, turrets and ornamental brickwork; former guests have included Offenbach and Dumas. The 'Oriental Room' has Chinese fittings, twin beds and a circular shower in a tower; the 'Suite de la Reine' is Napoleon III-style with two double beds. The palatial breakfast room has garden views. There is a no-children rule, as the antiques are just too breakable. *Open Easter–Oct, out of season by request.*

***Le Donjon**, Chemin de Saint Clair, t 02 35 27 08 23, *www.ledonjon-etretat.fr* (€€€–€€). Extraordinary 1860s concoction of neo-Gothic ivy-clad towers, turrets and battlements in landscaped gardens with views of the cliffs and the sea. The interior is a mix of ancient and modern, and the snug bedrooms vary in style – some have fireplaces and/or balconies, and most have whirlpool baths. There's a pool and an excellent restaurant (€€€). Dining areas are plush, with soul-soothing views: seasonal menus offer rich combinations of local mainstays like wild mushrooms, lamb, duck, seafood and Norman cheeses.

Manoir de la Salamandre (Hôtel La Résidence), 4 Bd Président René Coty, t 02 35 27 02 87 (€€€–€€). This gnarled old building with monster beams looks the essence of a Norman half-timbered house, but in fact it's a reconstruction of two separate 15th-century houses from Lisieux, brought here in the 1920s. The

staircase is superb. Rooms are comfortable, but vary a lot in size and quality. Three have four-poster beds. The restaurant (€€) makes up for what some of the rooms lack in charm with delicious, organically produced food: it specializes in fish and organic wines.

Villa Les Charmettes, Allée des Pervenches, t 02 35 27 05 54 (€€). Classic 19th-century Etretat villa with a wonderful wooded hillside garden with views down to the sea, and three very spacious B&B rooms. Full of character, they have a Belle Epoque feel, and one has an extra little bedroom attached for children. Breakfast is taken in the grand dining room, or if the weather is fine, on the lovely terrace.

**Ambassadeur, 10 Av Verdun, t 02 35 27 00 89, *www.hotel-ambassadeur.fr* (€€–€). Tranquil family-run hotel in an elegant 19th-century mansion set back from the busy road. It also has two well-priced family suites.

Les Courtines, 27 Avenue Georges V, t 02 35 29 14 55 (€€). Fine old brick and flint house 200 metres from the beach, with two stunning rooms decorated in Empire style. The owners are very friendly, and there's a lovely south-facing garden.

L'Huîtrière, Place du Général de Gaulle, t 02 35 27 02 82 (€€€–€€). Mainly-seafood restaurant in a prime position at the western end of the beach, with classic views of those famous cliffs.

The Pays de Bray

The Pays de Bray acquired its other name of *la boutonnière* or the 'buttonhole' because it occupies a soft geological 'hollow' between two great slabs of chalky stone, the Caux plateau and Picardy. It may not look consistently like a hollow, but its tiny, sleepy villages nestle down in rolling green valleys, with an air of remoteness that seems remarkable in an area just a short way from the Channel ports, Rouen or even Paris. It's best known for its cheeses, and especially Neufchâtel, a farm cheese that is said to be Normandy's oldest. The *Petit Suisse*, the mass-produced *fromage frais* beloved of children everywhere, was born here too. The Bray country's cheese-making traditions began to make its farmers a bit more prosperous in the 19th century, when railway lines opened up markets in Paris, but even this has not taken away the Bray villages' feel of old-fashioned rural tranquility. In the northwest of the Pays de Bray the vast **Forêt d'Eawy** beech forest offers spectacular trails for walking and horse-riding, and in among the villages are several of France's most extraordinary gardens.

Neufchâtel, Mesnières and the Gardens

⭐ Neufchâtel-en-Bray

The main town of the northern Pays de Bray, **Neufchâtel-en-Bray**, which gave its name to the cheese, had to be extensively rebuilt after being seriously damaged in 1940 and 1944. The centre, though, still has some houses dating from the 15th to the 17th centuries, and a short walk from anywhere in town will take you into lush countryside. Apart from the Saturday market – great for buying cheese – Neufchâtel's main attraction is its fine church of **Notre-Dame**, dating from the 13th century and with an impressive 15th-century Flamboyant Gothic porch. The long-windedly named **Musée J-B Mathon-A.Durand**, in a half-timbered 16th-century mansion down the street from the church, has exhibits on the rural life, customs, crafts and traditions of the Pays de Bray, including everything you might need to know about how to make cider and Neufchâtel cheese.

Musée J-B Mathon-A.Durand
t 02 35 94 31 66; open mid-June–mid-Sept Tues–Sun 3–6; Easter–mid-June and mid-Sept–Oct Sun 3–6; adm

A short way north of Neufchâtel along the picturesque valley of the River Béthune is the **Château de Mesnières-en-Bray**, a gleaming white Renaissance-style château built in 1500–50, and with vast fat drum towers that make it look as if it should be in the Loire rather than in rural Normandy. Today the château is a college, and its gardens *à la française* have been replaced by football pitches. The guided visit, however, takes you through the most interesting parts, like the 18th-century peacock-tail staircase that

Château de Mesnières-en-Bray
t 02 35 93 10 04; open July–Aug daily 2–6; Easter–June and Sept–Oct Sat–Sun 2–6; adm

---

Neufchâtel: The Food of Love

Neufchâtel's celebrated cheeses, with their chalky rinds and smooth, creamy texture, are believed to be Normandy's oldest. They are often made in a heart shape, which some say developed when farm girls wished to declare their affections for English soldiers in the Hundred Years' War: with no common language, the little cheeses became their gooey language of love. The whole-milk cheese, though, had already been enjoyed for centuries. Records suggest that as early as 1035 a local lord, Hugues of Gournay, was obliged to donate some cheeses as a tithe to the Abbey of Sigy. By the 18th century, Neufchâtel was exported to England and Belgium, although it was not granted an official *Appellation d'Origine Contrôlée* until as late as 1977.

Although the heart (*cœur*) is the best-known shape for Neufchâtel, it has traditionally been made in six different shapes, among them the *briquette* (little brick), *carré* (square) and cylindrical *bonde*. Drained cows' milk curds are packed into moulds by hand, then left to rind-ripen like Camembert so that they develop an (edible) white bloom. Flavour strengthens the longer the cheese is left to mature: it can be bought *jeune* (up to 12 days old), *demi-affiné* (one to three weeks old), or *affiné* (one to three months old). Neufchâtel still comes solely from local farms, and there are no large-scale producers.

Getting to Neufchâtel

. Neufchâtel is on the **train** line between Dieppe (45mins) and Gisors (1hr 10mins), from where there are connections to Paris. Auffay and Clères are both on the Dieppe–Rouen line, with a few trains daily.

CNA has two **buses** daily Mon–Sat between Neufchâtel and Rouen (55mins), and the SNCF runs buses to and from Dieppe and Forges-les-Eaux. There are no buses on Sun.

---

links the towers to the superb Italianate main courtyard, and which was meant to be ascended on horseback. Passing the beautiful *Galerie des Cerfs*, with its stag-hunting trophies and stag-motif floor tiles, you reach the intimate family chapel. Some of the images in its stained glass are distorted; the priceless Renaissance windows were dismantled to save them from destruction in the Revolution, and the jigsaw was obviously pieced back together in a rush. Even so, the chapel is superb, in contrast to the huge, grim neo-Gothic chapel erected next door in the 19th century, when the château housed an orphanage. It was recently damaged by fire. The *Salle des Cartes*, with hand-painted maps on the walls, was used to teach geography, but its main interest is its now-restored 17th-century painted ceiling. The finest room, though, is the *Salle des Quatre Tambours* (Room of the Four Drums), so called because of its drum-like ceiling motifs. The four buxom ladies of Mesnières who stare proudly from the portraits on its walls have been shabbily treated: their generous cleavages were considered too much for the orphans and were painted over. They've only recently been stripped of their prudish coverings and had their breasts reinstated. Incidentally, a pleasant way to get to the château from Neufchâtel is by bike or on foot along the *voie verte*, which follows a disused railway track (*see* p.85 for more on *voie vertes*).

To the west the largest village is **St-Saëns**, ancestral home of the composer. North of it stretch the grand beeches of the **Forêt d'Eawy**, criss-crossed with footpaths and bridle trails, including the 14km Allée des Limousins, a rider's favourite. To the south and west, on the other hand, you enter a remarkable 'triangle' of Normandy's most impressive recently-created private gardens. In **Grigneuseville**, 6km from St-Saëns, is **Agapanthe**, an immaculately neat garden dedicated, as its name suggests, to the agapanthus. A few kilometres west in Etaimpuis is the **Clos du Coudray**, a bigger and more luxuriant organic garden with 7,000-plus species, especially poppies, dahlias and flowering maples.

Most spectacular, though, are the **Jardins de Bellevue**, near Beaumont-le-Hareng. Created out of a wilderness by the dynamic Martine Lemonnier and her husband 30 years ago, the six-hectare estate holds hundreds of rare plants and trees from around the world, especially the Himalayas: blue poppies, hydrangeas, exotic hellebores and much much more. There are plants for every month of the year, and you can book a tour (in English) with Mme

Agapanthe
*t 02 35 33 32 05,
www.jardin-agapanthe.fr;
open April–Oct
Thurs–Tues 2–7; adm*

Clos du Coudray
*t 02 35 34 96 85,
www.leclosducoudray.
com; open April–Oct
daily 10–7, adm; nursery
open Nov–mid-Dec and
mid-Jan–Mar*

**Jardins de
Bellevue**
*t 02 35 33 31 37; open
daily 10–sunset, last
admission 6pm; adm;
free guided tours
June–Oct Sun 4pm*

Lemonnier or a member of her family. There's a small café, a garden shop and even an old carter's cottage, available as a *chambre d'hôte* (*see* below).

Another, completely different, garden surrounds the château at **Clères**, technically just outside the Pays de Bray's northwest border. The original 11th-century château that stood here – now an atmospheric ruin – apparently sheltered Joan of Arc. The current red-brick château dates from the late 15th century, and its 13-hectare park contains not only unusual plants but a wildlife park, with some 1,600 birds and around 200 animals. It's easy to get there by public transport: there are six trains daily from Rouen, and the park is around 500m from the train station.

Clères
t 02 35 33 23 08; open April–Sept daily 10–7; mid-Feb–Mar and Oct daily 10–6.30; Nov daily 1.30–5; adm

Tourist Information around Neufchâtel

Visit the tourist office for a leaflet that lists farms where you can taste and buy Neufchâtel cheese.

Market Days: Neufchâtel-en-Bray: Sat; St-Saëns: Thurs.

Post Office: 2 Place de la Libération.

Where to Stay and Eat around Neufchâtel

ⓘ **Neufchâtel-en-Bray ›**
6 Place Notre-Dame, t 02 35 93 22 96, www.ot-pays-neufchatelois.fr.

Neufchâtel-en-Bray ✉ 76270

**Les Airelles, 2 Passage Michu, t 02 35 93 14 60, *les-airelles-sarl@wanadoo.fr* (€). Neufchâtel's best traditional hotel, on the main street. Rooms are unexciting but comfortable, and there's a no-nonsense restaurant (€€). *Closed Sun eve and Mon exc July–Aug.*

Le Cellier du Val Boury, t 02 35 93 26 95, *www.cellier-val-boury.com* (€). A beautiful B&B in a huge farm within easy walking distance of the centre. The simply furnished bedrooms are in a 17th-century wine store, and there are two self-contained *gîtes* too.

Jardins de Bellevue, 76850 Beaumont-le-Hareng, t 02 35 33 31 37 (€). Deep inside these spectacular gardens (*see* above) is an ancient thatched cottage with two B&B rooms. They are pretty basic, but the location is magical. One of the Lemonnier family will bring you breakfast in the mornings.

ⓘ **St-Saëns ››**
Place Maintenon, t 02 35 34 57 75, www.ville-de-saint-saens.fr.

★ **Au Souper Fin ›**

Au Souper Fin, Place de l'Eglise, 76990 Frichemesnil, t 02 35 33 33 88, *http://souper.fin.online.fr* (€€€). This enchanting little place in a tiny village

4km north of Clères is primarily a restaurant, combining a homely atmosphere with Eric Buisset's sophisticated cooking. There are three comfortable rooms (€). *Closed Wed eve, Thurs and (Oct–Easter) Sun eve.*

Le Chardon Bleu, 20 Grande Rue Fausse Porte, t 02 35 93 26 64, *richarddye@wanadoo.fr* (€€). Scottish owners Pat and Richard Dye have done a fabulous job restoring this huge town house right in the centre of Neufchâtel. The five *chambres de luxe* are decorated in an eclectic mix of traditional and ethnic styles. Two of the rooms have interconnecting bathrooms. Non-smoking.

La Dranvillaise, 14 Rue de la Chapelle Dranville, Flamets Frétils, t 02 35 93 31 29 (€€). Lovely *longère* run as a *ferme-auberge* using produce from the farm. Try the *volailles au cidre et au calvados* and for dessert the *bavarois aux fruits rouges*. There are three rooms (€).

St-Saëns ✉ 76680

Le Logis d'Eawy, 1 Rue du 31 Aout 1944, t 06 19 15 52 04, *www.logisdeawy.com* (€€–€€€). Grand old half-timbered coaching inn in the heart of this pretty village in the forest. The four guest rooms have been done up with style and sensitivity, and there's a large double with disabled access on the ground floor. There's a courtyard and garden which guests can use, and breakfast is in the wonderful 18th-century panelled dining room.

Totes ✉ 76590

Auberge du Cygne, 5 Rue Guy de Maupassant, t 02 35 32 92 03

(€€€–€€). Savour a slice of history at this venerable coaching inn from 1611. Guests have included Guy de Maupassant (who wrote his *Boule de Suif* here). The grand beamed dining room has an amazing collection of French and English faïence. The setting and the food make this one of the region's most renowned eateries. There are seven rooms (€€–€).

Forges-les-Eaux

As its name suggests, iron and health-giving waters are what make this elongated town tick. Iron has been mined and worked here since Roman times, while its waters were first discovered in the 16th century. Their fame really took off in the 1630s, when the spa's guests included Louis XIII, Anne of Austria and Cardinal Richelieu, plus a retinue of 200 musketeers. In the following century the spa was endowed with a smart park where guests, who included Madame de Sévigné and Voltaire, could take their constitutionals. A casino was later erected to amuse visitors, but Forges was gradually eclipsed by other European waterholes. In the 1950s the spa was redeveloped into the current Grand Casino, which is now run by Club Med as a luxury health farm, although the natural springs have been blocked off, to the chagrin of local inhabitants. The (public) park alongside it has two placid lakes where you can hire pedalos, and leads to the **Bois d'Epinay**, a pretty forest with well-marked footpaths.

The rest of the town has a very different, workaday feel, but there are gems hidden among its uniform houses. Street names such as Rue du Bout de l'Enfer (Hell-End Street) recall Forges' other speciality, pottery, made here since Roman times. In the 18th century English potters arrived hoping that the local white clay would enable them to imitate Chinese porcelain, and in 1797 one, George Wood, set up the region's first earthenware factory. Early Forges earthenware is displayed in the Musée de la Faïence, housed in the Place Brévière. There are fine earthenware pots made of white clay, and the more typical heavy earthenware used to make *culs noirs* (black bottom) pots.

In the grounds of the Town Hall there's also the Musée des Maquettes J. Guillot, a quirky collection of models of horse-drawn carriages, hand-crafted by a retired man in the town, and Forges also has a small Musée Départemental de la Résistance et de la Déportation, on Rue Maréchal Leclerc, with a motley collection of war-related objects and documents. Other buildings of interest include the tourist office, in a 19th-century *relais de poste* (staging post), and an old convent in the Rue des Sources that in pre-casino days served as a gambling den for those taking the cure.

Cyclists and walkers may be interested in exploring a 40km-stretch of disused railway track that has been turned into a *voie verte* between Beaubec-la-Rosière, just north of here, and

Musée de la Faïence
open Tues–Fri exc public hols by appt through tourist office

Musée des Maquettes J. Guillot
open April–Oct Tues–Sat 2–5, Sun 2.30–6; adm

Musée Départemental de la Résistance et de la Déportation
open daily 2–6; adm

08 Dieppe, the Alabaster Coast and the Pays de Bray | Forges-les-Eaux

Getting to Forges-les-Eaux

There's a tiny **train** station at Forges, but it has only a couple of trains a day which go to Serqueux, 3km away, where you can change onto a train or an SNCF bus. Serqueux is a stop for local services on the Dieppe–Gisors–Paris and Rouen–Paris lines. SNCF **buses** run from Forges to Neufchâtel.

Saint-Aubin-le-Cauf, near Dieppe. It passes through Neufchâtel and Mesnières-en-Bray and is a great way to see this little-known part of Normandy. When finished, the *voie* will stretch all the way from Forges to Dieppe.

Northwest of Forges near Sommery is a remarkable local 'curiosity' very worth a detour, the **Ferme de Bray**. The ancient timber and brick farm buildings, assembled from the 15th to the 18th centuries and including a cider press, bread oven, dovecote and mill, have been magnificently preserved by the Perrier family, who have lived there for 18 generations. Until a few years ago they still worked it as a dairy farm, but have now turned it into a 'farm-museum' housing a fascinating range of old farm implements. There's a pond for trout fishing, too (tackle for rent). Best of all, you can stay here – a truly special experience (*see* below).

Ferme de Bray
t 02 35 90 57 27, http://ferme.de.bray. free.fr; open July–Aug daily 2–6; April–June and mid-Nov Sat–Sun 2–6; adm

ⓘ **Forges-les-Eaux ›**
*Rue Albert Bochet
t 02 35 90 52 10,
www.ville-forges-les-eaux.fr;
regional website
www.paysdebray.org*

★ **Auberge du Beau Lieu ››**

Tourist Information in Forges-les-Eaux

Market Days: Thurs, Sun
Post Office: Place Charles de Gaulle

Where to Stay and Eat in Forges-les-Eaux

Forges-les-Eaux ✉ **76440**

****La Folie du Bois des Fontaines, Route de Dieppe, t 02 32 89 50 68, *www.casinoforges.com* (€€€€€–€€€). The Pays de Bray's most luxurious option, with 10 emphatically opulent rooms in which no expense has been spared. Bathrooms are especially glitzy, with two-seater Jacuzzis, gold taps and classical statuary. The 'Folly' is a little 19th-century château in its own grounds on the smart side of town, near the Club Med spa.

**Hôtel de La Paix, 15 Rue de Neufchâtel, t 02 35 90 51 22, *www.hotellapaix.fr* (€). The red-brick façade of this classic small-town Logis hotel hides an entirely modern building with comfortable, if unexciting, bedrooms. The restaurant (€€) is a local institution. M. Rémy Michel's cooking is classic Norman,

with plenty of duck, ham and veal, fine fish and cream, cheese and cider sauces. There's a *menu végétarien*, too. *Closed Tues lunch and Fri lunch.*

Ferme de Bray, 76440 Sommery, t 02 35 90 57 27, *http://ferme.de.bray.free.fr* (€). This extraordinary old farm is an image of old Norman country life (*see* above). The large B&B rooms, equally traditional in style, have blissful views over the grassy courtyard and the fields beyond. If you're sensitive to crowing cocks or gobbling fowl, however, bring earplugs. Sommery is 6km northwest of Forges on the D915.

Auberge du Beau Lieu, Le Fossé, t 02 35 90 50 36, *www.auberge-de-beau-lieu.com* (€€€–€€). The matter-of-fact exterior of this inn, 2km southeast of Forges, reveals nothing of the stunning old dining room within. Specialities are fish and superb local duck, and tables need to be booked well ahead. There are three cottage-style bedrooms (€€–€). Despite a roadside location it's surprisingly quiet, and has a lovely garden.

Relais du Bec Fin, 76440 Sommery, t 02 35 09 61 30 (€€–€). Attractive little good-priced restaurant in Sommery, with a bargain set-lunch menu of local fare.

Le Havre and the Lower Seine Valley

Upstream from Normandy's foremost port of Le Havre, car plants and oil refinery chimneys give way to forests of beech and oak, which line the mighty River Seine. On its way to Rouen, the great river traces confident curves through surprisingly rural countryside, including the Forêt de Brotonne and the Marais Vernier wetland, famous for its birds, thatched cottages and rustic villages. The valley's dramatic chalk cliffs shelter the evocative remains of three of Normandy's finest and oldest abbeys: St-Wandrille, Jumièges and St-Georges de Boscherville.

09

Don't miss

⭐ **Bold architecture**
Le Havre **p.134**

⭐ **Birdlife and thatched cottages**
Marais Vernier **p.141**

⭐ **Tranquillity and tragedy**
Villequier **p.142**

⭐ **Magical monuments of the Middle Ages**
Abbeys of St-Wandrille, Jumièges and St-Georges **p.144**

⭐ **Fine food on the Seine**
La Bouille **p.147**

See map overleaf

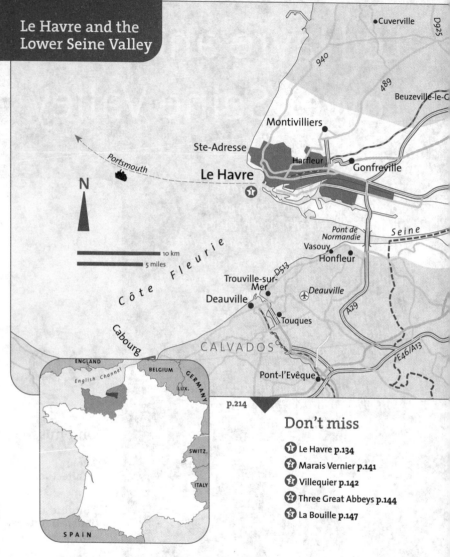

Cuverville

D925

940

489

Beuzeville-le-C

Montivilliers

Portsmouth

N

Ste-Adresse

Harfleur

Le Havre

Gonfreville

Pont de Normandie

Seine

Vasouy

Honfleur

10 km

5 miles

Côte Fleurie

Trouville-sur-Mer

D513

Deauville

Deauville

A29

Cabourg

Touques

CALVADOS

E46/A13

Pont-l'Evêque

ENGLAND

English Channel

BELGIUM

GERMANY

LUX.

SWITZ.

ITALY

SPAIN

p.214

Don't miss

Le Havre

1. Le Havre

Bombed to bits in the Second World War, Le Havre decided to look forward rather than back. It was re-created (locals prefer this word to 'reconstructed') by two radically different architects, a Frenchman, Auguste Perret, and, some years later, a Brazilian, Oscar Niemeyer. This was one of France's boldest post-war architectural experiments, and for many Perret's wide boulevards and apartment blocks create an exhilarating feeling of space and modernity. The city recently received international accolade when it was listed by Unesco as a World Heritage Site. And although Le

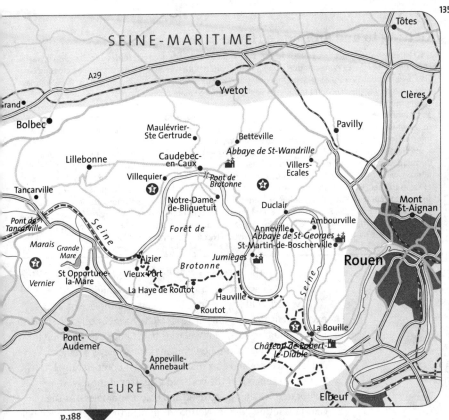

p.188

Havre is a ferry port and France's largest container terminal, it's not as dominated by industrial sprawl as you might imagine. It has a child-friendly two-kilometre beach in the middle of town (with imported palm trees in summer) and an excellent art museum, and makes an interesting place to spend a day on the way into or out of France.

Le Havre, which means 'The Haven', was created for King François I in 1517 because Honfleur and Harfleur, further up the river, were both silting up. After flooding in 1540 it was rebuilt on a grid plan. It grew from strength to strength, trading with the Americas and the French West Indies in cotton, sugar and tobacco. From the 19th century it entertained the *beau monde*, stepping off ocean liners en route between New York and Paris. One contemporary writer compared its grand boulevards to Paris, enthusing how 'the main street, the Rue de Paris, is truly worthy of the capital itself: straight, very wide, a paved highway decorated with sidewalks and edged with beautiful houses ...' Some of its grand Belle Epoque mansions still survive, particularly near the beach towards Ste-Adresse. Le Havre was also associated with many artists: Boudin lived here, Sisley and Pissarro were regular visitors, and Claude Monet grew up here from the age of five. He later returned to the city to paint

Getting to and around Le Havre

LD Lines (*www.ldlines.co.uk*, **t** UK 0870 428 4335, France **t** 0825 304 304) run **ferries** once daily each way Portsmouth–Le Havre (7½hrs for overnight crossing Portsmouth–Le Havre, 5½hrs for evening crossing Le Havre–Portsmouth). From May–September they also run ferries between Newhaven and Le Havre. Journey time each way is 5hrs. The ferry terminal is well connected to main roads.

Le Havre has a small **airport**, north of Ste-Adresse, with domestic flights (mostly to Lyon and Toulouse) and connections to several European destinations. You can fly direct to the UK with **Skysouth, t** (01273) 463 673, *www.skysouth.co.uk*, which flies Mon–Fri twice daily to and from Shoreham (Brighton; 45mins). **Airport information, t** 02 35 54 65 00, *www.havre.aeroport.fr*.

Le Havre has frequent **trains** to Paris (every 2hrs, journey time 2hrs), Rouen (55mins) and many other destinations, and a local line runs to Montivilliers (10mins). Local **rail information, t** 0836 35 35 35. Several **bus** companies serve the city. **Autocars Gris** (**t** 02 35 27 04 25) runs to Etretat and Fécamp, **Bus Verts** (**t** 08 10 21 42 14) to Caen, Honfleur, Deauville and other towns in Calvados, and Rouen's **CNA** (**t** 0825 07 60 27) has services to Rouen via Caudebec. For **bus enquiries, t** 02 35 22 34 00. Train/bus stations are on Quai Colbert.

For **taxis**, call **t** 02 35 25 81 81. You can also take a 2hr taxi tour of the city sites in English (up to 4 people; book at Tourist Office). For car hire try: **Avis**, Gare SNCF (train station), **t** 02 35 88 60 94; **Europcar**, 51 Quai de Southampton, **t** 02 35 25 21 95; **Budget**, 92 Rue Gustave Nicole, **t** 02 32 72 70 80.

several masterpieces such as *Impression, Soleil Levant*, the painting that gave its name to the Impressionist movement.

In the 20th century, Le Havre became the birthplace of existentialism: Jean-Paul Sartre is said to have conceived *La Nausée* in the Square St-Roch – between visits to Simone de Beauvoir in Rouen. When war came, however, Le Havre's role as a major industrial centre and port made it the most bombed target in France: 80 per cent of the port and a quarter of the city were obliterated, leaving 5,000 dead and 80,000 homeless. As the Germans retreated from Normandy in 1944 they attempted to hold onto Le Havre, and the Allies battered their way in with a massive bombardment. Many locals took refuge in the forests to the north.

The Modernist City

Modern architecture enthusiasts head first for the huge **Espace Niemeyer**, a sunken square containing Oscar Niemeyer's celebrated constructions from the 1970s – two gleaming white asymmetrical volcanoes that are home to a cultural centre. Locals nickname the larger one the 'elephant's foot' or the 'yogurt pot' or, ruder still, liken it to a cooling tower. A starker contrast with the concrete blocks by Perret would be hard to find. Whereas Perret loved straight lines, Niemeyer eschewed them, and while Perret liked his concrete as 'raw' as possible, often with shells or stones visible within it, Niemeyer's surfaces are painted and smooth. A good place to take in the clash of styles is the elegant footbridge across the **Bassin du Commerce**, one of several inland docks in Le Havre where you can rent rowing boats. The architects' showpieces are particularly dramatic when illuminated at night.

Heading towards the beach along Rue Voltaire, on the right is the Chicagoesque tower of Perret's **Eglise St-Joseph**, built in 1952 from his beloved reinforced concrete. Perret's last major work, it was

Eglise St-Joseph
open on request;
enquire at tourist office

built using deliberately low-cost, rough-cast materials and techniques. The church is somewhat grim and grey from outside, but inside stained-glass windows, coloured according to the direction they face (blue for north, mellow oranges for south) relieve the gloom. The altar stands below a 'Gothic-style' 106-metre lantern tower, designed to act as a beacon to liners approaching the port. To appreciate more of Perret's grand designs, wander along Avenue Foch, Rue de Paris and the nearby streets; his apartment buildings are characterized by neo-Gothic columns, arcades, and windows extending down to ground level. If you'd like to see what the apartments look like inside, the tourist office organizes tours to a show apartment designed by Perret in 1950 (book in advance). Perhaps his most impressive monument is the **Hôtel de Ville**, topped by a 17-storey tower and surrounded by walkways and fountains. Finished after Perret's death, it was extended in 1987.

Musée Malraux
t 02 35 19 62 62; open Wed–Fri and Mon 11–6, Sat–Sun 11– 7; closed Tues and some public hols; adm

On the seafront, south of the centre near the docks, the smart steel and glass block of the **Musée Malraux** forms a perfect setting for its fine collection of Impressionist art, second only to the collection in the Musée d'Orsay, Paris. It has recently been revamped, to make optimum use of natural light. Monet painted his Impression *Soleil Levant* (Impression, Sunrise) from a position just in front of the museum's site, and the Malraux has several of his finest works, including *Soleil d'hiver, Lavacourt*, a wonderful winter scene in pinks and purples; one of his evocatively murky paintings of London's Houses of Parliament; and in more abstract vein, *Les Falaises de Varengeville*. There is also one of the best of his Giverny waterlily paintings, unusual in that it's square. All the main Impressionists are here – Sisley, Manet, Pissarro – and there's a

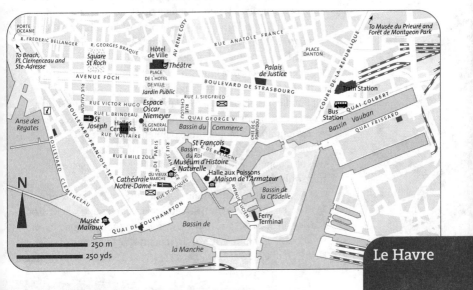

Le Havre

Auguste Perret: Crazy about Concrete

Perret's idea of beauty can be summed up in these simple words: do the best possible, with the least possible material and workforce.

Paul Jamot, 1926

Fulfil the programme – satisfy the need but without grand gestures.

Auguste Perret

'Concrete is stone that we craft, far prettier and nobler than natural stone,' declared Auguste Perret, 'natural stone is a stone that's dying.' One of the first architects to use concrete for whole buildings rather than just engineering structures like bridges, Perret believed that contemporary materials like reinforced concrete should be used because they are 'living'. In the case of Le Havre it was all he could afford, too: post-war reconstruction was a matter of making the best out of very little, and much of his work is unashamedly cheap. Born in Belgium in 1874, Perret was brought up in Paris, the son of a stonemason. With his brothers he built what was probably the first-ever apartment block entirely of reinforced concrete; other early constructions included Paris' Théâtre des Champs-Elysées and Orly airport. The destruction of Le Havre in 1944 presented him with the opportunity of a lifetime: the chance to design an entire city. It was also, though, Perret's swansong, for he died aged 80 in 1954, before his project was finished. Central to Perret's philosophy was the belief that the structure and aesthetics of a building should be one, an approach that became known as 'Structural Classicism'. 'The man who conceals any part of the structure deprives himself of the only legitimate, the most beautiful, ornament of architecture,' he wrote. He was particularly adamant about the neoclassical concrete pillars in his apartment blocks. 'The man who conceals a pillar commits a sin,' he declared, and fake pillars were 'a crime.' Perret's love affair with concrete was so complete that it excluded nature. Trees and flowers he saw as a distraction, which prevented people seeing beautiful buildings, and he opposed the planting of trees along Le Havre's Avenue Foch. The city authorities overruled him, though, and specks of green now dot the concrete expanses.

scattering of Fauvists, and a Tahiti landscape by Gauguin. The largest holdings are of two locals, Raoul Dufy and Eugène Boudin. The playful and vibrant Dufy collection was bequeathed by his widow, and includes both colourful renderings of *Havrais* relaxing and semi-abstracts like his red violin. On the upper floor there are over 200 canvases by Boudin who, though born in Honfleur, spent most of his life in Le Havre. Among many highlights are *Dame en blanc sur la plage de Trouville*, one of his best-known beach scenes, and *Entrée des jetées du Havre par gros temps*, a superb study of frenzied seas and menacing skies. There are also some 17th- and 18th-century works, including an enchanting Rembrandt-esque portrait of a young man by Fragonard.

If Boudin has given you a taste for Le Havre's past, stroll north along the seafront towards **Ste-Adresse**, Le Havre's answer to Nice, where Boudin and Monet often painted and where the intelligentsia built themselves mansions in the Belle Epoque. It was also popular with foreigners, especially the British, leading it to be dubbed '*la ville anglaise*'.

The 16th-century **Cathédrale Notre-Dame**, on Place du Vieux Marché, has been heavily restored, and its curves and yellow stone provide an odd contrast to the concrete symmetry around it. For something very different – and a haircut – head for one of Le Havre's hidden jewels: a barber's shop called **Salon des Navigateurs** on Rue du Petit Croissant, beside Rue de Bretagne, run by an amiable man who was once a barber on the ocean liner *France*. Clients wait outside in striped deckchairs (magazines supplied); inside, there's a treasure trove of antique hair-cutting kit and marine memorabilia. Women are welcome too.

Around Le Havre

Conveniently close to Le Havre, **Montivilliers** nonetheless has the feel of a small town. It's famous for its tanneries and for its **Abbaye de Notre-Dame**, an 11th-century Benedictine abbey that has been painstakingly restored. Like many abbeys upstream it was founded by St Philibert in the 7th century, destroyed by the Vikings, then rebuilt by the Normans. Montivilliers, however, was the only religious house in the area for women. The last nun left during the Revolution, and the beautiful honey-coloured buildings were used in turn as a prison, garrison, cotton mill and brewery. A visit leads through the abbey's various rooms, from the cloisters – rebuilt from scratch – to the dormitories and splendid Gothic refectory, accompanied by voices, music and written texts in French and English. It's an ideal place to begin the 'Seine Abbeys' route, with an excellent introductory display. The church of the **Abbatiale Saint-Sauveur** is also worth a visit: Romanesque and Gothic sit side by side, and there are traces of the bright colours in which it and the convent were once painted.

Sunday is the day to visit the village-suburb of **Harfleur**, 6km east of central Le Havre, with its cobbled streets, half-timbered houses and pretty waterways: it's market day, and the place springs to life as farmers from nearby villages bring in pungent cheeses and fresh vegetables. In the 13th century this was Normandy's largest port, but two centuries later it had silted up, and Le Havre was built in its place. Henry V of England landed here in 1415 and laid siege to the town before proceeding to Agincourt, and it was here that Shakespeare makes him utter his 'Once more unto the breach' speech. The **Eglise St-Martin** is a beautiful Gothic church built between the 12th and 16th centuries, and a 15th-century inn on Rue de la République houses the tiny **Musée du Prieuré**, with artefacts from Roman times to the present day, and work by local artists.

Abbaye de Notre-Dame
t 02 35 30 96 66; open April–Sept Mon–Fri 10–6 and Sat–Sun 2–6; Oct–Mar Mon–Fri 10–5 and Sat–Sun 2–6; adm

Abbatiale Saint-Sauveur
open Mon–Sat 9–6, Sun 2–6

Musée du Prieuré
open June–Sept Wed–Sun 2–6; Oct–May Sat–Sun and Wed 2–6; adm

09

Le Havre and the Lower Seine Valley | Le Havre

Tourist Information in Le Havre

The tourist office in Le Havre offers art and architecture weekends along with a wide range of guided or self-guided tours.

Internet Access: CyberMetro, 19/21 Cours de la République; Microminute, 7 Rue Casimir Perier.

Market Days: Le Havre, Mon, Wed, Fri, Av René Coty; Harfleur, Sun; Montivilliers, Thurs.

Post Office: 62 Rue Jules Siegfried.

Helicopter tours: Helistar runs 10min *Découverte de Perret* tours, minimum 4 people, departing from the airport and flying over Le Havre. Information, *t 02 35 54 13 13, www.helistar.fr.*

ⓘ **Le Havre >**
186 Bd Clemenceau, t 02 32 74 04 04, www. lehavretourisme.com

ⓘ **Harfleur**
1 Rue du Grand Quai, t 02 35 13 37 40

Shopping in Le Havre

For gourmet food products head for **Les Halles Centrales**, on Rue Voltaire. The **Comptoir des Arômes** at one end of the arcade has mouth-watering delicacies. For organic foods, there's a **Marché Bio** at 5 Rue St Jacques.

Where to Stay in Le Havre

Le Havre ✉ 76600

★★★**Vent d'Ouest**, 4 Rue de Caligny, **t** 02 35 42 50 69, *www.ventdouest.fr* (€€€). Sophisticated and brightly decorated, this is a real gem. Bedrooms have a luxurious feel; the owner's family set up the 'Interiors' department store. There's a bar, and simple meals are provided.

★★★**Novotel**, Cours Lafayette, **t** 02 35 19 23 23, *www.accor-hotels.com* (€€€). A chain hotel, but with an impressive glass-fronted design. It's the brainchild of architect Jean-Paul Viguier and has 136 super-modern rooms, a restaurant and a gym.

★★★**Les Voiles**, 3 Place Clemenceau, **t** 02 35 54 68 90, *www.lapetiterade. com* (€€€). You might need sunglasses to cope with the orange walls, but the seafront location is unrivalled. Ask for a balcony with sea view; there's also an enjoyable restaurant (€€).

★★★**Art Hotel**, 147 Rue Louis Brindeau, **t** 02 35 22 69 44, *www.bestwestern.fr/*

Vent d'Ouest >

arthotel (€€). Best Western hotel in the heart of Perret's Le Havre, bang opposite the *Volcan*. Its 31 business-like rooms are comfortable.

★★**Le Petit Vatel**, 86 Rue Louis Brindeau, **t** 02 35 41 72 07, *www.multi mania.com/lepetitvatel* (€). Basic but clean, quiet, central and good value.

Eating Out in Le Havre

La Villa, 66 Bd Albert 1er, **t** 02 35 54 78 80, *www.villaduhavre.com* (€€€€–€€€). Watch the breakers as you sample the gourmet delights created by much-admired chef Jean-Luc Tartarin. Housed in a Belle Epoque residence, with fairy-tale turrets. Book ahead. *Closed Sun eve, Wed eve and Mon.*

Le Bistrot des Halles, 7 Place des Halles Centrales, **t** 02 35 22 50 52, *www.bistrotdeshalles.com* (€€). A beautiful restaurant with first-rate food, specializing in meats. *Closed Sun.*

Les Trois Pics, Promenade des Régates, **t** 02 35 48 20 60 (€€). Nothing fancy, but for great for lunch right on the harbour. *Closed Sun eve and Mon.*

Le Lyonnais, 7 Rue de Bretagne, **t** 02 35 22 07 31 (€€–€). Lovely and cosy with a fireplace and traditional cuisine including fish *marmites*. *Closed Sun.*

Le Nuage Dans La Tasse, 93 Av Foch, **t** 02 35 21 64 94 (€). A good choice if you need vegetable matter after all those rich meals. Excellent salads. *Closed Sun.*

The Seine Valley between Le Havre and Rouen

East of Le Havre, three sleek bridges span the Seine, each a considerable feat of engineering: the graceful **Pont de Normandie**, completed in 1995, 856m long, and the most impressive; the more prosaic 608m **Pont de Tancarville**, the first bridge built across the Lower Seine; and the **Pont de Brotonne** cable-stay bridge, leading south into the Brotonne forest. There are tolls for crossing all three. Before they were built the only way of crossing the Seine below Rouen was by *bac*, a type of floating barge; most were grounded by the opening of the bridges, but some still operate at a few places on the river such as Duclair Jumièges and Vieux Port, quaint vestiges of a maritime past.

The Marais Vernier, the *Chaumières* and the Forêt de Brotonne

27 Marais Vernier

South of the Tancarville bridge the first bend of the Seine cradles the **Marais Vernier**, a horseshoe of marshland remarkable for its ancient thatched farmsteads and spectacular birdlife. Ringed by forested hills and crisscrossed by dykes and drainage channels, this watery wildness comes as a refreshing contrast after the industry around Le Havre. Enclosed by the Seine, the *marais* enjoys a microclimate of its own and contains a surprising diversity of plants and birds, which you can watch from lookouts on the main lake, the **Grand'Mare**. One can also walk or cycle along the marsh's southern rim via the GR23 footpath. This area was once common land on which locals raised cattle; this practice, rare in Normandy, is marked each 1 May when cattle are ceremonially branded before being let loose to graze. Many of the pastures are clad in apple trees, and **Ste-Opportune-la-Mare**, where you turn off for the birdwatching lookouts, has an orchard producing 50 apple

Maison de la Pomme
*t 02 32 20 27 11;
open July–Aug daily 1.30–6.30; April–June and Sept Sat–Sun 2–6.30; Mar and Oct Sun 2–6; Nov–Feb 1st Sun of month 10–6; adm*

varieties. There's also a **Maison de la Pomme**, and from October to April apple markets are held on the first Sunday in each month.

The *marais*'s most famous attractions, though, are its half-timbered cottages (*chaumières*), whose thatch roofs sprout pretty irises. Enchantingly run down, they seem almost to merge into the trees. They are at their manicured best, though, in **Le Vieux-Port**, east of the main marsh along the well-indicated 53km *Route des Chaumières* ('Thatched Cottage Route'). Many have gardens with holly hedges running down to the Seine. There are no shops, just a ferry across the river, and great tranquillity. Next along the Route, **Aizier** has a surprisingly large church, with a Neolithic funeral monument, believed to be from around 2000 BC.

Both the Marais Vernier and the villages to the east form part of the **Parc Naturel Régional des Boucles de la Seine Normande**, covering both banks of the Seine. As well as wetlands, the *Parc* contains 13,000 hectares of woods and forests, including the 7,000-hectare **Forêt de Brotonne**, an expanse of oak, beech, chestnut and pine crisscrossed by footpaths. You can find out more

09 Le Havre and the Lower Seine Valley | The Marais Vernier, the *Chaumières* and the Forêt de Brotonne

Birding in the Marais

The Marais Vernier is one of the best, and most beautiful, places in Normandy for birdwatching. From the two observation towers overlooking the Grand'Mare a feast of birdlife can be seen. Pride of place goes to the majestic **marsh harriers**, and in spring courting **great crested grebes** spar on the open water and feed their young on the abundant fish of the lake. **Cormorants** hang out their wings to dry, while **Cetti's warblers** chatter in the reedbeds. If you're lucky you might hear the rasping cries of **corncrakes**. Waders include the **black-tailed godwit**, with its conspicuous white bar on its wings and lapwing-like 'pee-oo-ee' call, the snub-billed **avocet** and white **spoonbill**. In winter large numbers of waterfowl gather in the *marais*, and at migration times it's possible to see virtually anything. (By John Voysey)

Maison du Parc
*t 02 35 37 23 16;
open July–Aug Mon–Fri
9–6.30; April–June and
Sept Mon–Fri 9–6 and
Sat–Sun 12–6; Oct–Mar
Mon–Fri 9–6*

Four à Pain
*t 02 32 57 07 99; open
July–Aug daily 2–6.30;
April–June and Sept Sun
2–6.30; Oct–Nov and
Mar Sun 2–6; adm*

Musée du Sabot
*same hours as
Four à Pain; adm*

Musée du Lin
*open July–Aug daily
2–6.30; April–June and
Sept Wed–Sun 2–6.30,
Oct Sun 2–6; adm*

Windmill
*open July–Aug
daily 2.30–6.30;
20 April–mid-Sept
Sun 2.30–6.30; adm*

about walks and other activities at the **Maison du Parc**, in an old manor in Notre Dame de Bliquetuit, near the southern end of the Brotonne bridge (and the point from which Boudin painted his *La Seine à Caudebec-en-Caux*). In the summer it lays on *Jeudis Naturalistes* – three-hour guided nature walks (in French).

The area's traditional crafts are presented in several small museums, two of which are in **La Haye-de-Routot**. You can watch bread being made in an 18th-century domed brick *Four à Pain*, or bread oven. Everyone leaves laden with *douillons aux pommes* apple pastries, *brioches* and crusty bread, and there are bread-making classes. The same building is also home to an unlikely fan club, the 'Friends of the Nettle' (*Amis de l'Ortie*). The stinging weed has, they argue, amazing medicinal and gastronomic properties, and the club holds a 'National Nettle Day' each April that attracts 5,000 visitors, culminating in a nettle-lovers' dinner. If that sounds too painful, the **Musée du Sabot** opposite contains an amazing collection of clogs of every shape, size and age. La Haye's other claims to fame are the 1,000-year-old yew trees in its churchyard, and its **Feu de Saint Clair** on 16 July, when villagers gather around a towering bonfire that's topped by a flower-decked cross.

Another local craft, linen-making, is represented in **Routot** by the **Musée du Lin**, and northeast in Hauville there is what is said to be the oldest functioning **windmill** in France, once one of six in the area that were owned by the monks at Jumièges.

Villequier

⭐ Villequier

*Now that, sitting beside the waves,
moved by this superb and peaceful horizon,
I can ponder on the profoundest truths
and look upon the flowers on the grass;
Now, dear God, that I have the sombre calm
to be able from now on
to look with my eyes on the stone where I know that in the shade,
she sleeps for ever;
Now that, softened by these divine sights
of plains, forests, rocks, valleys and silver river,
seeing my own littleness and your miracles,
I recover my sanity in face of the infinite.*

Victor Hugo, *Contemplations IV, 14*

Across from the Brotonne forest on the north bank stands pretty red-brick Villequier. It looks the picture of tranquillity, but for Victor Hugo it was steeped in tragedy, as it was here that on 4 September 1843 his beloved daughter Léopoldine drowned aged 19 while boating on the river with her husband, just seven months after their marriage. Hugo never really got over her death, which inspired his collection of poems *Les Contemplations*. The summer home of the family of Charles Vacquerie, Léopoldine's husband, is now the **Musée Victor Hugo**, which has an engaging collection of photographs, letters, mementos and such touching things as cartoons drawn by Hugo to amuse his children. Even if you don't linger long, the riverside setting of the house and its gardens is superb, and there's an attractive footpath along the river. Villequier also has an interesting church, **St-Martin**, with stained glass depicting a battle between Dieppois adventurer Jean Ango and a Spanish ship bringing back booty from Mexico.

Musée Victor Hugo
open April–Sept Wed–Mon 10–12.30 and 2–6; Oct–Mar Wed–Mon 10–12.30 and 2–5; adm

Caudebec-en-Caux

Caudebec, a few kilometres further east, is busier and less picturesque than Villequier, and the main town of this stretch of the Seine. Much of it was destroyed in 1944, and the modern town is pretty plain. The riverfront, though, is a pleasant place to wander or watch the water from one of its restaurants. In the past Caudebec witnessed a phenomenon known as the *mascaret*, a tidal wave that appeared from nowhere, drenching strollers unawares, but the river has since been reshaped to prevent this happening and make it safe for ships. In the 17th century Caudebec was famous for its hats and gloves, but most of their Protestant makers fled – many to England – after 1685.

Despite Caudebec's wartime destruction, a handful of old houses give an idea of how the fortified town once looked. The most ancient, the 13th-century **Maison des Templiers** on Rue de la Boucherie, houses a local history museum which has a Viking sword. Caudebec's most magnificent building is its Flamboyant-Gothic **Eglise de Notre-Dame**, which lords it over **Place du Marché**, where a market has been held every Saturday since 1390. Built between 1426 and 1539, its 18 chapels were sponsored by local guilds, who gave them superb stained glass. At the west end of town, the **Musée de la Marine de la Seine** recounts the part the river has played in local life, describes the various boats that have plied its waters, and ends with the Seine's new hi-tech bridges.

Maison des Templiers
t 02 35 96 95 91; open Wed–Thurs 2.30–6.30, Fri–Sun 10–12 and 2.30–6.30; adm

Eglise de Notre-Dame
open Easter–Oct 8–7; Nov–Easter 8–5

Musée de la Marine de la Seine
open April–Sept daily 2–6.30; Oct–Mar 2–5.30; adm

Le Havre and the Lower Seine Valley | The Marais Vernier, the *Chaumières* and the Forêt de Brotonne

ⓘ **Caudebec-en-Caux >**
Place Général de Gaulle, t 02 32 70 46 32, www.caudebec-en-caux.com

Tourist Information in Caudebec-en-Caux

Market day: Sat.
Post Office: Rue de la République

Where to Stay and Eat in Caudebec-en-Caux

Le Marais Vernier ✉ **27680**
L'Auberge de l'Etampage, t 02 32 57 61 51 (€). This simple village *auberge*, in

the midst of the Marais Vernier, offers a taste of the old rural France. It's named after the branding of animals that used to take place every year on 1st May. One of the three simple rooms has views over the Marais. From the restaurant (€€) you can watch Highland cattle.

Caudebec-en-Caux ✉ **76490**
Le Cheval Blanc, 4 Place René Coty, t 02 35 96 21 66 *www.le-cheval-blanc.fr* (€). If you stop over in Caudebec, this friendly family hotel

is the best bet, with comfortable rooms and a decent restaurant (€€–€). *Restaurant closed Sun eve.*

Au Rendez-Vous des Chasseurs, Maulévrier-Ste Gertrude, **t** 02 35 96 20 30 (€€). Pretty restaurant in a tiny village in the woods behind Caudebec. There are stone walls and fireplaces, and the menus are great value. *Closed Wed and Sun eve.*

Touffreville La Corbeline ⊠ **76190**

Château du Vertbosc, **t** 02 35 95 18 85, *http://chambrehotenormandie. orbispictura.com* (€). Each of its three rooms are furnished with smart antiques; from the window you will see orchids, deer and woods; and it's wonderfully quiet. Great value.

⭐ **The Three Great Abbeys**

St-Wandrille-de-Fontenelle
t 02 35 96 23 11, www.st-wandrille.com; ruins open daily dawn–1 and 2–dusk; tours Easter–Oct Wed–Sat and Mon 3.30; adm; accommodation available for retreats

The Three Great Abbeys of the Seine

St-Wandrille-de-Fontenelle

Westernmost of the Seine Valley's three great abbeys, St-Wandrille is the only one that still serves its original purpose behind its incongruously grand Baroque gate, and if you arrive at the right time you will be able to hear its 40-odd black-robed monks singing Gregorian chant (there are seven services a day). The abbey, which dominates the bucolic village of **St-Wandrille-Rançon**, was founded in the 7th century by Wandrille, a courtier of the Frankish king Dagobert. He abandoned the royal court to wander from monastery to monastery in Italy and study the rule of St Benedict, before returning to Normandy. His abbey became a great centre of learning and immensely powerful; then the Vikings arrived, destroying the precious buildings and sending the monks fleeing, but the abbey was rebuilt, and its fortunes rose again. You can wander freely among the ruins of the 13th-century abbey church, once decorated in bright colours. Precious little remains of it, though, as after the Revolution St-Wandrille, like so many other Norman abbeys, was plundered and used as a stone quarry.

The area where the monks now live is carefully protected, but parts of it are visited on the tour, including the ornate Gothic cloisters, and some 17th-century buildings in classical style. The most extravagant touches, like the entrance gate imitating the ones at Fontainebleau, were added by an Irish eccentric, the Earl of Stacpoole, who rescued St-Wandrille from oblivion in the 1860s and turned the magnificent refectory into a ballroom. Monks reclaimed the buildings 34 years later, continuing their 13-centuries-old tradition. In 1969 a 13th-century tithe barn from the Eure was dismantled and rebuilt at St-Wandrille to serve as a new church, and to house the relic of St Wandrille's head. The shop sells products crafted by monkly hands, from candles to furniture wax.

Jumièges
t 02 35 37 24 02, www.monum.fr; open July–Aug daily 9.30–6.30; mid-April–June and 1–15 Sept Mon–Fri 9.30–1 and 2.30–6.30, Sat–Sun 9.30–6.30; mid-Sept–mid-April daily 9.30–1 and 2.30–5.30; adm

Jumièges

Beside the next great loop in the Seine stand the evocative bleached towers of the Abbaye de Jumièges, against a backdrop of fields and forests. Like St-Wandrille it was founded in the 7th

Getting to the Three Great Abbeys

CNA **bus** 30A runs between Caudebec-en-Caux and Rouen bus station, via St-Wandrille, Jumièges, Duclair and St-Martin-de-Boscherville. It is quite frequent Mon–Sat, but there are few buses Sun. Bac **ferries** (*free*) run every 20mins or so between Duclair and Anneville-Ambourville on the left bank. There are also crossings at Le Mesnil-sous-Jumièges, Jumièges and Yainville. For timetables see *www.seinemaritime.net*.

century, but by Saint Ouen's protégé Philibert. It is one of the oldest monastic settlements in the Seine valley, and when first built was a symbol of Frankish civilization. Marauding Vikings destroyed the original building, but the vast abbey that rose from the ruins was one of the first and finest examples of Norman Romanesque. The twin-towered building that survives dates mostly from the 11th century, and William the Conqueror himself attended the abbey church's consecration on his way back from victory in England. In later centuries Jumièges slid into decline, and after the Revolution it was, like others, pilfered for its valuable stone. Mercifully this quarry enterprise was a financial flop, and Jumièges was rescued by a Parisian stockbroker, which thus allowed one of the most atmospheric sights in Normandy to survive.

It's a shame nothing remains of Philibert's great abbey, for it was a splendid affair. The great Romanesque building that remains today was begun in 1040 under Abbot Robert Champart, who would be Archbishop of Canterbury under Edward the Confessor. The next three centuries were a time of great prosperity, and the ruins of many abbey farm buildings can be seen. In the 17th and 18th centuries the Maurists, a Benedictine sect, renovated the abbey and added the vast library and an abbot's residence.

Visitors first enter the abbey church of **Notre-Dame**. Some 25 metres high, the Romanesque nave is Normandy's tallest; note the decorations on the capitals, like the delicate bird encircled by foliage. A lantern tower – typical of Norman Romanesque – once topped the transept, but only the western wall with its staircase turret remains. The south transept leads to the church of **St-Pierre**, with Romanesque façade and nave and a 14th-century choir with rib vaults decorated with carvings of men's heads. It is here that the *Tombeau des Enervés* (literally, tomb of the unnerved) is said to be. The *énervés* were, legend states, the two sons of Queen Bathilde, wife of King Clovis II, whom she punished for rebelling against their father by severing their leg nerves. Set adrift in a boat on the Seine, they landed at Jumièges, where the monks took them in. The porch and west 'tower' are believed to be the only pre-Viking remains at Jumièges.

Duclair

Draped along the Seine around the next loop in the river from Jumièges, Duclair is a pleasant place to stop for an afternoon and watch barges drift by from the shade of its lime trees. It was once an important port, but its river traffic nowadays mostly consists of pleasure steamers or stone barges. Its centre is the landing stage for the *bac*, the traditional ferry across the Seine. Duclair is also famous for its duck. Like its cousin the Rouen duck, the Duclair duck was born of a cross between domesticated and wild duck, and locals claim their *canard au sang* recipe for unbled duck is older than the more famous *canard rouennais* (*see* p.162). Duclair's other claim to fame is its Tuesday market, established by Richard the Lionheart on 7 June 1198 and held weekly ever since. The **Eglise St-Denis**, the oldest parts of which date from the 10th century, is notable for its triple gable and Romanesque belfry.

St-Georges-de-Boscherville

St-Georges-de-
Boscherville
*t 02 35 32 10 82,
www.abbaye-saint-
georges.com; open daily
April–Oct 9–6.30;
Nov–Mar 2–5; guided
tours Sun at 4; adm*

The third and least known of the trio of abbeys on this stretch of the Seine, the Abbaye de St-Georges-de-Boscherville, lords it over the tiny village of **St-Martin-de-Boscherville**, 12kms west of Rouen. Unlike St-Wandrille and Jumièges, it is pretty much intact, and even managed to escape the Revolution largely unscathed by converting itself into a parish church. Another contrast is that it is remarkably uniform in style, partly because it was completed in less than 30 years. Consequently it's one of the purest examples in existence of Norman Romanesque.

The first community of monks was established here in the 11th century by Ralph, William the Conqueror's tutor. His son, William de Tancarville, built the abbey church and monastery buildings between 1113 and 1140, using milky-white limestone from local quarries. The almost transparent quality of the stone and the light that floods in through the high windows and lantern tower create a breathtaking combination of luminosity and simplicity. There's delicious detail too: a host of creatures and odd stories lie in waiting at the tops of the capitals and above the transepts. The wall under the north transept, for example, harbours a bespectacled bishop, crook in hand, giving his blessing, and in the nave there's a carving of St Evroult, from whose abbey in the Ouche valley (*see* p.203–4) monks were sent to populate St-Georges in the 12th century. The exterior is also surprisingly ornate in comparison with stark Jumièges. Note the two monsters on the west front devouring a bird, and the serpent offering an apple to Eve.

St-Georges' finest carvings, though, are in the **Chapterhouse**. The capitals on its Romanesque arches are some of the richest in Normandy. The carvings that are there today, however, are actually copies; many of the originals are in the Antiquities museum in Rouen (*see* p.158), and others have not survived. There are ornate depictions of the childhood of Christ, while the so-called 'musicians' capital' has a wonderful bell-ringer beneath his row of bells, with his lute-player chum. The original chapterhouse was built around 1160, but in the 17th century Maurist monks stuck a classical-style building on top of it. Behind it are their kitchen gardens, recently replanted with medicinal plants, flowers and old varieties of fruit trees.

The Devil's Castle and La Bouille

South of St-Georges, the Seine is dominated by the crumbling ruins of the **Château de Robert le Diable**, on the south bank. It is named after William the Conqueror's father Robert, though there's no record of him having lived here. He got his nickname not because he was particularly evil but because, dying from the plague while on pilgrimage to Jerusalem, he was carried by four slaves to whom he allegedly declared 'When you return to Normandy, say that Duke Robert was taken to paradise by four devil slaves'. The 114-metre-deep well found here suggests that a fortress was probably first built on this site by the Romans, due to its strategic position. Successive versions were destroyed and reconstructed countless times on the same spot over the centuries.

✪ La Bouille

Below the château, just 10kms southwest of Rouen, the enchanting village of **La Bouille** stands perched on the Seine's sleepy southern banks. The beauty of its half-timbered houses and narrow stone lanes, enclosed by wooded slopes on one side and the glassy river on the other, has long attracted artists, writers, and folk from Rouen in search of a whiff of fresh air. It's famous too for its food, and has a phenomenal eight restaurants – one for every 100 inhabitants – which are packed with *Rouennais* at weekends, especially Sunday lunchtimes. There are frequent buses to and from Rouen.

Tourist Information around the Three Great Abbeys

Market Days: Jumièges: June–Sept, Sun, occasional markets at other times of year; Duclair: Tues.

Post Offices: Jumièges: 33 Rue Guillaume le Conquérant; Duclair: 95 Paul Ducros.

① **Jumièges >>**
Rue Guillaume le Conquérant, opposite the abbey,
t 02 35 37 28 97

Where to Stay and Eat around the Three Great Abbeys

St-Wandrille-Rançon ✉ 76490
Les Deux Couronnes, t 02 35 96 11 44 (€€). The name of this magnificent

17th-century *auberge-restaurant* recalls the generosity of two kings towards a neighbouring chapel. Meats are roasted over a huge fireplace, and it's a great place to relax after a day at the abbey across the road. *Closed Sun eve and Mon.*

Jumièges ✉ 76480
Le Clos des Fontaines, 191 Rue des Fontaines, **t** 02 35 33 96 96, *www.leclosdesfontaines.com* (€€). Bijou *hôtel de charme* that has been beautifully converted from an old farm building in the heart of the village. Beams and terracotta tiles abound, there are lovely views from the four bedrooms, and there's a great swimming pool.

Auberge des Ruines, 17 Place de la Mairie, **t** 02 35 37 24 05 (€€€–€€). This half-timbered building set round a courtyard was once a *relais de poste*; today's restaurant is smart, expensive but worth it for a treat. Always book. *Closed Sun eve, Tues eve and Wed.*

Auberge du Bac, t 02 35 37 24 16 (€€–€). A kilometre walk from the abbey, at the point where a *bac* ferry crosses the Seine, this relaxed little restaurant has a pretty terrace with lovely views. *Closed Mon and Tues.*

(i) **Duclair** >
Av Président Coty,
t 02 35 37 38 29,
www.duclair.fr.

Duclair ✉ 76480

Le Parc, 121 Av Président Coty, t 02 35 37 50 31, *www.restaurant-leparc.fr* (€€). On the banks of the Seine, this gastronomic (but sensibly priced) restaurant is famous for *canard au cidre fermier*, and has fine fish too. *Closed Wed.*

Bistro du Siècle, 75 Rue Jules Ferry, t 02 35 37 62 36 (€€–€). Meat and salmon are grilled over an open fire at this relaxed bistro. *Closed Sun and Mon.*

Villers-Ecalles ✉ 76360

Les Florimanes, 850 Rue Gadeau de Kerville, t 02 35 91 98 59 (€€). This 17th-century manor house in a village 7km north of Duclair, surrounded by gardens, is owned by a watercolour artist, and her talents have been put to exquisite effect in the furnishing of the B&B rooms, sitting room and breakfast room. A truly special place.

Pavilly ✉ 76570

La Croix d'Or, 4 Place près l'Esneval, t 02 35 91 20 09 (€€). One of those restaurants one goes to France to find: great hosts, fab food and imaginative décor – all at a reasonable price. A gem.

St-Martin-de-Boscherville ✉ 76840

(★) **Le Brécy** >

Le Brécy, 72 Route du Brécy, t 02 35 32 69 92 (€€). This 18th-century mansion with gardens and orchards takes some beating. B&B guests have a self-catering apartment, with its own

entrance. The furnishings reflect owners Jerôme and Patricia Lanquest's interest in interior decoration, and Madame brings breakfast to your private dining room. She's a fountain of knowledge about the abbey, where she's a guide. There's also a footpath leading to the banks of the Seine.

Canteleu ✉ 76380

Manoir de Captot, t 02 35 36 00 04, *www.captot.com* (€€). Drive through big iron gates up a long drive to this 18th-century manor, surrounded by woods. The pink *toile de jouy* room is beautiful, and breakfasts, served by the mistress of the manor in the primrose yellow drawing room, include her home-made jams.

La Bouille ✉ 76530

**Bellevue, 13 Quai Hector Malot, t 02 35 18 05 05, *www.hotel-le-bellevue.com* (€). At least half of the 18 rooms and the restaurant (€€€–€) have magnificent views over the Seine, and are light, contemporary and comfortable.

Les Gastronomes, 1 Place du Bateau, t 02 35 18 02 07 (€€€–€€). A little restaurant next to the church with the feel of a Belle Epoque bistro. *Closed Wed and Thurs.*

Hôtel de la Poste, t 02 35 18 03 90 (€€). With views over the Seine and the village square, this 18th-century *relais de poste* has one of La Bouille's best restaurants. Norman staples are imaginatively presented in an intimate setting. *Closed Mon eve, Tues and 22 Dec–12 Jan.*

Caumont ✉ 27310

8 Allée des Châteaux, t 02 35 18 03 11 (€€€). Perched above the Seine, this Second Empire villa is darkly atmospheric and is packed with intriguing artefacts. Dinner (€€) is available if you book ahead. Minimum stay two nights.

Rouen to Giverny

Rouen, the historic capital of Normandy, is a thriving city, industrial hub and, despite being miles from the sea, a major port. Its medieval half-timbered buildings and Gothic cathedral make it an essential stop on any tourist itinerary. Progressing along the Seine towards Paris, more attractions vie for your attention, from Richard the Lionheart's magnificent Château Gaillard, to Monet's home and exquisite garden at Giverny. Further inland is Emma Bovary country, the Forêt de Lyons and chocolate-box-perfect Lyons-la-Forêt. For watery tranquillity, head for the lush valley of the Eure with its groomed gardens spilling down to the river.

10

Don't miss

⭐ **A half-timbered medieval city**
Rouen p.151

⭐ **The perfect Norman village**
Lyons-la-Forêt p.168

⭐ **Richard the Lionheart's castle**
Château Gaillard, Les Andelys p.171

⭐ **Home of the waterlilies**
Monet's garden, Giverny p.176

⭐ **Placid villages and willow-draped rivers**
The Eure Valley p.181

See map overleaf

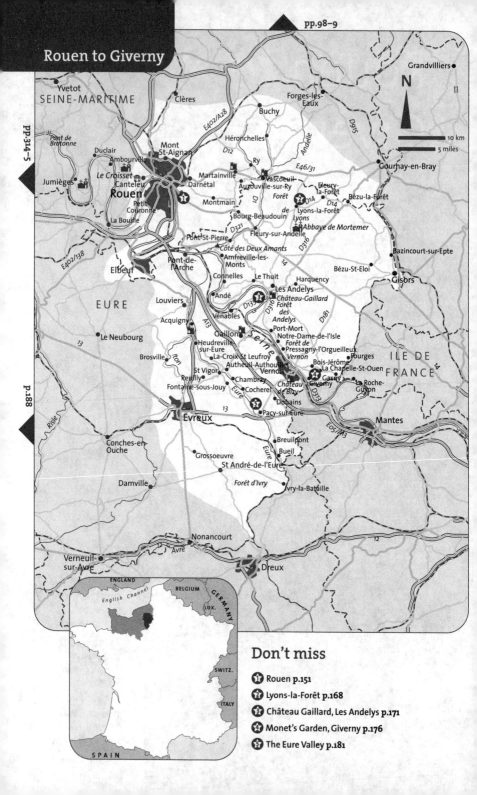

Rouen to Giverny

PP.314-5

p.188

Grandvilliers

N

10 km
5 miles

Yvetot
SEINE-MARITIME
Clères
Forges-les-Eaux
Buchy
Héronchelles
E402/A28
Duclair
Pont de Brotonne
Ambourville
D12
Mont St-Aignan
Ry
E46/31
Gournay-en-Bray
Jumièges
Le Croisset
Martainville
Vascoeuil
Andelle
Auzouville-sur-Ry
Fleury-la-Forêt
Bézu-la-Forêt
Rouen
Darnétal
Forêt
D14
Montmain
de
Lyons-la-Forêt
Petit Couronne
Bourg-Beaudoin
Lyons
Abbaye de Mortemer
La Bouille
Fleury-sur-Andelle
D321
Bazincourt-sur-Epte
Pont-St-Pierre
Côté des Deux Amants
Amfreville-les-Monts
Bézu-St-Eloi
Pont-de-l'Arche
Connelles
Le Thuit
Harquency
Gisors
Elbeuf
Louviers
Andé
Les Andelys
EURE
D135
Château-Gaillard
Venables
Forêt des Andelys
D181
Le Neuburg
Acquigny
Port-Mort
Notre-Dame-de-l'Isle
Gaillon
Forêt de
ÎLE DE FRANCE
Brosville
Heudreville-sur-Eure
Pressagny-l'Orgueilleux
La-Croix St Leufroy
Vernon
Fourges
St Vigor
Autheuil-Authouillet
Bois-Jérôme
La Chapelle-St-Ouen
Rewilly
Vernon
Giverny
Gasny
La Roche-Guyon
Fontaine-sous-Jouy
Chambray
Cocherel
Château de Bizy
D313
Evreux
Dobains
Mantes
Pacy-sur-Eure
E05/A13
Conches-en-Ouche
Breuilpont
Bueil
Grossoeuvre
St André-de-l'Eure
Damville
Forêt d'Ivry
Ivry-la-Bataille
Nonancourt
Avre
Dreux
Verneuil-sur-Avre

ENGLAND
English Channel
BELGIUM
GERMANY
LUX.
SWITZ.
ITALY
SPAIN

Don't miss

1. Rouen p.151
2. Lyons-la-Forêt p.168
3. Château Gaillard, Les Andelys p.171
4. Monet's Garden, Giverny p.176
5. The Eure Valley p.181

Rouen

 Rouen

Then, slightly buried in the morning mist, there appeared Rouen itself, its roofs gleaming in the sun and its thousands of spires, slender, pointed or squat, frail and elaborate, like giant jewels, its towers, square or round, crowned with armorial crowns, its belfries, its bell-towers, the whole host of Gothic church-tops dominated by the sharp-pointed spire of the cathedral.

Maupassant, *Bel Ami*

Victor Hugo called Rouen the city of a hundred bell towers, Monet was so entranced by its cathedral that he painted it over 30 times, and Flaubert's Madame Bovary bumped along its cobbled streets with her illicit lover in their horse-drawn cab. It was here too, that Joan of Arc – known locally as *La Pucelle*, the Maiden – met a sticky end, burned at the stake in the Place du Vieux Marché. Architecturally, the city's mix of beautifully preserved or restored half-timbered houses, Gothic churches and post-1945 concrete makes a potent cocktail.

Rouen's *raison d'être* was, and still is, its position on the Seine. The Romans built their port of *Rotomagus* at the first point upriver from the sea at which the river could be bridged. The Vikings pillaged it, but then cherished it after making their truce with the French king in 911, and it was here that the Duchy of Normandy really began. William the Conqueror died here and two of his successors as Kings of England, Richard and John, were crowned Dukes of Normandy in the great cathedral. Rouen's population boomed, building the magnificent churches and towering timber-framed houses that are the city's hallmark; by the 13th century Rouen was the second city in France. To protect themselves its inhabitants encircled the city with great walls, but these didn't stop the English from besieging Rouen during the Hundred Years' War and then occupying it for 30 years until 1449. When peace came at last, Rouen's trade blossomed, helped by its larger-than-life archbishop, Georges d'Amboise, who had close links with the French monarchs. It was a major centre for woollen trades, pottery, stained glass and printing. In the 18th century the town walls and some of its narrow streets were dismantled to make way for the boulevards we see today. The Seine is still a prime source of the city's wealth, through imports of oil products and exports of European foods. As a visitor, however, one could easily wander the streets for a day without realising a river ran through it at all, for the motorway-lined river frontage, created since 1945, is an undeniable eyesore.

Rouen's bleakest hour in recent memory was the night of 19 April 1944, which locals call the *nuit rouge*, red night, when the old centre went up in flames after a sadly misdirected Allied bombing raid. The war's shadow still looms large over the city, not just in memories but in the effects on its buildings. A great swathe of old Rouen between the cathedral and the Left Bank was flattened, and many edifices that were miraculously spared, such as the cathedral and the Eglise St-Maclou, are still being repaired today. We can only be relieved that so many architectural treasures survived. Rouen's restoration, masterminded by Basque architect Louis Arretche, was

Getting to Rouen

By Air

Rouen's **airport** at Boos, 10km to the southeast, has flights to Lyon and many European destinations, but currently no direct flights to the UK. However, you can get low-cost flights from Ireland to Beauvais, which is 80km away. **Boos airport information, t** 02 35 79 41 00, *www.rouen.aeroport.fr.* **Beauvais airport information, t** 08 92 68 20 66, *www.aeroportbeauvais.com.*

By Train

Rouen is a major rail hub, with frequent **trains** to/from Paris (1hr 15mins), Caen (1hr 50mins–2hrs 5mins), Lisieux (1hr 15mins), Le Havre (55mins) and Dieppe (1hr), all from the Gare Rive-Droite at the top of Rue Jeanne-d'Arc (Gare Rive-Gauche is mainly used for freight). There are fast TGV services to Paris and several other cities.

By Bus

The **bus station** (*Gare Routière*) in Rue des Charrettes has services to all the surrounding region. CNA runs regular services along the Seine valley to Caudebec via the Seine abbeys, to La Bouille and to Le Havre. There are also frequent services to Dieppe, Evreux (express), Fécamp, Les Andelys and other destinations. **Bus information, t** 08 25 07 60 27, *www.cna.fr.*

Getting around Rouen

By Car

Driving into Rouen, the main highways and *autoroutes* all tend to bring you onto the hectic *quais* along the north bank of the Seine. The best thing to do is to find Rue de la République, turn up it, and then follow the large 'P' signs to one of the several (reasonably priced) underground car parks, and leave your car there for the day. Place Général de Gaulle has the largest. On-street parking is very limited. A radio taxi can be called on **t** 02 35 88 50 50. Three **car hire** offices are **Budget**, 14–16 Av Jean Rondeaux, **t** 02 32 81 95 00; **Europcar**, 17 Quai Pierre Corneille, **t** 02 32 08 39 09; **France Cars**, 2 bis Av Jean Rondeaux, **t** 02 35 62 10 36.

By Bus and Metro

Central Rouen is compact enough to be easy, and pleasant, to **walk** around. To get around more quickly, there are plenty of **local buses**. Rouen's **metro** – more like a modern tram – is of more use for getting to and from the suburbs than for getting around the centre, with a main route up and down Rue Jeanne d'Arc. Bus and metro **tickets** and **timetable** information can be obtained from the tourist office and **Espace Métrobus**, 9 Rue Jeanne d'Arc, near the river (**t** 02 35 52 52 52; *open Mon–Sat 7–7*). A *Carte Découverte* ticket gives unlimited travel within the city for 1–3 days. There are numerous other passes available too.

---

cleverly executed – with a few exceptions like the brutalist Palais des Congrès, built next to the cathedral in the 1970s, and a *scandale*. The pedestrianization of the prettiest streets, like St-Romain, Damiette, Cauchoise and Gros Horloge, makes Rouen a very pleasant place to wander. For more orientation, consider the well-run walking tours from the tourist office (*see* p.164).

The Gothic City

A natural place to begin any tour of Rouen is the **Place de la Cathédrale**, from where many of the prettiest streets lead off. Running away to the north is the lively Rue des Carmes, leading to the main shopping area and museums; to the west is the ancient Rue du Gros Horloge with its giant clock, leading to the Place du Vieux Marché; and away to the east runs characterful Rue St-

Romain, packed with half-timbered houses, medieval alleyways and antiques shops.

The Tourist Office, right on the square, is housed in the **Bureau des Finances** (House of the Exchequer), built in 1509 for the city's chief tax-collector by Rouen's greatest Flamboyant Gothic architect, Roulland le Roux. Its fine proportions combined with ornate arabesque decoration mark a move from pure Flamboyant Gothic to more classical lines influenced by the Italian Renaissance. In the 19th century the building housed a lingerie shop on the first floor, from where, sitting among the stockings and lacy underwear, Monet did some of his many paintings of the cathedral across the square.

It's no wonder that the façade of **Notre-Dame Cathedral** so inspired Monet. Its mishmash of styles, spanning four centuries, is one of its most seductive features, and students of the different varieties of Gothic could well start here. The oldest part is the **Tour St-Romain**, on the left looking from the square, built in the 12th

Notre-Dame Cathedral

t 02 35 71 85 65; open April–Oct Tues–Sat 7.30–7, Sun 8–6, Mon 2–7; Nov–Mar Tues–Sat 7.30–12 and 2–6, Sun 8–6, Mon 2–7; Son et Lumière shows daily June–July 11pm, Aug 10.30pm, Sept 10pm

10 Rouen to Giverny | Rouen

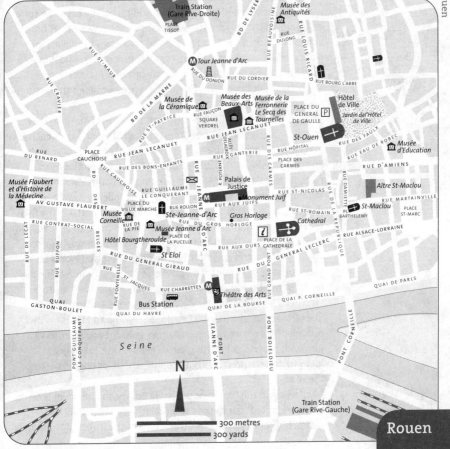

Rouen

century as part of the Norman Romanesque cathedral whose consecration had been presided over by William the Conqueror. Of the façade's three portals, the two smaller ones form a pair with celebrated 13th-century carvings: the one beside the Tour St-Romain has scenes of the life of John the Baptist and licentious Salomé. The unfortunate saint is sent to prison at Salomé's behest in revenge for his attempt to clean up the village morals – you see him behind bars on the far right of the portal – then executed by a hefty hangman and his head offered up on a plate. Herod, feasting on the left, is absorbed by an exquisite figure of Salomé standing on her hands. Continuing the façade's cheery themes, the other small portal to the right shows the stoning of St Stephen. The remarkable central portal, rising up to a Tree of Jesse, was the handiwork of Roulland le Roux, in the 16th century.

The simple lines of the Tour St-Romain contrast sharply with the lacy exuberance of the Flamboyant **Tour de Beurre** (Butter Tower) at the right of the façade, built from 1485. Its name stems from the fact that it was paid for by alms donated by parishioners who wanted to be allowed to eat butter during Lent. The cast-iron **spire** or *flèche*, which replaced two earlier attempts in wood, was only added in the 19th century. The spire, at 151 metres the tallest in France, brought howls of protest from Flaubert, who said it looked as if it had been designed by a whimsical boilermaker. His friend Maupassant dubbed it 'that strange bronze needle, enormous, ugly and odd.'

Inside, the cathedral's lofty 13th-century nave is illuminated by stained-glass windows, the earliest crafted in around 1230. Each glass jewel is encased by an iron surround, like a piece of mosaic. The windows' donors, usually trades guilds, left their 'logos' in pictorial form. The fishmongers donated the cathedral's most famous window, which tells the story of St Julien l'Hospitalier, the inspiration for one of Flaubert's *Trois Contes*, and portrays the fish-sellers themselves in its bottom panels. The story is to be read from the bottom: as a child Julien is told by a deer that he will one day kill his parents, and is so horrified he flees home and works for a *seigneur*. When his master dies, Julien marries his widow. One day he is out hunting, and his wife (dressed in red) receives visitors who need a bed for the night – Julien's parents looking for him. She offers them the marital bed. Julien returns and finds his bed occupied by a man whom he assumes to be an adulterer, so kills him with his sword. Realising what he has done, Julien goes away to do penance, founds a hospital and helps pilgrims across the river.

Following in the footsteps of Emma Bovary and her lover Léon on their celebrated visit to the cathedral (though hopefully less distracted), one can also visit the tombs of the Dukes of Normandy.

There's an idealized Rollo, the Viking first duke, and further on the 13th-century effigy of Richard the Lionheart, whose preserved heart is one of Rouen's treasures. In the Lady Chapel lie the famous tombs of Cardinal-Archbishop Georges d'Amboise and Louis de Brézé, Seneschal of Normandy. Reflecting the Renaissance fascination with death, De Brézé is shown both in his *forme glorieuse*, at the height of his powers, and his *forme de transit*, as a decomposing body. The Amboise tomb is thought to have been the work of Le Roux, while the De Brézé statues are believed to be by Jean Goujon, France's foremost 16th-century sculptor. Also of note are the 15th-century choir stalls, with delightful carvings of medieval tradesmen and some grotesque monsters. You can also visit the crypt, the only remaining part of the Romanesque cathedral, with a well that still works today.

A walk around the outside of the cathedral, with its rows of Gothic gables and two real jewels of Flamboyant Gothic in the north and south transepts, has as many fascinations as the interior. The north door leads to the **Booksellers' Courtyard**, where booksellers once sold their wares. Its 150 14th-century medallions are pure delight: in the top rows you can spot Adam and Eve fleeing the Garden of Eden, and Cain murdering his brother Abel. The rest depict vices and virtues – or seem to be simply a bit of fun, like the lovely philosophical sow, head cocked on hand and snout in the air, and the billy goat with bells.

Rouen's Half-Timbered Mansions

Towering and tottering, packed in cheek by jowl like pretty dolls houses, some 2,000 of Rouen's half-timbered houses have miraculously survived the ravages of war and fire, or been remarkably restored. Around 100 of these *maisons à pans de bois* date back to the Middle Ages. For centuries wood (mostly oak) was the cheapest local building material, while stone was expensive. The basic techniques were already used in Roman times: the framework of the house, including the roof, was pre-fabricated, then set on a foundation of stone. The space between the beams was packed with a mixture of straw and clay, or a kind of plaster. Tiled roofs were built steep to fend off the frequent rain. In contrast to half-timbered houses in most parts of England, which are usually just black and white, the Rouennais painted their homes any colour that took their fancy – ochres, baby blues, sage greens.

In a fortified city, space was always at a premium, so streets were narrow and houses extended upwards rather than sideways. Most had only one room on each floor. Street frontage – and thus light – was especially sought after, and if you were anyone you had to have *pignon sur rue*, a gable overlooking the street. The wealthy found a way to cheat: by making each successive storey overhang the one below you could increase floor space, a process known as corbelling. There are good examples in Rue St-Romain and the tiny alleyway off it, Rue des Chanoines. Gradually, though, the gap between houses on separate sides closed up, and the streets became increasingly dark, unhealthy and prone to fire. In 1520 the authorities decided to act, and corbelling was banned. This provides an effective way of dating half-timbered houses – if they overhang, they must be pre-1520.

Some wealthy owners crowned their houses with oriols, little stone towers. Originally these were probably defensive, but later they became penthouse rooms from where shipowners could keep an eye on ships coming into port. Few remain; the best are at 1 Rue de l'Hôpital, 48 Rue St-Patrice and 10 Rue St-Jacques.

From the Bookseller's Courtyard you emerge into **Rue St-Romain**, one of Rouen's oldest and prettiest streets, packed with half-timbered houses, many of which now contain *salons de thé* or shops selling the faïence ceramics for which the city is famous. No.9 and no.11, constructed in 1466, are particularly fine, with each storey protruding further than the one below. At no.74, look for the Gothic niches with carvings of St Nicholas resuscitating three children, and St Romain striking down a monster. On the same side is the **Archbishop's Palace**, still inhabited by the Archbishop of Rouen, where Joan of Arc's two trials were held.

St-Maclou
open Mon–Sat 10–5,
Sun 10.30–5.30

Lording it over the evocative Place Barthélémy is the church of **St-Maclou**, the second in Rouen's Gothic church triangle and a masterpiece of Flamboyant Gothic, built between 1437 and 1517. Although far smaller than the cathedral, St-Maclou – named after a 6th-century Welsh monk, St Malo – is no less awe-inspiring. The pentagonal west front is a fantasy of pinnacled ornament, disappearing into the air like a shimmering haze. The five-archway porch is typically Norman. There are ornate carvings of the Last Judgement above the central portal, and the wonderful carved wooden doors, which have miraculously survived since the 16th century, show Christ's baptism and circumcision. Much of the rest of the church was not so lucky and was seriously damaged in 1944. The lantern tower is still being restored. There's still lovely stained glass (kept in safekeeping during the war), and a Flamboyant Gothic staircase to the left of the Renaissance organ case, supported by columns attributed to Goujon.

Aître St-Maclou
open daily April–Oct
8–8; Nov–Mar 8–7

Heading eastwards from the church along Rue Martainville, a tiny sign and alleyway on the left-hand side leads to the enchanting **Aître St-Maclou**, a testament to the Black Death of 1348, which killed three quarters of the local population. A plot of land was hastily made into a graveyard, where the dead were slung into mass graves; subsequently it became a general cemetery for the poor, but when space ran out again in the 16th century half-timbered buildings were constructed around the courtyard as ossuaries to house the bones from re-used graves. The timber frames, carved with skulls, crossbones and gravediggers' tools, reveal their ghoulish purpose. On the west and east walls, Death is shown leading its victims – bishops, princes, the lot – in a macabre dance from which there is no return. A glass case near the entrance shows a cat's skeleton that was found in one of the walls, probably a black cat – an incarnation of the Devil – plastered into the masonry to ward off evil spirits. Today, the Aître houses Rouen's School of Fine Arts, whose students wander in and out of the bone rooms, seemingly oblivious to their spooky surroundings.

If you're in this area on a Sunday continue along Rue Martainville to **Place St-Marc**, site of a weekly flea market. Otherwise, head back towards St-Maclou and turn right up **Rue Damiette**, stuffed with antiques shops, to reach **Rue Eau de Robec**, so-called because a tributary of the Seine, the tiny Robec, once ran along it. The stream made this neighbourhood the hub of Rouen's textile trades, and special galleries were added to the tops of the houses where dyed cloth was dried. The stream regularly changed colour with the dyes that were thrown into it, with disastrous effects on locals' health. By the time Flaubert's Charles Bovary lodged there while studying medicine, the area had a foul reputation, and when Rouen's textile industry declined in the 20th century the Robec was diverted for sanitary reasons. It has been recently been 'reinstated' at the request of residents, but in a rather unromantic concrete bed. At no.185 is France's **Musée National de l'Education**, a beautifully and imaginatively presented collection of school memorabilia from the 16th century onwards.

A walk northwards along Rue du Pont de l'Arquet and through the tranquil gardens of the Hôtel de Ville will take you to Rouen's third great Gothic temple, the **Abbatiale St-Ouen**. A Benedictine abbey for over 1,000 years, it's named after an early bishop of Rouen, whose remains were buried here in 684, making it an important pilgrimage site. The present building, on the site of an earlier Romanesque one, took over 200 years to build, between 1318 and 1549. Even then, the façade wasn't finished, and would not be until the 19th century, with a mediocre pastiche. Luckily, while the main part was being built successive architects stuck to the original designs. The result was a jewel of *Rayonnant* Gothic, with a breathtaking sense of light and height. The nave's narrowness in relation to its height, and its sensuous clean white lines, makes it seem still loftier. All that remains today of the much larger abbey complex apart from the church itself are one gallery of the 15th-century cloisters, and the 18th century dormitory, which after the Revolution was turned into Rouen's imposing town hall. Its lovely gardens were once the monks' vegetable plots.

The entrance to St-Ouen is via the spectacular 14th-century Gothic portal on the south side, known as the 'Porch of the Marmosets' because its cheeky crouching carved figures are thought to represent monkeys. There are also medallions representing the life of St Ouen. Unlike other Norman abbeys like Jumièges, St-Ouen has no lantern tower; perhaps its architects thought the abbey was light enough already. Its greatest assets include its stained glass, mercifully put into safekeeping in 1939–45. The windows were created over three centuries. The oldest, begun in 1318, are in the choir. The rose windows above the transepts are both late 15th-century, and are among the earliest examples of Flamboyant Gothic, which appears again in the 16th-century windows along the nave, some with tracery patterns

Musée National de l'Education

t 02 32 82 95 95; open Wed–Fri and Mon 10–12.30 and 1.30–6, Sat–Sun 2–6; adm

Abbatiale St-Ouen

open mid-Mar–Oct Tues–Sat 10–12.15 and 2–6, Sun 9–12.15 and 2–6; Nov–mid-Dec and mid-Jan–mid-Mar Sat–Sun and Tues 10–12 and 2–5

10

Rouen to Giverny | Rouen

resembling leaping flames. At the west end you can see the remains of 16th-century towers which, in an act of barbarity in the 1840s, were knocked down to make way for the new façade. The rose window above them is modern.

The Museums, the Place du Vieux Marché and the Gros Horloge

From the giant square in front of St-Ouen and the Hôtel de Ville, Place Général de Gaulle, Rue Louis Ricard heads northwards, passing the Lycée Pierre Corneille, where Corneille, Flaubert and Maupassant all went to school. A turn off it along Rue Dulong leads to bustling **Rue Beauvoisine**, which Flaubert describes in *Madame Bovary* as 'full of boarding houses, churches and abandoned mansions.' Emma and her lover used to rendezvous every Thursday at the Hotel de la Croix-Rouge on Place Beauvoisine, but this busy junction's traffic means it has little charm today.

Musée des Antiquités
open Wed–Sat and Mon 10–12.15 and 1.30–5.30, Sun 2–6; adm

The **Musée des Antiquités**, housed in an old convent off Rue Beauvoisine, has ancient Egyptian and Greek collections, Gallo-Roman remains, medieval wood carvings and *objets d'art* and some fine Renaissance furniture and tapestries. The courtyard is a fantastical graveyard of statuary and stone carvings; inside, the museum's treasures include the famous Gallo-Roman Lillebonne mosaic showing the hunting of a deer, probably from the 4th century AD, and woodcarvings from old Rouennais houses knocked down to make way for the boulevards. There's also a magnificent 15th-century tapestry showing winged stags, and the originals of the lively carvings of the musicians from St-Georges-de-Boscherville (*see* p.146).

Tour Jeanne d'Arc
open April–Sept Wed–Sat and Mon 10–12.30 and 2–6, Sun 2–6.30; Oct–Mar Wed–Sat and Mon 10–12.30 and 2–5, Sun 2–5.30; adm

Heading back towards the centre down Rue Beauvoisine, turn right along Rue du Cordier to reach the **Tour Jeanne d'Arc**. This highly restored tower is all that remains of a moated castle built in the 1200s by King Philippe Auguste of France to strengthen his grip on the city he had only recently acquired. English nobles set up home here during the Hundred Years' War but, despite its name, Joan of Arc was actually imprisoned in the Tour de la Pucelle, demolished in 1809 (there are a few remains of it at 102 Rue Jeanne d'Arc). She may perhaps have spent at least a few hours in this tower in 1431, being threatened with various instruments of torture. Today the tower contains an interesting exhibition on medieval Rouen, reached via a winding staircase.

Musée de la Céramique
open Wed–Mon 10–1 and 2–6; adm

A short way south on Rue Fauçon is the **Musée de la Céramique** in a 17th-century mansion. It has a stunning collection of Rouen's distinctive decorated earthenware, *faïence de Rouen*. The man who started it all was Masséot Abaquesne, who in the mid-16th century borrowed techniques from Italy's majolica-makers and set up the city's first factory. Some of the magnificently colourful floor tiles in the museum bear his initials. Later, blue and white pottery from Nevers, Delft and China fuelled a craze for blue underglazes, and only around 1700 did red, then other colours, reappear. Rouen's industry flourished until the late 18th century, when English Wedgwood and a taste for porcelain sent it into decline, and the last factory closed in 1850. Star exhibits in the museum include dazzling tiles, all manner of ceramic follies, and a fascinating collection of 'propaganda' plates from the Revolutionary period.

Musée des Beaux-Arts
t 02 35 71 28 40, www.rouen-musée. com; open Wed–Sun and Mon 10–6; adm

Rouen's 'flagship' museum, the **Musée des Beaux-Arts**, presides over the expansive Square Verdrel, just across from the Musée de la Céramique. Its collection of European art from the 16th to the 20th centuries is highly impressive, although unfortunately the museum's own guidebooks are rather inadequate. Among its earlier masterpieces are Caravaggio's vivid *Flagellation of Christ*, its dark background in dramatic contrast with Christ's blood-red cloak, and *Demócrito*, Velázquez' penetrating portrait of a Spanish court jester. There are fine works by Perugino and Gérard David, and a whole room of giant canvases by Veronese. Closer to home, look out for Clouet's 16th-century *Diana Bathing*, and, three centuries on, the small paintings, many of horses, by Rouen-born Théodore Géricault. Many visitors come just for the excellent Impressionist collection, including (of course) one of Monet's renderings of Rouen cathedral, his general view of Rouen, and lovely works by Sisley, Degas, Boudin, Corot and Renoir. Later attractions include Modiglianis and several pieces by Marcel Duchamp, probably Normandy's greatest contribution to modern art. In the sitting area downstairs you can enjoy Dufy's bucolic rendering of the three cities of the Seine, Le Havre (his home town), Paris and Rouen.

Musée Le Secq des Tournelles des Arts du Fer
t 02 35 88 42 92; open Wed–Mon 10–1 and 2–6; adm

Heath Robinson enthusiasts will love Rouen's quirkiest museum, the **Musée Le Secq des Tournelles des Arts du Fer**, behind the Beaux-Arts in the 15th-century church of St Laurence. The name may be a mouthful, but it houses an enchanting collection of wrought ironwork collected by an eccentric called Henri Le Secq des Tournelles, the pieces dating from Gallo-Roman times to the present day. The setting is perfect: curly ironwork signs hang from the arches of the nave, and the cases in between have amazing collections of iron fantasies from keys and padlocks to door knockers in all manner of shapes. The locks are extraordinary – the largest nearly a foot high, the tiniest less than a centimetre – and with them are shoe buckles, corkscrews, sugar spoons, and much, much more.

From the museums walk a short way east along busy Rue Jean Lecanuet to return to Rue Beauvoisine (which just to the south becomes Rue des Carmes) and turn right to enter Rouen's main shopping area. A turn up Rue aux Juifs will take you to the breathtaking **Palais de Justice**, a lacy fantasy of Flamboyant Gothic stone. It was begun in 1499 as a merchants' hall, but when François I created Normandy's *Parlement* in 1514 the palace became its home. After the Revolution it housed the city's law courts. Its restoration after 1945 was one of the most painstaking, and you can still see bullet and bomb damage on the west façade. The interior can occasionally be visited: ask at the tourist office. The street on which the palace stands was the centre of one of France's oldest Jewish communities until their expulsion in 1306. During the restoration a room was discovered beneath the palais, a Romanesque chamber that was probably part of a synagogue, and is now called the **Monument Juif**. More than 900 years old, it is the oldest relic of Jewish life in France, but lately has been closed up again for security reasons.

Across Rue Jeanne d'Arc from the Palais de Justice, Rue Rollon leads to the second hub of Rouennais life after Place de la Cathédrale, **Place du Vieux Marché**, the old marketplace, which still resounds to the cry of market traders. One sound you won't hear is that of executions, which were still carried out here in Flaubert's day. Today this bustling square is ringed by a lively mix of cafés and restaurants, housed in its ancient half-timbered houses, where in summer you can drink in the atmosphere. These buildings were lucky survivors from the 1944 bombings, which demolished the church of St-Vincent in the centre. The square is most famous, of course, as the place where Joan of Arc was burned at the stake in 1431. The spot where this happened is marked with an iron cross, and the city commemorates her death on the Sunday nearest to 30 May, the anniversary of the execution, when flowers are tossed into the Seine at the point where her ashes were disposed of.

Eglise Jeanne d'Arc
open Mon–Thurs and Sat 10–12.15 and 2–6, Fri and Sun 2–6

Joan's statue, pale and pious, stands in the shelter of the **Eglise Jeanne d'Arc**, a post-war concrete construction with twisting fishscale-slated roofs in the form of waves, which people either love or loathe. Whatever you think of it you cannot fail to be impressed by the imaginative way architect Louis Arretche integrated into its structure the brilliantly-coloured Renaissance stained glass from the church of St-Vincent, which had been protected during the war. The sweeping wooden roof inside is built in the form of an upturned ship.

Musée Corneille
t 02 35 71 63 92; open during French school hols Wed–Sun 2–6; outside school hols Sat–Sun and Wed 2–6; adm

Next to the modern church are the remains of the **Eglise Saint-Sauveur**, where the playwright Pierre Corneille once worshipped. His birthplace across the square, on Rue de la Pie, is now the **Musée Corneille**. The author of the tragedies *Horace*, *Le Cid* and *Cinna*, born in 1606, grew up, went to school (at the *lycée* now named after him) and studied law while living between this house and another in Petit-Couronne (*see* p.164). His brother owned a tobacco shop next door. The museum, however, is a disappointment, as neither the façade nor the furniture is original.

The Place du Vieux Marché couldn't get away without an exhibit dedicated to Joan of Arc, but her memory is hardly well served by the **Musée Jeanne d'Arc** on the same side as the Musée Corneille. In the basement of a touristy shop, it's an old-fashioned exhibit with stilted waxworks of scenes from Joan's life. The best thing about them is the figures' hilarious pointy suede shoes. There's also some Joan of Arc memorabilia, and wildly romantic 19th-century portrayals of the warrior-saint. At the still-tackier end of the spectrum there are Joan of Arc snowstorms, soap bars and phone cards. She even has her own website, *www.jeanne-darc.com*.

Musée Jeanne d'Arc
open daily mid-April–Sept 9.30–7; Oct–mid-April 10–12 and 2–6, adm

La Pucelle's nickname graces the small square to the south reached via pretty Rue Panneret, which contains the **Hôtel de Bourgtheroulde**, an imposing 16th-century stone mansion whose

Hôtel de Bourgtheroulde
courtyard open Mon–Fri 9–12.30 and 1.30–6

La Pucelle: Joan of Arc

Inspired saint, determined patriot, or deluded hysteric? Although many facts are known about Joan of Arc, also known as *La Pucelle* (the Maiden), many aspects of her character and actions remain an enigma. The illiterate daughter of a ploughman from the Vosges, she was convinced from age 14 that she had been entrusted with a mission – to save France, then in the throes of the Hundred Years' War. Forcing her way into the court of King Charles VII, she persuaded him to let her join the fight against the English and their Burgundian allies. Inspired by the 'voices' of St Michael, St Catherine and St Margaret, she led 4,000 French troops to victory at Orléans. According to Bedford, leader of the English army, Joan's white armour so astonished his troops that they thought they were up against some kind of divine Amazon. French morale soared. Charles VII advanced to Reims, where he was crowned in 1429, his unlikely female comrade sitting beside him in the cathedral.

Joan went on to attack Paris, which was a disaster, and to relieve Compiègne, besieged by the Duke of Burgundy. Her luck, though, had turned. She was captured by the Burgundians and sold for an extortionate sum to the English, who attributed her victories to witchcraft. Joan appealed to her old friend Charles, but he was conspicuously silent.

Joan was imprisoned on Christmas Eve 1430 in the castle at Rouen, aged 19, and tried for witchcraft and heresy by a court led by the Bishop of Beauvais, Pierre Cauchon. Her defence was spirited. 'What do your voices say?' the Inquisitor asked. 'That I must be joyful and brave,' Joan replied. 'Which language do they speak?' he asked. 'A better one than yours,' she retorted. The judges ruled that she gave more importance to what she supposed were God's personal words than to the commands of the Church, and she was found guilty of heresy. Joan was told that if she refused to recant she'd be handed over to a secular court for punishment, and on 24 May 1431, before large crowds outside St-Ouen, she was intimidated into making a kind of recantation. Imprisoned again, she was then hauled up for wearing men's clothing. Reluctantly she agreed to wear a dress, but when she returned to her cell to find it, legend goes, the guards had hidden it. She was forced to resume her male attire, and a second trial sentenced her to death for her relapse into 'heresy and schism'. She was handed over for execution.

On 30 May Joan was led to the Place du Vieux Marché. The fire was lit and Joan died, her last word being 'Jesus'. According to legend the executioner found her heart intact among the ashes, but threw it into the Seine to prevent people venerating her relics. Around 20 years later, however, a papal commission quashed her death sentence and proclaimed Joan's innocence.

For the French Joan's greatness was in forging a sense of nationhood, and it's little surprise that the popularity of her cult has coincided with turbulent periods in French history. Still today she serves as a national heroine, although she's also been adopted as a mascot by the far-right National Front. Oddly, the Vatican only canonized her in 1920.

austere façade, as in most Norman Renaissance domestic buildings, gives little sign of the fantastically rich decoration within. It is believed to have been the first Rouen mansion built entirely of stone, and is some 200 years older, and in a much older style, than the other stone residences that survive in the city. The main rooms at the back of the inner courtyard were built in the Gothic style, with a sham turret and superb dormer windows. They, and the classical wing to the right, are now occupied by an insurance company. The most interesting section, though, is the Italianate gallery, built in 1520–32, with walls decorated with magnificent bas-reliefs depicting the *Triumphs of Petrarch* and the *Field of the Cloth of Gold* meeting between François I of France and Henry VIII of England in 1520.

Returning to the Vieux Marché, head east along Rue du Gros Horloge (known to locals simply as *Le Gros*), the historic pedestrianized street that links the city's two main squares. Always busy with shoppers and strollers, it's named after the **Gros Horloge**, the extraordinarily lavish Renaissance clock that straddles the street above an elegantly carved arch. It was installed in its prominent position in the 16th century, after townspeople complained that a previous clock, which for two centuries had hung in the adjacent belfry, was not visible enough. The giant clock has gleaming gilt faces on both its east and west sides, with one hand marking the hours. Around the base of the clock there are wooden carvings of divinities personifying the days of the week – the figures change every day at noon. The globe above, now immobile, used to show the phases of the moon. The clock is now powered by electricity, but the old mechanism, far older than the

The Mysteries of *Caneton Rouennais*

Every few months a group of Rouen's inhabitants meet to preserve one of the city's precious institutions. It's not a Gothic cathedral, or an age-old ceremony, but a dish dear to Rouennais' hearts: *caneton à la rouennaise*, or Rouen duckling. Its members, who sport duck-engraved medals that show they belong to the Order of the Duck, take their role very, very seriously.

Rouen duck's rich gamey flavour comes partly from the fact that the breed is a cross between a domestic and a wild duck, but also from the fact that to retain their blood, and so remain succulent, the ducks are killed by strangling rather than by having their throats slit. They are normally partly roasted, and the blood-rare breast meat sliced off, and then the rest of the carcass (except the legs) is crushed in an elaborate special press to extract the blood, which forms an important element in the finished sauce. This is enhanced with red wine, port and cognac, and often the liver is finely minced and stirred in at the last moment as well. The resulting dish is *caneton rouennais à la presse*. One of the restaurants that most keeps up this tradition is the Quatre Saisons (*see* p.166), with its *Maître Canardier* Pierre Guéret, whose family have been preparing duck this way for five generations.

The process of pressing duck was devised in the early 1800s by a Rouen restaurateur called Méchanet, and became a rapid success thanks to the enthusiasm of the Duc de Chartres, who spread the word in Paris. It was adopted by the famous chef Frédéric at the Tour d'Argent restaurant in Paris, and he began numbering all the pressed ducks he served. Today the number is over 600,000. Number 328 was served to Edward VII, then Prince of Wales, in 1890, and no. 253,652 went to Charlie Chaplin.

Belfry
*for opening times
ask at tourist office*

clock faces, is still stored in the adjacent **belfry**. There is talk of turning the belfry into a museum of time, but in the meantime visitors can climb up a staircase into it to enjoy awe-inspiring views of the city. One of the belfry's bells, cast in 1260, still rings 'the Conqueror's Curfew' at 9pm.

Flaubert and Medical Relics

One of Rouen's most fascinating museums is just outside the old centre. From Place du Vieux Marché, head west along Rue de Crosne, which after it crosses Boulevard des Belges becomes Avenue Gustave Flaubert. At the end of it is the **Musée Flaubert et d'Histoire de la Médicine**. It's housed in a wing of the Hôtel-Dieu, formerly the city's main hospital, which is now occupied by the regional council offices. If you're wondering why Flaubert and the history of medicine are rolled into one museum, this is because the novelist's father was chief surgeon at the hospital, and Gustave, born in 1821, spent his early years in this 18th-century house and its garden, which went with the post. It was an unusual childhood: the hospital's dissecting chamber was next door, and Flaubert describes 'how often my sister and I climbed up the trellis and, suspended between the vines, looked in at the laid-out corpses.' You need a strong stomach to visit some parts of the museum, with dessicated heads and corpses; but there are lighter touches too, like the hospital bed that accommodated six patients at once.

Musée Flaubert et d'Histoire de la Médicine
t 02 35 71 63 92; open Wed–Sat 10–12 and 2–6, Tues 10–6; adm

Specifically Flaubert-related exhibits include the stuffed parrot, immortalized by Julian Barnes' novel *Flaubert's Parrot*, which Flaubert supposedly 'borrowed' from the Natural History Museum to serve as inspiration in the description of a parrot in his story *Un cœur simple*, and there is also the simple room where Flaubert was born, with a first edition of *Madame Bovary* and other relics of the Flaubert family. The museum's magnetic highlight, though, is the series of rooms on the history of birth and childhood, with images of armies of babies being fed by proposed 'feeding machines', and such things as the extraordinary – and unique – cloth dummy showing the female anatomy, made in 1777 by a Madame Coudray as part of a campaign to improve the training of midwives. The hope was that this would help bring down appallingly high infant mortality rates. Daring stuff.

Le Croisset
18 Quai Gustave Flaubert, t 02 35 36 43 91; open July–Aug Wed–Sun 2–6; Sept–June Sat–Sun 2–6; adm; CNA bus 30A and city bus 9 both run here from Rouen

Around Rouen

Within the former village of Canteleu, now virtually a suburb of Rouen 9km west of the city, stands the estate of **Le Croisset**. The house that stood here was the riverside country home of the Flaubert family, to which they would 'retire from the city', and where the novelist spent most of his summers from 1844. Alas, today's industrial sprawl makes the location woefully different from the country idyll it was in his day. 'In summer I stay in my room at Croisset, alone with my mother and father, and in winter I stay in my room in Rouen. But at Croisset I have my boat and the garden,' he wrote to his friend Ernest Chevalier in 1845. After his nervous crises, and the death of his sister and father in 1846, Flaubert used it more and more as a refuge where he could write undisturbed. He died here in 1880. The house was later flattened to make way for an oil refinery; only the tiny garden pavilion, known as the **Pavillon Flaubert**, survived, and now houses a museum that includes the study where Flaubert conceived *Madame Bovary*, as well as some other memorabilia.

Petit-Couronne, on the south bank of the Seine and still more a part of Rouen's modern suburban sprawl, was one of the homes of another writer, Pierre Corneille. He inherited the lovely half-timbered house at 502 Rue Pierre Corneille, now the **Musée Pierre Corneille**. The furniture inside it is not original, but there's a moderately interesting collection of engravings, rare editions and writings connected with Corneille's life, and at the back of the house there is a lovely traditional thatched bread oven and an authentically 17th-century-style vegetable garden. Regular buses run there from Rouen.

Musée Pierre Corneille
open April–Sept Wed–Sat and Mon 10–12.30 and 2–6, Sun 2–6; Oct–Mar Wed–Sat and Mon 10–12.30 and 2–5.30, Sun 2–6; adm

Tourist Information in Rouen

(i) **Rouen >**
25 Place de la Cathédrale, t 02 32 08 32 40, www.rouen tourisme.com

The tourist office provides informative daily 2hr walking tours and various themed tours on topics such as Flaubert, Monet or the city's Jewish quarter. Children may enjoy the motorized **Petit Train**, which does an hourly 40min tour (April–Oct daily 10–12 and 2–5). There are also special tours for small children (usually in French) and boat trips on the Seine.

Internet Access: Cyber@net, 47 Place du Vieux Marché; Place Net, 37 Rue de la République.

Markets: Place du Vieux-Marché, Tues–Sun 6am–1.30pm; Place St-Marc, Tues, Fri and Sat 8am–6.30pm; Sun 8–1.30 (antiques and bric-a-brac).

Post Office: 45 Rue Jeanne d'Arc.

Shopping in Rouen

Faïence ceramics are available from several shops on Rue St-Romain; for antiques, head for Rue Damiette. The market in Place du Vieux Marché is the best place for fresh fruit and produce, and Rue des Carmes, Rue Ganterie and Rue St-Lô have the most fashion shops.

Fromagerie du Vieux Marché, 18 Rue Rollon. Friendly cheese merchant near the Place du Vieux Marché with a comprehensive selection of Norman (excellent Neufchâtel) and other French cheeses.

Boulanger Jean-Marie Viard, 23 Allée Eugène Delacroix. Baker with an impressive range of different breads.

Where to Stay in Rouen

Rouen ✉ **76000**

Several Rouen hotels adhere to the *Bon Weekend à Rouen* scheme, which gives you two nights for the price of one at weekends, bookable in advance. The tourist office has lists of hotels currently taking part. For places to stay in the countryside near Rouen, *see* p.147–8.

***Dandy, 93 Rue Cauchoise, t 02 35 07 32 00, *www.hotels-rouen.net* (€€). This small but elegant family-run hotel's greatest asset is its central location on the lovely Rue Cauchoise.

Its 18 small rooms are divided between the main house and a modern annexe, and there's a *salon de thé* downstairs. Parking available.

***Dieppe**, Place Bernard Tissot, **t** 02 35 71 96 00, *www.hotel-dieppe.fr* (€€). Opposite the railway station, this hotel is now affiliated to the Best Western chain, but has been run by the Guéret-Le Grand family ever since it opened in the 1880s. What the comfortable rooms lack in character is made up for by the friendliness of the staff and the excellent restaurant, Les Quatre Saisons (*see* below).

Anderson, 4 Rue Pouchet, **t** 02 35 71 88 51, *www.hotelanderson.com* (€€). You'll get a friendly welcome at this good-value hotel near the station. It occupies a white 19th-century mansion, and its bright rooms are stylishly furnished with a mix of antiques and modern furniture.

La Cathédrale, 12 Rue St-Romain, **t** 02 35 71 57 95, *www.hotel-de-la-cathedrale.fr* (€). Fine 17th-century townhouse in one of Rouen's most historic streets near the cathedral, with 26 attractive rooms. Rooms on the inner courtyard are best. Breakfast is in a manorial chamber, or in the lovely garden courtyard. Internet access for guests.

(★) Les Nymphéas >>

Le Vieux Carré, 34 Rue Ganterie, **t 02 35 71 67 70, *www.vieux-carre.fr* (€). The most stylish small hotel in town. Rooms, around a plant-filled courtyard, are simple but chic and comfortable. You take breakfast in the cosy sitting room, furnished with antiques and comfy leather armchairs, which at lunchtime turns into a restaurant (*see* below).

(★) Le Vieux Carré >

Les Carmes, 33 Place des Carmes, **t 02 35 71 92 31, *www.hoteldescarmes. fr.st* (€). Well-located Art Nouveau-style hotel with bright, attractive rooms and the same friendly owners as the Vieux Carré. Original artworks decorate the breakfast room.

Philippe Aunay, 45 Rue aux Ours, **t** 02 35 70 99 68 (€) This gorgeous half-timbered house, entered via a stone passageway from 1424, is a remarkable survivor of the 1944 bombing that destroyed many of its neighbours. Philippe Aunay's family have lived in the house ever since his great-grandfather had a fabric shop on the ground floor. He has three B&B rooms, which ooze character, and the house is packed with antiques and fascinating curios. Book in advance.

Eating Out in Rouen

Gill, 8–9 Quai de la Bourse, **t** 02 35 71 16 14, *www.gill.fr* (€€€€–€€€). If you want a taste of French food at its best, this stylish 2-Michelin-star restaurant on the quay is the place. Try the *pigeon rôti à la Rouennaise* and the langoustines. Be sure to dress accordingly as the atmosphere is as starched and spotless as the table napkins. *Closed Sun and Mon.*

L'Ecaille, 26 Rampe Cauchoise, **t** 02 35 70 95 52, *www.lecaille.fr* (€€€€–€€€). An elegant Michelin-starred fish and seafood specialist, once based in St Valéry-en-Caux. Try the *bouillabaisse*, or, for a real treat, the *Menu Homard* (€85), a set meal in which every course (desserts apart) is lobster. *Closed Sat lunch, Sun eve and Mon.*

Les Nymphéas, 7-9 Rue de la Pie, **t** 02 35 89 26 69, *www.les-nympheas.fr* (€€€). Reached via a little passageway off Place du Vieux Marché, this comfortable restaurant, in a stunningly restored half-timbered building, is one of the highlights of Rouen's cuisine. A speciality of chef Patrice Kukurudz is *canard sauvageon à la Rouennaise*, but he also produces fabulous fish. In summer, you can eat in the pretty enclosed courtyard behind. Booking essential. *Closed Sun eve, Mon and Tues lunch.*

Le P'tit Zinc, 20 Place du Vieux Marché, **t** 02 35 89 39 69 (€€€). This well-located and sophisticated brasserie-cum-*salon de thé* serves an imaginative range of dishes making good use of the market across the street. Very good for lunch, with tables outside in summer, and a mainly-young clientele. *Closed Sat eve and Sun.*

La Couronne, 31 Place du Vieux Marché, **t** 02 35 71 40 90, *www.lacouronne.com.fr* (€€€€–€€). Salvador Dalí, Queen Elizabeth and many other dignitaries have all eaten in this ancient building, as photos on the walls testify. It began serving food in 1345, making it the oldest *auberge* in France (according to its owners). Choose between floors: downstairs is snug and homely (with log fire), larger rooms upstairs are suitable for parties, and a tiny room is bookable for intimate gatherings. The food is typical Norman fare, with plenty of duck and oysters. Very popular with tourists, especially in summer when you can sit outside.

Les Quatre Saisons (Hôtel de Dieppe), Place Bernard Tissot, **t** 02 35 71 96 00 (€€€–€€). The Hôtel Dieppe's restaurant is celebrated as one of the best places to find a full-on, traditional *caneton Rouennais à la presse*, in the hotel's variant 'Félix Faure', which a Guéret forebear claims to have invented while working on a liner called *Félix Faure* in 1933. There are other classic Norman dishes too. *Closed Sat lunch.*

Les P'tits Parapluies, 4 Rue Bourg l'Abbé, Place de la Rougemare, **t** 02 35 88 55 26 (€€€–€€). Just off one of Rouen's prettiest squares, north of the Hôtel de Ville, this bistro has sunny yellow walls between black-oak beams. Its food, cooked by one of Rouen's up-and-coming young chefs, is refined and very enjoyable. *Closed Sat lunch, Sun eve and Mon.*

La Marmite, 3 Rue de Florence, **t** 02 35 71 75 55 (€€). This cosy family-run place in a side-street near Place du Vieux Marché is decent value, with a generous lunch menu. Their foie gras

in a cider jelly is wonderful. *Closed Sun eve, Mon and Tues lunch.*

Pascaline, 5 Rue de la Poterne, **t** 02 35 89 67 44, *www.pascaline.fr* (€€–€). Centrally placed, and owned by the same Guéret family as the Hôtel de Dieppe (*see above*), this is a bustling, friendly urban brasserie. If you're sick of meat and cream, this is the place: at lunchtime there's an excellent-value salad bar and self-service starter and dessert bars, as well as the usual brasserie favourites.

Le Chenevis, 43 Rue aux Ours, **t** 02 32 10 09 23, *www.lechenevis.com* (€). Vegetarians do not despair. This no-nonsense restaurant/store/tearoom serves wholesome organic food, including plenty of veg, which may make a welcome change after all that rich food. *Closed Sun and from 7pm Mon–Wed.*

Le Vieux Carré, 34 Rue de la Ganterie, **t** 02 35 71 67 70 (€). The attractive restaurant of this hotel (*see above*), calls itself a '*Gourmet Salon de Thé*', and specializes in light, imaginative lunches. There are interesting vegetarian choices, and funky salads with varied vinaigrettes. As a tearoom, it offers teas you never knew existed. *Open until 6.30pm only and closed Mon.*

Le Petit Cauchois, Rue Cauchoise, **t** 02 35 15 30 96 (€). A tiny place serving great-value, interesting dishes, with bargain lunch menus. *Closed Sat lunch, Sun and Mon.*

The Seine Valley Upstream from Rouen

A Diversion into Bovary Country: Ry and the Forêt de Lyons

Little **Ry**, in the valley of the river Crevon 20km east of Rouen, has been immortalized as the model for Yonville-l'Abbaye, the yawn-ville village that drove Emma Bovary wild for passion. If you're familiar with *Madame Bovary* you can feel remarkably at home here, walking along the Grande Rue 'about a gunshot in length, with a few shops on each side', past buildings like the one on

Getting around Bovary Country

CNA runs **buses** to and from Rouen and Vascoeuil approximately once an hour. To get around the *Circuit Bovary*, though, a **car** or **bike** is essential.

It's virtually impossible to get to and from Lyons-la-Forêt by public transport. There's just one CNA bus a day to and from Rouen – and that tends to be at an ungodly hour of the morning.

which Emma and Charles' wisteria-clad house was based (now a lawyer's office), 'with its convenient side entrance where Emma could come and go without being seen'. Further along, the fictional pharmacy run by the busybody Homais is now a souvenir and sewing shop called 'Emma', while the Crédit Agricole savings bank occupies the building that was the Hôtel de Rouen in Flaubert's day, and the Hôtel Lion d'Or in the novel. Unashamed of Yonville's reputation as the capital of tedium, locals have cashed in with such things as a 'Marché d'Emma' grocery and 'Le Bovary' restaurant, whose building featured in Madame Bovary as the Café

Galerie Bovary/Musée d'Automates
open July–Aug Tues–Sun 2.30–6; Easter–Oct Sat–Mon 2.30–6; adm

Français. Emma can be seen with her lovers in 3D at the **Galerie Bovary/Musée d'Automates**, in an old cider press, where automata made by a local clockmaker play out the novel's less provocative scenes. A monument outside Ry's 12th–16th-century church commemorates Delphine Couturier, whose suicide at an early age after marrying a local doctor almost certainly inspired *Madame Bovary*. Delphine's husband, Eugène Delamare, who was a student of Flaubert's father at the medical school in Rouen and died, heartbroken, shortly after his wife, is also buried in the churchyard. The church has a unique Renaissance wooden porch, with fabulous carvings of animals and warriors and a roof in the form of an upturned ship's hull.

You can follow Emma's wanderings and simultaneously explore this attractive part of Normandy by picking up a leaflet on the '*Circuit Bovary*', available from local tourist offices. The northernmost point is picturesque **Buchy**, which has held a market in its heavy-timbered *halles* every Monday since the 17th century. Descending back down to Ry along the **Héronchelles** valley, you pass through Héronchelles itself, with a 16th-century Renaissance manor, and the tiny nearby hamlet of **Yville**, two of the prettiest villages in the region. Even if you've never read *Madame Bovary*, the circuit is a good opportunity to penetrate little-known corners of deep Normandy.

Musée des Traditions et Arts Normands
t 02 35 23 44 79; open April–Sept Wed–Sat and Mon 10–12.30 and 2–6, Sun 2–6.30; Oct–Mar Wed–Sat and Mon 10–12.30 and 2–5, Sun 2–5.30; adm

A short way west of Ry, 15km from Rouen, is the exquisite red-brick **Château de Martainville**, built in 1485 for a wealthy Rouennais merchant. With its steep slate roofs and pepperpot towers, it's one of the earliest examples of the French Renaissance style. It now houses the excellent **Musée des Traditions et Arts Normands**, a fascinating collection of furniture, everyday and decorative objects, costumes and jewellery dating from the 15th to the 19th centuries.

Les Jardins d'Angélique
open May–June daily 10–7; July–Sept Wed–Mon 10–7; adm

A few kilometres further south, near Montmain, **Les Jardins d'Angélique**, in the grounds of a gorgeous 17th-century manor house, were created in memory of the owner's daughter, who died of cancer. It's an evocative place, noted for its roses, hydrangeas and dahlias.

Château de Vascoeuil
t 02 35 23 62 35; open July–Aug daily 11–6.30; mid-Mar–June and Sept–mid-Nov Tues–Sun 2.30–6; adm; family ticket available

From roughly the same era as Martainville, and less imposing but more inspiring, the turreted **Château de Vascoeuil** is 5km southeast of Ry. As well as shrubs its large gardens sprout an ever-expanding collection of sculptures by artists such as Dalí, Braque, Léger, Volti and Vasarely. More art is displayed inside the château, and in the stunning round dovecote. First-rate temporary exhibitions and musical evenings are held at the château each summer, and every two years it hosts the *Montgolfiades*, a magnificent balloon show. You can digest it all from the pleasant riverside restaurant-tea room, which also has a good view of Vascoeuil's most exuberant sculpture, the multi-coloured balloon-buttocked *Ludivine* by French sculptor Jacky Coville. For French visitors another point of vital interest is that Vascoeuil was the home of the 19th-century historian Jules Michelet, author of a vast *Histoire de France*, and there's a museum dedicated to him in a cottage in the gardens.

Lyons and its Exquisite Forest

East of Vascoeuil, the vast and undulating **Forêt de Lyons**, with ancient beeches and deep little valleys, extends over 10,000 hectares. The forest was a favourite hunting ground of William the Conqueror and his descendants, and many other kings and aristocrats in later centuries, which is why so much of it has survived. It's particularly lovely in autumn, when the trees turn. Wonderful for walking, it's intersected by a web of footpaths and cycleways, maps and details of which you can pick up at the tourist office in Lyons-la-Forêt, which also organizes guided walks.

 Lyons-la-Forêt

Few villages can be described as 'perfect' but **Lyons-la-Forêt**, with its ravishing 17th- and 18th-century half-timbered houses, gets as near as a place can get. There's scarcely a modern building in sight, and its uniform beauty has led to it being chosen as the set for numerous films, including the two French film adaptations of *Madame Bovary*. Lyons-la-Forêt (the 's' in which is pronounced), was originally the site of a Norman castle that reached its greatest importance under Henry I, the Conqueror's son, for whom it was a favourite residence. Henry died here in 1135, of a surfeit of lampreys eaten after a hunting expedition in the woods. Virtually nothing of his castle remains today, as the village was built on top of its ruins. This means there's little to do in Lyons other than sit in a café in the square, admire its variously coloured half-timbering and watch the world go by – which is all part of its charm. In the centre of the square is the 18th-century wooden *halles* or market hall, which still hosts a weekly market, and occasional antiques fairs in summer. Descending down the steep Rue d'Enfer (Hell Street), on the right at no.4 a plaque marks the house where Maurice Ravel came to compose in peace in the 1920s. At the bottom of the hill, across the little River Lieure, are the **Trois Moulins**, three quaint water mills that were owned by the French Crown until the Revolution, below a 17th-century Benedictine convent that is now a school. Curiously isolated from the village is the flint **Eglise St-Denis**, founded in the 12th century but given a Gothic transformation around 1500.

Abbaye de Mortemer
t 02 32 49 54 34, www.mortemer.fr; park open daily 1.30–6; guided tours of interior and St Catherine's Spring May–Aug daily 2–6, Sept–April Sat–Sun 2–5.30; adm

A short way south of Lyons is the ruined Abbaye de Mortemer, a Cistercian abbey built on marshland in 1134 under the protection of Henry I. After the Revolution most of its stones were removed to build the nearby village of Lisors. The ruins are surrounded by a park with three lakes and 'St-Catherine's Spring', where young women traditionally came to pray for a husband. Bachelors and spinsters still gather here in search of marital happiness a few times each year today, apparently with some results. There's also a 15th-century pigeon loft, with chestnut timbers, which at one time doubled up as a prison. Most visitors, however, come for Mortemer's distinctly commercial **Museum of Ghosts and Legends**, housed in the abbey's 17th-century buildings. The ghosts, with which the abbey is reputedly rife, include four monks whose throats were cut during the Revolution and Matilda, Henry I's daughter, who was confined here in punishment for her loose morals. The abbey cashes in on its spooky history with son-et-lumière shows, a medieval play and, on 15 August, a medieval *fête*.

Château de Fleury
guided visits mid-June–mid-Sept daily 2–6; mid-Sept–mid-June Sat–Sun 2–6; adm

On the eastern side of the Forêt de Lyons in Fleury-la-Forêt, the Château de Fleury stands in the woods like a hidden jewel. The Louis XIII-style château contains rooms with 18th-century décor, a doll museum and a stunning old kitchen. It was abandoned after World War II until 1978, when restoration began. Visitors can also wander around the four-hectare park and in summer can visit a maze and a collection of farm animals. The château also provides three truly memorable B&B rooms (*see* below).

Tourist Information in Bovary Country

The tourist office in Lyons-la-Forêt is very helpful, with details of organized walks and all the footpaths, cycling and riding trails within the forest.
Market Days: Buchy: Mon, also 1st Sun of month for organic farmers' market; Ry: Sat; Lyons-la-Forêt: Thurs, Sat and Sun.

Shopping in Bovary Country

La Boutique des Quatre Fermières, 22 Rue de l'Hôtel de Ville, Lyons-la-Forêt, t 02 32 49 19 73. Gourmet produce from local farms: preserves like foie gras, paté and *saucisson*, fresh meat (especially duck), and gastronomic ready-cooked meals.

Where to Stay and Eat in Bovary Country

Ry ✉ 76116 and area

ⓘ **Ry >**

*Maison de l'Abreuvoir,
t 02 35 23 19 90,
www.ot-ry-trois
vallees.com*

La Muette, 1057 Rue des Bosquets, Isneauville, **t** 02 35 60 57 69 *http://charmance-lamuette.com* (€€). This 18th-century half-timbered house in Isneauville has five attractive rooms, and one and a half hectares of colourful gardens. It's totally peaceful, yet only minutes from Rouen.

Ferme du Coquetot, 46 Rue du Coq, Bourg-Beaudouin, **t** 02 32 49 09 91 (€). Large Norman manor farm owned by a young couple who have created four lovely B&B rooms. There's access to a small kitchenette, and there's a *gîte* (sleeps four) in a converted dovecote.

Le Bovary, 14 Rue de l'Eglise, **t** 02 35 23 61 46, *le-bovary.la-table-doscar@ wanadoo.fr* (€€–€). This good-value traditional restaurant occupies the former Hôtel de France (the Café Francais in *Madame Bovary*), one of the prettiest half-timbered buildings on Ry's main street.

L'Hirondelle, 40 Grande Rue, **t** 02 35 02 01 46 (€€–€). The cooking here is a surprise: the style is not Norman but from southwest France, with dishes like *cassoulet, confit de canard* and Bayonne ham. There are also good salads, crêpes, omelettes and other one-course meals, and a nice outdoor terrace. *Closed Sun eve and Mon.*

Lyons-la-Forêt ✉ 27480 and Area

ⓘ **Lyons-la-Forêt >**

*20 Rue de l'Hôtel de
Ville, t 02 32 49 31 65,
www.lyons.tourisme.
free.fr; closed Mon*

***La Licorne, 27 Place Benserade, **t** 02 32 49 62 02, *www.licorne-hotel.com* (€€). Right on Lyons' ravishing square, this venerable half-timbered house has been an inn since 1610. There's a wonderful carved staircase and plenty of creaking corridors; the rooms are old-fashioned but comfortable, and there's a cosy bar with lots of red velvet. It's recently changed owners, and there are plans for a restaurant.

Château de Fleury la Forêt, **t** 02 32 49 63 91, *www.chateau-fleury-la-foret.com* (€€). Live like a French aristocrat of the *ancien régime* in this wonderful château with its Louis XVI décor. The three B&B rooms have wood panelling, antiques and wonderful views (one is a suite). Breakfast is served in the original kitchens, amid rows of copper pans.

Le Pré aux Biches, 11 Rue de l'Essart Mador, Les Taisnieres, **t** 02 32 49 85 52 (€). Longhouse in the woods near Lyons with three large and luminous B&B rooms, each with its own entrance. The owner's speciality is jam, and she runs jam-making courses throughout the year. Evening meals (€€) are also available Thurs–Sat, using produce from the extensive garden (book in advance).

La Halle, 6 Place Isaac Benserade, **t** 02 32 49 49 92 (€€). Intimate bistro-style restaurant in a half-timbered house on Lyons' lovely main square. Excellent-value menus feature novelties (for rural Normandy) such as seafood pasta, served in the dining room; salads, sandwiches, omelettes and other light dishes are also served in the bar or on the ample outside terrace. *Closed Sun eve and Mon.*

Les Lions de Beauclerc, 7 Rue de l'Hôtel de Ville, **t** 02 32 49 18 90, *www.lionsdebeauclerc.com* (€€–€). This place is an antique shop, restaurant and *hôtel de charme*. Its six elegant rooms – all furnished with antiques – include a family room. The garden terrace is great for summer breakfasts. The restaurant (€€) serves light dishes, like crêpes, and cakes at teatime. *Closed Tues.*

Following the Seine: Les Andelys to Vernon

South of Rouen, the stretch of the Seine between Pont-de-l'Arche and Normandy's southeast border near Vernon is, for the most part, magnificent. In the mornings, mists rise moodily from its dark waters, and by day its sensuous beech-clad cliffs are bathed in the

Getting to Les Andelys and Vernon

Vernon has frequent **train** services on the line between Paris-St-Lazare (45mins–1hr) and Rouen (30–55mins), and local trains on the same line also stop at Gaillon.

Cars Jacquemard runs regular **buses** to Pacy, Evreux, Gisors and Les Andelys. There are around five buses a day (April–Oct) to Giverny from Vernon train station, timed to link in with trains.

golden light that drew the Impressionist painters here like moths to a lamp. One of the most unspoiled sections is that between **Amfreville** and **Connelles**, where a rambling water mill has been transformed into a magical luxury hotel (*see* below). In **Andé** another stunning old mill has been turned into an arts centre where concerts and exhibitions are held in summer. Walkers can imbibe the atmosphere of the river by following the GR2 long-distance footpath, and there's an excellent circular walk from the riverside hamlet of **Le Thuit** (tourist offices have details).

Les Andelys and Richard the Lionheart's Castle

The highlight between Rouen and Vernon is **Les Andelys**, perched at the head of a dramatic loop in the Seine. It actually consists of two villages, Le Petit-Andely, originally a fishing village that was then fortified by Richard the Lionheart when he built his castle, and the older Le Grand-Andely, founded by the Romans, a short way up a valley inland. With riverside lawns, half-timbered houses and narrow streets, Le Petit-Andely is the prettier, and in the past attracted painters like Henri Lebasque, whose *La Promenade en Barque* was painted here. The 12th-century **Eglise St-Sauveur** was built for King Richard, and only narrowly escaped getting the same treatment at the hands of French troops as his castle above it. For shops (and the weekly market on Saturday), head up Avenue de la République to Le Grand-Andely.

Les Andelys is dominated by the Seine's most spectacular monument, Richard the Lionheart's **Château Gaillard**, perched on a spur above the river and reached via a steep footpath from behind the tourist office in Le Petit-Andely, or by car via a winding but well-signposted route through Le Grand-Andely. Its 5m-thick walls seem to grow out of the cliffs, and are still massive and awe-inspiring despite centuries of wars, pilfering and erosion. The castle was built for King-Duke Richard in just one year, 1196–7, after he returned from the Third Crusade to find that his childhood friend, and (the story goes) lover, Philippe Auguste of France was plotting to terminate the independence of the Duchy of Normandy. Using building techniques he'd learned in the Arab world, Richard resolved to build the most advanced fortification yet seen in Europe. It was a prodigious feat, and the Lionheart was justly proud of his 'beautiful, one-year-old daughter'. His satisfaction was brought to an abrupt end, though, by a crossbow wound.

⑧ Château Gaillard
t 02 32 54 04 16; open mid-Mar–mid-Nov Wed–Mon 10–1 and 2–6; adm for entry to keep and guided tours

Venerable Vénables

Little Vénables, a few kilometres west of Les Andelys in the middle of nowhere, may look nondescript, but for thousands of people across the world it's an ancestral home. Venables far and wide can claim descent from its most illustrious inhabitant, a thrusting young knight called Gilbert de Vénables who travelled with William the Conqueror to England. Every five years, Venables from as far afield as Canada return 'home' for a four-day jamboree consisting of a hectic round of mayoral handshaking, parties in the town hall, and visits to local archaeological sites. The first was held in 1986, the next is due in 2011. English soccer coach and pundit Terry Venables has apparently shown little interest, but Patrick Lequette, the convention organizer, is hopeful that once Terry has retired he may consider joining the ranks of his namesakes. Some 600 families are currently on the Venables mailing list, and they have a website (*http://venables.free.fr*), where they can exchange Venables gossip.

Richard's indecisive brother King John, who succeeded him, was a less formidable adversary. Philippe Auguste attacked Château Gaillard in 1203, beginning a six-month siege and finally launching an assault. Penetrating the thick-walled castle with its 15-metre-deep ditches looked all-but impossible, but Philippe's troops finally gained entry by stealth through a window in the chapel – a building injudiciously added by John (an alternative theory, that the French entered through the latrines, has been dismissed as bunk). The castle fell in March 1204, and with it the dual Anglo-Norman monarchy shuddered to an end. The loss of Normandy only added to the bite of John's nickname, 'Lackland'.

After a spell as a royal prison, Château Gaillard continued to be fought over during the Hundred Years' War and the 16th-century French Wars of Religion. In all, it was besieged seven times. After the last siege, Henri IV drew a line under the castle's military past and ordered its demolition.

Despite the ravages of time, and constant pilfering over the years, the buildings that remain – the keep, part of an outer bastion, and parts of the walls – are impressive. The techniques Richard the Lionheart learnt from Crusader castles can readily be seen. The walls facing the castle's most vulnerable point, the hill overlooking it, are pointed to deflect missiles, and the walls of the keep are sloped. Originally, they were seven metres taller, and topped by a tower. The excellent guided tours take you round the keep where you can see remains of the *grande salle*, with two fireplaces and ornate window openings overlooking the Seine, and stairs leading down to the food cellars, where up to a year's worth of supplies could be stored. The rest of the site is enchantingly wild, and you are free to wander around the chalky ruins. At sunset the views are difficult to beat, and there's also a superb 10-km circular walk that ends at the castle, beginning from Les Andelys tourist office.

An even earlier period of history is recalled in Le Grand-Andely's **Collégiale Notre-Dame** church, which stands on the site of a convent for the daughters of the nobility founded in the 6th century by Saint Clotilde, wife of Clovis, first of France's Frankish kings. The present church dates from the 12th and 13th centuries, although much of it was later rebuilt, including the fabulous Renaissance-style north façade. Inside, the main nave and chancel are plain Gothic, their simplicity illuminated by 16th-century stained glass windows depicting the life of Saint Clotilde. There are also three paintings by Quentin Varin, who inspired Les Andelys' most famous son, the Baroque painter Nicolas Poussin, born nearby in 1594. Poussin seems to have felt little attachment to his home town, however, and rarely returned after leaving to study in Paris in his twenties. His finest paintings were done in Italy, where he died in 1665. Nevertheless, one of his large paintings, *Coriolanus Answering the Tears of his Mother*, together with pictures by contemporary local artists, is exhibited in the small **Musée Nicolas Poussin**, on Rue Ste-Clotilde near the market square. There are also religious artefacts from the *Collégiale* and a 4th-century Gallo-Roman mosaic. Another museum, the **Musée Normandie-Niémen** on Rue Raymond-Phelip commemorates the feats of the Normandie-Niemen air group, set up by General de Gaulle in 1942 to fight in Russia. One of their 96 pilots, 46 of whom never returned, came from Les Andelys.

Musée Nicolas Poussin
open Wed–Mon 2–6, closed Tues; adm

Musée Normandie-Niémen
t 02 32 54 49 76; open June–mid-Sept Wed–Mon 10–12 and 2–6; mid-Sept–May Wed–Mon 2–6; adm

Following the D313 and D316 south across the Seine you come to **Gaillon**, a half-timbered town with the finest Renaissance château in Normandy, **Château Gaillon**, built at the beginning of the 16th century for Cardinal d'Amboise, Archbishop of Rouen, in imitation of mansions he had seen in Italy. The interior was badly damaged during the Revolution, but the elegantly ornate exterior, one of the earliest examples of Italianate influence in France, is by far its most important feature. Alas, the château is no longer open to the public. From Gaillon it's a quick drive down the N15 to Vernon. There's a prettier route, however, along the north bank of the Seine through the stone villages of **Port-Mort**, **Notre-Dame-de-l'Isle** and **Pressagny-l'Orgueilleux**. Strong walkers might be interested in the 24km **Circuit des Pigeonniers**, which tours local *pigeonniers* (*see* p.118). They include a rare square one at **Bourgoult**. The route starts at **Harquency** (tourist offices have details and maps).

Vernon

Most visitors use this town straddling the Seine just before it leaves Normandy as a jumping-off point for visiting Giverny. It's a busy little town, a centre of hi-tech industry. However, Vernon, whose origins go back to early Viking times, has other attractions too. Despite being badly knocked about in 1944, the town has some fine half-timbered houses, the most spectacular of which, the 15th-century **Maison du Temps Jadis** ('House of Bygone Days'), houses the local tourist office. Look out for the tiny carving of the *Annunciation* on its wooden corner post. Towering above the town, the **Eglise Collégiale Notre-Dame** has a Romanesque choir, a superb 15th-century Gothic façade with stunning rose window, and a rare 17th-century organ. There's a pleasant walk along the riverbank to the south, while just across on the east bank is the **Vieux Moulin**, a half-timbered mill-cottage on top of the last three surviving arches of the medieval bridge that carried traffic across the Seine until the 18th century. As an important river crossing Vernon was also well fortified: next to the Vieux Moulin is the **Château des Tourelles**, a dramatic 12th-century keep built by King Philippe Auguste to protect the bridge, and in the middle of the old town is the **Tour des Archives**, the only remaining part of the same king's castle. Two old mansions on Rue du Pont house a small museum, the **Musée A. G. Poulain**, which has sculptures, paintings and artefacts. Its highlights are paintings by Bonnard and Sisley and two Monets, *Nymphéas* and *Falaises à Pourville*.

Musée A. G. Poulain
open April–Sept Tues–Fri 10.30–12.30 and 2–6, Sat–Sun 2–6; Oct–Mar Tues–Sun 2–5.30; adm

On a hill on the southwest side of Vernon is the elegant **Château de Bizy**, begun in 1740 by one of the most fashionable architects of the era, Constant d'Ivry – who also designed the Palais Royal in Paris – for the Duc de Belle-Isle, an important figure at the court of Louis XV. The oldest part of the grand domain is the stables, modelled on those at Chantilly and Versailles. The central section of the main house, which was substantially altered towards the end of the 19th century with décor partly inspired by the Albani palace in Rome, houses some fine 18th-century panelling and Louis XIV Gobelin tapestries. There's also a fabulous 19th-century painted Erard piano, and a big collection of Napoleonabilia, gathered by the Dukes of Albufera, descendents of Marshal Suchet, one of Napoleon's generals, whose family have owned the château since the 1900s. Bizy's most attractive feature, though, is the wonderful vistas in the park outside, including splendid Baroque cascading fountains that once earned the estate the nickname 'Little Versailles'. The water garden is currently being restored, but even when they are not in operation there are pleasant walks in the extensive grounds.

Château de Bizy
t 02 32 51 00 82; open April–Oct Tues–Sun 10–12 and 2–6; Mar Sat–Sun 2–5; adm

Tourist Information around Les Andelys and Vernon

In Vernon, it's possible to hire kayaks for trips down the Seine. Contact **Stade de la Porte Normande, t** 02 32 51 14 93.

Market Days: Les Andelys: Sat; Gaillon: Tues; Vernon: Wed am, Sat all day.

Post Office: Les Andelys: 9 Av de la République; Vernon: 2, Place d'Evreux.

Where to Stay and Eat around Les Andelys and Vernon

Connelles ✉ **27430 and Pont St-Pierre** ✉ **27360**

★★★Le Moulin de Connelles, 40 Route d'Amfreville-sous-les-Monts, Connelles, **t** 02 32 59 53 33, *www.moulindeconnelles.com* (€€€€€–€€€). You may have to pinch yourself to believe this extraordinary half-timbered and turreted manor straddling the Seine is real. In the mornings, mists rise moodily from the water all around, and you can take a rowing boat to do some exploring. Part of the house is on an island, where paths lead to a swimming pool and tennis courts. Bedrooms are luxurious, and there's a lovely suite in a tower. The riverside restaurant (€€€) is also superb. *Oct–April closed Sun eve, Mon and Tues lunch.*

***Hostellerie La Bonne Marmite, 10 Rue René-Raban, Pont-St-Pierre, **t** 02 32 49 70 24, *ww.la-bonne-marmite.com* (€€). For a taste of old Normandy, this 18th-century coaching inn in a town near the junction of the Andelle and the Seine is ideal. Since 1966 it has been tended with devotion by Maurice and Denise Amiot, and their warmth and personal attention make a stay special. Rooms, around an ivy-clad courtyard, are traditionally furnished. The main attraction is the cosy brick and timbered restaurant (€€€–€€) where you can sample M. Amiot's inventive cooking, and his superb wine cellar. *Closed Sun eve, Mon, Tues lunch, 20 Feb–20 Mar and 20 July–10 Aug.*

Les Andelys ✉ 27700

***La Chaine d'Or, 25-27 Rue Grande, Le Petit Andely, **t** 02 32 54 00 31, *www.hotel-lachainedor.com* (€€€–€€). This elegant 18th-century hotel on the riverbank gets its name from a barrier across the Seine where river traffic paid tolls before proceeding to Rouen. Most rooms are large and luxurious, with fine views. The lovely riverside terrace restaurant (€€€) has hung on to its Michelin star despite changes of management. Cooking is a sublime blend of classic and Norman. *Closed Mon lunch and Tues lunch, Nov–Mar closed Sun eve–Tues lunch.*

Ferme de la Haye Gaillard, Route de Cléry, **t** 02 32 51 66 23, *www.la-haye-gaillard.com* (€). One of the B&B rooms at this old brick farm is on the ground floor, while the other is inside an ancient *pigeonnier* in the garden. On the tranquil plains by Château Gaillard above Les Andelys, it's a great place to unwind and, for walkers, the GR2 runs past the front door.

Gaillon ✉ 27600

Chez Claudine, 2 Chemin de Ste-Barbe, **t** 02 32 52 96 67, *c.lions@wanadoo.fr* (€). Situated on a hill above Gaillon town, Claudine Lions' house has exceptional views. There are three large B&B rooms, and breakfast is in the kitchen or in the huge garden. Great value.

Vernon ✉ 27201

Hôtel d'Evreux, 11 Place d'Evreux, **t 02 32 21 16 12, *www.hoteldevreux.fr* (€). Friendly old-fashioned Logis hotel in the centre of town. Rooms are comfortable if unexciting, and there's a pretty interior courtyard. The restaurant (€€) is a favourite with locals, providing Norman staples like duck and apples, alongside more unusual items. *Restaurant closed Sun.*

Les Fleurs, 71 Rue Carnot, **t** 02 32 51 16 80 (€€€–€€). This restaurant is really two: no.71 is a smart and serves refined Norman classics, while the Bistro at no.73 (**t** 02 32 21 29 19, €) is more easy-going, with bargain *plats du jour. Closed Sun eve, Mon, 2 wks in Mar and 3 wks in Aug.*

Bouafles ✉ 27700

Les Préaux, 2 Haute Rue, **t** 02 32 21 04 11 (€€). Grand 19th-century house, attractively restored by its artist owner. One of the two rooms has fabulous views of Château Gaillard and the cliffs of the Seine. There's a large and well-stocked garden too.

ⓘ **Vernon >>**
36 Rue Carnot,
t 02 32 51 39 60,
www.cap-tourisme.fr;
closed Mon

ⓘ **Les Andelys >**
Rue Philippe Auguste,
t 02 32 54 41 93

★ **La Chaine d'Or >**

Giverny

Sleepy little Giverny, across the Seine from Vernon, first caught Claude Monet's eye by accident as he travelled past it by train. He spotted *Le Pressoir*, a modest house with a large, neglected walled garden, and decided that this was the place to spend the rest of his days. On 24 April 1883 he arrived with Alice Hoschedé, a friend of

Getting to Giverny

There are frequent **buses** to Giverny from Vernon train station (*see* p.171) during the months when the Fondation Monet is open. Timings dovetail with train times, and there are around 10 buses daily each way Mon–Sat, and five daily on Sun and public hols.

his first wife , their respective children and their bags. After initial hiccups the move proved a success: 'I am filled with delight, Giverny is a splendid spot for me,' he wrote, barely one month later. Monet painstakingly tamed the house and garden, planting clumps of flowers to form intoxicating splashes of colour like those on an artist's canvas. Later, he created his Japanese water garden, whose waterlilies would become his trademark image. Despite years of neglect after Monet's death in 1926, the house and garden have been beautifully restored to their former glory, and now attract as many gardening fanatics as art lovers (no original art works are on display here, only copies). Miraculously, despite receiving over half a million visitors a year, Giverny village has retained its provincial charm, and makes a delightful day's outing from Rouen or Paris. To savour it at its tranquil best, visit in late afternoon when the tour buses have left, or midweek outside peak season. It's magical.

Monet's House and Garden

⭐ Monet's House and Garden
t 02 32 51 28 21,
www.fondation-monet.com; open April–Oct Tues–Sun 9.30–6; adm

Since 1980 Monet's house and garden have been administered by the Fondation Claude Monet, a private charity. Opinions differ as to which is the best time of year to enjoy the great man's garden: many rave about it in spring, when the wisteria over the curved bridge in the water garden is at its pristine best and azaleas, rhododendrons and clematis provide explosions of colour; others prefer the mellow autumn colours of the clusters of dahlias and carpets of dazzling trailing nasturtiums. Monet and his children originally planted and tended the garden themselves, but as it and the number of their visitors grew, six gardeners were eventually employed by the family full-time. The emphasis then, as now, was on creating exuberant and apparently unrestricted splashes of colour rather than on neatness and order.

In 1893 Monet bought another plot of land on the other side of the country road and the railway which then ran in front of his garden gate. Despite a thorny tangle of bureaucratic hurdles and local opposition, he managed to divert the Ru river, a tributary of the Epte to form a **water garden** with a Japanese-style footbridge. As this garden matured, the idea of painting it grew on Monet as well. 'I planted my water-lilies for pleasure,' he later wrote to a friend. 'I cultivated them without thinking of painting them... A landscape does not get through to you all at once... And then, suddenly, the magic of my pond was revealed to me.' Monet began to paint the lilies with a passion verging on obsession, in every possible light, at every possible angle; as he aged, the studies became increasingly abstract and impressionistic. A new studio had to be built to accommodate his waterlily paintings, which also grew steadily in size into the huge canvases he painted in his last years. One set of 48 waterlily pictures hung in his studio for six years, constantly touched up and improved, before being exhibited in 1909. Today a visit to the pond is slightly marred by the fact that the once-dusty track between the two gardens is now a fairly busy road, but crossing between them is facilitated by a pedestrian underpass funded, together with much of the restoration of the gardens, by the Texan millionaire Walter Annenberg.

The **house**, with its pink façade and ivy-green shutters, has been finely restored, making it feel, remarkably, almost as if Monet and family were still here. One can easily imagine the old artist with his long beard relishing the colours in his garden from the window of his modest, bright bedroom. The walls of most of the rooms are hung with one of the world's finest collections of Japanese prints, including works by Hokusai, Hiroshige and Utamaro, still arranged exactly as Monet hung them. On the ground floor is his comfortable studio, later replaced by another purpose-built one in the garden (which now contains the Foundation's shop). The summery yellow dining room and blue-tiled kitchen reflect another of Monet's passions: fine food. The artist-*bon vivant* spent countless hours eating, entertaining, cooking and copying out recipes into his cooking journals: dishes were based on whatever the garden or the local farmyards could supply. Monet's favourite lunch, which he ate every year on his birthday on 14 November, was home-caught woodcock, preceded by fish – usually pike or turbot – and followed by a rich, sweet pistachio cake laced with kirsch that he named *vert-vert* ('green-green').

The Village and the Musée d'Art Américain

After visiting Monet's house and gardens, the best way to absorb Giverny's unique atmosphere is to wander along the quiet main street – Rue Claude Monet – where you may spot the odd vine (they were once grown in abundance here, before being wiped out by phylloxera). Many of its pretty old houses were and still are inhabited by 'neo-Impressionist painters', who exhibit their works by the roadside. There are also some attractive cafés, the most famous of which is the **Hôtel Baudy**, where young American artists, in pursuit of inspiration from the master, stayed in the 1890s. It was originally a simple *café-épicerie*, but so many aspiring artists turned up looking for rooms that its owners Monsieur and Madame Baudy were obliged to turn it into a permanent hotel. An old shed was transformed into a ballroom, where dances were held each weekend. Pissarro raved about the Baudy after his visit, saying 'there you will find all that you need to paint, and the best company there is'; Renoir, Rodin, Cézanne and Sisley soon followed, spending hours in the café and its garden studios. Today it's more 'Hotel Gaudy' as the interior has been repainted bright yellow, but its walls are still coated with paintings, and it's a likeably relaxed place. The hotel part has long since ceased operation, but one of the studios has been preserved the way it once was, and there's a gallery hosting temporary shows by locally-based artists.

Musée d'Art Américain
t 02 32 51 94 65, www.maag.org; open April–Oct Tues–Sun 10–6; adm, but free 1st Sun of each month; guided tours by appointment

The many young American artists who came to Giverny hoping to follow Monet's example are now commemorated in the **Musée d'Art Américain**, also on Rue Claude Monet. Founded by a US businessman, Daniel Terra, and his wife, the museum, twinned with the Terra Museum of American Art in Chicago, displays the work of the Giverny painters and other American artists living in France, with works dating from around 1750 up to the present day. The core of the collection, though, is the paintings of American Impressionists such as Frederick Carl Frieseke, Willard Metcalf, Theodore Robinson, Lilla Cabot Perry and Theodore Butler – the last of whom married Monet's stepdaughter, and is buried with Claude Monet and others of the family in Giverny's little churchyard. The highlight of the museum is the fine set of paintings illustrating the domestic lives of women by Mary Cassatt, the 'first' woman impressionist, who lived in a château nearby at Le Mesnil-Théribus. The museum also has attractive gardens, including one that belonged to Lilla Cabot Perry, and a superb *salon de thé* – Les Saisons de Giverny – with good-value salads and set menus.

Where to Stay in Giverny

Giverny ✉ 27260 and area

There are surprisingly few places to stay in Giverny, and all of them need to be booked well in advance. Many are closed Nov–Mar. See also the village website: *www.giverny.fr*.

⭐ **La Réserve** >

La Réserve, t 02 32 21 99 09, *www.giverny.org/hotels/brunet* (€€€). Superb new house built in traditional style amid the woods and orchards above Giverny. The welcome is as delightful as the house, with its pine floors, beamed ceilings, huge beds and happy mix of ancient and modern furniture.

Le Moulin des Chennevières, 34 Chemin du Roy, **t** 02 32 51 28 14, *www.givernymoulin.com* (€€€–€€). Wonderful 17th-century half-timbered mill, set in three hectares of parkland. In 1850 the America painter Stanton Young turned the grain mill into a home and studio, and it stars in several of the paintings of fellow American artist Theodore Robinson. Downstairs rooms have oak panelling. There are three rooms in a medieval tower, including a suite.

Le Clos Fleuri, 5 Rue de la Dime, **t** 02 32 21 36 51, *www.giverny.org/hotels/fouche* (€€). Modern thatched house in idyllic gardens, run by the friendly Danielle, who can give plenty of tips about the area. Two of her three large B&B rooms, furnished in pine, are in a separate building in the garden.

Le Coin des Artistes, 65 rue Claude Monet, **t** 02 32 21 36 77 (€€–€). Four lovely B&B rooms, one a family room, above an art gallery. It's right in the heart of the village.

Eating Out in Giverny

Les Jardins de Giverny, Chemin du Roy, **t** 02 32 21 60 80 (€€€–€€). Belle Epoque mansion surrounded by rose gardens, with a lovely terrace. The cuisine of chef Serge Pirault is refined, including such things as a *croustillant* of cod garnished with seaweed, and there's a fine wine list. *Open mainly for lunch only; closed Mon, Sun eve, Wed eve and Nov–Mar.*

Auberge du Prieuré Normand, 1 Place de la République, 27620 Gasny, **t** 02 32 52 10 01 (€€€–€€). This mock-Norman building on a square in a little village above the Seine is a locals' favourite, and fills with families at weekends. The superb cuisine puts an original slant on Norman dishes. Good value. *Closed Tues eve and Wed.*

Le Moulin de Fourges, 38 Rue du Moulin, 27630 Fourges, **t** 02 32 52 12 12, *www.moulin-de-fourges.com*

(€€€–€€). This ancient mill on the banks of the Epte, 9km east of Giverny, is outstanding both for its ravishing location and its cuisine. The beautifully renovated dining rooms all have views over the water and the old mill wheel, while the cuisine makes inventive use of spices, herbs and mushrooms. The only downside is that in mid-season it gets hugely crowded – often with weddings and other events at weekends – so book well in advance. *Closed Nov–Mar.*

Ancien Hôtel Baudy, 81 Rue Claude Monet, **t** 02 32 21 10 03 (€€–€). For atmosphere and value for money this historic café-restaurant, where great painters once drank, ate and painted, is the place. The bright-yellow-walled, bohemian-style dining room is lined with pictures, and many locals meet here for a tipple. As well as a set menu, there are well-priced *plats du jour* and a selection of snacks. *Closed Sun eve, Mon and Nov–Mar.*

★ Le Moulin de Fourges >

Gisors

Like Les Andelys, Gisors, 30km to the east, was an important outpost of the Duchy of Normandy, and since the early Middle Ages it has been dominated by its towering white castle. From within vast and solid walls its defenders kept a watchful eye on the ambitious French to the east, and later on the English to the north. Remarkably, much of its ramparts are still intact, making this probably the best-preserved medieval castle in Normandy. The town that grew up in the valley below it is an attractive, lively place, despite being badly battered in 1940. Miraculously, both the castle and Gisors' other great treasure, its 16th-century church, were largely spared. Its liveliest day is market day on Monday.

Château
t 02 32 27 60 63;
*guided tours April–
Sept Wed–Mon;
Oct–Nov and Feb–
Mar Sat–Sun; adm*

The original **Château** was built by William the Conqueror's son William Rufus in 1097, but was expanded, equipped with a stone-fronted keep and enclosed within sturdy ramparts by Henry I in the 1120s. The keep would have been draped with paintings and tapestries, and you can still see traces of its old ovens and sinks. In 1161 the castle was strengthened further by Henry II, who made Gisors the region's key fortress – to no avail, as Philippe Auguste seized it for France 30 years later. Eager to assert his power, the French king lavished money on it, building the circular keep known as the *Tour du Prisonnier* that is the castle's most outstanding feature today, and inserting several new towers into the outside walls. Inside the main tower you can see graffiti carved by

Getting to Gisors

Train lines run from Gisors both south to Paris (1hr 10mins), and north to Dieppe (2hrs), via Forges-les-Eaux and Neufchâtel-en-Bray. Cars Jacquemard has **buses** to Evreux via Les Andelys or Vernon, TVS has buses to Rouen, while Cabaro operates buses to Beauvais.

prisoners who were held here. Again, the fortifications proved little use during the Hundred Years War, when Gisors was occupied on and off by the English until 1449. In the late 16th century, 500 years of continuous habitation came to an end, and the castle fell into ruin. In the keep, where you can see traces of a chapel built by Henry II to atone for the murder of Thomas à Becket, and the cool cellars where French kings later stored their food and wine.

Down in the town, the **Eglise St-Gervais–St-Protais**, clothed in a forest of pinnacles and buttresses, dates back to the 11th–12th centuries, but is best known as an example of the Renaissance architecture created by the Grappins, a local family of architects. The story of its evolution is told by the magnificent west façade, begun in Flamboyant Gothic style, then revamped in the 1530s in Renaissance mode. Many of its ornate statues lost their heads in the 1570s during France's Wars of Religion, but you can still see pilgrims' scallop shells carved over the doors. The church's opulence stems from the fact that after taking Gisors in 1193 the French monarchs gave the town special tax concessions to ensure its allegiance. Inside, it is a pleasing blend of Gothic and Renaissance, with richly carved decoration standing out against the pure, light walls of the nave. In 1540, however, Gisor's illusions of grandeur took a knock when money ran out; the church's builders downed tools, and so their work was never finished. The only remainder of the previous 11th century church is a small column crowned with acanthus leaves between the transept and the nave, which suggests the original church was far smaller. The side chapels were donated in the 16th century by the town's guilds, who vied with each other to provide them with the most splendid decoration. One of the finest carved pillars is that donated by the tanners, and there's a fine stained-glass window given by their rivals the cobblers. The Chapelle du Rosaire below the South Tower contains a spiral staircase and a fine bas-relief of the Tree of Jesse.

Gisors' other point of interest is a bronze statue of the Virgin, *La Vierge Dorée* (the Golden Virgin), on the Rue de Paris near the bridge across the River Epte, which people generally either love or hate. It's the latest of several statues that have replaced the first one that stood here, which was commissioned and coated in gold by King Philippe Auguste in thanks for his survival after nearly drowning in the Epte when his troops stormed the town. The virgin has had a rough ride: a 19th-century version was 'stolen' by the Germans, and its replacement was decapitated in 1979.

Tourist Information in Gisors

① Gisors ›
4 Rue du Général de Gaulle, **t** *02 32 27 60 63,* *www.ville-gisors.fr*

The tourist office in Gisors can provide guided tours of the town with advance reservation.

Market Days: Mon all day, Fri morning, both in Place des Carmélites.

Post Office: Rue du Général de Gaulle

Where to Stay and Eat around Gisors

Gisors ☒ 27140 and Area

***Château de la Rapée, 27140 Bazincourt-sur-Epte, **t** 02 32 55 11 61, *www.hotel-la-rapee.com* (€€€–€€). It's worth the tortuous drive along a forest track to reach this monument of Anglo-Norman architecture. It's a friendly and luxurious if eccentric place full of turrets, watchtowers and secret corners. The pink-toned restaurant has fine cuisine (€€€), and there's a swimming pool. Pissarro lived in Bazincourt from 1884. *Closed Feb; restaurant closed Tues.*

Hôtel Moderne, Place de la Gare, **t 02 32 55 23 51, *www.hotel-moderne-gisors.fr* (€). Old-fashioned small-town Logis hotel by the train station, with newly-refurbished rooms and a decent restaurant (€€–€).

Le Cappeville, 17 Rue Cappeville, **t** 02 32 55 11 08 (€€€–€€). Intimate, elegant restaurant offering refined versions of Norman staples. *Closed Wed, Thurs, 1–18 Sept and 5–15 Jan.*

Dangu ☒ 27720

Les Ombelles, **t** 02 32 55 04 95, *http://vextour.ifrance.com* (€). An old house with a garden running down to the River Epte. The three B&B rooms are elegantly furnished with antiques. Dinner available with advance notice. *Closed mid-Nov–mid-Mar.*

The Eure Valley and Evreux

 Eure Valley

The landscape around Evreux is one of contrasts. Just south of Rouen, flat prairies planted with cereals replace the meadows and orchards of northern Normandy, but as you continue south from the historic wool town of **Louviers** these plains give way to the picturesque Eure valley, which meanders lazily like a miniature version of the Seine. Less well-known than the mighty river that it joins at Rouen, the Eure valley has a special, unspoiled tranquillity. The prettiest stretch is between **Heudreville-sur-Eure**, about 9km south of Louviers, down to the market town of **Pacy-sur-Eure**. In the many charming small towns and villages that follow each other along the banks of the Eure, the stone or half-timbered houses have lawns that stretch down to the willow-draped river, where only fishermen and rowing boats disturb the peace.

Acquigny to Ivry

Château
park open July–Aug daily 2–7; May–June and Sept–mid-Oct Sat–Sun 2–6; adm

The pretty riverside town of **Acquigny**, just north of Heudreville-sur-Eure, has a good choice of restaurants and a fabulous Renaissance **château**, built in the late 16th century by Philibert Delorme for Anne de Montmorency Laval, lady-in-waiting to Queen Catherine de Medici. Its most distinguished feature is its attractive park, which has an orangery, a collection of citrus plants, and an impressive plantation of trees that dates back to 1768. South of

Getting around the Eure Valley

To explore the Eure valley it's pretty essential to have your own wheels. The nearest main **train** stations are at Vernon and Evreux, both of which are served by Cars Jacquemard **buses**.

The **Train Touristique** from Pacy runs Easter–Oct Wed and Sun, and sporadically during the rest of year. Trains run either south to Breuilpont (1½hrs return) or north to Chambray (2hrs return, including 1hr stop in Chambray). If you take the Chambray train, you can stop off at Cocherel for a guided tour and be picked up on the way back. For times, fares and Cocherel tours, t 02 32 36 04 63, *www.cfve.org*.

Acquigny, the village of **Cocherel**, known for a celebrated restaurant, was the site of a famous battle during the Hundred Years' War, when the French commander Bertrand du Guesclin defeated the combined forces of England and Navarre. More recently it was the home of Aristide Briand, several times French prime minister in the early 1900s and winner of the Nobel Peace Prize for his efforts toward Franco-German reconciliation. Further south, between Ivry-la-Bataille and Dreux, the Eure river forms the border of Normandy, and in the past served as an important line of defence.

Pacy-sur-Eure is the main centre of whatever's going on in the central Eure valley. Although there are few hotels along the Eure, there is an astonishing number of attractive restaurants and high-quality *chambres d'hôtes*, many of which have gardens by the river. From Easter to October you can explore the valley's picturesque narrow-gauge railway, or **Chemin de Fer de la Vallée de l'Eure** (part of the old Rouen–Orléans railway), by taking a ride in the *train touristique* that runs up and down from the tiny old station in Pacy-sur-Eure. Trains run north to Chambray (or Cocherel if you book onto a guided tour) or south to **Breuilpont**. At Breuilpont station there's a '*wagon-musée*' with an exhibition on the history of the line, and trips include a commentary by a guide.

Another option is to explore the river itself by canoe or rowing boat. The best place to hire boats is **Autheuil-Authouillet**, but there are landing-stages with boats in many of the villages along the Eure, including **La-Croix-Saint-Leufroy**. The Pacy tourist office has details of all the places with boats for rent in the valley.

Tourist Information around Acquigny

Boat and kayak hire: in Autheuil-Authouillet, t 02 32 35 16 46, or in La-Croix-Saint-Leufroy, t 02 32 67 82 87, *www.lacroix-ck.org* For a fee you can usually be accompanied and/or collected at the other end.
Market Day: Pacy-sur-Eure: Thurs.
Post Office: Pacy-sur-Eure: Place Dufay

Where to Stay and Eat around Acquigny

Acquigny ⊠ 27400
La Londe, 4 Sente de l'Abreuvoir, Heudreville sur Eure, t 02 32 40 36 89, *www.lalonde.online.fr* (€). Stay at this old farmhouse outside Acquigny for its huge garden, which runs down the banks of the Eure. There are two spotless rooms, amid total tranquillity.

① Pacy-sur-Eure >>
Place Dufay, t 02 32 26 18 21, information@ cap-tourisme.fr

⭐ L'Aulnaie >>

La Chaumière, 15 Rue Aristide Briand, t 02 32 50 20 54 (€€). The smartest of a surprising array of good-standard restaurants in this lovely riverside village, in a charming half-timbered thatched cottage. There are no set menus, only à la carte. *Closed Tues and Wed.*

L'Hostellerie d'Acquigny, 1 Rue d'Evreux, t 02 32 50 20 05 (€€). Light and airy restaurant on the Acquigny–Louviers road, serving good Norman cuisine at sensible prices. *Closed Mon and Tues.*

La-Croix-St-Leufroy ✉ 27490

La Boissière, Hameau de la Boissaye, La-Croix-St-Leufroy, t 02 32 67 70 85, *www.chambres-la-boissiere.com* (€). This 15th-century manor with its duck pond and colourful gardens is a real gem. In the middle of nowhere, it has five modern B&B guest rooms, and if you ask ahead you can get the chance to taste Madame's excellent home cooking (€€).

Brosville and St-Vigor ✉ 27930

Domaine de Broc Fontaine, 36 Rue St Fiacre, Brosville, t 02 32 34 61 78 (€€€–€€). The highlight of this 300-year-old farmhouse *gîte au jardin* in the Iton valley is its fabulous vegetable and flower garden, lovingly created by American owner Deborah. Rooms look over the rose and herb garden, the white garden or the orchard – take your choice. You can taste the (organic) produce, which includes some rare and exotic vegetables, if you order dinner in advance (€€). Deborah and her husband Olivier also run gourmet cooking weekends along with a seven-day Gourmet Tour of Normandy.

Le Moulin de la Côte, 8 Rue de Jouy, St-Vigor, t 02 32 34 66 88 (€€). The young owners of this 16th-century water-mill overlooking the Eure will take you canoeing, if you wish. It's a relaxed place with children and animals milling around, and the views from the two large, simply furnished B&B rooms are hard to beat. Dinner can be ordered, too, and there's a gîte.

Pacy-sur-Eure ✉ 27120 and Area

****Château de Brécourt, Douains, Pacy-sur-Eure, t 02 32 52 40 50, *www.chateaudebrecourt.com* (€€€€–€€). This 17th-century moated château in 20 hectares of tranquil grounds is perfect for a luxuriously relaxing weekend retreat or a visit to Giverny. The bedrooms, some of which have vast roof timbers and grand stone fireplaces, are all spacious and comfortable. The château's magnificently manorial restaurant (€€€–€€) is renowned for classic cuisine, and there's a lovely bar (in the former Salle d'Armes) and an indoor pool complete with frescoed ceiling.

L'Aulnaie, 29 Rue de l'Aulnaie, 27120 Fontaine-sous-Jouy, t 02 32 36 89 05, *http://chambre-fontaine.chez.tiscali.fr* (€€). Views from the two B&B rooms in this gorgeous 19th-century farmhouse are breathtaking. Languid lawns stretch down to a stream and merge into glorious beech woods, and there's a lovely sitting room with log fire. Fontaine is also a very pretty village, and the friendly hosts can give guests plenty of local information.

La Ferme de Cocherel, Hameau de Cocherel, Pacy-sur-Eure, t 02 32 36 68 27, *www.lafermedecocherel.fr* (€€€). This extensively modernized old house in a village a little north of Pacy along the river houses one of the Eure valley's finest restaurants. Menus are based on local produce, and combine sophistication with local tradition. Several former outbuildings around the pretty garden have been turned into comfortable bedrooms (€€€), which are only available to diners at the restaurant. *Closed Tues and Wed.*

Le Charolais, 17 Grande Rue, 27120 Chambray, t 02 32 26 05 78 (€€). This relaxed restaurant on the outskirts of Chambray, between Cocherel and La Croix, specializes in grilled meats, cooked traditional-style over a giant grill in an open kitchen. Diners can even bring along their own wine – a rarity in France. There's a log fire in winter and rustic, brick-and-beam décor, and the friendly owners speak good English. *Closed Sun and Mon.*

Evreux

Although it's the capital of the Eure *département*, Evreux actually stands not on the Eure river but on the smaller Iton, and this river and its offshoots snake their way lazily through the centre of the city. Evreux's history has been turbulent even by Norman standards, and its last thrashings, by German and Allied bombs in 1940 and 1944, destroyed much of what Madame de Sévigné once described as the prettiest town in Normandy. Nevertheless, the Gothic cathedral and bishop's palace (now a museum), largely spared in the war, give a taste of how the city once looked, and one can happily spend a day enjoying them and the riverside wash houses – or sampling one of Evreux's crop of excellent restaurants.

Cathédrale
Notre-Dame
open daily 8–12
and 2–7

The only remaining part of Evreux's medieval fortifications is the elegant 15th-century **Tour de l'Horloge** (clock tower), on the site of an earlier tower that stood beside the main gate into the town. To the south, overlooking the river, the Cathédrale Notre-Dame has a

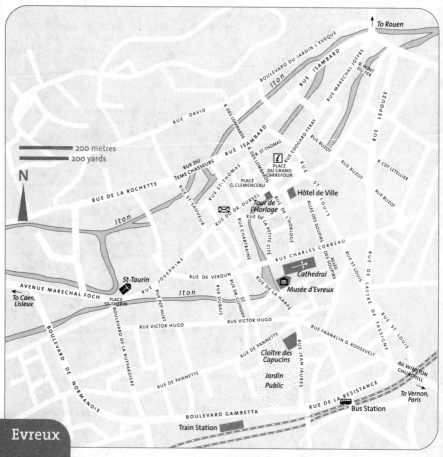

Evreux

Getting to Evreux

Evreux is on the Caen–Paris **train** line, and has frequent services in both directions. There are also good rail connections to Lisieux, Bernay and Conches-en-Ouche.

Cars Jacquemard provides **bus** services to Gisors via Pacy-sur-Eure, Vernon and Les Andelys. It also runs buses to L'Aigle, Conches and Le Bec-Hellouin. CNA connects Evreux with Rouen ten times a day and CFTI has services to Honfleur. Cariante also serves Verneuil sur Avre. Bus station, t 02 32 39 40 60.

lovely stone-lace-draped and pinnacled north door that is a perfect example of Flamboyant Gothic. Far older is the Romanesque arcading in the nave, built after Henry I of England razed the town's first cathedral in 1119. The choir boasts magnificent 14th-century stained-glass windows, some of the finest in France, and its 13 chapels display outstanding woodcarvings. Bears, foxes and monkeys squabble for your attention, but the best carvings are in the sixth, Gothic, enclosure, a menagerie of chained monsters and a porcupine designed to symbolize human vices.

Musée d'Evreux
t 02 32 31 81 90; open April–Oct Tues–Sun 10–12 and 2–6; Nov–Mar Tues–Sun 10–12 and 2–5; adm

The **Musée d'Evreux**, in the 15th-century former bishop's palace that nestles inside the ramparts beside the cathedral, has palaeolithic and Gallo-Roman domestic and religious objects in its archaeological room in the basement. The other floors contain a varied array of items, from 17th-century tapestries to paintings and a collection of apothecary jars in Nevers and Rouen faïence ware, originally from Evreux's hospital.

Further west, the **Eglise St-Taurin** is a weird mish-mash of styles from Romanesque to Baroque. Dedicated to the first bishop of Evreux, it probably began life as the abbey church of a Benedictine monastery, in the 10th century. Anglo-French wars reduced most of it to rubble, and it was rebuilt after 1200. Its greatest claim to fame is the **Châsse de St-Taurin**, an exquisite piece of craftsmanship made to house the relics of the saintly Taurinius. Constructed in the shape of a miniature Gothic cathedral, the reliquary is a fantastic concoction of gold, silver and precious stones. It's a miracle that such a delicate and extravagant piece survived both the Revolution and the Second World War. On the south side of the old town is the **Cloître des Capucins**, the former Capuchin cloisters.

An essential walk to take in Evreux is along the medieval streets bordering the river, from where you can see the old wash houses. The best bridges from which to see them are on Rue du Pont de Fer, Rue du Docteur Guindey, Rue Dubais and Rue du Président Huet. There are good views too from the path between Rue des 7ème Chasseurs and Rue Saint-Sauveur. Another good walk is the **Ligne Verte**, a 2.7km route that follows the track of the old railway from Evreux to Honfleur. For something more substantial, continue along the old railway all the way to Harcourt, in the Risle Valley (*see* p.193). The whole route is 31km long and is one of the Eure's three excellent *voies vertes*.

ⓘ **Evreux >**
*Place du Général de
Gaulle, t 02 32 24 04 43
www.ot-pays-evreux.fr*

★ **La Gazette >>**

Tourist Information in Evreux

The tourist office in Evreux organizes a wide range of monthly tours, covering subjects like gastronomy, heritage, gardening, geology and birds. Also offers guided taxi tours around town (book 48hrs in advance). The office has details and maps of walks and cycle rides on the Ligne Verte, the *voie verte* (*see* p.185) and elsewhere.

Internet Access: Cybernetics, 27 Rue Edouard Feray.

Market Days: main market, Sat, Place Clemenceau. Smaller market on Thurs.

Post Office: 25 Rue du Docteur Oursel.

On the last weekend of June, Evreux hosts a rock festival.

Shopping in Evreux

Chocolatier-Pâtissier Auzou, 34 Rue Chartraine, t 02 32 33 28 05. Gourmet chocolate-maker whose specialities include Pavés d'Evreux ('Evreux paving stones' – sugar coated almonds dipped in nougatine and chocolate). Customers can also visit the work-shops, and the owners are happy to let you taste before you buy. *Closed Mon.*

Les Jardins de Pomone, 15 Rue Feray. Great deli selling all kinds of Norman goodies from *pommeau* and calvados to cheeses and biscuits.

Where to Stay around Evreux

Evreux ✉ 27000

There are no outstanding hotels in Evreux itself, and if you are mobile it's often a more attractive proposition to stay in one of the many lovely B&Bs in the Eure valley (*see* pp.182–3).

*****Normandy**, 37 Rue Edouard Feray, t 02 32 33 14 40, *http://perso.wanadoo. fr/normandyhotel* (€€). Rooms in this old half-timbered building are reasonable, even if mostly compact and with hit-and-miss colour schemes. The attractive restaurant

(€€), with huge log fire, serves solid Norman fare, and there's a snug bar.

****Hôtel de France**, 29 Rue St-Thomas, t 02 32 39 09 25, *www.hoteldefrance-evreux.com* (€) Has a few simple rooms; the nicest is No.24 in the attic, with beams and antiques. The highlight is the restaurant (*see* below).

Eating Out in Evreux

Hôtel de France, 29 Rue St-Thomas, t 02 32 39 09 25, *www.hoteldefrance-evreux.com* (€€€). This gourmet restaurant is probably the best of Evreux's many eating places. Try the home-made *foie gras. Closed Sat lunch, Sun eve and Mon.*

La Gazette, 7 Rue St Sauveur, t 02 32 33 43 40 (€€). This intimate half-timbered house is Evreux's top culinary address. Chef Xavier Buzieux trained with the Roux brothers in London, and provides light, modern cuisine based on beautifully fresh local produce. Don't miss the *gâteau de pommes caramelisées. Closed Sat lunch, Sun and 3 wks in Aug.*

La Vieille Gabelle, 3 Rue de la Vieille Gabelle, t 02 32 39 77 13 (€€). Great restaurant serving traditional dishes with sophisticated touches, all based on what's fresh at the market that day. It's in an ancient Evreux house with beamed ceilings, and has three separate rooms (including a non-smoking one) which gives it an intimate feel. *Closed Sat lunch, Sun eve, Mon and 1st 3 wks in Aug.*

La Croix d'Or, 3 Rue Joséphine, t 02 32 33 06 07 (€€–€). Trayfuls of langoustines and oysters indicate that seafood is the speciality at this relaxed and good-value restaurant, but there are plenty of other fine dishes if seafood doesn't really float your boat.

Café Matahari, 15 Rue de la Petite Cité, t 02 32 38 49 88 (€). A funky café in a great location by the river, where Evreux's young crowd come to drink (there's Moroccan food too). Art exhibitions and concerts are often held here.

The Risle Valley and the Perche

Four rivers carve through the eastern département of Eure: the Eure, the Risle, the Iton and the Charentonne. The valley carved out by the Risle, which rises west of the fortress town of L'Aigle then flows through the plateau of the Pays d'Ouche, boasts some fine attractions, from the abbey of Le Bec-Hellouin to the châteaux of Beaumesnil and Champ-de-Bataille. South of the Risle, tucked away in the southeast corner of Normandy, lies the old – and little visited – province of the Perche. Its honey-coloured stone villages, understated manoirs and mild-mannered Percheron horses offer a taste of country traditions.

11

Don't miss

⭐ The old Oxbridge of Normandy
Le Bec-Hellouin p.190

⭐ An exquisite slice of the *ancien régime*
Château du Champ-de-Bataille p.194

⭐ Architectural pearls
Bernay p.195

⭐ Mighty horses and manor houses
The Perche p.204

⭐ Honey-stoned cottages
La Perrière p.208

See map overleaf

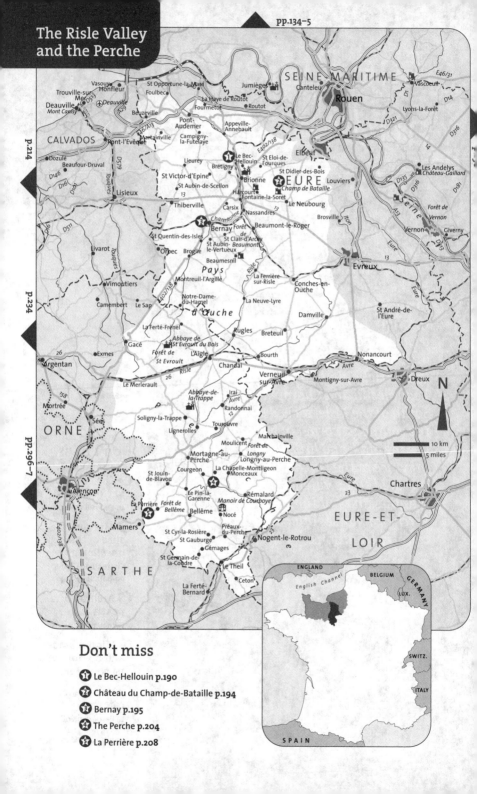

The Risle Valley and the Perche

p.214
p.234
pp.296–7

SEINE MARITIME

Rouen

CALVADOS

EURE

Pays

d'Ouche

ORNE

EURE-ET-LOIR

SARTHE

Vasouy
Honfleur
Trouville-sur-Mer
Deauville
Mont Canisy
Beuzeville
Pont-l'Évêque
Dozulé
Beaufour-Druval
Lisieux
Thiberville
St Victor-d'Épine
St Aubin-de-Scellon
St Quentin-des-Isles
Orbec
Broglie
Livarot
Vimoutiers
Camembert
Le Sap
La Ferté-Frênel
Gacé
Exmes
Argentan
Le Merleault
Mortrée
Sées
Alençon
Mamers

St Opportune-la-Mare
Foulbec
La Haye-de-Routot
Fourmetot
Pont-Audemer
Martainville
Campigny-la-Futelaye
Lieurey
Brétigny
Brionne
Harcourt
Carsix
Nassandres
Bernay
St Clair-d'Arcey
St Aubin-le-Vertueux
Beaumesnil
Montreuil-l'Argillé
Notre-Dame-du-Hamel
Rugles
Abbaye de St Evroult du Bois
Forêt de St Evroult
L'Aigle
Chandai
Risle
Abbaye de la Trappe
Irai
Avre
Randonnai
Soligny-la-Trappe
Lignerolles
Tourouvre
Moulicent
Mortagne-au-Perche
Courgeon
Longny-au-Perche
La Chapelle-Montligeon
Monceaux
St Jouin-de-Blavou
La Perrière
Forêt de Bellême
Le Pin-la-Garenne
Bellême
Nocé
Manoir de Courboyer
Rémalard
St Cyr-la-Rosière
St Gauburge
Gémages
Préaux-du-Perche
St Germain-de-la-Coudre
Le Theil
Ceton
La Ferté-Bernard
Nogent-le-Rotrou

Jumièges
Canteleu
Appeville-Annebault
Le Bec-Hellouin
St Éloi-de-Fourques
St Didier-des-Bois
Champ de Bataille
Fontaine-la-Soret
Le Neubourg
Beaumont-le-Roger
Brosville
La Ferrière-sur-Risle
Conches-en-Ouche
La Neuve-Lyre
Damville
Breteuil
Bourth
Verneuil-sur-Avre
Montigny-sur-Avre
Marchainville

Elbeuf
Louviers
Évreux
St André-de-l'Eure
Nonancourt
Dreux
Chartres

Les Andelys
Château-Gaillard
Forêt de Vernon
Vernon
Giverny

Wascoeuil
Lyons-la-Forêt

Don't miss

1 Le Bec-Hellouin **p.190**

2 Château du Champ-de-Bataille **p.194**

3 Bernay **p.195**

4 The Perche **p.204**

5 La Perrière **p.208**

ENGLAND

English Channel

BELGIUM

GERMANY

LUX.

SWITZ.

ITALY

SPAIN

10 km
5 miles

N

The Lower Risle

Pont-Audemer to Brionne and Le Bec-Hellouin

Pont-Audemer, only 24km southeast of Honfleur, owes its historical prominence, as its name suggests, to its bridge, the first substantial crossing point across the Risle as you head upstream from the Seine. The old town is crisscrossed by little canals, and while whoever dubbed it 'the Venice of Normandy' may have been more than a little over-enthusiastic, this ancient tanning town has a lot of charm. Along its lanes one can still see some of the old slate-roofed attics where skins were dried out, and the canals are lined with magnificent old houses where the wealthier merchants used to live. One of Pont-Audemer's most famous leather workers was Charles-Emile Hermès, whose luxury leather goods and silk scarves brought him worldwide fame and became a symbol of a certain kind of upper-crust French chic. On Mondays and Fridays the town buzzes with a vibrant market that's one of the region's best, especially for local cheeses and fresh produce.

The tourist office's map points you towards the prettiest *hôtels particuliers*, many of which have elaborately carved gateways. The **Eglise St-Ouen**, begun in the 11th century and enlarged (but never finished) in the 16th, has fine stained-glass windows, including one showing the saint after whom the church is named, and impressive Flamboyant Gothic decoration. Pont-Audemer is also a good base from which to explore the **Marais Vernier** marshlands in the Seine Valley (*see* p.141).

Brionne

The most dramatic moment in Brionne's history occurred in 1047, when William of Normandy (later the Conqueror) besieged the Duke of Burgundy here. The town was tossed from one side to another for many centuries, due to its commanding position over the Risle. An 11th-century keep, or **Donjon**, still dominates the town. It is one of the few Norman keeps that is square instead of round, a style that would be adopted in England after 1066. The climb up the tower is worth the effort for its views of Brionne and the Risle valley, with its apple orchards and half-timbered farmsteads. The town centre is also a tranquil place to wander, especially in the riverside park christened **Jardin de Shaftesbury** in honour of Brionne's twin town in England.

The **Eglise St-Martin** has 14th-century Gothic wood vaulting in the chancel, and an altarpiece from Bec-Hellouin abbey. On Sundays a great market fills the square beside it. The tourist office

Getting around the Lower Risle

The nearest mainline **train** stations are at Brionne, Deauville-Trouville or Rouen. Brionne has a few trains daily on the Caen–Rouen line, which also stop at Bernay.

EFFIA **buses** between Evreux and Honfleur stop in Pont-Audemer, Le Bec-Hellouin and Brionne. CNA bus No.31 runs to Rouen around six times daily. There are also good connections from Rouen to Lisieux and Bernay.

must have one of the choicest locations in Normandy: it's inside an old **cider press**, which still has the great round stone with which apples were crushed. The press forms part of the **Domaine de Lorraine**, a manor formerly owned by the Lorraine family, who lorded it over Brionne before the Revolution. Other parts of it, such as the laundry and the barn, can also be visited. Brionne also has a large lake, offering watersports in summer, and the tourist office can also inform you on horse-riding, fishing, hiking, mushroom picking and many other activities.

Le Bec-Hellouin

⭐ Le Bec-Hellouin
t 02 32 43 72 60, www.abbayedubec. com; guided tours Wed–Mon; adm; services Mon–Sat 11.45am and 6pm, Sun 10.30am and 5pm

The utterly picturesque village of Le Bec-Hellouin, in watermeadows beside the Risle, is dominated by the shimmering white bell tower of the Norman abbey that was once the ecclesiastical Oxbridge of Normandy. The **Abbaye de Notre-Dame du Bec** today houses some 20 Benedictine monks. It was founded by a local knight called Hellouin, who swapped his sword for a habit in 1034, and the abbey he created rapidly attracted the greatest brains in Europe. One of the first arrivals was Lanfranc, the great Italian theologian and scholar. In the 1040s William the Conqueror, who was in the area besieging Brionne, was so impressed with him that he made him his spiritual adviser, and once William had conquered England Lanfranc became his first archbishop of Canterbury. Many prominent clerics from Bec went to England, some taking Norman stone with them to build great monuments like Canterbury Cathedral. Gundulf, the Bishop of Rochester and architect of the Tower of London, was previously a monk at Bec. The English connection is reflected in the names of village streets, such as Rue de Canterbury, whose multicoloured timber-frame houses are a delight.

Virtually nothing remains of the original abbey apart from a few foundation stones that sketch its outline, but it must have been huge. The tower visible today was built separately from the abbey church around 1460. It somehow escaped the fate that befell the church and living quarters in the Revolution – the church was plundered for its stone, and the refectory and cloisters used for stabling army horses. The vast vaulted refectory, one of several buildings rebuilt in the 18th century, now serves as the abbey church, but you can still see horse-feeding troughs from its earlier incarnation. The army only left in 1940, and eight years later a group of monks were invited to return Bec to its original purpose. In the church there are some lovely 14th-century carved wooden statues from the original abbey church. At the top end of the nave lies Hellouin, in a sarcophagus beneath a sheet of glass. The story goes that during the Revolution looters pillaged everything they could find, but were superstitious about touching Hellouin.

The other highlight of the tour is the **cloister**, built in Italianate style in 1666, with bubbling central fountains. At the far end from the entrance an original medieval door has been remarkably preserved, thanks to its having been plastered over. Nobody knew of its existence until one day in the 1950s when, as the monks were processing around the cloister, a stone fell from the wall concealing the door, and a stonefaced virgin stared them in the eyes – a *vrai miracle*. The virgin's miraculous powers would also seem to have protected the grand 18th-century staircase behind the door: a bomb fell here in 1944, but never exploded.

The tour ends at the shop, which sells ceramics made by the monks. Members of the public can stay at the abbey on retreat, in simple rooms. On Sundays and festivals the monks hold joint services with local nuns and sing four-part harmonies, as well as singing Gregorian chant every day.

Tourist Information in Pont-Audemer and Brionne

ⓘ **Pont-Audemer >**
Place Maubert, **t** *02 32 41 08 21, www.ville-pont-audemer.fr.*

ⓘ **Brionne >**
1 Rue du Général de Gaulle, **t** *02 32 45 70 51, www.tourismecanton debrionne.com*

The Pont-Audemer tourist office organizes guided tours of the town July–Aug daily at 2.30 (in French; reserve in advance), as well as nocturnal 'theatrical' tours mid-July–mid-Aug Mon and Fri 9.30pm, which are rounded off with a glass of local cider.

Market days: Pont-Audemer: Mon, with a smaller one Fri; Brionne: Sun.

Post Office: Rue du 8 Mai 1945, Brionne.

Shopping around Pont-Audemer and Brionne

The Lower Risle is prime cider country. Some farms prefer visitors to reserve in advance for tastings.

Ferme de la Houssaye, Brétigny, **t** 02 32 44 87 75. Large cider producer offering tastings with advance reservation.

Ferme de la Bretterie, Carsix, **t** 02 32 46 16 25. Friendly small farm producing *pommeau*, cider and calvados. You can visit the 17th-century cellars and cider press, and of course, taste the produce. *Open by appointment 9–12 and 2–7.*

Ferme du Vieux Pressoir, St Eloi de Fourques, **t** 02 32 35 93 34. A smallholding producing not cider but foie gras and similar products.

Where to Stay and Eat around Pont-Audemer and Brionne

Appeville-Annebault ✉ 27920
Les Aubépines, Aux Chiffourniers, **t** 02 32 56 14 25, *http://perso.wanadoo. fr/lesaubepines* (€). This gorgeous *longère* (longhouse) is worth the drive along twisting lanes to get here. There's a well-tended garden, whose vegetables appear in the evening meal (€€, book in advance), and three pastel-coloured B&B rooms with

wonderfully tranquil views. *Closed Oct–Mar exc by arrangement.*

Beuzeville ✉ 27210

**Le Relais de Poste, 49 Rue C.Fouché, t 02 32 20 32 32, *www.le-relais-de-poste.com* (€). Utterly French Logis hotel in an old coaching inn on little Beuzeville's main square. Floral bedrooms are simple but comfortable, while the bistro-style restaurant (€€) provides hearty regional cuisine. There's a garden too. *Hotel closed Nov–Mar; restaurant closed Tues lunch, Thurs and Sun eve.*

Campigny-la-Futelaye ✉ 27500

****Le Petit Coq aux Champs, La Pommeraie Sud, t 02 32 41 04 19, *www.lepetitcoqauxchamps.fr* (€€€). A surprisingly large iris-clad thatched cottage in the countryside 6km south of Pont-Audemer. The 12 modern rooms are soothingly decorated, there are comfy lounges and a pool, and the hotel is run with a very personal friendliness. The restaurant (€€€) offers a lovely setting and fine food: in summer you dine outside, by the gardens; in winter you move into a snug dining room. *Hotel closed Jan; restaurant closed Sun eve and Mon (Nov–Mar).*

★ Le Petit Coq aux Champs >

Conteville ✉ 27210

Auberge du Vieux Logis, t 02 32 57 60 16, *www.auberge.conteville.free.fr* (€€€€). If you can afford it, eating here is one of Normandy's gastronomic experiences. With one Michelin star to his name, the chef makes the most of the local seafood to produce signature dishes like *gratin de homard, langoustines et Saint-Jacques. Closed Sun eve, Mon and (Sept–June) Tues.*

Epaignes ✉ 27260

Auberge du Beau Carré, 1 Routes des Anglais, t 02 32 41 52 42, *http://aubergedubeaucarre.monsite.wanadoo.fr* (18-45E). Chef Herve Deschamps cut his teeth at the Michelin-starred l'Auberge de la Butte at Bonsecours (now closed) and the superb l'Auberge des Ruines at Jumièges, and the result is a cuisine that's sophisticated, tasty and affordable. Ingredients are fresh and local, including plenty of seafood. Don't be put off by the unpromising furnishings, which would look more at home in a church hall; this is an address to watch.

Fourmetot ✉ 27500

Le Manoir de L'Aufragère, La Croisée, t 02 32 56 91 92, *www.laufragere.com* (€€€). Finely restored half-timbered manor in eight acres of orchards and farmland with five pretty bedrooms. The manor's English owner, Nicky, runs cookery courses, aided by French husband Régis, who organizes visits to local cheese merchants. While prices may be in the expensive band, this includes bed, breakfast and a superior dinner. Minimum stay 2 nights. Three-day cookery courses cost €600 full board.

Martainville-en-Lieuvin ✉ 27210

Le Mesnil, t 02 32 57 82 23 (€). This idyllic half-timbered cottage nestles in an exuberant garden. There are just two comfortable B&B rooms, and it's very peaceful. Dinner (€€) can be provided on request.

Brionne ✉ 27800

**Le Logis de Brionne, 1 Place St-Denis, t 02 32 44 81 73, *www.lelogisdebrionne.com* (€€). An old-fashioned Logis hotel in a quiet location 10 minutes' walk from the centre. The modern, glass-fronted restaurant is excellent (€€€–€€). *Restaurant closed Fri lunch, Sat lunch, Sun eve and Mon.*

**Auberge du Vieux Donjon, Place Frémont-des-Essarts, t 02 32 44 80 62, *www.auberge-vieux-donjon.com* (€). This grand half-timbered house faces a main road, but there are quieter rooms at the back. Its eight rooms are simple, in contrast to its fine restaurant (€€) with flower-filled terrace. *Restaurant closed Mon.*

Brasserie du Café de la Gare, 24 Place de la Gare, t 02 32 44 80 50 (€). For a glimpse of French everyday life, stop by to try the incredible-value set menu, laid on for workers at lunchtime during the week.

Le Bec-Hellouin ✉ 27800

***Auberge de l'Abbaye, Place Guillaume le Conquérant, t 02 32 44

86 02, *www.auberge-abbaye-bec-hellouin.com* (€€). Gorgeous old half-timbered hotel, a bit worn in places but in a ravishing location. A real taste of old France. It has a decent restaurant (€€) serving Norman favourites. *Hotel closed 15 Nov–15 Dec and 15–31 Jan; restaurant closed Tues–Wed.*

Restaurant Le Canterbury, Rue de Canterbury, **t** 02 32 44 14 59 (€€€–€€). One of the finest restaurants in the area, in a tiny side street near the Abbey. Chic. *Closed Sun eve, Tues and Wed.*

Berthouville ✉ 27800

Demeure d'Harsancourt, 342 Rue d'Harsancourt, **t** 02 33 44 02 49, *earl.harsancourt@wanadoo.fr* (€€). There are just two B&B rooms in this gorgeous manor, which dates back to the 13th century. You can also order dinner if you request in advance.

St-Eloi-de-Fourques ✉ 27800

Manoir d'Hermos, t 02 32 35 51 32, *www.hermos.fr.st* (€). Elegant and peaceful, this 16th-century house has large, wood-panelled B&B rooms with fine views onto meadows, woods and a lake. There's also a *gîte* available in the grounds.

St-Victor-d'Epine ✉ 27802

La Minardière, t 02 32 45 98 90, *clos-saint-francois@wanadoo.fr* (€). Wonderful black and white half-timbered farmhouse in the midst of a large and exuberant garden – Les Jardins du Clos St-François. There's just one smallish room on the end of the house, with its own access. Breakfast is brought to your room or served in the sitting room downstairs. The gardens themselves are open to the public May–Sept. Particularly gay friendly.

Harcourt to Beaumont: Two Châteaux

Domaine d'Harcourt

Domaine d'Harcourt
t 02 32 46 29 70; open mid-June–mid-Sept Wed–Mon 10–6.30; mid-Sept–mid-Nov and Mar–mid-June Wed–Mon 2–6; adm

If the 20-metre-wide moat hadn't been filled in with grass you'd almost expect a band of medieval knights to ride out from the great gateway of the Domaine d'Harcourt, a fairy-tale castle on the edge of the attractive village of Harcourt, about 6km southeast of Brionne. It stands, proud and aloof, on a mound in the midst of an arboretum containing 500 tree species from around the world, which gives the site an exotic touch. Remarkably well preserved, it was built around 1100 by Errand d'Harcourt, a pal of William the Conqueror from his English invasion days, who claimed to be descended from one of the most powerful Viking invaders, Bernard the Dane. His family lorded it over all the villages around, administering justice and gathering tithes and taxes. One of the most influential Harcourts, Robert II, was a companion of Richard the Lionheart.

The only remains of the first castle are a zig-zag-carved Norman archway above the well at the back. Most of the present castle dates from the 12th to the 14th centuries. In subsequent ages it gradually turned from fortress to country residence, but in the 18th century it had to be rescued from virtual ruin by a tree enthusiast from Paris, who planted the pines visible today. The estate is now run by the French Agriculture Academy. Inside the castle there's an exhibition on its history, with ceramics and other items excavated

Getting to Le Neubourg and Beaumont

Honfleur–Evreux **buses** stop at Le Neubourg, and Evreux–Bernay buses pass through Beaumont. Beaumont has a **train** station, on the Evreux–Caen (via Bernay) and Evreux–Rouen lines. Many journeys involve changing at Serquigny, where the Rouen and Evreux lines meet, 10km north of Beaumont.

here. The vast grounds include, as well as the spectacular arboretum, over 95 hectares of woods. Well-marked paths lead through them.

Château du Champ-de-Bataille

🎯 Château du Champ-de-Bataille
t 02 32 34 84 34, www.chateauduchamp debataille.com; house open July–Aug daily 3.30–5.30; April–June Sat–Sun 3.30–5.30; garden open June–Aug daily 10–6; April–May and Sept–Oct daily 2–6; guided tour of house and garden by appointment only; adm

It took designer Jacques Garcia ten years to restore this sumptuous 17th-century jewel near Ste-Opportune-du-Bosc, 5kms northwest of Le Neubourg. One of France's foremost – and most extravagant – interior designers, Garcia has carried out his task to perfection, and furnishings and fabrics are all in keeping with the 18th-century originals. Chandeliers, paintings, Flemish tapestries and carved panelling all contribute to the mood of pre-Revolutionary opulence; many items here actually came from palaces at Versailles or the Tuileries, having been rescued before the Revolutionaries got them, including a priceless chaise longue that belonged to Marie-Antoinette and an exquisite chair made for Louis XV to celebrate his affair with Madame du Barry.

The château itself, which Garcia rescued from long-term decline in 1992, was built as a country house for Count Alexandre de Créqui in 1653, and later passed to the all-powerful Harcourts. It has two virtually identical wings linked by a passageway, with a grand courtyard in between. The style is similar to that of châteaux at Vincennes and Vaux-le-Vicomte and the first royal château at Versailles, which were all built at around the same time by the great architect Louis Le Vau. Some have suggested Le Vau may have built Champ-de-Bataille, but this has never been proved. It is certain, however, that the gardens were designed by André Le Nôtre, the greatest figure in French garden design and architect of the gardens at Versailles. Bush by bush, Garcia has reinstated Le Nôtre's formal gardens using the original plans. At the same time, he has also been adding his own contemporary designs, carving out great tree-lined alleys and adding gold-leafed fountains, stone sphinxes and classical follies. Even if his theories sound rather airy, the gardens are a fun place to wander. In summer, open-air opera and theatre performances are hosted in the grounds.

Le Neubourg and Beaumont-le-Roger

The pleasant town of **Le Neubourg** has a large, appealing main square, dominated by the imposing (but never finished) 15th-century **Eglise St-Paul**. Around the town you can still see scraps of the castle that was built here around 1000, was stormed by Henry I

Tourist Information in Le Neubourg and Beaumont-le-Roger

ⓘ Beaumont-
le-Roger >
Rue de Belgique,
t 02 32 44 05 79

Market Days: Le Neubourg: Wed; Beaumont-le-Roger: Tues, Fri.

Post Office: Le Neubourg: Rue de la Paix.

Where to Stay and Eat around Le Neubourg and Beaumont-le-Roger

ⓘ Le Neubourg >
1a Route de
Beaumont, t 02 32
35 40 57, www.le-
neubourg.fr/tourisme

Le Neubourg ✉ 27110

★★Le Soleil d'Or, Place du Château, t 02 32 35 00 52, *http://lesoleildor.free.fr* (€). Solid, friendly hotel in a half-timbered house on the town square. The two single rooms are a bargain. The hotel also has a fireside bar and a good traditional restaurant (€€). *Closed Sun eve and Wed.*

Epigard ✉ 27110

La Paysanne, 8 Rue de l'Eglise, t 02 32 355 08 95, *lmauricelucas@club internet.fr* (€). Solid 17th-century farmhouse, offering five B&B en-suite rooms at a steal, and a lovely garden.

Nassandres ✉ 27550

Le Soleil d'Or, 1 Chaussée du Roy, t 02 32 45 00 08, *www.domainedu soleildor.com* (€€). Another Soleil d'Or, this one an elegant roadside hotel with large gardens beside the Risle. Room 8 has idyllic views over the river (and a higher price to match). The formal restaurant, Le Manoir du Soleil (€€€–€€) offers excellent *haute cuisine*. There's also a cheaper brasserie-style restaurant serving international dishes and, on certain nights, musical entertainment. *Restaurant closed Sun eve and Mon.*

St-Didier-des-Bois ✉ 27270

Chez Annick Auzoux, 1 Place de l'Eglise, t 02 32 50 60 93 (€). Timber-framed house in the centre of a quiet village, with four B&B rooms full of character and packed with antiques. With advance notice dinner can be provided (€€). There's also a self-catering *gîte*.

in the following century, and then was tossed between Normandy, England and France. If you are a cyclist or rambler, you can pick up the Voie Verte here which runs to Harcourt to the north, or to Evreux to the south, following the old Evreux-Honfleur railway track. **Beaumont-le-Roger**, 13km southwest, is another busy little old town. Close by is the **Prieuré de la Sainte Trinité**, a 13th-century ruined priory on a hill, slowly crumbling and with lovely views of the wooded valley below.

Bernay and the Pays d'Ouche

Bernay

🏛 Bernay

In the Second World War, Bernay was the town that got away – saved by dense fog that blanketed this crossroads at the meeting of the Charentonne and Cosnier rivers and meant the bombers couldn't see it. Hence its beautiful half-timbered medieval and Renaissance houses and cobbled streets were spared, making it today one of the most untouched historic towns in Normandy. The original town of Bernay grew up around a monastery that was founded by Judith of Brittany, wife of Duke Richard II of Normandy,

Getting to and around Bernay

Bernay has excellent **train** connections to Paris (1½hrs), Evreux (30mins), Rouen (1hr) and Caen (1hr). **Buses** run regularly to and from Pont-Audemer via Lieurey, leaving from beside Bernay train station. **Information**, *www.transports.cg27.fr*. **Bike hire**: Station Service Elan, 53 Blvd Sylla Lefèvre, **t** 02 32 43 08 68.

**Eglise Abbatiale
and Musée
Beaux-Arts**
*t 02 32 46 63 23;
church and museum
open mid-June–mid-
Sept Tues–Sun 10–12
and 2–7; mid-Sept–mid-
June Tues–Sun 2–5.30;
adm; free for under-16s,
and for all on Wed and
1st Sun of month*

in the early 11th century. The abbey church still survives. Bernay's other claims to fame are its wool and linen, the fact that it was the place where Edith Piaf spent her childhood (a street is named after her), and more bizarrely, its role as a centre of the sport of tractor-pulling (it hosts a national competition every June).

Give yourself a day to savour Bernay's quiet waterways and fascinating buildings, many of which have very fine, ornate carvings. Bernay's ebullient Saturday market also provides a fine glimpse of Norman provincial life.

The Eglise Abbatiale and Musée des Beaux-Arts

Built between 1017 and 1075, Bernay's vast Romanesque abbey church, chequerworked in flint and stone, is one of Normandy's oldest. It's famous for being one of the first churches in Normandy with three storeys, with a gallery or *triforium* above the nave

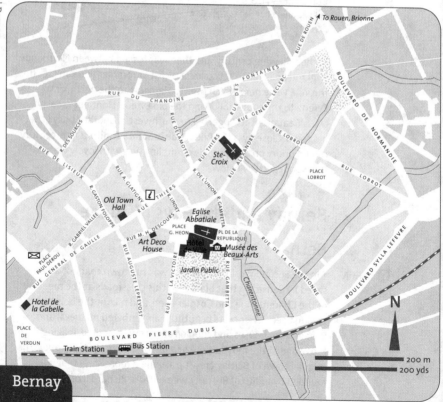

Bernay

arches, and above that a clerestory with windows that let in additional light. After the monks had been scattered by the Revolution, the abbey church became a prison, a courthouse and then a town hall. During the 19th century it lost its north transept to make way for the building of the Rue de l'Abbatiale. Today, stripped of furniture, its cream-coloured tuff stone has an awesome austerity, alleviated only by a few delicate carvings; look for the one by the side aisle of a crowned bishop or king with his left hand raised. The abbey's former living quarters now house the **Musée des Beaux-Arts**, a motley collection of paintings (Dutch, Flemish and Italian as well as French), ceramics and furniture. Its prize exhibit is the sarcophagus of Judith of Brittany, whose immense length suggests that she may have been dauntingly tall.

The Old Town

Bernay's other ecclesiastical pearl is the 14th-century **Eglise Ste-Croix**, with its extraordinarily wide nave and attractive carvings. If it looks rather comically squat from outside, it's because its original lantern tower, a graceful Gothic affair, blew down in a storm in 1687, killing 11 people and destroying part of the nave. The rebuilders decided to err on the side of caution, replacing it with a simple bell tower. In 1808 the church was the fortunate recipient of many treasures from Bec abbey (see p.190) after it had been dissolved in the Revolution, including the altar and a set of 14th-century statues of the Apostles and the Evangelists, which are now posted on the pillars of the nave. It also contains some remarkably ornate tombstones, including that of Guillaume d'Auvillars, Abbot of Bec, by the sacristy.

None of Bernay's **Renaissance houses** is open to visitors, but they can be seen from outside. One of the most remarkable is next to the tourist office. Note the ceramic *épis de faîtage* (gable-end statues), which grace the roof in the form of doves or cocks. There are more gems along the same main street, Rue Thiers. One, a blue-and-cream half-timbered affair hidden in a courtyard behind Coiffure Longchamp hairdressers', probably belonged to a royal official and later became the first **Town Hall**. It has some lovely carvings, including one of King François I, one of St Peter, key in hand, and another of a Virgin and Child. Similar colours were used to paint the **Art Deco house** on Rue M.H. Descours, built in the 1920s. Bernay's prettiest street is **Rue Gaston Folloppe**, which has a gorgeous collection of half-timbered houses, most of which now house antique, book and furniture shops, as well as some enticing bars and restaurants. At the north end of the street there's a picturesque bridge over the Cosnier, where you can spot the old washing platforms. At the west end of the main street (which in this stretch is not called Rue Thiers, but Rue De Gaulle) is the **Hôtel**

Tourist Information in Bernay

(i) Bernay >
29 Rue Thiers,
t 02 32 43 32 08,
www.bernay27.fr

Market Day: Sat.
Post Office: Place Derou.

Shopping in Bernay

J. P. Bernais, 21-23 Rue Gaston Folloppe. One of the most distinctive shops along this fascinating street: M. Bernais will show you round his 15th-century cellars where he stocks 50 types of calvados, 100 kinds of whisky and around 4,000 bottles of wine and champagne. He also sells all sorts of local produce. *Closed Mon.*

Where to Stay and Eat around Bernay

Bernay ✉ 27300

Moulin de Fouret >>

Le Bistrot du Bernais >

**Le Lion d'Or, 48 Rue du Général de Gaulle, t 02 32 43 12 06, *www.hotel-liondor-bernay.com* (€). Clean if conventional rooms in a central location. The 18th-century building was once Bernay's *relais de poste*.
Le Bistrot du Bernais, Rue Gaston Folloppe, t 02 32 46 23 60 (€€–€). Intimate, cosy and great value, and the most engaging eating place in town. The bistro specializes in local cheeses, and makes its own foie gras. In summer diners can sit in a tiny courtyard, the *Cour des Miracles*. *Closed Sun and Mon.*

Le Clos Normand, 5 Rue Robert Lindet, t 02 32 43 04 30 (€€–€). Simple restaurant in an old house serving traditional Norman fare. *Closed Mon, Tues and Sat lunch.*

St-Aubin-de-Scellon ✉ 27230

La Charterie, t 02 32 45 46 52, **mobile** 06 20 39 08 63 (€). A warmer welcome would be hard to find. This grand three-storey manor 4km north of Thiberville has four prettily decorated en-suite B&B rooms, and large gardens. Ask ahead and you can sample one of Marie-Hélène's fabulous dinners (€€).
Le Relais des Trois Chênes, Castelain, t 02 32 44 71 04 (€). This B&B is on one of the region's many *haras* (stud farms), and the two bedrooms are above the stables. There are plans to build a few *gîtes*, plus a massage centre, in the extensive grounds. Riding is available, of course. A taste of rural Normandy, in comfort.

St-Aubin-le-Vertueux ✉ 27300

Moulin de Fouret, t 02 32 43 19 95, *www.moulin-fouret.com* (€). Sleep to the sound of the rushing river that runs underneath this creeper-clad 16th-century mill, and by day wander in its leafy gardens. The modern rooms at this hotel, 3km south of Bernay, are great value and most have gorgeous views. The restaurant-bar (€€€–€€) is more plush, with a pretty terrace next to the river. *Closed Sun eve and Mon exc June–Aug.*

de la Gabelle, the 18th-century building where the royal collector of salt, once a major source of the town's wealth, used to live. It now contains the Ecole de Musique.

Travelling on from Bernay, you can follow the River Charentonne south to the little village of **Broglie** (pronounced Broy) with its 15th–16th-century **Eglise St-Martin**. A pleasant way to get there is by bike or on foot along the 13km *voie verte*, which passes through the metalworking village of **Ferrieres-St-Hilaire**.

The Ouche Plateau

Southeast of Beaumont and Bernay the upper waters of the Risle run across the broad plateau of the Pays d'Ouche. Still densely wooded, especially around the town of Conches-en-Ouche, the

Getting to and around the Ouche Plateau

It's easy to get to Conches by **train**: it's on the Paris–St-Lazare–Evreux–Caen line, with four trains daily each way. Verneuil has regular trains on the Paris–Montparnasse–Granville line, via Dreux, L'Aigle and Argentan, with several services each day. There are two **buses** daily each way between Verneuil and Evreux.

---

area is less populated than the lower valley, and its ancient villages are more widely dispersed and have a still stronger sense of rural quiet.

Beaumesnil to Conches

The little town of **Beaumesnil**, in apple country southeast of Bernay, is dominated by the Château de Beaumesnil, a fairy-tale concoction of 17th-century brick, stone, and shapely slate roofs whose ornate façade is mirrored in a surrounding moat. On one side, on an island, a labyrinth of box hedges perches on the mound of an old dungeon. A stronghold existed here from 1250, but the current château was built in 1633. Originally the château faced the other way, and it only took on its current orientation in 1759 after the villagers agreed to have one of their streets turned into the front drive. The 80-hectare park was probably landscaped by La Quintinie, a student of Le Nôtre at Versailles, prompting brochures to dub Beaumesnil the 'Versailles of Normandy'. The Revolution hit Beaumesnil hard: the then owner Armand de Béthune-Charost lost his head, and the buildings fell into disrepair.

The château contains a fabulous display on historic bookbinding, with some books dating back to the 15th century. Some of the exhibits are breathtakingly ornate, with fastenings of carved silver. Each summer special exhibitions are presented. The library has fine terracotta floor tiles bearing the arms of the past owners, the Montmorencys, and in the tiny chapel there are delicate wood carvings, including a 16th-century German portrayal of the Apostles with hauntingly lifelike expressions. The rooms with the best views are 'Madame's Apartments', named after Henrietta Maria, the daughter of Henri IV who married Charles I of England; she gazes haughtily down from the painting facing the door.

La Ferrière-sur-Risle, 7km east of Beaumesnil, is an outrageously pretty village with every possible colour and size of half-timbered house. The finest building of all is the 14th-century covered **market hall**. On Sundays it buzzes with a very rural market, but apart from that there's little to distract you while strolling along its single street, or ambling down to the meadows by the river. Its beautiful 13th-century **church** has interesting painted statues, including a stone St George allegedly invoked to cure eczema.

The 'capital' of the Ouche, **Conches-en-Ouche**, stands majestically on a spur above the River Rouloir, bordered by a huge park. Its centrepiece is its crumbling medieval castle, which looks as if it's

Château de Beaumesnil
*t 02 32 44 40 09,
www.chateaubeau
mesnil.com; open
Easter–June Fri–Mon
2–6; July–Aug daily
11–6; Sept Wed–Mon
12–6; adm*

gently tumbling into the valley. It was built to defend the town, which had rocketed in importance after local lord Roger de Tosny brought back relics of Saint Foy from Conques-en-Rouergue in southwest France in the 11th century. He also renamed the town after the similar-sounding *Conques*. The castle keep is now in too dangerous a state to visit, but there's a nice walk alongside it and down into the valley. There are more fine views from the stone balustrade outside the **Eglise Ste-Foy**, a gem of Flamboyant Gothic that replaced the church founded by Roger. It is a treasure chest of Renaissance stained glass, including one window showing a 'Mystic Wine Press', in which Christ – the eternal Vine – stamps the grapes, which produce a juice that also represents his blood.

Musée du Verre
Route de Ste-Marguerite; open Mar–Sept Wed–Sat 10–12 and 2–5.30, Sun 2.30–6; adm

Glass is the theme too of Conches' **Musée du Verre**, a collection of modern stained glass mostly by local glassmaker François Decorchement and his family. Back in the town, the house by the church that's now the St-Jacques gift shop (*see* below) contains a staircase down into staggering vaulted cellars from the 11th and 12th centuries, which once served as the lockup for local criminals.

On the north side of Conches there's an arboretum with 122 species of trees, and there are many fine walks in the surrounding woods, including a 3km signed trail.

Verneuil-sur-Avre

Brick, stone and water mingle in Renaissance harmony in this pretty fortified town on the upper reaches of the Avre. You can spot the soaring honey-coloured belltower of its church of La Madeleine from miles around, and its cobbled streets, crumbling town walls and half-timbered houses make little Verneuil one of Normandy's best-kept secrets. It has always been a border town: today it marks the transition from the Ouche to the Perche, but it was founded by Henry I in the 12th century to keep the French out of Normandy. As the nearby River Avre flowed through French territory he had a canal built to the Iton, 10kms to the north, to supply the town and to fill the moat surrounding it. In the Hundred Years' War Verneuil was a vital outpost on the line between English- and French-controlled areas, and its ramparts were the scene of a bloody battle in 1424 in which the Duke of Bedford thrashed Charles VII, confirming English supremacy north of the Loire.

The town's main square – alas, nowadays largely a car park – is dominated by the Flamboyant Gothic tower of **La Madeleine**, built in the late 15th century and awkwardly attached to a much older church, which it completely dwarfs. The building's wedding-cake-style four tiers are decorated with some fine statues, including a lively Adam, Eve and Serpent trio and, further up, a tiny kneeling figure in a cloak – a worthy local patron called Arthus Fillon, who footed the bill. Strangely, the tower can only be visited on the first

Sunday of each month between April and October, at 3.30pm (even then, check with the tourist office, as times change). The church contains some superlative statues: near the entrance, a spirited 15th-century St-Crépin, patron of shoemakers, knocks out some shoes on the lap of his apron, and further inside there's a touching St Gilles and his hound, jumping up affectionately as if to lick his master's bearded face.

Wandering out of the square down Rue du Canon and Rue de la Madeleine you pass some of Verneuil's finest houses, built from a mellow mix of flint, brick and stone. Most date from the 16th to the 18th centuries, though one of the finest, an ornate turreted residence on the corner of the two streets, is even older. To the right at the bottom of Rue du Canon is the **Tour Grise**, a 13th-century stone tower built for King Philippe Auguste once he'd grabbed the town for France. Behind it are the remains of the town walls, and the diverted Iton river. Further west, the enchanting Rue du Pont aux Chèvres takes you over the town's inland waterways to the venerable 16th-century **Maison à Tourelle**, with its intricately carved corner turret.

Eglise Notre-Dame
open June–Sept daily 9–7; Oct–May daily 9–6

By contrast the **Eglise Notre-Dame** further south, much of it built of local *grison* stone, looks heavy and forbidding. It has some fine carving, however, and as in La Madeleine the statues inside, mostly 16th-century, give fascinating insights into contemporary Norman life. There's Saint Fiacre, patron of gardeners, spade in one hand, a prayer book (or a gardening manual?) in the other; elsewhere, Sainte-Barbe mopes in her dungeon while donkeys and pig-faced lions frolic on the columns beside her. After visiting the church, wander up the square to the **Abbaye St-Nicolas**. There is also a shop selling local organic produce.

Abbaye St-Nicolas
t 02 32 32 02 94; church and abbey parlour open daily 2–6.30

Tourist Information in the Ouche Plateau

Market Days: Conches-en-Ouche: Thurs, smaller market Sun; La Ferrière-sur-Risle: Sun; Verneuil-sur-Avre: Sat.
Post Office: Conches-en-Ouche: 9 Rue St Foix; Verneuil-sur-Avre: Place de la Madeleine.

Shopping in the Ouche Plateau

Le Saint-Jacques, 12 Rue Ste-Foy, Conches-en-Ouche, **t** 02 32 30 20 50. The shop, which sells candles, glassware and ironwork, is on three levels, the lower two of which are medieval cellars. There's also a

teashop. *Shop closed Mon and Tues, teashop closed Mon–Thurs.*
La Pillerie, Route de Beaumesnil, 27330 La Barre-en-Ouche, **t** 02 32 44 37 87. Stock up on cider and apple juice at this family-run apple farm. Best to phone ahead.

Where to Stay and Eat in the Ouche Plateau

Beaumesnil ✉ 27410
Manoir du Val, St-Aubin-le-Guichard, **t** 02 32 44 41 04, *http://manoirduval. free.fr* (€). Magnificent 16th-century farmhouse with dovecote amid apple orchards just north of Beaumesnil. The three B&B rooms, all with bathroom, are comfortable, and cider,

ⓘ **Beaumesnil >>**
32 Rue du Château, t 02 32 46 45 68, http://tourisme beaumesnil27.free.fr

apple juice, jams and honey can be bought from the farm next door.

La Ferrière-sur-Risle ✉ 27760

Le Vieux-Marché, t 02 32 30 25 93 (€). In the heart of the village, with a view of the market, this bustling bar/restaurant also has pleasant rooms upstairs with shower or bath (€). Locals gather here at lunchtime, and there's a good set menu. *Closed Mon.*

ⓘ **Conches-en-Ouche >**
Place Aristide Briand, t 02 32 30 76 42, www.conches-en-ouche.fr

⭐ **Château de la Puisaye >>**

Conches-en-Ouche ✉ 27190

La Grand' Mare, t 02 32 30 23 30, *www.lerapporteur.fr/la-grand-mare* (€€). Excellent restaurant serving traditional dishes in a wood-panelled room with views over the park. As well as the main restaurant it also has a simpler bistro (€) for lighter meals. *Closed Sun eve, Mon and Tues eve.*

Le Donjon, 55 Rue Ste-Foy, **t** 02 32 30 04 75 (€€–€). A lovely old half-timbered building that bulges over the high street, where a dynamic young Paris-trained chef/owner creates original dishes that make a change from the standard, traditional Norman fare. *Closed Mon and Tues.*

ⓘ **Verneuil-sur-Avre >**
129 Place de la Madeleine, t 02 32 32 17 17, otsiverneuilavre@ wanadoo.fr

Verneuil-sur-Avre ✉ 27130

****Le Clos**, 98 Rue Ferté-Vidame, **t** 02 32 32 21 81, *www.hostellerieduclos.fr* (€€€€€). Smart antique-furnished rooms at sky-high prices in a turreted, black-and-white-checked château, with all kinds of health and fitness

facilities. The formal restaurant is equally opulent (€€€€€).

****Hotel du Saumon**, 89 Place de la Madeleine, **t** 02 32 32 02 36, *hotel.saumon@wanadoo.fr* (€). This old hotel – once a coaching inn – doesn't rate high on the friendliness stakes, but its location in the heart of town is great. Most rooms look onto La Madeleine, and the restaurant (€€–€) is good value. *Closed Sun eve in winter.*

Château de la Puisaye, t 02 32 58 65 35, *www.chateaudelapuisaye.com* (€€). This 19th-century château, amid vast parkland and woods, has been stunningly restored by its English owners. They offer five en-suite rooms, and you can also enjoy the huge dining room, library and living room, all with stone fireplaces and 19th-century woodwork. You get a full English breakfast in the morning.

Bémécourt ✉ 27160

Le Vieux Château, t 02 32 29 90 47 (€€). A deliciously eccentric place, full of artistic clutter downstairs and three impeccably clean classic bedrooms upstairs. The black and white half-timbered 'château' is in fact only 40 years old. Farm animals roam the courtyard, and the bohemian owner is a real character. The only snag: there's just one shared toilet. Dinner (€€) on request.

L'Aigle

L'Aigle's most exciting moment was when it was hit by a meteorite on 26 April 1803, and you can still see bits of the rocks that rained down on the area in the local museum. With a reputation as an industrial town thanks to a long tradition of metalworking, L'Aigle is often passed by, but this is a pity, as there are architectural gems in its old centre, and it hosts a celebrated – and huge –market every Tuesday.

The town got its name – 'the eagle' – from a Norman noble called Fulbert de Beina, who built a fortress here in the 11th century and found a nest of eagles on the same spot. In the 1690s his castle was replaced with the present sumptuous château, built to plans drawn up by Jules Hardouin-Mansart, Louis XIV's chief architect, who also built most of Versailles. Today it houses the Hôtel de Ville, which can be visited to see its monumental staircase and little

Getting to L'Aigle

L'Aigle has regular **train** services on the line between Paris-Montparnasse (1hr 20mins), Argentan and Granville (1hr 50mins). **Buses** run daily to Vimoutiers, Evreux and Mortagne (via Tourouvre), and on most days to Alençon.

Musée des Instruments de Musique
t 02 33 84 16 16; open Mon–Thurs 8.30–12 and 1.30–5.30, Fri 8.30–12 and 1.30–4.45

Musée de la Météorite
open April–Oct Sat–Sun and Wed 2–6, also Tues July–Aug; adm

Musée Juin 44
t 02 33 24 19 44; same hours as Musée de la Météorite; adm

Musée des Instruments de Musique, an engaging collection of venerable musical instruments, including a delightful 18th-century 'pocket violin'.

In a building alongside the main town hall there is the Musée de la Météorite, where you can see those pieces of rock for yourself, with exhibits on the scientist, Jean-Baptiste Biot, whose report into L'Aigle's meteorite was allegedly the first scientific proof such a phenomenon existed. L'Aigle also has its Second World War museum, in another wing of the château, the Musée Juin 44. It's called a 'talking waxwork museum', and uses original sound recordings to capture key moments of the Battle for Normandy. Visitors hear the BBC announcing the start of the invasion, General de Gaulle calling on his people to rise up, and Roosevelt trying out his atrocious French. It's old-fashioned, but informative.

On the other side of the historic Place St-Martin, near a house where Louis XIII stayed in 1620, looms the dark **Eglise St-Martin**, a hotchpotch of different stones and styles. Inside, it's so wide and squat it feels almost circular. During the Revolution four locals were decapitated in the square outside, and the church was turned into a 'Temple of the Goddess Reason'; a Robespierresque inscription under the windows still reads 'The French People believe in the Supreme Being and the Immortality of the Soul'. Inside there's also a 17th-century gilded altarpiece, dripping with grapes and vine leaves. The church is topped by a 500-year-old tower on whose pinnacles tiptoe an angel, a virgin, and the town's emblem, an eagle. One of its bells, which weighs two tonnes, is claimed to be the oldest in Normandy.

A walk around L'Aigle also reveals some fine stone and brick houses, many with lovely carvings. The best are in the streets behind the church, where the Risle drifts lazily through the town. There are more intriguing facades on Place de la Halle, once the wheat market, and since the 17th century the site of the celebrated Hôtel du Dauphin.

The Abbey of St Evroult–Notre-Dame-du-Bois

The haunting ruins of this 13th-century abbey 14km west of L'Aigle, on the edge of a man-made lake and encircled by thick woods, form one of the most evocative sites in the Pays d'Ouche. At sunset its dark red stones appear to glow, their shapes reflected in the still water. The ruins stand on the site of an earlier abbey

Tourist Information in L'Aigle

(i) L'Aigle >
*Place Fulbert de
Beina*, **t** *02 33 24 12 40,
www.paysdelaigle.com*

Market Days: Tues, one of the largest in Normandy.
Post Office: Place de l'Europe.

Shopping in L'Aigle

Les Caves de Normandie, 64 Rue Louis Pasteur, **t** 02 33 24 14 54. Offers tastings of fine calvados and *pommeau* inside the cellar.

Where to Stay and Eat in L'Aigle

L'Aigle ✉ 61300

***Le Dauphin, Place de la Halle, **t** 02 33 84 18 00, *www.hoteldudauphin. free.fr* (€). This wonderful old building on the market square has been a hotel since 1618. Rooms are traditional and comfortable, and it has two restaurants: one that's more traditional (€€) and a relaxed brasserie, Le Renaissance (€). *Restaurant closed Sun eve.*

Toque et Vins, 35 Rue Louis Pasteur, **t** 02 33 24 05 27 (€€). It's worth the short walk from the centre to this welcoming restaurant: the food is inspirational – including delicious salads – and there's a wide range of wines. *Closed Mon eve, Tues eve and Sun.*

La Ferté-Frênel ✉ 61550

Château de la Ferté-Fresnel, **t** 02 33 24 23 23, *http://chateau.fertefresnel.free.fr* (€€€). This 19th-century château, which stands in 20 hectares of parkland, is particularly famous for its great hall, which was adapted from a plan for the Paris Opera. It has four grand B&B rooms, and lovely landscaped gardens which are open to the public May–Oct. Occasional concerts are also held here in September as part of *Septembre Musical de l'Orne*. Dinner on request.

Le Paradis, Grande Rue, **t 02 33 34 81 33, *http://perso.wanadoo.fr/hotel. paradis*. Fun, good-value restaurant (€€) in a busy little village 14km northwest of L'Aigle. There are also 10 simple, gaudily-coloured rooms (€). *Closed Mon and (Sept–May) Sun eve.*

founded as early as the 6th century by St Evroult, a noble from the Bessin near Bayeux. It became an important centre of intellectual life under the Anglo-Norman dukes, and one of its monks was one of Normandy's most famous chroniclers, Orderic Vital. The edifice whose ruins you see today was huge – the nave alone was 11 metres wide and 41 metres long – but it must have had some fault lines as the central tower collapsed in 1802, just 11 years after the Revolution had closed the abbey. Visitors are free to wander among the ruins, and can also hire pedalos and boats for trips on the lake.

The Perche

 The Perche

Tucked away in the southeast corner of Normandy, and cloaked by great beech and oak forests, the old province of the Perche likes to keep itself slightly apart from the rest of the region. There's no drama here: fairy-tale manors nestle in lush valleys among gently rolling hills. Despite its appearance of fertility, however, the land is, by comparison with the rest of Normandy, relatively poor, which is why in the 17th century many of its inhabitants emigrated to Canada, forming much of the population of Quebec. The Perche's chalky phosphate-rich soils and grass, however, provide ideal pasture for the area's very special breed of horse, like an *appellation contrôlée* cider or cheese, the massive, placid and exceptionally strong Percheron. Breeding them became a lucrative business.

Historically too the Perche was a little world of its own, a separate territory or *comté* on the southern fringes of Normandy, with its own feudal lords and coinage. It was broken up after the Revolution and split between as many as four *départements*, only one of which, the Orne, lies inside Normandy. But, those who live in the Perche today still retain a strong sense of identity, and jealously hang on, even if by a thread, to their old country traditions and small-scale farms.

The Heart of the Perche and the *Manoirs*

As well as for Percherons, the Perche is known for its remarkable fortified manor houses, like extravagant miniature castles. Most of the Perche's *manoirs* were built after the region had been devastated in the Hundred Years' War. From 1450 local nobility and families from other parts of France who'd grown rich in royal

Mighty but Mild: The Percheron

Oncques si belle chose ne vis
Que ces chevaux de Normandy
(I never saw such a fine sight, as these horses from Normandy).
              Villehardouin, *History of the Conquest of Constantinople*, 1207

Solid, elegant and mild-mannered, the Percheron is the Rolls-Royce of horses. A horse like it has almost certainly existed here since the Ice Age. The story goes that from the 8th century onwards they were crossed with Arab stallions brought from Spain or back from the Crusades, producing a superb draft horse that thrived on the thick grass of the Perche. The Arab influence can be seen in its poise, fine skin and surprisingly free-flowing stride. The Percheron, with its small head and legs in proportion to its thickset muscular body, is remarkably agile for its weight (often as much as a ton) and has great stamina too: Percherons have been known to do 35 miles a day at a trot.

Over the ages the giant white or grey Percherons have been used as warhorses, coach horses and farm labourers. Their decline with the expansion of motorized transport was temporarily halted by the First World War, when they proved invaluable in coping with the battlefield mud. But, by the 1950s most had been replaced by tractors, except in the remotest corners of Normandy.

Those Percherons that have survived are often interbred with other breeds to improve their stock, or harnessed to the tourist trade. In Britain, where once they pulled London buses, they are now used as heavyweight jumpers or hunters. Percherons became particularly popular in the USA after a visit to France in 1815 by a certain Mr Morgan, who fell in love with the Percheron trotters harnessed to his carriage, and shipped them home. There they proved remarkably useful, and what started as the passion of a few enthusiasts turned into a major business: in 1889 a 28-wagon train was provided to take horses from the Perche to Le Havre to be shipped across the Atlantic, and between 1900 and 1910 over 10,000 made the journey. Before long, American breeders had created a 'bigger and better' American strain of Percheron. Today they have the honour of being the horse of choice to pull carriages at Disneyland.

Getting around the Heart of the Perche

The nearest **train** stations are at Nogent-le-Rotrou (22km from Bellême) and Le Theil, both on the Paris–Le Mans line. **Buses** run fairly frequently between Nogent station and Bellême, and there are also regular bus services between Bellême and Nocé, Mamers, Mortagne-au-Perche and Alençon. Buses from Bellême to La Perrière are much less frequent.

service began to build these wonderful stone homes, sandwiched between stone defensive towers. Most also had an extra octagonal tower, detached or attached at an angle, where the family could take refuge if under attack, and a moat gave further protection. The grander manors had their own chapel and that obligatory status symbol of the era, a dovecote (*see* p.118).

The greatest concentration of *manoirs* is in the central Perche, where around a hundred dot the lush countryside between Mortagne-au-Perche and Nogent-le-Rotrou. Much of their appeal today lies in the fact that they are still family homes, which depend on farming the land – *manoirs* rather than *châteaux*. As a result, though, many can only be viewed from outside. One of the finest, however, the gorgeous 15th-century **Manoir de Courboyer** 2km north of the village of Nocé, is visitable as it houses the **Maison du Parc**, headquarters of the **Parc Naturel Régional du Perche**. A very informative and well-organized centre, it makes a good first stop to get your bearings and find out about walking and cycling routes and facilities, as well as the area's history. There's also an excellent shop selling regional products, and a restaurant serving lunches and teas using local produce. If you're in search of the Percheron, there are plenty grazing on the manor's 65 hectares of land, where you are free to walk.

Maison du Parc
t 02 33 25 70 10, www.parc-naturel-perche.fr; open daily Jan–Mar 10.30–5.30; April–Oct 10.30–6; Nov–Dec 10.30–6.30; adm to manor, centre free

The area southwest of Courboyer and Bellême has some of the Perche's prettiest villages, including **Nocé** itself, whose great attraction is its fabulous restaurant, Auberge des Trois J (*see* below). A little way south of there is the 1565 **Manoir de Lormarin**, which you can view only on the outside, unless you stay in the B&B rooms (*see* below), and has a huge antiques store in its outbuildings. Right down on Normandy's southern border stands the lovely **St-Germain-de-la-Coudre**, with a church with an 11th-century crypt and a pleasing set of village shops; outside it stands the **Manoir de la Fresnaye**, claimed to be the oldest manor in the Perche. Back towards Bellême are **St-Cyr-la-Rosière**, whose church has a stunning Romanesque doorway, and nearby the imposing **Manoir de l'Angenardière**, a 15th-century *manoir* circled by austere-looking ramparts.

Manoir de la Fresnaye
t 02 33 83 57 64; open July–mid-Sept Tues–Fri 1–7; adm

Ecomusée du Perche
t 02 33 73 48 06, http://ecomuseedu perche.free.fr; open July–Aug daily 10–6.30; Sept–June Wed–Mon 2–6; adm

A short way southeast of St-Cyr, **Ste-Gauburge** houses the **Ecomusée du Perche**, a really happening place that's a regional folk museum, but also has exhibits on apples, cider-making, Percheron horses and local crafts, and also runs a variety of interesting courses. Temporary exhibitions are held in the converted church next door. Opposite the church, is the **Prieuré de Ste-Gauburge**, a 13th–15th-century Benedictine priory dedicated to Saint Gauburge, an 8th century English nun (Walburga, to the Saxons). After the Revolution, it was turned into a farm. Today the buildings are still fairly run down, but are under restoration by their private owners. The sumptuously carved prior's house contrasts starkly with the cramped former monks' quarters and the modestly-sized cloister; in one wall there's a tiny internal window through which the prior could keep watch on his charges to make sure they didn't grumble while they were in the chapel. The only things keeping an eye on the prior were a sheepish Adam and Eve (15th-century, and unfortunately now headless) and a monstrous human-headed serpent, which decorate a fireplace in his spacious living room. It's also possible to see the tomb of one of Ste-Gauburge's priors, Jacques Croquet, from the 14th century.

Prieuré de
Ste-Gauburge
1hr guided tours
during Ecomusée du
Perche opening hours at
weekends, bank hols
and school hols; adm

Another 5km east in **Préaux-du-Perche** is the **Jardin François**, planted around a stone farmhouse and looking like an Impressionist painting with its myriad colours. Named after its enterprising creator, it's particularly beautiful in spring, when the magnolias and azaleas are out, and art shows and concerts are held in the converted barns. There's also a *chambres d'hôtes* alongside (*see* below).

Jardin François
t 02 37 49 64 19,
www.jardin-francois.
com; open daily
sunrise–sunset, and to
11pm Fri; adm

Bellême

A solid stone gateway or *porche* is all that remains of the ramparts that once enclosed the walled town of Bellême, strategically perched on a spur overlooking the forests and pastures of the Perche. Today it houses not slings and arrows but books, as it contains the town library. The **Rue Ville-Close**, which leads away from the gate, is a gem, packed with elegant 17th and 18th-century houses in Neoclassical style. One wouldn't think so now, but in medieval times this town was a powerful fiefdom, the seat of the ruthless Bellême family, who controlled Normandy's southern border as far as Domfront. For years they were a thorn in the flesh of William the Conqueror, until he managed to sack Alençon and Domfront, and then placated the Bellêmes by marrying his friend Roger of Montgomery to the Bellême heiress, Mabel. Their downfall began in 1114, when much of the Bellêmes' lands were seized by the neighbouring Rotrou family, but the final sting came another century later, when their remaining wealth was taken from them by the King of France.

Nowadays Bellême is a low-key place, its main monument being the **Eglise Saint-Sauveur**, started in the 15th century but not completed until around 1712. Bellême also makes a good base for walking in the magnificent **Forêt de Bellême** and visiting the broad lake, the **Etang de la Herse**, hidden within the woods. In September the tourist office runs mushroom study days in the forest.

La Perrière

⭐ La Perrière

Just 12km or so west of Bellême, nestling among hills, is one of the prettiest of all Norman villages, La Perrière. Its name derives from the Latin *petraria*, or stone quarry, and its honey-stone cottages could almost be in the English Cotswolds. Several date from the 15th century, and among its most interesting buildings are the 13th-century **Prieuré** (priory) and the **Logis de l'Evêque** (bishop's house), with its fairy-tale turrets. The charming square also hosts a handful of chic cafés and a first-class *épicerie*.

If it all has a rather grand feel, it's because in La Perrière's 11th century heyday village life revolved around the great **Château d'Horbé**, which was controlled by the counts of Bellême until it was destroyed by the English in 1429. The present village square was actually the castle courtyard. La Perrière has fabulous views over the Perche countryside, with forests on two sides, and there are many good walks. With so much forest nearby, the village relied on wood for its survival and until recently clog-makers and cabinet-makers lined its backstreets. The other craft for which it's famous is a type of lace known as *filet*, claimed to be the oldest type of lace in the world. Confusingly, two museums display it, the **Maison du Filet** inside the tourist office, and the **Atelier du Filet**, in the Mairie, which also teaches the art of making *filet*.

Maison du Filet
*open July–Aug
Wed–Mon 2.30–6;
April–June and Sept
Sun 2.30–6; adm*

Atelier du Filet
*open Wed–Mon 10–12
and 2–6; adm*

Tourist Information in the Heart of the Perche

For information on the Parc Naturel Régional du Perche: Maison du Parc, Courboyer, 61340 Nocé, t 02 33 25 70 10, *www.le-perche.org*.

Market Days: Bellême: Thurs; Nocé: Tues.

Post Office: Bellêm: Place Boucicaut

Shopping in the Heart of the Perche

Cave de l'Hermitière, 61260 L'Hermitière, t 02 37 49 67 30, *www.cidrerie-traditionelle-du-perche.fr*. Tours available on request. Cider festival last Sun in Oct. *Open April–Oct 10–12 and 3–8, or by appt.*
Charles Bataille, 14 Bd Bansard des Bois, Bellême, t 02 33 73 41 02. High-class *chocolatier*.

Ferme de La Grande Suardière, La Perrière, t 02 33 83 53 29. Organic farm selling apple juice, tarts, home-grown veg and bread from home-grown wheat baked in a wood-fired oven. *Open Feb–Dec Thurs and Sun*. Guided tours *Feb–Dec Sun–Fri by appt*.
Les Aubinières, 61170 St Léger sur Sarthe, t 02 33 27 46 06. Farm selling home-made duck products, from foie gras to *confit* and *magret de canard*. *Open daily exc Sun pm*.

Where to Stay and Eat in the Heart of the Perche

Nocé and Préaux-du-Perche
✉ 61340
Manoir de Lormarin, t 02 33 25 41 89, *http://manoirdelormarin.free.fr* (€€€). Gorgeous B&B room in a recently-restored 17th-century outhouse of the *manoir*. The owner is an antique

dealer, so it's been refurbished and furnished with care and style. Breakfast is served in the bakehouse.

La Ferme & Le Jardin François, Préaux-du-Perche, t 02 37 49 64 19, *www.jardin-francois.com* (€€–€). Simple but stylish rooms in a converted farm building surrounded by the Jardin François gardens (*see* p.207). Breakfast, using produce from the farm, is deposited at your door.

⭐ **Auberge des Trois J >**

Auberge des Trois J, 1 Place du Dr Gireaux, Nocé, t 02 33 73 41 03 (€€€). Slick but intimate restaurant that's without doubt the best place to eat in the Perche – but not cheap. *Closed Sun eve, Mon and (Oct–June) Tues.*

Gémages and St-Germain-de-la-Coudre ⊠ 61130

⭐ **Le Moulin de Gémages >**

Le Moulin de Gémages, Gémages, t 02 33 25 15 72, *http://moulindegemages. free.fr* (€€–€). A hotel in a wonderful old mill surrounded by fishing rivers and rolling countryside. Rooms are simple but pretty, and the helpful owners offer heavenly evening meals (€€) on request. There's also a cottage for rent, and they run occasional courses in watercolour painting, fly fishing, and cooking.

Le Haut Buat, St-Germain-de-la-Coudre, t 02 33 83 36 00 (€). Idyllic farmhouse with its own apple orchards, owned by a friendly couple. B&B rooms are comfortable and stylish, and breakfast is home-made and home-grown.

ⓘ **Bellême >>**
Bd Bansard des Bois, t 02 37 73 09 69, www.lepaysbelle mois.com

Les Secrets de Jeanne, t 02 33 25 05 44 (€). About 2kms from St-Germain, this beautifully converted barn offers delicious crêpes and salads. There's loads of space, inside and out, so it's perfect for children.

Condeau, Rémalard and Moutiers-au-Perche ⊠ 61110

ⓘ **La Perrière >>**
La Grande Place, t 02 33 73 35 49, si-pays-pervencheres@ wanadoo.fr

****Château de Villeray,** t 02 33 73 30 22, *www.domainedevilleray.com* (€€€€€–€€€€). Luxury hotel in a 16th- and 18th-century château in 44 hectares of grounds, near Rémalard on the eastern edge of the Perche. There's a heated pool, tennis, horse-riding, and more. If you prefer a more rustic setting, you can stay at the Moulin de Villeray (€€€€€–€€€€) 100 metres walk away. In winter dinner

(€€€€) is served in the château, while from April to Oct it's served in the mill, on the banks of the Huisne.

Le Galion, 21 Rue de l'Eglise, t 02 33 73 81 77 (€€). Lovely village restaurant in Rémalard using local produce. Try the *filet mignon de porc au Petit Percheron* and the *poire farcie à la tomme de Perche. Closed Tues and Wed.*

La Villa Fol'Avril, 2 Rue des Fers Chauds, t 02 33 83 22 67, *www. villafolavril.fr.* Elegant hotel-restaurant in the centre of the attractive Percheron village of Moutiers. Its seven immaculate rooms (€€), some with beams, are stylishly decorated. It also has a first-rate restaurant (€€) which has an outdoor terrace area in summer. *Restaurant closed Mon, Tues and Sun eve.*

Domaine de la Louveterie, t 02 33 73 11 63, *www.domainedelalouveterie.com* (€€€–€€). This delicious 17th-century *longère* has it all: five B&B rooms, all decorated in different styles from fifties-retro to Chinese and Moorish; two gorgeous *gîtes*; evening meals (€€€); and 14 hectares of woods and meadows to wander in. There are also courses on themes like cooking, painting and riding.

Bellême ⊠ 61130

**Le Relais Saint-Louis, 1 Bd Bansard-des-Bois, t 02 33 73 12 21, *www.relais-st-louis.com* (€). Rooms at this hotel are far smarter than its slightly shabby façade suggests, and it's very central, with a decent restaurant (€€€–€€). *Restaurant closed Sun eve and Mon.*

La Perrière ⊠ 61360

Manoir de Soisay, t 02 33 25 02 35 (€). The B&B rooms at this fabulous 16th-century manor are unfussily elegant, and there's a terrace overlooking the Perche countryside. Owner Didier shows guests around the *manoir* explaining its intriguing historical details. There is also a *gîte* to rent.

La Maison d'Horbé, t 02 33 73 18 41, *horbe98@wanadoo.fr.* This historic village house, right on the town square, is a *salon de thé* serving lunch and evening meals (€), a *chambres-d'hôtes* (€), and an antique shop. One of the three rooms is done up in Moroccan style.

Mortagne and La Trappe

History and opulence ooze from the ancient stones of **Mortagne-au-Perche**, the largest town in the Perche. Many of its buildings were mansions inhabited by royal officials and their hangers-on under the *ancien régime*, when the town was capital of the Perche. This border town has always been vulnerable to attack, and it started life in the Middle Ages as a hilltop fortress. In the 17th century many of its people left for Canada, the most famous of them the enterprising Pierre Boucher, who founded Boucherville near Montreal (a window in the **Eglise Notre-Dame** shows him and his troop setting off). Mortagne's medieval streets, once encased by great stone defensive walls, are packed with surprises, from ancient sundials to turreted palaces with carved façades and crumbling convents.

The tourist office, housed in the old **Halle aux Grains** (grain market) has laid out an excellent tour around the town's historic buildings, marked with information panels. The 13th-century **Porte St-Denis**, one of the last remnants of the ramparts, contains the **Musée Percheron**, with collections of local coins and archaeological finds. Virtually opposite, the **Musée Alain**, housed in the beautiful 17th-century **Maison des Comtes du Perche**, pays homage to the philosopher-journalist-musician Alain, who was born in Mortagne and whose humanist attacks on the French establishment during the First World War were a rare voice of sanity. Mortagne's former affluence is testified to by buildings like the 16th-century **Maison Henri IV** – so-called because the king is supposed to have stayed here – on Rue de Toussaint, and the later **Hôtel du Receveur des Tailles**, which housed that most powerful of men, the tax collector. For a break, head for the **Ancien Couvent de St-François et Ste-Claire**, in Rue de Longny, founded as a convent in 1502 by Marguerite of Lorraine, Countess of Perche, and later turned into a hospital, which has deliciously tranquil cloisters and a tiny chapel.

Mortagne has another major claim to fame, as the capital of Norman *boudin noir*, blood sausage or black pudding. At the end of March each year it hosts a *Foire au Boudin*, when around 5km of the fat dark sausages are sold, and there's even a competition to see who can eat the most of the stuff. Judges also munch through *boudins* to award a prize to the best *boudin*-maker. There is also a bloodless white version, *boudin blanc*, made of meat, milk, eggs and flour, which Normans usually eat at Christmas. The black-pudding-makers belong to the 'Brotherhood of Black Sausage Tasters' (*Confrérie des Chevaliers du Goute-Boudin*), which takes the business of promoting *boudin* very seriously. Judging by the number of *charcuteries* in Mortagne, the residents need no convincing.

Musée Percheron
open mid-June–mid-Sept Tues–Sun 3–6

Musée Alain
t 02 33 25 25 87; open Thurs–Fri and Tues 3–6, Wed 10–12 and 2–6, Sat 10–12 and 2–5

Ancien Couvent de St-François et Ste-Claire
open daily 9–6

Getting to Mortagne

The nearest **train** station to Mortagne is at L'Aigle (32km away). **Buses** connect Mortagne with L'Aigle, Bellême and Nocé, Tourouvre and (Sat only) La Chapelle-Montligeon and Longny-au-Perche.

Villages around Mortagne

There are more beautiful villages and manors within a short radius of Mortagne. About 12km southeast past **Courgeon** is the **Manoir de la Vove**, one of the oldest in the Perche, with a beautiful chapel. The interior normally opens just for two days in September, but the grounds are open all year. A little north of there is **Monceaux-au-Perche**, at the confluence of two valleys, with the **Manoir de Pontgirard**, whose buildings and terraced gardens have been skilfully renovated by its owner, architectural historian Philippe Siguret. A line of little waterfalls connects the collections of plants and trees. They run occasional gardening courses (check the website for details).

In complete contrast, **La Chapelle-Montligeon**, back towards Mortagne, is dominated by a vast neo-Gothic **basilica** and a printing works, both erected at the end of the 19th century by an Abbot Buguet in an attempt to revive the village's flagging fortunes, both moral and economic. Basilica and printing press are still flourishing, and the church is a pilgrimage site. Some find more charm in the **Chapelle de Notre-Dame-de-Pitié**, at the entrance to **Longny-au-Perche**, a quaint 16th-century chapel that looks more like a *manoir* than a church.

To the north of the N12 highway, **Tourouvre** lost many of its inhabitants to Canada, from the 17th century onwards, and windows in the church relate the story of local families who helped found Quebec. A museum, the **Maison de l'Emigration Française en Canada** has recently opened to tell the story of emigration from the Perche to Canada. There are also plans to open a new **Maison du Commerce**, a museum about the history of shopping (contact Mortagne tourist office for details).

Abbaye de Notre-Dame de la Trappe

The first ever Trappist monastery, La Grande Trappe took its name from the Forêt de la Trappe in which it stands, 14km north of Mortagne. Its 30-odd white-robed monks belong to the Cistercian Order of the Strict Observance, a branch of the Benedictines, which is, as the name suggests, strict: they talk as little as possible, and certainly not to visitors. Unless you come here on retreat, the only chance you have of glimpsing the monks' austere existence (evocatively described by Leigh Fermor in *A Time to Keep Silence*) is by attending Mass. Unfortunately only a morsel survives of the

Manoir de la Vove
tours of exterior only, Mon and Sat 2–5

Manoir de Pontgirard
http://pontgirard. free.fr; garden open May–July and Sept Sat–Sun 10–12 and 2.30–6.30; Aug Thurs–Tues same hours; adm

Basilica
open daily 8.30am–9pm

Chapelle de Notre-Dame-de-Pitié
open daily 9–7

Maison de l'Emigration Française en Canada
t 02 33 83 30 64; open April–Sept daily 9.30–6.30; Oct–Dec and mid-Feb–end Mar Sat–Sun 10–5; adm

Abbaye de Notre-Dame de la Trappe
t 02 33 84 17 00, la.trappe@wanadoo.fr; closed except for attending Mass Mon–Sat from 9.30; Sun from 10.30; shop open daily

original 12th-century abbey, founded by an aristocratic cleric and crusader, Count Rotrou III of Perche. He did so to give thanks for his own safe passage across the English Channel, and as a memorial to his wife Princess Matilda, daughter of Henry I of England, who went down with the *Blanche Nef* at Barfleur (*see* p.296). The disaster had such an impact on him that he ordered the church to be built in the shape of an upside-down sailing vessel, with masts for pillars. By the 1660s the buildings and the monks' morals had lapsed into decadence – until an abbot called Abbé Rancé decided to pull the order up by the bootstraps, by establishing the Trappist rules of silence and austerity. The buildings were destroyed in the Revolution and the monks driven out, but as early as 1815 they managed to return and rise phoenix-like from the ruins.

The neo-Gothic creation erected in place of the old abbey looks, in the words of Leigh Fermor, more like a hospital or asylum than an abbey, but its setting is still magical. The shop sells an extraordinary range of monk-made goods and attracts coachloads of visitors, who also stroll in the forests. There's a lake, with boating and fishing facilities, nearby.

Tourist Information in Mortagne

(i) **Mortagne >**
Halle aux Grains,
t 02 33 85 11 18

Internet Access: 48 Rue des 15-Fusillés.
Market Days: Mortagne: Sat; Soligny-la-Trappe: Tues; Tourouvre: Fri.
Post Office: 16 Rue des 15-Fusillés.

Where to Stay and Eat around Mortagne

(★) **Le Tribunal >**

Mortagne-au-Perche ✉ 61400
Le Tribunal, 4 Place du Palais, t 02 33 25 04 77 (€€–€). Characterful old hotel on a historic square a stone's throw from the Porte St-Denis. The restaurant (€€) is the best in town. One thing to try is their *croustillant de boudin mortagnais,* made using the local black pudding.

Moulicent and Longny-au-Perche ✉ 61290
Château de la Grande Noë, Moulicent, t 02 33 73 63 30, *www.chateaude lagrandenoe.com* (€€€). A fascinating manor-house B&B, complete with oak panelling, antiques, ancestral portraits and chamber music in the drawing room, set in large grounds. *Open Mar–Nov, by arrangement Dec–Feb.*

Chez Nous, La Genetrie, Saint Hilaire le Châtel, t 02 33 83 92 57 (€€€). Stunning little restaurant in a tiny (and hard to find) village. In summer you eat in the garden by the pool. A la carte only in the evening, but there's a set menu for lunch. The décor and high-quality food make it worth the money. *Closed Sun eve and Mon.*

La Chapelle Montligeon ✉ 61400
Le Montligeon, t 02 33 83 81 19, *www.hotelmontligeon.com* (€€). This traditional hotel in the heart of the village is best known for its restaurant, which serves the best of Norman cuisine, using local produce. Try the scallops in a cider sauce. There's a fine log fire in winter, and a terrace in summer. *Restaurant closed Mon and Sun eve, exc in high season.*

La Ferté-Vidame ✉ 28340
Manoir de la Motte, t 02 37 37 51 69, *www.lemanoirdelamotte.com* (€€). This 19th-century chateau in three hectares of parkland on the Normandy border has just two delightful rooms, one of them a suite. Breakfast is in the oak-panelled dining room, and dinners can be provided on request.

The Norman Riviera

In the 1840s the coast between the mouths of the Seine and the Orne rivers was adopted by Parisians as their playground and dubbed the 'Norman Riviera' – and its delusions of grandeur have stuck ever since. Quaintly old-fashioned, deliberately exclusive, and a tad smug, Deauville and its less élitist neighbour Trouville are the Nice and Cannes of this shoreline, periodically prodded awake by an influx of film stars and horse-racing buffs. Today this stretch of coast is known as the Côte Fleurie (Flowery Coast). Further west are more sandy beaches and a dash of Belle Epoque seaside grandeur at resorts like Houlgate, Cabourg and Dives-sur-Mer.

12

Don't miss

⭐ 17th-century skyscrapers
Honfleur **p.214**

⭐ Normandy's zaniest museum
Maisons Satie, Honfleur **p.218**

⭐ *Moules* and prawns
Trouville **p.221**

⭐ Race-going and star-spotting
Deauville **p.221**

⭐ Belle Epoque grandeur
Cabourg **p.228**

See map overleaf

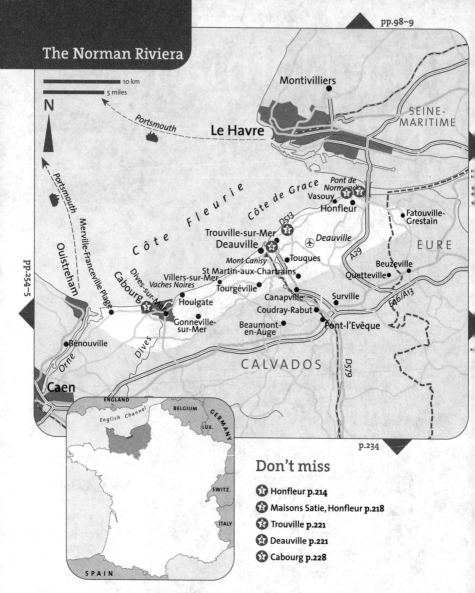

The Norman Riviera

10 km
5 miles

N

Portsmouth
Le Havre
Montivilliers

SEINE-MARITIME

Portsmouth

Côte Fleurie
Côte de Grace
Pont de Norman ⭐
Vasouy
Honfleur
Fatouville-Grestain

Merville-Franceville Plage
Ouistreham
Trouville-sur-Mer
Deauville
Deauville
EURE

pp.254–5
Mont Canisy
St Martin-aux-Chartrains
Touques
A29
Beuzeville
Quetteville

Dives-sur-Mer
Vaches Noires
Villers-sur-Mer
Tourgéville
Canapville
Surville
E46/A13

Cabourg
Houlgate
Coudray-Rabut
Gonneville-sur-Mer
Beaumont-en-Auge
Pont-l'Evêque

Bénouville
Orne
Dives
CALVADOS
D579

Caen

ENGLAND
English Channel
BELGIUM
GERMANY
LUX.

p.234

SWITZ.

ITALY

SPAIN

Don't miss

⭐ Honfleur **p.214**
⭐ Maisons Satie, Honfleur **p.218**
⭐ Trouville **p.221**
⭐ Deauville **p.221**
⭐ Cabourg **p.228**

Honfleur

⭐ Honfleur

Clustered around its enchanting inner harbour, the *Vieux Bassin*, with its lofty houses like 17th-century skyscrapers, Honfleur is unlike any other town in Normandy. It seems to stand in its own little world, with little regard for industrial Le Havre just across the Seine estuary, the beach towns to its west or the Pays d'Auge to the south. Honfleur's beauty and the quality of its light have attracted many painters, and Boudin, the father of Impressionism, was born here. He, Monet, and others like Corot, Daubigny and the

Getting to and around Honfleur

The nearest **train** stations are at Lisieux and Deauville (15kms), both well connected by bus.

Calvados' Bus Verts **bus** No.20 between Le Havre and Caen stops at Honfleur and other coastal towns. Bus No.50 runs between Le Havre and Lisieux, also via Honfleur. Buses leave from the *Gare Routière*, on Rue des Vases. **Bus Verts information, t** 0810 214 214.

Like many towns Honfleur has a **Petit Train Touristique**, a (tractor-drawn) child-friendly 'train' around the sights (May–Sept daily), departing from the *Gare Routière*. For **taxis**, call **t** 02 31 98 87 59.

Dutchman Jongkind often painted Honfleur and its skies while staying just outside the town at the Ferme St-Siméon, then a simple *auberge*, now a very grand hotel. At any time of year Honfleur is a wonderful place to wander, to explore its winding alleys, watch the yachts gliding in and out of the old port or just settle down for a long, boozy lunch in one of its many restaurants (apparently, there's one for every 80 inhabitants).

Honfleur's strategic position at the mouth of the Seine made it an important port from the 11th century onwards. During the Hundred Years' War, Charles V of France gave it fortified walls to keep out the treacherous English, who nonetheless managed to occupy Honfleur for 32 years beginning in 1419. It grew in importance throughout the 15th century, as rival Harfleur across the Seine silted up. Shipbuilding took off, and the town spawned many celebrated navigators, sailors and captains, among them Samuel de Champlain, whose voyages, beginning in 1608, led to the founding of Quebec and French Canada. By the 18th century, the shipping magnates of little Honfleur had mounted well over 100 expeditions.

The Vieux Bassin and L'Enclos

Honfleur's extraordinary inner harbour, the **Vieux Bassin**, was built from the 1660s on the orders of Louis XIV's minister Colbert, to provide a safer inner harbour for the port. Its fabulous quayside houses date from this same era. The real jewels are in the row along **Quai Ste-Catherine**. With their slate roofs and slate or half-timbered façades, the buildings, some ten storeys high, look as if they might topple over at any time. They had to extend upwards, as space was at a premium, and in order to compensate for being built against a slope – so that each house is narrow in depth as well as width. Each one, though, is a different height and colour, which is an essential part of their enormous charm. This is the heart of Honfleur, and the *quai*'s many cafés and restaurants are ideal for watching the yacht-crews in the *Bassin*, or the odd traditional Norman sailing boat. At the seaward end of the quay is the rugged stone **Lieutenance**, the 16th-century former residence of the Lieutenant-Governors of Honfleur, straddling the bridge between the Vieux Bassin and the more functional **Avant Port**.

Honfleur map

- Maison Satie
- Jardin Public
- BOULEVARD CHARLES V
- Phare de la Jetée Est
- R. ADOLPHE MARAIS
- RUE HAUTE
- RUE DE L'HOMME-DE-BOIS
- R. DLARUE MARORUS
- RUE VARIN
- RUE BUCAILLE
- R. J. DOUBLET
- RUE DES CAPUCINS
- R. ALBRETIER
- R. BARBEL
- R. BOULANGER
- Musée Eugène Boudin
- RUE DES LINGOTS
- PLACE HAMELIN
- PLACE CATHERINE
- St Catherine
- PLACE BERTHELOT
- Quai de la Lieutenance
- QUAI DES PASSAGERS
- JETÉE OUEST
- Avant Port
- JETÉE DE L'EST
- JETÉE DE TRANSIT
- PLACE DU PUITS
- RUE DU PUITS
- R. E. BOUDIN
- R. BRÛLÉE
- R. DU DAUPHIN
- R. ST-CATHERINE
- Vieux Bassin
- R. ST-ÉTIENNE
- Q. DE LA QUARANTAINE
- PLACE A BOUDIN
- RUE DE LA VILLE
- Q. DE LA TOUR
- Musée de la Marine/ Musée d'Ethnographie
- COURS DES FOSSÉS
- R. MONTPENSIER
- R. DE LA CHAUSSÉE
- Greniers à Sel
- Bus Station
- QUAI TOSTAIN
- R. JEAN DE VIENNE
- QUAI DE LA CALE
- Bassin de l'Est
- CHARRIÈRE DU PUITS
- RUE DE LA BAVOLE
- LE GRAND BOULOIR
- RUE DE LA RÉPUBLIQUE
- RUE CACHIN
- NOTRE DAME
- Q. LEPAULMIER
- R. DES VASES
- R. SAINT NICOL
- LE PETIT BOULOIR
- RUE SAINT
- RUE DES BUTTES
- PLACE ST-LÉONARD
- St-Léonard
- RUE SAINT LÉONARD
- R. VILLEY
- R. PESTEL
- CHARRIÈRE ST-LÉONARD
- PLACE ALBERT SOREL
- R. A. DUBOURG
- RUE BOURDET
- RUE AUX CHATS
- To Paris, Rouen
- N
- 200 metres
- 200 yards

Attached to it is the Porte de Caen, an old town gate that is one of only two surviving sections of Honfleur's medieval ramparts, demolished when the Vieux Bassin was built (the other bit is outside the Musée d'Ethnographie). Inside the gate a plaque commemorates Champlain's departure for Quebec from this same spot. In the evenings fishing boats come up to the Quai de la Lieutenance to unload their prawns, which can only be sold here by fishermen's wives, a historic right that is jealously guarded.

The tangle of delightful alleyways east of the Bassin is known as **L'Enclos** ('The Enclosure'), since this was the original medieval town of Honfleur, 'enclosed' within its first town walls. It's crossed roughly from north to south by the Rue de la Ville, once known as the King's Way, on which stands the remarkable **Greniers à Sel**, the great royal salt stores built in 1670, using stone from the recently-dismantled ramparts. Salt was hugely important in those days – for local consumption and for the Atlantic fishing fleets, to preserve cod and herring – and at one time these stores held 10,000 tonnes of the stuff. Trading in salt was a royal monopoly, and the heavy tax laid on it, the *Gabelle*, was an important cause of the 1789 Revolution. The stores' oak-timbered roofs are superb, and today the building hosts concerts and exhibitions.

A few streets away on Rue de la Prison is the **Musée d'Ethnographie et d'Art Populaire**, in the former town prison. Visitors can see the communal cell where prisoners eked out a grim existence, sleeping chained to bare boards – although this was luxury compared to the solitary confinement cells, which had no furniture at all and just a slit in the door for air. At the back of the yard is a remnant of the old town walls. The museum's other rooms, divided between two old houses, contain reconstructions of Norman interiors, with fine collections of antiques, costumes and china. Many represent different trades, from sailor to haberdasher to weaver; more unusual items include a copper bath in the shape of a slipper, a beautiful box-bed from the Pays de Caux, and a stunning oak marriage wardrobe carved in 1783, which is unusual in that it shows the name of the bride.

Musée d'Ethnographie et d'Art Populaire
open April–Sept Tues–Sun 10–12 and 2–6.30; mid-Feb–end-Mar and Oct–mid-Nov Tues–Fri 2.30–5.30, Sat–Sun 10–12 and 2.30–5.30; adm, joint ticket with Musée de la Marine

Virtually next door, on Quai St-Etienne, stands the equally traditional **Musée de la Marine**. The best thing about it is its setting, the 14th century St-Etienne church, which since the Revolution has undergone numerous transformations from warehouse to theatre to fish market. It still retains, though, a lovely oak-timbered roof and carved columns. The contents are a tribute to Honfleur's maritime history, including paintings, scores of ship models, and a fine 17th-century mariner's chest, believed to be from Nuremberg. At Whitsun Honfleur still stages its *Fête des Marins*, a maritime jamboree during which boats are bedecked with flowers and fishermen bless the sea.

Musée de la Marine
same opening times as the Musée d'Ethnographie; adm on separate or joint ticket

South of L'Enclos across Quai Lepaulmier – site of the tourist office – is **St-Léonard**, a late 15th century church with a fine Gothic portal. An organic food market is held in front of it every Wednesday morning.

The Faubourg Ste-Catherine, Boudin and Satie

Honfleur's finest architectural jewel is the **Eglise Ste-Catherine**, northwest of the Vieux Bassin in the **Faubourg Ste-Catherine**, traditionally the sailors' district, which grew up outside the walls of medieval Honfleur. Ste-Catherine is the finest timber-frame church in France, but it shouldn't really still be here, as the building was only meant to be temporary. An earlier church in stone had been destroyed by the English, but when it came to rebuilding in the 1460s stone was scarce, and needed to rebuild the port. Wood on the other hand was plentiful, and a material local shipbuilders were familiar with. The two vaulted naves are, in effect, upturned ship's hulls. The naval craftsmen's tools were crude, as can be seen in the irregularities of some of the pillars; below the grand organ, though, there's a wonderful wooden balustrade carved with

16th-century musical instruments. During the Revolution Ste-Catherine was used as a 'Temple of Reason'; and later attempts were made to 'improve' it by coating the beams in plaster and adding a classical-style porch, but it's now been restored to its wooden simplicity. The belfry, across the lovely Place Ste-Catherine, had to be built separately as the wooden church couldn't take the weight of cast-iron bells. The belfry itself is now closed to visitors, but there is an exhibition in the room below it, known as the **Clocher Ste-Catherine**. On Saturdays, Place Ste-Catherine hosts Honfleur's main market, and off the square a tangle of passageways and steps lead down towards two streets that contain a high proportion of Honfleur's restaurants, the Rue de l'Homme de Bois, and, below it, the misnamed Rue Haute.

The sailors' church provided ample inspiration for artists like Monet, Jongkind and Dufy, whose renditions of it are exhibited in the **Musée Eugène Boudin**, off Rue de l'Homme de Bois. It was founded by Honfleur's best known artist himself, in 1868, as a showcase for the 'Honfleur school' of painters, who also included Corot and Jongkind. It has one of the best collections anywhere of Boudin's own works, including his *Personnages sur la plage de Trouville vers 1865* and *Plage de Trouville – Conversation 1876*, and the wonderful *Port de Dieppe*, which has touches of both Turner and Monet. There are also some pleasing Impressionistic paintings by other artists, like Courbet's *Rivage de Normandie près de Honfleur* and the several works by Boudin's fellow Honfleur-born artist Louis-Alexandre Dubourg, including his attractive *Marché aux Poissons*. Other rooms in the museum have displays of Norman furniture, dress and headgear. From the upper floor there are stunning views over the Seine, while the rooms contain some nice but wildly contrasting Dufys, including *Champs de Blé en Normandie*, with its mellow cornfield against rich blue skies.

Honfleur was also the birthplace in 1886 of the maverick musician, artist and writer Erik Satie, and you can immerse yourself in his quirky world at the **Maisons Satie**, one of Normandy's must-sees. The old half-timbered house is the place where Satie was born in 1866, and lived until he was 12. 'Museum', though, isn't really the word to describe this all-engrossing experience: armed with an electronic headset, in French or English, you are led from one room to another to the accompaniment of Satie's music, extracts from his writings and a series of imaginatively Satie-esque visual effects. It's visually stunning, and the sets in each room are works of art in themselves. The first room, totally black, has an ominous row of black umbrellas in the corner, an invisible ticking clock, and in the centre an enormous illuminated pear with wings; in the background, you hear Satie's *Danse pour un Enterrement*. Even if you know little about Satie, you may well come out of the

---

Clocher Ste-Catherine
open mid-Mar–Sept Wed–Mon 10–12 and 2–6; Oct–11 Nov Wed–Fri and Mon 2.30–5, Sat–Sun 10–12 and 2.30–5; adm

Musée Eugène Boudin
t 02 31 89 54 00; open mid-Mar–Sept Wed–Mon 10–12 and 2–6; Oct–mid-Mar Wed–Fri and Mon 2.30–5, Sat–Sun 10–12 and 2.30–5; adm

Maisons Satie
t 02 31 89 11 11; open May–Sept Wed–Mon 10–7, Oct–Dec and mid-Feb–April Wed–Sun 11–6; adm

house feeling passionately about him, having discovered such things as the fact that for a time he dressed only in black and ate only white food. You finish the tour riding a kind of giant basketball on a crazy musical merry-go-round. It's all so endearingly eccentric and wittily humorous that it's a trial returning to the world outside.

For somewhere to digest it, the **Jardin Public** is just across Boulevard Charles V, and beyond that there's a rather plain beach. Nature lovers and anyone with children may also want to visit **Naturospace**, also on Boulevard Charles V, proclaimed as the largest tropical butterfly house in France, and which also contains a dazzling array of tropical plants. For more invigorating exercise, climb to the top of the cliff of the **Côte-de-Grâce** above Honfleur, where you'll find the lovely chapel of **Nôtre-Dame-de-Grâce**, built in 1600 to replace an earlier one built by Duke Richard II of Normandy. For centuries Honfleur's mariners have come here to pray before and after voyages and to give thanks for safe passages, and the chapel walls are coated with ex-voto plaques to Our Lady of Mercy. The view from here inspired Boudin and his troupe of young Impressionists, who stayed at the (now gentrified) Ferme St-Siméon, but two sights they would not have seen are the oil refineries of Le Havre or the huge, sleek **Pont de Normandie**, which gracefully straddles the Seine.

Naturospace
open daily July–Aug 10–7; April–June and Sept 10–1 and 2–7; Oct–Nov 10–1 and 2–5.30; Feb–Mar 10–1 and 2–5.30; adm

Tourist Information in Honfleur

(i) **Honfleur >**
Quai Lepaulmier, t 02 31 89 23 30, www.ot-honfleur.fr

The tourist office organizes guided tours in English from May–mid-Oct on Wed at 3pm (tours in French Wed 11am, Thurs and Sat 9pm). The office's *Passe Musées* gives combined entry to four of Honfleur's museums.
Internet Access: Le Jardin des Peintres, 11 Bd Charles V; Cyber Pub, 55 Rue de la République.
Market Days: Sat, Place Ste-Catherine; Marché Bio (organic market) Wed, in Cours des Fossés.
Post Office: 7 Cours Albert Manuel.

Where to Stay in Honfleur

Honfleur ✉ 14600

All along the Côte Fleurie accommodation prices vary substantially by season, and in peak season (July–August) can be extortionate. Book well ahead.

****Ferme Saint-Siméon**, Rue Adolphe Marais, t 02 31 81 78 00, *www.fermesaintsimeon.com* (€€€€€). Honfleur's top hotel, in huge grounds overlooking the Seine. As well as opulent rooms and suites, a gorgeous indoor pool and a health spa, the half-timbered 'farm' offers fading memories of the Impressionists who painted here when it was a far humbler place. There's a top-of-the-range restaurant too (€€€€). The same owners also run the Manoir du Butin and La Chaumière, two other luxurious hotels on the edge of town.

La Maison de Lucie, 44 Rue des Capucins, t 02 31 14 40 40, *www.lamaisondelucie.com* (€€€€) A really stunning hotel, based in an 18th-century mansion in the historic centre, with five stylish bedrooms and two suites looking onto a courtyard garden, along with five more rooms in the adjoining building. Moroccan tiled bathrooms and oak panelling add to the charm, and there's a neo-Moorish spa in the vaulted cellars. A truly special place.

Le Clos Bourdet, 50 Rue Bourdet, t 02 31 89 49 11, *www.leclosbourdet.com* (€€€€). Owners Fan and Jean-Claude Osmont have turned this *maison de maître* into a deliciously eclectic mix of Baroque and contemporary. There's lots of mock-zebra skin and old photographs, and wonderful home-made tarts and jams. Painter Eugene Boudin was born in the same street.

***Les Maisons de Léa, Place Ste-Catherine, t 02 31 14 49 49, *www.lesmaisonsdelea.com* (€€€€–€€). Gorgeous, stylish hotel spread between four houses on Place Ste Catherine. Rooms vary in size (and so price), but all have the latest comforts.

***L'Absinthe, 1 Rue de la Ville, t 02 31 89 23 23, *www.absinthe.fr* (€€€). Stunning small hotel in a 16th-century presbytery in L'Enclos, whose seven bedrooms have beams, antique furniture, and Jacuzzis in the bathrooms. Its harbourside location is unbeatable, and there's a restaurant opposite (*see* below).

Hôtel des Loges, 18 Rue Brûlée, t 02 31 89 38 26 *www.hoteldesloges.com* (€€€–€€). Owner Catherine Chouridis has put all her artistic flair into converting this historic Honfleur house into one of the town's most stylish hotels. The décor of the 14 rooms is calming and contemporary, and there's a self-catering cottage too. Breakfasts are served in the no-less appealing dining room. If you've fallen in love with the designer fittings and accessories, you can now buy them downstairs. Babysitting also available.

La Cour Sainte Catherine, 74 Rue du Puits, t 02 31 89 42 40, *www.giaglis. com* (€€). Friendly B&B in a restored 17th-century convent bang in the middle of Honfleur. There are nine pleasant rooms, some with beams, and breakfast is in the courtyard garden or the converted *pressoir*. WIFI and internet available too. A bargain.

Eating Out in Honfleur

The Manoir du Butin (*see* above under Ferme Saint-Siméon) has the best of Honfleur's hotel restaurants.

Sa Qua Na, 22 place hamelin, t 02 31 89 40 80, *www.alexandre-bourdas.*

com (€€€€). If the name sounds Japanese, it's no coincidence: young chef Alexandre Bourdas lived in Japan for three years. Both the minimalist décor and the food have Asian touches, but you'll also find Norman staples with an original twist. The restaurant has just won its first well-deserved Michelin star. Unmissable.

L'Absinthe, 10 Quai de la Quarantaine, t 02 31 89 39 00, *www.absinthe.fr* (€€€). With the same owners as the similarly-named hotel (*see* above), L'Absinthe has stunning dining rooms in a 15th-century house. The food is innovative, if pricey.

La Terrasse et l'Assiette, 8 Place Ste-Catherine, t 02 31 89 31 33 (€€€–€€). Michelin-starred, and Honfleur's foremost gourmet restaurant. Specialities include lobster omelette and a mouth-watering warm chocolate gâteau. *Closed Mon, mid-Nov–mid-Dec and (Sept–June) Wed.*

Entre Terre et Mer, 12–14 Place Hamelin, t 02 31 89 70 60 (€€€–€€). One of the best in town, central, with stunning décor and tables outside in summer. Ask for the catch of the day. *Closed Wed (Oct–May only) and 20 Jan–10 Feb.*

Le Bréard, 7 Rue du Puits, t 02 31 89 53 40 (€€). Norman cooking with an original international twist, reflecting chef Fabrice Sebire's worldwide travels. Fish is particularly good – try the cod roasted with *ras al hanout* and the tuna with a soya and wasabi sauce. Service and décor are both stylish and relaxed. *Closed Wed and (Sept–June) Tues and Wed lunchtimes.*

L'Homme de Bois, 30-32 Rue de L'Homme de Bois, t 02 31 89 75 27 (€€). The kind of restaurant we all dream about: old beams, log fires, a friendly welcome, excellent food, superb value.

La Petite Chine, 14-16 Rue du Dauphin, t 02 31 89 36 52 (€). Enchanting little tearoom in one of the old town's most idiosyncratic buildings, off the Vieux Bassin. The décor is chic, and the food is wonderful: come for coffee, fresh light lunches or tea, accompanied by one of co-owner Jean Claude's fabulous home-made cakes. *Closed Mon, end June and end Nov.*

⭐ Sa Qua Na >

The Côte Fleurie

Trouville-sur-Mer

 Trouville-sur-Mer

Let us take the air on the beach And contemplate the Ocean so tranquil.

Ah! If Paris only had the sea, It would be a little Trouville!

From *Niniche*, an 1878 vaudeville set in Trouville

The greatest events of my life have been some thoughts, readings, a few sunsets on the sea at Trouville...

Flaubert

Aquarium

open July–Aug daily 10–7.30, Easter–June and Sept–Oct daily 10–12 and 2–7, Nov–Easter daily 2–6.30; adm

Divided only by the river Touques, at first glance Trouville and Deauville appear to be two halves of the same resort town. Scratch the surface, though, and you soon spot the differences. Deauville is chic, artificial and has a life that's largely seasonal; Trouville, while no less picturesque, is a more down-to-earth, gutsy place with a year-round life of its own and river quaysides smelling of fresh fish. And, as its inhabitants are quick to tell you, Trouville was a favourite with Parisians before Deauville was even thought of. The first beach huts appeared here in the 1840s, and Napoléon III brought his court here in the following decade. Opulent villas lined the seafront, and Parisians flocked here to indulge in bathing, gambling and parading up and down. 'It is between the casino and the water...,' wrote an 1868 guidebook, 'that you can see coming and going, rivalling one another in luxury, bathing in order to undress, dressing again an hour later in order to change costumes, all these elegant Parisians, English, Spanish, Russians or Americans, for whom life is a perpetual fair.' With the tourists came writers and artists. Flaubert had met his first love Elisa on Trouville's soft sands at the age of 15; later, Monet painted *Boardwalk at Trouville* and the *Hôtel des Roches Noires*, while Boudin's *Beach at Trouville* is among his best work.

Today the beach is as lovely as ever, with its sweeping vistas, villas and ice-cream stands. In contrast to Deauville's methodically planned avenues, Trouville, away from the promenade, is an organic tangle of twisting lanes and houses, its streets packed with curiosity shops, restaurants and cafés. The liveliest spot is the quay along the Touques, where fishermen sell their catch each morning, and where bustling brasseries provide some of the best (and cheapest) seafood and fish on the coast. On Wednesday and Sunday mornings it's the site of a wonderful **market**. In July and August some stalls are there every day. For indoor entertainment there's an **Aquarium**, or of course you can try a flutter at the casino.

Deauville

 Deauville

Poodles, racehorses, film stars and well-heeled Parisians with impeccable skins – they're all here in plush Deauville, which glares at its rival Trouville across the Touques. Its lightning transformation from fishing hamlet to Parisians' playground was the brainchild of Napoléon III's half-brother, the Duc de Morny, who in the 1860s wandered across the river from Trouville and decided he could

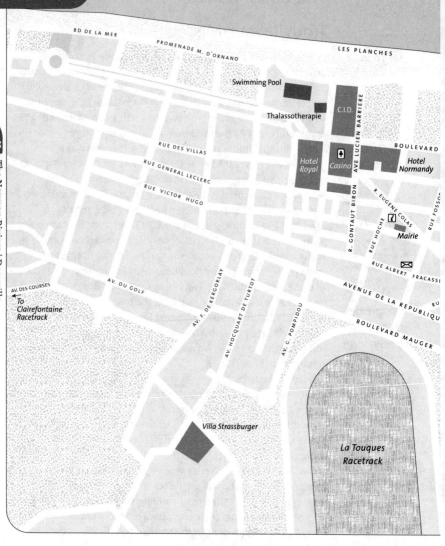

build something bigger and better on the dunes on the other side. He was joined in this enterprise by his physician Dr Joseph Oliffe, a wealthy British émigré based in Paris, and between them they spent a fortune dredging the marshes beside the Touques, creating a yacht basin and erecting a bridge across the river. Streets were laid out as broad avenues where Parisian visitors would feel at home, and over-the-top 'Anglo-Norman' villas with lashings of mock timbering sprang up as fast as their speculative builders could erect them. In just three years 250 mansions appeared,

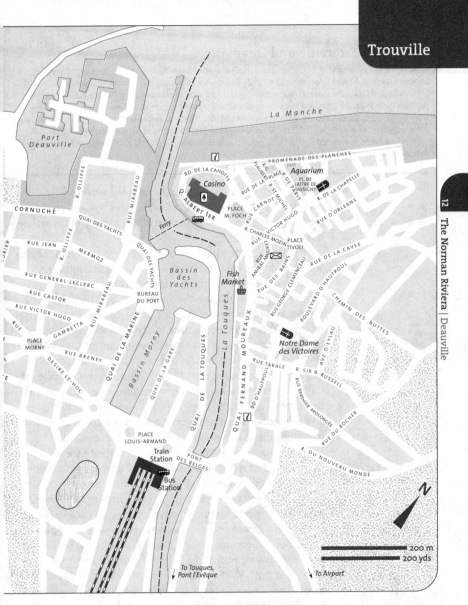

La Manche

Port Deauville

CORNUCHÉ

R. OLLIFFE
RUE MIRABEAU
QUAI DES YACHTS
R. OLLIFFE
MERMOZ
RUE JEAN
RIER
QUAI DES YACHTS
Ferry
BD. DE LA CAHOTTE
Casino
Q. ALBERT 1ER
PLACE M. FOCH

PROMENADE DES PLANCHES
R.G. FLAUBERT
RUE DE LA PLAGE
R. ST-MICHEL
R. DE PARIS
Aquarium
PL. DE LATTRE DE TASSIGNY
R. DE LA CHAPELLE
RUE CARNOT
RUE D'ORLEANS

RUE GENERAL LECLERC
RUE CASTOR
RUE VICTOR HUGO
RUE
GAMBETTA
PLACE MORNY
RUE BRENEY
DESIRE LE-HOC
'E

RUE MIRABEAU
BUREAU DU PORT
Bassin des Yachts

QUAI DE LA MARINE
Bassin Morny
QUAI DE LA GARE

QUAI DE LA TOUQUES
La Touques
Fish Market

R. CHARLES VICTOR HUGO
RUE CHARLES MOZIN
RUE AMIRAL MAGRET
RUE DES BAINS
PLACE TIVOLI
RUE DE LA CAVEE
RUE GEORGE CLEMENCEAU
BOULEVARD D'HAUTPOUL
CHEMIN DES BUTTES

QUAI FERNAND MOUREAUX
Notre Dame des Victoires
RUE TARALE
BD D'HAUTPOUL
AVE D'EYLAU
R. SIR B. RUSSELL
RUE BERTHIER PROLONGÉE
RUE DU ROCHER

PLACE LOUIS-ARMAND
Train Station
PONT DES BELGES
Bus Station

R. DU NOUVEAU MONDE

N

To Touques, Pont l'Evêque

To Airport

200 m
200 yds

followed by a casino and a racecourse, and Deauville already had a special clinic for dogs in the 1870s. Deauville's winning stroke was the railway, which through Morny's influence was routed to newly-born Deauville rather than Trouville. By the 1900s anyone who was anyone made a point of being seen on the promenade or *Planches* at Deauville, which began to be dubbed 'Paris' 21st *arrondissement*'.

Today Deauville is a sedately ritzy – and expensive – place, frequented most loyally by the elderly wealthy citizens of France and their small canine companions. Its more youthful and

Getting to Trouville and Deauville

Deauville has an **airport** at St-Gatien-des-Bois, 8km east of town. Ryanair offers three flights weekly to London Stansted. **Airport information, t** 02 31 65 65 65, *www.pays-auge.cci.fr/aeroportdeauville*.

Trouville and Deauville share a **train station**, by the Pont des Belges (*see* p.223). There are frequent trains to/from Paris-St-Lazare (2hrs), via Pont-l'Evêque and usually Lisieux (20mins). There is also a coastal line from Deauville to Dives-Cabourg, with infrequent services, mostly in summer (Sat–Sun only mid-Sept–late June, daily late June–early Sept). A **Petit Train Touristique** runs Easter–Sept from the Deauville town hall.

Both towns are also served by Bus Verts' **bus** No.20, which links the train station with Caen and Le Havre. **Bus information, t** 0810 214 214.

fashionable credentials are given a shot in the arm every September with Deauville's American Film Festival, and you can see the visiting stars' names painted on the bathing huts that line its giant beach.

When you've done your share of glitterati-spotting from the bars and cafés on the *Planches*, there's a luxurious thalassotherapy centre and a host of designer boutiques to provide further entertainment. There's also the casino, and Deauville's two lavish **racetracks**, which together form one of the major centres of horse-racing in France. **La Touques** track, built by Morny in 1864, is used for flat racing, while the less élite **Clairefontaine** mainly hosts steeplechases and trotting. Two events held at La Touques each August, the polo tournament and the Grand Prix de Deauville – the traditional end to Deauville's racing season on the last Sunday in the month – attract the *crème* of French society. Millions of euros also change hands in the August Yearling Sales, and in an attempt to prolong the season, winter racing during October and November has recently been introduced. Along with the rest of Normandy, the town stages a week of **Equi'days** in October, with races, sales and parades of horse-drawn carriages.

La Touques
free guided visits Sun, on race days only

Clairefontaine
free guided tours 10am on race days

Equi'days
www.equidays.com

Anyone interested in Deauville's often bizarre *Anglo-Normand* architecture should venture down to the town's most extravagant creation, the geranium-decked **Villa Strassburger**, a half-timbered concoction of pepperpot towers, pagoda cornices and Swiss-chalet roofs one above the other. It was built in 1907 for Baron Henri de Rothschild, but his wife never took to it as it lacked a sea view, and in 1924 the family sold the mansion to a wealthy US lawyer and *bon vivant*, Ralph Beaver Strassburger. Its proximity to the racetrack was ideal for the horse-mad American, and he was equally able to indulge his other love – lavish entertaining. The mansion became a magnet for every well-heeled visitor to the Deauville social scene, who dined, danced and drank in its sumptuously furnished rooms. Today, the walls are plastered with a fascinating collection of portraits of Strassburger's prize-winning pure-breds and cartoons of his high-living guests, the international social and racing élite of the 1920s and '30s.

Villa Strassburger
open July–Aug, check with tourist office for exact times; adm

The quirkiest of Deauville's Anglo-Norman edifices is the half-timbered **1913 railway station**, next to the Pont des Belges between Deauville and Trouville, and a short walk from the town's two main yachting marinas. There's more architectural excess on the seafront, in the form of the *grandes dames* of Deauville hotels, the Normandy and the Royal, built in 1912 and 1913 respectively. Despite the efforts of local officials to keep it alive throughout the year, Deauville is pretty quiet outside *La Saison*. From November to Easter its grand mansions are tightly shuttered, and the lines of beach umbrellas stand tied up like brightly coloured palm trees along the beach. But, if you're after peace and quiet, you'll find both in plentiful supply.

Tourist Information in Trouville and Deauville

The Trouville tourist office organizes *Promenades Littéraires* (in French; May–Sept), visiting the Trouville haunts of the writers who have passed through, like Flaubert, Proust or Duras. In July and Aug there are weekly guided tours of the town.

In summer the Deauville tourist office organizes a host of free walking tours of the town, looking at its architecture and/or history. There are also 'Horse Tours' (in French; normally Wed) led by a professional horse trainer, which take you behind the scenes of Deauville's famous racecourse. **Bookings, t** 02 31 63 47 34 or **t** 06 07 25 47 23.

Children may enjoy the **Petit Train Touristique** which runs Easter–Sept, starting at Ciro's restaurant or the Town Hall in Deauville.

Market Days: Trouville: Wed and Sun, Quai Fernand Moureaux, fish market daily; Deauville: Tues, Fri, Sat, and daily July–Aug, Place Morny–Rue Breney.

Post Office: Trouville: 16 Rue Amiral de Maigret; Deauville: Rue Robert-Fossorier.

Where to Stay in Trouville and Deauville

Trouville-sur-Mer ✉ 14360

As everywhere along this coast, prices and availability vary by season.

Le Flaubert, Rue Gustave Flaubert, **t 02 31 88 37 23 *www.flaubert.fr* (€€€). One of few Trouville hotels on the beach, this old place is one of the most comfortable in the town. Try to get a room with a balcony overlooking the sea. *Closed 11 Nov–mid-Mar.*

***Saint James, 16 Rue de la Plage, **t** 02 31 88 05 23 (€€€–€€). Cosy *hôtel de charme* conveniently between the beach, the casino and the riverside quay. Characterful rooms are furnished with antiques, and the lounge has a wonderful fireplace.

Le Fer à Cheval, 11 Rue Victor Hugo, **t 02 31 98 30 20 *www.hotellefera cheval.com* (€€). Mid-range hotel in an attractive old building; rooms are plain but comfortable, the owners are especially friendly, and fresh pastries arrive for breakfast.

La Maison Normande, 4 Place de Lattre de Tassigny, **t 02 31 88 12 25, *www.maisonnormande.com* (€). In an Anglo-Norman villa, this is Trouville's best budget option. Its basic, characterful rooms are all different, so ask to look at a few before you make your choice.

Deauville ✉ 14800

More than in any other of the towns along the Côte Fleurie, Deauville prices vary hugely by season, and many places are closed entirely Nov–Mar.

****Normandy Barrière, 38 Rue Jean-Mermoz, **t** 02 31 98 66 22, *www.normandy-barriere.com* (€€€€€). To splurge on the full Deauville

ⓘ **Deauville >>**
Place de la Mairie,
t *02 31 14 40 00,*
www.deauville.org

ⓘ **Trouville >**
32 Quai Fernand
Moureaux,
t *02 31 14 60 70,*
www.trouville
surmer.org

experience, head for the town's most extraordinary grand hotel. With its sister-hotels the Royal and the Golf, it's owned by the Lucien Barrière empire. The Normandy, a cream and moss-green half-timbered fantasy mansion looking out to sea, is the largest, with 290 rooms and suites, and the only one open year-round. The Royal is almost next door, while the Golf stands in manicured grounds on top of Mount Canisy next, naturally, to the golf course, one of France's finest. Comforts and service at all three are fabulous, including a choice of gourmet restaurants, health and beauty centres, pools and tennis courts. The Normandy's sumptuous lobby pays tribute to the Second Empire founders of Deauville, with great glass chandeliers like golden fireworks.

Villa Josephine, 23 Rue des Villas, t 02 31 14 18 00, www.villajosephine.fr (€€€€€). This half-timbered 19th-century villa is both a piece of history and a work of art. It used to belong to the Duke of Morny's doctor, and each of the nine rooms is named and styled after members of the Duke's family. The result is a *hôtel de charme* that's sophisticated and luxurious – as you'd expect at the price. There's a great garden too.

***L'Augeval, t 02 31 81 13 18, www.augeval.com (€€€–€€). Luxurious, stylish hotel in a turreted Belle Epoque mansion near La Touques racetrack. There's a pleasant garden with a pool, and a gym.

**La Côte Fleurie, 55 Av de la République, t 02 31 98 47 47 (€€). An attractive cream villa that's a good cheaper option. Rooms are simple but stylish, and breakfast is served in the garden or a pretty dining room.

Eating Out in Trouville and Deauville

Trouville-sur-Mer ✉ 14360

Brasserie Les Vapeurs, 160 Quai Fernand Moureaux, t 02 31 88 15 24 (€€€). You may spot Gérard Depardieu here, or the odd Hollywood star –

their photos cover the walls of this bustling brasserie right on the quai. Fish and seafood are natural favourites – served within hours of being caught – but for something lighter there are plenty of salads and local classics. As it's a true brasserie there are no set menus, but they are available in the same owners' Les Voiles restaurant, next door.

Bistrot Les Quatre Chats, 8 Rue d'Orléans, t 02 31 88 94 94, www.les4chats.com (€€€). Cosy hip-bohemian bistro with wooden tables, old prints and intriguing bric-a-brac, including an amazing old coffee machine. A sizeable choice of tapas-style dishes is chalked on a blackboard (there's no set menu) and there's a fine wine selection. *Closed Mon, Tues and Wed.*

Brasserie Le Central, 5–7 Rue des Bains, t 02 31 88 80 84, www.le-central-trouville.com (€€). It's hard to distinguish between this 1930s brasserie and Les Vapeurs alongside, and their terrace tables merge into each other. The emphasis is also on fish and seafood, including *moules* cooked every which way. Above the brasserie, the Central is also a comfortable hotel with 21 rooms (€€). The same owner has recently opened another good restaurant, Les Annexe, on Rue des Bains, t 02 31 88 10 27 (€€).

Tivoli Bistro, 27 Rue Charles Mozin, t 02 31 98 43 44 (€€). Family cooking in simple, friendly surroundings, at very reasonable prices.

Cocotte Café, 58 Rue des Bains, t 02 31 88 89 69, www.cocottecafe.com (€€–€). Down-to-earth, convivial bistro with a big local clientele: the atmosphere is bohemian, the prices modest, and menus are based on whatever's freshest at the market. *Closed Mon and Tues.*

Deauville ✉ 14800

Le Ciro's Barrière, Bd de la Mer, t 02 31 14 31 31 (€€€€). It's chic, the beach, the sea and the casino are a dice's throw away, and the food is exquisite. It naturally isn't cheap, but if you want to indulge in people-watching Ciro's is a big part of the Deauville scene. The dining room is best known for its range of superb seafood, including *lobster à l'armoricaine* or utterly extravagant *plateaux de fruits de mer*. *Closed Tues and Wed.*

Le Spinnaker, 52 Rue Mirabeau, **t** 02 31 88 24 40 (€€€). One of Deauville's best-known restaurants. Specialities include scallops with boletus mushrooms and *salade de* *langoustines aux truffes*; dress smartly. *Closed Mon and Tues.*

Chez Marthe, 1 Quai de la Marine, **t** 02 31 88 92 51, *www.chezmarthe.com* (€€). Trendy but relaxed, without the formality of many Deauville restaurants, this intimate bistro is next to a marina. Menus highlight the day's catch. *Closed Wed and Thurs.*

Houlgate to Cabourg

Houlgate

Little seems to have changed in demure Houlgate since it was built in the mid-19th century as one more Paris-by-the-sea, with its own mini-Bois de Boulogne in an attractive park. A graceful procession of villas, a showcase of French *architecture balnéaire*, lines the promenade above the sandy beach, and visitors still drift to the Casino each evening to try their luck in a respectable manner. The villas are a real mishmash of styles, with touches of Swiss chalet, English manor and Italian villa, but somehow they rub happily along together. The largest were mostly built between 1870 and 1880, and the best are in Rue des Bains, Rue Amédée-René and Rue Baumier. The imposing domed edifice that stands above the eastern end of the beach, once the **Grand Hôtel** but now converted into holiday flats, gives an idea of the splendour of Houlgate in its golden era. The era became even more golden with the arrival of the Paris railway line in 1882, turning Houlgate into one of Normandy's most popular bathing resorts.

Now as then Houlgate is a strictly seasonal town, and often spookily quiet outside the months from June to September. Even in high season, though, it's a relaxing place to stop for a while (and cheaper than other Côte Fleurie resorts). Your most energetic activity may well be popping to the shops on Rue des Bains for a baguette or taking a turn along the promenades, but should you feel more energetic, there's a rewarding walk from Houlgate to the **Vaches Noires** (Black Cows), a dramatic line of strange-looking black-clay cliffs halfway between Houlgate and Villers-sur-Mer to the east. You can walk along the cliffs or along the beach beneath them, but the sea is wilder here, and you need to keep an eye on the shifting tides.

Dives-sur-Mer

If the other Côte Fleurie towns are known for their beaches, Dives-sur-Mer, centuries older than any of the 1860s resort towns

Getting to Houlgate, Dives and Cabourg

Dives and Cabourg share a **train station** (Dives-Cabourg) at the end of the line from Deauville, and there's also a second smaller station in Dives (Dives-Port Guillaume). Trains run up from Paris via Deauville all year on Fri and Sat, and back to Paris via Deauville on Sat and Sun, but from late June to early Sept there are services daily. For all other destinations, change in Deauville.

Bus Verts' Caen–Le Havre **bus** No.20 stops at Houlgate, Dives, Cabourg and most other points along the Côte Fleurie.

around it and slightly inland between Houlgate and Cabourg, is famous as the starting point for the biggest event in Norman history, the invasion of England. William the Conqueror and his men waited for a favourable wind here for four long weeks before setting out for Hastings. At that time the port was one of the largest in the Duchy of Normandy and in the centre of the town, but as the River Dives has silted up in succeeding centuries what harbour there is left has shifted downstream towards the sea. Today Dives' 'Port Guillaume' is populated not by Viking ships but by yachts moored in a modern marina. Further downriver there's still a tiny fishing harbour, where fishermen sell their catch, and at the start of August Dives stages a *Fête de la Mer*.

Just as Cabourg cashes in on Proust, Dives is not shy about William the Conqueror. Just off Rue d'Hastings the ancient collection of half-timbered structures that once formed the village inn – whose guests included Alexandre Dumas – have been made into a **Village Guillaume le Conquérant**, with artists' workshops and, in a geranium-clad courtyard, two enjoyable restaurants. Nearby is the lovely **Place de la République**, which every Saturday hosts a lively market in Dives' vast timber-roofed 15th-century **Halles**, or market hall. Inside, wrought iron signs ensure every stallholder knows his place. The market spills over into the square, around which there are some pleasant, unpretentious bars where you can sit back from the bustle over a café. On the opposite side of the square is a 17th-century mansion, the **Lieutenance**, and just off the *place* is the massive, mostly Gothic church of **Notre-Dame de Dives**, which served as Proust's 'land's end church of Balbec'. Look out for the list of William the Conqueror's comrades, etched on the west wall in the 19th century; you might find an ancestor among them.

Cabourg

⭐ Cabourg

All Cabourg's streets lead to the **Grand Hôtel** (*see* below), the great Belle Epoque edifice in the middle of the seafront from where Marcel Proust watched fashionable holidaymakers parading on the grand promenade – now named the Promenade Marcel Proust. He used their comings and goings as material for his *A la*

Recherche du Temps Perdu, loosely modelling his imaginary town of Balbec on Cabourg. Today the hotel cashes in shamelessly on its Proustian associations with outrageously expensive teas – including madeleines, of course – in its Le Balbec restaurant, and the chance to stay in a room reconstructed to look as it would have when the novelist padded its carpets (his actual room is now occupied by the hotel manager).

Like so many towns along this now neatly-domesticated coast, Cabourg consisted of little more than fishermen's shacks until 1853, when a Parisian lawyer, Henri Durand-Morimbau, decided to flatten the dunes and build a bathing resort, complete with the necessary grand hotel and casino. In the 1880s, when rail links slashed the journey time from Paris to three hours, the resort took off in earnest. Beaux-Arts and Anglo-Norman-style villas sprang up like mushrooms, and in 1907 Cabourg gained still more social cachet when the Grand Hôtel was expanded, revamped and reopened in still more opulent form. It remained fashionable through the 1920s and 1930s, and many French entertainment stars, including Edith Piaf and Jean Richard, graced the stage of its casino-music hall.

With its grand hotel, villas, casino, racecourse and neat gardens, Cabourg hasn't really changed much since Proust's time. It's sedately tranquil, except in July and August, when Parisian families

In Search of Proust

As a child in the 1880s Marcel Proust spent part of each summer in Cabourg, Trouville or Dieppe, with his grandmother. From the dining room of Cabourg's Grand Hôtel (in its first, pre-1907 incarnation), he'd watch the world go by outside its vast windows. 'Whether they were going home to some unknown villa or coming out, racquet in hand, to meet for a game of tennis...', he wrote, 'I watched with passionate curiosity in the blinding light of the beach.' Years later, in 1907, he returned to Cabourg to the recently-reopened Grand to help get over the death of his mother, and his asthma. 'Having heard that there was a hotel in Cabourg reputed to be the most comfortable on the coast, I went there', he told a friend. 'Since I got here I've been able to get up and go out every day, the first time in six years that I've been able to do that'.

Returning year after year, he immersed himself in his favourite activity: people watching. Dressed in his old twill overcoat, he'd sit in the vast chandeliered dining room, observing old ladies walking their poodles and elegant *Parisiennes* sporting their hats and parasols, more interested in being seen than in seeing. At night the same room became the 'aquarium', as locals pressed their faces against the windows, awed by the luxury within, 'as extraordinary to the poor as the life of strange fishes or molluscs.' Cabourg's petty snobberies fascinated Proust, and late at night he'd lure hotel staff into his room to play draughts and fill him with gossip about the other guests, before he settled down to a night's writing. The view from his rooms never failed to thrill him, a feeling reflected by the narrator in *A l'ombre des jeunes filles en fleur*, so excited that he keeps putting down his hotel towel to gaze at the emerald waves.

Today, Proust enthusiasts in Cabourg can join in a range of activities – including talks and guided walks – organized by the Cercle Littéraire Proustien de Cabourg-Balbec (contact Mme Yvette Le Roux, **t** 02 31 91 06 69).

and their dogs return to open up their *maisons secondaires*. Staid Cabourg did manage a brief moment of notoriety in the swinging '60s, when a young lady went topless on the prom, displaying what's said to be the first 'monokini' seen in France. You're unlikely to find such excitement nowadays, but Cabourg can still boast of its 4km beach, one of the best in Normandy, and in June, to compete a little with Deauville's big and glitzy American Film Festival, Cabourg hosts a 'Festival of Romantic Film'. The town's streets, built in a fan pattern around the Grand Hotel, are intersected by a central street, Avenue de la Mer, with most of the shops and restaurants. In summer, children can enjoy a *Petit Train Touristique*, and there's a mini sports complex called **Le Sporting** towards the west end of the prom with a swimming pool, tennis and squash courts, mini-golf and more.

Some 3km west of Cabourg along the coast, at the mouth of the River Orne, is **Merville-Franceville-Plage**, another small, neat seaside town with a long, attractive prom above a fine beach. Seafood restaurants and other French beach pleasures aside, it has another point of interest as the site of a German Second World War gun battery that is now the **Musée de la Batterie de Merville**. The battery consisted of four massive concrete bunkers, built in 1943 and each with a 155mm gun, and would have been in a prime position to bombard the Allied ships and the British beach landings at Sword Beach just to the west on D-Day in 1944. Putting the battery out of action was one of the main objectives of the British paratroop drops on the night of 5–6 June, but the attack on the bunkers almost ended in disaster. Many of the aircraft carrying the men of the 3rd Parachute Brigade to Merville lost their way – in part due to all the smoke and dust thrown up by bombing raids intended to make their job easier – and far fewer than half the intended force of 750 men landed near the target, and then with hardly any of their equipment. Nevertheless, an assault was quickly improvised, and in an hour of savage fighting around 4am the battery was taken and rendered useless, in one of the most remarkable – and bloodiest – incidents of D-Day, with dreadful losses on both sides. The small museum in one of the bunkers tells the story very effectively.

Musée de la Batterie de Merville
www.mairie-merville franceville.fr;
open April–Sept daily 10–6; Oct and 15–31 Mar Sat–Mon and Wed 10–5; adm

Tourist Information in Houlgate, Dives-sur-Mer and Cabourg

In July and Aug the Houlgate tourist office organizes an inspired selection of guided tours (all in French, except by request) on subjects from architecture and archaeology to flora and fauna. They also provide leaflets for a series of self-guided architectural walks.

The Dives-sur-Mer tourist office lays on guided tours, too, during the summer months.

① Dives-sur-Mer ››

9 Rue Général de Gaulle, t 02 31 91 24 66 (July–Aug), otherwise t 02 31 28 12 50, www.dives-sur-mer.com

① Cabourg ››

Jardins du Casino, t 02 31 91 20 00, www.cabourg.net

① Houlgate ›

10 Bd des Belges, t 02 31 24 34 79, www.ville-houlgate.fr

Market Day: Houlgate, Thurs and daily July–Aug; Dives-sur-Mer, Sat, Place de la République; fish market, Fri–Sun am, daily July–Aug, in the port; Cabourg, Wed, Sat–Sun and July–Aug, Place du Marché.

Post Offices: Houlgate, 2 Bd des Belges; Dives-sur-Mer, 2 Rue du Général de Gaulle; Cabourg, 66 Av de la Mer.

Shopping in Houlgate, Dives-sur-Mer and Cabourg

Cave de l'Abbaye, Place du Marché, Dives-sur-Mer, t 02 31 28 04 37. A wonderful wine merchant set in the caves beneath the Lieutenance in Dives-sur-Mer.

A la Recherche du Temps Perdu, 3 bis Av du Cdt Touchard, Cabourg. This place in Cabourg sells vastly overpriced Proustian memorabilia, but it's still a fun shop to wander around, all the same.

Where to Stay and Eat in Houlgate, Dives-sur-Mer and Cabourg

Houlgate ✉ 14510

**Hotel Santa Cecilia, 25 Av des Alliés, t 02 31 28 71 71, *www.hotel-santa-cecilia.com* (€). Friendly family-run hotel in an 1880s villa. The sitting room, where you have breakfast, has been kept just as it was when the villa was built.

1900, 17 Rue des Bains, t 02 31 28 77 77, *www.hotel-1900.fr* (€€€–€€). This vintage brasserie with old-fashioned bar is an architectural gem. The emphasis is on local produce, especially fish and seafood. It also has 18 basic guest rooms (€).

L'Eden, 7 Rue Henri Fouchard, t 02 31 24 84 37 (€€). Lovely décor and superb food, this is Houlgate's best restaurant. The specialities are fish and seafood. *Closed Mon and Tues exc in July and Aug.*

Dives-sur-Mer ✉ 14160

Guillaume le Conquérant, 2 Rue Hastings, t 02 31 91 07 26 (€€€–€€). The more upmarket of the two restaurants in the Village Guillaume le Conquérant. The dining room is cosy and full of beams, in summer you can dine in the courtyard, and the food is excellent. The Ecurie Guillaume le Conquérant, t 02 31 24 08 14, alongside (€€), is more modest but equally scenic, with tables outside in summer. It has a pretty *chambre d'hôtes* too (€). *Restaurant closed Mon eve and Tues.*

Chez Le Bougnat, 27 Rue Gaston Manneville, t 02 31 91 06 13 (€€). Tuck into hearty Norman cuisine surrounded by bric-a-brac and an intriguing range of old posters at this genial restaurant. The atmosphere is very congenial, and the food satisfying and enjoyable. *Closed evenings Sun–Wed exc during July and Aug.*

Cabourg ✉ 14390

****Grand Hôtel, Promenade Marcel Proust, t 02 31 91 01 79, *www.grandhotel-cabourg.com* (€€€€€–€€€). It's impossible to miss this wedding-cake-like palace, dominating the seafront. Prices of its 68 rooms and two suites (including the 'mock-Proust' room) vary according to sea view and amount of luxury. There's also a *salon de thé*, and Proust aficionados will want to dine in the first-class restaurant, Le Balbec (€€€). *Closed Mon and (June–Sept) Tues.*

L'Argentine, 3 Jardins du Casino, t 02 31 91 14 25, *www.argentine-cabourg.com* (€€€–€€). A characterful 1890s villa near the Grand Hôtel, which its owners dub a *chambre d'hôtes de caractère*. Rooms, all with Proustian names, have been elegantly redecorated by the amiable young owners, and in summer you breakfast on a small outside terrace. In the afternoons it turns into a *salon de thé*.

Le Beau Site, 30 Av Maréchal Foch, t 02 31 24 42 88 (€€€–€€). In a 1900s villa, the best restaurant in Cabourg for fresh fish and seafood with a sea view. *Closed Mon.*

Le Champagne, 11 Place du Marché, **t** 02 31 91 02 29 (€€–€). A popular restaurant with locals, providing tasty good-value Norman cuisine. *Closed Sun eve and (June–Sept) Mon.*

Dupont Avec un Thé, 6 Av de la Mer, **t** 02 31 24 60 32 (€). Superb *pâtisserie* that has tables where you can sample its mouth-watering delights, savoury and sweet. There's a branch in Dives (42 Rue G. Manneville).

Le Home-Varaville ✉ 14390

Manoir de la Marjolaine, 5 Avenue du Président Coty, **t** 02 31 91 70 25, *http://manoirdelamarjolaine.free.fr* (€€€–€€). Village and beach are within easy walking distance, but all is tranquil at this attractive 1850 manor surrounded by a leafy park. The four B&B rooms – two classic French, two *exotiques* – have Jacuzzi bathrooms and very luxurious furnishings.

Lisieux and the Pays d'Auge

With its lush landscape of apple orchards, half-timbered farmsteads and harvests of creamy cheeses and fiery calvados, the Pays d'Auge, in the département of Calvados, embodies the essence of what most people think of as Normandy. Three of the four classic Norman cheeses – Pont-l'Evêque, Livarot and Camembert – come from here, as do the area's finest ciders. In the south of this region you'll also find ancient manor houses, the timber-frame market hall of St-Pierre-sur-Dives where a weekly market has been held since the Middle Ages, and some intriguing gardens.

13

Don't miss

⭐ **Cider Country**
Cambremer **p.240**

⭐ **Home of a modern saint**
Lisieux **p.243**

⭐ **The thousand-year-old market**
St Pierre-sur-Dives **p.247**

⭐ **Aristocratic quirkiness**
Château de Vendeuvre **p.247**

⭐ **Normandy's cheese route**
Livarot to Camembert **p.249**

See map overleaf

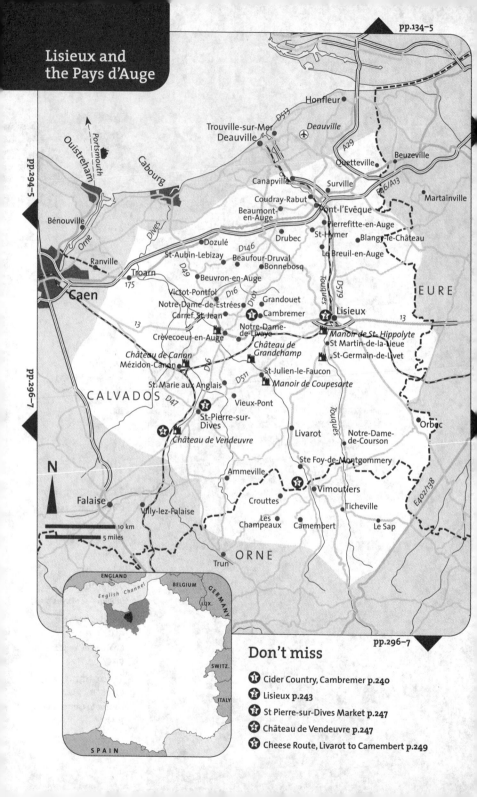

Lisieux and the Pays d'Auge

Honfleur

Trouville-sur-Mer
Deauville
Deauville

Ouistreham
Portsmouth
Cabourg

Quetteville
Beuzeville

Surville

pp.294–5

Canapville
Martainville

Coudray-Rabut
Pont-l'Evêque

Beaumont-en-Auge
Pierrefitte-en-Auge

Bénouville
Drubec
St-Hymer
Blangy-le-Château

Dozulé
Le Breuil-en-Auge

Orne
Dives
St-Aubin-Lebizay
D146

Ranville
Beaufour-Druval

Troarn
Bonnebosq

175
Beuvron-en-Auge

Caen
D49
Victot-Pontfol
D16
Grandouet

Notre-Dame-de-Estrées
Cambremer
Lisieux

Carref. St-Jean
Notre-Dame-de-Livaye
Manoir de St-Hippolyte

EURE

13
St Martin-de-la-Lieue

Crèvecoeur-en-Auge
Château de Grandchamp
St-Germain-de-Livet

13

Château de Canon
D16

Mézidon-Canon
St-Julien-le-Faucon

St-Marie aux Anglais
D511
Manoir de Coupesarte

pp.296–7

CALVADOS
D47

Vieux-Pont

St-Pierre-sur-Dives
Orbec

Livarot
Notre-Dame-de-Courson

Château de Vendeuvre
Touques

Ste-Foy-de-Montgommery

N

Ammeville

Vimoutiers

Falaise
Crouttes
Ticheville

Villy-lez-Falaise
Les Champeaux
Camembert
Le Sap

10 km
5 miles

ORNE

Trun

Don't miss

1. Cider Country, Cambremer **p.240**
2. Lisieux **p.243**
3. St Pierre-sur-Dives Market **p.247**
4. Château de Vendeuvre **p.247**
5. Cheese Route, Livarot to Camembert **p.249**

The Northern Pays d'Auge

Beaumont-en-Auge and Pont-l'Evêque

[It is] the shadiest, wettest country I know... You see no horizon, but only a few copses, filled with mysterious shade, a few cornfields, but chiefly pasture, soft, quietly sloping meadows, where the rich grass is mown twice yearly, where when the sun is low the apple trees give deep shadows, where untended flocks of sheep and herds of cows graze. Every hollow is filled with water: pond, pool, river. On every side streams constantly murmur...

André Gide,
L'Immoraliste

Perched on a rocky outcrop, **Beaumont-en-Auge** straddles the lush rolling landscape of the Pays d'Auge and the flat Touques valley. Climb up to the top of the village, by the castle, and you can see both. Today Beaumont is a peaceful village of some 500 inhabitants with a vibrant artistic community, but in the past it was a pilgrimage site, thanks to a cousin of William the Conqueror's wife, Robert Bertrand, who founded a Benedictine priory here in 1060. Parts of the priory church, **St-Sauveur**, still remain. From the 13th century the priory harboured a military academy, whose star pupil would be the 18th-century mathematician Pierre-Simon Laplace. The Revolution brought the closure of both priory and the academy, but Beaumont has hung onto its architectural treasures, and its houses are an interesting mix of stone, timber and slate, many now occupied by art galleries and chic little shops.

A few kilometres south of Beaumont, just north of the pretty village of **Bonnebosq**, is the 16th-century **Manoir du Champ-Versant**, a small but perfect picture of a Pays d'Auge manor house, with cider press, stables, bakery and barns. It is a showcase of all the region's building styles, with 16th-century towers, 18th-century half-timbered frontage, and checkerboard flanks and chimneys in brick and stone. There are even traces of an old *château-fort* on the site that pre-dated the manor. The splendidly ornate chimneys inside were only recently unveiled by accident during restoration work. Two bedrooms in the manor are rented as *chambres-d'hôte*, with wonderful views over the grounds (*see* p.238).

Pont-l'Evêque

The town of Pont-l'Evêque has become synonymous with its creamy tile-shaped cheese. It's made from the rich milk of Norman cows grazing in the lush countryside around the town, so affectionately described by André Gide, whose family owned the nearby Château de La Roque-Baignard and whose mother lived in Pont-l'Evêque itself. The town itself is an odd mix. Enter from the west along Rue St-Michel and the half-timbered houses suggest another picture-postcard spot like Beuvron or Beaumont – among the finest is the old coaching inn the Aigle d'Or, which now houses one of the region's best restaurants. Alas, however, thanks to its strategic bridge over the Touques the centre of Pont-l'Evêque was badly bombed in 1944, and has mostly been rebuilt. It's still not lacking in provincial charm, though, especially on market day (Monday), when local farmers display mountains of cheeses in the

Getting to the Pont-l'Evêque Region

Pont-l'Evêque has a **train** station on the Paris–Lisieux–Deauville line, although many journeys involve changing at Lisieux. Some journey times are Deauville (10mins), Lisieux (12mins) and Paris-St-Lazare (2hrs 10mins).

Bus Verts' No.50 **bus** route between Le Havre and Lisieux calls at Pont-l'Evêque and Le Breuil-en-Auge, and also Honfleur and several other towns. Route No.36 runs between Pont-l'Evêque and Caen (1hr) around three times daily. **Bus Verts information, t 0810 214 214.**

square beside the river. During Easter, Whitsun and July and August there's also a farmers' market *à l'ancienne* on Sunday mornings, where locals don traditional costumes.

Historically, Pont-l'Evêque has been an important staging post between Bayeux, Caen, Rouen and Lisieux. Its lack of defensive walls often left it vulnerable to attack, however, particularly from the English, who ransacked the town three times. The 13th-century church, **St-Michel**, was partly destroyed at that time and subsequently rebuilt in Flamboyant Gothic style. The town's half-timbered Dominican convent, which now houses exhibitions, dates from around the same period, as do many of the surviving half-timbered houses.

South from Pont-l'Evêque

A couple of kilometres south of town on the D48, a remarkable 12th-century tithe barn in the grounds of the **Château de Betteville** houses a **vintage car museum**, with over a hundred cars dating from 1900 to 1950, from Bugattis to Chevrolets, all smelling of lovely old leather. Wonderfully elegant waxwork ladies step out of the historic vehicles, and there's also an assortment of motorcycles, horse-drawn carriages, some 500 model cars and, if cars don't fire your engine, the château next door holds a display of traditional costume from around the world. In a totally different vein, virtually opposite the château there's a leisure centre on Pont-l'Evêque's ample lake, offering canoeing, tennis, riding or boating.

Vintage car museum
t 02 31 65 05 02; open daily July–Aug 10–7; April–June and Sept 10–12.30 and 1.30–7, Oct–mid-Nov 2–6; adm

The Cheese of Pont-l'Evêque

The first Pont-l'Evêque cheese is believed to have been made by 12th century monks, who called it 'Angelot' (from *Augelot*, meaning 'cheese from Auge'). The earliest written reference to the cheese was made by one Guillaume de Lorris, who in his 1236 *Roman de la Rose* wrote, 'All good tables are equipped with Angelons cheeses as dessert.' It did not acquire its current name until the 17th century. The cheese, which must be made from full-fat unpasteurised milk from Normandy cows, is produced by first packing curds into square moulds, then rind-washing them in salt, leaving them to dry, and stacking them up like books on a shelf to age and acquire their characteristic yellow-orange rind and delicate flavour. Three and a half litres of milk are needed to make a 350g cheese.

Pont-l'Evêque has enjoyed AOC (*Appellation d'Origine Contrôlée*) status since 1976. Standards are maintained by the *Confrèrie des Chevaliers du Pont-l'Evêque*, a select group of local residents who taste different cheeses throughout the year and each May judge a competition in the town. According to the experts in the matter, Pont-l'Evêque should 'smell of earth, but not of manure'.

As you continue south, the countryside gets ever more lush and varied. Up above the Touques valley, **Pierrefitte-en-Auge** – found via a meandering detour off the main Lisieux road – has a church with an interesting 17th-century painted ceiling. Over the top of the next hill, gorgeous **St-Hymer** sits in its own tiny valley beside a babbling brook. It is famous for its ancient priory, founded by Hugues de Montfort in 1066. There are many fine footpaths and bridlepaths from St-Hymer if you want to explore, or an extremely pleasant inn if you just want to watch the world go by.

Château du Breuil
*t 02 31 65 60 00,
www.chateau-breuil.fr;
open daily 9–12
and 2–6; adm*

A little further south, the 17th-century Château du Breuil, outside **Le Breuil-en-Auge**, has been renowned for 50 years as the home of one of the foremost calvados producers in the Pays d'Auge. It's a large, commercial operation, but its slick tours (in French, English or German) are a good introduction to the art of making calvados. The highlight is the *cave*, where ancient oak casks are lined up in a 17th-century barn, giving off delicious vapours that make the air quite intoxicating. Visitors get to taste calvados aged from two to 15 years at the end of each tour.

Tourist Information in the Pont-l'Evêque Region

ⓘ Pont-
l'Evêque >
16 bis Rue Saint-
Michel, Pont-l'Evêque,
t 02 31 64 12 77,
www.blangy-pont
leveque.com

Market Days: Pont-l'Evêque: Mon; also farmer's market Easter Sun, Whitsun and Suns in July–Aug.

Post Office: Pont-l'Evêque, Place Henri Féquet.

Shopping in the Pont-l'Evêque Region

Atelier Fromager de Pont-l'Evêque, Route de Lisieux, Pont-l'Evêque, t 02 31 64 61 96. Cooperative *fromagerie* where the local cheese is made with entirely traditional methods. As well as buying, in July–Aug you can watch it being made. *Closed Sat and Sun.*

Calvados Cœur de Lion, Rte de Trouville, RN177, Coudray-Rabut, t 02 31 64 30 05, *www.coeur-de-lion.com*. Ancient distillery in a stunning half-timbered manor just north of Pont-l'Evêque. There are free guided tours, with the usual *dégustation*. *Closed Sun.*

Calvados Père Magloire, Rte de Trouville, Pont-l'Evêque, t 02 31 64 30 31, *www.pere-magloire.com*. Another big calvados name on the north side of town. Guided tours in several languages. It also has a nice restaurant (*see below*). *Open Easter–Oct daily; adm for guided tour.*

Château du Breuil, Le Breuil-en-Auge, t 02 31 65 60 00, *www.chateau-breuil.fr*. Fine ciders and calvados can also be bought here (*see* also above).

Where to Stay and Eat in the Pont-l'Evêque Region

Beaumont-en-Auge and St-Etienne-la-Thillaye ✉ **14950**

La Maison de Sophie, Le Presbytère, t 02 31 65 69 97, *www.lamaisonde sophie.fr* (€€€€). A stunning *chambres d'hôtes* in an 18th-century presbytery, run by France's top TV chef and best-selling cookery writer Sophie Dudemaine. The five themed rooms are exquisite and at weekends you can order dinner (€€€€), cooked by Sophie's staff. Cookery weekends are often held here. There's a lovely garden too. Minimum stay 2 nights at weekends.

Auberge de l'Abbaye, 2 Rue de la Libération, t 02 31 64 82 31, *www.aubergelabbaye.com* (€€€–€€). Classy restaurant in a smart 18th-century house, presenting Norman cuisine with a sophisticated touch. *Closed (Sept–June) Tues and Wed.*

Bonnebosq ✉ 14340

Manoir du Champ-Versant, D16 road, **t** 02 31 65 11 07 (€). The rooms are simple, and the one in the tower has an outside bathroom, but the experience of staying in this ancient Pays d'Auge manor (*see* p.235) is hard to beat. There are two B&B rooms: breakfast is brought to you in the vast dining room, with a stone fireplace and oak table. There is also a *gîte*, which you can rent by the night (€).

Drubec ✉ 14130

La Haie Tondue, **t** 02 31 64 85 00 (€€€–€€). A huge, famous old coaching inn on the N175 Caen–Pont-l'Evêque road outside Drubec. Menus feature classic Norman dishes with some adventurous touches like delicate fruit sauces. Packed on summer weekends. *Closed Tues and Mon eve exc Aug and public hols; also 1 week Feb–Mar, 1 wk June and most of Oct.*

Pont-l'Evêque and Blangy-le-Château ✉ 14130

Auberge de l'Aigle d'Or, 68 Rue de Vaucelles, Pont-l'Evêque, **t** 02 31 65 05 25 (€€€–€€). This stunning old *relais de poste* is one of the Pays d'Auge's top gastronomic restaurants – with prices to match. Its three dining rooms are separated by vast beams, and there's a fine fireplace. *Closed Tues exc in Aug, Wed and (Nov–Easter) Sun eve.*

Les Tonneaux du Père Magloire, Route de Trouville, **t** 02 31 64 65 20, *www.les-tonneaux-du-pere-magloire.com* (€€). At this restaurant, opposite the distillery, you eat inside ancient cider casks and are served by waitresses in local costume. It may be a tad kitsch but the food here – based on local cheese and cider of course – is good, especially the *fondues normandes*. If you're drinking the cider, be sure to choose the draft, which is superb.

La Galerie d'Art, Le Mesnil sur Blangy, **t** 02 31 64 77 13 (€). Eat while you enjoy the art. There are just five tables at this art gallery-cum-restaurant, whose owner is both a sculptor and a chef. The dishes all use local produce and often have unusual twists. It gets popular in the evenings (but usually closes at 9.30pm) so it's best to book. *Closed Mon, also Tues and Wed in low season.*

St Martin-aux-Chartrains and Surville ✉ 14130

Le Prieuré Boutefol, Surville, **t** 02 31 64 39 70, *www.prieureboutefol.com* (€€). Each of the four B&B rooms in this huge old half-timbered priory northeast of Pont-l'Evêque symbolizes one of the seasons. The autumnal one, in russet reds and oranges, is in the main house, while others are in an outbuilding in the extensive gardens. The owner, Mme Colin, is as charming as her rooms. An exceptional place.

Manoir Le Mesnil, RN177, St Martin-aux-Chartrains, **t** 02 31 64 71 01, *www.manoirlemesnil.com* (€€). An imposing 1900s manor house with large, originally furnished B&B rooms, each one decorated following a theme. It's set back from the main Pont-l'Evêque-Deauville road, and there are two self-catering *gîtes* in the garden at the back.

Pierrefitte-en-Auge and St-Hymer ✉ 14130

Auberge Des Deux Tonneaux, Pierrefitte-en-Auge, **t** 02 31 64 09 31, *www.aubergedesdeuxtonneaux.com* (€€). The Norman classics here are unsophisticated but very tasty, though the best thing about this famous place is its setting, at the top of a hill overlooking one of Normandy's prettiest valleys. In summer, you can survey the scene from check-clothed tables under cherry trees; in winter, you can appreciate the interior of the 17th-century oak-beamed *auberge*. *Closed Sun eve and (Nov–Mar) Mon.*

Auberge du Prieuré de St-Hymer, Le Bourg, St-Hymer, **t** 02 31 64 07 82 (€€). Another half-timbered hostelry, once part of the village's priory. It serves simple meals at reasonable prices, plus one-course dishes, including salads. *Closed Mon and Tues exc public hols.*

The Heart of Cider Country: Beuvron and Cambremer

Beuvron-en-Auge, in the lush heart of the Auge countryside, is one of those places where you have to pinch yourself to believe it's quite real. Its absurdly pretty half-timbered houses clustered around a market square make this one of the most appealing villages in Normandy – even though its good looks attract the coachloads on summer weekends. The oldest of its houses are 16th century, notably the gorgeous **Vieux Manoir** with its fine, gargoyle-like carvings. Others were built two centuries later, when the village was important for tanning and weaving, as streets like **Ruette d'Enfer** (Little Hell Street) recall. Today Beuvron's main income is due, apart from tourism, to horse breeding, as you can see from the stud farms dotting the countryside. It also has a surprisingly sensible range of shops: the usual gift shops are accompanied by a good number of places selling local produce like calvados, cider and cheeses.

Cambremer

The little town of Cambremer, perched on top of a steep hill, is the very heart of cider country. The central Pays d'Auge is the only area in the whole of Normandy that has an official *Appellation Contrôlée* for its cider, and cider produced within the AOC is properly known and labelled as *Cidre de Cambremer* or *Cru de Cambremer*. Cambremer itself is less postcard-pretty than some Auge villages, but also less touristy. With an attractive, steeply-sloping central square and a likeable array of shops, cafés and restaurants, it's a pleasant place to sit for a while and absorb the small-town atmosphere. The best time to see the town is during the *marchés a l'ancienne*, held on Easter Sunday, Whit Sunday and on every Sunday morning during July and August, when small-scale producers from all the nearby villages dress up in traditional

Apple Magic

Apples have flourished in Normandy as long as anyone can remember. The Celts and Romans were equally entranced by the wild apple trees that grew here. In the 13th century, ships from the Bay of Biscay brought in the first grafts of cider apple trees, and varieties like Bisquet and Marin Onfroy made their appearance. As cider-drinking caught on from the 14th century more types of cider apple were developed. Today experts have counted a staggering 100 varieties in Normandy, a tiny selection of which are seen in local markets. Queen of the eating apples is the *Reinette*, sweet, crisp and russet streaked with yellow. *Calville* apples are used in baking, for making Norman apple desserts. Cider apples are quite different, often small, rich in tannin and unsuitable for eating. In the Pays d'Auge, with its AOC for ciders, only 48 apple varieties – all locally grown – are authorized for making cider and calvados. The stars of the bunch are the *Bedan*, the *Frequin Rouge*, the *Mettais* and the *Noël des Champs* (so called because it's picked late, in December). A good calvados generally blends apples of varying sweetness and bitterness.

Getting around the Cider Country

The nearest mainline **train** station for most of this area is Lisieux, with connections to Paris, Rouen and Deauville (*see* p.215). Mézidon-Canon also has a station, on the Caen–Argentan–Alençon and Caen–Lisieux lines, with several trains daily.

Bus Verts' **bus** No.58 between Lisieux and Carrefour St-Jean stops at Cambremer, and route 52 between Lisieux and St-Pierre-sur-Dives goes through Crèvecœur. Some smaller villages have very infrequent bus services. **Bus Verts information, t** 0810 214 214.

Norman costume and display all their farm-produced cheeses, meats and ciders at their very best. On Wednesday afternoons in July and August the tourist office organizes excellent *circuits découverte*, guided tours which take you around manors, stud farms and cider cellars that you would not otherwise get a chance to see.

Jardins du Pays d'Auge
t 02 31 63 01 81; open May–mid-Sept daily 10–6.30; Oct–mid-Nov Mon–Fri 10–5; adm

If you're interested in gardens, it's worth visiting the **Jardins du Pays d'Auge**. Built around a 17th-century half-timbered farm and its outbuildings, it has several themed gardens (including an Angels' Garden and Devils' Garden) and a cute museum of garden tools.

This is also the place to do some serious cider and calvados tasting. One of the most attractive venues is the grand manor just outside Cambremer, by the road south towards Crèvecœur, of Pierre Huet, one of the biggest names in calvados. A lovely way to explore ciders is to follow the **Route du Cidre**, a well-signposted 40km circular route through tiny villages and green, beech-shrouded lanes that takes in around 20 cider producers, large and small, which are open to visitors and sell direct to callers, each one locatable by the official sign of an apple and *Cru de Cambremer*. Most have apple juice, cider vinegar and often calvados as well as ciders, and even if you don't buy at every stop, it's a lovely way to discover some of the most beautiful parts of the Auge countryside. If you fancy a first-hand experience of how cider and calva are produced, in October and November you can join in a *weekend au pressoir*, at which you help gather apples in return for a heart-

🕕 Route du Cidre

The Craft of Calvados

In September, appley vapours pervade the Pays d'Auge, as producers embark on the historic process of making cider and calvados. The first apples are picked between 15 September and the end of October. If they're due to be turned into calvados, they must be washed, crushed and pressed within 48 hours. The juice is left to ferment for one to six months, and then distilled twice using a traditional copper still to separate the alcohol (outside the Pays d'Auge calvados is only distilled once). The first distillation extracts what are called the *petits eaux* ('little waters'), which have an alcohol content of around 30 per cent; the second distillation of the 'little waters' produces a colourless and very strong spirit with 68–72 per cent alcohol.

It must then be aged in oak casks for at least two years, by which time it's gained a rich amber hue, which darkens as the calvados gets older, and a mellow, woody taste, which gets smoother with age. Once the angels have taken their share (in other words, when some has evaporated), the alcohol content drops to between 40 and 45 per cent. The producer then marries calvados from different years, choosing each for its complementary qualities. Once bottled, calvados stops ageing.

warming look at how cider and calvados are made – and of course you're allowed as much cider as you can drink. The tourist office in Cambremer can provide details both of the weekends and of the Cider Route.

Crèvecœur and Canon

From Cambremer a road runs south to St-Laurent-du-Mont and then to the crossroads village of **Crèvecœur-en-Auge**, on the Caen–Lisieux road. Just to the west is the **Château de Crèvecœur**. Since the 1970s it has been owned by the Alsatian Schlumberger engineering family, who have immaculately restored its Norman motte-and-bailey castle and half-timbered outbuildings. No-one quite knows Crèvecœur's origins, although three 11th-century ivory chesspieces unearthed here, believed to be Saxon, have led some to believe that the local lord accompanied William the Conqueror to England. Today, as well as an informative permanent exhibit on medieval building techniques, the castle hosts a range of medieval-themed activities, from concerts in the chapel (where there's a superb collection of medieval instruments) to medieval summer fairs. Another highlight is a 15th-century square dovecote, with accommodation for 1,500 birds. Of more specialist appeal is the owners' **Musée Schlumberger**, dedicated to oil exploration.

A few kilometres to the southwest, the **Château de Canon** on the outskirts of **Mézidon-Canon**, provides a complete contrast to rustic Crèvecœur. The honey-coloured stone mansion was built in the 18th century for Jean-Baptiste-Jacques Elie de Beaumont, a free-thinking lawyer and friend of Voltaire. The château itself is closed to visitors but Canon is best known for its wonderful gardens, virtually as they were when laid out by Elie de Beaumont in line with Enlightenment philosophical ideas. A mix of formal French and untamed English in style, they are budding with follies, fountains, Italianate sculptures and other curiosities, such as the **Chartreuses**, an enchanting series of interconnected walled gardens and orchards. A separate building was used to host the *Fêtes des Bonnes Gens*, 'Festivals of Good People', begun by Elie de Beaumont and his equally liberally-minded wife in 1775, at which deserving local villagers were given prizes for being good head of the family, mother, old man, or whatever. This largesse virtually ruined the family, but stood them in good stead in the Revolution,

Château de Crèvecœur
t 02 31 63 02 45, www.chateau-de-crevecoeur.com; open July–Aug daily 11–7; April–June and Sept daily 11–6; Oct Sun 2–6; adm

Château de Canon
t 02 31 20 05 07, www.chateaude canon.com; open June–Sept Wed–Mon 2–7; Easter–May Sat–Sun 2–6; adm

13 Lisieux and the Pays d'Auge | The Heart of Cider Country: Beuvron and Cambremer

Le Trou Normand

Trou normand means 'Norman hole'. The hole in question occurs about midway through a big Norman meal, when all eating ceases so that diners may quaff a small – or not so small – glass of calvados, to open up a space for the next courses. That done, the meal may recommence.

Normans defend this old tradition with the claim that calvados aids digestion. Nowadays, some restaurants serve the *trou* in the much more refined (and exquisite) form of an apple sorbet, drenched in calvados.

when the château was spared. Its liberal traditions are continued by its current owners, descendents of the Elie Beaumonts, who run the estate as an organic farm. Their produce is on sale in the estate shop.

Tourist Information in Beuvron and Cambremer

ⓘ Beuvron-en-
Auge >>
t 02 31 39 59 14, open
June–Sept only

Market Days: Beuvron-en-Auge: Sat; Cambremer: Fri, also *Marché à l'ancienne* Sun at Easter, Whitsun, July–Aug.

Shopping in Beuvron and Cambremer

Calvados Pierre Huet, Manoir La Brière des Fontaines, 14340 Cambremer, t 02 31 63 01 09, *www.calvados-huet.com*. This classic manor amid 60 hectares of orchards has been home to four generations of calvados-makers. Tours are informative and entertaining, and naturally end with a *dégustation* of calvados of varying ages. You can also picnic in the grounds. *Shop open Mon–Sat and (Easter–Sept) Sun; guided tours (in English on request) Easter–Sept daily, adm, which is deducted from any purchases*.

★ Le Pavé
d'Auge >>

Cidre de Cambremer Grandouet, 14340 Grandouet, t 02 31 63 08 73. Another traditional apple farm producing cider, calvados and *pommeau*, just north of Cambremer. Guided tours (*adm*) are in French, and there's a video in English. *Open daily*.

La Ferme de Beuvron, Beuvron-en-Auge, t 02 31 79 29 19. A farm cooperative that takes over a brick building on the north road out of Beuvron for direct sales of a range of local produce. *Open Sat–Sun all year, and usually daily June–Sept*.

Ferme de la Mimarnel, 14340 Cambremer, t 02 31 63 00 50. Jacques-Antoine Motte makes and sells superb goat's cheese, and with advance notice gives farm tours (any day except Thurs or Sat am). He also makes organic bread, and runs fun days for children. The entrance is on the D50 just east of the crossroads with the D101 from Cambremer.

Where to Stay and Eat around Beuvron and Cambremer

Beuvron-en-Auge ✉ 14430

Aux Trois Damoiselles, Place Michel Vermughen, t 02 31 39 61 38, *www.manoirdesens.com* (€€). The smart, slightly chi-chi, B&B rooms are all the same in this new house, which somehow manages to blend perfectly in the village square. No medieval nooks and crannies, but the house also contains a *salon de thé*, a shop selling local produce, and picnics can be provided on request.

Chez Mme Hamelin, Place de Beuvron, t 02 31 39 00 62 (€). Lovely half-timbered L-shaped house around a flower-filled courtyard. It's in the heart of the village, but the two B&B rooms are very quiet. Nothing is too much trouble for Mme Hamelin, who serves excellent home-made breakfasts. *Closed Nov–Easter*.

Le Pavé d'Auge, Halles Anciennes, t 02 31 79 26 71, *info@lepavedauge. com* (€€€). One of a growing band of Michelin-starred Norman restaurants, the Pavé, in Beuvron's market hall, is a treat, with many succulent specialities. *Closed Mon and (Sept–June) Tues; also first week July and 24 Nov–28 Dec*.

Auberge de la Boule d'Or, Place de Beuvron, t 02 31 79 78 78 (€€). This half-timbered house, opposite the Pavé d'Auge, has a lovely rustic feel, and tasty, solid regional cooking. *Closed (Sept–June) Tues eve and Wed, and all Jan*.

La Forge, Place de Beuvron, t 02 31 79 29 74 (€€). Another mid-budget restaurant inside another wonderful half-timbered house. The menu offers good Norman meat-and-cider classics, and brasserie-style lighter dishes. *Closed Tues and Wed (Mar–Sept), Wed and Thurs (Oct–Feb)*.

Cambremer >
Rue Pasteur,
t *02 31 63 08 87,*
www.cambremer.com

Cambremer ✉ 14340

***Château Les Bruyères**, Route du Cadran, **t** 02 31 32 22 45, *www.chateaulesbruyeres.com* (€€€). Stylish 19th-century residence in quiet countryside east of Cambremer. Bedrooms vary a lot in size (and price – which also changes by season) but all are pretty, with period furniture. There's a garden with a swimming pool, and refined meals can be provided with advance reservation (€€€). They also run occasional cookery weekends.

Manoir de Cantepie, Le Cadran, **t** 02 31 62 87 27 (€€–€). With its myriad turrets and gables, this timber-framed mansion east of Cambremer looks like a dolls' house, but is genuinely from the 1600s. Breakfast is served by your kindly hosts in a fabulous panelled dining room, and the big B&B rooms have many antique touches. The views are superb and the peace is complete; a truly special place to stay.

Au P'tit Normand, Rue Pasteur, Cambremer, **t** 02 31 32 03 20 (€€–€). Attractive little *restaurant–saladerie* on the main square. If you don't want a three-course meal, there's a good choice of entrecôtes, crêpes and salads. *Closed Sun eve and Mon.*

Beaufour-Druval ✉ 14340

Les Puces Gourmandes, Route de Dozulé, **t** 02 31 65 12 91 (€). A cute *salon de thé* and restaurant in the middle of nowhere, northeast of Beuvron. There's a good mix of salads and light dishes, and a mind-boggling list of posh teas. It's mainly open for lunch, but dinners are served with advance reservation, and occasionally there are literary or musical evenings. *Open July–Aug daily, Sept–June Sat–Sun and public hols only.*

Notre-Dame-d'Estrées
✉ 14340

Aux Repos des Chineurs, Chemin de l'Eglise, **t 02 31 63 72 51, *www.au-repos-des-chineurs.com* (€€€–€€). If you like the furniture in your room, say the word: Madame deals in antiques, and most of the furniture in this gorgeous old hotel between Cambremer and Crèvecoeur is for sale. The bedrooms are unfussily elegant, and breakfast is taken in an old dining room that turns into a *salon de thé* for the afternoons. *Hotel closed end Dec–early Mar.*

Notre-Dame-de-Livaye
✉ 14340

Aux Pommiers de Livaye, RN13, **t** 02 31 63 01 28, *http://bandb.normandy. free.fr* (€€). Attractive half-timbered house amid gardens on the N13 road east of Crèvecœur. Rooms, most in a separate little cottage, are packed with pretty knick-knacks, and there's a three-room family suite in the main house, where a truly Norman dinner is served with advance notice. The friendly owners will also fill in any gaps in your knowledge of calvados, cider, or the area. *Closed Dec–Mar.*

Lisieux

⭐ **Lisieux**

Whether its inhabitants like it or not, Lisieux, largest town in the Pays d'Auge, has been pretty much hijacked by a devout country girl with a Mona Lisa smile and a will of iron named Thérèse Martin. Thérèse, who died young a little over a century ago, became a saint, and today makes her presence felt in the form of a monstrous basilica on one of the hills dominating the town, which no one can fail to notice on arrival. The other major recent event that has marked Lisieux was the Second World War, which ripped the heart out of the old city. Post-1945 reconstruction was uninspired and drab. Mercifully, the fine 12th–13th-century Gothic cathedral was largely spared.

Saint Thérèse and her Little Way

Single-minded, sensitive, spirited, and some say sentimental, Thérèse Martin was convinced from an early age that she would become a saint. Almost from the time she learned to talk her goal was to enter the convent of Carmel in Lisieux, following in the footsteps of her elder sisters. Ironically, though, it was not until after her tragically early death that she became famous.

Born in 1873, Thérèse lost her mother to cancer at the age of four, an event that profoundly affected her. The family moved from Alençon to Lisieux, where she was raised by her father and an aunt in an atmosphere of fairly conventional, traditional piety.

There were traits in Thérèse's character, though, which singled her out. At age three she was already pathetically anxious to be good, saying '*Je vais être bien mignonne*'. Her mother had described her as 'of an almost invincible obstinacy'. The main focus of her stubbornness was the convent: she first asked to enter Carmel when she was nine. When she lost her favourite sister to it, she fell ill and nearly died, but was miraculously pulled back from the brink by an apparition of the Virgin. When another sister left for Carmel, her resolve became stronger than ever. She was turned down by the Convent but then went to see the Bishop of Bayeux; when this got her nowhere she secured an audience with the Pope at the Vatican – no mean feat for a 14-year-old country girl.

By the age of 15 she had got her way, giving up soft beds for an unheated cell at Carmel. There she developed her philosophy of the 'Little Way' (Thérèse always loved diminutives: she had been her father's 'Little Queen', and in the convent described herself as a 'Little White Flower' and 'Jesus' little wife'), which can best be summed up by 'I will be good.' Hers was no original or mystical thought, but rather a Way that ordinary souls could grasp. 'In my Little Way,' she wrote, 'there is nothing but very ordinary things; little souls must be able to do everything that I do.' Her aim was not to do extraordinary things but to do ordinary things extraordinarily well.

A couple of years before her death, Thérèse told a fellow nun that 'I shall die soon... I shall send down a rain of roses. I feel that my mission is about to begin, my mission of making others love God as I love Him, of giving my Little Way to souls....' At the age of 24, in 1897, the 'little flower' was felled by tuberculosis.

The most remarkable chapter of Thérèse's life opened after her death. She would probably have disappeared into oblivion had it not been for the posthumous publication of her brief spiritual biography, *L'Histoire d'une Ame* (Story of a Soul). Its impact was mind-blowing: people from all over the world queued up at Carmel's doors asking to enter. Miracles started to happen. A certain Abbé Anne in Bayeux was cured of consumption after pressing a relic of Thérèse to his heart, and other remarkable cures were attributed to her. The Bishop of Bayeux contacted Rome, who looked into the case. She was canonized in 1925, in a ceremony that drew half a million pilgrims.

Saint Thérèse's legacy lives on. In the First World War the French forces adopted her as their protector, and in the 1920s a vast and opulent basilica was begun in Lisieux, while all over Normandy statues appeared of the nun clutching her trademark white roses. Coachloads of pilgrims come to Lisieux today to see her relics. And even those who find her cult treacly admit that Thérèse was extraordinary in her ordinariness.

Basilique de Ste-Thérèse
open daily April–Sept 8–8; Oct–Mar 9.30–6

Diorama
open daily Easter–Oct 11–1 and 2–6; Nov–Easter 2–5; adm

Le Carmel
open daily April–Oct 7–7; Nov–Mar 7–6.30

Les Buissonnets >>

The stone and concrete neo-Byzantine **Basilique de Ste-Thérèse**, consecrated in 1954, is one of the largest churches built in France since the Middle Ages. Capable of holding 4,000 people, it has vast domes lined inside with colourful mosaics reflecting on the message of the 'little saint'. The gentle dramas of Thérèse's life are recounted by waxworks in the **Diorama** in Rue Jean XXIII. Thérèse was buried in the chapel of **Le Carmel**, the convent in Rue de Carmel, where she lived until her death. The final bead in the Sainte-Thérèse rosary is **Les Buissonnets**, the bourgeois house where Thérèse lived between the ages of four and 15. You pass a handful of trinket shops to get to the house on Rue des

Getting to and around Lisieux

Lisieux is the main rail junction between Rouen and Caen: there are frequent **trains** to/from Caen (30mins), Rouen (1hr 30mins), Deauville (20mins) and Paris (1hr 45mins). **SNCF information**, t 0836 35 35 35. Bus Verts has efficient services to Le Havre (route 50) via Honfleur, and there are also regular **buses** to Deauville, Vimoutiers, St Pierre-sur-Dives and Orbec. Inside Lisieux, from in front of the Cathedral, Lexobus No.3 runs to Les Buissonnets, and No.1 to the rail station.

<< **Les Buissonnets**
open Easter–
Sept daily 9–12 and
2–6; Feb–Mar and Oct
10–12 and 2–5; Nov–Jan
10–12 and 2–4

Cathédrale
St-Pierre
open daily 9–6

Musée d'Art et
d'Histoire
open Wed–Mon
2–6; adm

Buissonnets, where elderly ladies show you around, aided by tape recordings on key episodes of saint's life.

If you've overdosed on saintly kitsch, the sobriety of Lisieux's **Cathédrale St-Pierre** comes as a breath of fresh air. It was begun in 1035 but struck by fire in 1136, and then rebuilt from around 1160. It is famous for being the first cathedral in Normandy to have used flying buttresses to support its vaults. The Lady Chapel was built in 1432 on the orders of Pierre Cauchon, the Bishop of Lisieux who sentenced Joan of Arc to death. This is where Thérèse, who, not surprisingly idolized Joan, took first communion. Cauchon's tomb is to the left of the altar. There are other pleasing carvings as well, whose (often irreverent) details contrast with the cathedral's austere lines – look out for the cheeky jester dancing above the headless statue of a bishop in the south transept.

Also worth visiting is the **Musée d'Art et d'Histoire** on Boulevard Pasteur, which tells the story of Lisieux's wartime devastation and also has an interesting collection of the famous *Pré d'Auge* ceramics which decorate so many of the region's manors.

Tourist Information in Lisieux

(i) **Lisieux >**
11 Rue d'Alençon,
t 02 31 48 18 10,
www.lisieux-
tourisme.com

As well as the Lisieux tourist office, there's a **Pilgrims' Information Centre** at 31 Rue du Carmel, **t** 02 31 48 55 08, *www.therese-de-lisieux.com*
Internet Access: Web Café, 6 Place de la République
Market Days: Sat, Place de la République; in July–Aug there's also a *marché à l'ancienne* in Place François Mitterrand, Wednesday pm, selling crafts and gourmet foods.
Post Office: Place François Mitterrand

Where to Stay and Eat in Lisieux

Lisieux ✉ 14100
***Azur Hotel**, 15 Rue au Char, **t** 02 31 62 09 14, *www.azur-hotel.com* (€€).

Newly refurbished and centrally located hotel with friendly staff. Rooms are spotless and light, and some have the odd beam or too as a reminder of old Lisieux.
***La Place**, 67 Rue Henry Chéron, **t** 02 31 48 27 27, *www.lisieux-hotel-delaplace.com* (€€). On the central square, this hotel's greatest asset is its views of the cathedral. Rooms are unexciting but well-equipped.
La Baronnière, 14100 Cordebugle, **t** 02 32 46 41 74, *www.labaronniere.connectfree.co.uk* (€). Wonderful old house in large grounds which include a lake. It's run by English Christine and her French husband who cooks regional meals using local produce (€€€, order in advance). The double room in the old pantry has a Louis XIV bed; the other double is in an outside barn with its own entrance.
Les Acacias, 13 Rue de la Résistance, **t** 02 31 62 10 95 (€€€–€€). The cream

and pale green colour scheme gives this traditional restaurant a pleasant airy feel, and there's a good range of set menus including many satisfying Norman classics. *Closed Sun eve, Mon and (Nov–April) Thurs eve.*

Le Relais des Quatre Routes, 14100 Ouilly le Vicomte, **t** 02 31 32 91 66 (€).

If you want excellent unpretentious food at excellent prices, this is your place. Working locals eat here at lunchtime – no frills but a jolly good three-course meal with wine and coffee is yours for a mere €11. *Closed Sat eve and Sun; evenings by reservation.*

The Southern Pays d'Auge

Grand Châteaux and St-Pierre's Celebrated Market

Domaine de St Hippolyte
open Easter–Sept daily 10–6, adm

South of Lisieux there is a landscape of more open, gently undulating lushness, dotted with more apple orchards and farmsteads. Just outside **St-Martin-de-la-Lieue**, 4km from the city, is the **Domaine de St Hippolyte**, a slickly-run manor farm where Norman cows gently munch beneath apple trees. The 16th-century house is closed to the public, but what's special about the *domaine* is that all the other half-timbered buildings, its dairy, cider press, bread oven and dovecote, are still intact, and are used to explain how a self-supporting Norman farm was once run. In the morning you can get a glimpse of white-bonneted milkmaids pressing curds into cheese moulds, and at the end of the day can watch the cows being milked. Visitors can also taste the produce and cider (which can be bought in the shop), and picnic in the grounds.

St-Germain-de-Livet
open Feb–Sept and mid-Oct–Nov Wed–Mon 11–6, last admission 1hr before closing time; adm

Another 5km south, the fairy-tale château of **St-Germain-de-Livet** stares serenely from behind flower-filled gardens and its moat, on which swans gracefully glide. The original 15th-century manor, built on the site of a 12th-century moated castle, was a half-timbered affair; the exquisite turreted castle we can see today with its checkerboard of glazed bricks and stone was mostly added between 1561 and 1588. The central archway leads to an arcaded courtyard with delicate Renaissance decoration, off which the *Salle des Gardes* has remarkable 16th-century biblical frescoes. Vast beams dominate, and the Louis XV room has more superb *Pré d'Auge* glazing, this time on floor tiles. Delacroix lived here for a time, and there are souvenirs of him in the *Chambre de Delacroix*.

To the west, the unspoilt village of **St Julien-le-Faucon** is sandwiched between two of the Pays d'Auge's loveliest half-timbered manors, neither of which, alas, is open to visitors. North of St-Julien, the **Château de Grandchamp** was built in two stages in the 16th and 17th centuries, with oriental-looking turrets. To the south is the 15th-century **Manoir de Coupesarte**, with a placid moat and half-timbered turrets on all four corners. The rambling manor is slightly dilapidated in places, but that adds to its charm.

Getting around the St-Pierre Region

St-Pierre-sur-Dives has a **train** station, on the Caen–Argentan–Alençon–Le Mans line, with several trains daily. Most trains also stop at Mézidon-Canon (*see* p.240). Bus Verts' **bus** No.62 runs between Mézidon-Canon and Falaise via St-Pierre, and route 52 links St-Pierre to Lisieux.

St-Pierre-sur-Dives

This small town on the banks of the Dives is the main hub of the southern Pays d'Auge thanks to its famous market, held every week since the early Middle Ages. The central stage for this colourful theatre is the **Halles**, the vast timber-frame market hall which was first built in the 11th century and has been rebuilt several times since, most recently after being bombed in 1944. Its solid wood-beam frame rests on low stone walls, and the whole 70-metre-long construction is held together by chestnut pegs. Inside on market day (Monday), the Halles offers a rare window onto rural Norman life. Country folk set up stalls laden with rustic riches from live chickens, ducks and fat *saucissons*, to fruit and veg and the very best Camembert and Livarot cheeses. Outside the Halles, the market oozes like a runny Camembert across the surrounding squares, where you can find more farm produce and anything from shoelaces to second-hand car parts. Then, at midday, the market disappears and the ancient stone town returns to its sleepy self.

The market was created by monks at **St-Pierre's Abbaye**, originally founded by Comtesse Lesceline, William the Conqueror's aunt. After the Revolution its church became the town's parish church, and the monastery buildings were sold off. Today only the **Abbatiale** church, part of the cloisters, and the lovely 13th-century **Salle Capitulaire** (Chapterhouse) can be visited, but the town is slowly restoring other buildings. Most of the church is Gothic, although a 12th-century Norman tower, topped by an octagonal spire, still remains, known as the **Tour St-Michel**. The highlights are its delicate 14th-century Gothic façade, its harmonious triple-deckered nave, and the Flamboyant Gothic north tower.

One of the old monastery buildings, south of the church, contains the tourist office and the **Musée des Techniques Fromagères**, which tells you everything you ever wanted to know about cheese-making in painstaking detail, coagulable proteins and all. The best bit is the robotic cow, whose innards light up as they convert grass into milk. St-Pierre is also famous for leather, and there's an interesting walk to follow around the old **Quartier des Tanneries** with water mill and wash house.

Château de Vendeuvre

Most French châteaux manage to be either elegant or entertaining (a few do neither), but Vendeuvre is one of the few that succeed in being both. Original, quirky, and full of sedate

Halles
open on non-market days Easter–Oct 8–7

St-Pierre's Abbaye
abbey and cloister open 9–6; salle capitulaire open daily 9.30–12.30 and 1.30–6

Musée des Techniques Fromagères
open May–Oct Mon–Fri 9.30–12.30 and 1.30–6, Sat 10–12 and 2–5; Nov–April Mon–Fri 9.30–12.30 and 1.30–5.30, Sat 10–12; adm

Château de Vendeuvre
t 02 31 40 93 83, www.vendeuvre.com; open May–Sept daily 11–6; April daily 2–6; Oct Sun 2–6; 1st half Nov daily 2–6; adm

surprises, it's a château where the owners' evident wealth has been put to stylish use. The Count and Countess of Vendeuvre's enthusiasm is boundless, whether expressed in miniature furniture, dog kennels ancient and modern, or extravagant water gardens. This is not to mention the splendid house itself, owned by the family since it was built in 1750.

The *orangerie* contains the **Museum of Miniature Furniture**, a collection that began when the current Countess, aged seven, admired a miniature 18th-century writing desk in the home of an elderly aunt. The old lady gave it to her as an 18th birthday present: the tiny desk is a gem, with La Fontaine's fables daintily illustrated in exotic woods. There are around 750 items in the collection (still-expanding), dating from the 16th century to the 1930s. They range from 'masterpieces', made by apprentices to qualify as craftsmen, to models of larger furniture and pieces made expressly for children. Exquisite works of craftsmanship, they often have light-hearted touches that children enjoy, such as tiny mice or other animals crouching in corners.

The **château** itself was designed by Jacques-François Blondel, a noted architectural teacher of the era, in a restrained, Louis XV style. Its lovely period furnishings escaped the wrath of the Revolutionaries; the château was less lucky in 1944, and has had to be painstakingly restored. There are plenty of interesting oddities in the spacious rooms, like a 19th-century fish-shaped chandelier, syringes used to powder wigs and a collection of automated life-size puppets, which include haughty ladies whose bosoms puff in and out like robin's breasts as they pour tea or write letters. There's more aristocratic quirkiness in the basement, in a **collection of animal kennels**, which often mimic the furniture of their owners: the most over-the-top is an 18th-century marquetry bed-kennel, trimmed with damask. The Count's passion, meanwhile, is outside the house in the **Jardins d'Eau 'Surprises'**, a fanciful water garden with concealed fountains that spring to life when you're least expecting them. There's also a collection of exotic birds and animals, and the gardens are as entertaining as the château.

Tourist Information in St-Pierre

(i) **St-Pierre-sur-Dives >**
Rue Saint-Benoist,
t *02 31 20 97 90,*
www.mairie-saint-pierre-sur-dives.fr

(★) **L'Auberge de la Levrette >>**

Market Days: St-Pierre-sur-Dives: Mon; 1st Sun of month the *Halles* host an antiques market; mid-July–Aug the Abbey cloisters host *Les Animations du Cloître*, a farmers' market with displays of local produce, craft skills and folklore, held every Friday 5–8pm.

Post Office: St-Pierre-sur-Dives, Place du Marché.

Where to Stay and Eat around St-Pierre

St-Julien-le-Faucon ✉ **14140**
L'Auberge de la Levrette, **t** 02 31 63 81 20 (€€). Originally a hunting lodge for the Marquis de Grandchamp, lord of the nearby château. The restaurant is a local favourite. Be sure to try chef Georges Fayet's famed *variation sur le thème de la pomme. Closed Mon and Tues, exc on public hols.*

Ste-Marie-aux-Anglais
✉ 14270

L'Auberge du Doux Marais, Ste-Marie-aux-Anglais, 14270 Mézidon, t 02 31 63 82 81 (€€). At this ancient farm deep in the countryside, diners sit at wooden tables while home-reared meats are grilled over a wood fire. Specialities include *galette au Camembert* as starters. Always book in advance.

Vieux-Pont-en-Auge ✉ 14140

Le Manoir du Lieu Rocher, t 02 31 20 53 03, *www.castleinnormandy.com* (€€). Splendid old half-timbered manor run by a vivacious singer and her pianist husband. Its *chambres-d'hôte* rooms are exceedingly comfortable, and there's an apartment for five. A

perfect place to relax, and the little hamlet of Vieux-Pont is a gem.

St-Pierre-sur-Dives ✉ 14170

Château des Roches, 37 Rue du Bosq, t 02 31 20 60 80, *www.chateaudesroches.com* (€€). Elegant mansion – scarcely a 'château' as such – in a quiet back street in St-Pierre with large, smartly furnished B&B rooms. The friendly young owners also provide dinner (€€) on request.

Ferme de l'Oudon, Berville-L'Oudon 14170, t 02 31 20 77 96, *www.fermedeloudon.com* (€€). Beautifully converted stone farm with three fabulous B&B rooms, and three *gîtes*. In summer you eat your gourmet breakfast in the garden. Evening meals (€€€) available Mon–Wed if booked. A gem.

The Cheese Route

⭐ The Cheese Route

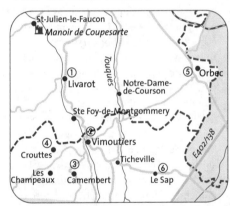

Every Norman is familiar with **Livarot**'s ① famous cheese, with its orange-ribboned rind, and you can buy it in any of the little town's many excellent food shops. To see how Livarot cheese is made, head for the

Village Fromager
42 Rue du Général Leclerc; open Mon–Fri 9.30–12 and 1.30–5, Sat 9.30–12

Village Fromager dairy on Rue du Général Leclerc, which also has a mini-museum and shop. During the first weekend of August the village stages a whiffy two-day *Foire aux Fromages* at which hundreds of the pungent cheeses are displayed and tasted. Otherwise, there's little to detain anyone in Livarot, another Norman town that was badly hit in the Second World War.

Continuing south through the verdant countryside studded with apple and pear orchards below Livarot you reach **Vimoutiers** ②, whose main square is dominated by statues of a cow and Marie Harel, the farm girl credited with 'inventing' Camembert cheese. The town's endearingly old-fashioned **Musée du Camembert** has a unique collection of milking and cheese-making implements, cheese labels and photos of milkmaids laden like oxen with milk churns, which well convey what a back-breaking job this was. In

Musée du Camembert
Avenue Général de Gaulle; open Mar–Oct Mon–Sat 9–12 and 2–6, Sun and public hols 10–12 and 2.30–6; adm

Getting around the Cheese Route

Bus Verts' **bus** No.53 runs regularly between Lisieux and Vimoutiers, via Livarot, and STAO bus No.51 links Vimoutiers and L'Aigle, via Ticheville and Le Sap.

the third week of October, Vimoutiers hosts an **Apple Fair**, including a competition to make the longest apple peel.

Camembert and Crouttes

Around Vimoutiers the landscape becomes still lusher and more undulating, dotted with ancient half-timbered farmsteads and milk-heavy cows. In spring, when the apple trees are in blossom, it's very near to paradise. Don't let this beauty distract you from finding the tiny turning to **Camembert** ③, a village so small you could miss it if you blink. The church and the *Mairie* are the main buildings in this mythical village of 185 souls, most of whom live in farms around it. Unlike the farms that make the authentic cheese, the **Ferme Président** and neighbouring **Maison du Camembert** are unashamedly commercial outfits, run by the largest factory manufacturer of camembert cheese, Président. Nonetheless it's an entertaining place to visit, in two parts. The first is a museum with every kind of information on the manufacture of the cheese, and full of fascinating, information-heavy facts such as the statistic that some 560 million camemberts are produced in France each year. The second section is the cheese-shaped shop, selling all manner of cheesabilia from cheese knifes and boards to cheese itself. Visitors can also begin the all-important task of tasting.

Maison du Camembert
t 02 33 12 10 37; ferme open June–Aug daily 10–12.15 and 2–6; adm; Maison du Camembert open May–Aug daily 10–6.30, Mar–April and Sept–Oct Wed–Sun 10–5.30

At the top of Camembert village is the splendid 16th-century **Manoir de Beaumoncel**, home of Marie Harel (*see* opposite), where she once hid her priestly cheese expert. Unfortunately, because of strict hygiene regulations it's virtually impossible to blow in on a Camembert farm and watch any cheese being made – with the exception of **Ferme de la Héronnière** (*see* under 'Shopping' below).

Manoir de Beaumoncel
open sometimes in the afternoon June–Aug; check with tourist office

Perched on a hilltop a few kilometres northwest of Camembert, **Crouttes** ④ boasts a 12th-century church where Harel was christened, a couple of cider farms, a great *ferme-auberge* (*see* p.252) and the beautiful **Prieuré St-Michel**. This Benedictine priory,

Prieuré St-Michel
open May–Sept Wed–Mon 2–6; adm

Lovely Livarot

The uninitiated may be startled by Livarot's pungent odour, orange-brown crust, and deep, but not overly strong, flavour, but persevere, as the cheese grows on you. Its distinctive feature is the five bands wrapped around the sides of the cheese to preserve its shape, giving it the nickname *le colonel*. Once made of sedge grass, the bands are now usually made of paper. The cheese, matured for four to six weeks, has been made on a select handful of farms around the town of Livarot since the 13th century, and one of its early promoters was Thomas Corneille, brother of the famous playwright Pierre. In the 19th century Livarot, was Normandy's best-known cheese, and dubbed 'the workman's meat', but only since 1975 has it enjoyed an *appellation d'origine contrôlée*.

The Legend of Camembert

New York is like a Gothic Roquefort cheese. San Francisco makes me think of a Roman Camembert.
Salvador Dalí

Not Normandy's oldest, but its most famous cheese, Camembert was 'invented' by a farm girl from the village of the same name called Marie Harel in 1791. A priest fleeing the Revolution hid in her house, and suggested changes in the way she made cheese, using techniques from his own native region of Brie. The new rich cheese was an instant hit in the weekly market at Vimoutiers, and Harel passed her secret on to her son-in-law Thomas Paynel, who developed the cheese's shape, consistency and taste. Its biggest marketing coup occurred by chance when Napoléon III, passing through to open a railway, tasted the cheese and loved it. He asked for more, and named the cheese after the first village where it was made. Camembert reached Paris for the first time in 1863.

The invention shortly afterwards of the characteristic round wooden box, made from poplar, further enabled the gooey cheese to be transported to cheeseboards around the world. Early camemberts often bore names such as *Camembert de la République* or *Camembert du 14 Juillet* in homage to its Revolution-era origins, but over the years Joan of Arc and all sorts of other figures have made their way onto cheese boxes. In 1983 true *Camembert de Normandie* was endowed with an AOC denomination, to help differentiate it from the pallid imitations that have sprung up worldwide. The real things are made with unpasteurized milk, curdled with rennet, moulded with a ladle then drained, salted, turned, removed from the mould, and left to mature for a month in a dry cellar, so that the skin forms naturally.

once a dependent house of the Abbey of Jumièges in the Seine valley (*see* p.144), dates from the 13th century, but an older priory stood here even before that. It has a delightful park and gardens, and an enormous tithe barn where concerts, exhibitions and workshops are held between April and September. There's also an intimate chapel, a huge cider press which in summer hosts a tea-room and restaurant, and B&B rooms in the priory's lovely half-timbered cottages (*see* p.252).

Orbec and Le Sap

On the eastern edge of the Pays d'Auge, **Orbec** ⑤ is an attractive town with a good bunch of medieval houses, in one of which Claude Debussy stayed when he wrote *Jardin sous la Pluie*. To the southwest is **Le Sap** ⑥, a pleasant village with an ancient cider farm in its outskirts that has been beautifully restored and converted into a community-run complex that includes a quite sophisticated restaurant (*see* p.252), library, exhibition hall and, in the old cider press, the **Ecomusée de la Pomme au Calvados**, a fabulous collection of ciderabilia, from rickety wooden apple-presses to old stills and *cigares*, small elongated calvados barrels that Normans hid under their carriage seats at times in the 19th century when the French tax authorities made it illegal to transport alcohol without paying stiff duties. There's also an orchard displaying around 40 varieties of apple trees, and a kitchen garden with vegetables and herbs that have long disappeared from conventional shop displays. In November the museum hosts a very popular *Fête du Cidre*.

Ecomusée de la Pomme au Calvados
www.le-grand-jardin. asso.fr; open June–Sept Tues–Sun 10.30–12.30 and 2–6.30; Oct–Dec Wed–Sat 10–12 and 2–6, Sun 10–12; Mar–May Sun 2–6; adm

(i) **Vimoutiers** >
21 Place de Mackau,
t *02 33 67 49 42,*
otpaysducamembert@
orange.fr

(i) **Livarot** >
1 Place Georges
Bisson, **t** *02 31 63 47 39,*
www.ot-livarot.org

Tourist Information along the Cheese Route

Market Days: Livarot: Thurs;
Vimoutiers: Mon pm, Fri am.

Shopping along the Cheese Route

Ferme de Cutesson, Route de Gacé,
Vimoutiers, **t** 02 33 39 18 53.
Picturesque organic farm selling first-
rate cider and *poiré. Closed Sun.*

Fromagerie Durand de La Héronnière,
Camembert, **t** 02 33 39 08 08. The
only farm where you can watch
Camembert being made, 2km outside
the village on the road towards Trun.
Guided tours July–Aug Mon–Sat.

La Galotière, Crouttes, **t** 02 33 39 05
98. Half-timbered manor 5km west of
Vimoutiers producing organic cider,
poiré, pommeau and calvados.

Where to Stay and Eat along the Cheese Route

Livarot ✉ 14140

Manoir de Courson, Notre-Dame-de-
Courson, **t** 02 31 32 30 69 (€€€).
Splendid half-timbered manor in
tranquil gardens, 10km east of Livarot.
The exquisite suites are mostly in a
separate building, but you breakfast
in the main house with hosts Gérard
and his Cambodian-born wife
Sopheakna, whose origins inform
much of the décor. A swimming pool
completes the picture. *Closed Nov.*

Manoir de Belleau-Belleau, Notre-
Dame-de-Courson, **t** 02 31 32 32 57,
accueil.decouverte@wanadoo.fr (€€).
Attractive red-brick manor in large
grounds on a quiet back lane. The
B&B rooms are smart without being
ostentatious. There's also a *gîte.*

**Hôtel du Vivier, Place de la Mairie,
Livarot, **t** 02 31 32 04 10 (€). Old-style
Logis hotel in the town centre with
unsophisticated but comfy rooms. The
hotel is best known, though, for its
impressive restaurant, Le Cottage (€€).

Crouttes ✉ 61120

Le Prieuré St Michel, **t** 02 33 39 15 15,
www.prieure-saint-michel.com (€€€).

There are five plush, traditionally-
styled rooms in the outhouses around
the priory courtyard. Dark gnarled
beams and terracotta-tiled floors
abound. There are also two self-
catering *gîtes,* housed in the former
bakery and dairy.

Ferme-Auberge 'Du Haut de Crouttes',
t 02 33 35 25 27 (€€). Crouttes' other
major attraction, this rambling half-
timbered farm, offers hearty dinners
in a converted barn looking on to the
courtyard. Typical fare is country
favourites like *poulet au camembert,*
yummy apple puds and *teurgoule* (rice
pudding). Book ahead. *Closed Sun eve.*
There are also two simple rooms (€).

Les Champeaux-en-Auge ✉ 61120

La Camembertière, **t** 02 33 39 31 87
(€€–€). Not surprisingly given its
name, cheese is king at this friendly
roadside restaurant – but there are
plenty of other Norman goodies too,
including fine local meats. Everything
you eat is produced within a 10km
range of the restaurant. *Closed
(Oct–April) Sun eve and Wed.*

Ticheville ✉ 61120

La Maison du Vert, **t** 02 33 36 95 84,
www.maisonduvert.com (€). Run by
two Brits, with two simple yet smart
B&B rooms. Below them there's a
great rarity in Normandy, a vegetarian
restaurant (€€). Dishes are colourful
and innovative, using their own
garden produce wherever possible,
and there are delicious fruit desserts.
Closed Oct–Mar.

Le Sap ✉ 61470

Les Saveurs du Grand Jardin, **t** 02 33
36 56 88, *www.le-grand-jardin.asso.fr*
(€€–€). Elegant restaurant in Le Sap's
beautifully restored cider farm and
community centre. Traditional
Norman classics are served with some
original touches, and local produce is
used wherever possible. *Closed Sun
eve and Mon, (Oct–May) Mon–Thurs.*

Les Glycines, 2 Rue Hubert Laniel,
t 02 33 39 41 59 (€). Lovely down-to-
earth restaurant in the centre of the
village whose menu, chalked on a
blackboard, changes every day
according to what's at the market.
Closed Mon lunch, Tues and Wed lunch.

The D-Day Coast,
Caen and Bayeux

The coast between Caen and the Cotentin peninsula contains some of the best-known beaches in the Western world, thanks to their role in the Allied invasion of German-occupied France on 6 June 1944. Remnants and memories of the D-Day landings pervade this shoreline, the eastern stretch of which is known today as the Côte de Nacre or 'Mother of Pearl Coast', with its old-fashioned seaside resorts. Inland is the Bessin, a region where fortified medieval farms lord it over rolling expanses of farmland. Then there are the cities Caen and Bayeux, the former home to an imposing pair of abbeys, the latter known across the world for its extraodinary medieval tapestry.

14

Don't miss

⭐ **A profoundly moving museum**
Mémorial de Caen **p.262**

② **A beach and a floating harbour**
Arromanches **p.268**

③ **Wide sands and memories**
Omaha Beach **p.273**

④ **A watery wilderness**
The Bessin-Cotentin Marshes **p.276**

⑤ **The longest cartoon strip in history**
Bayeux **p.284**

See map overleaf

Iles St-Marcouf

Cotentin

D902

D2

p.326

St Martin-de-Varreville

Utah Beach

La Madeleine

Ste-Mère-Eglise

St Sauveur-le-Vicomte

Ste-Marie-du-Mont

Grosse-Fontenay

Grandcamp-Maisy

Pointe du Hoc

Vierville-sur-Mer

St-Laurent-sur-Mer

Moitiers-en-Bauptois

Douve

E3-E46

D913

La Rive

Baie des Veys

D514

900

St Côme-du-Mont

Appeville

St-Germain-du-Pert

E46/13

D903

Carentan

Isigny-sur-Mer

Bessin

Vouilly

Parc Naturel des Marais du Cotentin et du Bessin

Lison

Le Breuil-en-Bessin

Lessay

Vire

Le Molay-Littry

D15

Forêt de Cerisy

650

Périers

D2

Cerisy-la-Forêt

Abbaye de Mondaye

Balleroy

Vire

D72

N

St-Lô

D11

MANCHE

Coutances

Torigni-sur-Vire

10 km

5 miles

D7

p.290

Caen

Caen was the child of Normandy's greatest love affair, between William the Bastard (Conqueror to be) and Matilda of Flanders. William had already built himself a stronghold there. Then, when William made Matilda his bride the Pope excommunicated them on the grounds that they were distant cousins, and to placate him and their consciences William and Matilda each built an expiatory abbey, a sort of His and Hers, a few kilometres apart. Residential districts sprang up around them. Caen had been born.

Miraculously, those abbeys, the Abbaye-aux-Dames and the Abbaye-aux-Hommes, were spared during the 1944 battles, which

E n g l i s h   C h a n n e l

Côte   de   Nacre

Portsmouth

Omaha Beach

Colleville-sur-Mer
Port-en-Bessin
Longues-sur-Mer
Tracy-sur-Mer
Arromanches
Gold Beach
Ver-sur-Mer
Courseulles-sur-Mer
Bernières-sur-Mer
St-Aubin-sur-Mer
Langrune-sur-Mer
Luc-sur-Mer
Juno Beach
Sword Beach
Merville-Franceville plage
Cabourg

D514
Maisons
Magny-en-Bessin
Ryes
D65
D514
Crépon
Seulles
Reviers
Douvres-la-Delivrande
Ouistreham
Riva Bella
Dives
Sully
D12
Creully
Fontaine-Henry
Thaon
Mathieu
Bénouville
Ranville
Dozulé

Bayeux
St Loup-Hors
N13-E46
D22
Orne
D49

D15
Subles
Rots

Juaye-Mondaye
Audrieu
Carpiquet
Airport
Caen
Troarn

D13
D9
175

Tilly-sur-Seulles
Tessel
Eaor/A84
13

Caumont-l'Eventé
St Louet-sur-Seulles
D675
CALVADOS
Château
de Canon

D54
D71
Villers-Bocage
Orne
Mézidon-Canon
D16

N175
St-Georges-d'Aunay
Bretteville-sur-Laize

pp.296–7
p.214
p.234

ENGLAND
English Channel
BELGIUM
GERMANY
LUX.
SWITZ.
ITALY
SPAIN

Don't miss

- Mémorial de Caen **p.262**
- Arromanches **p.268**
- Omaha Beach **p.273**
- The Bessin-Cotentin Marshes **p.276**
- Bayeux **p.284**

> *The three steeples [of Saint-Etienne and Saint-Pierre] were still alone ahead of us, like three birds perched on the plain, immobile, visible in the sunlight. Then, distance tearing itself to pieces like a fog that lifts to reveal in every detail a form still invisible a moment earlier, the towers of the Trinité appeared...*
>
> Marcel Proust, 1907

pretty much obliterated the rest of the historic city (*see* p.259). Many other churches and buildings have been intelligently restored or rebuilt, with the result that Caen – as well as being the near-unavoidable transport hub for this area – is far more interesting than a glimpse of its postwar blocks might suggest. Caen is also the location of one of Normandy's most moving Second World War museums, the Mémorial de Caen (*see* p.262).

Duke William's Castle and the Place St-Pierre

Apart from its mighty walls, little remains of William's castle, the **Château Ducal**, on a rocky outcrop dominating the city. But the grassy expanses within them provide a welcome haven, as well as having excellent views. The earliest walls were probably made of wood, so the stone ramparts there today probably date from the time of Henry I. They are interrupted by 13 towers, including the **Tour de la Reine-Mathilde** and the **Tour Puchot**, both constructed by King Philippe Auguste after he'd got his hands on Normandy in 1204. One of the oldest surviving buildings is the **Echiquier** (Exchequer), a rare example of civilian architecture from the reign of Henry I. It probably had two floors, the ground floor serving as kitchens, while the one above was a banqueting hall, where it's rumoured that Richard the Lionheart threw a party on his way to the Crusades.

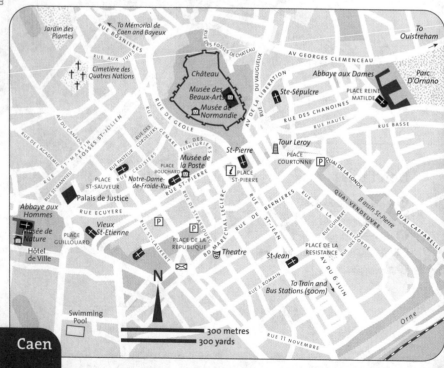

Caen

Getting to Caen

By Air

Caen's Carpiquet **airport** has flights to Corsica, Lyon, Bulgaria and Malaga, as well as twice daily weekday flights on 8-seaters to Brighton with **Skysouth** (t (01273) 463 673, *www.skysouth.co.uk*). **Airport information**, t 02 31 71 20 10, *www.caen.aeroport.fr*.

By Sea

Brittany Ferries (t France 0825 828 828, *www.brittanyferries.com*; see also p.80) sails 3 times daily each way year-round between Portsmouth and Ouistreham, Caen's port, 14km north of the city. Daytime crossings take about 6hrs, night sailings 7hrs, or there's a high-speed ferry mid-March–end Oct Fri–Sun that takes 3½hrs. Ouistreham is a compact port, and drivers can make a quick getaway on the D514 road, which links with roads to Caen and the D-Day coast. Bus Verts' No.1 runs from the ferry terminal to Caen.

By Rail

There are excellent train connections to Paris (2hrs, less by high-speed TGV), via Lisieux, and to Cherbourg (1hr 15mins). There is also a line from Caen via St-Pierre-sur-Dives, Argentan, Alençon and Le Mans to Tours (3hrs). The **station** is south of Caen centre, on the south side of the River Orne.

Getting around Caen

By Car

Anyone driving into Caen, whether from Ouistreham or by motorway, has to join the *Périphérique* ring road. Before following signs for *Centre-Ville* into town it's advisable to have an idea of which exit to take. Inside the city **parking** is only really difficult in the old centre, where there are reasonably-priced car parks. **Car hire** offices include: **Budget**, 54 Place de la Gare and Ouistreham Ferry Terminal, t 02 31 83 70 47; **Europcar**, 36 Place de la Gare and Ouistreham Ferry Terminal, t 0825 89 54 70; **RentaCar**, 40 Rue d'Auge, t 02 31 84 10 10. For **taxis**, try **Abeilles**, t 02 31 52 17 89, *www.taxis-abeilles-caen.com*.

By Bus

Caen has excellent **local buses** and **trams**: the tourist office has maps. There is a regular service between the train and bus stations and the tourist office, and No.2 runs from the office to the *Mémorial*. **Local bus information**, t 02 31 15 55 55, *www.twisto.fr*. The **bus station** (*Gare Routière*) is next to the railway station. Calvados' Bus Verts runs throughout the *département*, including a 'D-Day Line' bus along the beaches. **Bus Verts information**, t 0810 214 214, *www.busverts.fr*.

Musée de Normandie
www.musee-de-normandie.caen.fr;
open Wed–Mon 9.30–6

Within the castle walls the former Governors' Lodge houses the **Musée de Normandie**, a collection of treasures from Gallo-Roman times to the present day. Early items include a statue of a 1st century AD mother goddess found at the bottom of a well, and remarkable offerings from a 6th-century tomb. From later eras there are fine Viking relics and jewellery, and exhibits on Norman country life such as clogs carved with the shape of the wearer's toes and a 19th-century biscuit-seller's box with a lottery game on the lid to tempt buyers.

Musée des Beaux-Arts
open Wed–Mon 9.30–6

Nearby, in a concrete and glass bunker, the **Musée des Beaux-Arts** has a rich collection especially strong in Italian, Flemish and Dutch art. The paintings, which survived the war by being secreted in a château on the Loire, include Perugino's graceful and highly influential *Marriage of the Virgin*, the same artist's very different *St Jerome in the Desert*, and Veronese's gruesome 1581 *Judith and Holophernes*. One of the Flemish highlights is Rogier van der

Weyden's 1464 *Virgin and Child*, a radiantly beautiful virgin with ruby robes and bejewelled cuffs. There's a good display of French 19th- and 20th-century art, from Courbet's *La Mer* to Edouard Vuillard's bold yet intimate portrait of Suzanne Desprez, and Normandy's Impressionists are naturally well represented, including an empty Deauville beach by Boudin, and one of Monet's waterlilies. The museum also has a first-rate café-restaurant, Le Café Mancel (*see* p.263).

Heading downhill into the city, the blackened old stones of the **Eglise St-Pierre**, heavily restored after wartime bombardments but still with its marvellous Gothic steeple, loom up. It has a slightly bent nave, not because the workmen had a bad day but because the church, built over several centuries, had to be slotted in between the other buildings of the town centre. The Renaissance decoration of the apse is unashamedly pagan: you're more likely to see scenes from fables and romantic poetry than biblical figures.

A few yards to the east is the **Tour Leroy**, which once formed part of the city's ramparts. The tower dominates the broad **Place Courtonne**, which is sadly now more car park than square, although some of Caen's best restaurants line its edges. On the southeast side of the square is the **Bassin St-Pierre**, an inland marina at the end of the canal linking Caen to the sea, which provides a welcome breath of fresh air. **Rue du Vaugueux**, off Place Courtonne to the north, is the centre of a historic old neighbourhood with cobbled streets, crooked houses and lively restaurants and bars.

Almost next to St-Pierre church is the tourist office, which is based in another of Caen's architectural treasures, the **Hôtel d'Escoville**. Looking at its austere façade one has no idea of the ornate decoration in its courtyard, reached via a door to the left of the office entrance. The Italianate mansion was built in the early 16th century for one of the town's wealthiest merchants, Nicolas Le Valois d'Escoville, and has exquisite stonework and carvings.

Tragically, the war destroyed virtually all Caen's timber-framed houses, but there are two remaining ones in the pleasant Rue St-Pierre (Nos.52 and 54). The timber frames are actually fake: the main structures are made of Caen's celebrated fine limestone – *pierre de Caen* – so only the façades were of wood, decorated with intricate carvings. Rather incongruously, No.52 now houses the **Musée de la Poste** , with esoteric collections of stamps, postcards, postboxes and telegrams.

Musée de la Poste
open mid-June–mid-Sept Tues–Sat 10–12 and 2–6, mid-Sept–mid-June Tues–Sat 1.30–5.30; adm

St-Sauveur to the Abbaye-aux-Hommes

The area just to the west of the postal museum was, from the 15th to the 18th centuries, famous for its printing; Caen was one of the first French towns to develop a printing industry, and books are

The Battle for Caen

Thanks to its strategic location and transport links, Caen was a prime target for the invading forces in 1944, and consequently suffered some of the worst destruction seen anywhere in Normandy. The build-up to D-Day brought heavy bombing, which reduced much of the medieval quarters of St-Pierre and St-Jean to rubble. As fires raged for 11 days, survivors were tortured by the cries of hundreds entombed in cellars of collapsed houses. Still the Allied bombings continued, joined once the invasion had begun by bombardment from ships out at sea, and on 9 June the spire of St-Pierre was felled by a shell from *HMS Rodney*, 14 miles offshore. Another casualty was the mental hospital of Le Bon Sauveur, whose 1,500 women patients had been swelled by 4,000 refugees who believed its status would protect it from bombardment. With phenomenal bravery, the Mother Superior led them in a mass exodus. The sane found refuge with another 10,000 fugitives in the caves of Fleury-sur-Orne, just south of Caen, from where the stone used to build Westminster Abbey and the Tower of London was quarried. The mentally ill were taken in a straggling column to Pont-l'Abbé, 40 miles west. Nevertheless many of Caen's people hung on in the city, camping on the flagstones of St-Etienne, eerily untouched.

The final and most terrible wave of bombing began on 7 July. Over 450 RAF bombers pounded the city. A British rifleman, watching from the fields across which he was to advance the next day, wrote 'colossal raid on Caen. Marvellous and awe-inspiring sight. Terrible to watch. Dust obscured the sun.' Inside the city a refugee mother felt 'the whole earth shudder. It went on and on for 50 minutes, with a single break of five minutes.' When the bombers left, very little of the northern half of Caen was still standing. It had received as many bombs in an hour as had fallen on Hamburg, a city 20 times its size, in each of the great fire-storm raids of a year before. A British soldier who entered the city on 9 July, after another day of bitter fighting for possession of the ruins, found 'just a waste of brick and stone, like a field of corn that has been ploughed. The people gazed at us without emotion of any kind; one could hardly look them in the face, knowing who had done this.' One of the doctors who had stuck it out wrote, 'the bombardment...was absolutely futile. There were no military objectives...All the bombardment did was... to choke the streets and hinder the Allies in their advance through the city.'

(Abridged from John Keegan, *Six Armies in Normandy*, Jonathan Cape, 1982)

still a passion today – there are several fine old bookshops (some with teashops) on Rue St-Pierre and Rue des Croisiers. The **Place Pierre Bouchard**, behind the church of **Notre-Dame-de-Froide-Rue**, housed one of the town's most important early presses, owned by printer Jean Macé. **Rue Froide**, where the majority of printers and booksellers lived, retains much of its 16th-century atmosphere; look at No.35, with its ornately-carved stone windows.

The streets around **Place St-Sauveur**, with their cobbles and ornately carved façades, form Caen's traditional heart. Executions were held in the square (the last, of three priests, in 1793), and the city's largest market has since time immemorial been centred every Friday on the space in front of the old St-Sauveur church (mostly destroyed in 1944). The most striking thing about the square is the uniformity of its white stone buildings, very different from the jumble of most Norman squares. This is because a 1735 edict forced owners of timber-frame houses to replace them with stone ones, mostly in the orderly styles fashionable in the reign of Louis XV.

St-Etienne
open Mon–Sat 8.15–12 and 2–7.30, Sun 2.30–7.30

In the western corner of the old city soar the grey towers of Caen's most famous church, **St-Etienne**, attached to William the Conqueror's **Abbaye-aux-Hommes**. The 11th-century towers are topped with entirely different octagonal 13th-century Gothic spires. Having miraculously survived the 1944 bombardments by becoming a refuge for the homeless, church and monastery seem to be indestructible. William the Conqueror was less lucky. He chose St-Etienne as his final resting place, but his burial in 1087 was a fiasco: his servants stripped him almost naked on the way from Rouen, where he had died; then, finding the grave too small for his great bulk, the pallbearers tried to bend the rotting corpse in half, causing his stomach to burst open and scatter its contents onto the crowd. His remains took another beating during the Wars of Religion, and only a thighbone was left. Today, it has won the dignified resting place it deserves, beneath a black stone slab before the altar.

The speed at which the church was built – between 1066 and 1077 – gave it a unity of style. A key player in its construction was the prior of Bec abbey, Lanfranc, St-Etienne's first abbot and later Archbishop of Canterbury. Architecturally it was ground-breaking, with a monumental façade supported by four powerful buttresses. Most of the interior, equally austere, is pure Norman Romanesque, but the three different levels prefigure northern Gothic. Light floods in above the crossing through an extraordinary lantern tower, rebuilt in the 17th century after the original, taller one in wood had collapsed. The choir is one of the oldest in Normandy, with wonderful 17th-century satirical woodcarvings. In the 19th century some were judged too risqué, and removed.

Abbaye-aux-Hommes
t 02 31 30 42 81;
guided tours daily 9.30,
2.30 and 4; July–Aug
Mon–Fri 11, 1.30 and 4;
tours in English; adm

Little remains of the original **Abbaye-aux-Hommes**, for which St-Etienne was built, founded by William in 1060 to house 120 Benedictine monks. In the 18th century the abbey was given a major revamp by the Maurist monk-architect Guillaume de la Tremblaye, who rebuilt the cloisters and changed its square plan to an H, and much of these later abbey buildings now contain Caen's Hôtel de Ville. The abbey's immense wealth can be seen from the opulent furniture and solid panelling; particularly fine is the vaulted **Salle Capitulaire**, now used for marriages. In case anyone had forgotten who started it all, there's a statue of William in the Sacristy next door. It's actually a waxwork of Charlton Heston, borrowed from Paris' wax museum; somebody thought Heston looked Conqueror-like, and Christian Dior ran him up a dapper tunic and cloak. The grand staircase in white Caen stone, is a masterpiece of engineering, appearing almost suspended in the air. The visit ends in the richly carved **refectory**, used as a hospital in 1944; it's easy to see how narrowly it escaped destruction from the pockmarks in the stone. The 11am tour includes the misnamed **Salle des Gardes**, which never held guards but was built in the 14th century to receive important visitors. Its floor is paved in stunning ceramic tiles displaying coats of arms.

**Musée d'Initiation
à la Nature**
*open Easter–Oct
Mon–Fri 2–6,
Nov–Easter Wed 2–6*

Tucked behind the abbey, in the former bakery, is the tiny **Musée d'Initiation à la Nature**, an old-fashioned natural history museum with plenty of stuffed birds and animals. The best part is its delightful garden, which has themed areas on scented, medicinal, or poisonous plants, and an engaging 'geological path'.

The Abbaye-aux-Dames and the Trinité

**Abbaye-aux-
Dames**
*t 02 31 06 98 98,
www.cr-basse-
normandie.fr;
free guided tours
daily exc some public
hols at 2.30 and 4*

A suitable distance away on the opposite side of Caen stands the equally imposing **Abbaye-aux-Dames**, which was founded by Matilda, consecrated in the year of the Conquest, and finished after both William and his queen were dead. Not surprisingly, its history mirrors that of William's abbey: like the Abbaye-aux-Hommes it owes its survival to the fact that in June 1944 it sheltered the homeless and wounded. Matilda's original buildings were also given a facelift by Guillaume de la Tremblaye, but work was still going on when it was interrupted by the Revolution, so a fourth side of the cloisters was never built. The convent buildings have also undergone various transformations, and today most are occupied by the Basse-Normandie regional council.

One of the most fascinating edifices is the neoclassical oval **Lavatorium**, where the nuns washed their hands in huge black marble basins before going into dinner. The entrance hall with its voluptuous Caen stone double staircase has a portrait of the Abbey's most notorious daughter, Charlotte Corday, who in 1793 made her way to Paris and stabbed the revolutionary extremist Marat in his bath, and was guillotined within a week for her pains. Visitors can also see the convent library, now called the Matilda room, where Corday perused the works of Rousseau and Voltaire.

Eglise de la Trinité
*open daily 8–12
and 2–7*

The abbey church where Matilda was buried, the **Eglise de la Trinité** is a masterpiece of Norman Romanesque. It's recently been given a scrub, so the interior looks incongruously new, but the exterior is even starker than that of St-Etienne. The nave has the usual three storeys, the top admitting light to illuminate its gorgeous cream-coloured stone. The ceiling, built in 1130, was one of the first in Normandy to be vaulted rather than made of timber. In the choir is Matilda's tombstone, of black Tournai marble. She died at 50 – not a bad age at the time, especially considering she'd borne 10 children. In the 16th century Protestants had a go at the tomb, but left more behind than in that of her husband. In 1959 her casket was opened to find out more about the queen, and it was discovered she was less than 1.5 metres tall.

The highlight of the Trinité is its **crypt**, a forest of squat columns probably built in the 12th century to support the choir above. It's not truly a crypt, as it has windows on three sides. It has fascinating, slightly crude carvings, including some grim ones of the Last Judgement. A far more experienced hand clearly produced the fantastical carvings in the church's **apse**, including one of an elephant, whose driver is holding his trunk with two hands. One theory goes that William the Conqueror's son Robert described elephants from memory, after taking part in the First Crusade in 1096. Behind the stone rose at the centre of the vault in the 13th-century **chapterhouse** there is another curious feature, a tiny statue of the architect, silently watching over his handiwork.

The Mémorial de Caen

⭐ **Mémorial de Caen**
Esplanade Dwight Eisenhower, t 02 31 06 06 44, www.memorial-caen.fr; open daily mid-Feb–5 Nov 9–7; 6 Nov–mid-Feb Tues–Sun 9.30–6; closed 3 wks in Jan; adm, but free for WW2 veterans, war widows and under-10s; to reach the museum by car, do not enter central Caen but follow signs from the Périphérique, exit 6; by bus, take Twisto bus No.2 from opposite the tourist office

Set amid lawns on a plateau named after General Eisenhower on the northern edge of the city, Caen's foremost monument to the events of 1944 is not, its creators insist, another war museum, even though much of it deals with the horrors of the two world wars. It focuses both on the causes of war and on peace, using a mixture of moving film footage, recorded testimonies (which you listen to in booths), animated maps, visual effects and other interactive means as well as an incredible collection of photographs. The experience can be challenging, as the Mémorial's aim is not only to inform but also to pose questions. One of its strongest points is that it presents world events as experienced by individuals – both famous and ordinary. The result is profoundly moving.

Architecture and theme are cleverly intertwined, thanks to the efforts of architect Jacques Millet: the outside of the building appears as if it's been rent in two, symbolizing the destruction of war and the sword cut that opened up the Atlantic wall. The message engraved on the building is appropriate to war-wrecked Caen: 'Grief had wrecked me; my brothers raised me from the ruins, and a river of freedom sprang from my wound.' The descent into war history is designed as a downward spiral, a sort of descent into hell. On the lower floor you enter a dark globe where Hitler's oppressive speeches reverberate, before the darkest display, a mortuary of hundreds of candles flickering in the darkness, representing the Holocaust. Sketches made by one camp inmate on scraps of paper are particularly touching. Further on there are more detailed exhibits on the events in Normandy itself in 1944, and rooms on the consequences of World War II and the Cold War. Explanations are multilingual, and three films are shown at various stages of the visit (check times as you enter): two deal with World War II, while the final one treats later conflicts.

On the upper level there are exhibits on different models for peace today, with some interactive (if sometimes slightly obscure) electronic screens and games. A tunnel takes you to the Nobel Peace Prizewinners' Gallery, housed in a former German bunker, and peace gardens provide welcome space for contemplation. The Mémorial has an excellent bookshop, café-restaurant and other facilities. Allow half a day for a full visit.

Tourist Information in Caen

ⓘ Caen >

Place Saint-Pierre,
t 02 31 27 14 14,
www.tourisme.caen.fr

ⓘ **Calvados**

8 Rue Renoir,
t 02 31 27 90 30,
www.calvados-
tourisme.com

Internet Access: L'Espace, 1–3 Rue Basse, Place Courtonne; Le Systénium, 130 Rue St-Jean.

Market Days: Fri, Place St-Sauveur and Fossés St-Julien; Sun, Place St-Pierre–Place Courtonne. Some stalls daily, Place Courtonne.

Post Office: Place Gambetta.

Where to Stay around Caen

Caen ✉ 14000

All the hotels listed, except Château d'Audrieu and Les Cordeliers, are part of a local scheme offering a 30% discount on two-night stays during winter months.

****Château d'Audrieu, 14250 Audrieu, **t** 02 31 80 21 52, *www.chateaudaudrieu.com* (€€€€€). Luxurious hotel in an 18th-century château in a village 12km west of Caen. It has a fine restaurant (€€€) and 30 hectares of parkland.

***Le Dauphin, 29 Rue Gemare, **t** 02 31 86 22 26, *www.le-dauphin-normandie.com* (€€€–€€). Now affiliated to Best Western, this family-run former priory nevertheless has a lot of character, with lovely wooden stairs and stone walls, and oak beams in some of its 37 rooms. There's free parking, and one of the city's best restaurants (€€€–€€), presenting traditional Norman cuisine in elegant form. *Restaurant closed Sun eve from Oct–May.*

★ Le Clos Saint Martin >

Le Clos Saint Martin, 18 bis Place Saint Martin, **t** 02 31 50 09 71, *www.le-clos-saint-martin.com* (€€€–€€). From the outside it looks like a heavily modernized 18th-century mansion, but inside is a haven of taste and luxury. Owners Sylvie and Jean-Noël have created four elegant bedrooms (including a suite), making this one of the nicest places to stay in the region.

*Bernières, 50 Rue de Bernières, **t** 02 31 86 01 26, *www.hotelbernieres.com* (€). Run by the same able and welcoming owner as the Bristol, with 17 rooms each with bath or shower.

★ Café Mancel >>

The breakfasts are a feast. A good budget choice.

Bristol, 31 Rue du 11 Novembre, **t 02 31 84 59 76, *www.hotel-bristol-caen.com* (€). Don't be put off by the location a little distant from the centre (although handy for the train or bus stations): inside, the Bristol is a welcoming haven. The bright, stylish rooms are a bit grander than those at the same owner's Bernières. Breakfasts are excellent value.

Les Cordeliers, 4 Rue des Cordeliers, **t 02 31 86 37 15 (€). This hotel occupies a lovely 18th-century house on one of Caen's most historic streets. Rooms are basic, but some, in a modern annexe, look out onto a roof garden.

*Saint-Etienne, Rue de l'Académie, **t** 02 31 86 35 82, *www.hotel-saint-etienne.com* (€). Rooms at this simple hotel are tiny, but the elm stairs are fabulous, the owner is hospitable and the quiet, old-town location is perfect.

Eating Out in Caen

Le Pressoir, Avenue Henri Chéron, **t** 02 31 73 32 71, *www.restaurant-le-pressoir.com* (€€€). Probably Caen's finest *restaurant gastronomique*: Ivan Vantier has earned himself a Michelin star with his imaginative cooking. *Closed Sat lunch, Sun eve and Mon.*

Le Bouchon du Vaugueux, 12 Rue Graindorge, **t** 02 31 44 26 26 (€€–€). This tiny informal place serves great classic Norman food and has stacks of atmosphere, but to enjoy it you musn't mind rubbing elbows with your neighbours, at convivial tables. A gem. *Closed Sun and Mon.*

Dolly's Café, 16/18 Av de la Libération, **t** 02 31 94 03 29 (€). If Norman food is all too much, come here for some solid English fare. There are home-made scones and cakes at teatime, and a shop too. *Closed Mon.*

Hémisphères, 15 Rue des Croisiers, **t** 02 31 86 67 26 (€). An attractive tearoom above a bookshop; on sunny days you can sit on the small roof terrace. *Closed Sun.*

Café Mancel, Musée des Beaux Arts, **t** 02 31 86 63 64 (€€). Stylish décor, imaginative modern cuisine and a lovely setting in the heart of the

Conqueror's castle make this an exceptional place. It often holds jazz or poetry evenings, and it's non-smoking. *Closed Sun eve and Mon.*

L'Insolite, 16 Rue du Vaugueux, t 02 31 43 83 87 (€). Elegant good-value restaurant in the prettiest part of town, serving Norman specialities, especially fish and seafood.

Archidona, 9 Rue Gemare, t 02 31 85 30 30 (€€). This new stylish restaurant has taken Caen by storm. Great food, great value. And it's hip. *Closed Mon.*

Le Petit B, 15 Rue du Vaugueux, t 02 31 93 50 76 (€€). Another mid-budget choice in the popular Rue du Vaugueux. Sit out on the terrace in summer. *Closed Sun and Mon.*

The D-Day Coast

When the British troops landed on Sword Beach on 6 June 1944, it was hoped that Caen itself would be taken on the first day, so close did it seem to the landing beaches. However, it would take over a month of fierce fighting before the city was securely in Allied hands, by which time much of it was in ruins (*see* p.259). The nearest of the invasion beaches is only 14 kilometres (9 miles) north of Caen, at Ouistreham. This guide to the D-Day landing sites goes from east to west, beginning, fittingly, with the first piece of French territory taken on 5–6 June, the bridges across the River Orne and the Caen Canal between Bénouville and Ranville. For an introduction to the events of 1944 and more on visiting D-Day sites around Normandy, *see* pp.39–46.

Pegasus Bridge

Mémorial Pegasus
Av Major Howard, Ranville, t 02 31 78 19 44, www.normandy 1944.com; open daily Feb–Mar and Oct–Nov 10–1 and 2–5; April–Sept 9.30–6.30; adm

Beside the road between Caen and Ouistreham, a modern bridge now crosses the Caen Canal and the Orne at **Bénouville**. The old iron bridge that stood across the canal in 1944, named *Pegasus* for ever after in honour of the winged-horse emblem of the British airborne troops, is famous for being the first objective liberated in France. It now sits in the grounds of the **Mémorial Pegasus**. The museum tells the story of how the British 6th Airborne Division,

The First Landing

The Parachute Field Ambulance attached to the 6th Airborne Division landed near Varaville, between Pegasus Bridge and Cabourg. The following is the account of one of their number, James Bramwell.

'The land west of Varaville consisted of orchards and fields divided by thick hedges. The sight at dawn was unforgettable. The lanes and ditches were strewn with equipment. Green silken canopies, and here and there the brilliant red or orange of a container chute, draped the apple trees and hedges, their flaccid rigging lines drawing attention to the empty harness suspended beneath them. And thereby hung many a tale of midnight suspense, of rescue by French civilians, of food and shelter and care where bones were broken. During the first 12 hours we frequently ran across French peasants who said they had hidden an injured parachutist in a barn or knew where one was hiding. They were as excited as children making the most of some interruption in the dull routine of life at home; they wanted to tell us all about the last four years in the space of four minutes; and they wanted us to stay and celebrate the day of liberation in calvados or cognac. It's ironic to reflect that for those people around Varaville, it was the beginning of the worst two months of the German occupation.'

Extract from the privately printed war diary of the Parachute Field Ambulance

Getting around the D-Day Coast

The D514 **road** runs the length of this coast, only turning slightly further inland west of Arromanches. There is no local **bus** along the whole coast (except for the D-Day Line), but Bus Verts No.1 runs from Caen to Luc-sur-Mer via Ouistreham; No.3 runs on from Luc to Courseulles; and No.74 from Courseulles to Arromanches before turning inland to Bayeux. From there, bus No.70 runs to Port-en-Bessin and Omaha Beach.

The nearest **train** stations are Caen and Bayeux. For information on Portsmouth–Ouistreham ferries, *see* p.232. Heading inland from the beaches, it's naturally difficult to tour the area without a car. However, the No.74 bus between Courseulles and Bayeux does stop at Crépon.

---

combining paratroopers and glider-born infantry, seized the bridge just after midnight on 5–6 June. It was the only crossing point between Caen and the sea, so its capture intact was crucial. The Division's other tasks were to destroy bridges over rivers further east, and to obstruct a German counterattack on the landing beaches from the east.

Preceded by pathfinder gliders to mark the way, five platoons of the Oxfordshire and Buckinghamshire Light Infantry and Royal Engineers successfully landed by glider beside Pegasus Bridge. 'Even after crossing the coast,' recalled their commander Major John Howard, 'everything was so quiet that it seemed we were merely carrying out an exercise in England.' As they reached the bridge the Germans immediately opened fire, but the troops managed to secure the crossing within 15 minutes. At the Bénouville end of the bridge is the little **Café Gondrée**, the 'First House Liberated in France', where the Gondrée family, who still run it today, uncorked 97 bottles of champagne for the paratroopers to celebrate the triumph. They still had to hold onto the bridge for many hours against fierce German attacks, though, until at around 1pm the sound of bagpipes playing *Highland Laddie* heralded the arrival of commandos led by Brigadier Lord Lovat, advancing from Sword Beach. Losses were heavy: more than 1,000 men were killed, and now lie in the British cemetery at **Ranville**. Survivors hold a memorial ceremony each year, although their numbers are getting fewer and fewer. Visitors to the museum can see a Bailey Bridge, of the kind built across the canal shortly after 6 June to supplement the permanent bridge, and a replica of a Horsa glider, as well as films and battlefield relics. From May to September there's also a **son et lumière** at the bridge, evoking the events of 1944.

Son et lumière
Tues–Sun, enquire at museum for times

Sword, Juno and Gold

Ouistreham-Riva Bella

People tend to regard Ouistreham as a place to pass through on their way to or from a ferry, but it's not without its charm, in an old-fashioned way. Belle Epoque mansions near the sandy beach

For the Fallen

They shall grow not old, as we that are left grow old:
Age shall not weary them, nor the years condemn.
At the going down of the sun and in the morning
We will remember them.

They mingle not with their laughing comrades again;
They sit no more at familiar tables at home;
They have no lot in our labour of the day-time;
They sleep beyond England's foam.

Laurence Binyon, 4th and 5th stanzas from *For the Fallen*, September 1914

recall the days when this was a popular seaside resort, and there's still a spa and a casino. There are reminders of another episode in its past along the beach, too, in the shape of concrete bunkers. Ouistreham was the first French town liberated on 6 June 1944. Today the main shopping street, Rue de la Mer, has pleasant cafés and shops, and there's an excellent **market** on the quayside. The best beach, Riva Bella, is huge at low tide. Also, largely ignored and inside the town, Ouistreham has a superb fortified Norman church, from the 12th century.

Le Musée du Mur de l'Atlantique
Av 6 Juin, t 02 31 97 28 69; open daily April–Sept 9–7; Feb–Mar and Oct–Dec 10–6; adm

Musée No. 4 Commando
t 02 31 96 63 10; open 15 Mar–Oct daily 10.30–6; adm

The town has two World War II museums. **Le Musée du Mur de l'Atlantique** is housed in an old German bunker, and is interesting perhaps as one of few museums to present the battle more from a German point of view. It's incredible how much was squeezed into a tiny space: a radio room, with statue of Hitler, sleeping quarters, an ammunition store, an infirmary. Opposite the casino is the **Musée No. 4 Commando**, which covers the role of a French commando unit that landed at this point on D-Day, with original film material from the day.

From Ouistreham to Courseulles

The rather romantically-named **Côte de Nacre** ('Mother of Pearl Coast') stretches west from Ouistreham, lined with holiday homes and modest old seaside towns where you can watch the waves over a plate of *moules-frites* – Colleville, Lion-sur-Mer, Luc-sur-Mer, Langrune, Bernières, Courseulles. In June 1944 the fine beaches roughly between Ouistreham and Luc-sur-Mer formed Sword Beach, while from St-Aubin to Courseulles was the Canadian beach, Juno. Most of the time, though, there are now few reminders of 1944, other than the odd tank with a plaque. Old-fashioned French seaside pleasures, from casinos to trinket shops, have regained the upper hand.

Musée Radar
open April–Oct daily 10–6; adm

A few kilometres inland from **St-Aubin-sur-Mer**, on the south side of **Douvres-la-Délivrande**, is one of the more unusual D-Day memorials, the **Musée Radar**, a vintage-1943 German radar station with a small museum of special attraction to anyone interested in early electronics. Beyond St-Aubin the first larger resort is **Courseulles-sur-Mer**, a slightly more modern port with a pretty marina. The five-mile stretch of beach between St-Aubin and La Rivière, just west of Courseulles, was where Canadian troops landed on D-Day. Their contribution is commemorated by the gleaming new maple-leaf-shaped **Centre Juno Beach**. This totally bilingual, state-of-the-art museum is inspiring and moving. It is unusual in that it seeks to evoke the whole experience of Canada in World War II, so that nearly half is dedicated to Canadian society at the outbreak of war and the efforts made by civilians and military alike. The visit begins with a film montage – aimed to represent the thoughts and impressions of Canadian troops as they reached France – which you watch from inside a simulated landing craft with a guide, before you emerge into the museum. The 'Road to Victory' room, with huge film screens flanked by TV screens on which veterans, politicians and academics comment on what is going on, makes an imaginative change from the usual collections of military hardware. The final, totally blackened, room is the most moving, with Laurence Binyon's famous World War I poem *For the Fallen* on one wall (*see* p.266), and a silent list of the Canadians who died in 1939–45 on another. The centre also has a special circuit for children, including games and quizzes. If the experience has given non-Canadians a taste for the country, they can stock up on Canadian goodies in the shop. The museum also lays on a fascinating bilingual tour of the Juno beach itself.

Centre Juno Beach
Voie des Français Libres, **t** *02 31 37 32 17, www.junobeach.org; open daily April–Sept 9.30–7; Nov–Feb 10–1 and 2–5; Mar and Oct 10–6; adm, but free for WW2 veterans, war widows and under-10s*

14 The D-Day Coast, Caen and Bayeux | Sword, Juno and Gold

The Taking of Juno Beach

Nearly two years after their debacle at Dieppe (*see* p.104), the Canadians returned to Normandy's shores on D-Day. Although conditions were less treacherous and the German opposition less daunting, the difficult terrain, and poor weather, would make it the deadliest of the D-Day beaches after 'bloody Omaha'. Of 14,000 Canadian troops who landed or were parachuted in on 6 June, 340 lost their lives and nearly 600 were wounded. Many were killed by German mines and 'C elements', massive iron obstacles that tore the bottom out of landing craft as they attempted to beach. This was the kind of trap the troops had trained to avoid, but on Juno bad weather and an offshore reef prevented the Canadians from landing at low tide, so there was no option but to plough through the obstacles, festooned with mines.

The landing craft headed for the few gaps that clearance groups had managed to open up. Once ashore, the troops had to get past concrete and steel bunkers, which were particularly strong around Courseulles. A company of the Royal Winnipeg Rifles reached the town with only 26 of its 120 men still standing; the ghosts of Dieppe seemed close. However, another company that landed further west managed to move into open country and capture the little village of Graye-sur-Mer, where only a few days afterwards Churchill, Montgomery and later King George VI would all come to view the beachhead. There were more casualties as the struggle went on in the ruined houses around the harbour at Courseulles, and in Bernières and St-Aubin, before the Canadians ventured 16km inland, nearly reaching the Caen–Bayeux road. At the end of 6 June, the Canadians had forged deeper into France than any other Allied forces.

West of Courseulles the holiday resorts largely come to an end, and cows take over the fields just inshore behind the wilder stretch of coast leading to Arromanches, centre of the other British landing beach, Gold.

Gold Beach: Ver-sur-Mer and Arromanches

Ver-sur-Mer, 5km from Courseulles, was the easternmost point of Gold Beach on 6 June 1944, and the landing zone of the 69th Brigade of the British 50th Northumbrian Division. Today, it's another small beach town, but a couple of streets back from the seafront on Place Amiral Byrd it has the **Musée America-Gold Beach**. This modern museum has two separate parts: one commemorates the first transatlantic mail flight, made by the US aviation pioneer Admiral Byrd in June 1927 in his plane the 'America', which landed in Ver, while the second, as the name suggests, deals with the events of D-Day on Gold Beach, with a particular emphasis on the planning of the assault and the special weaponry used to help clear the way through the mines and other defences for the troops.

Musée America-Gold Beach
t 02 31 22 58 58; open July–Aug daily 10.30–1.30 and 2.30–5.30; May–June and Sept–Oct Wed–Mon 10.30–1.30 and 2.30–5.30; adm

 Arromanches

Strollers and bathers on the lovely sandy beach at **Arromanches** cannot avoid being reminded of the dramatic events here in June 1944; ringing the bay, like grotesque flotsam, are the weathered concrete remains of the artificial harbour, known as 'Mulberry', which started as a madcap idea but turned out to be a key to the Allies' success. For a few weeks, Arromanches became the busiest port in the world. The story of the harbour is told in meticulous detail at the **Musée du Débarquement**, overlooking the beach. The floating harbour concept was born of the fact that the Germans occupied all the established ports along the coast, so an alternative way of landing troops and supplies had to be found. The solution came in a memo written by Churchill, exhibited in the museum: 'They must float up and down with the tide. The anchor problems must be mastered. Let me have the best solution worked out. Don't argue the matter. The difficulties will argue for themselves.'

Musée du Débarquement
t 02 31 22 34 31; open daily May–Aug and Easter 9–7; Sept 9–6, Mar and Oct 9.30–12.30 and 1.30–5.30 ;Nov–Dec and Feb 10–12.30 and 1.30–5; April 9–12.30 and 1.30–6; adm

His determination paid off. Eight months were spent secretly constructing the components of the harbour in Britain, and its 146 concrete caissons or foundations, some as tall as five-storey buildings, were towed across the Channel as the invasion began. Engineers worked around the clock to assemble the breakwater, sinking the concrete pillars off the rocks in front of Arromanches and linking them with floating roadways and wharfs. They finished in a phenomenal 12 days, but the next day a freak storm began that very nearly blew the chances of success out of the water. It raged for three terrifying days. An American Mulberry at Omaha was destroyed completely, along with nearly 100 landing craft, but while the British one at Arromanches lost many of its breakwaters and roadways, it was still usable to get desperately-needed supplies ashore. Arromanches' Mulberry harbour kept going until November 1944, by which time two and a half million men and half a million vehicles had passed through it.

This dramatic operation is well recounted at the museum – but the best exhibit is the bay below you, now named 'Port Winston', where it all happened. Items of interest include ships models, a British chaplain's 'Field Communion Case' and a bewildering array of military uniforms and hardware, and a couple of brief films.

A short walk to the east on Chemin du Calvaire is another 1944 exhibit, **Arromanches 360**, which hosts a film presentation, *The Price of Liberty*, in a circular nine-screen theatre. It's a mix of archive footage, specially-shot modern footage and visual effects, aimed, as the blurb says, at 'plunging you into the heart of the action'. World War Two aside, Arromanches is a pleasant low-key little town with some decent cafés and restaurants and a fine beach. At low tide you can walk out to parts of the Mulberry, but the best view of 'Port Winston' is from the hill above town.

A few kilometres from Arromanches is **Longues-sur-Mer**, where, high on the cliffs, remains a battery of four German 152mm guns, which threatened ships landing at Gold Beach to the east and Omaha to the west. It was here that a German lookout first spotted the Allied ships on D-Day; the first German shots were fired at 5.37am, and the battery – after sending to Bayeux for more ammunition – continued firing until early evening. Sixty years on, some of the bunkers survive largely as they were when the Germans abandoned them, and the guns, now pointing impotently skywards, are the only heavy guns still in place in Hitler's 'Atlantic Wall'. It's also a hauntingly beautiful spot, with heather and gorse-lined paths and great views out to sea.

Inland from the Beaches

D-Day associations aside, the area immediately behind the Invasion coast is the rolling green plain of the **Bessin**, one of the most productive farming areas in Normandy, especially for cattle and dairy products. As well as its fruitfulness and tranquillity, the other things that characterize the Bessin are its quiet stone – not half-timbered – villages, and its huge, extraordinary fortified medieval farms, built with high walls and towers to resist earlier English invaders, in the Hundred Years' War. Just 7km southeast of Arromanches, the farming village of **Crépon** has been on the map since Norman times. A close associate of William the Conqueror became lord of the manor after 1066, and Crépon's grand church of **St-Gildard-et-St-Médard** built in the 12th century and rebuilt in the 15th, is celebrated for its magnificent Louis XV wood panelling. Crépon's aristocratic roots explain its special abundance of

Arromanches 360

t 02 31 22 30 30; www.arromanches 360.com; open daily June–Aug 9.10–6.40, April–May and Sept–Oct 10.10–5.40; Feb–Mar and Nov 10.10–5.10; Dec 10.10–4.40; adm but free for WW2 veterans

14

The D-Day Coast, Caen and Bayeux | Sword, Juno and Gold

fortified manors, the most notable of which is the Ferme de la Rançonnière (*see* p.272). On the village green there's a memorial to the Green Howards regiment, which liberated Crépon in 1944.

Château de Creully

t 02 31 80 67 08; open daily July–mid-Sept 10–12.30 and 2.30–5.30; adm

Another 4km south are the impressive towers of the **Château de Creully**, built in stages from the 11th to the 16th centuries. In 1944 the château housed the first BBC radio transmitter set up on French soil, and there's a small radio museum in one room. From its terrace you can see the **Château de Creullet**, on the Arromanches road, a smaller 18th-century house that General Montgomery officially took as his headquarters after D-Day, and where he received George VI and Winston Churchill. Montgomery himself, however, actually preferred to keep his real headquarters in a truck-caravan parked in the grounds, camouflaged as hay stacks.

Château de Fontaine-Henry

t 02 31 80 00 42, www.chateau-de-fontaine-henry.com; open mid-June–mid-Sept Wed–Mon 2.30–6.30; Easter–mid-June and mid-Sept–2 Nov Sat–Sun 2.30–6.30; adm

This area's most remarkable historic house, however, is a few kilometres to the east, the **Château de Fontaine-Henry**. With its extraordinarily steeply pitched Renaissance slate roofs towering above a delicately chiselled stone façade, Fontaine-Henry has the feel of a château of the Loire transported to rural Normandy. The château was built from around 1450 on the ruins of a medieval fortress, first erected by the powerful Tilly family to safeguard the routes to the coast. The only traces of this fortress today are two buttresses that supported the huge stone ramparts, and the fine vaulted cellars beneath the main house. In 1944 the castle regained its protective purpose, when the village's inhabitants took refuge in the cellars. Canadian tank shells decapitated one tower, but by 6 June Fontaine-Henry had been taken, relatively unscathed.

The castle's stunning façade is a stonemason's jaunt through history. The sober 15th-century south gable contrasts starkly with the over-the-top Flamboyant Gothic square tower next to it. Around the well, the style changed again in the later 16th century as the castle was enlarged. Inside, the entrance hall, originally the kitchens, has an unusual fireplace with three separate hearths, above which are the nine coats-of-arms of the families who have made Fontaine-Henry their home. In the drawing rooms, austerity gives way to 19th-century opulence. The main focus of interest are the paintings: the first drawing room has works by Philippe de Champaigne and a celebrated Correggio, *The Education of Love*, and the second has a fine portrait of Louis XIV as a child.

The **chapel**, with its superb stone choir stalls, was built in the 13th century by Henri de Tilly, in atonement to the Pope for some 'misdoings' (we're not told what) after he took part in a crusade. The guided tour ends with tea by the fire, or a taste of local apple juice and cider, which you can buy. In July and August the château runs *Nocturnes*, night-time tours by torchlight with medieval music and costumes, and in mid-August a *Grande Fête Renaissance* is held.

A short way down the Caen road in an isolated valley is **Thaon**, with a deconsecrated 11th-century Norman church that's very much worth a visit (ask at the house next door for permission). The unusual belfry is topped by a pyramid roof.

Tourist Information along Sword, Juno and Gold Beaches

Market Days: Ouistreham: Tues, town centre; Fri (and July–Aug Wed–Sun), Riva Bella; also Sun (May–Sept, Riva Bella), and fish market daily all year on the quay. Courseulles: Tues, Fri, fish market daily, on the harbourside. Creully: Wed.

Post Offices: Ouistreham: 11 Route de Lion; Arromanches: Ave de Verdun.

Internet: Courseulles-sur-Mer: Omac, 56 Rue de la Mer; Arromanches: Place Trémoulet; Ouistreham: Eclairtel, Rue de la Mer, and Appy Informatique, Rue Gambetta.

Shopping along Sword, Juno and Gold Beaches

La Ferme de Billy, 31 Rue de l'Eglise, 14980 Rots, t 02 31 26 50 51, *www.vauvrecy.com*. This farm was built in 1651 by the Billy family who owned most of Rots. Since 1851 it's been owned by the Vauvrecy family who produce some very tasty apple juice, cider and calvados. You can also do tours of the cider press, cider house and cellar.

Where to Stay and Eat along Sword, Juno and Gold Beaches

Ouistreham ✉ 14150

**Le Normandie-Le Chalut, 71 Av Michel Cabieu, t 02 31 97 19 57, *www.lenormandie.com* (€€). Chef-owner and local personality Christian Maudouit has been running this celebrated hotel-restaurant just off the seafront for over 25 years. He produces regional specialities with a personal touch, such as lobster cooked with green lentils, or duck foie gras with a five-berry fruit jelly. Compared with the plush restaurant (€€€–€€), the hotel rooms are simple, but well kept. *Restaurant closed (Nov–Mar) Sun eve and Mon.*

Bernières-sur-Mer ✉ 14490

L'As de Trèfle, 420 Rue Léopold Hettier, t 02 31 97 22 60. (€€€–€€). Don't be put off by the rather banal exterior of this building, a few streets inland in Bernières: the food here is superb, innovative and fresh, and it's renowned as one of this coast's best eating places. *Closed Mon, Jan and (Oct–May) Tues.*

Courseulles-sur-Mer ✉ 14470

**La Crémaillère, Av de la Combattante, t 02 31 37 46 73, *www.la-cremaillere.com* (€€–€). The pleasant, smallish, recently refurbished rooms in this modern hotel are decorated in nautical navy and yellow. Most have sea views, but there are cheaper rooms in a separate annexe without them. Prices vary by season. The lovely panoramic restaurant (€€€–€€), with tables inside and out, specializes in fresh fish and seafood.

La Chaumière, Domaine de l'Ile de Plaisance, t 02 31 37 45 48 (€€). The best thing about this restaurant in a mock-old building by a windmill is its tranquil location, overlooking marshes by the sea. There are tables outside in fine weather, and the fish-based menus vary according to the catch.

Ver sur Mer ✉ 14114

Le Mas Normand, t 02 31 21 97 75, *http://perso.wanadoo.fr/ lemasnormand* (€€) Tall, characterful 1778-built stone house which has been restored by a young couple, Mylène and her chef husband Christian. The three quiet bedrooms

ⓘ **Courseulles-sur-Mer >>**

5 Rue du 11 Novembre, t 02 31 37 46 80, www.courseulles-sur-mer.com

ⓘ **Ouistreham >**

Jardins du Casino, t 02 31 97 18 63, www.ville-ouistreham. fr; information point too in Place Charles de Gaulle, near the ferry terminal

(i) **Arromanches >**
*2 Rue du Maréchal
Joffre, t 02 31 22 36 45,
www.arromanches.com*

have beams and modern comforts and are furnished with fabrics and soaps from Mylène's native Provence. You'd be daft not to dine (€€) and try Christian's Norman specialities.

Arromanches and Tracy-sur-Mer ✉ 14117

La Marine, Quai du Canada, t 02 31 22 34 19, *www.hotel-de-la-marine.fr* (€€). The sound of the waves lull you to sleep at this classic, friendly hotel bang on the seafront. With great views of the beach and Mulberry harbour, it's long been a Veterans' favourite. The 28 smart rooms have recently been refurbished to a high standard, although they vary in size. The comfortable restaurant (€€€–€€) has panoramic views and good fish specialities. *Closed Nov–mid-Feb.*

Crépon-Creully ✉ 14480

Ferme de la Rançonnière, Route d'Arromanches, Crépon, t 02 31 22 21 73, *www.ranconniere.com* (€€€–€€). The oldest part of this magnificent fortified farm is 13th-century. It's run by the quietly delightful Isabelle Sileghem and her husband. Rooms, around a broad courtyard, range from basic with shower to baronial suites with ample bathrooms, beamed ceilings and wonderful hand-carved Norman armoires. There are good half-board rates if you eat in the excellent restaurant (€€€–€€), which serves fine Norman fare (especially poultry). For total tranquillity, stay at the family's nearby 18th-century manor house, the Ferme de Mathan (€€€–€€), with fewer beams but sumptuous antiques.

Manoir de Crépon, Route de Caen-Arromanches, Crépon, t 02 31 22 21 27, *www.manoirdecrepon.com* (€€). This lovely rust-coloured old manor belongs to the village's mayor, Anne-Marie Poisson. Her light and spacious B&B rooms are tastefully decorated with antiques, and include two suites with private bathroom. There's a great garden too.

Hostellerie St Martin, Place Paillaud, Creully, t 02 31 80 10 11, *www.hostelleriesaintmartin.com* (€). The 12 rooms are clean but unexciting, but this venerable hotel's charm is its location at the heart of this pretty village. Its excellent restaurant (€€–€) in the 16th-century market serves Norman staples, including plenty of duck and goose.

Reviers ✉ 14470

La Malposte, Patricia & Jean-Michel Blanlot, 15 Rue des Moulins, t 02 31 37 51 29 (€). The three B&B rooms here, in a 'hunting lodge' next to an old mill in Reviers, less than 4km from Courseulles, are modern and colourful, and have views over a garden and rushing stream. The young owners are friendly and welcoming.

Sully, Maisons ✉ 14400

Château de Sully, Route de Port-en-Bessin, t 02 31 22 29 48, (€€€€–€€€). Opulent hotel in a magnificent 18th-century mansion in vast grounds just northwest of Bayeux, with fitness centre, indoor pool and a Michelin-starred restaurant (€€€). *Hotel and restaurant closed Dec–Feb.*

Manoir du Carel, Maisons par Bayeux, t 02 31 22 37 00, *manoirducarel@ yahoo.fr* (€€€). This 16th-century fortified manor, off the road between Bayeux and Port-en-Bessin, combines the austerity of its stone outside with luxury within. There are three comfy rooms, and copious breakfasts are served in the beamed dining room. There's also a *gîte*, with its own garden, which can be let by the night or for longer.

Omaha and the Marais

Unlike many towns along this coast, **Port-en-Bessin**, 11km west of Arromanches and 9km from Bayeux, is a real working fishing port: colourful boats, fishy smells and an excellent Sunday market take the place of the usual casino and thalassotherapy centre. Get up early and you can see the fish auction, where weather-gnarled

Getting around the Omaha Region

Bus Verts' route 70 runs from Bayeux to Grandcamp-Maisy, via Port-en-Bessin and all the Omaha Beach villages; and No.30 goes from Grandcamp to Carentan via Isigny.

Musée des Epaves Sous-marines du Débarquement
open June–Sept daily 10–12 and 2–6; adm

🚩 **Omaha Beach**

Musée D-Day Omaha
t 02 31 21 71 80, www.dday-omaha.net; open daily June–Sept 9.30–7.30; Mar–May and Oct–Nov 10–12.30 and 2–6; adm

fishermen dispose of their catch: Port-en-Bessin is famous for scallops, and naturally has its choice of seafood restaurants in which to try them. The other point of interest is one of Normandy's oddest private museums, the **Musée des Epaves Sous-marines du Débarquement**, which is, in effect, a scrapyard of wrecks retrieved from the D-Day landings. Collected by owner Jacques Lemonchois, who has the official salvage concession for the beaches, the objects run from whole tanks to pennies and safety pins. Some of the finds are for sale. Some find it ghoulish, others fascinating.

Moving west, the coast becomes hillier and the cliffs steeper, and inland the landscape turns into *bocage*, scrub-covered grassland between tall hedges. Partly because of this terrain, the 4km **Omaha Beach**, where the US Army's 5th Corps landed on D-Day, saw the worst casualties (*see* overleaf for an eye-witness account). The long beach runs past three villages, from east to west Colleville, St-Laurent and Vierville (all 'sur-Mer'). It's a very broad, open beach: those of the attackers who managed to land at low tide and avoid obstacles like 'Rommel's asparagus' and 'hedgehogs', and who had not been drowned by the weight of their equipment as they jumped from their vessels, had little defence against the Germans on top of the cliffs. As the invaders struggled forward they were cut down by withering small-arms fire, leaving a scene of devastation. Ultimately sheer numbers, toughness and heroism, backed by naval gunfire, allowed American forces to edge inland. The cost was high: of the 30,000 due to land on Omaha on D-Day, nearly 1,000 were dead by the end of the day. A memorial marks the site of the first US military cemetery on French soil, where those who died on the beach were buried. Given all this agony, it can feel incongruous to see summer sunbathers here topping their tans.

It was at Omaha, at the western end near Vierville, that the Americans assembled their own Mulberry harbour. No sooner was it afloat than it was shattered by the sudden storm. While the British repaired their less damaged harbour, the Americans, many of whom had been sceptical about Churchill's idea in the first place, abandoned the project and resorted to beaching craft to get supplies to shore. There are examples of landing craft outside the **Musée D-Day Omaha** in Vierville, near the site of the artificial harbour. The museum is privately-run and a bit worn, but has some everyday objects that make the war come alive, like coffee sachets, toothbrushes and shaving soap issued to US soldiers. There are

Omaha: the Landing from Hell

In the early hours of 6 June 1944, the mighty engine of the ship ceased and it was as quiet as the grave and everyone on board stopped what they were doing and gazed at each other, knowing full well the time had come. I could just make out the French shoreline in the distance. Above our craft the sky looked very hazy and the stars instead of being dim were a dull red, but worst of all we were being tossed about like a cork in a bottle.

The only noise I heard this night was the occasional rubbing of cloth against cloth and the heavy breathing of the soldiers as they found a place to sit, and just in front of me, a skinny soldier was bending forward, and although he was only speaking softly, I heard him saying the Lords prayer.

A mile away from the coastline all the great ships had been moored, and as each of the landing crafts were loaded, they pushed away from the mother ship to travel very slowly shoreward. On this landing we had drawn the short straw. The Germans were prepared and waiting for us and as the cold damp mist lifted from the shoreline we were sitting ducks.

The mist began to clear and one was able to see the brightness of the sun just clearing the edge of the horizon. This was when we heard the machine guns; the Germans were shooting at the first wave of boats to try landing on the beach. Two boats to the right of ours were blown completely out of the water, leaving debris and body parts floating on the sea. It would be impossible for me to describe the yells of pain and the death cries, and to make matters worse, there was nothing we could do about it for we all were the intended target. Every so often I would hear an explosion nearby and see pieces of metal fly through the air. Everyone in the boat was thinking, 'When will it be our turn?'.

The sky became quite light and we saw a haze of smoke as one of the crafts floated in flames on the sea. We were getting closer to the brownish white sands and we could make out the barbed wire and sea defences. Then all hell broke loose as the gunners onshore homed in on our boat. All at once the front of the landing craft disappeared, breaking in half and killing those at the front. The rest of us were left fighting for our lives in the wreckage.

I found myself in water up to my neck, just able to reach the sand on tip toes. The dead were floating all around me and I had to push them away as I and a few of my buddies made our way toward the sands. I had lost my rifle but at least I was alive.

About a dozen of us made it to the waterline, where we threw ourselves down among the dead bodies that had been washed up by the windswept sea. Just beside me, and huddled in a ball, was the young soldier I'd seen praying; he seemed to be crying like a baby boy. I lay amongst the dead. In fact, I played dead, for it did not take too much working out what the machine gunners were doing.

As each landing craft approached the sands, the gunners lying in concealment on the shoreline opened fire, killing or wounding everyone on board. This had not happened to the landing craft I was on, for an artillery shell had found our boat and soldiers in the sea are not very good targets. Each landing craft missed by the artillery had the machine gunners to reckon with. There were corpses everywhere. My leg was paining me, aching like hell, and I turned on my side and put my hand down to touch something very wet. Looking at my open hand I found it was covered in blood.

On this day I would suppose one man in every twenty reached the beach alive, but at least these men stood a chance of survival. Each of us knew we could not help our chums, only listen to the voices that gradually faded away. I put my hands over my ears to drown out the yelling and groaning of soldiers either dying or mortally wounded. I swear to God I never thought I'd ever see the day where I would be in this type of mess. To this day, I wonder why it was me that survived. Only God knows.

Then the battle became hand-to-hand combat, something I had been dreading. We were so incensed about the killing of our friends that we fought like demons, and believe me, prisoners were only taken towards the end of the conflict. I believe that when we breached the enemy's line, it opened up the chance for many of our soldiers to also breach the enemy's stronghold. Thus the battle for Omaha really began. I cannot remember every detail of the battle because I was too busy trying to stay alive. On this day, however, I knew what it was like to stare a man in the face and kill him – and this stays with me for the rest of my life.

CPL W. H. Nelson, 315th Infantry Division, United States Army; abridged by Clare Hargreaves.
Reproduced by kind permission of WW2 People's War, *an online archive of wartime memories:*
www.bbc.co.uk/ww2peopleswar.

chunks too of a British Lancaster Bomber and a US P47 Thunderbolt fighter, and the usual uniforms and hardware.

Musée-Mémorial d'Omaha Beach
t 02 31 21 97 44, www.musee-memorial-omaha.com; open daily July–Aug 9.30–7.30; mid-May–June and Sept 9.30–7; mid-Mar–mid-May and Oct–mid-Nov 9.30–6.30; mid-Feb–mid-Mar 10–12.30 and 2.30–6; adm

Omaha's other museum, the **Musée-Mémorial d'Omaha Beach**, is in St Laurent-sur-Mer, back towards the eastern end of the beach. Confusingly similar in name to the other museum but far larger and more organized, it's run by a passionate enthusiast, who for the past 30 years has been collecting D-Day memorabilia. He's been given items by veterans and farmers, and the museum has a good mix of German and Allied hardware, and an evocative recreation of Omaha beach as it would have been just before the landing. One of the most touching exhibits is a British helmet, covered in barnacles, dug up from the seabed by a diver. Outside, there's a US 155mm gun, and a Sherman tank.

American Military Cemetery
t 02 31 51 62 00, www.abmc.gov; open daily 9–5

Overlooking Omaha, on a magnificent clifftop location at Colleville, is the 70-hectare **American Military Cemetery**, a deeply moving sight with its pristine white marble crosses lined up in perfect rows. If they look bare, it's because they are all inscribed on the 'back' so they can face the US. It is a piece of transplanted America, with its White House-style monumental architecture and ever-so-trim lawns. And it's so huge that any individual gets lost in the sea of crosses, painfully underlining the grim reality of the landings. The 9,387 graves include four women nurses, Theodore Roosevelt Junior (the oldest soldier in the US troops, who died not in action but of a heart attack in July 1944), and two of the brothers of the soldier who inspired Spielberg's film *Saving Private Ryan*. There are also 307 graves to soldiers whose identity is unknown. The semicircular memorial contains a bronze statue that represents 'the spirit of American youth rising from the waves.'

Some kilometres beyond the western end of Omaha beach is **Pointe du Hoc**, a huge outcrop of rock with sheer 30-metre-high cliffs that Colonel James Rudder and his US 2nd Ranger Battalion scaled on the morning of 6 June in a bid to silence a German gun battery on top. The action was considered vital as the guns had both Omaha and Utah beaches within range. Unfortunately the assault started half an hour late, with the result that the men had to scramble up the cliffs amid a hail of German bullets. Of the 225 men who began the climb, only 90 were fit to fight by the end of the day, and 77 of them lay dead. In a tragic irony, it turned out the battery was a dummy, as the Germans had decided the point was too vulnerable and had moved their guns inland. Pointe du Hoc's eerily cratered landscape is a fit testimony to the ferocity of the fighting, although grass and broom have now healed over many of the earth's wounds. It's a strangely tranquil spot for watching the gulls fishing in the bay, or catching the sunset over the Cotentin.

West of the point is a charming little fishing port, **Grandcamp-Maisy**, with old boats in its harbour and fresh fish for sale on the

Musée des Rangers
open June–Aug daily 10–7, mid-Feb–May and Sept–Oct Tues–Sun 3–6; adm

quayside each morning. The Pointilliste painter Georges Seurat painted some of his first seascapes here, including a rendering of the Pointe du Hoc, which he called *Le Bec du Hoc*. The horrific drama that took place on Pointe du Hoc is recounted at the **Musée des Rangers**, an old-fashioned little museum with a video in English or French.

The Bessin-Cotentin Marshes

🔸 **The Bessin-Cotentin Marshes**

From Grandcamp-Maisy the D514 coast road veers south, as the Bessin is separated from the Cotentin Peninsula and Utah Beach by a giant *marais* or marshland, extending over 27,000 hectares and crisscrossed by rivers and ditches. It's now the centre of a national park, the **Parc Naturel Régional des Marais du Cotentin et du Bessin**, which in total covers 140,000 hectares and extends as far as the dunes on the west coast of the Cotentin. It's divided into lots of smaller reserves, with a series of local information centres scattered around the park (*see* p.278).

The narrow lanes that lead west from Grandcamp through tranquil **Géfosse-Fontenay** (with its fabulous bed and breakfasts, *see* p.279) peter out on the shores of the **Baie des Veys**, an atmospheric expanse of mud flats and oyster beds that looks out towards the St-Marcouf islands. Occasionally you can spot seals here. The *marais* are seasonally flooded, and are also on the migration route from northern Europe to Africa, so the range of birds varies according to the seasons. At any time, though, the wetlands contain an abundance of birdlife, including rare white storks, yellow wagtails, bitterns, buzzards and red-breasted mergansers. There are numerous observatories to allow you to see birds from close quarters. The park headquarters, Les Ponts d'Ouve, at **St-Côme-du-Mont** near **Carentan** (*see* p.278) provides ample information on walks and wildlife, shows videos, and gives nature tours, some specially for families. Marked trails you can walk on your own include the attractive 5km path through inland wetlands from **St-Germain-du-Pert** (signposted from the D514), and there are also cycling and riding trails. It's also possible to see the marshes by flat-bottomed boat (*see* below).

In June 1944, the *marais* proved hostile terrain for US paratroops, many of whom drowned in the floodwaters, weighted down by their equipment. Others gathered in the village of Graignes, where they were spotted by the Germans and surrounded. On 11 June, many Americans and the village priest were killed, the houses

Marais Boat Tours

For flat-bottomed boat tours through the marshes of the Marais, contact **Barbey d'Aurevilly II**, t 02 33 71 55 81 / t 02 33 71 65 30; or **La Rosée du Soleil**, t 02 33 55 18 07 / t 02 33 71 65 30. The former leaves from the Port Jourdan landing stage by Les Ponts d'Ouve information centre, the latter from La Taute landing stage. Phone or mail in advance for bookings May–Sept.

Wildlife Watching in the Marais du Cotentin

I spot a distant white stork stabbing its massive orange bill into the shallows, hunting frogs. And then a swallowtail butterfly shoots past. Such species are common here, and this 1,400-square-kilometre wetland holds a greater diversity and density of wildlife than anywhere I've been in Britain.

There's water everywhere – from the mighty River Vire, which drains western Normandy, to the streams, ditches and canals that riddle the open landscape. Water is slowly drawn to the sea around the town of Carentan, and each shallow river valley creates a mosaic of reeds, ponds, lakes and wild expanses of marsh known as *le marais*. These low-lying meadows flood in winter, creating a sullen landscape of slumped willows that is hugely attractive to wildfowl and waders. The floods recede in spring, leaving fertile farmland and flower-rich water meadows teeming with frogs, toads and newts. The coastline is a key stopping-off point for migrant birds on their way from southern Europe to Scandinavia. More than 40,000 ducks and waders turn up here each winter, resting on the flats and meadows by day and heading inland to feed in the *marais* at night.

You can walk along the Parc's byways and paths for many kilometres rarely meeting another human, though occasionally you come across ancient *maisons de marais* constructed of *torchis* – ochre-coloured wattle and daub farmhouses, smothered in creepers and as much home to house martins and sparrows as to Norman farmers.

Every step of the way, you can have encounters with wildlife. In spring, for example, I walked for 10km along the Canal de Vire et Taute, counting 37 species of birds along the way. By this time, I was getting blasé about the storks, egrets and myriad butterflies. But then, as I approached a vast reedbed, my first-ever bittern flew up just three metres in front of me, obviously feeling its reed-like disguise was about to be blown. Much bigger than I expected, it settled further away, deep within the reeds to begin blowing across the top of an empty bottle – or that's what its eerie, booming call sounded like.

Five minutes later, birds I'd assumed were buzzards turned out to be marsh harriers making their sky-dance courtship flights above the tussocky grassland of the floodplain.

Carentan is a good base from which to explore these rich habitats. From here you can take a boat up the River Taute deep into parts of the *marais* that are hard to reach on foot. And just north of the town is the small reserve of Les Ponts D'Ouve, where you can spy on the inhabitants of the *marais* from the comfort of numerous hides.

White Stork
When: March onwards each year, vanishing in autumn.
Where: If you're driving through the *marais* region, stop regularly wherever the landscape opens up. Those white blobs in the distance might not be sheep after all.

Swallowtail
When: Flies from mid-spring to midsummer.
Where: You're most likely to see the butterfly in unimproved marshland. However, I've also spotted it flying in gardens and over farmland.

Marbled Newt
When: Late March to June.
Where: Look in ponds and ditches almost anywhere, particularly in early spring when adults display their jagged crests.

Coypu
When: All year, but best when the water is lower in spring, summer and autumn.
Where: Look for them in the Cotentin's sluggish rivers and canals, where their large tunnels undermine the banks.

Marsh Harrier
When: Mostly migratory and so easiest to see in spring and summer.
Where: Marsh harriers are unmistakable during their slow hunting flights just above the reedbeds or water meadows. Look out for the golden-flecked head and mantle.

Fergus Collins. Reprinted by kind permission of BBC Wildlife Magazine

Dead Man's Corner Museum
t 02 33 42 00 42, www.paratrooper-museum.org; open daily 10–6; adm; guided tours on request

UCL Isigny
2 Rue Docteur Boutrois, t 02 31 51 33 88; www.isigny-ste-mere.com; guided tours in French and English July–Aug Mon–Fri 10, 11, 2, 3 and 4, rest of year by appointment; adm

pillaged and those taken prisoner executed. The harrowing story of the first clashes between the paras of the 101st Airborne and the Green Devils of the 6th Fallschirmjäger German Parachute Regiment is recounted at the new **Dead Man's Corner Museum** in **Saint-Côme-du-Mont**. The site has remained mainly intact.

Isigny-sur-Mer, at the western end of the Bessin, is famous for its dairy products, and above all *crème fraîche*. Isigny butter and cream even hold an *appellation d'origine contrôlée* (AOC) label, just like fine wines. EU hygiene regulations have become so strict now that it's virtually impossible to see cheese being made: however, the vast **UCL Isigny** factory, which makes fine cheeses as well as butter and cream, is a rare exception. Staff in white coats and bonnets stir the white sludge to be turned into cream or cheese, and there's a chance to taste and buy at the end.

(★) **L'Ecailler >>**

(i) **Grandcamp-Maisy >>**
118 Rue A. Briand, t 02 31 22 62 44, grandcamp.maisy @wanadoo.fr

(i) **Port-en-Bessin >**
Quai Baron Gérard, t 02 31 22 45 80, www.bayeux-bessin-tourism.com

Tourist Information around Omaha

For information on the Parc Naturel Régional des Marais du Cotentin et du Bessin, contact Les Ponts d'Ouve Information Centre, St-Côme-du-Mont, t 02 33 71 65 30, *www.parc-cotentin-bessin.fr*. A useful joint website for all the communes listed here (other than Port-en-Bessin): *www.cc-isigny-grandcamp-intercom.fr*.

Market Days: Port en Bessin: Sun; Vierville-sur-Mer: Mon; Grandcamp-Maisy: Tues, also Sat, or Sun in July–Aug; Isigny-sur-Mer: Wed, Sat.

Shopping around Omaha

Ferme du Lavoir, Formigny t 02 31 22 56 89. Small organic cider farm selling cider, calvados, apple juice and apple jelly. In summer they serve crèpes and *galettes* under the apple trees.

Ferme de la Sapinière, Saint-Laurent-Sur-Mer, t 02 31 22 40 51. Large farm selling cider, apple juice and calvados. They also run cider tours.

Where to Stay and Eat around Omaha

Port-en-Bessin ✉ 14520

★★★★La Chenevière, Escures Commes, t 02 31 51 25 25, *www.lacheneviere.fr*

(€€€€€). Successful marriage of country home and first-class hotel, just inland of Port-en-Bessin. All of its 27 rooms overlook a magnificent park, and it has a great restaurant (€€€€).

L'Ecailler, 2 Rue Bayeux, t 02 31 22 92 16 (€€€€). Fresh fish and lobster are kings at this sophisticated restaurant near the quayside. You can even (if your pocket allows) choose a menu in which every course – bar the dessert – is based on lobster. Chef Stéphane Carbonne's innovative cuisine has justifiably earned him a Michelin star, and the restaurant's stylish design provides a relaxing backdrop while you savour his dishes. *Closed Mon and (Sept–June) Sun eve and Tues lunch.*

Le Bistrot d'à Côté, 18 Rue Michel Lefournier, t 02 31 51 79 12, *www.barque-bleue.fr* (€€). A popular mid-budget restaurant, just off the harbour, where you'll find fish and *moules* cooked every which way, as well as vast platters of *fruits de mer*. *Closed Tues and Wed.*

Grandcamp-Maisy and Saint-Pierre-du Mont ✉ 14450

Le Château, Grandcamp Maisy, t 02 31 22 66 22 (€€). Two of the comfy bedrooms are in the ancient château that was built in 1580, and which owners Alain and Marion have skilfully restored. The other two B&B rooms are in the main house, and all around is a large garden and attractive outbuildings. Alain is a trawler master and will take you shrimp-fishing if you book. He's also passionate about birds.

Le Château, Saint-Pierre-du-Mont, **t** 02 31 22 63 79 (€€). Another place known as 'Le Château', with four grand rooms, some with views of the sea, set in an old stone château in a coastal hamlet 4kms east of Grandcamp. One has a private entrance. Great value.

La Marée, Quai Henri Chéron, **t** 02 31 21 41 00 (€€). Elegant little place on the harbour in Grandcamp-Maisy, where fishy menus are based on the daily catch. You can sît inside or out. *Closed Sun eve and (Sept–May) Mon.*

Géfosse-Fontenay ✉ 14230

⭐ Ferme-Manoir de la Rivière >

Ferme-Manoir de la Rivière, **t** 02 31 22 64 45, *www.chez.com/manoirdela riviere* (€). Stunning fortified farm with stone floors and sumptuous fabrics run by the enthusiastic Isabelle Leharivel and her farmer husband Gérard. The B&B rooms are huge; one has a little window looking out to sea, and the rest have views of cows in the fields. Home-made breakfasts are served beside the inglenook fireplace, and evening meals are available outside summer months (not Sun) with prior notice. In the garden there are barns, a *pigeonnier*, and a little watchtower made into a self-catering *gîte* for two. The owners also sell the work of local artists and craftsmen, and have bikes for hire.

L'Hermerel, **t** 02 31 22 64 12, *lemarie hermerel@aol.com* (€). Another equally magnificent fortified farm B&B, with its own *pigeonnier* and chapel. Parts of the building dates from the 15th century. The stylish beamed rooms are beautifully furnished, and the welcome is warm. *Closed Nov–Mar.*

St-Laurent-sur-Mer ✉ 14710

La Sapinière, 100 Rue de la 2ème Division d'Infanterie US, **t** 02 31 92 71 72, *www.chez.com/lasapiniere* (€). A hotel with a difference: the 15 bright and well-equipped rooms are in individual wooden cabins in the dunes behind Omaha beach. Each has a terrace at the back, and a sea view from the front. There's also an excellent restaurant (€) in another cabin, offering tasty *plats du jour* as well as the usual seaside *moules-frites* and crêpes. *Closed Nov–Mar.*

Longueville ✉ 14230

Le Roulage, **t** 02 31 22 03 49 (€€). One of Normandy's most stunning *gîtes au jardin* in an 18th-century stone farmhouse surrounded by a cluster of secret gardens with apple, pear and apricot trees, roses and hydrangeas. The two en-suite rooms are beautifully furnished with antiques, and breakfast (using home-made jams of course) is in the dining room overlooking the garden. A real find.

Utah and Ste-Mère-Eglise

North of the Marais and the Baie des Veys the coastline resumes as a seemingly endless stretch of sands and dunes along the southwest of the Cotentin Peninsula. Just beyond Carentan and the densest marshes a road turns east towards the little village of **Ste-Marie-du-Mont**, and after meeting the sea becomes a narrow coast road that runs along the edge of the thinly-populated dunes, through tiny beach villages. The expanse of sand between La Madeleine, east of St-Marie, and St-Martin-de-Varreville, where mussel-bed stakes now stand in place of German defences like 'Rommel's asparagus', formed the westernmost of the D-Day beaches, **Utah Beach**, landing zone for the US 7th Army Corps. It was just off here that the D-Day seaborne landings started, at 4.30am, with the capture of the **Iles St-Marcouf** (still a military

Getting around the Utah Beach Region

STN **bus** No.5 from Cherbourg to St-Lô stops at Ste-Mère-Eglise, Carentan and other points.
STN information, t 02 33 88 51 00.

zone), followed a couple of hours later by the first landings on the beach itself.

The main focus, for visitors to the massive sweep of dunes and marshes that is Utah, is by the beach itself, 6km from Ste-Marie-du-Mont, the **Musée du Débarquement-Utah Beach**. It was built on the exact site where, at 6.30am on 6 June, the first American soldiers landed on Norman soil. Part of it is also contained in an old German bunker. Like the one at Arromanches, the Utah museum makes effective use of the beach, of which it has a panoramic view, together with models, equipment and other relics. Touchingly, the museum was founded by the then-mayor of Ste-Marie-du-Mont, who was shot in error by US paratroops as they stormed a German battery, and then dedicated the rest of his life to ensuring the world would know the true and horrific story of what happened here. On 6 June, some 23,250 men and 1,700 vehicles landed on this beach. There are guided tours and a film in English.

Musée du Débarquement-Utah Beach
www.utah-beach. com; open June–Sept daily 9.30–7; April–May and Oct 10–6; Feb, Mar and Nov 10–5.30; adm

Around the Utah museum there are several monuments, many commemorating individual soldiers, and at Varreville there is a large memorial marking the return to French soil here, a few weeks after D-Day, of the French division under the legendary General Leclerc. Next door to the museum you cannot miss the lively beachside bar/restaurant (with Net access), **Le Roosevelt**, which has an engaging collection of war memorabilia assembled by the owner. He naturally welcomes veterans, who automatically get a

Le Roosevelt
*t 02 33 71 53 47,
www.le-roosevelt.com*

Utah Beach: The Least Costly Landing

In the first plans for the Normandy landings they were to be confined to three beaches, codenamed Omaha, Gold and Juno, but when this front appeared too narrow another was added to the east, Sword. The Allies then decided they needed to acquire a deep-water harbour as soon as possible and Cherbourg seemed an ideal candidate, so a fifth landing beach was included, Utah.

In advance of the sea landings, US paratroopers from the 101st and 82nd Airborne divisions dropped onto French soil a few minutes after midnight on the night of 6 June. Their aim was to take German gun batteries, cut roads and telephone lines and to secure the routes from the beaches. Meanwhile, US and British warships were mustering 10 miles off the coast. At 5.30am the ships began their bombardment of German defences. At 6.30am, men of the 8th Regimental Combat Team of the US 4th Infantry Division landed at Utah. Surprised by the lack of opposition, they discovered they'd come ashore 2km wide of their intended mark. Brigadier-General Theodore Roosevelt, the only general to land with the first wave of troops, was unfazed, and declared 'we'll start the war from here'. The beach was secured easily, and by 9am was under US control; by midday, tanks had reached Ste-Marie-du-Mont. In complete contrast to the carnage at Omaha, casualties among the seaborne troops were relatively light, and the 4th Division lost fewer than 200 men on D-Day – although the paratroopers inland, many of them cut off and still without any idea of just where they were, were having a far, far tougher time. The 4th Division's next task was to link up with the airborne divisions, and then to advance to cut the Carentan–Cherbourg road as part of the plan to isolate the Cotentin.

free drink and are invited to etch their signatures on the walls. Below the bar there's a bunker that served as a US Navy communications centre; to his delight, on the 50th anniversary in 1994, two veterans who had been radio operators here found their names scratched on its walls.

Halfway between the museum and Ste-Marie-du-Mont, the tiny beachside chapel of **La Madeleine** miraculously survived bombing in 1944 – in part, at least. It owes its existence to the anxiety of a Norse chieftain. The sea was so choppy that he promised that if he landed safely on the Norman coast he'd convert to Christianity and build a chapel; he did all three, and was baptised in the font that's still there today (the rest of the chapel was later rebuilt). Ste-Marie-du-Mont itself has a fascinating church, as well as a pleasant crêperie and a restaurant, all on the village square. There are also many fine walks from Ste-Marie into the Marais nature park (*see* p.276).

Ste-Mère-Eglise

The pretty stone town of Ste-Mere-Eglise, by the Cherbourg road 12km inland from Utah, is one of the most visited of all the Normandy sites, having been the hub of the US airborne landings on the night of 5–6 June. At the centre of the town is its 13th-century church, on whose tower a US paratrooper and his parachute were trapped as he tried to land. As anyone who has seen the 1960s film *The Longest Day* will recall, the poor paratrooper, John Steele, got caught on the tower as he fell and hung there throughout the night and much of the next day, ignored by the Germans around the church who assumed he was dead. Steele used to revisit Ste-Mère regularly until his death, and an effigy of him dangles incongruously from the tower to this day – one of Normandy's oddest war memorials. Many of his colleagues were less lucky, and were killed as they fell on the well-defended town, or speared by its chestnut trees. Their exploits are recounted inside the church, in a modern stained-glass window. Otherwise, the church is a fine example of pure Gothic, vaulted in the form of an upturned ship, and has magnificent carvings of animals that provide a welcome dash of humour in a town with so many grim memories.

Animals have always played an important part in the life of Ste-Mère-Eglise, and today, war associations aside, it's also known as the home of Normandy's biggest livestock market. In former times a huge hiring fair (*louerie*) was held in the town each 1 August, to which farm workers would come to get work for the following year. Today this has been replaced by the *Fête de la Grand' St Pierre* on the first weekend of August, a showcase of country crafts and a variety of animal contests.

Musée Airborne

t 02 33 41 41 35,
www.airborne-
museum.org; open daily
April–Sept 9–6.45;
Feb–Mar and Oct–Nov
9.30–12 and 2–6; adm

Across the square is the **Musée Airborne**, in two buildings both shaped (more or less) in the form of the parachutes used by the US 82nd and 101st Airborne Divisions in 1944. The first building houses a Waco glider, which you can climb inside, and a display of photos, letters, diaries, guns and equipment. There's also a 'cricket', a gadget that imitated the sound of the insect and with which the paratroopers were supposed to be able to identify friend or foe. Surprisingly for a museum focused on US troops, the documentation is only in French. The second part of the museum displays a genuine C-47 Dakota plane, just like the ones that dropped paratroopers or towed gliders on D-Day. There are interactive screens describing the operation in mind-blowing detail, and a 15-minute film on the C-47, but overall this museum – despite being one of Normandy's 'most popular' – doesn't tell its story very well. Just as useful, and highly enlightening, is the well-laid-out guided walk around the town, which leads to information boards at various points where crucial events unfolded. They give clear step-by-step accounts, with remarkable photos of the places where you stand as they looked during the battle.

Ste-Mère-Eglise also has a non-war-related attraction, especially enjoyable for children, in the first-class **Ferme Musée du Cotentin**, a stunning 17th-century farm housing traditional animal breeds like Cotentin donkeys and Norman Cob horses. Farm life in past times is also recreated in the kitchen, cider press and bread oven, and the museum organizes activities around themes like harvesting or bread-making.

In the middle of the countryside between the Cherbourg road and the sea around 9km north of Ste-Mère-Eglise, near the village of Azeville, is another hefty surviving relic of Hitler's Atlantic Wall, the **Batterie d'Azeville**, a set of giant bunkers on a hill that once housed heavy guns that sought to fire on the ships landing at Utah, until they were taken by US troops on 9 June. Unlike the Longues battery it no longer has its guns in place, but nevertheless the labyrinthine bunkers can still inspire awe, and there's a video exhibit on the battles in the area.

Ferme Musée du Cotentin

t 02 33 95 40 20,
musee.sainte-mere@
wanadoo.fr; open
July–Aug 11–7,
April–May 2–6; June
and Sept 11–6; adm

Batterie d'Azeville

www.cg50.fr; open
daily July–Aug 11–7;
April–May 2–6; June
and Sept 11–6; adm

Tourist Information around Utah Beach

Market Day: Ste-Mère-Eglise, Wed.

(i) **Ste-Mère Eglise >**
23 Place Abbé St
Pierre, t 02 33 21 00 33,
www.sainte-mere-
eglise.info

Where to Stay and Eat around Utah Beach

Ste-Mère-Eglise ✉ 50480

Manoir de Juganville, 39 Les Mezières, St-Martin-de-Varreville, t 02 33 95 01

97, *www.juganville.com* (€€). Four kilometres inland from the beach, this ivy-clad 16th-century stone manor has been stylishly restored to provide four attractive bedrooms with swish bathrooms. There's a relaxing lounge and library downstairs, and breakfast is in the dining room overlooking the large garden.

Les Quatre Etoiles, Turqueville, t 02 33 10 27 70, *www.quatre-etoiles.net* (€€). The oldest part of this turreted stone manor dates from the 18th century,

ⓘ **Carentan**
Boulevard de Verdun,
t 02 33 71 23 50,
www.ot-carentan.fr

but since then it's been used as a farm and had several additions. It's been cleverly converted into a *chambres d'hôte de charme* by its Dutch owners Francis and Tonnis Muntinga (he a publisher, she an interior designer) who moved here in 2002. Its four rooms are extremely elegant, there's a library in the old cider barn and huge gardens to relax in. Dinner is available on request.

Le John Steele, 4 Rue du Cap de Laine, **t 02 33 41 41 16 (€) An unspoiled inn with a pretty courtyard, named after the paratrooper who got snarled on the village tower. Its best rooms are in the main house; those in a modern annexe are more functional. The excellent restaurant (€€–€) gets busy, so book. *Restaurant closed Sun eve and Mon exc July–Aug.*

Ferme Musée du Cotentin, Chemin de Beauvais, **t** 02 33 95 40 20, *musee.sainte-mere@wanadoo.fr* (€). Four B&B rooms in a wing of the beautiful old farm that houses the farm-museum (*see* above). They have gorgeous beams and panelling, and the views and setting are superb. *Closed Dec–Jan.*

Bayeux

Everybody has heard of Bayeux's great tapestry, the only pictorial account of William the Conqueror's invasion of England. There's much, much more, though, to detain you among this old city's immaculately preserved grey-stone buildings, an engagingly varied mix with fine examples from the Middle Ages and each of the 16th, 17th and 18th centuries. They were miraculously spared destruction in the war: 10km from the landing beaches, Bayeux was the first sizeable town in France to be liberated, just one day after D-Day and without severe bombing, and briefly became the capital of Free France. With one of the largest and most comprehensive of Normandy's D-Day museums and the largest British war cemetery in the region, Bayeux has long been a favourite with British visitors. It has all the advantages of a town but few of the snags: the centre has largely escaped the gaudy street signs and bland new buildings that blight many other historic town centres, and its gardens and lazy river provide many peaceful havens for taking stock of it all.

Historically, Bayeux is one of the oldest and most important towns in Normandy. Over 2,000 years ago it was already an important Gaulish settlement, which then became a significant Roman town, which was attacked and sacked by Saxon raiders in the 4th century. After the departure of the Romans Bayeux, still the main town in the region, passed to the newly-arrived Franks, until Rollo, the famous Viking founder of Normandy (*see* p.29), married the daughter of the town's Frankish governor, and went on to produce the dynasty of the Norman Dukes. Rollo's son, William Longsword, was born in Bayeux in 905, and here too Harold swore he would accept the right of William the Bastard, Longsword's great-great-grandson, to the English throne. The story of what happened next is told by the town's most precious treasure, the tapestry, which attracts 400,000 visitors a year.

😊 Bayeux Tapestry

Centre Guillaume-le-Conquérant, Rue de Nesmond, t 02 31 51 25 50; open daily May–Aug 9–7; 15 Mar–April and Sept–2 Nov 9–6.30; 3 Nov–14 Mar 9.30–12.30 and 2–6; closed 2nd week Jan; adm, ticket includes Musée Baron Gérard

The Bayeux Tapestry

For centuries the Bayeux tapestry was known in France as the *Tapisserie de la Reine Mathilde*. The story went that while William was conquering England Matilda spent her lonely hours like a medieval Penelope, embroidering this memorial to her husband's deeds. In fact, Matilda was too busy raising their ten children, was in Caen and not Bayeux, and, as far as we know, had no particular penchant for sewing. It makes a good story all the same, and it's one that Napoleon made much of when he took the tapestry to Paris to whip up anti-English feeling.

If Matilda did not make the tapestry, who did? The definitive answer is lost in time, but this hasn't stopped historians arguing over it for centuries. The most likely explanation is that it was commissioned by Odo de Conteville, William's megalomaniac half-brother and Bishop of Bayeux, after 1066 but long before 1082, when he and William fell out and William had him imprisoned. Odo took part in the invasion, so had first-hand knowledge of the events depicted in the tapestry, and on his return to Bayeux he may have been looking for something to embellish his new cathedral. Being a man of large ego, he made sure to inflate his role in the conquest: no other Norman cleric is depicted, for example, and he placed himself at the centre of the action in critical moments. It's

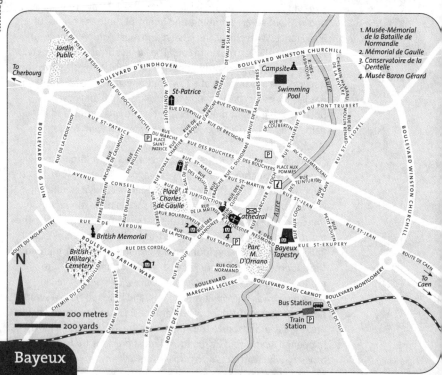

1. Musée-Mémorial de la Bataille de Normandie
2. Mémorial de Gaulle
3. Conservatoire de la Dentelle
4. Musée Baron Gérard

Bayeux

Getting to and around Bayeux

Bayeux has frequent **trains** on the Paris–Caen–Cherbourg line, and there are also trains to St-Lô, Coutances, Avranches and destinations in Brittany. **Train information, t** 0836 35 35 35, *www.ter-sncf.com*.

From the **bus station**, by the train station, Bus Verts No.74 runs to/from Courseulles-sur-Mer via Arromanches, and No.70 runs to/from Grandcamp-Maisy via Port-en-Bessin and Omaha Beach. There are also regular buses to Caen. Buses are infrequent on Sundays. **Bus Verts information, t** 0810 214 214, *www.busverts.fr*.

Like many Norman cities, Bayeux has a **Petit Train** which tours the old town April–Oct and visits the Battle of Normandy museum, the British cemetery and the British memorial. It departs at regular intervals from 11am from the corner of Rue Larcher and Rue Leforestier, by the cathedral.

also significant that the tapestry is the only source that presents Harold's supposed oath of loyalty to William as taking place in Bayeux – which may just have been more propaganda for Odo and his town.

The actual stitching, however, was probably done on the other side of the Channel. Pre-Conquest Normandy had no tradition of large-scale embroidery, but the Anglo-Saxons did, so it's believed that the tapestry was made by a team of English women, probably under the direction of monks in Winchester or Canterbury, and completed in time for the dedication of Bayeux cathedral in 1077. One of the tapestry's greatest qualities is its uniformity of style: the whole tapestry was clearly designed by a single, talented and well-informed eye.

The Great Comic Strip

Strictly speaking, the tapestry is not a tapestry at all, but an assembly of nine embroidered strips of linen, showing 58 panels, skilfully divided by trees or buildings. The last section is almost certainly missing, and most historians agree that it originally included a further three metres of post-Hastings scenes dealing with William's coronation. The embroidery we do have is a staggering 68.38 metres long, making it far the longest comic strip in history. The story is generally told in chronological order, but some events appear out of sequence, such as the burial of Edward the Confessor, which in the tapestry precedes his death. Although the tapestry is always described as an account of the Norman Conquest, in fact only just over half of it deals with the invasion; the rest portrays political events before the Conquest and, along the way, everyday life of the time, including enchanting scenes of places in Brittany and Normandy, among them the bay of Mont-St-Michel, where Harold has to rescue two of William's men from the tides and shifting sands.

The tapestry's delight is its naturalism, vigour and earthy detail. This naturalism is not literal – horses, for example, might be gold, yellow or blue. But we are given the minutest details about how people lived and acted, whether it's their hairstyles and clothes, the

The Tapestry's Own Story

The story of the Bayeux Tapestry is as colourful as the tapestry itself, and it's nothing short of miraculous that it survives today. The first known mention of it dates from 1476, when it was listed in an inventory of Bayeux cathedral. It describes how a 'very long and narrow hanging on which are embroidered figures and inscriptions comprising a representation of the Conquest of England' was displayed on the Cathedral's annual day of the Relics. The rest of the year it was presumably rolled up and stored away, which is probably why it survived fires and wars for the next 500 years. The next mention of the tapestry was in 1724, when a drawing of part of it was sent to Paris and used by Bernard de Montfaucon as the basis for the engravings of some scenes from the tapestry published in his *Monuments de la Monarchie Francaise* in 1729. It was also around this time that, for no apparent reason, the tapestry became known in France as Queen Matilda's Tapestry. Its survival during the Revolution was a close shave: it was grabbed from the cathedral, and would have been used as a wagon cover or cut up to provide material for a carnival float if a local magistrate had not intervened. In 1803 it was sent to Paris as propaganda for Napoleon's plans to invade England. When these were abandoned, the tapestry was sent back to Bayeux, relined, and then exhibited in the public library. During the 1939–45 war it passed through a number of hiding places, including the cellars of the Paris Louvre. It returned home to Bayeux in 1945.

carpenters' tools they use, or catering arrangements during the invasion – shields were turned into makeshift trays, for instance. Even the horses are overflowing with life: over 200 of them gallop across the tapestry, tossing their heads and pawing the ground, charging in battle, or somersaulting over one another. In contrast, the emaciated soldiers look limp and miserable. Harold, of course, looks every inch the double-dealer, with his drooping moustache and shifty expression.

A lot of the fun occurs in the borders. These disappear when the dramatic tension is high, as when William's brightly coloured Viking-prowed ships set sail. Towards the end, when the Battle of Hastings rages, the lower border becomes a dumping ground for dead and maimed bodies and for looters looking for pickings. Before this, though, there are delightful scenes of 11th-century agricultural life, from hunting and farming to seed-sowing. The menagerie of dogs, birds and fantastical griffins and dragons is charming, but also echoes the scenes they frame; look out for the lone dog beneath Edward's funeral procession. Unexplained, seemingly irrelevant, stories lurk in the borders too, like the lady who seems to be involved in a scandal with a priest. The inscription states enigmatically 'Where a clerk and Aelfgyva', and provides no verb to tell us what they were doing. The well-endowed male nude in the margins suggests it was something lewd.

Viewing the Tapestry

The Guillaume-le-Conquérant visitor centre in which the tapestry is housed provides a very comprehensive – and entertaining – range of information to place the embroidery in context, and a full visit can easily take 2½ hours or more. All the labelling, audio guides and so on are in English and some other languages as well as French. The visit begins with an in-depth introductory exhibition, with a timeline explaining William's dispute with Harold, commentaries and audiovisual displays. It's an invaluable preparation for the real thing, on a separate floor. There are a couple of films too, shown on the second floor. The tapestry is beautifully exhibited in a U-shaped darkened room, to protect it, and *autoguides* (headphones) in several languages are provided with a very informative scene-by-scene commentary.

Cathédrale Notre-Dame

Cathédrale Notre-Dame
open daily July–Sept 8.30–7, April–June 8–6, Oct–Dec 8:30–6, Jan–Mar 9–5

Begun around 1050, and completed under the patronage of Bishop Odo, Bayeux's cathedral was consecrated in 1077. This ceremony was Odo's greatest moment, and was attended by all the major figures of the Norman court, including William and Archbishop Lanfranc. Not only did Bishop Odo show off the magnificent cathedral he'd helped build but he almost certainly also displayed his spectacularly colourful tapestry, hung around the nave. In subsequent years it would be brought out on feast days, a visual treat for the illiterate masses. A fire ravaged the cathedral in the 12th century, however – although the tapestry survived – and the only bit of Odo's original building that is intact today consists of part of the front towers and the **crypt**, a gem of Norman architecture, with acanthus-leaf-clad carved capitals and lively frescoes of angels playing lutes and trumpets.

The rest of the church is a mix of Norman Romanesque and Gothic, the highlight being the highly decorated nave, which has some Middle Eastern-style tracery and outstanding late 12th-century stone carvings. Two women clasping hands are a touching portrayal of fidelity and friendship, another carving shows a stout bishop proudly clasping his crook, and elsewhere there's a juggler with a monkey. The lovely choir stalls date from the Renaissance era, and were made by a Caen cabinetmaker. The many depictions of Thomas à Becket, like the carvings on the tympanum of the portal in the south transept, are a reminder of the links between England and Normandy. The 12th-century Gothic **Chapterhouse**, next to the north tower, has a lovely blood-red 15th-century fresco of the Virgin, and consoles from which monsters and grotesque figures precariously hang.

After the 1789 Revolution the cathedral was converted into a Temple of Reason and the Supreme Being, but witnessed violent scenes when a crowd of destitute women dashed a bust of Rousseau to the floor to cries of 'When the good Lord was there we had bread!' The Revolutionaries, however, did have time to plant a 'Tree of Liberty', next to the old Bishop's Palace, by the cathedral's north side. This huge plane tree, now over 200 years old, still survives, giving welcome shade on hot summer days.

Around Old Bayeux

**Conservatoire de
la Dentelle**
*t 02 31 92 73 80;
open Mon–Sat 10–
12.30 and 2–6*

The **Conservatoire de la Dentelle,** just opposite the cathedral's west front at 6 Rue Bienvenu, is one of the last locations in Normandy where you can watch the making of bobbin lace, for which Bayeux has been famous since the 17th century. The art largely died out in the Industrial Revolution, but has recently been by resuscitated by lacemaker Mylène Salvador, who decoded the old designs by looking at antique lace through a magnifying glass. It's a fascinating place with a congenial atmosphere: groups of demure women, young and middle-aged, crouch over their clusters of pins, around which the threads and their bobbins are painstakingly wound. There's a permanent display of exquisite pieces, ancient and modern, including some amazing designer pieces, one in the form of a spider's web, another patterned like a brain. Anyone can enrol to learn this ancient art, too, as the Conservatoire provides a range of courses. It's also worth visiting just to see the building, the 16th-century **Maison d'Adam et Eve**, one of Bayeux's few remaining half-timbered houses. Carved on the façade are some magnificent naïve woodcarvings of Adam, Eve and a menacing-looking snake (the carvings of the plump Child Jesus and of St Michael and the dragon are much more recent).

More outstanding old town houses are spread around the nearby streets. There's a massive 14th-century timber-framed mansion at the corner of Rue des Cuisiniers and Rue de Saint-Martin, but the finest is the ornate **Grand Hôtel d'Argouges**, at 4 Rue St-Malo, where François I is said to have rested his head in 1532. These beautiful houses once stood within protective town walls surrounded by a moat, but only fragments of these walls remain. Much of Bayeux was obliterated in the Hundred Years' War, and then replaced in subsequent centuries by the stone houses we see today, but those were still dangerous times, which is why many houses have tiny windows and doors, and are topped by watchtowers. One of the most extraordinary is the four-storey **Hôtel du Croissant**, at the end of a narrow alleyway at right angles to Rue St-Jean.

**Mémorial du
Général de Gaulle**
*t 02 31 92 45 55; open
daily June–Aug
9.30–12.30 and 2–6.30;
Mar–May and Sept–Nov
10–12.30 and 2–6; adm*

The grandly baronial **Hôtel du Gouverneur** in Rue Bourbesneur, which dates from the 15th century, houses the **Mémorial du Général de Gaulle**. It celebrates the day General de Gaulle gave his first speech on liberated French soil from the Préfecture in Bayeux on 14 June 1944, with an unashamedly hagiographic movie showing the ecstatic crowds who greeted the French leader in Place du Château (now Place de Gaulle) just up the street, and the General conducting them in singing the *Marseillaise*. If the Gaullist fervour gets a bit much, look out for the views of what's left of Bayeux's medieval ramparts.

Musée Baron Gérard
*t 02 31 92 14 21;
open daily July–Aug
10–12.30 and 2–7;
Sept–June 10–12.30
and 2–6; adm, but
included in Bayeux
Tapestry ticket*

The **Musée Baron Gérard** in the lovely Hôtel du Doyen on Rue Lambert Leforestier beside the cathedral is best known for its collection of the decorated porcelain for which Bayeux became famous in the 19th century. The pieces are glazed in red, gold and blue, and lavishly decorated with flowers and exotic birds. The museum has some pleasing paintings too, including some Boudins, a small Corot, and a lovely work showing women embroidering by Gustave Caillebotte, an Impressionist friend of Degas, perfectly encapsulating the tranquillity of a hot summer's afternoon. There are also more examples of Bayeux's famous lace, including some outrageously tall lace headdresses.

Bayeux's War Museum and the British Cemetery

Musée-Mémorial de la Bataille de Normandie
Blvd Fabian Ware, t 02 31 51 46 90; open daily May–Sept 9.30–6.30; Jan–April and Oct–Dec 10–12.30 and 2–6; English film times: Oct–April 10.30, 2.45 and 4.15; May–Sept 10.30, 12, 2, 3.30 and 5; adm

The **Musée-Mémorial de la Bataille de Normandie** stands on one of the boulevards that ring Bayeux, southwest of town. It has recently been completely renovated, making it one of the largest and most important Normandy D-Day museums. Using an effective combination of sound, still and moving images and interactive activities, it retells the history of the Battle of Normandy from 7 June to 29 August 1944. The story is told chronologically, but also looks at themes such as war correspondents, the Resistance and the destruction of Normandy's towns. There's also a 25-minute film in French or English. Allow one to two hours for the visit.

On the other side of the same boulevard and a little to the east is the largest of the many **British war cemeteries** in Normandy, its simple white tombstones surrounded by a mass of bright flowers and manicured lawns. In line with Commonwealth War Graves Commission practice, the families of the dead were invited to suggest inscriptions, and many are deeply moving. The majority of the 4,868 graves are British, but in total 11 nationalities are represented here, and in a gesture of reconciliation several hundred of the graves are German. Across the road there's also a monument commemorating the 1,837 British and Commonwealth personnel lost in Normandy with no known grave.

Tourist Information in Bayeux

(i) **Bayeux >**
Pont St Jean, t 02 31 51 28 28, www.bayeux-tourism.com

The tourist office provides details of some excellent walking routes around the town centre.

In the first weekend of July, Bayeux gets into medieval mood at the *Fêtes Médiévales de Bayeux*, a commemoration of the Battle of Formigny in 1450, which ended the Hundred Years' War in Normandy.

Market Days: Sat, the principle market, Place Saint Patrice; Wed, a smaller market, Rue Saint Jean.

Post Office: 14 Rue Larcher
Internet: Hotel Novotel, 117 Rue St Patrice.

Shopping in Bayeux

Cidre et Calvados des Remparts, 4 Rue Bourbesneur-Place de Gaulle, t 02 31 92 50 40, *www.lecornu.fr.*

Francois Lecornu's apple orchards are on the outskirts of town, but his *caves* are in the middle of Bayeux in his large 17th-century stone house. Visitors can take a tour as well as tasting and buying calvados, excellent ciders and apple juice, and calvados apple jam. They also have *chambres-d'hôtes*, the Logis des Remparts (*see* below). *Closed Mon.*

Au Comptoir des Saveurs, 45 Rue St-Martin, **t** 02 31 21 57 99. A gorgeous store packed with local delicacies, from *pommeau* and cider to fine patés and biscuits. *Closed Sun and (Sept–June) Mon.*

Where to Stay around Bayeux

Bayeux ✉ 14400

★★★Château de Bellefontaine, 49 Rue de Bellefontaine, **t** 02 31 22 00 10, *www.hotel-bellefontaine.com* (€€€). Smart hotel in an 18th-century mansion in lush wooded grounds by the River Aure, on the southern edge of town. There's a lovely sitting room with fireplace, and it's very tranquil.

★★★Grand Hôtel de Luxembourg, 25 Rue des Bouchers, **t** 02 31 92 00 04, *www.bestwestern.fr* (€€€). Central, international-style hotel in a 17th-century mansion that's now affiliated to the Best Western chain. The rooms smack of chain hotels, but are nicely furnished. There's a smart restaurant, Les Quatre Saisons (€€€–€€). The same owners have another hotel next door, also affiliated to Best Western but slightly cheaper, the **★★★Hôtel de Brunville**, Rue Genas-Duhomme, **t** 02 31 21 18 00 (€€), with more 'mass-produced' rooms, and also with its own restaurant (€€).

★★★Lion d'Or, 71 Rue St-Jean, **t** 02 31 92 06 90, *www.liondor-bayeux.fr* (€€€–€€). This former coaching inn has been owned by the same family for 75 years. Rooms are decorated in traditional style, although some have recently been renovated in dazzling stripes. There's an excellent restaurant (€€€–€€). *Restaurant closed Sat lunch and Mon lunch.*

★★Argouges, 21 Rue St-Patrice, **t** 02 31 92 88 86, *www.hotel-dargouges.com*

(★) Logis des Remparts >>

(€€). Elegantly comfortable hotel in the 18th-century former mansion of the Argouges family, in a walled garden near Place St-Patrice. Rooms are divided between the main house, and a less grand house next door. Rooms combine modern comforts with château style, and the staff are charming.

Clos de Bellefontaine, 6 Rue de Bellefontaine, **t** 02 31 22 73 63 (€€). A really outstanding B&B in a honey-coloured stone manor with just two exquisite rooms, each on their own separate floor. The bright double on the first floor has a separate sitting room. Downstairs there's a stunning *salon* with a vast fireplace, which guests are free to use. The place is unusual in that it has a large garden. The delightful young owners make you feel totally at home.

Family Home, 39 Rue Général de Gaulle, **t** 02 31 92 15 22 (€). A cross between a hotel and a youth hostel, in a wonderful old building off Place de Gaulle. Guests can choose between beds in basic dormitory-style rooms, and a smarter single/double, which costs more. It's a friendly budget option, and pleasant as long as you don't mind rubbing elbows with school groups around the large table for dinner (€) or breakfast. Picnics can be provided, and non-guests can eat here too with advance notice.

Les Glycines, 13 Rue aux Coqs, **t** 02 31 22 52 32 (€). This attractive stone town house, run by a friendly farming couple, is ideally central. The three pretty guest rooms, furnished with antiques, look over the tiny garden.

Logis des Remparts, 4 Rue Bourbesneur, **t** 02 31 92 50 40, *www.lecornu.fr* (€). The friendly couple who run this B&B, as well as Bayeux's cider farm (*see* above) have done a superb job converting their old stone house. There are three bedrooms, one a two-room suite, all with antique furniture and original touches.

Le Petit Matin, 2 bis Rue de Quincangrogne, **t** 02 31 10 09 27, *www.lepetitmatin.com* (€). Fifteenth-century mansion on a quiet alley in the centre of town. There are three attractive rooms, and breakfast is in the antiques-filled dining room or in the garden. Dinner (€€) is on offer if you book in advance, and bikes are available for hire. A relaxing and welcoming place.

Les Trois Pierre, 22 Rue des Bouchers, t 02 31 92 34 38, *www.vinadom.com* (€). On a quiet side street in the centre of Bayeux, this pleasant little *chambres-d'hôtes* has four great-value rooms, including a family room. There's a little garden at the back.

St-Loup-Hors ✉ 14400

Manoir des Doyens, t 02 31 22 39 09, *m-jp.chilcott@tiscali.fr* (€). A lovely golden 17th-century stone house with its own orchard, in a village 2km south of Bayeux owned by a British military historian and his wife, who makes wonderful jams and croissants for breakfast. They have three spacious, comfortably casual B&B rooms.

Subles ✉ 14400

Moulin du Hard, Route de St-Paul-du-Vernay, t 02 31 21 37 17 (€€). Large old stone mill beside its own river (where you can fish). The friendly owners have restored it beautifully, making full use of natural materials. There are two B&B suites, each with two rooms, bathroom and lovely views. Subles is 5km south of Bayeux.

Eating Out in Bayeux

La Coline d'Enzo, 2–4 Rue des Bouchers, t 02 31 92 03 01 (€€€). Don't be misled by the name – there's nothing Italian about the cooking at this delightful restaurant, which is fast earning the accolade as the town's top gourmet choice. Chef Nicolas Marie delights in combining Norman traditions with international ideas. *Closed Sun and Mon.*

La Rapière, 53 Rue Saint Jean, t 02 31 21 05 45, *www.larapiere.net* (€€€–€€). Another must-try for foodies. This cosy beamed restaurant in the centre of town offers great-value Norman classics. Meat and fish are equally flavoursome and exquisitely prepared. For dessert try the mouth-watering *chaud-froid de fruits du marché sur lit croustillant.* Book a table upstairs. *Closed Wed and Thurs.*

L'Amaryllis, 32 Rue St Patrice, t 02 31 22 47 94 (€€). Small, pretty restaurant at the western end of Bayeux's main street run by a charming husband and wife team. Chef Pascal Marie offers refined, Norman dishes using fabulously fresh local ingredients. The duck, for example, is from down the road. Fantastic value. *Closed Sun eve and Mon.*

Le Petit Bistrot, 2 Rue du Bienvenu, t 02 31 51 85 40 (€€). Bijou place in a bijou location, opposite the cathedral. Imaginative cooking, including sea-food specials. Book ahead, as there are only a few tables. *Closed Sun and Mon.*

L'Assiette Normande, 3 Rue des Chanoines, t 02 31 22 04 61 (€€–€). Small, good-value restaurant near the cathedral, with good low-price menus. *Closed Mon.*

Le Pommier, 38/40 Rue des Cuisiniers, t 02 31 21 52 10, *www.restaurantle pommier.com* (€€–€). The location opposite the cathedral, means plenty of tourists find this place, but that doesn't detract from its friendly service, attractive interior and great-value Norman food. *Closed Tues and Wed.*

South and West of Bayeux

Château de Balleroy
t 02 31 21 60 61, www.chateau-balleroy. com; open daily mid-Mar–mid-Oct 10–6; Jan–mid-Mar and mid-Oct–20 Dec 9.30–12 and 2–5; adm

The attractive 80km (50-mile) -wide triangle of land between Caen, Bayeux and St-Lô contains two remarkable treasures: the château at Balleroy, and the Abbaye de Cerisy-la-Forêt. To reach either, you really need your own wheels.

Balleroy

If you approach Balleroy from the east you see the neat, grandiose façade of the **Château de Balleroy** long before you get

Getting around South and West of Bayeux

It's difficult to see this area without a **car**, but Bus Verts' infrequent **bus** No.71 bus runs from Bayeux to Balleroy, and No.8 runs from Caen to Tilly-sur-Seulles.

there, in the distance at the end of a long, straight tree-lined road. There's no discretion here, rather a blatant flaunting of the owner's wealth and power. That this was considerable can be seen from the fact that the entire village was rebuilt around his château. The designer behind this grand scheme was none other than François Mansart, one of the greatest architects of his time, who built Balleroy in 1631–6 for Jean de Choisy, Chancellor to Gaston d'Orléans, brother of Louis XIII. The gardens, originally at the back rather than the front, were designed by the equally prestigious André Le Nôtre, who crafted the gardens at Versailles. In 1704 the château passed by marriage to the Balleroy family, ennobled by Louis XIV, who managed to keep it through the Revolution and right up to 1970. The most famous member of the line was Albert de Balleroy, a 19th-century painter and friend of Manet and other Impressionists. Due, perhaps, to his wealth the poor man has been relegated by history to the rank of second-rate artist.

In 1970 Balleroy was jolted from its provincial sleepiness when the château was bought by American multimillionaire Malcolm Forbes, owner of *Forbes Magazine*, and pal of numerous US presidents. He restored and furnished the place, and decorated it with photos of himself hobnobbing with celebrity friends like Elizabeth Taylor or Ronald Reagan, many of whom visited here. But above all he used Balleroy to indulge one of his passions, ballooning, and set up a balloon museum and organized balloon meets. These meets have been less frequent since Forbes' death in 1990, but the museum is still aloft and his son Christopher still visits the house occasionally for glitzy weekend parties.

The house consists of a three-storey central block flanked by single-storey wings, all topped by mansard roofs. The moat was for fun rather than function, and was never filled with water. Through the hallway, whose lovely staircase appears to be suspended in air, the first room on the tour is the *Salon Louis XIII*, with a stunning wood ceiling and wall panelling in matching grey. Here and in the smoking room next door you see Albert de Balleroy in full flow – all the paintings, most of them gory hunting scenes showing hounds tearing stags to pieces, are his work. In utter contrast, the smoking-room ceiling, painted with brightly coloured balloons, gives a foretaste of Forbes' playful originality. On the far wall there is a portrait of one of the Balleroy brothers who was guillotined in the Revolution – indicated by the black scarf around his neck. Also of interest are the fine carvings of scenes from La Fontaine's *Fables* in the 18th-century oak panelling. The next three 'themed' rooms reflect the Forbes family's passion for European history. The first two are dedicated to Queen Victoria (though there's still a balloon-shaped chandelier) and Louis-Philippe, while the third is rather grandly called the Waterloo suite, with a wacky juxtaposition of Napoleonic memorabilia with items associated with his enemy the Duke of Wellington. The last room in the visit is the *salon d'honneur*, the most authentic room in the château, which still has its original magnificent, and beautifully restored, parquet floor.

Around the château are the ornamental gardens, made by Duchêne to La Nôtre's designs. The stable blocks house the bookshop and the **Balloon Museum**, stuffed with balloonabilia of every kind. At the end of it there may be little you don't know about balloons, or about the ballooning adventures of Forbes and his chums. To come down to earth, wander in the park behind the house and visit the tiny church, also designed by Mansart in 1651, or sit in a café on the peculiarly grand village square.

Cerisy-la-Forêt and Mondaye

Heading northwest from Balleroy, through the beautiful natural beech forest of the **Forêt de Cerisy** – wonderful for walks – you reach one of the most impressive but least-known of early Norman

Abbaye de Cerisy-la-Forêt
t 02 33 57 34 63; open Easter–Oct daily 9–6.30; guided tours Easter–Sept daily, Oct Sat–Sun; adm

abbeys, the **Abbaye de Cerisy-la-Forêt**. It was founded by William the Conqueror's father, Robert the Magnificent, on the site of an existing monastery, and most of it had been built by the time William invaded England. It's on the edge of the tranquil village, with cows in the fields around it and grassy slopes on one side that drop down to a lovely pond, which used to supply the monks with fish and water, and is now surrounded by interesting modern sculptures. The waters haven't always been so calm: in 1562 the abbey was ransacked by Protestants, and during the abbey's centuries of decline it was often knocked about, and even partly demolished. The most important parts, though, remain remarkably intact, including the **Abbatiale** (abbey church), the **Salle de Justice** (courtroom) and the Gothic **Chapelle de l'Abbé**, added in 1260. The church's simple interior is a gem of Norman Romanesque, and contains an exhibition on Norman architecture.

Abbaye de Mondaye
t 02 31 92 58 11, www.mondaye.com; open daily 9–12 and 2.30–6; guided tours daily July–Aug; adm

Further east in Juaye-Mondaye is the **Abbaye de Mondaye**, a classical-style monastery and church in large grounds. Unusually, the whole complex was erected at the same time, in the early 18th century, which gives it a restrained harmony, although the fourth side of the cloisters was never built because the monks ran out of money. It's still inhabited by monks of the Prémontré or Norbertine Order, which emphasises work in the community. The church is open for services, and accommodation is available for retreats. In summer the abbey also hosts concerts.

Tilly-sur-Seulles

Tilly's cheerful-sounding name belies the agony suffered by this little village in 1944. Virtually all of its buildings were destroyed, one in ten of its population perished and entire families were wiped off the face of the earth. Even the dead got no peace: bodies were laid to rest in the school, but that was then burned by the Germans, prompting locals to say they had 'died twice.' As the Germans and British fought for control, poor Tilly was tossed like a football between the two sides – 23 times, to be precise, in the space of 12 days. In the fierce fighting around the school and the aptly named Rue d'Enfer (Hell Street), soldiers from the British 50th Division and German Panzer Lehr Division faced each other bayonet to bayonet. The tiny **Musée de la Bataille de Tilly-sur-Seulles**, in a restored 12th-century chapel, is a poignant display that was set up by the villagers themselves, with many contributions from British veterans. It stands out from other war museums in that it's about ordinary people, rather than hardware. A memorial lists the villagers who died: unlike the inhabitants of cities, Tilly's were trapped and couldn't get away. The list includes six members of the family of one of the excellent guides who lead tours. Outside the chapel is a statue of Joan of Arc, which was hit by a shell. Incredibly, it tore out her heart but left the rest intact. Outside Tilly, there's another **British war cemetery**, with 1,224 graves.

Musée de la Bataille de Tilly-sur-Seulles
open Sat–Sun 2–6; adm for non-veterans

Where to Stay and Eat South and West of Bayeux

Balleroy ✉ 14490

Manoir de la Drôme, 129 Rue des Forges, t 02 31 21 60 94, *www.manoir-de-la-drome.com* (€€€€–€€€). Michelin-starred restaurant in a pretty old stone house beside the River Drôme. Among chef Denis Leclerc's impressive creations are *turbot aux épices douces* (turbot with sweet spices) or *fricassée de sole au foie gras et pâtes fraîches* (sole with foie gras and home-made pasta). *Closed Sun eve, Mon, Tues lunch, Wed and Feb.*

Le-Breuil-en-Bessin ✉ 14330

***Château de Goville**, t 02 31 22 19 28, *www.chateaugoville.com* (€€€€–€€€). Set in lush parkland, this 18th-century manor 12km southwest of Bayeux has been in the same family for 300 years. The current head of the house, Jean-Jacques Vallée, is a passionate collector – of buttons, Wedgwood china, toy soldiers – and each of the rooms, furnished in antiques and with lovely views, has its own character and name: 'Pink Adeline', with windows on three sides, is especially fine. There's an elegant restaurant (€€€) with garden views. *Restaurant closed Tues and Wed.*

Tessel ✉ 14250

La Londe, Paul & Eliane Amey, t 02 31 80 81 12, *paul.amey@wanadoo.fr* (€). A 19th-century house 3km southeast of Tilly, with a pretty garden and furnished in simple country style. The three rooms all have basins, but share a bathroom and loo.

Bricqueville ✉ 14710

Le Relais du Marais, t 02 31 51 74 71, *www.relais-du-marais.com* (€). The three impeccable guest rooms in this old stone manor have been prettily decorated by owner Mireille Dufour. Breakfast is in the airy dining room, with views of the large gardens.

The Suisse Normande and Southern Normandy

The hills of La Suisse Normande may not quite be the Alps, but the rocky peaks and craggy gorges of this enchanting stretch of the River Orne are certainly dramatic compared to the rest of Normandy. In summer, canoeists, hang-gliders and rock-climbers flock here, while the less energetic take it easy on the willow-clad riverbanks.

Lace, horses and pear orchards are the highlights of the region further south, most of which falls within the département of the Orne. Great forests clothe the undulating landscape and the lace-making town of Alençon is a surprisingly relaxing departmental capital.

15

Don't miss

⭐ **Rocky outcrops, willows and winding lanes**
Clécy **p.298**

⭐ **Birthplace of William the Conqueror**
Falaise **p.303**

⭐ **Equestrian paradise**
Le Haras National du Pin **p.309**

⭐ **French home of lace**
Alençon **p.312**

⭐ **Pears and perry**
Domfront **p.321**

See map overleaf

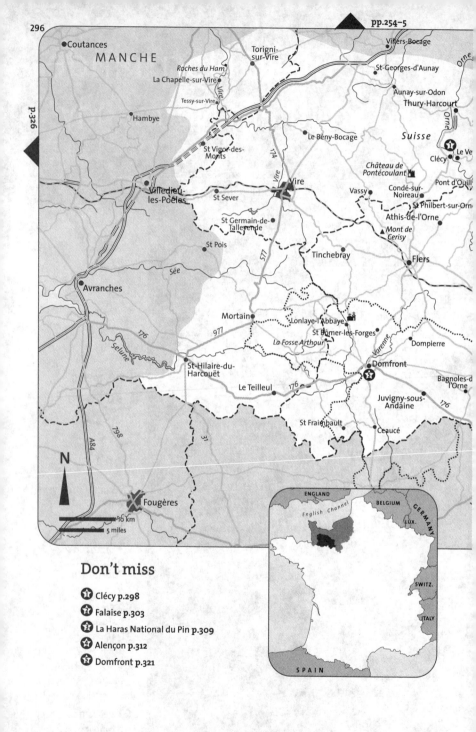

pp.254-5

p.326

Coutances

MANCHE

Torigni-sur-Vire

Villers-Bocage

Roches du Ham

La Chapelle-sur-Vire

St-Georges-d'Aunay

Tessy-sur-Vire

Aunay-sur-Odon
Thury-Harcourt

Hambye

Le Bény-Bocage

Suisse

St Vigor-des-Monts

Le Ve
Clécy

Château de Pontécoulant

Pont d'Ouill

Vire

Condé-sur-Noireau

Villedieu-les-Poêles

St Sever

Vassy

St Philbert-sur-Orn

St Germain-de-Talleyende

Athis-de-l'Orne

Mont de Cerisy

St Pois

Tinchebray

Flers

Sée

Avranches

Mortain

Lonlaye-l'Abbaye

St Bomer-les-Forges

Dompierre

La Fosse Arthour

St-Hilaire-du-Harcouët

Domfront

Bagnoles-d
l'Orne

Le Teilleul

Juvigny-sous-Andaine

Selune

Ceaucé

St Fraimbault

N

Fougères

26 km
5 miles

ENGLAND

English Channel

BELGIUM

GERMANY

LUX.

SWITZ.

ITALY

SPAIN

Don't miss

Map labels:

CALVADOS

Bretteville-sur-Laize

St-Pierre-sur-Dives · Livarot · Orbec

Potigny

Le Petit Coulibœuf · Vimoutiers

Normande · Falaise · Morteaux-Coulibœuf

Villy-lez-Falaise

Camembert

Rouvrou · Roche d'Oëtre · Montormel

Gorge de St Aubert

Trun

Chambois

Putanges · Le Bourg-Léonard · Gacé · L'Aigle

Orne · 26 · Exmes

924 · Argentan · Silly-en-Gouffern · Haras du Pin

Briouze · Écouché · Château de Médavy · Risle · 26

St Cristophe-le-Jajolet · Abbaye-de-la-Trappe

Château de Sassy · Macé

Rânes · Boucé · Mortrée

La Ferté-Macé · Sées · Soligny-la-Trappe

Magny-le-Désert · 908 · Carrouges · ORNE

Forêt · Essay

Parc Naturel Normandie-Maine d'Écouves

St Denis-sur-Sarthon

St-Céneri-le-Gérei · Alençon

St Léonard des Bois · Champfleur

p.188

The Suisse Normande

This area's grandiose postcard-label of 'Suisse Normande'
apparently arose out of a throwaway remark by a French
government minister on a visit to the area in 1932, but somehow
the name has stuck. Certainly by Norman standards, it does have a
ruggedness that you cannot find elsewhere. With the exception of
pretty Clécy, the area's towns were badly mangled in the war, so
visitors come here not for urban architecture but for inspiring
landscapes. For anyone remotely active, there are countless
possibilities; to find out what's on offer, consult the region's
website: *www.suisse-normande.com*.

Getting around the Suisse Normande

Bus Verts' No.34 bus between Caen and Flers stops at Thury-Harcourt, Clécy, Condé-sur-Noireau and other points en route. **Bus Verts information, t** 0810 214 214, *www.busverts.fr*.

Thury-Harcourt

Thury, northernmost point of 'Norman Switzerland', adopted the second part of its name from the Harcourt family, who in 1700 made Thury their ancestral seat. They built the fine **Château d'Harcourt**, which was later home to the Governors of Normandy, but both château and town were devastated in 1944. The town has been rebuilt in the usual modernist style but all that's left of the château is its chapel and 70 hectares of delightful **parks and gardens**. The gardens, along the banks of the Orne, are spectacular in spring, when the grassy alleys are carpeted with narcissi and tulips. There's a lovely walk, too, around the big, wild lake.

Château d'Harcourt
t 02 32 45 07 11; parks and gardens open July–Aug daily 10–8; Mar–June and Sept–Nov Wed–Mon 2.30–6; adm

Clécy and the Orne Gorges

⭐ **Clécy**

Grey-stone **Clécy**, perched above the rushing Orne, is the Suisse Normande's most scenic stop. From its winding lanes you get breathtaking views of the dramatic **Pain de Sucre** (Sugarloaf), a rocky outcrop overhanging the river, and of the tiny farmsteads that dot the hills. Most people come here for the restaurants and boats, which pack the riverbanks below the town around its popular sister village, **Le Vey**. It's a pleasant place to sip coffee under the willows. In a local legend, some thieves stole a church bell from Pont d'Ouilly, but as they galloped off to Clécy, their horses stumbled and the bell tumbled into the river. It's said that from beneath the waters the bell still tolls every Christmas Eve, summoning the faithful to mass.

Clécy village, with its granite hilltop houses, has quite a different atmosphere from Le Vey. The helpful tourist office will equip you with information on walks and other activities in the area, including a delightful two-hour circuit around the Pain de Sucre. The office also houses the **Musée Hardy**, a collection of local landscape paintings by artist André Hardy. Halfway between the village and the river, the **Musée du Chemin de Fer Miniature** delights train and modelling buffs with a specially-built hangar containing some 250 model locomotives and 400 metres of track. The collection has been assembled and cherished over 35 years by Yves Crué and his son, Emmanuel, and includes a complete model town. In the gardens there's a miniature train children can ride in, and a snack bar serving farm cider and crêpes.

Musée Hardy
open Mon–Sat 10–12.30 and 2.30–6.30

Musée du Chemin de Fer Miniature
t 02 31 69 07 13, www.chemin-fer-miniature-clecy.com; open July–Aug daily 10–12 and 2–6.30; Easter–June daily 10–12 and 2–6; Sept Tues–Sun 10–12 and 2–6; Oct Sun 2–5; Mar–Easter Sun 2–5.30; adm

From Le Vey an idyllic country road follows the river southeast to **Pont-d'Ouilly**, at the confluence of the Orne and the Noireau. Much of it was destroyed in 1944, so it lacks Clécy's charm, but the 15th-century **Chapelle St Roch** was mercifully spared. The village is most popular, though, for watersports, and as a jumping-off point for climbers and walkers. The most spectacular point nearby is the **Roche d'Oëtre**, a giant crag dominating the densely forested valley below. From the viewing table at the top there are stupendous views. The escarpment below is said to look like a human face, and the rock also contains a cave used in the 1790s as a hideout by Normandy's counter-Revolutionaries, the Chouans. A wonderful two-hour walk starts and finishes at the Roche d'Oëtre, passing through **St-Philibert-sur-Orne** and **Rouvrou**. For something shorter, there's an easy stroll from Rouvrou to the **Méandre de Rouvrou**, a shady bend in the river. There are also great walks along the **Gorges de St-Aubert**, south of the Roche d'Oëtre towards Putanges.

Condé and Pontécoulant

Southwest of Clécy, **Condé-sur-Noireau** was largely rebuilt after 1945, but has a good array of shops where you can stock up for walks. It's also famous in France as the birthplace of Admiral César Dumont d'Urville, who explored New Guinea, the Pacific islands and Antarctica in the 1820s and 30s. Condé is within reach of some of the Suisse Normande's prettiest countryside, including the tranquil valley of the Druance, on whose wooded banks stands the turreted **Château de Pontécoulant**. The Le Doulcet family lived there from the 14th century, but the current buildings date from the 16th and were substantially enlarged later as the family moved up the social scale. The dovecote bears witness to their wealth and status. The house was left to the Calvados *département* in 1896 after the last member of the family died, and it is now a museum with a fine collection of old furniture and family portraits. Equally attractive is the huge wooded park around the house.

Château de Pontécoulant
t 02 31 69 62 54; open mid-April–Sept Wed–Mon 10–12 and 2.30–6; Nov–mid-April Wed–Sun 2.30–4.30; adm

Tourist Information in the Suisse Normande

The listed tourist offices organize guided walks and provide information on all kinds of outdoor activities. Also useful is the area's joint website, *www.suisse-normande.com*.

Market days: Thury-Harcourt: Thurs; Pont d'Ouilly: Sun; Athis de l'Orne: Tues; Condé-sur-Noireau: Thurs.

ⓘ *Clécy* »
*Place du Tripot,
t 02 31 69 79 95*

ⓘ *Thury-
Harcourt* ›
*2 Place St-Sauveur,
t 02 31 79 70 45, otsi.
thury@wanadoo.fr*

Where to Stay and Eat in the Suisse Normande

Thury-Harcourt ✉ 14220
***Relais de la Poste, Rue de Caen, **t** 02 31 79 72 12, *www.ohotellerie.com*

(€€–€). Horse-drawn carriages used to pull up outside this old *relais de poste*, but it's now a welcoming hotel. Rooms are elegant and comfortable, and there's also a sauna, sun bed and large garden. A barn-style outhouse accommodates a fine restaurant (€€€–€€) where you can choose your lobster or crayfish from the aquarium. *Closed Sun eve and Mon in Oct–April and 23 Dec–Jan.*

Clécy, Le Vey ✉ 14570
***Moulin du Vey, Le Vey, **t** 02 31 69 71 08, *www.moulinduvey.com* (€€€–€€). This ancient flour mill on the tranquil banks of the Orne has been turned into a smart hotel with a lovely garden and also a *salon de thé*. The

(i) **Pont d'Ouilly >>**
Bd de la Noé,
t 02 31 69 29 86

hotel also owns two other establishments nearby, the Manoir de Placy and the Relais de Surosne, which have similar prices, and also have apartments to suit families. The Moulin has a formal restaurant (€). *Restaurant closed Sun eve and Mon lunch in winter. Hotel closed Dec–Jan.*

**Au Site Normand, Clécy, t 02 31 69 71 05, sitenormand@voila.fr (€). Traditional Logis hotel in the middle of the village opposite the church. Rooms are calm if unexciting, and there's a thoroughly old-style Norman restaurant (€€).

La Ferme du Vey, Le Vey, t 02 31 69 71 02, www.la-ferme-du-vey.com (€). Old stone farmhouse a few yards from the bridge at Le Vey, with three simple but pleasant B&B rooms. Ceilings have beams and one room has lovely views over the countryside. It's also a working cider farm.

(i) **Condé-sur-Noireau >>**
29 Rue du 6 Juin,
t 02 31 69 27 64,
www.conde-sur-noireau.com

Le Manoir de Miette, Le Vey, t 02 31 69 45 80 (€). Stunning stone manor with lovely stone carvings in colourful gardens. The three rooms don't really do the house justice, but are clean and quiet and the location makes up for any lack of sophistication. There's also a tiny cottage in a dovecote, with its own entrance and kitchen.

Pont-d'Ouilly ✉ 14690

**Auberge Saint Christophe, t 02 31 69 81 23, aubergesaintchristophe@wanadoo.fr (€). Old stone house accommodating both a traditional hotel and one of the best restaurants in the area (€€€–€€). *Closed Sun eve and Mon.*

Arclais, t 02 31 69 81 65 (€). Three-room B&B in a modern house with fabulous views of the hills. It's run by a kind nature-loving couple who will cook you organic dinners (€) using garden produce. Book ahead. They can provide information on walking or hang gliding in the area.

Condé-sur-Noireau ✉ 14110

Le Bouquet de Saveurs, 4 Rue Dumont d'Urville, t 02 31 66 99 09 (€€). Excellent gastronomic choice in the centre of Condé just next to the St Sauveur church. *Closed Wed, Thurs eve and Sun eve.*

The Vire Valley

The steep-sided upper valley of the River Vire winds south from St-Lô, through the lush area known as the **Bocage Virois**. The term *bocage* comes from the Norman *bosc*, or wood, and the region is characterized by fields enclosed by deep ditches and high hedges and woodlands (for more about the *bocage*, see pp.357–64). The most spectacular stretch of the Vire valley is between the **Roches de Ham**, a pair of sheer schist promontories, and **Tessy-sur-Vire**. The village between these two points, **La Chapelle-sur-Vire**, has been a pilgrimage centre since the 12th century. At the eastern end of the gorge, 10km north of Vire town, stand the remains of the **Viaduc de la Souleuvre**, designed by Gustave Eiffel. Only the six supporting granite pillars of Eiffel's original structure remain, and the last train chugged across them in 1970. The half-bridge is now a magnet for **bungee-jumpers**, who leap off it into the gorge. Climbers and canoeists love the gorge too.

Viaduc de la Souleuvre
*open for bungee-jumping April–mid-Nov;
minimum age 13,
advance reservation
essential, t 02 31 66 31
66, www.ajhackett.fr*

An old railway track along the Vire valley is currently being cleared to create a *Voie Verte* footpath from Carentan through St-Lô and down to Pont-Farcy, just south of Tessy. It will provide an excellent way of exploring the Vire valley on foot, by horse or by bicycle.

Getting around the Vire Valley

Vire has regular **train** services on the Paris-Montparnasse–Granville line, which also stop at L'Aigle, Argentan and Villedieu-les-Poêles.

Bus Verts' No.32 **bus** links Vire with Caen via Aunay-sur-Odon, and Villers-Bocage, and Les Courriers Bretons connects Vire with Fougères.

Vire

The hilltop town of Vire was virtually obliterated in the Second World War, but it's managed to hang on to its most cherished tradition, a knobbly, lightly smoked, tripe sausage known as *andouille de Vire*. The chubby sausages hang from every butchers' shop in the town like bunches of meaty grapes, and competitions are held regularly to find out whose *andouille* is the tastiest. The sausage is served thinly sliced and cold, in salads, or cooked inside tasty tarts, next to chunks of Calvados-drenched apples. *Andouilles* naturally feature strongly in local restaurants as well.

If you don't like the thought of pigs' intestines, the moody ruins of the **castle**, around which Vire grew up in the 8th century, make a pleasant place to stroll, with fine views over the Vire valley. The castle was strengthened in the 12th century by Henry I, and a square keep added, but Henry's handiwork was undone by Richelieu five centuries later. The valley, the **Vaux de Vire**, was once famous for textile mills and tanneries. It's also where *vaudeville*, or light stage comedy, was born, based on bawdy drinking songs written by the 15th-century poet Olivier Basselin at his home in the Vale of the Vire.

The centrepiece of Vire's main square is the ancient **Tour de l'Horloge** (clock tower), originally the main gate to the fortified

It Takes Some Guts...

One of them would call it her little dille, her staff of love, her quillety, her faucetin, her dandilolly... And some of the other women would give it these names – my bunguetee, my stopple too, my bush-rusher, my gallant wimble, my pretty borer, my coney-burrow-ferret, my little piercer, my augretine, my dangling hangers, down right to it, stiff and stout, in and to, my pusher, dresser, pouting stick, my honey pipe, my pretty pillicock, linky pinky, futilletie, my lusty andouille, and crimson chitterling.
François Rabelais, *Gargantua and Pantagruel*, 1534

Traditions die hard in Normandy, and one of the oldest is Vire's famous chitterling sausage, the *andouille*. The earthy Renaissance writer Rabelais has his comic hero Gargantua feast on the stuff, but pokes fun at its phallic shape. Methods have changed little since his day, and *véritable andouille* is still made by hand. The sausages are made of carefully washed, cleaned and shredded pigs' guts – belly, small and large intestines and sometimes heart and head as well – which are salted and left in brine for a few days, then strained in a *robe* (a 'dress'), a piece of large intestine. The fresh *andouille* is then smoked over a beechwood fire for six to eight weeks, to give it its sooty flavour. If you buy any, be sure it's labelled '*véritable andouille de Vire*', as counterfeiters abound.

On All Saints Day (1 November) locals get a chance to eat as much as they like at the *Festival Andouille de Vire*, organized by the 200-strong 'Brotherhood of the *Véritable Andouille de Vire*', whose motto is *Viro veni edi* ('I came to Vire and I ate [*andouille*]').

town, flanked by twin towers and later topped with a belfry. Temporary exhibitions are held in the tower, and there is also a room commemorating the 500 inhabitants of Vire who perished in Allied bombings on 4 June 1944. There are good views if you climb the spiral stairs to the top. Nearby there's an interesting church, **Notre-Dame**, built in the 13th and 15th centuries on the site of a Romanesque chapel. At the foot of the town, beside the river on Place Ste-Anne, the fine 18th-century hospital the Hôtel Dieu now houses the **Musée des Arts et Tradition Populaires de Vire**, which has a well-presented collection of 18th- and 19th-century bonnets, jewellery, costumes and furniture, including some fabulously carved marriage wardrobes topped with amorous turtle doves. There are good walks along the river by the little *écluse* (reservoir) which once supplied the castle, and a racetrack on the outskirts of town.

Some 20km north of Vire in the hamlet of **St-Martin-des-Besaces** (between Le Bény-Bocage and Torigni-sur-Vire) is one of the more individual small Normandy war museums, the **Musée de la Percée du Bocage**. The 'museum of the Bocage breakthrough' concentrates very specifically on the events around St-Martin itself on 30 July– 1 August 1944, when the village and 'Hill 309' (now named 'Coldstream Hill' in honour of the Coldstream Guards) was taken in fierce fighting by the British 11th Armoured Division.

Musée des Arts et Tradition Populaires de Vire
t 02 31 68 10 49; open May–Sept Wed–Mon 10–12 and 2–6; Oct–April Wed–Fri and Mon 2–6, Sat–Sun 10–12 and 2–6; adm

Musée de la Percée du Bocage
open June–mid-Sept Wed–Mon 10–12 and 2–6; May Sat–Sun 10–12 and 2–6; adm

Tourist Information in Vire

ⓘ **Vire >**
Square de la Résistance,
t 02 31 66 28 50,
www.vire-tourisme.com

Market Days: Fri; smaller market Tues, Place de la Mairie; foie gras markets are held on various dates Nov–Dec.
Post Office: 17 Rue aux Fèvres.

Shopping in Vire

Jean-Paul Lesouef, 35 Rue Armand Gasté, **t** 02 31 67 70 32. Everyone in Vire has their favourite butcher, which they swear is the best place for getting true *andouille de vire*. M. Lesouef has a high reputation.

Where to Stay and Eat in the Vire Valley

Vire ✉ 298 14500
Hôtel de France, 6 Rue d'Aignaux, **t 02 31 68 00 35, *www.hoteldefrance vire.com* (€). A solid Logis hotel with a warm atmosphere and comfortable,

prettily decorated rooms with showers or baths. It's known for its restaurant (€€), serving fine local fare. There's a sister hotel, the Hôtel Saint-Pierre, around the corner.
Au Vrai Normand, 14 Rue Armand Gasté, **t** 02 31 67 90 99, *www.au-vrai-normand.com* (€€–€). Friendly little restaurant in the centre of town run by a young couple. Cooking is traditional Norman. *Closed Sun eve, Tues eve and Wed*.

St-Germain-de-Tallevende
✉ 14500
Auberge Saint-Germain, **t** 02 31 68 24 13 (€€–€). Enchanting restaurant in a beautiful stone house in a quiet village 6km south of Vire. Specialities include *andouille de Vire*, of course, but if you're not a chitterlings fan there are delicious alternatives like the leek and haddock *tarte*, and excellent fruity desserts. Great value. *Closed Sun eves and Mon*.
Ferme-Auberge La Petite Fosse, **t** 02 31 67 22 44 (€). Home-produced fare

which you eat at the farm. Reserve in advance.

Roullours ✉ 14500

Le Manoir de la Pommeraie, Route de Flers, **t** 02 31 68 07 71 (€€€). If you're after a gastronomic treat, this ancient manor, a couple of kilometres from Vire, is the place. *Closed Sun eve and Mon.*

Guilberville ✉ 50160

Le Châpeau Rouge, Carrefour du Poteau, **t** 02 33 56 77 82 (€€). A rustic restaurant with an attractive fireplace. Try their scallops, and their home-made *foie gras de canard*. *Closed Thurs.*

Sourdeval ✉ 50150

Le Val, **t** 02 33 59 64 16 (€). A rural home run by rural folk – the owner was born here. The rooms are simple, with views of the farmyard or the valley, and there's also a separate cottage with a family room. You are welcome to watch the milking too.

Falaise to Argentan

Falaise

 Falaise

The strategically prominent chalky cliff after which the town is named (*falaise* just means 'cliff') made this the ideal site for the castle where William the Bastard (later Conqueror) breathed his first. His father, Robert, when still merely the younger son of the Duke of Normandy, had allegedly spotted Arlette, William's mother, washing clothes in the river below the château at the spot now dubbed **La Fontaine d'Arlette**. Smitten by the 16-year-old Arlette, he invited her to the ducal castle; however, instead of sneaking in the back door, the sassy teenager rode triumphantly through the main gate to meet her assignation. Nine months later, in 1027, baby William's squawks resounded through the castle's corridors, Robert's father and brother both died a short time afterwards so that he inherited the Duchy, and the rest is history.

Château Guillaume-le-Conquérant

t 02 31 41 61 44, www.chateau-guillaume-le conquérant.fr; open Feb–Dec daily 10–6; guided tours July–Aug daily at 10 and 2; Sept–June Sat–Sun 3.30; last ticket sold 1hr before closing; adm

You spot Falaise's dramatic castle atop its seemingly impregnable rock long before you reach the town. A remarkable amount of the fortress survived the bombing that decimated the rest of the town in 1944, and it remains one of the best examples of medieval military architecture in France. From its keep and ramparts you can survey Falaise's two fine Romanesque churches, precious historical remnants in the modern town, which mushroomed post-war on the flat valley of the River Ante below.

The ship-shaped castle that William was born in was probably built in the first decades of the 11th century by Duke Richard II. Little remains of that stronghold however, and the square keeps that are visible today were built by William's successors Henry I and Henry II, while the barrel-shaped **Tour Talbot** was added for the French king, Philippe Auguste, after he seized Normandy in 1204. In 1417 Falaise castle fell into the hands of Henry V of England, and it

Getting to Falaise and Argentan

By a twist in railway design the Caen–Argentan–Alençon–Le Mans–Tours **train** line does not pass through Falaise but Coulibœuf, 7km east. There are buses to the station, but trains are infrequent. The station is just south of Le Petit Coulibœuf. Argentan has good **train** connections on the Rouen–Tours (via Lisieux) and Caen–Le Mans–Tours lines. From Lisieux there are frequent connections to Paris.

Bus Verts' No.35 **bus** runs more frequently between Falaise and Caen (but with no service on Sun). STAO buses have one route (TER A) from Argentan railway station to Flers and another (TER B) to Bagnoles-de-l'Orne via La Ferté-Macé. **Bus information**, t 02 33 36 07 11.

was besieged for the last time in 1590, by Henri IV of France during the French Wars of Religion.

It took the destruction of World War II to bring forth the next castle builder, architect Bruno Décaris, who took charge of the restoration of the ruined castle in 1986. He was adamant that rather than attempting a pastiche of medieval constructions, whatever restored sections were added between the crumbling walls should be clearly identifiable as modern. And clear it certainly is. Foremost among Décaris' handiwork is a stone box-shaped edifice tacked onto one side of the keep, which looks like a block of flats, with shiny steel escalators inside. This futuristic 'restoration' raised howls of protest at the time, but is now firmly part of Falaise's skyline. Whether you like it or not, it's difficult not to admire the use of illuminated glass floors inside, which expose the original structure of the keep and give a feel for its height. The internal restoration is a mixture of traditional, as in the Talbot Tower, and avant-garde, with extensive use of modern materials like Teflon, glass and steel. The self-guided tour takes you on an intriguing and colourful, if at times slightly obscure, journey through the castle's bloody history. As an appropriate conclusion the visit ends with a more conventional exhibition on William, in the oldest part of the castle near where he was probably born.

Falaise Town

Outside the castle is a broad, sloping square, dominated by a ferocious statue of William. On the other side of the square is the church of the **Ste-Trinité**, a masterpiece of Gothic with a stunning 15th-century triangular porch. Inside, don't miss the scenes of martyrdoms and medieval life on the nave capitals, the Flamboyant window with its wild petal tracery, and the raised ambulatory on tubular columns. The church has only recently reopened after long post-war restoration. Another of Falaise's churches, **St-Gervais** at the bottom of Rue Trinité, once a dependence of Caen's Abbaye-aux-Dames, managed to hang onto its 12th-century façade and lantern tower despite a battering by Philippe Auguste in 1204. Inside the church there are fine 15th-century Flamboyant windows, while howling gargoyles guard the exterior.

Musée des Automates
*t 02 31 90 02 43,
www.automates-avenue.fr; open
April–Sept daily 10–6,
Oct–Mar Sat–Sun 10–6;
closed from 2nd week
Jan–1st week Feb; adm*

In the town centre, there's a curious attraction in Musée des Automates, on Boulevard de la Libération, one of the two intersecting main streets. It houses 300 automata that were made over many decades for the window displays of big Parisian department stores: for years these mechanical toys were considered the ultimate lure to entice shoppers, especially at Christmas. The tradition apparently began in 1909, after Peary's expedition reached the North Pole, and the Bon Marché store reconstructed the feat as part of their Christmas display. Other key moments in French history are told, the most entertaining of which is the time in 1936 when cyclists in the Tour de France race ran into a herd of piglets. The museum is heart-warming and fun, and a tonic if you've overdosed on World War history.

Musée Août 1944
*t 02 31 90 37 19,
www.normandie-museeaout44.com;
open June–Sept daily
10–12 and 2–6; April,
May, Oct and 1–15 Nov
same hours but
closed Tues; adm*

As a major battlefield in 1944, though, Falaise naturally has its war museum. The Musée Août 1944, housed in an old cheese factory on the Chemin des Rochers, reached by continuing west from the town centre along Bd Libération past the castle. It recalls the battle of the Falaise pocket with a collection of military hardware, uniforms and models, and some graphic photos, models and film footage of Falaise before, during and after the battle. Eisenhower described Falaise as 'one of the biggest slaughter fields a war sector ever knew'. The capture of the road to Falaise was identified as early as 1943 as one of the Allies' key goals in the

15 The Suisse Normande and Southern Normandy | Falaise

The Battle for the Falaise Gap

'Should this be a success,' wrote a diarist at First Canadian Army Headquarters, 'the war is over. The rest will be a motor tour into Germany.' He was referring to the plan, in August 1944, for the Canadian Army, including a Polish division, to launch a powerful drive southwards from Caen to Falaise, to link up with American troops moving northeastwards towards Argentan. The hope was that the Allies would thus close off the 'pocket' west of Falaise that the German armies still held after General George Patton's US 3rd Army had broken out of Normandy at the end of July to Le Mans and the Loire. Against heavy resistance, by 12 August the Allied forces had advanced far enough to be a major threat to the German divisions. Just 30km separated the Americans south of Argentan and the British and Canadians north of Falaise. Between them was the 'Falaise Gap', the Germans' only means of escape.

With 20 German divisions, numbering around 155,000 men, trapped inside the noose, a desperate Hitler described 15 August as the 'worst... of my life.' The following day he reluctantly agreed – too late – to a withdrawal. Field Marshal van Kluge, the German commander in Normandy, committed suicide two days later. On 17 August the Canadians finally took Falaise, just 12 miles north of the Americans, and on 19 August Polish troops confronted the Germans on the long whale-like ridge of the Macé at Mont-Ormel. After two days and nights of bitter fighting, the gap was closed on the 21st, a moment Montgomery would describe as 'the beginning of the end of the war.'

The battle was one of the war's bloodiest, causing carnage that is hard to comprehend: one soldier from the French 2nd Armoured Division compared it to 'hell, where the stench of corpses was unbearable, and long bones of dead animals and men were crunched beneath the caterpillar tracks of the armoured vehicles.' Eisenhower likened the inside of the 'pocket' to a 'massive carpet of dead and rotting flesh'. Some 10,000 Germans died, while around 50,000 were taken prisoner; of 38 German divisions committed to the battle, 25 had been completely destroyed. Nobody dared count the number of dead horses. However, large numbers of German troops had also escaped through the gap, and the war would continue for another nine months.

invasion of Normandy, yet it took 77 difficult days for Allied troops to reach William the Conqueror's birthplace. Encircled, the desperate Germans defended Falaise against Allied efforts to close the so-called Falaise Gap, and the town and virtually all the surrounding villages were reduced to rubble.

Mémorial de Montormel

Mémorial de Montormel
t 02 33 67 38 61,
www.memorial-montormel.org; open May–Sept 9.30–6; Oct–Mar Sat–Sun and Wed 10–5; April daily 10–5; adm

Looking at the lovely countryside around this hill between Argentan and Vimoutiers, some 25km southeast of Falaise, it's hard to imagine the slaughter that took place here in August 1944. The hill, also known locally as the Macé, was the site of the final battle that closed the Falaise Gap and so brought the Battle of Normandy to a close. Final victory was clinched by the Polish Division led by General Maczek – but only after 325 Poles had lost their lives. A huge stone memorial commemorates the battle, with a museum alongside that tells the story hill by hill. Headphone commentary is provided in English, French, Polish or German.

Tourist Information in Falaise

(i) Falaise >
Le Forum, Bd de la Libération, t 02 31 90 17 26, www.otsifalaise.com

Market Day: Sat.
Post Office: 25 Rue Champ St Michel

Where to Stay and Eat around Falaise

Falaise ✉ 14700
Manoir de Lentaigne, 1 Rue du Sergent Goubin, t 02 31 40 95 86, www.bandb-falaise.com (€€€–€€). A beautiful 18th-century town mansion that's been turned into a very special chambres d'hôtes. There are five attractive high-ceilinged rooms and there is also a library/sitting room, garden and pool.
**Hotel de la Poste, 38 Rue Georges Clemenceau, t 02 31 90 13 14, hotel.delaposte@wanadoo.fr (€€–€). This Logis hotel on the main street is the best bet inside town. Rooms are attractive and modern, and to avoid traffic noise ask for rooms at the back. There's a restaurant (€€), or the Fine Fourchette (see below) is next door. Hotel and restaurant closed Sun eve, Mon and (Oct–May) Fri eve.
★ L'Attache >
L'Attache, Route de Caen, t 02 31 90 05 38 (€€€–€€). Intimate restaurant on the outskirts of town. Chef Alain Hastain makes sophisticated use of Norman staples like camembert and

andouille, mingling them with wild herbs, woodland mushrooms and edible flowers. There's a good choice of fish or meat. Booking essential. Closed Tues and Wed.
La Fine Fourchette, 52 Rue Georges Clemenceau, t 02 31 90 08 59 (€€€–€€). Central Falaise's top eating option, even if a tad touristy, with innovative cooking with subtle touches amid chic décor. Excellent value, and with a wide range of prices.

Villy-lez-Falaise ✉ 14700
Ferme La Croix, t 02 31 90 19 98 (€). This solid Norman stone house in a quiet village 4km east of Falaise has been in the same family for over a century, and has a lovely garden. The two B&B rooms, furnished with antiques, are pleasing and comfortable. A totally tranquil experience.

St-Germain-le-Vasson ✉ 14190
Ferme-Auberge des Massinots, t 02 31 90 54 22 (€€). Fine old courtyard farm 15kms north of Falaise where the Tocheport family produce great meals using their own produce, washed down with home-produced cider or calvados. You eat in a convivial dining room, where there's a fire during winter months. Book in advance. There's a farm shop too. Closed Sun eve and mid-Dec–mid-Jan.

Argentan

Lace, the Battle of Normandy and Thomas à Becket have all played a part in the history of this ivory-stone fortified town on a hill above the Orne. It was here that Thomas and Henry II tried to resolve their differences, and it was here, after talks had collapsed, that the king casually remarked that he'd be well rid of his turbulent priest – a throwaway comment four of his knights were only too pleased to turn into action in the archbishop's cathedral of Canterbury. The more recent violence of the Second World War hit Argentan badly, and since the battle of the 'gap' (see p.305) the whole of the lower town has been rebuilt. In the upper town, however, much of the 12th-century town walls and 17th- and 18th-century houses remain intact, making it an agreeable stopover. The best days to visit are Tuesday and Friday, when the market square, Place du Marché, springs to life. Most of the town's sights are here or nearby too: the tourist office occupies part of the 18th-century **Chapelle St-Nicolas**, the original model of which was part of the castle next door, which now houses the Law Courts.

Eglise St-Germain
open on request: ask at the tourist office

Across the square stands the twin-towered 15th-century **Eglise St-Germain**, which even now is still being repaired from war damage. When first built it was the centre of a political wrangle between its builders and Argentan's royal governor, who complained that its tower would dwarf the town's castle. Building plans were put on ice, and the tower was only finished in the 1630s. The new stonemasons got their revenge with a bit of fun: look carefully and you'll see a statue of a woman bending over exposing her ample posterior – probably a reference to a recognizable prostitute of the time. Above her, leans another buxom wench, whose melon-sized breasts are pierced with holes through which the rainwater drains. Inside, the nave has a distinctive stone carving of a donkey, a reference to St Germain's preferred means of transport.

At the far end of the **Rue Griffon**, which has some of Argentan's finest old mansions, the 15th-century **Eglise Saint-Martin** is an impressive example of Flamboyant Gothic with a pierced octagonal tower, which still bears the mark of wartime bombings. There's a magical square behind it, Place Jean-Louis Castets. Lace enthusiasts will want to head to the **Maison des Dentelles**, an attractive mansion which stands in a park beside a lake in the Rue de la Noë. Inside are 200-odd exhibits of lace made by various techniques, as well as examples of the needlepoint lace for which Argentan, Alençon and Falaise were famous from the late 17th century. In its 18th-century heyday Argentan had more than 1,200 lace-makers, some based in the fine houses that grace Rue St Martin. You can also see examples of work by the town's surviving

Maison des Dentelles
t 02 33 67 50 78; open June–mid-Oct Tues–Sat 9–12 and 2–6, Sun 9–12; adm

Tourist Information in Argentan

(i) **Argentan >**
Place du Marché,
t 02 33 67 12 48,
www.argentan.fr

Market Days: Tues, Fri, Place du Marché; Sun, Place St-Martin.
Post Office: 2 Rue Charles Léandre.

Where to Stay and Eat around Argentan

Argentan ✉ **61200**

**La Renaissance, 20 Avenue de la 2ème DB, t 02 33 36 14 20, *www.hotel-larenaissance.com* (€€–€). Chic, light and airy rooms with bath or shower. There's a contemporary restaurant (€€), whose young chef Arnaud Viel won a national competition for his *moelleux au chocolat noir*, an ethereal chocolate mousse.

Le Bistro de l'Abbaye, 25 Rue Saint Martin, t 02 33 39 37 42 (€). Delightful small family restaurant in an ancient chapel in the centre of town, serving Norman specialities. *Closed Sun, Mon eve and Tues eve.*

Silly-en-Gouffern ✉ **61310**

***Pavillon de Gouffern, t 02 33 36 64 26, *www.pavillondegouffern.com* (€€€–€€). Built 200 years ago by a gentleman to entertain his hunting friends, this elegant 'pavilion' stands in 80 hectares of gardens and forest (with tennis courts), 7km east of Argentan. Newly refurbished rooms, some in the well-converted outbuildings, display a simple elegance, and there's a fine restaurant (€€€€).

Survie-Exmes ✉ **61310**

Les Gains, Survie, t 02 33 36 05 56, *www.lesgains.co.uk* (€€). Superb manor farm with a *pigeonnier* and duck stream tastefully converted by English farmers Christopher and Diana Wordsworth, who live here with their daughters. The three B&B rooms in the old dairy are simple and pretty. Dinner (€€) – under the pergola if it's fine – can be provided with advance notice. It's about 10km north of Exmes, on the road towards Vimoutiers. *Closed Dec–Feb.*

Abbaye des Benedictines
Rue de l'Abbaye; open Mon–Sat 2.30–4; adm

lacemakers today, and admire the flowerbeds in the gardens outside which are designed to imitate the patterns of the lace. You can view Argentan's needlepoint lace being made at the town's convent, the **Abbaye des Benedictines**, south of the town centre. A lace-making school was set up here in 1874 by the mayor who wanted to resuscitate the industry, which had been killed off by the Revolution. Today the nuns still carry out their eye-straining work in the afternoons. You can round off your visit with Vespers, when the nuns sing Gregorian chant.

Around Argentan

Le Bourg-Saint-Léonard
t 02 33 36 68 68; open July–Aug daily 2.30–5.30; May–June and early Sept Sat–Sun 2.30–4.30; adm

Argentan is encircled by a surprisingly large number of attractive, little-known, châteaux, the nearest of which is the glistening white **Le Bourg-Saint-Léonard**. There's something a touch sad about this glorious but human-scale stately home, silent compared to the days when guests rolled up the gravel drive ready for a calvados after a hectic day's hunting. The house and its pretty orangery and stables were built in 1763 by a wealthy courtier of the future Louis XVIII. The dining room is still laid as it would have been in the 18th century, with Limoges china, and there's more classical elegance in the Music Room and the *Grand Salon*, with lovely Louis XV panelling. Outside, you can wander in the vast gardens, modelled on those of English landscape architects like William Kent and Capability Brown.

Le Haras National du Pin

⭐ **Le Haras National du Pin** t 02 33 36 68 68, www.haras-nationaux. fr; open daily April–Sept 10–6 (includes 1hr guided tour of stud); Thursday Horse Shows (last 1hr) June–Sept at 3pm, also occasional Tues in July and Aug; visit to Forge July–Aug Tues 3–5; visit of paddocks with horses July–Aug Wed 3–5; visit to Saddlery July–Aug Fri 3–5. Occasional horse races Sept–Oct (ring for details); adm

If you have equestrian leanings, France's official national stud farm or *haras*, in the heart of Normandy's most important horse-breeding region, is paradise. Horses are bred, raced, even buried here, and on summer Thursdays the great beasts strut their stuff with carriages to music around the magnificent courtyard. Even non-horse-lovers can enjoy the evocative atmosphere of the historic salmon-pink brick stables, grand château and lush, immaculate grounds.

A national stud farm was the brainchild of Louis XIV's minister Colbert, although he did not live to see it built. He decided that imported stallions, like lace (*see* p.315), were bankrupting the country, so France should breed its own. Le Pin's design was entrusted to Robert de Cotte, who built it from 1715 to 1730. If it makes you think of Versailles it's no coincidence, as De Cotte had designed the great stables at Louis XIV's palace. The formal gardens were also designed by a pupil of the royal gardener Le Nôtre. The stud is proud of its royal connections, and is dubbed, somewhat cornily, 'the horses' Versailles.'

This five-star accommodation houses up to 60 equally magnificent equine residents, although the number drops to a couple of dozen in the breeding season (mid-February to mid-July) when many are sent to neighbouring farms. Breeds kept at the *Haras* include local ones, like grey Percherons and Normandy cobs, and others like French trotters, Arab and English thoroughbreds, and the odd New Forest and Connemara. In September the *Haras* hosts a national Percheron competition (*see* p.205 for more on Percheron horses).

The guided tour takes in the stables and their priceless occupants, collections of saddlery and 19th-century carriages; and even the tomb of *Furioso*, an English thoroughbred who managed to sire over 300 offspring, including many champions. The château, whose white stone looks oddly out of place against the brick stables, can also be visited (albeit with restrictive opening times), and on some days each summer there are tours of the blacksmith's workshop, tack room and paddocks.

Château de Médavy

Château de Médavy t 02 33 35 54 54; open July–Aug daily 2–7; April–June and Sept–15 Oct Sat–Sun 2–6; adm

In the 17th century Médavy was the site of one of Normandy's juiciest scandals. The owner, François-Bénédict de Rouxel de Médavy, took a fancy to one of his neighbours, a country girl called Mlle Nonant. Unfortunately she didn't reciprocate François-

Bénédict's feelings, so he kidnapped the girl and her mother and locked them both up in the château. Soldiers were sent and local dignitaries intervened, but all to no avail. It finally took an act of the Rouen parliament to give the maiden back her liberty. A century later, perhaps wishing to extirpate all memory of this affair, another Rouxel de Médavy replaced the old castle with the honey-grey stone house you see today. The only remains of the old building are the red-brick gate towers that studded the corners of a once-formidable moat.

Médavy's origins go back far further: it was built as a fortress in the 11th century to defend the crossing over the Orne. It's recently been through hard times but is now being restored room by room. The best thing about the château's interior is its floors: there's a fantastic sun-shaped oak and walnut floor in the great sitting room, created in homage to the Sun King Louis XIV, and a beautiful oak floor in the study.

Château de Sassy

Château de Sassy
St-Christophe-le-Jajolet, t 02 33 35 32 66; open mid-June–mid-Sept daily 10.30–12 and 2.30–6; mid-April–mid-June and 1st half Sept Sat–Sun 2.30–6; adm

Unlike its neighbouring châteaux, red-brick Sassy, perched in classical splendour at the top of a hill, is a home, and at weekends you'll see assorted grandsons on horses galloping through the park. Inside, the 18th-century house has a warmer feel than Normandy's many unoccupied residences.

Since 1850 it's been lived in by descendents of Chancellor Pasquier, who escaped the Revolutionary guillotine by a cat's whisker. The current family are horse breeders, and well-known in the racing world. Many visit Sassy for the formal French-style gardens, with a lacework of box hedges that contrasts with the salmon-coloured sand, which in turn echoes the tones of the grand façade. They are surprisingly modern, and were planted only in 1925 by Achille Duchêne.

The Heart of the Orne

Sées

With its abundance of ruined abbeys and medieval atmosphere, sleepy Sées feels like the town that time – and the world – forgot. No wonder French director Luc Besson used it as a set for several scenes in his film *Joan of Arc*. This unexpected gem is a treasure trove of architectural wonders, but somehow it's not got onto a tourist route, with the bonus that you can feel you are discovering it for yourself.

Sées' pretentions to religious grandeur, and its name, date back to AD 400, when it became the episcopal see of St Latuin, who had

Getting to Sées

Sées has a few **trains** daily on the Caen–Alençon–Tours line. The **station** is east of town on Bd Pichon. STAO **buses** have services to Argentan and (less frequently) Alençon.

Cathedral
open daily 9–6; for tours enquire at the tourist office

converted the district to Christianity and built the first cathedral. Luck, though, has not been on Sées' side: the superb **cathedral** that stands today, one of the finest examples of 13th-century Norman Gothic, is the fifth one to occupy the spot. The fourth was razed in 1174 during battles with the English, while the third was the casualty of downright carelessness by its own bishop, Ivo of Bellême, who burnt it down by mistake in 1048, a mere 42 years after the last stone had been laid, while trying to evict thieves from houses next door.

Today the cathedral's 70-metre-high spires look incongruously tall against the rest of the town, and are particularly impressive when illuminated at night. Inside, the purity of its lines and gleaming white stone is exquisite, as are its two rose windows, like stonework lace. The choir, based on that at Amiens, is a delight, and around the altar there's a stone menagerie of animals, men and women with a mischievous array of expressions and postures, amid an abundance of leaves and trees.

Beside the cathedral is the 13th-century **Chapelle Canoniale**, a beautiful Romanesque building with pretty cloisters, later converted into a market hall. Next door is the **Musée Départmental d'Art Religieux**, a museum of religious art and vestments housed in an ancient canon's residence.

Musée Départmental d'Art Religieux
open July–Sept Wed–Mon 10–6; adm

Northwest of the cathedral is **Rue Charles Forget**, lined with ancient seminaries, and, on the right, the square where every December Sées holds a famous turkey fair. Past the remains of the old city gates, the atmospheric **Cours des Fontaines**, the town's 18th-century wash house, is bordered by a shady park. There's another equally evocative wash house in **Allée Saint-Benoît**, reached via Rue du Vivier, where you can stroll beside the Orne. On the way you pass the remains of **Notre-Dame du Vivier**, a 13th-century church allegedly built on the site of an oratory erected by Saint Latuin.

One of the town's more striking features is **Les Halles**, the circular 19th-century corn market, now the library. Further east on Place St-Pierre are the remains of the 10th-century **Eglise Saint-Pierre**, and of a feudal *motte*. Also worth a visit is the **Abbaye de St-Martin**, though it is only open irregularly to visitors, so check with the tourist office before visiting. The abbey is situated on the southeast edge of town, built in the 7th century, subsequently rebuilt, deconsecrated in the Revolution and now inhabited by an insurance company.

Tourist Information in Sées

(i) Sées >
Place Général-de-Gaulle, t 02 33 28 74 79, sees.tourisme@ wanadoo.fr

Market Days: Sat, Cathedral square; small markets Wed and Sun in Place des Halles.
Post Office: 1 Rue de la République.

Where to Stay and Eat around Sées

Sées ✉ 61500

**Le Dauphin, 31 Place des Halles, t 02 33 80 80 70, *dauphinsees@wanadoo.fr* (€€). Next to Les Halles, this former coaching inn is the pick of the bunch. The owners are friendly, and the seven cosy rooms are prettily furnished with antiques. There's an excellent restaurant (€€€–€€), with some wonderful things like *escalope de foie gras chaud au cidre et à la crème*. Restaurant closed (Oct–May) Sun eve and Mon.

**L'Ile de Sées, 61500 Macé (5km from Sées), t 02 33 27 98 65, *www.ile-sees.fr* (€€–€). Comfortable country hotel where you can enjoy open fires in winter and spacious grounds, including tennis courts, in summer. All 16 rooms have baths. There's a gourmet restaurant (€€). *Hotel closed 15 Nov–15 Feb; restaurant closed Sun eve and Mon.*

Essay ✉ 61500

Château de Villiers, t 02 33 31 16 49, *http://chateau-normandie.com* (€€€–€€). Stone, space and silence are all yours at this fine but unassuming 16th-century château, 6km southeast of Sées, which has been carefully restored and furnished by its friendly young owners, who live here with their children. There are just three B&B rooms to date, with stone fireplaces and views over the park. Breakfasts include plenty of home-made goodies.

Alençon

✪ Alençon

Perched on the borders of Normandy and Maine, Alençon escaped much of the destruction that ravaged so many nearby cities in 1944, and many of its quaint streets, sandstone or half-timbered mansions and waterways have kept their medieval charm. Its greatest claim to fame – and source of wealth – is its lace-making tradition, which dates back to the 17th century and is still painstakingly maintained (just) by eleven ladies at the state-funded National Needlepoint Workshop, the last of its kind in France. This is no easy option: it takes around 10 years to perfect the art of making *Point d'Alençon* (needlepoint lace), and around 30 eye-straining hours are needed to make a piece of lace the size of a postage stamp.

Historically, Alençon owed its importance to its position on the crossroads of key trading routes. In 1048 it was besieged by William the Bastard/Conqueror, who, the legend goes, was so miffed by the jokes made by the city's defenders about his illegitimate origins that he had the hands and feet of 30 prisoners cut off and flung into the castle. Realising the grim fate that awaited them if they continued to resist, the garrison surrendered. A more likely explanation is that William was simply securing the southern borders of his Duchy with his usual ruthless vigour. More recent horrors were meted out here in 1940 by the Germans, who bombed and occupied the city. Four years later, Alençon became the first town in France to be liberated by French troops, when Leclerc's Second Armoured Division drove in.

Around Old Alençon

The wide junction of **Place du Général de Gaulle** marks the northern limit of old Alençon, and greets anyone driving into the city from the north, or walking to the centre from the railway station. From there, Rue Saint-Blaise heads into the city. The **Préfecture**, on the right, inhabits the 17th century red-brick building formerly known as the Hôtel de Guise, since from 1676 it was lived

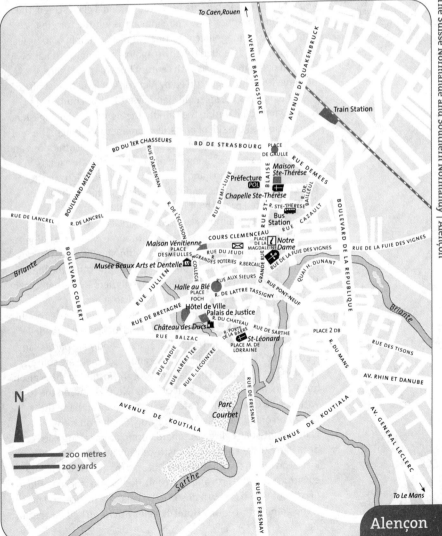

To Caen, Rouen

AVENUE DE QUAKENBRUCK

AVENUE BASINGSTOKE

Train Station

BD DU 1ER CHASSEURS

BD DE STRASBOURG

PLACE DE GAULLE

RUE D'ARGENTAN

RUE DEMEES

BOULEVARD MEZERAY

RUE DE LANCREL

R. DE LANCREL

R. DE L'ECUSSON

RUE DEMI-LUNE

Préfecture POL

Maison Ste-Thérèse

RUE ST-BLAISE

Chapelle Ste-Thérèse

R. STE-THÉRÈSE

R. DU BAILLEUL

RUE CAZAULT

Bus Station

BOULEVARD DE LA REPUBLIQUE

COURS CLEMENCEAU

Maison Vénitienne

PLACE DESMEULLES

PLACE DE LA MAGDALEINE

Notre Dame

RUE DE LA FUIE DES VIGNES

RUE DE LA FUIE DES VIGNES

R. DU JEUDI

GRANDES POTERIES

R.BERCAIL

GRANDE

Musée Beaux Arts et Dentelle

COLLEGE

RUE AUX SIEURS

RUE PONT-NEUF

QUAI H. DUNANT

Briante

BOULEVARD COLBERT

RUE JULLIEN

Halle au Blé

PLACE FOCH

R. DE LATTRE TASSIGNY

RUE DE BRETAGNE

Hôtel de Ville

Palais de Justice

R. DU CHATEAU

RUE DE SARTHE

PLACE 2 DB

RUE DES TISONS

Château des Ducs

RUE BALZAC

R. PORTE DE LA BARRE

St-Léonard

PLACE M. DE LORRAINE

R. DU MANS

RUE CANDIE

RUE ALBERT 1ER

RUE E. LECOINTRE

AV. RHIN ET DANUBE

Briante

N

AVENUE DE KOUTIALA

Parc Courbet

RUE DE FRESNAY

AVENUE DE KOUTIALA

AV. GENERAL LECLERC

200 metres
200 yards

Sarthe

RUE DE FRESNAY

To Le Mans

Alençon

Getting to Alençon

Alençon has fairly regular **train** links to Paris (usually via Le Mans), Tours, Granville, Argentan and Caen. TIS provides **bus** services to Le Mans, and STAO links Alençon with destinations throughout the Orne (Sées, Argentan, L'Aigle, Mortagne-au-Perche, Bagnoles-de-l'Orne, La Ferté-Macé, Carrouges, Flers and others).

in by Elisabeth d'Orléans, Duchesse de Guise. Napoleon slept here, in 1811.

Virtually opposite is the **Chapelle Ste-Thérèse** and, next door at No 50, the house where St Thérèse of Lisieux was born in 1873:

Maison Natale de Ste-Thérèse
t 02 33 26 09 87; open June–Sept daily 9–12 and 2–6; Feb–May and Oct–Dec Wed–Mon 9.30–12 and 2.30–5

Maison Natale de Ste-Thérèse. For the story of St Thérèse, *see* p.244. Plaques giving thanks to the saint cover the walls of the chapel, and various memorabilia are exhibited behind a glass screen. The **Grande Rue** continues south, passing on the left the turreted **Maison d'Ozé**, a magnificent fortified mansion built in 1450 by Jean du Mesnil, who defended the town against the English. It narrowly escaped demolition in the 19th century, but was mercifully preserved, and is now occupied by Alençon's helpful tourist office.

Next to it soars the splendid Flamboyant-Gothic church of

Notre-Dame
open daily 9–12 and 2–5.30

Notre-Dame, built during the Hundred Years' War under English domination, on the site of an earlier Romanesque church. The English influence is visible in the style of the small Gothic dogs and dragons that scamper along the ribs of the elaborate vaults. Unfortunately the choir and transepts were rebuilt in 1745 after a fire, creating rather a hotchpotch of styles. The highlight is the richly decorated porch, built in 1506, an example of pure Flamboyant style, almost like needlepoint lace in stone. The Renaissance puts in an appearance with some extremely refined stained glass windows above the triforium, showing illustrations of Old Testament stories on one side, and on the other the life of the Virgin Mary, that clearly suggest the glaziers – whether local or not – were familiar with German and Italian styles.

Fine 18th-century ironwork balconies adorn many houses on the Grande Rue and in streets like Rue du Jeudi or Rue des Grandes-Poteries (those in the latter at Nos. 41, 42, 33 and 7 are particularly elegant). Walking south along the Grande Rue, there are some stunning half-timbered houses on the right, including the **Maison aux Piliers**, adorned with a coat of arms (No. 123), and, on the corner with Rue du Château, the **Café des Sept Colonnes**, where the hangman once lived. All are 15th century. Further on is the Flamboyant-style **Eglise St-Léonard**. Turning right along Rue Porte de la Barre there are more fine 15th-century houses on the way to Place Foch, with the **Château des Ducs** – a magnificent building constructed in the 14th and 15th centuries by an associate of Joan of Arc, but which is now a prison – the **Palais de Justice**, and next to it the grand 18th-century **Hôtel de Ville** with its arched façade. Just to the north is the lovely metal- and glass-domed circular corn market, the **Halle au Blé**, based on the design of the Paris Stock Exchange. The roof so enthralled the ladies of the town that they dubbed the new building the 'crinoline of Alençon'. The ground floor has lately been turned into an internet café, and exhibitions are held on other floors. A short walk further north, into the Cour Carrée de la Dentelle, will take you to the town's largest museum of its lace traditions.

Musée des Beaux-Arts et de la Dentelle

Musée des Beaux-Arts et de la Dentelle
t 02 33 32 40 07; open July–Aug daily 10–12 and 2–6, Sept–June Tues–Sun 10–12 and 2–6; guided visits July–Aug daily 2.30 and 6; lace-making demonstrations July–mid-Sept Mon, Wed and Fri 2.30 and 4.30; adm

The museum has taken over a former Jesuit college off the Place Commandant Desmeulles to display its pleasing collections of lesser-known European art and painting (including some nice Courbets) and first-rate lace, which includes examples from all the main lace-making centres of Europe – Venice, Bruges, Le Puy, Bayeux and Argentan, as well as Alençon itself. Rock'n'Roll fans will be heartened to see a collection of black (machine-made) Chantilly lace. The three main lace-making techniques are shown: needlepoint, bobbin and machine-made lace. Pride of place, however, is reserved for Alençon's own 'Point d'Alençon', and one

15 The Suisse Normande and Southern Normandy | Alençon

Queen of Laces: Alençon Lace

In the mid-17th century fashionable courtiers and their ladies at Versailles couldn't get enough lace: they wanted the stuff for collars, cuffs, handkerchiefs, brollies, bonnets, for virtually anything. The only problem was that France couldn't afford it, as lace was then manufactured almost exclusively in Venice, and was seriously dear. Lace was plunging France into bankruptcy.

Louis XIV's finance minister, Jean-Baptiste Colbert, had an idea: why not bring Venice's lace-making tradition to France, so that fashionable needs could be met at home? Twenty or so Venetian lace-makers were brought to Alençon, which already had some tradition in lacemaking, to teach local needlewomen. In 1655 Colbert set up a royal school of lace-making in Alençon, and soon some 8,000 women were applying themselves to the eye-straining art. Imports from Venice were banned.

An important development in the growth of lace-making was the introduction of *point de France* (French needlepoint), an adaptation of the Venetian technique, which uses up to 6,000 buttonhole stitches per square inch. This French technique permitted a wider variety of patterns. Mme de la Perrière, the woman charged with overseeing the Alençon school, also introduced more efficient production methods, so that instead of one woman seeing a piece through from start to finish she carried out just one stage, almost in an early form of production line. Louis XIV's courtiers were delighted; one of Alençon lace's greatest fans was Marie-Antoinette.

The Revolution, however, dealt the industry a near-mortal blow, for with the nobility went their lace and the demand for it. A few years later, though, Napoleon realised that unless something was done the tradition would disappear, and so insisted on the wearing of lace in court. In 1851 Alençon lace received a special boost when it was designated 'the queen of laces and a lace for queens' at the Great Exhibition in London. Techniques were improved, and a new method was invented to give lace a more shaded effect, in contrast with the comparative simplicity of earlier pieces.

However, one more blow came in the last decades of the 19th century, with the introduction of machine-made lace. To help resist the pressure in 1903 a lace-making school was established, and then, in 1976, the National Needlepoint Workshop was set up, allowing the tradition to hang on by a thread. The labour involved is so great that the Workshop's 12 hard-working lace-makers rarely produce pieces larger than a postage stamp.

central exhibit demonstrates the ten separate stages required in its manufacture. During the guided tours, a member of the Alençon Needlepoint Workshop also demonstrates how a piece of lace is made. Other examples of their handiwork are for sale at the entrance, but their exorbitant prices are a reflection of the extraordinary amount of work required to make each tiny, delicate piece.

Coming out of the museum, if you cross Rue du Collège and head eastwards back towards the town centre along the charming Rue du Jeudi, you will pass more of Alençon's architectural gems, most of them dating from the 18th century, including two real mansions, the **Maison Vénitienne** at No. 62, and the **Hôtel Le Rouillé** at No. 42.

Tourist Information in Alençon

(i) **Alençon >**
Maison d'Ozé, Place de la Madeleine,
t 02 33 80 66 33,
www.paysdalencon
tourisme.com

The tourist office has a good accommodation booking service and also rents out audio-guides in English to help you navigate the town's sites. The Orne Tourist Board has its office in Alençon, at 86 Rue St-Blaise, t 02 33 28 88 71, *www.ornetourisme.com.*

Internet Access: La Rotonde, Rue des Filles-Notre-Dame.

Market Days: Thurs, Sat, Place Madeleine.

Post Office: 16 Rue du Jeudi.

Shopping in Alençon

Jacky Pedro, 39 Grande Rue, t 02 33 26 00 47. This *chocolatier* and *salon de thé,* run by the same family for three generations, has a mouth-watering array of hand-made chocolates.

Vins et Tradition, 7 Rue de la Halle aux Toiles (near the post office), t 02 33 32 15 07. Wonderful old-fashioned shop stocking calvados, *poiré,* cider, and *pommeau.*

Where to Stay and Eat around Alençon

Alençon ✉ **61000**

**Le Grand Cerf, 21 Rue St Blaise, t 02 33 26 00 51, *www.hotelgrandcerf-61.com* (€). This traditional 19th-century hotel, with a grand façade, is the smartest in town and is ideally situated near the Chapelle St-Thérèse

and the centre of Alençon. Specialities in the restaurant (€€€–€€) include *foie de canard au torchon. Restaurant closed Sun eve.*

La Hulotte, 47 Rue Albert Premier, t 02 33 32 28 11 (€). The friendly couple who own this ancient building, near a park, are passionate about vintage cars. The two pleasant guest rooms are normally let out as a suite, suitable for a family.

Au Petit Vatel, 72 Place Commandant Desmeulles, t 02 33 26 23 78 (€€€–€€). A little gem of a restaurant on a central *place,* and the place to eat in Alençon. It's worth going for the *menu gastronomique. Closed Sun eve and Wed.*

L'Escargot Doré, 183 Av du Général Leclerc, t 02 33 28 67 67 (€€€–€€). This popular restaurant is 2km south of central Alençon. Once a farm, it retains its rustic feel, and you can watch your fish or meat being barbecued over the ancient fireplace. *Closed Sun eve, Mon and 1st week Jan.*

Le Bistrot, 21 Rue de Sarthe, t 02 33 26 51 69, *lebistrot.alencon@free.fr* (€€–€). The check tablecloths and framed posters on the walls give this great-value place the feel of a busy Parisian bistro. The *menu du marché* is excellent. *Closed Sun and Mon.*

Champfleur ✉ **72610**

La Garencière, t 02 33 31 75 84, *http://monsite.wanadoo.fr/garenciere* (€). This delightful converted farmhouse B&B, about 6km southeast of Alençon on the D19 road, has five rooms, a swimming pool and a wonderful collection of eggcups. Meals can be provided (€€).

Saint Paterne ✉ 72610

Château de Saint Paterne, t 02 33 27 54 71, *www.chateau-saintpaterne.com* (€€€€). Few châteaux are quite perfect, but this white stone château, just 2kms from Alencon, gets as close as possible. The owners are genuinely friendly, the seven rooms are stunning, and the park around is a delight. There's a restaurant (€€€) if you don't feel like stirring. If you feel active, there are tennis courts, golf, and a heated outdoor swimming pool (May–Sept). A truly chic retreat.

Alençon-Valframbert ✉ 61250

Château de Sarceaux, t 02 33 28 85 11, *www.chateau-de-sarceaux.com* (€€€–€€). This 18th-century hunting lodge, set in 12 hectares of parkland just north of Alençon, has been in the family for generations. The five rooms, all furnished with antiques, have recently been refurbished and range in price to suit all pockets. Breakfast included in price. Candelit dinner in the Salon Quatrebarbes (€€€).

★ Château de Saint Paterne >

Around Alençon and Carrouges

The Alpes Mancelles

The name Alps may seem a bit exaggerated to describe this region of heather and broom-clad hills, shared between Normandy and Maine, but they certainly have a rugged charm. The story goes that two saintly brothers from Italy, Céneri and Cénéré, settled here in the 6th or 7th century, because it reminded them of the Alps. They were obviously a persuasive pair. The region is now part of the extensive **Parc Naturel Normandie-Maine**, and offers good walking, canoeing and cycling.

The absurdly picturesque village of **St-Cénéri-le-Gérei**, perched above a hairpin bend in the Sarthe river on the borders of the Orne, Sarthe and Mayenne *départements*, could almost be in the English Cotswolds, with its honey-stoned cottages and stone-tile roofs. Numerous painters have been drawn to its charms, including Corot and Courbet, and every Pentecost bank holiday weekend (May/June), the village hosts a three-day arts festival. Since it's been dubbed 'one of the prettiest villages in France', in summer you have to share it with the crowds, but out of season it's as lovely as ever.

St-Cénéri lost its castle to the English in the Hundred Years' War, but its 11th–12th-century **church** survived, although it's undergone some severe surgery in the past 200 years. Inside, its medieval frescoes have endured heavy-handed restoration, but still have charm, particularly a Virgin who protects a clock under her cape and looks rather cross-eyed with anxiety. Wander down across the fields to the meander in the river and you'll fine the delightful, tiny 14th-century **Chapelle du Petit-Saint-Cénéri**, against a backdrop of woods. This has traditionally been a pilgrimage site, and inside there is the stone where St Cénéri is said to have prayed and meditated. It also has atmospheric multi-themed gardens,

Les Jardins de la Mansonière
t 02 33 26 73 24; open June–mid-Sept Wed–Mon 2.30–6.30, end-April–May Fri–Sun 2.30–6.30; adm

Les Jardins de la Mansonière. In the summer months, candlelit musical evenings are held in the gardens. Some 6km southwest of St-Cénéri and in Mayenne is the pretty village of **St-Léonard-des-Bois**, crouching beneath high cliffs, and a good base for exploring the Alpes Mancelles by foot.

Carrouges

Northwest of Alençon, on the road towards La Ferté-Macé, the appealing little town of Carrouges boasts a pretty square, a good range of shops and a couple of simple hotel-restaurants, and a grand old château. This is not really cheese country, but Carrouges produces a very passable *Gruyère de Carrouges*, which you can pick up in the town. It is also the administrative centre of the Normandy-Maine Regional Park, and has a good visitor's centre, the **Maison du Parc**, in some former outbuildings of the château. As well as providing comprehensive information it organizes demonstrations and events on a range of themes, from mushrooms to apples to pottery, and from April and October runs 'nature expeditions' into the park. The park has a total of 2,500km of signposted paths, and for anyone interested in walking, cycling or riding, there are wonderful possibilities just east of Carrouges in the magnificent, surprisingly mountainous **Forêt d'Ecouves**, within the Normandy-Maine park.

Château de Carrouges
t 02 33 27 20 32, open daily mid-June–Aug 9.30–12 and 2–6.30; April–mid-June and Sept 10–12 and 2–6; Oct–Mar 10–12 and 2–5; adm

The enchanting 14th-century moated **Château de Carrouges**, standing serenely in 10 hectares of gardens and orchards, comes as a surprise: it's built not of stone but little red bricks, each one moulded by hand. They're combined in playful zigzags and chevrons with black bricks that match the severe slate roofs, and in their time set a trend mimicked by other grand houses of Normandy. The Le Veneur family, who inherited the castle in the 16th century, made their fortune from ironworks fired by wood from the abundant forests, and you'll see some lovely 17th-century wrought-iron gates in the grounds.

You approach the castle through the fairy-tale gatehouse, with pepperpot roofs and sumptuously carved windows, a caprice of

The Legend of Carrouges

Carrouges's red bricks have a deeper significance too. The colour red, from which the château and the first lords of the manor got their name, has, according to popular legend, sinister origins: centuries ago, the story goes, Evelyne du Champ de la Pierre married Ralph, sire of Carrouges. After months of waiting, an heir was on the way and seven days feasting began, including a hunt in the neighbouring forests. Ralph, however, never returned from the hunt, having been smitten by a fairy with whom he made love by the light of a golden moon. One night his wife discovered the couple and slayed her rival with a golden dagger. The next morning Ralph's bloodspattered body was discovered in the courtyard. Evelyne gave birth to a son – a redhead of course – who bore a bloodstain on his forehead which never healed. He was baptised Karl the Red, or Carouge. For seven generations, the Carrouges would be redheads and bear bloodstains on their foreheads.

Getting around the Carrouges Region

It is difficult to get around this region without a **car**. **Buses** run infrequently from Alençon to St-Céneri. There are better services from Alençon to Carrouges (on the route to La Ferté-Macé), and Carrouges also has buses to/from Argentan and Sées.

Cardinal Le Veneur, a confidant of François I and a friend of Rabelais. Carrouges is one of the first examples of Renaissance architecture in Normandy, and it was here that Le Veneur first experimented with making geometric patterns with bricks. His family inhabited the château right up until 1936, when it was bought by the French state. The Veneurs may have got their name from one of their line said to have been master of the royal hounds (*grand veneur*) under William the Conqueror. Whether that's true or not, the Le Veneurs were a cheery lot: their family motto is *Sic sic licet esse beatis* (I like it the way it is).

The oldest part of the château is the 14th-century keep, built as a stronghold in the Hundred Years' War. The guided tour, however, concentrates on the more opulent residential chambers, built around a central courtyard in the 15th–16th centuries. The kitchens have paraphernalia used to prepare sumptuous feasts, and on an upper floor is a bedroom where Louis XI stayed in 1473 while on a pilgrimage to Mont-St-Michel. The North Hall still retains the entrance to the chapel, which Alexis Le Veneur destroyed in the last years of the *ancien régime* with a view to building a monumental bridge leading to a new entrance. He ran out of money, however, so the bridge was never built.

The wing housing the main apartments is reached via a square-shaped open-well staircase, built in 1579, with unusual 'painted on' fake-brick walls. The final section includes the dining room, the portrait hall – with portraits of 14 generations of Le Veneurs – and the great hall, all with tapestries, painted beams and great stone fireplaces. The only one of the castle's 150 rooms to have no fireplace is the light and airy *salon de thé*, by the lovely courtyard and gardens. On the first weekend of August the château hosts a *Fête de la Chasse et de la Pêche*, a massive hunting jamboree of hounds, horses and hunting horns. It's well worth visiting if you're in the area at the time.

Tourist Information in Carrouges

(i) **Parc Naturel Normandie-Maine**
Maison du Parc, Carrouges, t 02 33 81 75 75, www.parc-naturel-normandie-maine.fr

For online visitors' information on the area, see *www.paysdalencon tourisme.com*.
Market Day: Carrouges: Wed.
Post Office: Carrouges: 7 Place de Gaulle.

Where to Stay and Eat around Carrouges

St-Cénéri-le-Gérei ✉ 61250

La Dent de Loup, 2 Rue Saint Germain, Héloup, t 02 33 28 41 09 (€€–€). You'll only find the best local ingredients at this lovely little village restaurant, between Alençon and St Cénéri. *Closed Sun eve and Mon.*

L'Auberge des Peintres (also known as Le Lion d'Or), t 02 33 26 49 18 (€). This restaurant was – and still is – an artists' hangout, and you can admire the paintings on the walls while you enjoy honest Norman cooking, at sensible prices. *Closed Mon and Tues outside high season.*

Carrouges ✉ 61320

**Nord, Rue de Ste-Marguerite, t 02 33 27 20 14 (€). Simple hotel with cosy bedrooms whose excellent restaurant (€€–€) bustles with locals at lunchtime. *Restaurant closed Fri from Sept–June.*

Au Petit Germance, Ciral, t 02 33 28 07 16 (€). Enjoy traditional locally produced food at this lovely *ferme-auberge* in the village of Ciral, due south of Carrouges. *Closed Mon–Thurs, reserve in advance.*

Rânes ✉ 61150

**Hôtel Saint Pierre, 6 Rue de la Libération, t 02 33 39 75 14, *www.hotelsaintpierre.com* (€). A solid stone hotel opposite the castle and park at Rânes, 11km north of Carrouges, with a wonderful restaurant (€€–€) and 12 pleasant rooms. Food is strictly Norman, including excellent local beef with camembert sauce.

La Ferté-Macé to Domfront

La Ferté-Macé

French gourmets flock to this town west of Carrouges in search of its celebrated *tripes en brochette* (tripe grilled on skewers), but even if cattle stomachs aren't your thing it's a pleasant place to stop off, particularly on Thursdays, market day, when farmers bring in calvados and *boudin noir* from surrounding villages. The town began life as a fortress in the 11th century (whence the name *Ferté*), which was expanded in the next century by one Mathieu Macé. Once an important textile centre, it retains many interesting 18th- and 19th-century buildings. In summer, locals and visitors head for its man-made lake to swim, sail, windsurf, fish, play golf or ride in the surrounding woods.

Musée du Jouet

32 Rue de la Victoire, t 02 33 37 47 00, open July–Aug daily 3–6; April–June and Sept Sat–Sun 3–6; adm

La Ferté's visitor attraction is the **Musée du Jouet**, or toy museum, an intriguing collection of 19th and 20th century games, toys, electric trains and musical instruments. On Ascension Thursday La Ferté holds a *Fête à l'Andouille* (gut sausage festival) and tripe competitions are staged throughout the year.

Bagnoles-de-l'Orne

If you suffer from varicose veins, or are a fan of Belle Epoque architecture, this old-fashioned spa town, set around a lake amid pretty forests, will be ideal. The pace is still as sedate as in the 1870s, when Europe's wealthy began to come to this out-of-the-way spot in search of its healing waters, and you can picture ladies in their bonnets and crinolines promenading beside the lake. As well as relaxing one can wander through the forest (decent hikes, and great mushrooms in autumn) or, to boost the circulation, take out a pedalo on the lake or have a flutter at the Casino.

Getting around the Domfront Region

Public transport is scarce: the nearest **train** station to Domfront is at Flers (20km), on the Granville–Argentan line. For La Ferté-Macé and Bagnoles-de-l'Orne, the nearest stations are at Briouze and Argentan, from where the SNCF runs bus services.

STAO **bus** TER B runs to and from Argentan via both towns. Meanwhile, STAO bus No.24 links Domfront with Flers via Lonlay l'Abbaye, and No.22 runs to La Ferté-Macé and Bagnoles.

From April to October Bagnoles gently buzzes with *curistes*, who visit the **Grande Source** (the Great Spring), inside the thermal treatment centre, which spews mildly radioactive waters said to do wonders for circulatory and glandular disorders. The spa is big business, attracting the sick from all over France. It's a costly one too: hotels and restaurants are pricey, and the atmosphere tends to be seriously formal.

The tourist office organizes guided tours of the town's quaint **Belle Epoque mansions**, built in the town's golden era. Under a local bylaw they had to conform to the style in vogue at the time, with turrets, balconies and bow windows. In the huge grounds of the **Château de la Roche**, now the **Hôtel de Ville**, are a bird reserve and arboretum, and the **Roc au Chien**, a rocky promontory with great views. For children there's a 'little train' that runs around town during the summer months from the **Centre d'Animation**, which also has a busy programme of entertainment. For a complete change, visit the **Musée des Sapeurs Pompiers**, which has a display of horse-drawn fire engines.

Musée des Sapeurs Pompiers
*t 02 33 38 10 34;
open April–Oct daily
2–6; adm*

Domfront

Domfront

Perched on a sandstone ridge in the midst of the Passais, an area known for its pears and perry, little Domfront is a medieval gem, with quaint lanes, half-timbered houses and a ruined castle where Henry II and envoys of his estranged archbishop Thomas à Becket thrashed out their differences. It still has the feel of a fortress – built on the site of a hermitage founded by a 6th-century monk, St Front – and the ramparts and some of the original towers still stand. One alongside Rue des Fossés-Plisson, which also has the best views, is still crowned with its original battlements. Domfront became an English possession in 1100, after its people had revolted against their overlord, Roger de Montgomery, and sought the protection of William the Conqueror's youngest son Henry, later Henry I. He built the **castle**, with stunning views of the valley, the ruins of which, still with its dungeons inside four-metre-thick walls, can be visited. Later Domfront was a favourite residence of Henry II and his queen Eleanor of Aquitaine. In the Hundred Years' War poor Domfront was tossed back and forth between the French and English, and it wasn't until 1450 that the French got their hands on it for good.

Musée Charles Léandre
open Mon 2–4, Tues–Fri 9–12 and 2–4, Sat 9–12

The Hôtel de Ville houses the small **Musée Charles Léandre**, with paintings and lithographs by the local artist of the same name. Domfront's main draw, though, is its lovely half-timbered houses and hidden courtyards and mansions, many of which lie on the pedestrianized **Grande Rue** and **Rue Docteur Barnabé**, which turns into Rue de l'Hôpital.

Eglise Notre-Dame-sur-l'Eau
open daily 8–6, guided tour by appointment

A couple of kilometres west and downhill from the medieval centre, nestled among trees on the banks of the River Varenne, stands the squat 11th-century **Eglise Notre-Dame-sur-l'Eau**, a jewel of Norman Romanesque where pilgrims used to stop en route to Mont-St-Michel. Its visitors are said to have included Richard the Lionheart, Louis XI of France and, more recently, Flaubert and Mérimée. Two legends cling to this tiny church, the first that Eleanor of Aquitaine's daughter was baptised here, the second that Thomas à Becket celebrated Mass here in 1166 while exiled in France, though neither has been backed up by facts. If the church appears a little truncated, this is because it was once over 40 metres long, but 19th-century authorities butchered four of its six bays to make way for a road. The little church endured more devastation in 1944, and has only recently been restored. Mercifully its greatest treasures survived: its superb 12th-century frescoes, representing nattily-dressed apostles, and a 14th-century statue of the Virgin and Child.

Around Domfront

West of Domfront you enter pear-growing territory, with orchards grazed by spectacled Norman cows, and a signposted *Route de la Poire* around perry-tastings and fruit museums. Around 9km north of Domfront a bucolic valley provides the setting for

Lonlay-l'Abbaye
open daily 8–7

Lonlay-l'Abbaye. The abbey church, founded as part of a Benedictine monastery in the 11th century, was never finished, and the Wars of Religion, the Revolution and Second World War all wreaked havoc on the abbey buildings, but you can still visit the church, which has a fine Romanesque transept and 15th century porch. What really takes the biscuit though is the **Biscuiterie de l'Abbaye** next door, which churns out *sablés de l'Abbaye*, shortbread biscuits made to a secret recipe. South of Lonlay, legend has it that King Arthur was tossed into a ditch at the foot of an awesome sandstone gorge since known as **La Fosse-Arthour**, as punishment for trying to rejoin his wife Guinevere before sunset. Afterwards Guinevere, overcome with grief, killed herself. Today the gorge is frequented by rock-climbers, canoeists and fishermen.

Biscuiterie de l'Abbaye
t 02 33 30 64 64, www.biscuiterie-abbaye.com

Flower show
for tours of farms in bloom, and special events, contact t 02 33 30 69 60, st.fraimbault@ wanadoo.fr

In summer, picturesque **St-Fraimbault**, on Normandy's southern border, holds a perpetual **flower show**. Flowers have been a speciality here for over 30 years, and the village has 8,000 square metres of flowerbeds.

Tourist Information around La Ferté-Macé and Domfront

The La Ferté-Macé tourist office organizes a 'mushroom day' in the third weekend of October. In summer the Domfront tourist office runs occasional guided tours of the castle.

Market Days: La Ferté-Macé: Thurs; Bagnoles-de-l'Orne: Tues, Sat, Place du Marché; Wed, Fri, Allée des Anciens Combattants; Domfront: Fri.

Post Office: La Ferté-Macé, 32 Rue aux Cordiers; Bagnoles-de-l'Orne, Av de l'Hippodrome; Domfront, Place de la Liberté.

Shopping around La Ferté-Macé and Domfront

Manoir de Durcet, 61600 Magny-le-Désert, t 02 33 37 16 47. The friendly owners of this attractive manor sell their own calvados, cider, *pommeau* and *poiré*.

Chais du Verger Normand, Rue Mont-St-Michel, Domfront, t 02 3 38 53 96. Tastings and a full range of Norman apple tipples.

Le Clos Normand, Les Martellières, 61330 Sept-Forges, t 02 33 38 30 95. M and Mme Boisgontier produce a superb range of pear beverages, and speak English. Sept-Forges is 15km south of Domfront near Ceaucé.

L'Yonnière, 61330 Torchamp, t 02 33 30 84 76. Cider farm 6km southwest of Domfront selling *poiré Domfront*, *calvados Domfrontais* and *pommeau*.

La Poulardière, 61350 Saint Fraimbault, t 02 33 38 31 96. Organic farm that produces *poiré*, apple and pear juice.

Where to Stay and Eat around La Ferté-Macé and Domfront

La Ferté-Macé ✉ 61600

**Auberge de Clouet, Chemin de Clouet, t 02 33 37 18 22 (€). A small place with a colourful garden, fine views over the lake, and a good restaurant (€€€–€€). *Hotel closed Sun eve and Mon from Oct–Mar; restaurant closed Sun eve all year.*

Auberge de la Source, La Peleras, t 02 33 37 28 23 (€). The young owners built this *auberge* on the site of their parents' apple press. Cosy pristine B&B rooms, furnished with antiques, have views of the lake, just in front of the house, where you can sail, windsurf or try many other sports. There are several self-catering cottages and a bunkhouse too, which gives the place a young sporty atmosphere. There's also a great restaurant (€) next door, with a huge chimney where they grill locally-produced meat. You sit on long tables with the other guests.

Boucherie Châtel, t 02 33 37 11 85. If you want to do as the locals do, come and taste the local (cooked) tripe at this old-fashioned family butchers in the village centre.

Bagnoles-de-L'Orne ✉ 61140

There are some surprisingly zany places to stay here. Many hotel restaurants are happy to cater for special diets, but many are also mainly geared to full- or half-board guests.

***Le Manoir du Lys, Route de Juvigny, La Croix Gauthier, t 02 33 37 80 69, *www.manoir-du-lys.fr* (€€€€). An imaginatively converted manor house with 25 rooms in the Andaine forest, by a golf course. The hotel and its excellent restaurant (€€€–€€) are the pick of the Bagnoles bunch. *Hotel closed 2 Jan–14 Feb, restaurant closed Nov–Easter Sun eve and Mon.*

***Bois Joli, 12 Av Philippe du Rozier, t 02 33 37 92 77, *www.hotelboisjoli.com* (€€€–€€). Floral themes dominate the smart rooms in this 19th-century Anglo-Norman mansion, on the edge of the woods. The owners are friendly and in October organize mushroom weekends. The restaurant (€€€–€€) has superb views over the lake.

**Le Celtic, 14 Rue Dr Pierre Noal, t 02 33 37 92 11, *www.leceltic.fr* (€). This newly refurbished hotel-restaurant, in a lovely Belle Epoque mansion, is famous as much for its stylish, calming rooms as for its great

(i) **Bagnoles-de-l'Orne >>**
Place du Marché,
t 02 33 37 85 66,
www.bagnoles-de-lorne.com

(i) **La Ferté-Macé >**
11 Rue de la Victoire,
t 02 33 37 10 97,
www.tourisme-lafertemace.fr.st

restaurant (€€). The chef has recently built up a strong reputation and you can see him at work as you eat. Great value. (If the hotel is full, try its sister hotel, Bagnoles Hotel, 6 Place de la République, **t** 02 33 37 86 79, which charges similar prices and also has a restaurant, Le Bistro Gourmand.) *Closed mid-Jan–5 March; restaurant closed Sun eve and Mon outside high season.*

(i) **Domfront** >
12 Place de la Roirie,
t *02 33 38 53 97,*
www.domfront.com

Domfront ✉ 61700

Château de La Maigraire, Saint Bômer-les-Forges, **t** 02 33 38 09 52 (€€€–€€). This 1870s château 6km north of Domfront town has been brilliantly restored by its interior-designer owner Jean Fischer. There are just two rooms, one a suite for 2 or 3, and both furnished with antiques.

Belle Vallée, 5kms from Domfront, **t** 02 33 37 05 71, *www.belle-vallee.net* (€€–€). Beautiful 19th-century *maison de maître* in 18 acres of land, including a walled garden, a pond and a paddock. It's owned by an English couple who have done a great job restoring and decorating its five luxurious en-suite rooms, all with beams. If you reserve in advance, you can get an evening meal too (prices on request).

Hotel de France, 7 Rue du Mont-St-Michel, **t 02 33 38 51 44 (€). The best option inside Domfront town, although *madame* can appear a bit ferocious. Rooms are simple, slightly worn, and all have bathrooms. Those at the back have wonderful views of gardens, the river and Notre–Dame sur L'Eau. The homely *auberge*-style restaurant (€€) serves hearty Norman cuisine beside a grand fireplace, and there's also a Grill (open daily) serving huge steaks. *Restaurant closed Sun eve and Mon.*

Le Bar Normand, Place de l'Eglise, **t** 02 33 38 51 29. This bar-restaurant, in a lovely half-timbered house in the heart of the town, serves crêpes and light meals which you can wash down with *poiré* or cider.

Chanu ✉ 61800

Les Huttereaux, **t** 02 33 66 83 32 (€). Although it's officially a *chambre-d'hôte* you get a whole converted dairy-house to yourself, complete with tiny kitchen and living room. It's set amid a lovely garden, with a pond, and beyond that, woods. Sylviane brings breakfast to your cottage in the morning. She'll cook you dinner (€) in the main house if you ask in advance.

Cherbourg
and the Cotentin

With its jagged granite coastline, picturesque ports and sandy beaches, the finger-shaped Cotentin Peninsula in many ways seems closer in character to wild Brittany or Ireland than sedate Normandy. At the top of the finger stands Cherbourg, the largest man-made harbour in the world. On the east coast are two enchanting granite ports much loved by the English, Barfleur and St-Vaast, the latter famous for its oysters. The Cotentin's west coast is blessed with miles of white sandy beaches, culminating in the spectacular Bay of Mont St-Michel and its extraordinary pinnacle-top monastery.

16

Don't miss

⓫ *Moules* and bobbing boats
Barfleur **p.332**

⓬ Giant cliffs and ocean views
Cap de la Hague **p.340**

⓭ The perfect fishing village
Portbail **p.341**

⓮ Soaring granite ruins among the trees
Abbaye de Hambye **p.359**

⓯ France's magic mountain
Mont-St-Michel **p.368**

See map overleaf

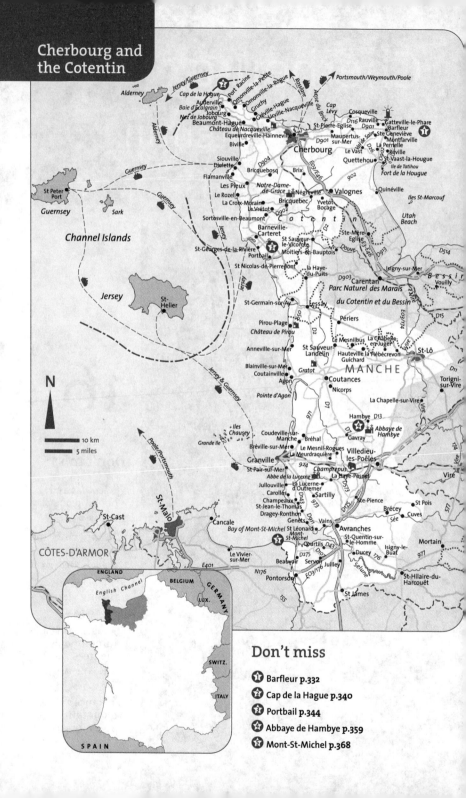

Cherbourg and the Cotentin

Portsmouth/Weymouth/Poole

Jersey/Guernsey
Alderney
Cap de la Hague
Baie d'Ecalgrain
Jobourg
Nez de Jobourg
Beaumont-Hague
Château de Nacqueville
Equeurdreville-Hainneville
Biville

Port Racine
Omonville-la-Petite
Omonville-la-Rogue
Gruchy
Cléville-Hague
Urville-Nacqueville

Auderville

Anse du Brick
Rosière

Cap Lévy
Cosqueville
Rauville
Catteville-le-Phare
Barfleur
St-Pierre-Eglise
Maupertus-sur-Mer
Ste Geneviève
Montfarville
La Perrelle
Réville
St-Vaast-la-Hougue
Ile de Tatihou
Fort de la Hougue

Cherbourg
Le Vast
Quettehou

St Peter Port
Guernsey

Sark

Channel Islands

Jersey

St-Helier

Siouville
Diélette
Flamanville
Les Pieux
Le Rozel
La Croix-Morain
Le Vrétot
Sortosville-en-Beaumont

Bricquebosq
Brix
Notre-Dame-de-Grâce
Négreville
Bricquebec
Yvetot-Bocage
Valognes
Quinéville
Iles St-Marcouf

Cotentin
Utah Beach

Barneville-Carteret
St-Georges-de-la-Rivière
Portbail
St Nicolas-de-Pierrepont
St Sauveur-le-Vicomte
Moitiers-en-Bauptois
la Haye-du-Puits

Ste-Mère-Eglise
Douve
Isigny-sur-Mer

Bessin
Vouilly

D903
Carentan
Parc Naturel des Marais du Cotentin et du Bessin

St-Germain-sur-Ay
Lessay
Périers

Pirou-Plage
Château de Pirou
Anneville-sur-Mer
St Sauveur-Landelin
Le Mesnilbus
La Chapelle-en-Juger
Hauteville la Flébécrevon Guichard
St-Lô

Blainville-sur-Mer
Coutainville
Agon
Gratot

MANCHE
Torigni-sur-Vire

Coutances
Nicorps
La Chapelle-sur-Vire

Pointe d'Agon

Iles Chausey
Grande Ile
Coudeville-sur-Manche
Bréhal
Gavray
Hambye
Abbaye de Hambye

Bréville-sur-Mer
Le Mesnil-Rogues
La Meurdraquière
Villedieu-les-Poêles

Granville
St-Pair-sur-Mer
Abbe de la Lucerne
Champrepus
La Haye-Pesnel
Viré

Jullouville
Lucerne-d'Outremer
Carolles
Champeaux
St-Jean-le-Thomas
Dragey-Ronthon
Genêts
Sartilly
Ste-Pience
Brécey
Cuves
St Pois

St Léonard
Mont-St-Michel
Vains
Avranches
St-Quentin-sur-le-Homme
Ducey

Bay of Mont-St-Michel
Courtils
Julley
Isigny-le-Buat
Mortain

CÔTES-D'ARMOR
St-Cast
St-Malo
Cancale
Le Vivier-sur-Mer
Beauvoir
Servon
Pontorson
St James
St-Hilaire-du-Harcouët

Poole Portsmouth

ENGLAND
English Channel
BELGIUM
GERMANY
LUX.
SWITZ.
ITALY
SPAIN

N
10 km
5 miles

Don't miss

Cherbourg

Hub and capital of the Cotentin, Cherbourg is another ferry port that many regard as a utilitarian place to head straight out of. The city's golden era as an arrival point for great transatlantic liners ended with the Second World War; it was then heavily fought over and damaged and bombarded by both sides in 1944, and post-war much of the town around the port area has been rebuilt. The maze of streets in Cherbourg's centre, however, survived the war surprisingly intact, and is a pleasant place to wander. In the attractive cafés lining the inland harbour, the **Bassin de Commerce** and the **Avant-Port**, you can sample the local seafood and watch the fishing boats chugging in and out. If possible, make time to visit the city's most modern attraction, the **Cité de la Mer**, an imaginative museum recreating the experience of the ocean, on the site of the old Transatlantic Terminal. Children can also explore Cherbourg aboard the *petit train*, which tours the city in summer.

Cherbourg first became something more than a fishing hamlet under William the Conqueror, who built a fortress here. In 1145 his granddaughter Matilda built a much larger abbey, the **Abbaye du Vœu**, on one of the hills just west of the modern town. It was devastated in 1944 but has been restored. The Norman castle was given new fortifications in 1300 by King Philippe IV le Bel, and during the Hundred Years' War Cherbourg was the scene of constant skirmishing between the French and English. In the 1670s, under Louis XIV, the idea began to be put forward that Cherbourg should be transformed into a vast port and naval base by means of artificial breakwaters, to make up for the lack of a good deep-water port on France's Channel coast. The old castle was pulled down and work began in 1688, but this would be one of the most long-drawn-out projects in French history. After years of stop-start under the *ancien régime*, it was given decisive impetus by the first Napoleon, as a weapon in his wars with Britain, but the naval port was only completed under his grandson Napoléon III in the 1850s.

This giant new harbour, though, also made Cherbourg such an important stopping off point for transatlantic liners: in 1929 some 300,000 passengers passed through, and even in the 1950s celebs like Rita Hayworth or Elizabeth Taylor stepped onto Cherbourg's grand quay. On 26–29 June 1944 Cherbourg became the first large French city to be liberated, as US troops battered their way into the town in vicious fighting. The Germans besieged in Cherbourg had resisted ferociously in order to deny the Allies the use of the port, and, before surrendering, comprehensively sabotaged the docks. Salvage and repair work was carried out around the clock, and by late 1944 Cherbourg was able to take over from the Arromanches Mulberry (*see* p.268) as the busiest port in the world. Today

Abbaye du Vœu
*t 02 33 87 89 26;
gardens open year
round, abbey open
July–Aug Sat–Sun*

16

Cherbourg and the Cotentin | Cherbourg

Getting to Cherbourg

By Sea

Brittany Ferries sails three times daily (twice daily outside high season) from Poole on the high-speed Condor hovercraft (5hrs); and twice daily from Portsmouth (3hrs). **Irish Ferries** and **Celtic Link Ferries** have services from Rosslare (between one and three times weekly) which take around 18hrs. For more on Channel ferries, including contact details, *see* p.79.

All companies use the same **terminal**, on the east side of the harbour. There are frequent buses from there to the city centre. For drivers who don't want to linger in Cherbourg, it's easy to get out of town by following the '*Toutes Directions*' and 'Caen–Paris' signs on the N13 main road south.

By Air

You can also fly to Cherbourg's tiny **airport** at Maupertus, 11km east, from Southampton with **Flybe**, t 0871 700 0535, *www.flybe.com* (flights May–Sept Mon, Wed and Fri). There are also daily scheduled flights to Paris-Orly and Jersey with **Twin Jet**, t 0892 707 737. **Airport information**, t 02 33 88 57 60, *www.aeroport-cherbourg.com* There's no public transport from the airport into town.

By Train

There are frequent train links to Cherbourg's **station** in Av Jean-François Millet from Paris (3hrs, or less by TGV) via Bayeux and Caen, and from Avranches, Brittany and the Loire via Coutances.

Getting around Cherbourg

By Bus

Cherbourg's *Gare Routière* (**bus station**) is opposite the railway station at the south end of the port. **Zephir Bus** (t 0810 810 050, *www.zephirbus.com*) provides buses inside the city and also has some routes to the Cap de la Hague and villages east of Cherbourg. **STN-Verney** (t 02 33 44 32 22) runs buses to other parts of the Manche *département*.

By Car and Bike

Car hire offices include **ADA**, 10–12 Av de Paris, t 02 33 20 65 65; **Avis**, 5 Rue de la Saline, t 02 33 88 66 99; **Budget**, 62 Quai Alexandre III, t 02 33 94 32 77; **Europcar**, 4 Rue des Tanneries, t 02 33 44 53 85; **Hertz**, 43 Rue du Val de Saire, t 02 33 23 41 41; **RentaCar**, 48 Quai Alexandre III, t 02 33 20 14 06.

To phone for a **taxi**, call t 02 33 53 36 38 or t 02 33 53 17 04. For **bike hire**, try **Cycles Peugeot Kerhir**, 31 Bd Schuman, t 02 33 53 04 38 (*closed Mon*).

Cherbourg's chief business is as an industrial and commercial port, and a French navy town, manufacturing submarines, and the luxury liners have been mostly replaced by cross-Channel ferries.

Visiting Cherbourg

Visitors can see both submarines and the once-fashionable Art Deco railway station (*Gare Maritime*) where the world's rich boarded transatlantic liners at the **Cité de la Mer**. This centre, conveniently close to the ferry terminal, took 10 years to build but the result is a fascinating experience (which needs 2–3 hours to take in properly). It's divided into two parts: the first is the more traditional, with an impressive aquarium housing a huge range of often-weird sea creatures, a pool where you can touch the fish, and another 'bottomless' aquarium, 10 metres deep, designed to show changes in fish and flora as you plumb the depths. It's suitable for adults and children alike, and there are plenty of interactive TV

Cité de la Mer
*t 02 33 20 26 69,
www.citedelamer.com;
open daily July–Aug
9.30–7, last entry 6;
May–June and Sept
9.30–6; Feb–April and
Oct–Mar 10–6; closed
some public hols and
most of Jan; adm*

PORT MILITAIRE

Port de Plaisance de Chantereyne

La Cité de la Mer

AVENUE DE CESSART

To Abbaye du Vœu

RUE DE L'ABBAYE

Musée d'Histoire Naturelle, d'Ethnographie et d'Archéologie

PLACE NAPOLEON

Parc Emmanuel Liais

RUE DE LA BUCAILLE

RUE EMMANUEL LIAIS

RUE GRANDE VALLÉE

Basilica Ste-Trinité

RUE TOUR CARRÉE

RUE DE L'ÉGLISE

BD FÉLIX AMIOT

ALLÉE DU PRÉSIDENT MENUT

To Ferry Terminals

AVENUE ARISTIDE BRIAND

QUAI CALIGNY

QUAI GENERAL LAWTON COLLINS

Avant Port

RUE DE LA MARINE

PLACE DES CAVALIERS

RUE CHRISTINE

Market

PLACE CENTRALE

RUE DU COMMERCE

GRANDE RUE

RUE DU PORT

RUE NOTRE DAME

RUE EMMANUEL LIAIS

RUE G FOUACE

RUE DU CHATEAU

RUE MONTEBELLO

RUE EMILE ZOLA

RUE EMILE ZOLA

PONT TOURNANT

RUE DU VAL DE SAIRE

RUE TOURVILLE

RUE MAL R. FOCH

R. J-BAPTISTE BIARD

Théâtre

Musée Thomas Henry

RUE VASTEL

RUE DES HALLES

RUE LOUIS XVI

QUAI ALEXANDRE III

Bassin du Commerce

QUAI DE L'ENTREPOT

AV. CARNOT

RUE DE L'HERMITAGE

AVENUE DELAVILLE

BOULEVARD MENDES FRANCE

Shopping Centre

AV. LEMONNIER

Bus Station

AVENUE JEAN

FRANCOIS MILLET

DES PANNERIES

Train Station

AVENUE DE PARIS

Jardin des Plantes

AVENUE ETIENNE LECARPENTIER

BOULEVARD DE L'ATLANTIQUE

MONTÉE

Musée de la Guerre et de la Libération

Fort du Roule

RESISTANTS

DES

BOULEVARD DE L'ATLANTIQUE

N

250 m
250 yds

To Caen

screens where you can test or expand your knowledge. The second part of the visit takes you aboard a nuclear submarine, *Le Redoutable*, launched by General de Gaulle in Cherbourg in 1967 and decommissioned in 1991. Weapons-fans can see the launchers for its 16 lethal missiles, and get an insight into everyday life down below by touring the 130-man crew's living quarters and gym. Alongside, a room offers you the chance to navigate a (simulated) submarine yourself. As you leave the Cité you pass a relic of Cherbourg's bizarre participation in the American Civil War. In 1864 two rival warships, the *Confederate Alabama* and the *Union Kearsage*, fought a pitched battle off the rocks of Cherbourg. The *Alabama* had crossed the Atlantic to obstruct shipping to the northern states, and the *Kearsage* had followed in pursuit. The wreck of the Alabama was discovered by a minesweeper in 1984, and since then various parts have been retrieved, including the cannon displayed in the Cité.

Musée Thomas Henry
Rue Vastel, t 02 33 23 39 30; open May–Sept, Tues–Sat 10–12 and 2–6, Sun–Mon 2–6; Oct–April Wed–Sun 2–6; adm free

For a more conventional museum, head for the centre of town and the Musée Thomas Henry, a superb collection of art begun by the 19th-century collector and connoisseur Thomas Henry. Its most outstanding works are 15th- and 16th-century Italian paintings like Filippino Lippi's *The Entombment* and Fra Angelico's tiny but powerful *Conversion of Saint Augustine*, but there are also superb Flemish paintings from the same period. Normandy-born Nicolas Poussin is represented by a touching *Pietà*. More local still are the paintings of Jean-François Millet, born a few miles away at Gruchy (*see* p.341), and who taught himself to paint by copying works in the Henry collection, which he knew well (some of his copies are now in the museum as well). The museum's Millet collection is one of the best there is, and is unusual in that it consists mainly of portraits rather than the landscapes for which he is better known. Two of the most touching are those of his young wife – she looks little over 15 – which is Cherbourg's answer to the *Mona Lisa*. The first, *Portrait of Pauline Ono in Blue*, shows a demure if slightly melancholy girl, head slightly cocked, hair immaculately groomed and her mouth half-smiling, half-serious; the second, *Pauline Ono en Deshabillé*, is a shocking contrast: her hair is strewn carelessly over a silk nightgown, and the haunted look in her tearful eyes is more pronounced still. She was suffering from tuberculosis, and died a few weeks after Millet painted her, at the tender age of 22. Other local talent is exhibited in the form of Eugene Boudin's *Retour de Pêche au Soleil Couchant*, and a big collection of still lives by Guillaume Fouace.

Musée d'Histoire Naturelle et d'Ethnographie
t 02 33 53 51 61; open May–Sept Tues–Sat 10–12 and 2–6, Sun–Mon 2–6; Oct–April Wed–Sun 2–6; adm free

A walk northwest from the Thomas Henry museum takes you to the Musée d'Histoire Naturelle et d'Ethnographie, also known as the Musée E. Liais, a lovely old-fashioned museum within the city's **botanical gardens**. It's housed in the 19th-century house of

Emmanuel Liais, an astronomer and savant who was for a time mayor of Cherbourg. As well as the predictable glass cases of sharks' jaws and Melanesian masks, the museum has one special treasure: an Egyptian mummy, discovered in 1832.

On the southwest side of the city, beyond the railway station and the pleasant park of the **Jardin des Plantes**, with its statue of Millet, a steep walk uphill will take you to the excellent Musée de la Guerre et de la Libération, housed in the glowering **Fort du Roule**, perched on a hill with spectacular views of the harbour. The scars of the June 1944 battle – when German troops tried to hold out in the fort to the last – are still easily visible on the walls of the mid-19th-century fortress, and inside maps, photos and films recount the story of the bitter fighting that liberated the town. There is also a particularly moving exhibit, of an urn containing ashes and earth taken from concentration camps.

Musée de la Guerre et de la Libération
t 02 33 20 14 12; open May–Sept Tues–Sat 10–12 and 2–6, Sun–Mon 2–6; Oct–April Wed–Sun 2–6; adm

Tourist Information in Cherbourg

Cherbourg >
2 Quai Alexandre III, t 02 33 93 52 02, www.ot-cherbourg-cotentin.fr

In addition to the main tourist office, there is a smaller information centre inside the Cité de la Mer (*closed Jan*), and one at the ferry terminal.
Internet Access: Net Phone, Rue Grande Rue; Archésys, Rue de l'Union.
Market Days: Tues, Thurs, Sat; Sun (Octeville).
Post Office: Rue Paul Doumer.

Where to Stay in Cherbourg

Cherbourg ✉ 50100
Hotels in the centre are functional. If you want something with more character, head for one of the lovely *chambres d'hôtes* listed below, all of which are in the outskirts.

La Maison du Chevreuil >

La Maison du Chevreuil, 36 Av du Chevreuil, 50120 Equeurdreville-Hainneville, t 02 33 01 33 10, *http://perso.wanadoo.fr/maison-duchevreuil* (€€). Gorgeous 18th-century manor house, with walled gardens back and front where in summer you eat breakfast. It's hidden away in the westerly suburbs, yet it's only five minutes' drive to the ferry port. The three en-suite rooms (one a suite) are in the outhouses.
**Moderna, 28 Rue de la Marine, t 02 33 43 05 30, *www.moderna-hotel.com*

(€). South American hangings give a homely atmosphere to this friendly central hotel owned by a Colombian family. It's popular with cyclists who can put their bikes in the central courtyard. Pristine top-floor rooms have views over the port.
**La Renaissance, 4 Rue de l'Eglise, t 02 33 43 23 90, *www.hotel-renaissance-cherbourg.com* (€). Good-value hotel near the Eglise de la Trinité, whose bright clean rooms look over the port. Beautiful Norman *armoires* in the corridors.
Manoir Saint Jean, Tourlaville, t 02 33 22 00 86 (€). Ancient stone manor 6km southeast of Cherbourg. Right on the coast path, it's blissfully quiet, and there's a room with an outside entrance for those with early ferries to catch.

Eating Out in Cherbourg

Cherbourg ✉ 50100
For seafood and a view over the port, head for the many restaurants on and around the Quai Caligny.
L'Aigue Marine, 16 Quai de Caligny, t 02 33 23 95 69, *www.laiguemarine.com* (€€). Seafood restaurant with pavement terrace on the harbour front. If a plate of *fruits de mer* is what you're after, this is the place. *Closed Sat lunch and Sun.*

Le Pommier, 15 bis Rue Notre-Dame, t 02 33 53 54 60 (€€). Attractive little restaurant with a sun-drenched terrace to sit in summer. Meat and fish, both local and fresh, take equal place on the simple menu. There's an equally easy-going restaurant next door. *Closed Sun and Mon.*

L'Ambroisy, 39 Rue Grande Rue, t 02 33 10 19 29, *lambroisy@wanadoo.fr* (€€). Don't be put off by the funky purple exterior: this is one the best eateries in Cherbourg. Its interesting menu combines classical French with exotic spices and flavours, using local ingredients. Try the foie gras with Sichuan peppers and rhubarb. *Closed Mon lunch, Sat lunch and Tues.*

Sel & Poivre, 17 Rue du Port, t 02 33 01 24 09 (€€–€). A tiny place just off the Quai de Caligny, whose minimalist décor belies its innovative menu, a fusion of French and and Oriental flavours. Try the mixed plate of hors d'oeuvres, and for main course the spiced roast lamb with a gratin of potatoes and roasted peppers. *Closed Tues eve and Wed.*

Anse-du-Brick/Maupertus

✉ 50100

La Maison Rouge, 16 Anse du Brick, t 02 33 54 33 50, *delsautp@aol.com* (€€€–€€) This modern glass-fronted restaurant's clifftop location, overlooking the bay of the Anse du Brick 12km east of Cherbourg, is difficult to beat. Classic French cooking using fresh local meat and fish. *Closed Mon and Tues.*

The Tip of the Peninsula

Barfleur, the Val de Saire and St-Vaast

🏅 **Barfleur**

It's hard to fault the perfectly self-contained fishing harbour of Barfleur, 25km east of Cherbourg. Fishermen deposit their catch on the old granite flagstones of the harbour, quaintly elegant medieval houses line its streets, and the pace of life is idyllically slow. Barfleur's tranquillity, however, belies a busy and turbulent history. In medieval times its streets buzzed with the comings and goings of dukes and kings, and for a time it was the biggest port in Normandy, as the main harbour for traffic to and from the Normans' new possessions in England. The ship the *Mora* in which William the Conqueror sailed to England was built at Barfleur, and his helmsman, Etienne, came from here. A bronze plaque fixed to a rock by the quayside commemorates the momentous voyage. Later, English pilgrims en route to Mont-St-Michel and Santiago de Compostela disembarked here. In 1120 tragedy hit when the ship carrying Henry I's son, William Atheling, foundered on the rocks (*see* opposite). Barfleur also witnessed crucial episodes in the dispute between Henry II and Thomas à Becket; Becket visited Barfleur several times and founded a small monastery here, and years later, Henry II stopped here en route to see the Pope to ask him to lift his excommunication due to Becket's murder.

By the 12th century Barfleur's population had reached around 9,000. In 1346, however, at the start of the Hundred Years' War, Edward III of England sacked the town and slaughtered most of its inhabitants, and then the Black Death polished off many of the

Getting around the Barfleur Region

STN **bus** No.1 runs between Cherbourg and Barfleur and St-Vaast, calling at Montfarville, Réville and other Val de Saire villages. No service Sundays.

survivors a few years later. It 's been downhill ever since, and it now has fewer than 600 people.

Tucked behind the tourist office at the left end of the quay is the squat schist-roofed **Eglise St-Nicolas**, which took a phenomenal 223 years to build, starting in 1630. Inside, it has a remarkable 16th-century *Pietà*. From the church it's worth wandering along **Rue St-Nicolas** and **Rue St-Thomas-Becket**, where you'll find some of Barfleur's finest houses, with *oeil-de-boeuf* attic windows and delicate ironwork and schist roofs topped by ceramic *épis de faîtage*, or roof statues. In the pottery at Rue du Vast you can see how the latter are made. Barfleur's oldest house, from medieval times, is in the **Cour Ste-Catherine** in the middle of the village, reached via a low granite arch.

Barfleur has three small beaches, but a better bet is to walk the scenic 3km-stretch of the GR223 coastal footpath north to the rocks on which William Atheling's ship foundered, now protected by the **Gatteville lighthouse**. At 75 metres high, it is the second tallest lighthouse in France, and its guiding beams can be seen 50 kilometres away. The energetic can scale its 365 granite steps and admire this engineering feat, which took five strenuous years to build from 1829 to 1834. On the way back, stop to enjoy the lovely stone village of **Gatteville-le-Phare**, with its rambling central square and monumental Norman church with 12th-century belfry.

Gatteville lighthouse

t 02 33 23 17 97; open daily May–Aug 10–12 and 2–7, April and Sept 10–12 and 2–6, Mar and Oct 10–12 and 2–5; adm

The Val de Saire

This name of this area comes from the little river valley that runs through the northeast corner of the Cotentin, but the label 'Val de Saire' is used to describe the whole of the bulge of land east of

The White Ship, a Shipwreck that Changed History

In 1120 Henry I, King of England and Duke of Normandy, was returning to England with his two sons and, it is said, was approached in Barfleur by the son of Etienne, the helmsman who had navigated William the Conqueror to England. He asked the King to travel in his ship the *Blanche Nef*, the White Ship. The King declined, but entrusted his sons and the flower of the Norman court – around 300 nobles – to his care. The *Blanche Nef* had barely left the harbour when it hit a rock, due, it's thought, to the carelessness of the crew, who had imbibed several calvados too many. William and the noble passengers were drowned – everyone except for a butcher from Rouen named Berold, who survived by clinging to a plank of wood. It is from him that we have a first-hand account, related by Robert Wace in his *Roman de Rou*. It is said, too, that Henry I never smiled again.

The tragedy changed the course of English history, for Henry was left without an heir, and on his death the rights of his daughter Matilda to the Crown were challenged by her cousin Stephen. After years of civil war, the Anglo-Norman monarchy was passed to the House of Plantagenet, descendants of Matilda and her husband Geoffrey of Anjou.

Cherbourg. It's a beautiful area of woodlands and pastures, dotted with tiny, quiet granite villages which in the past gained a livelihood from the mills along the River Saire. In the 19th century there were 37 of them, producing cotton, grain and iron. The centre of activity was the village of **Le Vast**, which in the 19th century had 1700 inhabitants (compared to its current 300). The river was channelled to power a huge cotton mill, built in 1795 and employing 600 villagers; all that remains today are the mill ponds, the waterfall, and mill-workers' cottages. To get the most out of the area, you need to explore on foot or bicycle – there are plenty of good footpaths and quiet lanes, and you can pick up details of circular routes at the helpful tourist office in Barfleur.

Other than Le Vast, the prettiest villages include **Réville**, with its manor houses and 11th-century church, and **La Pernelle**, whose main street runs steeply up to a little granite church from where there are fabulous views as far as Gatteville lighthouse to the north and Grandcamp-Maisy to the south. It's also a pilgrimage site, with an image of the Virgin of Lourdes. La Pernelle's views were not missed by the German army, who installed an observation post and gun battery here that in June 1944 bombarded the US troops at Utah Beach, 30km south. Retaliation followed and one of the casualties was the church, of which only the 14th-century stone tower survived. Much of the building you see today is a reconstruction.

Another of the Val de Saire's gems is **Montfarville**, an idyllic village with solid granite houses, winding streets and an unusual **church**, whose awesome bell tower dates from the 13th century. The main church was rebuilt in 1763, and contains two very different treasures: first, a 12th-century Virgin and Child woodcarving, *Notre Dame de Consolation*, which was hidden from the wrath of the Revolutionaries in 1793 to escape destruction; second, a remarkable series of 18 frescoes in the choir representing the life of Christ, painted by local artist Guillaume Fouace at the end of the 19th century. There's a pleasant bar-restaurant too, for sitting down and absorbing the atmosphere.

St-Vaast-la-Hougue and Tatihou

The strangely-named St-Vaast (pronounced '*san-va*') competes with Barfleur, 10kms north, for the prize of prettiest port in the eastern Cotentin. Barfleur perhaps just wins, as Saint-Vaast has a bit more of the feel of a working town. Its lifeblood today is its busy marina, where cross-Channel yachties hang out, and its oyster beds south of the town, as *huîtres de Saint-Vaast* are renowned all over France. One can watch the action and sample local oysters in the many bars and restaurants that line the attractive waterfront, and there are some nice if rugged beaches to the north. Forts to the south of town and on the offshore island of Tatihou give a military feel to the place; they were erected in 1694 by Louis XIV's fortress-builder Marshal Vauban after the Battle of La Hougue two years earlier, in which the French navy, mustered to carry a French-Irish army to Britain to restore the deposed James II to the English throne, was defeated off St-Vaast by an Anglo-Dutch fleet. The fate of other unlucky sailors is remembered in the tiny Romanesque **Chapelle des Marins** at the south end of the pier. Topped by a Virgin who keeps watch over the sea, this isolated landmark has guided sailors into the bay since the 11th century. There are great views of the coast from the grassy terrace around it.

The **Fort de la Hougue** on the spit south of St-Vaast remains largely in military hands, but you can visit the **Ile de Tatihou** by boat and you can even stay there. The sandy island gets its strange name from a Viking leader, Tati. It's a great excursion, whether you are interested in birds and plants, for which Tatihou is famous, or history, or just the scenery. Vauban's **fort** now contains a hotel, bookshop, café and restaurant, as well as the former *lazare*, the quarantine hospital for crews struck by the plague or other infectious diseases. There is also a **Musée Maritime**, which has objects retrieved from wrecks and a workshop that restores traditional Norman fishing vessels, and also hosts weekend courses in fish cookery.

In August Tatihou hosts an annual festival of 'maritime' music from around the world, the **Festival des Musiques du Large**, which includes the *Traversée* (Crossing), when crowds walk the 2km-strait across to the island, known as *le Rhun*, at low tide. The rest of the year you can stroll through the dunes and grassy moorlands to spot a rich variety of seabirds, with many cormorants and terns. To enjoy the peace of the island, you can also stay in one of the island's simple guest rooms (*see* below), and in July and August there are cruises around the island in a sailing boat, tickets for which are available at the Maritime Museum. To preserve its precious environment, a maximum of 500 visitors a day are allowed onto Tatihou, so it's wise to book in advance.

Quinéville

This low-key beach village between St-Vaast and Utah Beach, with a couple of bars and hotels, houses the excellent **Musée de la Liberté**. This is another 'war museum', but you won't find any weapons or uniforms. Instead, it portrays life in France under the Occupation, with the aid of waxworks, posters, photos and documents. There are graphic illustrations of the exodus of eight to 10 million refugees from the Normandy battlefields, and the museum describes how, from August 1940, French people were forbidden to eat fresh bread – it was too good and left you wanting

Ile de Tatihou
boat tickets can be bought and accommodation booked (at least three days in advance) at Acceuil Tatihou on the Quay Vauban, t 02 33 23 19 92; crossings April–Sept daily 10–12 and 2–4; last boat back leaves the island at 6, or 7 in July–Aug

Musée Maritime
open April–mid-July and mid-Aug–Sept 10–12 and 2–6; mid-July–mid-Aug 10–12 and 2–7, adm

Festival des Musiques du Large
book in advance, t 02 33 23 19 92, www.tatihou.com

Musée de la Liberté
t 02 33 95 95 95, www.memorial-quineville.com; open daily June–Sept 9.30–7.30; Oct–Nov 10–6; adm

more, so bakers were obliged to let it go stale to make it less appetising – and ate nettles and dandelions to keep themselves going. The highlight is a reconstruction of a complete 1940s street, and there's a film in French. The most touching exhibit is a baby's gas mask, so huge it virtually swallows up the baby.

Tourist Information around Barfleur

Market Days: Barfleur: small market on Sat; St-Vaast: Sat.

Shopping around Barfleur

Maison Gosselin, 27 Rue de Verrue, St-Vaast-la-Hougue, **t** 02 33 54 40 06. Superb *épicerie*, founded in 1889, where you can find luxury foodstuffs from calvados to jams, pâtés, cheeses and wines. They deliver to yachts. *Closed Mon from Sept–June.*

Where to Stay and Eat around Barfleur

Barfleur ✉ 50760

Le Conquérant, 18 Rue St-Thomas Becket, **t 02 33 54 00 82 (€€). This 17th-century stone manor, perfectly positioned 50 metres from the harbour, is Barfleur's choice hotel. Rooms, which look over the attractive and tranquil walled garden at the back, have recently been refurbished. The hotel offers simple suppers around the fireplace for residents. *Closed mid-Nov–end-Mar.*

Le Manoir de l'Epine, Hameau Denneville, 50760 Gatteville-Le-Phare, **t** 02 33 22 04 55, *www.manoirdelepine. com* (€€). Fabulous 16th-century fortified farm in a sleepy hamlet just outside Barfleur with four en-suite rooms. Its lively owners also offer delicious dinners (€€; order in advance) which are roasted on a spit in the massive granite fireplace in the dining room.

M Leterrier, Hameau de Quenanville, 50760 Gatteville-Le-Phare, **t** 02 33 23 10 19 (€€–€). There are three pretty bedrooms in this solid granite house

in a hamlet just outside Barfleur, and there's a large walled garden you can relax in.

Le Moderne, 1 Place du Général de Gaulle, **t** 02 33 23 12 44 (€€€–€€). It's the restaurant that gives La Moderne its reputation, as the three rooms (€) are functional. The atmosphere is formal without being stuffy, and the cooking – based on finest local ingredients – is exquisite. *Open daily July–Aug; Sept–June closed Tues eve and Wed.*

Brasserie Café de France, 12 Quai Henri Chardon, **t** 02 33 54 00 38 (€). This place virtually next to the tourist office is a simple brasserie, but it serves the best *moule-frites* for miles. *Closed Wed out of season.*

Cosqueville ✉ 50330

Au Bouquet de Cosqueville, Hameau Remond, **t** 02 33 54 32 81, *www.bouquetdecosqueville.com* (€€€€). This place is renowned for its restaurant, one of the best in the Cotentin. Chef Eric Pouhier, has been cooking there for three decades. Being on the coast, fish and seafood are the speciality. Try the lobster and herb salad. There are seven modest rooms (€) if you don't feel like driving after an evening feast. *Restaurant open daily in Aug, closed Tues in July, and Tues–Wed from Sept–June.*

La Pernelle ✉ 50360

Le Panoramique, **t** 02 33 54 13 79, *www.le-panoramique.fr* (€€–€). The location and view at this big modern glass restaurant are breathtaking: it's next to the old German gun battery at the top of La Pernelle hill and you can see right along the coast. It's recently become a significant name on the foodie circuit, with seafood a speciality. Try the scallops with apples and calvados. *Closed Thurs exc July–Aug.*

ⓘ **Barfleur >**
2 Rond Point Guillaume le Conquérant, **t** 02 33 54 02 48, *www.ville-barfleur.fr*

★ **Au Bouquet de Cosqueville >>**

(i) **St-Vaast-la-Hougue >>**

1 Place Général de Gaulle, t 02 33 23 19 32, www.saint-vaast-reville.com

(★) **France et des Fuchsias >>**

(★) **La Fèvrerie >**

Montfarville, Réville and Ste-Geneviève ✉ 50760

Clemasine, 48 Rue de la Grand'ville, Montfarville, t 02 33 22 08 63, *www.clemasine.com* (€€). This old stone farmhouse has been skilfully converted by its friendly owner M. Gancel to provide four light and stylish bedrooms, with painted beamed ceilings, antiques and pretty bedcovers. All are split level so that children can sleep semi-separately.

La Fèvrerie, Ste Geneviève, t 02 33 54 33 53, *caillet.manoirlafevrerie@wanadoo.fr* (€€–€). One of the best B&Bs in Normandy, this stunning and ancient farm has three pretty rooms. Madame is passionate about interior decoration, while her husband breeds racehorses. Great breakfasts too, including local specialities.

La Tourelle, 20 Rue Landemer, Montfarville, t 02 33 23 18 35 (€). Owners M and Mme Lebeaut are both ex-actors (she is English) and they have left an artistic mark on the bedrooms which have a distant view of the sea. There's a pretty walled garden behind.

Manoir de Cabourg, Réville, t 02 33 54 48 42 (€). Vast 15th-century fortified farm, reached via an imposing driveway. Madame is a welcoming and gentle soul who serves breakfasts in her flagstoned kitchen.

St-Vaast-la-Hougue ✉ 50550

***France et des Fuchsias, 20 Rue Maréchal-Foch, t 02 33 54 42 26, *www.france-fuchsias.com* (€€). Long a British visitors' favourite, this lovely old inn is a few minutes' walk from the harbour. The courtyard is, as its name suggests, covered in climbing fuchsias. Rooms vary: the best are in the garden annexe, some with nice decking balconies. There's a self-catering cottage for four too. Equally famous is its restaurant (€€€–€€), which has fuchsia-pink traditional décor and offers every imaginable seafood dish, including, of course, the local oysters. *Closed Jan and Feb, Mon (exc July–Aug), also Tues from Nov–Mar.*

Hôtel de l'Île Tatihou Acceuil, Tatihou, t 02 33 54 33 33, *www.tatihou.com* (€). Atmospheric guesthouse in a former barracks in the fort on Tatihou island, with 34 very simple en-suite rooms. There are two simple restaurants, the Intra Muros (€), and Le Fort Carre, t 02 33 54 07 20, which offers salads, *moules-frites* and *plats du jour* (€). *Open July–Aug only; restaurants open April–Sept.*

Le Chasse Marée, 8 Place du Général de Gaulle, t 02 33 23 14 08 (€€). Neat little place on the harbour front specializing in fresh fish. *Closed Mon and Tues (Sept–June), closed Mon lunch (July–Aug).*

Inland from Cherbourg

Valognes

At the time of Louis XIV, Valognes' abundance of grand town houses, with their mullioned windows and stone façades, led it to be called 'Normandy's Little Versailles'. It was said that if you wanted to get into the court at Versailles, you had to do Valognes first. There were over a hundred beautiful stone mansions, owned by the wealthy nobles who administrated the then-'capital' of the Cotentin. Alas, 1944 bombings destroyed over half these old houses, but there are enough mansions and churches left to make a stop here worthwhile, and a walk alongside its quiet waterways gives a flavour of what the town was once like. One of Valognes' most celebrated past visitors was the maverick Norman novelist and ardent royalist Jules Barbey d'Aurevilly, who wrote some of his novels here.

Getting around the Valognes Region

Hôtel de Beaumont
t 02 33 40 12 30; open Easter weekend and July–mid-Sept Wed–Mon 2.30–6.30 and Tues 10.30–12; rest of year groups only on request; adm

Hôtel Grandval-Caligny
t 06 98 89 31 64; open on request only

Musée du Cidre
t 02 33 95 82 00; open April–Sept Mon–Sat 10–12 and 2–6, Sun 2–6; Sept–June closed Tues; adm

Musée de l'Eau-de-Vie et des Vieux Métiers
same hours as Musée du Cidre; adm

Abbaye de Valognes
8 Rue des Capucins; closed lunchtime

The only mansion you can easily visit is the 18th-century **Hôtel de Beaumont** in Rue du Versailles Normand. It has a splendid curved main façade with a fine wrought iron balcony, while at the back a contrasting classical façade overlooks the gardens. In the state rooms upstairs, reached via an imposing double carved staircase, one can see how the Norman aristocracy lived. The **Hôtel Grandval-Caligny** in the picturesque Rue des Religieuses, is a good deal older, but can unfortunately only be visited on request. One of its tenants was Barbey d'Aurevilly who completed his collection of stories, *Les Diaboliques*, here and dined at the Grand Hôtel du Louvre next door. Perhaps the best way to experience the mansions is to stay overnight – two have been turned into hotels/B&Bs (*see* listings).

Opposite the Hôtel de Beaumont is Valognes' **Musée du Cidre**. The best thing about it is the old stone house it occupies, built in 1480 as a workshop for dyeing wool and leather, with the Merderet river meandering peacefully behind it. The museum has a good collection of presses, exotic cider cups, and a cider barrel transformed into a bed (which became a target for a local amateur woodcarver's erotic fantasies, which always leaves visitors smirking). If calvados is your preferred tipple, a few doors down inside the 17th-century Hôtel de Thieuville, there is the **Musée de l'Eau-de-Vie et des Vieux Métiers**, which displays calvados-related and other trades carried out in the Cotentin from the 11th to 20th centuries. On the east side of Valognes town are the remains of some **Gallo-Roman baths**, a remnant of the Roman colony of *Alauna* that stood here. The tourist office supplies a map showing various circuits around the main sights, and will also encourage you to visit the restored 17th-century **Abbaye de Valognes**, whose nuns churn out sugar-coated sweets, *pâtes de fruits*.

Bricquebec

Midway between the peninsula's east and west coasts, in rolling countryside, the pretty country town of Bricquebec is dominated by its mighty medieval **castle**, whose ramparts and keep (visitable on foot) remain remarkably intact. The castle's origins and name (from the Norse *brekka*, meaning slope, and *bekkr*, a stream) are Viking, and the man who masterminded its foundation was a pal of William Longsword, William the Conqueror's great-great grandfather, a Scandinavian called Anslech. It was rebuilt in the Conqueror's time, and again in the 14th century. Bricquebec castle was occupied for over 30 years by the English under Henry V, and owned for a time by the Earl of Suffolk; in the 19th century, part of the castle was converted into one of the Cotentin's first hotel-restaurants, still there today, whose previous guests include Queen Victoria. Each Monday Bricquebec hosts the largest market in the northern Cotentin, infusing with life the attractive stone streets and the Place Ste-Anne in front of the castle. On the last weekend of July it also holds an important festival, the *Fête de Ste-Anne*. Just north of town is the **Abbaye de Notre-Dame-de-Grâce**, a Trappist monastery which is open to the public in the afternoons in summer. Its shop, which sells *charcuterie* made by the monks from their own pigs, is open daily throughout the year.

Tourist Information around Valognes

Market Days: Valognes: Fri; Bricquebec: Mon.
Post Office: Valognes: Place du Château; Bricquebec: Place Gosnon Verger.

Shopping around Valognes

Brasserie Artisanale d'Alauna, Le Bas Castelet, Valognes, t 02 33 95 14 98. Not so much a brasserie as a brewery, located near the Gallo-Roman ruins. Apparently Romans drank beer here, a tradition that's been 'revived' with enthusiasm by owner Luc Léonard, who is happy to let you taste (and buy!) his lagers and beers, including *Alauna* lager and *La Trinquette*, a blonde beer with a dash of calvados.

Cidrerie La Chesnaie, Route de St-Joseph, 50700 Yvetot-Bocage, t 02 33 40 17 71. The Couppey family have been making cider at this farm, 3km west of Valognes, since 1896, and have it down to a fine art. Apart from cider you can taste and buy calvados, *pommeau*, *poiré* and their special *liqueur de pomme. Open Mon–Sat 9–12 and 2–6.30; also Sun mid-July–mid-Aug.*

Where to Stay and Eat around Valognes

Valognes ✉ 50700
Hotel Grandval Caligny, 34 Rue des Religieuses, t 02 33 95 27 96,

derenouf@wanadoo.fr (€€). A more authentic Norman B&B experience would be hard to find: your hosts are a wonderful elderly couple, and the remarkable 17th-century mansion is full of antiques including some fabulous armoires. The larger room has a four poster, and a Jacuzzi in the bathroom; the second room has an exterior bathroom. If it's fine, you take breakfast looking over the tranquil courtyard at the back.

Manoir de Bellauney, 3½kms north of Valognes near Tamerville, t 02 33 40 10 62, www.bellauney.com (€€). This lovely turreted stone manor was built in the 15th and 16th centuries on the site of a monastery and has three en-suite rooms, decorated in the styles of different periods. The medieval bedroom has a fireplace with the coat of arms of the original owners.

Manoir de Savigny, off road to Savigny, t 02 33 08 37 75, www.manoir-de-savigny.com (€€). Run by a friendly young couple who have recently completely refurbished this 16th-century manor, 3km southeast of Valognes. There are five en-suite guest rooms (including a 'Moroccan' one), some with antiques, all with views over the extensive grounds.

**Grand Hotel du Louvre, 28 Rue des Religieuses, t 02 33 40 00 07, grand.hotel.du.louvre@wanadoo.fr (€). All the rooms in this friendly 17th-century coaching inn in the town's most historic street have recently been refurbished. Some have antiques, others are more basic. The grand room No.4, where famous guests have slept, needs to be booked well in advance. The restaurant (€€)

offers solid, if at times bland, Norman cooking. *Closed Mon lunch, mid-Dec–mid-Jan and (Oct–May) Sun eve.*

Brix ✉ 50700

Château Mont Epinguet, t 02 33 41 96 31, *www.chateaulemontepinguet.co.uk* (€). Not a place to go if you're after formality or luxury: the atmosphere is casual and furnishings quirky, but the welcome from your English hosts is warm and genuine. You can also rent self-catering cottages in the grounds, or the château itself.

Yvetot-Bocage ✉ 50700

La Forge d'Yvetot, t 02 33 40 13 01 (€). Formerly the village forge, this roadside inn, 3km west of Valognes, serves meat and fish cooked over a vast fireplace in the old-fashioned way, plus lighter dishes like crêpes, *galettes* and pizzas. *Closed Mon eve, Tues and Sept.*

ⓘ **Bricquebec** ›
13 Place Ste-Anne,
t 02 33 52 21 65,
www.ville-bricquebec.fr

Bricquebec ✉ 50260

Château de Saint Blaise, Route des Grosmonts, **t** 02 33 87 52 60, *www.chateaudesaintblaise.com* (€€€€€). Elegant 18th-century château in ample grounds, including an 'English garden.' Rooms are grand and comfortable – as you'd expect at the price. Breakfast included. *Open April–Oct.*

***L'Hostellerie du Vieux Château, 4 Cours du Château, **t** 02 33 52 24 49, *www.lhostellerie-bricquebec.com* (€€). A unique place: part of Bricquebec castle, overlooking the keep and a garden-filled courtyard. Its 17 rooms vary in style but are all attractively furnished. The 'Knights' Hall', with massive stone fireplaces, imposing arches and tiled floors, houses an enjoyable restaurant (€€€–€€). *Closed mid-Dec–Jan.*

La Lande, Les Grosmonts, **t** 02 33 52 24 78, *www.lalande-bricquebec.com* (€€). Characterful Norman house owned by an English couple. There are two double rooms and a twin, and guests can order dinner (€€) in advance. Ted, whose father was a famous photographer in WW2, runs D-Day tours which take in both classic sites and less known places, plus some of his father's photos.

Négreville ✉ 50260

Le Mesnilgrand, t 02 33 95 09 54, *www.lemesnilgrand.com* (€€). Buried in leafy lanes north of Negreville, this converted 18th-century cider farm is truly tranquil. It's recently been bought by an English couple,who are refurbishing the five bedrooms and have also set up a restaurant (€€, order in advance). The owners are both professional musicians, and run occasional music weekends.

Le Vrétot ✉ 50260

Manoir du Val Jouet, t 02 33 52 24 42 (€). Fabulous little 16th-century manor at the end of a narrow leafy lane between Bricquebec and Barneville-Carteret, set in large gardens. There are three comfortable bedrooms, two sharing a bathroom so they would be suitable for a family. There's also a *gîte* to rent in the grounds.

La Croix Morain, t 02 33 52 22 64 (€). Don't be put off by the unassuming exterior of this old inn at a crossroads; within you'll find an authentic taste of old Normandy, and guests sit on benches at long communal tables. Lunch consists of local meats grilled over a wood fire, and on Sundays they cook a roast. There are lovely home-made puds too. Be sure to book on Sundays. *Closed evenings exc groups with reservation.*

The Cap de la Hague

⭐ **The Cap de la Hague**

One of the best things about Cherbourg is the ease and speed with which you can get out of town: heading west from the city, within ten minutes you can be on the immense sandy beach at **Urville-Nacqueville**, a fashionable bathing spot for 19th-century Cherbourgeois, who built themselves fancy seaside villas there. The GR223 footpath follows the coast all the way around the La Hague

Getting around the Cap de la Hague

STN **bus** No.2 runs a few times daily to the towns and villages around the Cape from Cherbourg, and there's also a useful local taxi company, **Taxi Beaumont, t** 02 33 08 46 46.

Château de Nacqueville
t 02 33 03 21 12; open mid-April–Sept Wed–Thurs and Sat–Mon for guided visits at 2, 3, 4 and 5; adm

peninsula, with fabulous views. Just inland from Urville is the **Château de Nacqueville**, first built in 1510 as a fortified manor, although most of it was rebuilt in the 18th and 19th centuries. It's set in English-style romantic gardens, with a lake, azalea-fringed lawns, and waterfalls. For something to eat or drink and a fine sea view, head for the point of **Landemer**, famous for its vistas and characterful old hotel-restaurant between the road and the cliffs.

From Landemer there's an especially lovely stretch of the GR223 footpath west to tiny **Gruchy**, a hamlet of the larger village of **Gréville-Hague**, where the artist Jean-François Millet was born. Gruchy's Cornish-like cluster of granite houses, fuchsia-filled gardens and sleepy lanes leading down to heather-clad cliffs falling away abruptly down to the sea has enormous charm. The

Maison Millet
t 02 33 01 81 91; open daily April–May 2–6, June and Sept 11–6; July–Aug 11–7, French school hols exc Christmas 2–6; adm

small **Maison Millet** is the artist's birthplace, a plain cottage where he lived with his eight brothers and sisters, with an engaging little museum on his life and art. Across the lane you can see the well that featured in many of Millet's works. Visitors can see a short film about Millet's life, and as you drive back up through the pretty village of Gréville-Hague you pass Millet's bronze statue presiding over the little square.

Continuing west towards the cape – the winding road sometimes follows the cliffs, sometimes twists inland – the tiny fishing village of **Omonville-la-Rogue** has attractive granite houses, an 18th-century fort, and a few seaside bars and restaurants. It also has a venerable 16th-century farm recently

Le Tourp
t 02 33 01 85 89, www.letourp.com; open Easter–mid-Nov daily 2–7

converted into a stylish museum and cultural centre, **Le Tourp**. Still more enchanting is the sister village of **Omonville-la-Petite**, whose ancient buildings sit in a valley amid lush vegetation, and where another famous artist, the poet and film scriptwriter Jacques Prévert, spent the last 10 years of his life. The **Musée Jacques**

Musée Jacques Prévert
t 02 33 52 72 38; open daily April–May 2–6; June and Sept 11–6; July–Aug 11–7; adm

Prévert is in a lovely setting, and a very evocative place for anyone with an interest in French literature or cinema. Prévert's grave is in the churchyard. Just west is **Port Racine**, which boasts, rather nonsensically, of being the smallest port in France. Apart from watching fishing boats bobbing up and down, there's little to do here other than continue along the coast towards the spectacular **Goury lighthouse**, on a rocky cove below the larger village of **Auderville** that has its own little community, including a tourist office and the excellent Auberge de Goury restaurant.

Around the Cape, and after the wild and beautiful **Baie d'Ecalgrain**, the gorse-clad cliffs become dramatic around the

La Hague's Nasty Secret

Few French people forget the images in 1980 of the Greenpeace boat *Rainbow Warrior* harrying a ship carrying Japanese spent nuclear fuel into Cherbourg harbour to be delivered to La Hague's nuclear reprocessing plant. The *Rainbow Warrior*'s crew were arrested, but charges were dropped after Cherbourg's dockers threatened to strike in support. The French Government got its revenge when it sank the *Rainbow Warrior* in Auckland, New Zealand, in 1985. The 1980 protest failed to stop the activities of the plant, operated by the government-owned COGEMA, which is today the biggest importer of foreign spent nuclear fuel in the world – although it only really has one competitor, the Sellafield plant in Britain. The Beaumont-Hague plant reprocesses waste from Germany, Japan, Belgium, the Netherlands and Switzerland, and stands accused of dumping around 230 million litres of its own waste in the Atlantic each year. Contamination from the plant has been shown to spread northwards along the coasts of Europe, and Greenpeace has labelled it one of the largest sources of atmospheric radioactivity in the world, and says discharges have risen alarmingly in the past few years. Some official reports say children living near the plant face an increased risk of leukaemia.

Central to Greenpeace's campaign is the discovery in 1997 that an exposed waste pipe on the beach of Les Moulinets had left radioactive contamination 3,000 times higher than normal. It sued COGEMA to stop further discharges. The company carried out an operation to clean up the residue, but it's claimed that instead of reducing radioactive levels this has actually increased them, as radioactive material is dispersed around the sea floor.

The battle between COGEMA and Greenpeace has raged on, despite efforts by the company and the French government to portray the environmentalists as marginal extremists. On numerous occasions Greenpeace's monitoring equipment has 'mysteriously' disappeared, and it has accused COGEMA of theft. Greenpeace scored a psychological victory in 2000 at the conference of the Oslo-Paris Commission (OSPAR) set up to protect marine life in the northeast Atlantic; a webcam was attached to an underwater discharge pipe and the images relayed directly to the conference – until the cable link was 'accidentally' cut. The Conference adopted a resolution condemning the dumping of nuclear waste into the sea and called for an end to the practice by 2020, but since the two main offenders, France and the UK, abstained and are not obliged to abide by it, this has little real effect. Greenpeace hopes that the drip-drip of pressure on the French government will eventually force it to limit discharges and one day, close the plant. So far, though, there is little sign that France's love affair with nuclear power – which produces three quarters of its electricity – and its offshoots will come to an early end.

Nez de Jobourg (literally the 'Jobourg Nose'), the highest cliff in continental Europe. On a clear day you can easily see Alderney, the closest of the Channel Islands. Looking the other way, however, the forbidding towers of the Beaumont-Hague nuclear reprocessing plant (*see* above) are a blight on the horizon, an unforgivable piece of central government planning – although local tourist offices have been well-trained to brush over both the eyesore and any potential threat to health. It used to be possible to take a deliberately-reassuring free tour of the vast plant, but since 9/11 these have been abandoned (although there is still an information point, and interested visitors can still take a tour around the *outside* of the plant). There are more things nuclear at **Flamanville** to the south (a power station). Sadly, the stretch between the two nuclear installations contains some of the Cotentin's finest beaches, such as **Biville**, **Siouville** and **Diélette**. This may deter you from swimming, but locals don't seem to worry, so you can make your mind up for yourself. Other things to be aware of, though, are the fierce tides and undertows on this windblown, exposed coast.

Tourist Information on the Cap de la Hague

(i) Beaumont–
Hague ›
45 Rue Jallot,
t 02 33 52 74 94,
www.lahague.org

The COGEMA Beaumont-Hague nuclear reprocessing plant (t 02 33 02 73 04, *www.cogemalahague.fr*) has an information office by the main entrance to the plant. You can also join a free 2hr bus tour, which includes a talk and video on the virtues of nuclear reprocessing (*April–Sept; by reservation otherwise*). **Market Days**: Beaumont-Hague: Sat.

Where to Stay and Eat on the Cap de la Hague

Urville-Nacqueville ✉ 50460

(i) Auderville-
Goury ››
t 02 33 04 50 26;
open daily July–Aug,
and in French school
hols exc Christmas

*Le Landemer, 2 Rue des Douanes, Landemer, t 02 33 03 43 00, *www.le-landemer.com* (€). Perched on the cliffs overlooking the beaches at Landemer, 12km west of Cherbourg, this old-style, slightly scruffy hotel – where Millet often painted from the terrace – oozes character. Its nine rooms are simple but pleasant, many with sea views, and downstairs there's a cosy restaurant (€€). *Hotel closed last 2 wks Nov and 1-15 Jan; restaurant closed Mon lunch exc public hols.*

La Blanche Maison, 874 Rue St-Laurent, t 02 33 03 48 79, *blanche maison@infonie.fr* (€). Although it's a mere 10km from Cherbourg, this converted farmhouse is tucked away in a pocket of green lushness between Urville-Nacqueville and Dur-Ecu manor. There is just one guest room, in a separate part, with access to a small kitchen.

(★) Auberge de
Goury ››

Omonville-la-Petite ✉ 50440

**La Fossardière, Hameau de la Fosse, t 02 33 52 19 83 (€). Ancient stone house hidden among idyllic gardens on the outskirts of Omonville-la-Petite – the perfect romantic hideaway. The ten rooms are split between two cottages, and breakfast is served in the old village bakery, which also serves as a bar. There's also a sauna. *Closed mid-Nov–mid-Mar.*

**St-Martin des Grêves, 50440 Omonville-la-Petite, t 02 33 01 87 87, *www.hotel-st-martin.fr* (€). This hotel, in a grand stone house overlooking the Anse St-Martin bay and Port Racine, makes a good alternative if you can't get into the Fossardière. Rooms are basic but comfortable, there's a large garden, and the welcome is friendly.

St-Germain-des-Vaux ✉ 50440

Le Moulin à Vent, Hameau Danneville, t 02 33 52 75 20 (€€) Get to this restaurant perched on a spectacular height above Port Racine early to get a table with the best view. Seafood and fish are the specialities at this granite inn, on the road inland to St-Germain-des-Vaux, with a long-disused stone windmill alongside. One of the Cape's best restaurants.

Auderville-Goury ✉ 50440

**Du Cap, Le Bourg, t 02 33 52 73 46, *www.hotelducap.org* (€). Relaxed hotel in a traditional stone house in the heart of tiny Auderville, on the edge of fields that drop down to the sea. There are eight comfortable en-suite rooms, seven with fine sea views through the eaves, and there's a room equipped for disabled guests on the ground floor.

Auberge de Goury, Port de Goury, t 02 33 52 77 01, *www.aubergedegoury.com* (€€€–€€). Choose your seafood as you come in, then settle down by the huge log fire and prepare yourself for a solid gastronomic experience. The food is simply prepared – much is grilled over a wood fire – but it's stunningly fresh, whether it's fish or Cotentin lamb. The excellent desserts and cheeses round the meal off nicely, washed down by fine wines. *Closed Jan.*

La Malle aux Epices, t 02 33 52 77 44, *lamalleauxepices@wanadoo.fr* (€€–€) Tucked away in the back of Auderville's auberge, this tiny restaurant transports you to the Far East: owner Christophe learned the art of putting an Eastern spin on local produce in New York and does it to great effect here. Try the great-value *menu decouverte* which includes a selection of the best dishes. Be sure to book, as the place has become very popular. *Closed Mon eve, Tues and Sat lunch.*

The Western Cotentin

Barneville-Carteret

The view stretches ten leagues. From there you can see a reasonably wide bay between two promontories on two opposing headlands, from whose mists the belltowers of Port-Bail and Barneville emerge like two great nails on the ends of a horseshoe. A great red haze, into which the fishing boats set forth, stretched out to sea and disappeared into the limits of the gulf.

Victor Hugo, letter to his wife, 7 July 1836

Deserted sand dunes and long, long beaches stretch south from La Hague all the way to Barneville-Carteret, the first resort of any size on the west Cotentin coast. Despite being bracketed together under a single name, Barneville-Carteret consists of three quite distinct parts.

A couple of kilometres inland, **Barneville**-proper is a historic little town with a superb Romanesque church, **St-Germain**, which doubled as a watchtower against English marauders in the Hundred Years' War (look for the fantastical animal carvings on the columns inside). The town now extends a warmer welcome to its many Anglophone visitors, who flock to the lively market in the square on Saturday morning. Downhill by the sea, on the north side of a neat bay, **Carteret** is a pleasing marina and fishing port nestling under the impressive Cap de Carteret, topped by a lighthouse. If you walk around the headland for around 20 minutes, following the narrow but well-marked *Sentier des Douaniers*, you reach mile upon mile of deserted sands on the **Plage de la Vieille Eglise** (the beach can also be reached by driving to the lighthouse and heading right to a car park).

In the opposite direction, on the south side of the estuary of the River Gerfleur, the neat holiday villas of sedate **Barneville-Plage** extend along the beach. It's popular with French families each summer, and there are plenty of watersports on offer. Barneville-Plage took off as a bathing resort at the end of the 19th century with the arrival of the railway, and some elegant villas remain. Today all three parts of the Barneville-Carteret *ménage* have some chic restaurants, bars and shops, but Carteret probably comes out tops. On fine days you can spot Jersey, which lies 22km southwest of Barneville-Carteret.

✪ Portbail

A few kilometres south at the mouth of the river Ollonde, picturesque **Portbail** is as near to the perfect fishing village as you can get. A sandy spit leads to the quay for ferries to Jersey and to a sand and shingle beach, while around the ancient village fishing boats glisten in the pure, limpid light. The lovely 11th-century village church of **Notre-Dame**, with its pyramid-topped monolithic tower, is believed to be one of Normandy's oldest, and in summer hosts art shows and concerts. Beside it are the remains of an even older place of worship, a 4th-century **Gallo-Roman baptistry**. On Tuesdays Portbail's streets spring to life with a busy market, where you can buy anything from oysters to doorknobs. Flying enthusiasts may also be interested to know that **Lindbergh-Plage**,

Gallo-Roman baptistry
t 02 33 04 03 07;
guided tours of church and baptistry July–Aug

Getting to Barneville-Carteret and Region

STN **bus** No.3 from Cherbourg is the main public transport to this area, calling at Barneville-Carteret and Portbail (*Mon–Sat only*).

High-speed **catamarans** to Jersey, Guernsey and Alderney are run by **Manche Isles Express, t** 08 25 13 30 50, *www.manche-isles-express.com*, departing from Barneville-Carteret and from Diélette, 23km north.

the little beach community on the southern side of the Ollonde estuary, is so-called because Charles Lindbergh crossed the French coast here during his first solo transatlantic flight in 1927.

In summer a small tourist train runs along the dunes between Carteret and Portbail; it's a great way to get to the markets in both towns (timetable information available from tourist offices).

Tourist Information around Barneville-Carteret

(★) Les Ormes >>

Market Days: Barnveille village:Sat; Carteret: Thurs (July–Aug); Barneville-Plage: Sun; Portbail: Tues.

Post Offices: Barneville village: Rue Guillaume-le-Conquérant; Portbail: Rue Philippe Lebel

Shopping around Barneville-Carteret

La Maison du Biscuit, 50270 Sortosville-en-Beaumont, t 02 33 04 09 04. Manufacturers of traditional Norman biscuits, with a small factory, shop and teashop on the Valognes road 8km northeast of Barneville. *Closed Mon, Jan and 1 wk in Sept.*

Where to Stay and Eat around Barneville-Carteret

(i) Barneville-
Carteret >

*Barneville village:
10 Rue des Ecoles,
t 02 33 04 90 58,
www.barneville-
carteret.fr; provides info
on local walks;
Carteret: Place
Flandres-Dunkerque,
t 02 33 04 94 54*

Barneville-Carteret ✉ 50270
   There's a fine selection of high-quality hotels and restaurants here in all price ranges. All restaurants offer freshly caught fish and seafood.
***La Marine, 11 Rue de Paris, t 02 33 53 83 31, *www.hotelmarine.com* (€€€€–€€€). The 29 rooms in this attractive harbourside hotel have just been renovated, providing a luxurious place to stay where you can enjoy fabulous views of the ocean. The smart restaurant (€€€) offers high-quality fish and seafood dishes under guidance from its famous chef Laurent Cesne. *Hotel closed mid-Nov–early Mar; restaurant closed Mon and Tues lunch, exc in July–Aug.*
***Les Ormes, Quai Barbey d'Aurevilly, t 02 33 52 23 50, *www.hoteldesormes.fr* (€€€). Based in an elegant 19th-century mansion opposite the marina, this hotel has a more personal feel than the Marine, but offers similar comforts. It also has the advantage of having a large and idyllic garden where you can eat when it's fine. Its 12 rooms are chic and characterful, and there's a fine restaurant Le Rivage (€€€) which is one of the best in the area. Try the oysters in a creamy Camembert sauce.
**Le Cap, Promenade Abbé Lebouteiller, t 02 33 53 85 89, *www.hotel-le-cap.fr* (€€) Another excellent hotel which has just received a makeover. Choose your view – sea, port or countryside. Its excellent restaurant (€€€) is a favourite with locals.
**Les Isles, 9 Bd Maritime, t 02 33 04 90 76, *www.hoteldesisles.com* (€€). Another great-value hotel in a smart white building in a prime location on the front in Barneville-Plage. All rooms have recently been refurbished, and some have terraces overlooking the ocean. There's a heated swimming pool and Jacuzzi, and a decent restaurant (€€). *Closed Jan–Mar.*

Le Rozel ✉ 50340

Le Château, t 02 33 52 95 08 (€€). Several kilometres north of Barneville-Carteret, this fairy-tale granite château is 1km from the sand dunes and a vast, windswept beach. It originally belonged to Bertrand du Rozel, a companion of William the Conqueror, but was extended in the 18th century. It has just one elegantly furnished suite which can sleep 3-4 people and has a toilet in the turret! Guests can make their own breakfast from home-reared produce, and there's also a fully self-catering wing.

ⓘ **Portbail >**
26 Rue Philippe Lebel,
t 02 33 04 03 07,
www.portbail.org

Portbail ✉ 50580

La Roque de Gouey, Rue Gilles Poirier, **t** 02 33 04 80 27 (€). A delightful old farm building on the edge of the village with lots of character, run by a friendly retired couple. The part set aside for B&B guests has a huge fireplace, attractive furniture and even a small kitchen. There's a large ground-floor room (suitable for disabled guests) and two smaller ones up steepish outside stairs.

Le Cabestan, 3 La Caillourie, **t** 02 33 04 35 30 (€€–€). First-rate fish and seafood restaurant on a sandy spit overlooking the sea, near the quay for ferries to Jersey. The atmosphere is friendly, the fish couldn't be fresher, and it's great value. *Closed Mon, Tues and Jan.*

St-Nicolas-de-Pierrepont ✉ 50250

La Ferme de l'Eglise, t 02 33 45 53 40, *www.normandie-cottages.com* (€). Two large, simply furnished B&B rooms in a large farmhouse run by a friendly English couple near a village a few miles inland from Portbail. It's a tranquil place with big gardens and rambling barns, and there are also three *gîtes* to rent.

Lessay and Magic Castles

Abbatiale de la Ste-Trinité
t 02 33 46 37 06;
church open daily 9–7;
abbey buildings open
for guided tours on
certain days in
July–Aug; adm for tours

South of another fine historic village, **St-Germain-sur-Ay**, a road cuts inland off the coast road to **Lessay**, an important centre for processing food from the Cotentin farms, with some attractive streets at its heart. *Lessay* means 'standing on the waters', since the land here was originally only swamp, and occupied only by the isolated **Abbatiale de la Ste-Trinité**. The abbey is a remarkable monument to dedication and architectural purism. Built in 1064, it was the church of an important abbey with around 50 monks and 40 dependent parishes extending as far as Jersey and Britain. The abbey was closed by the Revolution, and its huge church became Lessay's parish church. On 11 July 1944 this priceless treasure was virtually demolished when the Germans exploded 25 mines there to improve their defences.

Faced with the decision as to how to rebuild the abbey, the town voted to rebuild it stone by stone, to restore it to its Norman Romanesque glory. The painstaking 13-year job has been done to such perfection that some say the abbey is finer now than it was when the Germans came. It's certainly closer to the way it was when it was first built, as later elements like a tower and some over-the-top Baroque chapels have been deliberately left out, and original Romanesque features reinstated. The grimacing gargoyles that clutch the squat central tower – the restorers counted 70 – have been particularly well-returned to their original beauty. The living quarters and cloisters next door, built in classical style in the

Getting around the Lessay Region

STN **bus** No.7 from Cherbourg to Coutances and Granville stops in Lessay, but it's very difficult to get to the castles without a car.

18th century under the guidance of Guillaume de la Tremblaye, were less damaged by the war and are now in private hands.

Inside, the abbey is a feast of purity, simplicity and light. The only ornamentation is the exquisite carvings on the tops of the columns, each one different. It also displays one of the earliest experiments in rib vaulting, from the late 11th century. It took some time to perfect the technique, and one can see places where the architects hadn't quite grasped it: the earliest columns are too narrow to receive the ribs, whereas they slot perfectly into the later built columns. The church holds two interesting gravestones, one of the abbey's founder, Eudes au Capel, whose bones were discovered here during the rebuilding work, the other of the enthusiastic priest who oversaw the church's post-1945 restoration. The chapel on the south side of the abbey is Gothic, built after the Hundred Years' War destroyed an earlier one, although its wooden ceiling is Romanesque in style. In complete contrast, at the back of the church there are a stunning, if slightly moth-eaten, 13th-century stone statue of Ste-Opportune, and a unique and fascinating 14th-century stone frieze that once decorated the abbey tombs. The latter depicts ladies, alternately sitting or standing beneath Gothic-style arches, mourning their dead – their tear-drenched hankies can still be seen, delicately etched in the stone. It's a miracle that such a carving survived. In July and August a series of concerts are held in the church.

Château de Pirou

Château de Pirou
t 02 33 46 34 71,
www.chateau-
pirou.org; open
July–Aug daily 10–6.30;
April–June and Sept
Wed–Mon 10–12 and
2–6.30, Feb–Mar and
Oct–Nov Wed–Mon
10–12 and 2–5;
adm, joint ticket with
Abbaye de la Lucerne
(see p.360); guided
visits on request

From Lessay, if you follow the D650 road back towards the coast, you can continue south through a flat plain of marsh, *bocage* and moorland, with dunes, the sea and a string of modest beach villages on one side. Amid this landscape you come to two unmissable romantic, fairy-tale castles that have remained remarkably unchanged since the Middle Ages: Pirou and Gratot.

The 12th-century Château de Pirou, reached via a winding lane off the coast road, was entirely forgotten until the 1960s when its present owners discovered it as a neglected farm, mostly buried under creepers. It's since been cleaned and restored, and work is still continuing, but without destroying the magic of this old, old place. The castle is just like in fairy-tale books, with a moat, forbidding granite walls, turrets and battlements, and you pass through three ancient gateways, each of which once had its own moat and drawbridge, to reach it. Pirou claims to be the oldest of

The Legend of Pirou

When the Vikings invaded Normandy they tried to storm Pirou, but in vain. Thwarted, they then tried to force its inhabitants to surrender by blockading the castle and starving them to death. Eventually a deathly calm reigned over the place. Suspecting a ruse, the invaders waited a whole day. The next day, with the castle still silent, they scaled the walls. Inside they found an old man whose life they promised to spare if he told them what had happened to the Lord of Pirou and his family. He told them that with the help of a magic book, they'd turned themselves into geese to escape their assailants. The Norsemen remembered they had indeed seen a flock of geese flying over the castle the previous day.

Some time later, the wild geese returned to their castle to turn themselves back into their human selves. Alas, the invaders had burned the book of magic spells, so they had to remain as geese for ever after. But to this day they return every spring in the hope of finding the spell book. Look carefully, and you may spot some geese around Pirou too.

all the castles in Normandy, for there was probably a stronghold here before the first Viking attacks in the 9th century. At that time it stood alone on a schist island in the marshes, whose waters fed into the moat. A knight from the Pirou family accompanied William the Conqueror to England, and the Pirous were rewarded with an estate in Somerset, where they founded Stoke-Pero in the village of Stoke. The castle was besieged countless times in the Hundred Years' War, and it was subsequently inhabited by families of minor nobles, including the knight Jehan Falstolf, renowned for his bravery, who was (possibly) reincarnated by Shakespeare as the beer-swilling Falstaff. By the 19th century Pirou had been effectively been abandoned to the weeds, ghosts and tobacco smugglers from Jersey. In 1966 it was finally bought by a private owner, who gave it to a charitable foundation so that restoration could begin.

You see the castle in its full glory only after doing an almost complete circuit of the moat. An arched stone bridge replaces the old drawbridge, which was dropped or hoisted through the slots you see above the gateway. The fortress in front of you had six turrets, of which only one remains. Anyone who attacked the castle would be greeted with a rain of projectiles hurled from the top. One of the oldest parts is the guardroom, with heavy beamed ceiling and an immense fireplace with a one-piece stone lintel. Beyond it there's a small inner courtyard, from where you can climb up precipitous stone steps to the ramparts. Cavities are visible in the walls where gargoyles allowed rainwater to escape, and there's a fabulous, magic-castle-like slate roof. From the top of the ramparts and the tower there are also wonderful views across the marshes, out to sea and, on a good day, even as far as Jersey – excellent for spotting approaching enemies.

Outside the enclosure, the pretty chapel of St-Laurence has a wooden roof in the shape of an overturned boat, similar to the one in Ste-Catherine in Honfleur. Next door to it is the courtroom, where the lord of the castle judged disputes, now hung with a modern tapestry (in the style of the Bayeux one) depicting the Normans' 12th-century conquest of Sicily and southern Italy, in which the Pirou clan also took part. Occasional tours of Pirou are run in summer, including special ones for children; enquire at the tourist office in Coutances (*see* p.352).

Château de Gratot

If Pirou captivates, the castle of Gratot, about 15km due south towards Coutances, takes the breath away. Its evocative ruined turrets encircled by a large moat are just like in the picture books, and part of their charm is that you're likely to have them all to yourself as you explore. Around the château you can stumble across ancient stone fireplaces, terracotta floor tiles and stone carvings that let your imagination roam, and the setting among trees behind the quaint village church is idyllic.

Most of the castle dates from the 14th century, when Gratot was the stronghold of the Argouges clan, the most famous of which was the maverick Chevalier Jean d'Argouges who won eternal condemnation in France by handing over Granville to the English for a bribe. It took a succession of diplomatic marriages for the family to prove their loyalty to the kings of France. The last Argouges sold up in 1777, and it began to be used as a farm. In 1914 a wedding party was being held here when part of the roof collapsed onto the banqueting tables – before the guests had arrived – which led the then owner to abandon the place. It remained derelict until 1968, when teams of volunteers came to the rescue and began Gratot's conservation. Justifiably proud of what they've achieved, they've composed an information booklet in several languages. In summer, Gratot hosts concerts and festivals in its grounds.

The most romantic part of the castle is its **Tour à la Fée** (Fairy Tower) with its time-worn spiralling steps and slit windows. It is so-called because, according to one of the legends attached to the castle, one of the lords of Gratot fell hopelessly in love with a beautiful maiden he'd encountered at the fountain. When he asked her to marry him she announced that she was a fairy and she could only marry if he vowed never to utter the word 'death'. The lord promised. One day during a party at the château, he grew impatient of waiting for his ladyship, stormed up to her boudoir and, in his temper, let out the fateful word. She uttered a terrible cry, clambered onto the window sill and disappeared for ever.

The Coast south from Pirou

Travelling south from **Pirou-Plage**, a little traditional resort with a clutch of seafront restaurants, the next two coastal towns, **Anneville** and **Blainville** are two of the quietest points on this

Where to Stay and Eat around Lessay

ⓘ **Lessay**
11 Place St-Cloud,
t 02 33 45 14 34,
www.canton-lessay.com

ⓘ **Blainville-sur-
Mer >**
Place de la Marine,
t 02 33 07 90 89,
www.ot-blainville
surmer.com

Gratot ✉ 50200

La Tournebride, t 02 33 45 11 00 (€€€–€€). Cosy intimate restaurant in a granite house virtually opposite Gratot castle. The food is solidly Norman-traditional, the atmosphere friendly, and it's very popular with locals. Closed Sun eve and Mon.

Blainville-sur-Mer ✉ 50560

Village de Grouchy, 11 Rue du Vieux Lavoir, Grouchy, **t** 02 33 47 20 31, www.jr.sebire.free.fr (€). Large 17th-century granite house in tranquil Grouchy, 1½ km inland from Blainville-sur-Mer, which the family has lived in since 1797. There are four cheerfully decorated B&B rooms in the attic and a double en-suite room downstairs. Breakfast is served in a gorgeous kitchen/dining room. There's a large garden, where in summer guests are free to use the barbecue (and the fridge).

Périers ✉ 50190

Le Pont Sanson, t 02 33 07 79 00 (€€). Gorgeous old house with two antique-filled bedrooms reached via a spiral staircase. It's owned by a Scottish woman and her French husband. There's a fabulous garden too, which even has a summer room for guests.

unassuming stretch of coast. All these communities are famous for their cultivation of mussels and oysters, and have a handful of restaurant-bars where you can taste the local seafood during the summer season.

Agon-Coutainville, the largest, is still a low-key place with a rather desolate beach that's deserted except in July and August, when holidaymakers arrive in droves. At low tide, locals set off in search of cockles and clams. There's a good walk south to the **Pointe d'Agon**, a headland offering fine views. There's also one hotel, and a couple of bars where you can sit out on a terrace by the beach.

Coutances

Coutances, capital of the central Cotentin, perches quietly on a mound of rock, and you can spot the shimmering twin towers of its cathedral from miles around. A Gothic masterpiece, this cathedral was miraculously spared in the onslaught that destroyed two thirds of Coutances in 1944. On Thursdays farmers from surrounding villages bring their cheeses and vegetables to sell at Coutances' market, and the evocative **Jardin des Plantes**, in the Rue Quesnel Canveaux, is one of the loveliest parks in Normandy with its vibrant beds, mazes, Italianate terraces and lovely views. The gardens, on the edge of an old artisan quarter spared by the war, are open and illuminated on summer nights.

Jardin des Plantes
open daily July–mid-
Sept 9–8.30pm,
April–June and late Sept
9–8, Oct–Mar 9–5

Cathédrale de Notre-Dame

Despite its fame as a showcase of Norman Gothic, Coutances cathedral hides a remarkable secret: it is in fact two cathedrals rolled into one, and its graceful soaring columns conceal a Norman

**Cathédrale de
Notre-Dame**
open daily 9–7; for
tour details see p.352

Getting to Coutances

Coutances has good **train** connections, with several daily each way on the Cherbourg–Avranches line, many of which also call at Granville, Pontorson-Mont-St-Michel, Rennes or other destinations further south, and several via St-Lô to Bayeux and Caen.

STN **bus** No.7 (Cherbourg–Granville– Avranches) stops at Coutances. In July–Aug there are extra services to resorts on the coast.

All the churches in this part of Normandy, St-Lô, Carentan, Périers (in that order of importance) are styled on the church at Coutances. The appealing spires of Coutances are austere like the main bell tower of Chartres, yet as discreet as the spire of St-Denis... When one of these spires... suddenly emerges from behind a hill, it's a magnificent adventure into the countryside.

Victor Hugo, letter to his, wife, 1 July 1836

Romanesque cathedral, 200 years older, that remains virtually intact. It's a hard job to make this out, except in the transept, unless you take one of the guided tours (*see* p.352): they're an unmissable experience – but be warned, if you've ever suffered from vertigo, that the narrow passageways along the edge of the lantern tower are seriously high.

The bishops responsible for it all are lined up in a modern window near the entrance: on the left, William the Conqueror's friend Geoffroy de Montbray, who built the Norman cathedral in 1056; on the right, Hugues de Morville, whose Gothic reincarnation was completed in 1274; and in the centre, St-Ereptiole, who probably built the first church on this site. The Gothic cathedral, which enveloped the old Romanesque one like a fashionable overcoat, was the fruit of Philippe Auguste's integration of Normandy into France in 1204 and his desire to experiment with '*architecture française*' – the new-found Gothic style. It was not unusual for a cathedral to graft Gothic onto Romanesque – the two sitting side by side at Bayeux and Evreux, for example – but at Coutances the reclothing was virtually complete. The cathedral recovered from damage in the Religious Wars in 1562 but took another serious battering in the Revolution, when it underwent various transformations from grain store, to theatre, to Temple of Reason. Restoration began shortly afterwards, but some of the work was heavy-handed, to say the least; when Victor Hugo visited in 1836 he complained that much of it had been painted yellow.

The Cathedral's highlight is its Gothic nave, whose succession of parallel arches and pillars gives an exhilarating feeling of lightness, height and graceful elegance. Crafted from local limestone, they are in stark contrast to the squat round-arched nave of the Romanesque church, which skulks behind its blind triforium; look carefully and you can see small windows in the triforium that lead from one cathedral to the other. A walkway runs along the clerestory above it, which you can follow on the guided tour.

A similar impression of ethereal airiness is given by the lantern tower, also skilfully grafted onto a Romanesque one, and whose pencil-line arches are delicately interwoven to increase the feeling of sweeping verticality. It's built on three levels, two of which you can see from inside. Suspended at these dizzy heights, the stonemasons clearly had a field day: there are some lovely details, including an apple tree thought to be the personal stamp of one of the architects or stonecarvers.

The stained glass rivals that of Rouen cathedral, especially the windows in the north transept, from the 13th century. They're pretty grimy, but among the blackened faces you can just make out Thomas à Becket, whose life story is told as a comic strip – the kneeling figure of Becket as Henry's henchmen prepare to fell him with their swords is visible in the fourth panel from the bottom, while above it, Thomas lies on his deathbed. There are more 13th-century jewels in the **Chapelle St-Lô**, with rich blues and reds. The window tells the story of St Lô, who was appointed bishop while still a 12-year-old boy, and has lovely detail like the helper holding the hem of his robes while he celebrates Mass. A panel above it depicts a picnic, which is brought to an abrupt end by a devil and thuggish friends who pounce on St-Lô and his party from a tree. Miraculously the windows survived the war.

Tourist Information in Coutances

(i) **Coutances >**
Place Georges Leclerc,
t 02 33 19 08 10,
www.coutances.fr

Cathedral tours (in French) July and Aug Sun–Fri at 11 and 3 (in English Tues 11.45); May, June and early Sept Tues and Sun at 3; Jan–April and Oct–Dec last Sun of month at 3; adm; tickets via tourist office.
Internet Access: OCEP, Rue Nicolas.
Market Days: Thurs. There are also special *marchés de pays* on some Fridays in July–Aug, specializing in local products.
Post Office: Rue St-Dominique

Where to Stay and Eat around Coutances

Coutances ✉ 50200

Manoir de l'Ecoulanderie, t 02 33 45 05 05, *www.l-b-c.com* (€€). This old white house, on the outskirts of Coutances, has three elegant rooms, two of them suites, and is set amid spacious, carefully tended gardens with good views of the cathedral. There's even a heated indoor pool.
Les Hauts Champs, La Moinerie de Haut, Nicorps, t 02 33 45 30 56 (€). Farmhouse among hills, woods and fields about 2km outside Coutances, whose owners breed horses. Madame makes bread and croissants for breakfast and offers dinner too (€€).

Le Clos des Sens, 55 Rue Geoffroy de Montbray, t 02 33 47 94 78 (€€–€). Great, tiny family-run restaurant with low beamed ceilings and imaginative dishes based on local ingredients. A real find. *Closed Wed eve and Sun.*

Le Mesnilbus ✉ 50490

Auberge Les Bonnes Gens, t 02 33 07 18 23 (€€). Giant old granite inn in the middle of nowhere offering hearty Norman classics, with a good choice of beers, wines and ciders. It also has four simple rooms (€). *Closed Sun eve and Mon (June–Aug), Mon and Tues (Sept–May).*

Montpinchon ✉ 50210

Le Castel, t 02 33 17 00 45, *www. le-castel-normandy.com* (€€€). A stunning 1870s *petit château* in four acres of parkland with six bedrooms all furnished with stone fireplaces, chandeliers and period furniture. The owners are English, and offer a four-course evening meal (€€) which you eat by candlelight around an Edwardian walnut dining table. There's even llama trekking on offer, and there's a two-bedroomed *gîte* for rent. Unmissable.

Orval ✉ 50660

Catherine Simon, t 02 33 45 59 29 (€). Wonderful ancient stone farmhouse in a small village south of Coutances. with four rooms of varying sizes, and a kitchen and sitting room for guests.

Granville

Somebody with a vivid imagination once dubbed Granville the 'Monaco of the North'. Like Monaco, its old town huddles on a rocky promontory overlooking the sea, while the port and commercial district sprawls along the reclaimed land below. But there the similarities end: the Belle Epoque architecture of Granville's beachside villas is distinctly Norman, there are no tax exiles and very few (at least, visible) millionaires, and you're more likely to find Cotentin oysters and *sole Normande* than *bouillabaisse* in its harbourfront restaurants. Whatever the hype, Granville, the largest and one of the most interesting towns along the west Cotentin coast, is an engaging place to spend some time. There's a fine beach, complete with sea-water swimming pool, and you can get a bird's-eye view of the action from the footpath following the line of the old ramparts above the beach.

The Haute-Ville

The most interesting part of Granville is the Haute-Ville, the old 'upper town', which grew from nothing when the giant spit of rock on which it stands, projecting into the sea, was chosen by the English as a base to do battle with the French in the Hundred Years' War. The man in charge, Sir Thomas Scales, just had time to erect fortifications and lay the first stones of the massive church of **Notre-Dame** when in 1442 the French grabbed Granville, eager to control this natural fortress with its far-reaching views right out to Mont-St-Michel. The remarkable pepperpot-towered house built into the rock known as **Le Guet** (the lookout) dates from around that time. Today, old Granville, with its tightly packed 16th- and 17th-century granite buildings clinging to steep cobbled streets, is an atmospheric place, and its main streets, Rue Cambernon and the Rue des Juifs, have some fascinating antiques and art shops. Many of the grand houses were built for shipbuilders and privateers, such as Pléville Le Pelley, who later became Minister for the Navy in one of the governments that followed the Revolution.

Musée du Vieux Granville

t 02 33 50 44 10; open April–Sept Wed–Mon 10–12 and 2–6; Oct–Mar Sat–Sun and Wed 2–6; adm

The Haute-Ville also has a couple of attractive museums, the **Musée du Vieux Granville**, which is set inside the city walls and contains paintings, model boats and a poster spelling out the local rules for bathing in 1837 (strictly segregated, ladies were to bathe on the north side, men on the south); and the **Musée d'Art Moderne Richard Anacréon**, a personal collection of mostly Fauvist and Pointillist paintings assembled by the bookseller and art collector of the same name. Born in Granville in 1907, Anacréon ran a shop and gallery in Paris for many years through which he got to know a great many figures in the literary and artistic worlds, and when he died in his home town in 1992, he left Granville his books

Musée d'Art Moderne Richard Anacréon

t 02 33 51 02 94; open June–Sept Tues–Sun 11–6; Oct–May Wed–Sun 2–6; adm

To Coutances

N

250 metres
250 yards

HAUTE-VILLE
Musée Richard Anacréon
Casino
Musée du Vieux-Granville
Notre-Dame

Musée et Jardin
Christian Dior

Parc du Val

Train Station

PLACE
ALSACE- LECLERC
LORRAINE

BASSE-VILLE

Bassin à
Flot

Avant-
Port
Ferry
Terminal

Jersey/Guernsey and the Chausey Is.

and paintings. Among the artists represented in this very individual collection are Derain, Vlaminck and Picasso. One of his closest literary friends was Colette, and one corner of the museum holds the writer's bureau, pictures and rare personally signed editions.

Granville's other noted son, Christian Dior, is far better-known, and his former summer home, the grand salmon-pink clifftop Villa Les Rhumbs, is now the delightful **Musée et Jardin Christian Dior**. It's possible to walk up to the 19th-century villa from the beach, via a staircase cut into the cliffs. Dior began by making costumes for himself and his friends for the Granville carnival, and although the family moved to Paris, the couturier often returned here for the summer. The museum is an unashamedly indulgent extravaganza of sequins, taffeta, lace and silk, including many of Dior's sketches and *haute couture* dresses that help tell the story of 20th-century fashion. Specific exhibits change, but among those you might see are an impressive full-length evening cape inspired by the coats worn by fishermen's wives in Granville, a pair of the couturier's scissors, and predictably over-the-top pieces like a hat the shape and size of a drinks tray. Each year the museum holds a special exhibition. The hydrangea-filled gardens outside, planted by Dior's mother Madeleine, have wonderful views of the bay.

Musée et Jardin Christian Dior

t 02 33 61 48 21, www.musee-dior-granville.com; open end May–Sept daily 10–6.30; adm

Getting to and around Granville

Granville is well-connected by **train**, as it's the end of a line from Paris-Montparnasse via Vire and Argentan, and has connections to the Cherbourg–Rennes and Caen–Rennes lines (although these involve changing trains, usually in Coutances or Lison, near St-Lô).

Buses are quite frequent between Granville and Coutances, Avranches, Mont-St-Michel and other destinations; STN bus No.7 runs between Cherbourg and Avranches via Granville, and No.12 to Mont-St-Michel via Avranches.

Manche Iles Express, t 0825 133 050, runs a daily **ferry** service (*April–Sept*) to Jersey, Guernsey, Sark and Alderney. Between Oct and Mar, ferries run to Jersey and Guernsey at weekends and school hols. Several companies run ferries/catamarans to the Chausey Islands. Times vary due to the tides, so check with the tourist office. **Corsaire, t** 0825 138 050, *www.compagniecorsaire.com*, operates April–Sept. More reliable is **Jolie France, t** 02 33 50 31 81, *www.ileschausey.com*, which operates year-round (daily April–Sept, then two or three times week).

You can also take a half-day or **day trip** on *La Granvillaise*, a converted oyster fishing boat; tickets and info at Maison de la Bisquine, 43 Blvd des Amiraux Granvillais, **t** 02 33 90 07 51, *www.lagranvillaise.org*.

The Basse-Ville

Granville's Basse-Ville brings you firmly down to earth with its modern, traffic-filled shopping streets. Walk seawards from the centre for a few minutes, though, and you are in the lively commercial fishing port, where fish merchants and attractive seafood restaurants line the harbour front. It also contains the **Gare Maritime**, from where ferries depart to Jersey and the Iles Chausey. Around the north side of the cape, Granville's atmosphere changes again, to that of a traditional French bathing resort, with villas and obligatory casino.

The Chausey Islands

The barren Iles Chausey, a 50-minute boat-ride from Granville, are famous for their massive tides, and for quarries that provided granite used to build Mont-St-Michel and pave the streets of Paris. In legend the islands were said to have been part, like Mont-St-Michel, of the mythical Scissy Forest, said to have been submerged by freak tides in 709. The surviving granite outcrops became hideouts for smugglers and pirates, and later saw many scuffles between the French and the English. Today the quarries lie dormant and the islands are inhabited by huge numbers of sea birds (notably great cormorants and shags) and a handful of hardy fishermen and lighthouse-keepers who live on the main island of

Carnival in Granville

Granville's Shrove Tuesday carnival is one of Normandy's most colourful, with four days of floats, funfairs and jollity. Festivities begin on the Saturday before Shrove Tuesday. The carnival's origins stretch back to the time when many local men disappeared for months at a time to fish for cod in Newfoundland. They would spend their last few days as landlubbers squandering their money on booze, and dressing up in costumes that hid all manner of licentiousness. Still today, on the last day of the carnival, residents don masks and costumes to surprise their friends, and a carnival effigy is burned on the beach to mark the end of the party.

Grande Ile (the only island that can be visited). Each summer the population swells to about 500, and a single hotel opens up, as well as some self-catering cottages.

There are three excellent sandy beaches, including the wild **Plage de Port Homard** on the southwest side, dominated by the **Château Renault**, built in 1923 by the car-construction family. A footpath south towards the lighthouse takes you past a **fort**, built in 1860 and now a fisherman's shelter. Other activities are likely to be watching for dolphins or birds – or rocks. The weirdly-shaped granite rocks on the northwest side of Grand Ile have nicknames like the 'monk' and the 'elephant', and legend has it that at low tide 365 rocks – or mini-islands – are visible, one for every day of the year.

Tourist Information in Granville

(i) **Granville** >
4 Cours Joinville,
t 02 33 91 30 03,
www.ville-granville.fr

The tourist office organizes tours of town July–Aug Thurs–Sat.
Internet Access: Café La Citrouille, Rue St Sauveur.
Market Days: Sat; smaller market Wed, Place du 11 Novembre.
Post Office: Cours Joinville.

Where to Stay and Eat around Granville

Granville ✉ 50400

All hotels are in the Basse-Ville, or in the outskirts. Most of Granville's best restaurants are around the port and specialize, not surprisingly, in fish and seafood. Most have outside terraces and a *salle panoramique* for watching the boats coming in and out.

***Les Bains, 19 Rue G Clemenceau, t 02 33 50 17 31, *www.hoteldesbains-granville.com* (€€). The reception area has the feel of a chain hotel, with piped music and plastic flowers, but the rooms at this hotel are a pleasant surprise with fresh coloured fabrics and great sea views. It's ideally placed, a stone's throw from the casino.

**Le Michelet, 5 Rue Jules Michelet, t 02 33 50 06 55 (€). Lovely big villa with 19 comfy rooms looking over either the town or the sea (in the distance), run by a welcoming couple. An excellent budget option.

Le Cabestan, 70 Rue du Port, t 02 33 61 61 58 (€€). Large brasserie-style harbour-front restaurant with terrace. *Out of season closed Tues eve, Thurs and Sun eve.*

Le Phare, 11 Rue du Port, t 02 33 50 12 94 (€€). Seafood restaurant at the very end of the quay, right under the Haute-Ville. *Out of season closed Tues and Wed; also closed mid-Dec–10 Jan.*

Bréville-sur-Mer ✉ 50290

***Domaine de la Beaumonderie, 20 Route de Coutances, t 02 33 50 36 36, *www.la-beaumonderie.com* (€€€€–€€). General Eisenhower clearly had good taste, as for a time he made this hotel, just north of Granville and overlooking a bay, his headquarters. There are rooms to suit different budgets, most with lovely views over the gardens and sea. The hotel has a swimming pool and tennis courts, and its restaurant, L'Orangerie (€€€€–€€€) is the most prestigious around Granville. The setting is stunning, and it offers a fine range of Norman cuisine and seafood.

Iles Chausey ✉ 50400

Le Fort et Les Isles, t 02 33 50 25 02 (€). Listen to the waves as you sleep in the simple rooms of this white house in a pretty garden, the only hotel in the Chauseys. It has a restaurant (€€) serving local seafood, with great views. *Minimum stay of 2 nights in July, Aug and during long weekends; closed end-Sept–mid-April.*

Inland Cotentin: The Bocage

Away from the sea, the region sweeping from the central Manche around St-Lô across to Vire and the Suisse Normande is known as the **Bocage Normande**. Essentially, the *bocage* is shaped like a vast waffle. Its crinkly, wooded countryside is carved into thousands of pocket handkerchief-sized fields, divided by tight, high hedgerows rooted into walls of earth that are often over a metre high, which meander up and down over the rolling, sometimes steep hills. The narrow, deep lanes between the fields are often barely wide enough to let a tractor through. In short, the landscape is utterly impenetrable, as Allied soldiers found to their cost during the Normandy battles. Mention the word *bocage*, and anyone who fought in Normandy will turn pale, for the terrain and the hedgerows gave defending Germans the perfect cover from which to launch surprise attacks on the approaching Allies, causing slaughter and horror on an unprecedented scale.

Wars aside, at other times it's a distinctively intimate, tranquil, utterly green landscape. In the Middle Ages, many monasteries chose the *bocage* for its remoteness and isolation. Today, there are also plenty of interesting farms, producing cider or rearing the famous Cotentin lamb, tempting *fermes-auberges*, and many other elements of an unchanging, very rural atmosphere.

Villedieu-les-Poêles and the Bocage Abbeys

The name of this appealing little town deep in the *bocage* means 'City of God of the Cooking Pots', because its inhabitants' passion has long been the beating of copper, pewter and other metals into the form of saucepans, church bells – or copper pigs, like the one over the entrance to the butcher's shop on the main square. The tradition started in the 1100s, when Villedieu's founder Henry I of England and Normandy gave the town to the Knights of St John, along with trading privileges to boost industry and cut rural poverty. The Knights took advantage of this to encourage metal-working, and the habit stuck, so that by 1740 some 139 workshops were crammed into Villedieu's stone and slate houses. Today, one can still watch giant cathedral bells, the size of juggernauts, being lovingly crafted in Villedieu's bell foundry, one of the last completely traditional foundries in Europe. The town is undeniably touristy, especially in summer, with a line of souvenir shops along the main street and copper pans and trinkets you never knew you wanted on sale at every corner, but somehow Villedieu manages to be a living, vibrant town as well.

Getting to Villedieu-les-Poêles

Villedieu has a **train station** on the Granville– Argentan–Paris line, but only some trains stop there. Some STN **bus** routes stop at Villedieu, but to get to the abbeys a **car** is essential.

Atelier du Cuivre
54 Rue Général Huard, t 02 33 51 31 85, www.atelierducuivre. com; open Mon–Fri 9–12 and 1.30–5.30, Sat 9–12 and 1.30–4.30; July–Aug also open Sun 10–12 and 2.30–5.30; adm; joint ticket with Maison de l'Etain

Maison de l'Etain
15 Rue Général Huard, t 02 33 51 05 08; open July–Aug Mon–Sat 9–12 and 1.30–6; June and Sept Tues–Sat 9–12 and 1.30–6; adm, joint ticket with Atelier du Cuivre

Musée de la Poeslerie et Maison de la Dentellière
25 Rue Général Huard, t 02 33 90 20 92; open April–mid-Nov Wed–Sat 10–12.30 and 2–6, Tues 2–6; adm

Fonderie des Cloches
t 02 33 61 00 56, www.cornille-havard.com; open July–Aug daily 9–6; Feb–June and Sept–mid-Nov Tues–Sat 10–12.30 and 2–5.30; adm

Parc Zoologique de Champrépus
t 02 33 61 30 74; open April–Sept daily 10–6; Feb and Oct–mid-Nov daily 1.30–6; Mar Sat–Sun 1.30–6; adm

Abbaye de Hambye >>

At the centre are two main streets, the elongated Place de la République and, parallel to it, Rue Docteur Huard (turning into Rue Général Huard). Running off the latter are attractive stone courtyards housing old copperworkers' homes and workshops, many of which can be visited, like the **Atelier du Cuivre** (Copper Workshop) and the **Maison de l'Etain** (Pewter House). Also of interest is the **Musée de la Poeslerie et Maison de la Dentellière** (Museum of Copperworking and Lace-making). The most interesting workshop, though, is the great bell foundry, the **Fonderie des Cloches**, on Rue du Pont-Chignon. Methods and materials have changed little since medieval times, right down to the clay, horse dung and goat's hair used to make the moulds on which the bells are formed. Around 100 bells are turned out each year, of which about a quarter go abroad, especially to the States. Since it is a real live workshop, the activity you're likely to see there varies from day to day but you might, if lucky, see the furnaces alight, decorative inscriptions being crafted in Plasticine, or moulds being made. At the end of the tour you can buy a set of the pewter-lined copper pans, or have a bash at playing a few of the bells in the yard outside.

Every four years on the fourth Sunday after Pentecost, Villedieu holds a religious festival called the ***Grand Sacre***, commemorating the town's founders, the Order of St John of Jerusalem. As many as 30,000 people process through the town, and neighbourhoods erect altars on special themes. The next *Grand Sacre* will be in 2008. On a less spiritual note, there is another attraction nearby that children particularly enjoy, the **Parc Zoologique de Champrépus**, a wildlife park 8km west of Villedieu, with 7 hectares of grounds and all kinds of exotic animals to watch as well as other features like a scented garden and mini-farm.

To the north and west of the 'City of God' are two extraordinary relics of medieval Normandy, the abbeys of Hambye and La Lucerne-d'Outremer.

Abbaye de Hambye

With its soaring granite ruins silhouetted against the sky and crows whose eerie cries echo through the surrounding trees, the lichen-draped Benedictine abbey of Hambye has a certain feel of rural Yorkshire. The abbey's English flavour is not just a coincidence, as it was founded in 1145 by Guillaume or William Paynel, whose ancestor had been a Sheriff of Yorkshire and a bigwig in the

✪ **Abbaye de Hambye**

south of Hambye village, 12km north of Villedieu-les-Poêles, t 02 33 61 76 92, www.cg50.fr; open daily April–Oct 10–12 and 2–6; Nov–Mar by appointment; adm; guided tours in French Wed–Mon, included in adm; English-speaking visitors are given an information sheet to follow the tour; detailed guided tours July–Aug Mon at 2pm

Domesday survey. It had close links with England, especially Norwich, and its later benefactors included Henry II and Eleanor, Countess of Salisbury. One of the best-preserved medieval abbeys in Normandy, Hambye has an idyllic sylvan setting and excellent guides that make a visit unmissable.

The first monks to tread Hambye's stones were brought here from the Perche, and the abbey flourished until the 14th century, when corruption set in and numbers started to dwindle. After the Revolution the **abbey church** was sold off and quarried for its stone, leaving it in the ruined state you see it today. Even from the ruins, though, one can see that the abbey was built in different styles, because the two chief architects couldn't agree. The odd thing is that the styles are chronologically back to front: the choir, which was constructed first, was built in Gothic style on three levels topped with pointed arched windows and supported by hefty flying buttresses, but the architect who then took over clearly didn't buy the new-fangled style and reverted to the Norman Romanesque, that locals were more familiar with, in the round-arched lantern tower. The stone carvers had some fun here too: the central pillar in the north transept depicts a lively hunting scene with a huntsman blowing a trumpet and a stag being chased by two snarling dogs.

The other abbey buildings, in far better condition, are a showcase of restoration, thanks to the unflagging efforts of a remarkable woman, Mme Beck, who bought Hambye in 1956 and has been restoring the abbey bit by bit ever since. While you can visit the church independently, this part of the abbey can only be seen with the guided tour (which is included in the admission price). In the old kitchens the huge juggle-jointed granite stones above the fireplace are a real feat of Norman engineering, and you can see the effective system whereby waste water collected in a large basin and from there crossed the courtyard into the stream. The 12th-century Romanesque **Parlour** doubled as a 'speaking room' (*parloir*) and funerary chapel, where monks were laid before being buried in the cloisters. Note the red fleur-de-lys painted on the ceilings (at that time a symbol of the Virgin) and the magnificent 15th-century wooden *pietà*.

The **Chapterhouse**, next door, was built later and is typical of Norman Gothic, with delicately moulded arches and fine fan vaulting. The typically Norman twin entrance is similar to the lady chapel at Kirkstall in Yorkshire, while the vaulting is similar to that of Norwich Cathedral, with which Hambye once had close links. On one side is a carving of a monk with big ears – a reflection of the fact that this was where the monks listened to readings and discussed them.

**Abbaye de la
Lucerne-
d'Outremer**
4½km west of
La Lucerne-d'Outremer,
west of D7 road from
La-Haye-Pesnel,
t 02 33 48 83 56,
www.abbaye-lucerne.fr;
open April–Sept daily
10–12 and 2–6.30; mid-
Feb–Mar and Oct–Dec
Wed–Mon 10–12 and
2–5; closed for visits
during Mass on Sun at
11.15; adm, joint ticket
with castle of Pirou

Abbaye de la Lucerne-d'Outremer

It's devilishly difficult to find, but when you finally reach La Lucerne's evocative ruins nestling in a wood-clad valley you'll be glad you made the effort. It is the most atmospheric – you often have the chance to wander around on your own – and the most intact of the Cotentin abbeys, having better escaped the post-Revolutionary barbarity that afflicted so many others. Above all, though, it's the centre of a remarkable project, not just to restore it, but to rebuild it and re-establish a monastic community. Hence 'restoration' has gone beyond shoring up the ruins to actual rebuilding in significant parts of the abbey.

The abbey's site was chosen in 1161 by the Blessed Achard, then Bishop of Avranches, a prominent Norman churchman who had also been Canon of Bridlington in County Durham. It gained its subtitle 'd'Outremer' (from across the sea) by showing persistent loyalty to England. In 1204, when Philippe Auguste seized Normandy, the monks of La Lucerne remained stubbornly faithful to their previous master, King John, and when the English reappeared during the Hundred Years' War, the abbey provided a chaplain for Edward III. This didn't prevent the abbey from becoming one of the largest religious houses in France, until its dissolution in 1791. The main church was built from 1164 to 1178 in a simple, unadorned Norman Romanesque. Its very plainness gives it strength, and its crossing tower set the model for many churches in the region. Even simpler is the **Chapel of the Blessed Achard**, a beautifully austere space that is one of the oldest parts of the abbey. Towards the back of the church a door leads to the slightly later, Gothic-style **Chapterhouse** and **cloister**, still in ruins but due for restoration. Clearly visible and in better condition is the **Lavatorium**, the monks' washing area, with classic Norman carving. Another door off the cloister leads to the giant 18th-century **refectory**, built on top of a 12th-century vaulted cellar. Its centrepiece is a spectacular original timber staircase. The restored church contains a superb 1780 organ, which is regularly used for concerts (mainly in July and August) and weekly Sunday services.

Behind the abbey to the east is a stretch of the **Forêt de la Lucerne**, the thick woodland that once covered most of the valley of the Thar. The forest and the land beside the abbey are crossed by the GR226 long-distance footpath, which follows the line of one of the **Chemins aux Anglais**, the old tracks used by medieval English pilgrims going to Mont-St-Michel and Santiago de Compostela. Using the footpath and a path off to the south (free map available at the abbey), it's an easy 3km-walk to the pretty village of La Lucerne-d'Outremer, where there's an enjoyable *auberge* (see opposite).

(i) **Villedieu-les-
Poêles >**
*Place des Costils,
t 02 33 61 05 69,
www.ot-villedieu.fr*

Tourist Information in Villedieu

Market Days: Tues.
Post Office: Place des Costils.

Where to Stay and Eat around Villedieu

Villedieu-les-Poêles ✉ 50800

La Ferme de Malte, 11 Rue Jules Tetrel, **t** 02 33 91 35 91, *www.lafermedemalte. fr* (€€€). An ancient farmhouse, once owned by the Knights of St John, in extensive grounds on the outskirts of town. It's now a ritzy hotel, with two smart bedrooms, a *gîte* for rent, and a superb restaurant (€€€–€€) which uses produce from the garden. *Closed Sun eve, Mon and Dec–Jan.*

Manoir de l'Acherie, Ste-Cécile, **t 02 33 51 13 87, *www.manoir-archerie.fr* (€€). Old granite house with carefully tended gardens and an ancient cider press, 2km north of the town centre. Bedrooms are carpeted, with plenty of antiques, and there's a flagstoned and beamed restaurant (€€) which has won awards for its cuisine.

St-Pierre et St-Michel, 12 Place de la République, **t 02 33 61 00 11, *www.st-pierre-hotel.com* (€). A traditional hotel on the town square. Don't be put off by the sombre corridors: the rooms are prettily decorated. Ask to look at a few, as they're all different. There's a first-rate restaurant serving solid Norman fare (€€).

Château des Boulais, Saint-Martin-le-Bouillant (12km from Villedieu), **t** 02 33 60 32 20, *www.chateau-des-boulais. com* (€€–€). Mme Drouas and her Dutch partner offer four guest rooms in their vast stone château. If you book in advance you can also enjoy one of Mme's delicious dinners (€).

Le Mesnil-Rogues ✉ 50450

L'Auberge du Mesnil-Rogues, t 02 33 61 37 12 (€€). This welcoming *auberge* occupies a granite building in a tiny village in the heart of the *bocage*. The centrepiece is the huge stone fireplace, where succulent local meats are grilled by the owners. There are plenty of more sophisticated dishes too, all amazing value. Book well in advance, as it's always packed. *Closed mid-Sept–April Mon and Tues; May–June Mon and Tues eve; and closed Jan–Feb and 3 wks in Sept–Oct.*

Hambye ✉ 50450

Auberge de l'Abbaye, 5 Route de l'Abbaye, **t 02 33 61 42 19 (€€–€). Gorgeous hotel-restaurant on the banks of the River Sienne, close to the abbey. The 7 rooms have a romantic feel, and there's a pretty garden. Best known for the enthusiasm of owners Micheline and Jean Allain, and their excellent restaurant (€€€–€€). It's very popular with British visitors, and hotel and restaurant need to be booked well ahead. *Closed 2 wks late Feb and late Sept; restaurant also closed Sun eve and Mon.*

La Lucerne-d'Outremer ✉ 50230

Le Courtil de la Lucerne, t 02 33 61 22 02 (€€–€). Country restaurant in an imposing 18th-century former presbytery of Cotentin granite and slate, set in a garden and with a neat dining room. The cuisine is hearty Norman with touches of sophistication: there's lots of cheese and calvados, rounded off with the speciality calvados ice-cream soufflé. *Closed Wed and Feb.*

St-Lô

In the Battle of Normandy, the old hill town of St-Lô became known as the 'Capital of the Ruins' and the grim photographs of its devastated streets have become one of the classic images of the campaign. Five hundred of its people died, and 95 per cent of its buildings were destroyed. The web of mostly-brutalist concrete buildings erected in their place since 1945 is unlikely to detain you

Getting to St-Lô

St-Lô is on the Rennes–Caen train line, and has good services to Coutances and Avranches. STN bus No.5 runs regularly between St-Lô and Cherbourg via Carentan and Valognes.

for long – unless, of course, your aim is to retrace the terrible story of St-Lô's hard-fought-for liberation by the US Army. Among those who helped at a temporary hospital set up among the ruins by the Irish Red Cross was novelist Samuel Beckett, whose tasks included procuring rat poison for the maternity unit. You can visit the **Mémorial de la Madeleine**, a small exhibition in memory of the liberator US Army divisions which is in the old leprosy hospital in the Square du 11 Septembre 2001. A signposted route devised by the tourist office takes you past the key flashpoints, including remnants of old St-Lô, such as the bizarre half-destroyed Gothic church and the castle ramparts. It also leads to the entrance to the prison, whose inmates – including a large number of Resistance fighters – perished when the building was bombed on the night of 6 June 1944. An urn containing their ashes stands grimly at the doorway, which is all that survived of the building.

Mémorial de la Madeleine
t 02 33 77 60 35; open July–mid-Sept Sat–Sun 3–6

If you're not a war enthusiast there's another reason to stop at St-Lô: its impressive new **Musée des Beaux-Arts**, housed in a modern white building. Its *pièce de résistance* is a series of Flemish tapestries, woven in the early 17th century, which tell the sentimental love story of shepherds Gombault and Macée. There's plenty of spanking, kissing and skirt-lifting in the bucolic scenes, which show peasants dancing, tilling the fields, feasting, chasing butterflies and playing a type of *boules*. The series ends, amid plenty of sighing and weeping, with poor Gombault getting old, clearly worn out by all the frolicking. Other exhibits in the museum include a couple of works by Corot, who painted St-Lô and its surrounding countryside several times, an ever-so-tiny picture of two women on the beach with umbrellas by Charles-François Pécrus, and a lovely Boudin of a sunset at low tide. The museum is completed by a series of paintings and photographs of St-Lô before and during the war. There's more art in the unlikely setting of the **French-American Memorial Hospital**, which displays a peace mosaic by Fernand Léger. It was meant to encircle the entire hospital, but money ran short.

Musée des Beaux-Arts
t 02 33 72 52 55; open Wed–Mon 10–12 and 2–6; adm

The church of **Notre Dame**, begun in the 13th century and added to on and off for the next four, is now a moving testimony to St-Lô's wartime agony. Its ornate façade was brutally amputated in the fighting, and after the war the town decided not to rebuild it but to replace it with a stark wall of green schist, which stands like a huge gaping scar. You can also see shells embedded in the church's medieval stone outside. Otherwise, the church has been

Notre Dame
t 02 33 77 60 35; open daily 8.30–6.30; free tours of stained glass July–Aug Tues and Fri at 3.30

conventionally restored, and has regained much of its Flamboyant Gothic glory. It has fine 15th and 16th-century stained glass, including a window showing St-Laud, an early Bishop of Coutances, after whom the town was named in the 6th century. One of the church's most interesting features is its external pulpit, complete with miniature spire, which greatly impressed Victor Hugo when he visited in 1836. For a further taste of the medieval town, head down from the ramparts past the **Tour des Beaux-Regards** and its war memorial, and along Rue H Dumanoir to the Rue Falourdel. If you are in St-Lô on Saturday, there's a huge market.

Horsey folk may like to visit St-Lô's official stud, the Haras National, on Rue Maréchal Juin on the northern edge of the city. It lacks the architectural splendour of the Haras du Pin in the Orne (*see* p.309), but the horse-and-carriage parades around its 19th-century courtyards on summer Thursday afternoons are just as entertaining for horse-lovers. The stud is famed for its native Normandy cobs and its *selles français* (French saddle horses), the most productive of which is a mighty stallion called Rosire, whom you'll meet during the tour. During the breeding season in spring and early summer many of the stud's 110 stallions disappear to local farms.

In summer, boats and canoes can be hired on the Vire, and there's a pleasant walkway along its banks, which is part of the new *Voie Verte* that follows an old railway track from Carentan down to Pont-Farcy, just north of Vire. Tourist offices have maps.

Haras National
t 02 33 77 60 35, open for guided visits July–Aug 11, 2.30, 3.30 and 4.30; June and Sept 2.30 and 4.30; adm; from last Thurs July–first Thurs Sept, there are horse and carriage parades every Thurs at 3pm; adm

16 Cherbourg and the Cotentin | St-Lô

Tourist Information in St-Lô

Internet Access: La Passerelle, 9 Av de Briovère.
Market Day: Sat.
Post Office: Place du Champ de Mars.

Where to Stay and Eat around St-Lô

St-Lô itself has little attractive accommodation, and it's a better bet to find a *chambre d'hôtes* in the countryside nearby.

St-Lô ⊠ 50010

**Mercure, 5-7 Av de Briovère, Place de la Gare, t 02 33 05 10 84, *www.mercure.com* (€€). This modern hotel beside the Vire is pretty much a soulless concrete carbuncle, but it's about St-Lô's best. Its redeeming factor is its first-rate restaurant, Le

Tocqueville, (€€€–€€), which is comfortable, has excellent Norman cuisine and is very popular with locals. *Restaurant closed Sat lunch, Sun eve and 15 Dec–5 Jan.*

Bistrot Paul et Roger, 42 Rue du Neufbourg, t 02 33 57 19 00 (€). The quintessential family-run French bistro, complete with check tablecloths, photographs and a collection of old radio sets. The copious servings are good value. *Closed Sun and Mon eve.*

Hébécrevon ⊠ 50180

***Château d'Agneaux, Av. Ste Marie, t 02 33 57 65 88, *www.chateau-agneaux.com* (€€€€). Plush 13th-century granite castle 5km west of St-Lô, with 12 superb oak-beamed rooms, some with four-poster beds. Four simpler ones are in a 16th-century square tower. There's a pricey restaurant (€€€€) in a medieval-style panelled dining room.

St-Lô ›
Place Général de Gaulle, t 02 33 77 60 35, www.saint-lo.fr

Manche
Maison du Département, t 02 33 05 98 70, www.manchetourisme.com

Château de la Roque, t 02 33 57 33 20, *www.chateau-de-la-roque.fr* (€€). Fabulous 16th-century stone manor house with its own lake and 15 large, light bedrooms beautifully furnished with antiques and plush rugs. Breakfast, including home-made bread, is included, and dinner, using organic, home-reared meats, is available on request (€€). There's also a hammam and gym, while cycling, riding and tennis are all possible in the 18-hectare grounds. *Closed 2 wks in Jan.*

Cavigny ✉ 50620
La Vimonderie, t 02 33 56 01 13, *http://perso.wanadoo.fr/sigrid. hamilton* (€). Elegant 18th-century granite house in five acres of garden, run by Sigrid, previously a potter in England. The three bedrooms have

original beams, interesting antiques and lots of lace. Cream teas available, and dinner (€) on request. Minimum stay 2 nights. *Closed Jan–Feb.*

Villiers-Fossard ✉ 50680
Le Suppey, t 02 33 57 30 23, *http://perso.wanadoo.fr/nancy.buisson* (€). Fine 18th-century farmhouse with stables and outbuildings around a flower-filled courtyard. It's owned by Nancy, an American, and her French husband Jean. There are two rustically-furnished double bedrooms, a garden and even a spring.

Quibou ✉ 50570
Saint Léger, t 02 33 57 18 41 (€). Lovely farmhouse in quiet hamlet, with two double rooms, and a garden where you can picnic or barbecue.

The Bay of Mont-St-Michel

Approaching the Bay

Heading south along the coast from Granville you pass through **St-Pair-sur-Mer**, **Jullouville** and **Carolles**, low-key traditional beach resorts of varying degrees of tackiness with huge sandy Atlantic beaches. The asset of these and other coastal settlements is their magical views across to Mont-St-Michel, seen sharply-etched on bright days, or as a mysterious, shadowy presence when the ocean mists close in. The neat little resort of **St-Jean-le-Thomas** describes itself optimistically as 'le petit Nice de la Manche', but, again, its biggest attraction is the stunning view.

Walks to Mont-St-Michel, Bird-watching and Other Activities

Several guide agencies take groups across the sands at low tide, following the old pilgrim routes to the abbey, or to other parts of the bay, such as the Mount's sister island of **Tombelaine** (uninhabited, but full of birds). Some provide special-interest walks (for bird-watching, for seeing the sunset) and walks for children, and with some it's also possible to cross the Bay on horseback. *No one should try any walks in the bay without an expert guide.*

Most guides are based in Genêts, where most walks begin, although some start from the car park at Mont-St-Michel. Guided walks are usually organized only April–Oct, but some run all year. The schedule, naturally, depends entirely on the weather and tides. Groups to the Mount follow the old pilgrim route, through the **Bec d'Andaine**, a point just north of Genêts. This walk (barefoot, and in shorts) takes about 45mins each way, with 1–2hrs on the mount before returning.

Reliable guide organizations include: **Chemins de la Baie**, 34 Rue de l'Ortillon, Genêts, **t** 02 33 89 80 88, *www.cheminsdelabaie.com*; **Maison de la Baie de Genêts**, *see* under 'Tourist Information' opposite; **Maison du Guide**, 1 Rue Montoise, Genêts, **t** 02 33 70 83 49, *www.decouvertebaie.com*: a big range of walks, and crossings on horseback; **Didier Lavadoux**, Genêts, **t** 02 33 70 84 19 or **t** 06 75 08 84 69.

Genêts and the Walk to Mont-St-Michel

Far more of a place in its own right than the resorts to the north, Genêts is an attractive old stone village with wonderful views of Mont-St-Michel, with which it has been linked since time immemorial. It grew up as the principal departure point for pilgrims walking to the abbey, in the centuries when there was no causeway linking it to the mainland. It's mind-blowing to imagine what an exciting, and terrifying, journey reaching the Mount on foot must have been, risking one's life in the face of quicksands and racing tides. It's still possible to get a taste of how this must have felt with the guided walks across the sands to the Mount, which are mostly run from Genêts (*see* opposite). On a bright day, it's a wonderful experience. **On no account should anyone attempt the journey without a guide**: legends abound about pilgrims who were lost to the mists, the sands and the tides.

Tourist Information in the Bay of Mont-St-Michel

The official **Maisons de la Baie** are the best sources of information on walks and all other ecology-related activities in the Bay. Genêts is the place to find out about walks across the sands to Mont-St-Michel, and Courtils has an excellent interactive exhibition (*see* p.378). The centres have a joint website: *www.baiedumontstmichel.com*.

Maison de la Baie de Courtils, Route de Roche Torin, 50220 Courtils, **t** 02 33 89 66 00. South side of Bay.

Maison de la Baie de Genêts, 4 Place des Halles, **t** 02 33 89 64 00. North side of the Bay.

Maison de la Baie de Vains, Route du Grouin du Sud, 50300 Vains, **t** 02 33 89 06 06. North side of the Bay, just west of Avranches.

Maison de la Baie du Mont St-Michel, 35960 Le-Vivier-sur-Mer, **t** 02 99 48 84 38, *www.maison-baie.com*. South side of the bay, just inside Brittany.

⭐ Le Haute Gilberdière >>

Where to Stay and Eat around Genêts

Genêts ✉ 50530

Le Moulin, **t** 02 33 70 83 78 (€). Four simple attic-style B&B rooms in a wonderful old water mill on the edge of Genêts. The beds were made by Monsieur: it's not luxurious, but the welcome is genuine and friendly.

Chez François, Rue Jérémie, **t** 02 33 70 83 98, *www.chezfrancois.fr* (€). Great village café-bistro specializing in grilled meats (and some fish) cooked on an open wood fire in a massive stone fireplace. It's simple but real, and an excellent (and very popular) place to come after the walk across from Mont St-Michel. *Closed Wed and Thurs (Sept–June)*.

Dragey ✉ 50530

Belleville, Route de Saint Marc, **t** 02 33 48 93 96, *www.mt-st-michel.net* (€€). Grand old stone house whose owners train racehorses and bring up five children. Dragey is just inland from the bay, but you can see Mont-St-Michel from the roof windows of the minimalist B&B rooms. Breakfasts in the farmhouse kitchen are great. There are two *gîtes* to rent too.

Sartilly ✉ 50530

La Haute Gilberdière, **t** 06 80 87 17 62, *www.champagnac-farmhouse.com* (€€€–€€). This 19th-century *longère* farmhouse, in the countryside behind the bay, is bliss: there are roses in the garden, fat beams inside, home-made jams for breakfast and soothing views. Cosy B&B rooms have antiques and classy bed linen, and the artistic owners are a delight. *Closed Nov–Mar*.

Avranches

Friend, do you remember? When we left Avranches a beautiful setting sun was shining through the branches. As we journeyed, our wheels rustled the green bushes; We admired the sky, the fields, and the sea, all three, And for a moment our ecstasy made us speechless.

Victor Hugo, letter to his wife, 30 June 1836

Eglise St-Gervais
t 02 33 58 00 22; open June–mid-Oct daily 10–12 and 2–6

Scriptorial d'Avranches »

Perched on a cluster of granite hills that fall dramatically down to the Bay of Mont-St-Michel, Avranches has been inextricably bound up with the abbey on the rock ever since Aubert, then Bishop of Avranches, had the visionary dreams in the 8th century that led to Mont-St-Michel's foundation. You can see his skull, complete with the hole where the archangel Michael poked his imperious finger, in the town's 19th-century **Eglise St-Gervais**. It's now gold-plated, and an amazing sight. There are spectacular views of Mont-St-Michel from the so-called **Plate-forme**, a square with a paving stone where, kneeling for a whole day dressed only in a shirt, Henry II did penance for the murder of Thomas à Becket, at the instigation of one of the greatest abbots of Mont-St-Michel, and also bishop of Avranches, Robert de Torigni. That was on 22 May 1172, when the 'platform' was in front of the great door of Avranches cathedral. However, the edifice crumbled away in the 1790s, helped by local Revolutionaries, and the stone, enclosed by chains, is all that's left of Henry's dramatic gesture.

Avranches' proudest treasure, though, is its collection of some 200 illuminated medieval manuscripts from Mont-St-Michel in the newly-opened **Scriptorial d'Avranches** in the Place d'Estouteville. The manuscripts, which cover a host of subjects from classical works by Plato and Aristotle, to science, history and biblical texts, were rescued from Mont-St-Michel's library during the Revolution. Considered some of the finest illuminated pieces in the world, they are beautifully presented in the Salle du Trésor within the Scriptorial. Other rooms cover the history of Avranches' links with the Mount, plus exhibits of the materials used to execute the manuscripts, including inks, pigments, tools (from feathers to cow horns and parchment made from a sheep's gut) and plenty of interactive displays. For more on the manuscripts *see* p.371.

Avranches' Famous Poet: Turold

One of Avranches' major claims to fame is as the birthplace of the 12th-century Norman poet Turold, who – most probably – wrote the oldest and most famous epic poem in the French language, *Le Chanson de Roland* (The Song of Roland). The epic, which recounts the dramatic story of the Battle of Roncesvalles in 778, in the era of Charlemagne, is a masterpiece of the *chanson de geste* (song of deeds), used to recount great episodes of history. Turold's name is muttered almost as an afterthought in the last line of the poem. He is a shadowy figure and little is known about his life, but he gets a mention in the Bayeux Tapestry and is thought to have taken part in the Conquest, becoming Abbot of Peterborough after the English defeat. His pupil, the troubadour Taillefer, is said to have declaimed stanzas of the *Chanson* to rouse Norman soldiers before the Battle of Hastings. The *Chanson*, a 1080 manuscript of which is preserved in Oxford, refers early on to 'great St Michael of Peril-by-the-Tide', the name by which Mont-St-Michel was originally known.

Getting to Avranches

Avranches has **train** connections to Rennes (via Pontorson) and, going north, to Coutances, St-Lô, Lison (change for Cherbourg), Caen and points further afield.

STN **bus** No.12 links Avranches with Granville. Courriers Bretons links Avranches with Pontorson (from where there are buses to Mont-St-Michel).

<< Scriptorial d'Avranches
t 02 33 79 57 00; open July–Aug daily 10–7, May, June and Sept Tues–Sun 10–6; Oct–April Tues–Fri 10–12.30 and 2–5, Sat–Sun 10–12.30 and 2–6; adm

Musée Municipal
t 02 33 58 25 15; open June–mid-Oct 10–12.30 and 2–6; adm

Musée de la Second Guerre Mondiale
t 02 33 68 35 83; open July–Aug 9.15–7, April–June and Sept–mid-Nov 9.15–12.15 and 2–6; adm

If you'd like to find out more about how the manuscripts were made, head for the newly revamped **Musée Municipal** in the former bishop's palace in Place Jean de Saint-Avit, which has a model of a monastic *scriptorium* (with inks and pigments), as well as replicas of the interior of a Norman country home and of craft workshops. Also worth discovering are the **Jardin des Plantes**, a haven of peace with particularly fine views across the Bay of Mont-St-Michel, and the ruins of the old **castle**, which overlooks the tourist office. Avranches' old town has some tranquil squares and fine old buildings, such as the **Hôtel des Trois Marchands** on Place du Marché, one of few 16th-century half-timbered mansions still standing in the town, and the 17th-century **Maison aux Gargouilles** ('Gargoyle House') on Rue Challemel-Lacour, formerly quaintly known as the Rue des Quatre Oeufs ('Four Egg Street').

Avranches was also a critical point in the 1944 battles: a monument to General George Patton, southeast of the centre, commemorates the spot where he spent the night before his crucial Avranches breakthrough on 31 July 1944, which smashed through the German lines to the Loire. The statue stands on US soil – literally, as it was shipped across the Atlantic to form the memorial garden. Near the same junction, by the main road south, there's also a **Musée de la Second Guerre Mondiale**, an eccentric private collection with a big range of old equipment, uniforms and other war relics.

Tourist Information in Avranches

ⓘ Avranches >
2 Rue du Général de Gaulle, t 02 33 58 00 22, www.ville-avranches.fr

Internet Access: Cyber Espace du PIJ, 24 Place du Marché; Cyber Café O'Baryo, 42 Rue St-Gervais.
Market Day: Sat, Place du Marché
Post Office: Rue St-Gervais.

Where to Stay and Eat around Avranches

Avranches ✉ 50300
***La Ramade**, 2 Rue de la Côte, Marcey-les-Grèves, t 02 33 58 27 40, *www.laramade.fr* (€€€–€€). There are 11 romantic-style rooms in this large stone mansion set in extensive grounds, just west of Avranches. *Closed Jan.*

****Croix d'Or**, 83 Rue de la Constitution, t 02 33 58 04 88, *www.hoteldelacroixdor.fr* (€€–€). Deliciously old-fashioned half-timbered hotel with lovely gardens, rustic décor, elegant bedrooms and an excellent restaurant (€€€–€€). *Closed Jan.*

La Renaissance, Rue des Fossés, t 02 33 58 03 71, *www.hotel-renaissance-avranches.fr* (€). Half the eight rooms in this hotel-bar share bathrooms and toilet, while the others have a toilet in the room but share showers. The rooms, however, are pleasingly clean and the location is central, making this a good choice if you're on a rock-bottom budget.

Le Bistrot de Pierre, 5 Rue du Général de Gaulle, t 02 33 58 07 66 (€€–€). Chic, central bistro, and the food's good value. In winter, they make a good choucroute. *Closed Sun.*

La Belle Epoque, 1 bis Place Saint-Gervais, t 02 33 58 00 55 (€€–€). Enchanting little eatery on a pretty square specializing in crêpes and grilled meats. At lunchtime there are bargain menus and *plats du jour*. *Closed Mon.*

Ste-Pience ✉ 50870

Le Manoir de la Porte, t 02 33 68 13 61, www.manoir-de-la-porte.com (€). Beautiful old stone manor in large

★ **Le Moulin de Jean** >>

gardens in tranquil countryside, 10km north of Avranches. The three prettily furnished B&B rooms are comfortable, charming and have wonderful views.

St-Pois ✉ 50670

Le Moulin de Jean, La Lande, Cuves, t 02 33 48 39 29, www.lemoulindejean. com (€€). Distinctly sophisticated but relaxed restaurant hidden deep in the *bocage* 26km northeast of Avranches, in a stunningly restored old water mill. The dishes are works of art: the style is heavily influenced by that of well-known Michelin-starred London-based chef Jean-Christophe Novelli, who used to co-run the mill. Desserts come with his trademark caramel coil and other '*fantaisies*'.

Mont-St-Michel

⊕ **Mont-St-Michel**

Above them, apparently miraculously suspended in the sky, rose a massive tangle of spires and belfries, of granite sculpted into flowers, of flying buttresses, of arches stretching from one tower to another, a stunning masterpiece of massive yet delicate architectural lace, adorned with a crazy army of menacing gargoyles...

Maupassant,
Notre Cœur

Standing proud and mysterious above an apparently unending waste of sands carved by glistening curving rivers, the island and abbey of Mont-St-Michel has over the centuries inspired, intimidated and intrigued – and continues to do so today. Artists, novelists, religious visionaries and pilgrims have all flocked here to see one of the most awe-inspiring and improbable sites in the world. Today it holds the dubious honour of being the most-visited site in France outside Paris – around three million people come each year. Maupassant likened its sheer-sided abbey to an 'imaginary manorhouse, stupefying as a dream palace, improbably stange and beautiful,' Stendhal wrote how the mount 'issued from the waves like an island with the shape of a pyramid,' while for Victor Hugo the vast seas surrounding the island were both 'terrible and charming', mirroring the heaviness of his heart. Even the embroiderers of the Bayeux Tapestry depicted the Mount and the treacherous quicksands around it; Harold, accompanying Duke William on a campaign in Brittany, generously rescued some of the Norman soldiers from sinking into the sands, temporarily earning William's affection and respect.

Settlement of the Mount was a triumph of faith over reason: the inhospitable rock stands in the middle of a 100,000-acre bay that is swept by Europe's highest tides, with a reach of up to 50 feet at spring tides. When the tides are low, the sands, seemingly so peacefully picturesque with their streams and pools shining like burnished metal, hide menacing quicksands and shifting banks that have swallowed many a fisherman or pilgrim. And when the tide comes in, it races 'at the speed of a galloping horse', as locals say – at 200 feet per minute. The first thing that greets you as you arrive on the rock is up-to-the-minute information about the tides, which you need to know if you've left a vehicle in the car park as parts of it flood at high tide. It all adds to the feeling of being part of a maritime adventure.

The improbability of the Mount as a place to live was, of course, the very reason why Christian hermits first settled here in the 6th century, and built two sanctuaries. The arid rock was too inhospitable to produce food, so when they were hungry they lit fires. When people on shore saw smoke they would load food onto donkeys, which were guided by 'the hand of God' to the doors of the hermits' retreats.

Then came a man called Aubert, the Bishop of Avranches. One night in 708 he had a dream in which the Archangel Michael commanded him to build a church on the rock. Aubert dismissed the dream and his heavenly visitor was obliged to call again. When, on the third visit, Aubert still seemed to be taking no notice, the

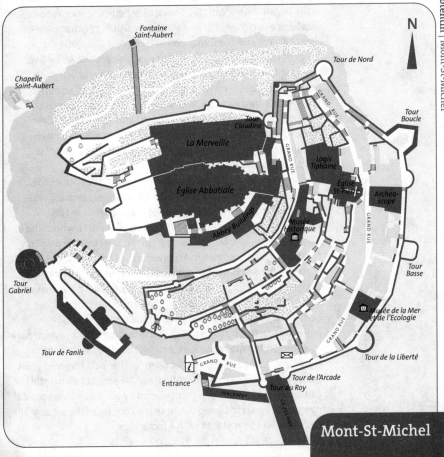

Mont-St-Michel

Getting to Mont-St-Michel

There is a **single ticket** that takes you by **train** and **bus** to Mont-St-Michel all the way from Paris, via Rennes (train to Rennes, then bus via Pontorson). There are five services daily, three on Sun.

Other buses link up with trains arriving from Caen and St-Lô at Pontorson. The Courriers Bretons bus company runs local services between Mont-St-Michel and Pontorson, via Beauvoir, and also has services from Avranches and St-Malo. **Bus information, t** 02 99 19 70 80, *www.lescourriersbretons.com.*

archangel, so the story goes, was forced to bang a hole in the bishop's skull with his finger to drive the message home (there's a wonderful 12th-century drawing of this in the abbey manuscripts, and you can still see his finger-pierced skull; *see* p.366). Aubert finally swung into action and built a small chapel which was a replica of Monte Gargano, a cavern sanctuary in southern Italy where Saint Michael was said to have appeared in 492. The cult spread rapidly and pilgrims, keen to seek the archangel's protection in unsettled times, flocked to the rock, which became known as Mont-St-Michel. Successive generations enlarged the sanctuary, but the creation of the giant, intricate structure that exists today really began in 966, with the arrival of Benedictine monks to establish a permanent abbey. Successive Dukes of Normandy – especially William the Conqueror and Henry II – and, after 1204, Kings of France all favoured the abbey, which grew layer by layer.

During the Hundred Years' War, high ramparts and defensive towers were hastily constructed on the south side to repel the English, and the island became a symbol of French national identity. In the Revolution, it was turned into a prison, which ironically probably saved it from destruction. In 1863 the prison was finally closed, and in 1874 the abbey became France's first official national monument.

A symbolic spiritual presence still remains on the rock (made up of around five monks and nuns, who hold regular services), and some pilgrims still make their way across the sands in the traditional manner. But the main influx is of tourists, who come in hordes, choking the Mount's single narrow street to the point of bursting in high summer. To experience the Mount that Maupassant described as 'lonely on the limitless sands' you need to visit in winter, or at least outside of July or August. It retrieves some of its magic in the evening, when the trinket shops have closed and the coaches have gone on their way. The rock is currently reached by a 1.9km-causeway leading past a vast car park to a strip on the mainland with a gaggle of motel-style hotels. However, because the bay is silting up – in the past hundred years the bay floor has risen by 10 feet – there are plans to dismantle the causeway to allow the sediment carried by the area's three coastal rivers once again to sweep out to sea. According to the scheme the causeway will be replaced with a footbridge.

The Village

Wedged between the ramparts and the rock supporting the great abbey, Mont-St-Michel's one-street village is reached via the 16th-century gate the **Porte de l'Avancée**, a fairly late addition to the island's defences. To the left as you approach the gate, the **Burghers' Guard Room**, built around the same time, now houses the tourist office. The Mont's one street, the medieval cobbled **Grande Rue**, leads up to the Abbey in an anti-clockwise spiral, and has some beautiful houses – provided you can see them through the crowds. The **Hôtellerie de la Lycorne** has an annexe clad in chestnut wood tiles straddling the street, while the **Auberge de la Sirène** boasts a handsome 15th-century timber-frame façade. The prime spot is hogged by the **Mère Poulard** hotel and restaurant, whose visitors have included Henry James, Margaret Thatcher and Leon Trotsky (fortunately not all at the same time). The original Mère Poulard made such creamy omelettes that people made pilgrimages to the rock just to taste them. When she died in 1931, some say she took her recipes to the grave, but the family who bought the restaurant claim she passed them on. Whatever the truth, the sight of white-capped kitchen staff whipping the hell out of hundreds of eggs makes good theatre, and you can make up

The Mont-St-Michel Manuscripts

Given the isolation of their rock in the sea, it may seem a paradox that Mont-St-Michel's monks were better informed about what was happening in the outside world than virtually anyone on the mainland. Firstly, because pilgrims visited them from all over Europe, bringing ideas and learning; secondly, because their famous library, which at its peak contained perhaps 700 to 800 manuscripts, became a place where ideas and books were continually exchanged. And it was here, in the *scriptorium*, that some 70 manuscripts were created, including some of the finest in Europe.

The *scriptorium* was created in 966. Books were produced for worship and as tools for study, and would often be read aloud at mealtimes. But the *scriptorium*'s heyday came a century later, at around the time when William the Conqueror was invading Britain. Some 30 dated and signed manuscripts reflect the intense activity of this time, which continued under William's successors. In 1154 the Mount's book-loving abbot Robert de Torigni commissioned the famous *Cartulary*, containing a stunning illustration in gold of St Aubert's dream and another with an idealized vision of the foundation of the abbey. Many other manuscripts, alas, have not survived.

In the 13th century, everything changed. Philippe Auguste annexed Normandy to France, and later the Hundred Years' War and the plague disrupted activity, while the *scriptorium* slowly ceased production. With the invention of printing, books began to be produced in urban workshops run by lay people, although the monastic workshops struggled on until the 16th century. In the following 200 years many of the remaining manuscripts disappeared into the hands of thieves and 'art lovers', with little to stop them carrying away these treasures.

Come the Revolution, Dom Dufour, the abbey's last librarian, watched with a heavy heart as the last of his priceless books were carried across the sands to Avranches, to be stored in the bishops' palace. He counted out 255 manuscripts. But even in 'safekeeping' their number fell further, as thefts continued. Miraculously they survived the bombing that razed much of Avranches in 1944, having been stored in a castle in the Loire valley. Housed in their new museum, they provide a superb insight into the vigour of intellectual life on Mont-St-Michel.

your own mind about whether the omelettes rank as high in the fluffiness stakes as their reputation promises.

Mont-St-Michel has some entertaining, if small, museums, and you can buy a reduced ticket for all four of them. Near the bottom of the main street, the **Musée de la Mer et de l'Ecologie** has a large collection of old model boats, presented by a jovial ship's captain on a porthole-shaped video screen (in French and English). Upstairs there's an exhibition about the bay's ecology and its phenomenal tides. Virtually opposite the lovely 15th–16th-century **Eglise Saint Pierre**, the **Archéoscope** tells the history and legends surrounding Mont-St-Michel through a 20-minute sound and light show. The commentary is in French, but the special effects and helicopter-shot film footage make it entertaining even if you can't follow it completely. **Le Logis Tiphaine** is the residence built in 1365 by Bertrand Duguesclin, a leading French commander during the Hundred Years' War, for his wife Tiphaine. And finally, virtually next door to the entrance to the abbey is the **Musée Historique**, an eclectic collection ranging from watch cases and seals to medieval torture instruments recalling the period when the abbey was used as a prison, housing up to 600 prisoners at a time. Waxworks are used to recreate the lives of famous prisoners who languished in the Mount's inhospitable cells.

If you've had enough of museum-visiting, shopping, or eating in the village's overpriced and often disappointing restaurants, you can get a change of perspective by following the footpath along the line of the ramparts from the **Tour du Roy** as far as the **Tour du Nord** – one of the island's oldest towers, from the 13th century – which offers stunning views of both the steeply-pitched slate rooftops of the village and the ever-changing sea and sands. One of the most spectacular sights is watching the tide coming in and seeing the Mount become an island once again, a reminder of how isolated it must have been before the causeway was built.

Musée de la Mer et de l'Ecologie
open mid-Feb–11 Nov 9.30–5.30; Christmas hols 10–5; adm

Archéoscope
same hours as the Musée de la Mer et de L'Ecologie, above

Le Logis Tiphaine
same hours as the Musée de la Mer et de l'Ecologie, above

Musée Historique
same hours as the Musée de la Mer et de l'Ecologie, above

The Abbey

The abbey, whose tangle of spires and belfries seemed to Maupassant to be miraculously suspended in the sky, appears even more austere and forbidding as you climb the dauntingly steep stone steps, the *Grand Degré*, to its huge doors. The buildings were made from granite quarried locally and on the Chausey Islands, out in the bay; and one can only marvel at how the great stones were heaved up such steep rock, 80 metres above sea level. Because of the pyramidal shape of the Mount, the abbey's structure is unique: the buildings had to be wrapped, quite literally, around the granite rock. The abbey church, which used to extend right the way across the terrace from where you can now get stupendous views of the bay, stands on crypts that create a platform to take the weight of a

The Abbey
t 02 33 89 80 00, www.monum.fr; open daily May–Aug 9–7, Sept–April 9.30–6; visits include 1hr guided tour in French/English; last entry 1hr before closing time; 2hr lecture tour in French also available July–Aug 10.30, 11.30, 2 and 3; Sept–June Sat–Sun at 10.30 and 2; nocturnal visits of abbey and gardens available July–Aug Mon–Sat 7–midnight, though changeable so enquire at the tourist office for times; adm

church 80 metres long. The section known justifiably as the *Merveille* (Marvel), showed even greater mastery: its 13th-century builders succeeded in perching two blocks of three-storey buildings on a steep rocky slope, a procedure that needed great technical mastery. The structures become progressively lighter towards the top, and on the outside the building is supported by awesomely massive buttresses.

The tour of the abbey begins with the **church**, built mainly in three stages in the 11th, 12th and 13th centuries. The chief remaining parts of the early, pure Norman Romanesque church, completed in 1058, are the massive pillars around the crossing, and the eastern bays of the nave on the south side with their rounded arches. Alas, parts of this first structure proved too weak, and in 1103 the north side collapsed onto the monks' dormitory – fortunately most of them were attending Matins at the time. Beginning in the 1440s the choir was rebuilt in Flamboyant Gothic style, a triumph of soaring verticality. Its luminous triforium and the huge windows above it bathe the choir in glorious light, a marked contrast to the sombre nave. The monks intended to rebuild the rest of the church in the same style as well, but never got around to it as money ran out: pilgrim numbers had dwindled, and Mont-St-Michel's medieval popularity was waning. The outside of the church is supported by two layers of flying buttresses, lavishly decorated with leafy pinnacles and a superb Flamboyant Gothic lacework staircase. In 1897 the abbey church's spire was topped by a copper statue of the Archangel Michael made by one Emmanuel Frémiet, and the gleaming figure still keeps watch over the bay today.

The Merveille

A door leads from the church to the beautiful slender-columned **Cloisters**, which provided a place of prayer and meditation, away from the crowds of pilgrims. Today they offer lovely views over the gardens and the sea, as well as still being decorated by remarkable stone carvings in fine Caen stone: dragons, harvest scenes, luxuriant vine leaves, a badly damaged St Francis. The delicacy of its carving and the cloisters' structure have strange echoes of the Moorish Alhambra in Granada. Look carefully in the southeast corner and you'll spot a seated monk – perhaps the cloisters' builder – flanked by two others, perhaps two stone-carvers. They'd have been scandalized when, five centuries later, Victor Hugo's mistress wantonly carved her initials on one of the stones, an act of vandalism later obliterated by restorers.

The cloister is the uppermost part of the section of Mont-St-Michel known as the **Merveille** (the Marvel), a complex three-storey wing constructed in several levels on a steep slope at the start of the 13th century to provide new living quarters for the monastery. It was built at breakneck speed between 1212 and 1228, and its tiering reflects the division of medieval society into those who worked with their hands, those who waged war and those who prayed. In the huge **refectory** where the monks ate their meals in silence, the architect created an interesting optical illusion: as you enter, the walls appear to be solid granite, and yet the hall is surprisingly light. The walls are pierced by scores of slender-columned windows that helped to support the wide ceiling while also providing soft, even light. The only disruption to the perfect harmony of the windows is the pulpit, in the south wall, from where one of the monks read from scripture as the others ate.

A stairway leads down to the light and airy **Salle des Hôtes** (Guest Hall), beneath the refectory, where royal and aristocratic pilgrims munched their way through roasts cooked in the great fireplaces at one end of the room. The hall's austere appearance today is very different from the richly ornate room it would have been when first built, with its delicate columns ornamented with finely carved foliage, its walls hung with splendid tapestries and the floor tiles vividly painted. From there you enter the two **crypts**, which were actually built to support different sections the choir of the church above them; the second, the St-Martin crypt, is the older of the two, built in 1000 as a foundation for the south transept. The next room, the **monks' ossuary**, originally held the exhumed bones of monks, but much later housed a wheel that hoisted provisions during the time when the abbey was a prison. The prisoners stood inside the wheel like caged rats.

The **Chapelle St-Etienne**, the funeral chapel, leads to one of the most interesting features of the abbey, the **Promenoir** (covered walk), a double-naved hall built at the end of the 11th century, through which the monks walked to their dormitories, and where they took exercise during the long days of winter when ocean storms might make it almost impossible to go outside. Its original plain wooden ceiling was replaced first with Romanesque groined vaults and then, a few decades afterwards, with intersecting ribbed vaults that represented an early tentative – and somewhat clumsy – experiment in Gothic style.

The Promenoir leads to the misleadingly named **Salle des Chevaliers** (Knights' Hall), which far from housing knights was actually the hall where the monks who were skilled as scribes did their work of painstakingly copying and illuminating manuscripts. It has its comforts – which were very necessary given the long hours monks spent toiling here: two large fireplaces kept their fingers from freezing up completely, and along the same wall latrines were fitted between the buttresses. The room is a classic

Tourist Information on Mont-St-Michel

(i) **Mont-St-Michel >**
t 02 33 60 14 30,
www.ot-montsaint
michel.com

The tourist office is impossible to miss, next to the main gateway onto the Mount. For details on the Maisons de la Baie information centres dotted around the Bay, *see* p.365. The **post office** is on Rue Grande.

Where to Stay and Eat on Mont-St-Michel

Hotels and restaurants on Mont-St-Michel itself are often extortionately expensive for what they provide, and it's often better to stay and eat in a village nearby. If you don't mind motel-style places, there are also cheaper options at the entrance to the causeway.

***La Mère Poulard, t 02 33 89 68 68, *www.mere-poulard.com* (€€€€€–€€€). The walls are plastered with photographs of the famous who have stayed here; rooms are beautifully furnished with plush carpets and antiques, and some have stunning views of the sea (you pay accordingly). The still more celebrated restaurant (€€€€–€€€) serves its famous fluffy omelettes, which you can watch being made in the kitchen next door, from 11.30am onwards. There's also a selection of set menus,

mostly at also-lofty prices. It's a tourist trap, but fun all the same.

***Les Terrasses Poulard, t 02 33 89 02 02, *www.terrasses-poulard.com* (€€€€–€€). Owned by the same family as La Mère Poulard, this is the other luxury option on the island, just below the abbey. It also has a fine restaurant (€€).

***St-Pierre, t 02 33 60 14 03, *aubergesaintpierre@wanadoo.fr* (€€€–€€). Ancient building with small, comfy rooms, some with amazing views. Even its restaurant (€€) is a historic monument. A decent bet provided you can stomach the kitsch, which includes waitresses in regional dress, but still a tad expensive for the level of the food.

***La Croix Blanche, t 02 33 60 14 04 (€€€–€€). Rooms have the feel of an international chain hotel, with mass-produced furnishings, but the views are breathtaking. There's a reasonable restaurant (€€).

**Le Mouton Blanc, t 02 33 60 14 08, *www.lemoutonblanc.com* (€€). The nearest thing to a budget option on the Mount, although hardly cheap. Rooms have rather tacky furniture but also some nice beams, and the location is great. The restaurant (€€€€) serves the usual omelettes and seafood, or there's a cheaper cafeteria-style place alongside.

piece of 13th-century Norman architecture, with its pointed vaulted arches and squat capitals exuberantly carved with plants. The last room visited in the *Merveille* – reflecting the descent through the medieval hierarchy – is the **Almonry** on the lowest level, which now serves as the abbey's book and souvenir shop, but where once the monks distributed charity to poor pilgrims – sometimes in hundreds at a time – who had made their way to Mont-St-Michel.

Around Mont-St-Michel

Once you've disentangled yourself from the hotels at the end of the Mont-St-Michel causeway, driving due south along the banks of the Couesnon (past the point where it is believed Harold is depicted rescuing the Norman soldiers in the Bayeux Tapestry) you pass through the little village of **Beauvoir** to arrive in **Pontorson**, a

Getting to Pontorson

Train services link Pontorson with Rennes, Avranches, St-Lô and some other destinations, including Paris. The Courriers Bretons **bus** company runs 14 buses daily Mon–Sat (nine, Sun) between Pontorson and Mont-St-Michel, stopping at Beauvoir. **Bus information, t** 02 99 19 70 80, *www.lescourriersbretons.com.*

low-key, likeable town with two superb hotels, which makes it a good base for visiting the Mount. One of the hotels, the **Montgomery**, is a 16th-century mansion that once belonged to the Counts of Montgomery, distant relatives of the British Field-Marshal, one of whom killed King Henri II in 1559. Guests can even sleep in the Count's bedroom with advance booking. Pontorson also has a fascinating 12th-century church, the **Eglise Notre-Dame**, said to have been founded by William the Conqueror himself in gratitude to the Virgin Mary for having got his army successfully across the treacherous Couesnon quicksands. On Wednesdays a lively market is held in the town square, providing a refreshing dose of normality after the sometimes theme-park atmosphere of Mont-St-Michel.

Some 15km southeast of Pontorson near **St-James**, in Normandy's southwest corner, is the second of the large World War II **American military cemeteries** in the region. It contains 4,410 graves, and in the chapel there are several individual and regimental memorials and an exhibit on the fighting that took place in the area in 1944.

Back towards Mont-St-Michel, another good centre in which to base oneself while visiting the Abbey and the Bay is **Ducey**, 15kms east of the Mount, which has pleasant shops, a decent hotel and many good walks beside the lovely, fast-flowing Sélune river. In summer, it's brimming over with geraniums. Between there and Pontorson there are several more pretty villages, such as **Servon**, with some extremely attractive bed and breakfasts and a great restaurant, and, with a small detour, **Courtils**, right on the edge of the salt flats with superb views of Mont-St-Michel. A wonderful base for short walks and birdwatching excursions into the marshes, Courtils also contains the southern **Maison de la Baie**, a very informative and enjoyable information centre with a great, interactive exhibition on the unique geography of the Bay of Mont-St-Michel and the many legends that have gathered around it over the last 3,000 years.

While in this area, be sure to taste its local speciality, *agneau pré-salé*, lamb raised on the salt marshes. In the 11th century the monks at Mont-St-Michel discovered that lambs which had grazed on marshes that were washed by the sea were particularly tasty and tender, and they are still savoured today. The flavour stems in part from the nearly 70 different species of plants that are found in the marshes, and which are grazed by the lambs. At various points around the Bay, such as Courtils, Vains and St-Léonard, you can also see the flocks of sheep scattered across the bay flats, munching the marsh grasses.

Tourist Information around Mont-St-Michel

Market Days: Pontorson: Wed; Ducey: Tues, also Sun July–Sept.

Post Office: Pontorson, 18 Rue St-Michel; Ducey, Rue du Génie.

Where to Stay and Eat around Mont-St-Michel

Beauvoir ☒ 50170

✶✶Hotel Le Beauvoir, 9 Route du Mont-St-Michel, **t** 02 33 60 09 39, *www.le-beauvoir.com* (€). A very simple traditional village hotel-restaurant very close to the Mount – a useful fallback if you can't afford to stay there. They serve local favourites from *agneau pré-salé* to *moules marinières*. There are 18 basic rooms (€) upstairs.

Pontorson ☒ 50170

✶✶✶Montgomery, 13 Rue du Couesnon, **t** 02 33 60 00 09, *www.hotel-montgomery.com* (€€€€€–€€). This 500-year-old stone mansion, once owned by the Counts of Montgomery and now affiliated to Best Western, is a real gem, with a spectacular 1550s oak staircase. The Earl's room has a four-poster bed, but all the 32 rooms have beams, Jacuzzis and attractive antiques and fabrics, and some have views of Mont-St-Michel. There's a pretty terrace, and a cosy bar and restaurant (€€), which is open to residents only.

✶✶Bretagne, 59 Rue du Couesnon, **t** 02 33 60 10 55, *www.lebretagne pontorson.com* (€). No less characterful than the Montgomery, although in a totally different way, as you'll see from the purple painted mock beams on the front. Rooms are equally quirky, with a mix of cheap modern and antique furniture. The hotel is best-known locally, however, for its restaurant (€€€–€€), with a grand Art Nouveau dining room and

menus that make inventive use of local ingredients like *agneau pré-salé*.

Ducey ☒ 50220

✶✶Auberge de la Sélune, 2 Rue Saint-Germain, **t** 02 33 48 53 62, *www.selune.com* (€). The rooms are comfortable but unexciting at this hotel, but its major assets are its gardens and its location on the Sélune river, which makes it popular with fishermen. It has a fine restaurant (€€), with light, modern décor and innovative, delicious food, making fine use of fresh salmon and trout from the river. *Closed mid-Nov–mid-Dec.*

Servon ☒ 50170

✶✶Auberge du Terroir, **t** 02 33 60 17 92, *aubergeduterroir@wanadoo.fr* (€€–€). There are six stylish, colourful and very comfortable rooms B&B rooms at this inn in the middle of a quiet old village, three in the main house and the others in an annexe. The auberge is best-known, though, as a restaurant (€€€–€€). The chef and his wife hail from Limoges, but are enthusiasts for the produce of the Bay, especially salt-marsh lamb and seafood. The dining room is bright and elegant, and it's definitely one of the Bay's best restaurants. *Closed Wed, Thurs lunch, Sat lunch, and mid-Nov–mid-Dec.*

Le Petit Manoir, 21 Rue de la Pierre du Tertre, **t** 02 33 60 03 44, *agedouinmanoir@tiscali.fr* (€). There are stunning antique bedheads and Norman wardrobes in the two B&B rooms in the main farmhouse, decorated in pastel colours. There are also three other more modern rooms, including one fitted for wheelchair access. The farm's greatest selling point, though, is its fantastic views of Mont-St-Michel in the distance. *Closed mid-Nov–early Feb.*

St-Quentin-sur-le-Homme ☒ 50220

✶✶✶Le Gué du Holme, 14 Rue des Estuaires, **t** 02 33 60 63 76, *www.le-gue-du-holme.com* (€€). This smart

---

ⓘ **Ducey** ››
4 Rue du Génie,
t 02 33 60 21 53,
www.ducey-tourisme.com

★ **Auberge du Terrior** ››

ⓘ **Pontorson** ›
Place de l'Hôtel de Ville, **t** *02 33 60 20 65,*
www.mont-saint-michel-baie.com

★ **Montgomery** ›

① **Courtils >**

Maison de la Baie de Courtils, Route de Roche Torin, t 02 33 89 66 00, www.baiedumontst michel.com; excellent centre with a bird-viewing platform on the bay and a great, interactive exhibition on all aspects of the Bay's history, ecology and legends

hotel in the centre of the village of St-Quentin has ten unexciting but comfy rooms looking out onto a gorgeous garden. Its restaurant (€€€) is one of the most prestigious around the Bay. The tone is smart, the menu, which changes with the seasons, elaborately *haute cuisine. Closed May–Aug Mon lunch, Sat lunch; Jan–April Mon, Sat lunch and Sun eve.*

Courtils ✉ 50220

***Manoir de la Roche Torin, t 02 33 70 96 55, www.manoir-rochetorin.com** (€€€€–€€€). One of the most luxurious options around the Bay, a grand, ivy-clad 19th-century house superbly placed on the edge of the marshes north of Courtils village. Its 15 rooms are plushly comfortable, and three have fabulous views of the Mont. There's a great lush garden, and the restaurant (€€€) – also with great views from its tables – has a high reputation. The mainstay of the menu is *pré-salé* lamb, served in many ways, along with fine seafood. A very relaxing place. *Closed mid-Nov–mid-Dec and Jan–mid-Feb.*

Juilley ✉ 50220

Les Blotteries, t 02 33 60 84 95, *www.les-blotteries.com* (€€). Old converted farm overlooking fields, with three stunning guest rooms furnished with antiques, one with whirlpool bath. There's a lovely granite fireplace in the white breakfast room downstairs. Pets are welcome, and there's even a baby-sitting service.

Language

Throughout France a certain level of politeness is expected: use *monsieur, madame* or *mademoiselle* when speaking to everyone (never *garçon* in restaurants!), from your first *bonjour* to your last *au revoir*.

For **food and drink** vocabulary, *see* the Menu Reader on pp.66–70.

Useful Words and Phrases

hello *bonjour*
goodbye *au revoir*
yes *oui*
no *non*
good evening *bonsoir*
good night *bonne nuit*
please *s'il vous plaît*
thank you (very much) *merci (beaucoup)*
good *bon (bonne)*
bad *mauvais(e)*
excuse me *pardon/excusez-moi*
Can you help me? *Pourriez-vous m'aider?*
My name is... *Je m'appelle/Je suis...*
What is your name? *Comment vous appelez-vous?* (formal)
How are you? *Comment allez-vous?*
Fine *Ça va bien/Bien*
I don't understand *Je ne comprends pas*
I don't know *Je ne sais pas*
Can you speak more slowly? *Pourriez-vous parler plus lentement?*
entrance *entrée*
exit/way out *sortie*
open *ouvert*
closed *fermé*
push *poussez*
pull *tirez*
WC *les toilettes*
men *hommes*
ladies *dames/femmes*
Help! *Au secours!*
doctor *le médecin*
hospital *un hôpital*

police station *le commissariat de police*
bank *une banque*
post office *la poste*
stamp *un timbre*
phone card *une télécarte*

Accommodation

Do you have...? *Est-ce que vous avez...?*
I would like... *J'aimerais...*
How much is it? *C'est combien?*
It's too expensive *C'est trop cher*
Do you have any change? *Avez-vous de la monnaie?*
Do you have a room? *Avez-vous une chambre?*
I want to book a room *Je voudrais réserver une chambre*
Can I see the room? *Puis-je voir la chambre?*
How much is the room per day/week? *C'est combien la chambre par jour/semaine?*
single room *une chambre pour une personne*
twin/double room *une chambre à deux lits/ pour deux personnes*
shower *douche*
bath *salle de bain/baignoire*
cot (child's bed) *un lit d'enfant*

Transport

Where is/are...? *Où est/sont...*
left *à gauche*
right *à droite*
straight on *tout droit*
here *ici*
there *là*
close *proche*
far *loin*
up *en haut*
down *en bas*
I want to go to... *Je voudrais aller à...*
What time does it leave (arrive)? *A quelle heure part-il (arrive-t-il)?*

a ticket (single/return) to... *un aller (aller simple/aller et retour) pour...*
bus *l'autobus*
bus stop *l'arrêt d'autobus*
bus/coach station *la gare routière*
railway station *la gare*
delayed/late *en retard*
on time *à l'heure*
platform *le quai*
timetable *l'horaire*
car *la voiture*
driver *chauffeur*
breakdown *une panne*
give way/yield *céder le passage*
driving licence *permis de conduire*
motorbike/moped *la moto/le vélomoteur*
no parking *stationnement interdit*
petrol (unleaded) *l'essence (sans plomb)*

Time

What time is it? *Quelle heure est-il?*
It's 2 o'clock (am/pm) *Il est deux heures (du matin/de l'après-midi)*
...half past 2 *...deux heures et demie*
morning *le matin*
afternoon *l'après-midi*
evening *le soir*
night *la nuit*
today *aujourd'hui*
yesterday *hier*
tomorrow *demain*
now *maintenant*
soon *bientôt*

Days

Monday *lundi*
Tuesday *mardi*
Wednesday *mercredi*
Thursday *jeudi*

Friday *vendredi*
Saturday *samedi*
Sunday *dimanche*

Numbers

one *un*
two *deux*
three *trois*
four *quatre*
five *cinq*
six *six*
seven *sept*
eight *huit*
nine *neuf*
ten *dix*
eleven *onze*
twelve *douze*
thirteen *treize*
fourteen *quatorze*
fifteen *quinze*
sixteen *seize*
seventeen *dix-sept*
eighteen *dix-huit*
nineteen *dix-neuf*
twenty *vingt*
twenty-one *vingt-et-un*
twenty-two *vingt-deux*
thirty *trente*
forty *quarante*
fifty *cinquante*
sixty *soixante*
seventy *soixante-dix*
eighty *quatre-vingts*
eighty-one *quatre-vingt-et-un*
ninety *quatre-vingt-onze*
hundred *cent*
two hundred *deux cent*
thousand *mille*
million *million*

Further Reading

Allen Brown, R., *The Normans and the Norman Conquest* (Constable, 1969). The growth of Norman power, and how the Conquest impacted on Normandy and England.

Ardagh, John, *France Today* (Penguin, 1987). A thoroughly readable journalistic account of modern France.

Ardagh, John, *Writers' France* (Hamish Hamilton, out of print). An informative and entertaining study, covering literary themes in France.

Bernstein, David, *The Mystery of the Bayeux Tapestry* (Weidenfeld & Nicolson, 1986). An interesting book that tackles many of the mysteries and disagreements surrounding the famous tapestry.

Chibnall, Marjorie, *The Normans* (Blackwells, 2000). Interesting academic study on the rise and expansion of Normandy.

Dannenberg, Linda; Le Vec, Pierre; Moulin, Pierre; and Bouchet, Guy; *Pierre Deux's Normandy* (Random House, 1988). A beautifully illustrated coffee-table book.

David, Elizabeth, *French Provincial Cooking* (Michael Joseph, 1960, 1997) Delightful anecdotes about a provincial France that's fast disappearing.

Guermont, Claude, with Paul Frumkin, *The Norman Table* (Charles Scribner's Sons, 1985). Very readable recipe book.

Hastings, Max, *Overlord* (Pan, 1999). A first-rate and balanced account of D-Day and its aftermath.

Herbert, Robert L., *Impressionism: Art, Leisure and Parisian Society* (Yale, 1988). A fascinating exploration of the themes behind Impressionist painting, and especially interesting on the influence of the Norman seaside.

Joyes, Claire, *Monet's Table: The Cooking Journals of Claude Monet* (Simon & Schuster, 1989). Original and beautifully illustrated book, with usable recipes.

Keegan, John, *Six Armies in Normandy* (Jonathan Cape, 1982). A moving military history of D-Day and the Normandy campaign. Obligatory reading to get a clear overview of the events of 1944.

Kemp, Anthony, *D-Day: The Normandy Landings and the Liberation of Europe* (Thames & Hudson, Abrams, 1994). Well illustrated guide first published to mark the 50th anniversary.

Leigh Fermor, Patrick, *A Time to Keep Silence* (John Murray). The veteran travel writer immerses himself in the lives of the monks of St Wandrille and La Trappe.

Lottman, Herbert, *Flaubert* (Methuen, 1989). A readable and thoroughly researched biography of Flaubert.

McLynn, David, *1066, The Year of the Three Battles* (Jonathan Cape, 1998). Dispels a number of commonly-held myths surrounding William the Conqueror, and gives an insightful account of his early life.

Miller, Russell, *Nothing less than Victory: The Oral History of D-Day* (Pimlico, UK, William Morrow/Quill, USA). A moving compilation of veterans' recollections, letters and diaries.

Millon, Marc and Kim, *The Food Lover's Companion to France* (Little, Brown, 1996). User-friendly guide to French food.

Pelatan, Jean, *The Percheron Horse Past and Present* (Association des Amis du Perche, 1985). A thoroughly researched history of the Percheron horse and its decline.

Russell Taylor, John, *Claude Monet: Impressions of France* (Collins & Brown, 1995).

An exploration of Monet's world, portrayed through letters, sketches, rare photographs and cartoons.

Sackville-West, V., *The Eagle and the Dove* (Michael Joseph, 1943). A study of two Saint Theresa's: the Spanish Teresa of Avila, and the French one from Lisieux.

Warner, Marina, *Joan of Arc: The Image of Female Heroism* (Univ. of California, 1999). A meticulous study that seeks to sort the myths surrounding the life of Joan of Arc from the truth.

Watkin, David, *A History of Western Architecture* (Laurence King, 1986). Solid and readable introduction.

Wilson, David, *The Bayeux Tapestry* (Thames & Hudson, 1985). A ravishing book with the tapestry in full colour, and a good background text.

Zeldin, Theodore, France 1845–1945 (Oxford UP, 1980). Five thematic volumes on this vitally important century in French history.

Index

Main page references are in **bold**. Page references to maps are in *italics*.

Author's Acknowledgements

My thanks remain to all those who helped with the first edition. For the second edition, I should like to thank Rebecca Spry and Roxanne Besse, who helped with research and editing, my editor James Alexander, and Sarah Gardner and Antonia Cunningham at Cadogan. I am also deeply grateful to Brittany Ferries, who got me across the water. In Normandy, I would like to thank those people in tourist offices who went out of their way to provide updated information; there are too many to list them all, but I should like to mention by name Armelle Le Goff at the Calvados regional tourist office, Caroline Boscher at the Bayeux office, Anne-Marie Coulon in Alençon, Carole Raubert at the Orne regional tourist office, Capucine d'Halluin at the Eure regional tourist office, Isabelle Chollet at the Manche regional tourist office, Marie Carel in Bernay, Aline in Domfront, Elizabeth Potel in Dieppe, Chantal Trevidic at the Ecomusée du Perche, Mme Leclerc in Duclair, Sandrine Chardon in Deauville, Patrice Belliot at Le Havre, and Sandra Parnisari at the Seine Maritime tourist office. I also owe thanks to Julia Mclean, cider producer in Blangy-le-Château, and Clive Saville for restaurant recommendations; Amanda Monroe at Rail Europe for updates on rail to and through Normandy; Sorrel Everton who provided information about gardens and B&Bs in the Seine-Maritime; Ceri Crump, Cyril Huet and the Haras du Pin who helped with pictures; Mme Christiane Allix Desfauteaux, Eric Bonnifet and Mme Lebault who generously provided accommodation; and Steve and Emma Grant who kindly spent their honeymoon testing out some of Calvados' top restaurants. Last but certainly not least, I should like to thank my friends who offered encouragement and support throughout, especially Jo Walsh, Fiona Everton and Anne and John Voysey. This edition is dedicated to them.

Credits

John Keegan and his publishers Jonathan Cape for permission to reproduce the excerpt from from *Six Armies in Normandy* on p.259.

Katherine Campbell from *WW2 People's War*, the BBC's online archive of war-time memories, for permission to reproduce an excerpt from the diary of W. H. Nelson on p.274. The archive can be found at *www.bbc.co.uk/ww2peopleswar*.

BBC Wildlife Magazine for permission to reproduce their article on the wildlife of the Cotentin, by Fergus Collins, on p.277.

Picture Credits

With many thanks to: Pierre Huet; Père Magloire; Fromagerie Graindorge; Haras du Pin/Jean Eric Rubio; Deauville Tourist office/Olivier Houdart; CDT Orne; H Guermonprez; Kicca Tommasi.

Second Edition Published 2007

Cadogan Guides
2nd Floor, 233 High Holborn,
London WC1V 7DN
info@cadoganguides.co.uk
www.cadoganguides.com

The Globe Pequot Press
246 Goose Lane, PO Box 480, Guilford,
Connecticut 06437–0480

Copyright © Clare Hargreaves 2004, 2007

Cover photographs: © Vladimir Pcholkin,
 Martial Colomb
Introduction photographs: © Pierre Huet;
 © Père Magloire; © Fromagerie Graindorge;
 © Haras du Pin/Jean Eric Rubio; © Deauville
 Tourist office/Olivier Houdart; © CDT Orne;
 © H Guermonprez; © Kicca Tommasi
Maps © Cadogan Guides, drawn by
 Maidenhead Cartographic Services Ltd

Art Director: Sarah Gardner
Managing Editor: Antonia Cunningham
Editor: James Alexander
Assistant Editor: Nicola Jessop
Proofreading: Elspeth Anderson
Indexing: Isobel McLean

Printed in Italy by Legoprint
A catalogue record for this book is available
 from the British Library
ISBN: 978-1-86011-355-0

Normandy touring atlas

N

10 km
5 miles

English Channel

Côte d'Albâtre

Veules-les-Roses
St-Valéry-en-Caux
Mesnil-Durdent
Ingouville
Les Grandes Dalles
Château Mesnil-Geoffroy
Sassetot-le-Mauconduit
Cany-Barville
Ermenouville
Notre Dame de Salut
Ouainville
Grainville-la-Teinturière
Fécamp
Valmont
Doudeville
St-Léonard
Yport
Ganzeville
Oherville
Etretat
Héricourt-en-Caux
Angeville-Bailleul
Bennetot
Cuverville
Pays de Caux
Fauville-en-Caux
Goderville
Bréauté
Beuzeville-le-Grand
Yvetot
Bolbec
Maulèvrier-Ste Gertrude
Betteville
Montivilliers
Abbaye de St-Wandrille
Lillebonne
Ste-Adresse
Harfleur
Gonfreville
Caudebec-en-Caux
Villequier
Pont de Brotonne
Tancarville
Notre-Dame-de-Bliquetuit
Forêt de Brotonne
Le Havre
Pont de Normandie
Aizier
Jumièges
Honfleur
Pont de Tancarville
Hauville
Vasouy
Marais
St Opportune-la-Mare
Foulbec
Grande Mare
Vieux-Port
Trouville-sur-Mer
Fatouville-Grestain
Vernier
La Haye de Routot
Deauville
Touques
Beuzeville
Fourmetot
Routot
St Martin-aux-Chartrains
Quetteville
Côte Fleurie
Côte de Grace
Villers-sur-Mer
Surville
Pont-Audemer
Appeville-Annebault
Tourgéville
Martainville
Campigny-la-Futelaye
Le Bec-Hellouin
Ouistreham
Houlgate
Coudray-Rabut
Pont-l'Evêque
Riva Bella
Gonneville-sur-Mer
Beaumont-en-Auge
Pierrefitte-en-Auge
Lieurey
Brétigny
St Eloi-de-Fourques
Mathieu
Bénouville
Blangy-le-Château
Brionne
Drubec
Beaufour-Druval
Le Breuil-en-Auge
St Victor-d'Epine
Ranville
St-Aubin-Lebizay
Bonnebosq
Harcourt
Troarn
Beuvron-en-Auge
Grandouet
St Aubin-de-Scellon
Fontaine-la-Soret
Caen
Victot-Pontfol
Carref. St. Jean
Cambremer
Lisieux
Nassandres
CALVADOS
Notre-Dame-de-Livaye
Manoir de St-Hippalyte
Thiberville
Carsix
Crèvecœur-en-Auge
St Martin-de-la-Lieue
Beaumont-le-Roger
Château de Grandchamp
St-Germain-du-Livet
Mézidon-Canon
St-Julien-le-Faucon
Château de Coupesarte
St Quentin-des-Isles
Bernay
Forêt de Beaumont
Ste-Marie aux Anglais
Bretteville-sur-Laize
Vieux-Pont
Livarot
St Clair-d'Arcey
St-Pierre-sur-Dives
Orbec
Broglie
St Aubin-le-Vertueux
Château de Vendeuvre
Notre-Dame-de-Courson
Beaumesnil
Potigny
Pays
Ammeville
Le Petit Coulibœuf
Ste Foy-de-Montgommery
Vimoutiers
Montreuil-l'Argillé
La Ferrière-sur-Risle
Falaise
Morteaux-Coulibœuf
Crouttes
Ticheville
Notre-Dame-du-Hamel
La Neuve-Lyre
Villy-lez-Falaise
Les Champeaux
Camembert
Le Sap
d'Ouche
Rugles
Montormel
Trun
La Ferté-Frênel
Chambois

Juno Beach
Portsmouth
Portsmouth
Bernières-sur-Mer
St-Aubin-sur-Mer
Langrune-sur-Mer
Merville-Franceville-Plage
Luc-sur-Mer
Sword Beach
Dives-sur-Mer
Cabourg

Seine
Côte de Grace

2
3

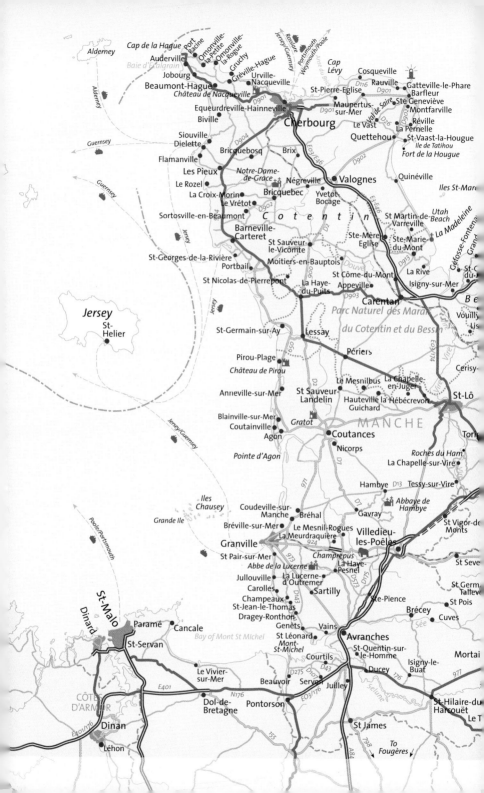

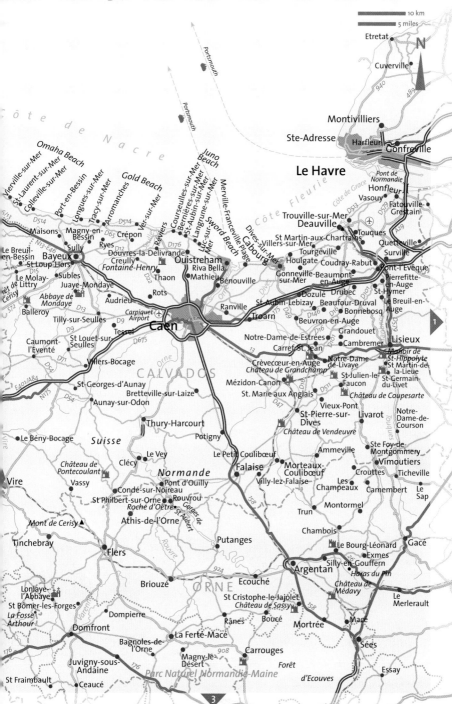

English Channel

Côte de Nacre

10 km
5 miles

N

Etretat

Cuverville

Portsmouth

Montivilliers

Ste-Adresse   Harfleur   Gonfreville

Le Havre

Pont de
Normandie

Honfleur

Côte de Grace

Vasouy

Côte Fleurie

Fatouville-
Grestain

Omaha Beach

Vierville-sur-Mer
St-Laurent-sur-Mer
Colleville-sur-Mer

Port-en-Bessin

Longues-sur-Mer
Tracy-sur-Mer

Gold Beach

Arromanches

Ver-sur-Mer

Juno
Beach

Courseulles-sur-Mer
Bernières-sur-Mer
St-Aubin-sur-Mer
Langrune-sur-Mer

Merville-Franceville Plage

Sword Beach

Luc-sur-Mer

Dives-sur-Mer

Cabourg

Trouville-sur-Mer

Deauville

Touques

St Martin-aux-Chartrains

Villers-sur-Mer

Tourgéville

Houlgate

Coudray-Rabut

Quetteville

Surville

Pont-l'Evêque

Pierrefitte-
en-Auge

St-Hymer

Le Breuil-en-
Auge

Lisieux

Maisons

Magny-en-
Bessin

Crépon

Rèviers

Le Breuil-
en-Bessin

Bayeux

Sully

Ryes

Douvres-la-Délivrande

Ouistreham

Gonneville-Beaumont-
sur-Mer

Dozulé

Drubec

Beaufour-Druval

Bonnebosq

St Loup-Hors

Creully

Fontaine-Henry

Riva Bella

Le Molay-
Littry

Subles

Thaon

Mathieu

Bénouville

St-Aubin-Lebizay

Abbaye de
Mondaye

Juaye-Mondaye

Audrieu

Rots

Ranville

Troarn

Beuvron-en-Auge

Grandouet

Balleroy

Tilly-sur-Seulles

Carpiquet
Airport

Caen

Notre-Dame-de-Estrées

Cambremer

Manoir de
St-Hippolyte

St Martin-de-
la-Lieue

Caumont-
l'Eventé

St Louet-sur-
Seulles

Tessel

Carref St. Jean

Notre-Dame-
de-Livaye

St-Julien-le-
Faucon

St-Germain-
du-Livet

Villers-Bocage

Crèvecœur-en-Auge

Château de Grandchamp

Château de Coupesarte

St-Georges-d'Aunay

Bretteville-sur-Laize

Mézidon-Canon

St. Marie aux Anglais

Vieux-Pont

Livarot

Notre-
Dame-de-
Courson

Aunay-sur-Odon

St-Pierre-sur-
Dives

Château de Vendeuvre

Ammeville

Ste Foy-de-
Montgommery

Vimoutiers

Le Bény-Bocage

Suisse

Thury-Harcourt

Potigny

Le Petit Coulibœuf

Crouttes

Ticheville

Le Vey

Clécy

Falaise

Morteaux-
Coulibœuf

Les
Champeaux

Camembert

Le
Sap

Château de
Pontécoulant

Normande

Villy-lez-Falaise

Vire

Vassy

Condé-sur-Noireau

Pont d'Ouilly

St Philbert-sur-Orne

Rouvrou

Roche d'Oêtre

Montormel

Trun

Athis-de-l'Orne

Mont de Cerisy

Chambois

Gacé

Tinchebray

Putanges

Le Bourg-Léonard

Exmes

Flers

Silly-en-
Gouffern

Haras du Pin

Briouzé

Ecouché

ORNE

Argentan

Château de
Médavy

Le
Merlerault

Lonlaye-
l'Abbaye

St Bômer-les-Forges

St Cristophe-le-Jajolet

Château de Sassy

Dompierre

Château
Arthour

Rânes

Boucé

Mortrée

Mace

Domfront

La Ferté-Macé

Sées

Bagnoles-de-
l'Orne

Juvigny-sous-
Andaine

Magny-le-
Désert

Carrouges

Forêt

Essay

St Fraimbault

Ceaucé

Parc Naturel Normandie-Maine

d'Ecouves

CALVADOS

3

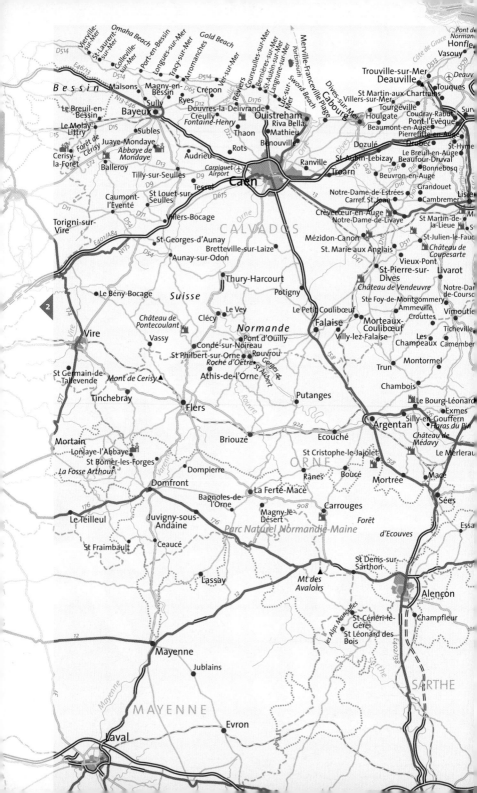